D1710076

ERITREA

Titles in ABC-CLIO's *Africa in Focus* Series

Eritrea   Mussie Tesfagiorgis G.

Ethiopia   Paulos Milkias

Titles in ABC-CLIO's *Asia in Focus* Series

China   Robert André LaFleur, Editor

Japan   Lucien Ellington

The Koreas   Mary E. Connor, Editor

ERITREA

Mussie Tesfagiorgis G.

ABC-CLIO

Santa Barbara, California • Denver, Colorado • Oxford, England

Library of Congress Cataloging-in-Publication Data

Tesfagiorgis G., Mussie.

  Eritrea / Mussie Tesfagiorgis G.

    p. cm. — (Africa in focus)

  Includes bibliographical references and index.

  ISBN 978–1–59884–231–9 (hard copy : acid-free paper) — ISBN 978–1–59884–232–6 (ebook)
1. Eritrea. 2. Eritrea—Social life and customs. I. Title.

DT393.T47   2010

963.5—dc22   2010021773

ISBN: 978–1–59884–231–9

EISBN: 978–1–59884–232–6

14 13 12 11 10   1 2 3 4 5

This book is also available on the World Wide Web as an eBook.

Visit www.abc-clio.com for details.

ABC-CLIO, LLC

130 Cremona Drive, P.O. Box 1911

Santa Barbara, California 93116-1911

This book is printed on acid-free paper ∞

Manufactured in the United States of America

This book is dedicated to my beloved son Natan
My wife Mehret Mesfin
And my parents

Contents

About the Author

Mussie Tesfagiorgis G., a researcher in African environmental and political history, was born in Eritrea where he also completed his undergraduate studies in history. He accomplished his post-graduate studies at Hamburg University, Germany and was awarded his doctorate in history from the same university in 2007. His earlier publication is *A Fading Nature: Aspects of Environmental History of Eritrea (1800–1991)*. He has also published several other articles in journals and books.

Acknowledgments

I am indebted to many people who assisted me in different ways throughout the preparation of this book. I am very grateful to my former university mentor Professor Dr. Bairu Tafla from Hamburg University for his unequaled guidance and advice on many aspects of Eritrean history. I also owe many thanks to Professor Abebe Kifleyesus from the University of Asmara, whose suggestions about many aspects of Eritrean culture proved enormously helpful.

My former instructor at the University of Asmara, and my close friend, Dr. Jonathan Miran of Western Washington University deserves special thanks for his morale boosts and academic assistance throughout my time working on this book. I would like to thank him profusely for his important insights on themes related to Eritrea's history, his proofreading, and comments on issues related to the history of Islam in Eritrea, as well his generous offer of his Eritrean photo collection. I would also like to express my deepest gratitude to my close friend Dr. Christine Matzke of the Humboldt University Berlin; her kindness and assistance have been very essential throughout this work. I am also very thankful to her for the proofreading and advice on themes related to Eritrea's visual and performing arts.

Another close friend, Dr. Getie Gelaye of Hamburg University, deserves my special thanks for his constant encouragement as well as his academic assistance on various subjects related to literature in the Horn of Africa. My special thanks also go to my friend Dr. Hartmut Quehl of the University of Hannover for his unflagging support, suggestions about the source material related to postcolonial Eritrea, and for making his private collection available to me. David Paige and Kim Kennedy-White as well as Lynn Jurgensen of ABC-CLIO deserve my special thanks for their constructive suggestions and valuable assistance during the writing of this book. Moreover, I would like to thank ABC-CLIO for commissioning this work. I owe engineer Kibreab Teweldeberhan of Ottawa special thanks for his insightful comments on various subjects of Eritrean history and culture. My thanks also go to Beemnet T., Mulugeta G., and Iyob of Ottawa who provided me with some source materials for the book. I also owe many thanks to Mahlet A., Tesfagabir M. and Nebiat A., and Elsa M. for their guidance and support during the writing of this book.

I would like to extend my warmest gratitude to my parents, whose moral assistance stimulated courage in me and has always bolstered my morale over the years. They raised me in a warm and supportive atmosphere, and they have inspired my enthusiasm for education and learning since childhood. My warmest thanks to my wife, Mehret Mesfin, and my beloved son Natan for making my work on this book so pleasant. Their company has always been my strength. I dedicate this book to them. My brother, Semere, deserves special thanks for his unlimited help in gathering data and collecting photographs for this book from Eritrea.

Without preparing a long list of appreciation, it will be impossible for me to mention the names of all the people whose contributions to this book have been crucial. However, I would like to express special thanks to my best friends and relatives in Hamburg: Kudusan Okbu and Karlo Kidane, Freweyni, Gebriela, Lula, Selam and James, Kiros and Aida, Weyzero Beserat Misgena, Liya Moges Ketema, Samuel Araya, Yodit, Tesfalem, Wongiel, Billy, Sven Mathiessen, Abeba, Fitsum and Yirgaalem, Samson and Fitsum Gidey and Mersha Alehegn. My special thanks also to my relatives and friends for their moral support over the years: especially the Matzke family, Dr. Francesca Locatelli, Dr. Richard Reid, Dr. Uoldelul Chelati, Mrs Saba Gebrehiwot, Ms Simret Solomon, Ken. Asfaha Sebhat, my aunts Abeba Gebremeskel, Ogba Gebremeskel and Lentenkiel Teklemariam, Mehret Hagos, Weizero Desta Sebhat, Selam Alem, Asmelash Gebregziabher and Dehab Yosief, Mrs Akberet Woldu and Ainalem Afaha. I owe an apology for any person whose name has unintentionally been excluded from the above list. However, I would like to acknowledge that no one else is responsible for the content of the book but me.

Mussie Tesfagiorgis G.
Winnipeg, March 2010

Introduction

Eritrea is located on the Red Sea coast of Africa that is commonly known as the Horn of Africa. More precisely, the area of the Horn of Africa where Eritrea is located is also known as northeast Africa. This region comprises a group of countries, namely Eritrea, Sudan, Ethiopia, Djibouti, and Somalia. Eritrea is the youngest and one of the smallest countries on the continent. Its total landmass is estimated at 125,320 square kilometres (48,262 square miles). The Eritrean coastline along the Red Sea, which extends to about 1,200 kilometers (745.6 miles), consists of over 350 islands, and this part of the Red Sea is the habitat of a great diversity of fish and coral reef populations. In sum, Eritrea is located at one of the most strategic positions of the Red Sea, which is characterized by busy maritime and commercial routes of ships passing to and from the Mediterranean Sea.

The country's geographical features can be broadly divided into three climatic regions: the arid and semiarid eastern and western lowlands (comprising the eastern coastal plains, which include the Semhar Plains, the Dankalia region, and the Barka and Gash territories); the cool and mild plateau (comprising the former Akkele Guzay, Seraye, and Hamasien provinces); and the temperate and mild northern highlands of the country.

The main economic activity of the greater part of Eritrea's population is agriculture. Although pastoralism and agro-pastoralism are dominant economic activities in most lowland areas, sedentary farming is practiced as a main economic activity by a majority of the population in the plateau. Pastoral economic activity is characterized by the seasonal migration of livestock and their owners from one grazing area to another throughout the fragile lowland ecosystems. Most peasants in the plateau depend on rain-fed farming for living. They cultivate varieties of grains such as sorghum, maize, millet, barley, and wheat. Lowland agro-pastoralists also cultivate grains such as millet and sorghum. Some small lowland sedentary farming communities such as Kunama and Nara also cultivate varieties of grains.

Seen from the economic and climatic point of view, rainfall is one of the most decisive environmental factors countrywide. Rainfall is decisive for crop production and animal husbandry. However, the amount of rainfall varies across the climatic regions of the country. The eastern escarpments and plateaus receive higher annual rainfall but most lowlands receive less annual rainfall. The amount of rainfall decreases eastward and southeastward of the eastern escarpments and the coastal areas. Similarly, it also decreases from the northern and western parts of the plateau further toward the plains of Barka lowlands and Gash-Setit. Therefore, Eritrea is characterized by four main ecological zones: the arid coasts of the Red Sea and the Dankalia territory; the mild and cool central plateaus; the temperate northern highlands; and the semiarid western lowlands.

Eritrea comprises striking ethnolinguistic diversity. There are nine ethnolinguistic groups distributed in different parts of the Eritrean territory: the Afar, Bilen, Hedareb, Kunama, Nara, Rashaida, Saho, Tigre, and Tigrinya. Common historical experiences and long-standing commercial as well as cultural interactions among these groups resulted in the formation of modern multicultural Eritrea.

Eritrea's history is characterized by prevalent conflicts, movement of people, and external intervention. The troubled history of the country can largely be attributed to its strategic location along the Red Sea and at the crossroads between the Nile Valley and the south. Foreign involvement that includes persistent intervention of some European, African, and Asian powers during the last centuries turned the whole territory into a battlefield. The people of this territory have suffered throughout many turbulent centuries; however, thanks to their assorted strategies of survival, community-based rules of livelihoods, and their socioeconomic organizations, they have survived all the hardships caused by natural and manmade disasters.

Eritrea's coastal territories were occupied by Arab (Muslim) forces in the eighth and fifteenth centuries. By the sixteenth century, the Arab control of the coastal region was replaced by Ottoman Turks who sought control over the Red Sea and the Horn of Africa at large. Yet, Ottoman presence in this area was confined to the coasts of the Red Sea, especially Massawa and its vicinities. Although the Ottomans attempted further expansion into the Eritrean and Ethiopian highlands, they suffered repeated defeats by local forces. Therefore, they remained on the coastal areas until the second half of the nineteenth century. Ottoman power on the Eritrean Red Sea was substituted by Khedival Egypt, which attempted further expansion toward the Eritrean highlands in the mid-1870s. Egyptian forces in Eritrea sustained significant defeats by Ethiopian forces under Emperor Yohannes IV.

Once more, the Ethiopian presence in Eritrea did not last long and was often confined to the Eritrean plateau. In the 1880s, Mahdist forces seized military momentum and attempted to invade the Horn of Africa. Ethiopia was targeted and invaded by the Mahdists, and Emperor Yohannes IV was killed by these forces. The death of Yohannes resulted in a power vacuum in the territory. By the mid-1880s, Italian forces, who had sought control of the territory ever since they occupied Assab, used the opportunity to occupy Eritrea. By 1890, Italy declared that Eritrea had become its first-born colony in Africa.

Italy ruled Eritrea until 1941; during its occupation a number of significant changes took place in the territory. In addition to the creation of a politically integrated Eritrea, the Italians were also engaged in massive construction of transport and communication services. Italian presence in the territory also resulted in relative peace for most Eritrean ethnolinguistic groups who suffered from external and internal strife during the pre-Italian period. However, Italy's internal policies in the colony were often erratic and inconsistent, especially toward issues related to land and other resource-exploitation principles.

The colonial state applied policies of land expropriation immediately after its occupation of the territory. It also applied harsh treatment against local chiefs who the state accused of intending to rebel against the colonial government. Using these abusive methods, the colonial government executed and imprisoned many Eritrean notables. Most of the detained chiefs languished in the island prison of Nakura. The main idea behind this action (which some scholars consider as "Italian genocide in Eritrea") was that the colonial government wanted to eliminate potential rebellion in the colony.

The expropriation of massive farm and grazing lands as well as Italy's native policies in the colony also resulted in the marginalization of indigenous populations. The government's native policies resulted in the remarkable dominance of the colonizers over the local population. Policies of racial segregation were introduced in the public sphere. Justice was also administered on the basis of racial segregation. The Italian colonial government's educational policies were also repressive. Eritreans were permitted to attend only four grades of elementary school. Even then, the educational provisions were not based on meaningful technical and academic training for Eritreans. The colonial government considered Eritreans merely as main resources for the colonial army. By the end of its rule in Eritrea, the colonial government had recruited around 60,000 native soldiers. The colonial government engaged the greater part of these Eritrean forces in its struggle for the Italian colonial establishment in Libya, Ethiopia, and Somalia.

The combination of all these ill-guided internal policies resulted in a profound dissatisfaction among the indigenous population. Local unrest resulted in repeated resistance and rebellion. One of the most significant mass- and elite-based rebellions against the colonial government was demonstrated under the leadership of a local notable, *Degiat* Bahta Hagos in 1894. Bahta's rebellion mustered about 2,000 local army troops who attempted an overt military confrontation against the colonial army. The rebellion lasted only a few days, during which Bahta himself was killed in the battle of Halai and his followers disbanded. Yet, the impact of this rebellion on colonial thinking was remarkable. At least in principle, the colonial government was compelled to reconsider its land policies, and land expropriation and Italian settlement was slowly discouraged.

In 1941 (during the midst of World War II), the Italian forces in Eritrea were defeated by the Allied Forces. Britain occupied Eritrea and restored a status quo that existed in the colony during the pre-war period. Meanwhile, Ethiopia, which was invaded by the Italian fascist forces in 1935, was given its independence while the British Military Administration (BMA) was established in Eritrea. Although the greater part of the Eritrean population expected the presence of the BMA to liberate them from the Italian colonizers, the British allowed an active Italian economic and social presence to remain in the colony. Most of the economy and administration was still to be controlled by the Italians—to the dissatisfaction of the native population. Moreover, BMA's postwar economic policies further increased the dissatisfaction of the local population. The British in Eritrea sold or relocated a number of industrial plants in the territory.

Yet, BMA's educational policies in the country were remarkably constructive. The British followed a liberal stand in the educational sector, and so Eritreans were admitted to attend elementary and middle schools. Moreover, a teachers' training institution was opened. The number of schools and pupils dramatically increased during British rule in the country. The British also allowed the creation of local political parties, which played significant roles in the development of the Eritrean identity.

The postwar political situation became complicated. Ethiopia's claims over Eritrea and the British political attitude in the region further complicated the Eritrean postwar question. Unable to solve the problem of whether Eritrea should be granted independence or be given to Ethiopia, the Four Victorious Powers (Britain, France, the United States, and the Soviet Union) presented the issue to the United Nations (UN). The UN sent a commission to Eritrea from among member states to come up with a proposal on Eritrea's future. Finally, the UN passed a resolution to federate Eritrea with Ethiopia. In 1952, Eritrea and Ethiopia established federal governments as defined by the UN constitution for Eritrea. Ethiopia's continuous intervention in the internal domains of the Eritrean government resulted in persistent conflict between the two governments. By the mid-1950s, Ethiopia increasingly gained control of the economic and military spheres of Eritrea. By 1962, Ethiopia officially declared that Eritrea had been annexed to the Ethiopian territory.

Eritrea's annexation by Ethiopia resulted in popular discontent across the country. The Eritrean armed struggle for independence started in 1961. The Eritrean war of independence was to last for the next thirty years. First the Eritrean Liberation Front (ELF) and later the Eritrean People's Liberation Front (EPLF) became two rival but highly organized military forces in the Eritrean fields. By the 1970s, these forces defeated the Ethiopian army in most battles and were able to almost wholly occupy Eritrean territory. However, the Ethiopian communist regime under Mengistu Haile Mariam received massive military support from the Soviet Union. Moreover, the internal strife and civil war between the ELF and EPLF also significantly affected the military might of both fronts and changed the balance of power on the battlefields. The Eritrean forces were compelled to withdraw to the Sahel Mountains where they defended their positions until the mid-1980s. By 1988, the EPLF army started to launch military offensives against the Ethiopian army and occupied Afabet (one of the most strategic military positions for Ethiopian forces). By 1990, the EPLF liberated Massawa and greater parts of the Eritrean plateau. On May 24, 1991, the EPLF army occupied Asmara, which signified a complete military victory of Eritrean fighters over the Ethiopian army.

Immediately after Eritrea's liberation, the EPLF established the Provisional Government of Eritrea (PGE). In 1993, the PGE organized a national referendum by which Eritrean citizens were asked to vote for or against independence of the country. The referendum, which was supervised by the UN, was concluded by overwhelming majority vote for Eritrea's independence. Eritrea formally declared its independence on May 24, 1993.

The PGE implemented a number provisional laws related to various aspects of the country. The government also enjoyed massive support from the majority of Eritrea's population. Eritreans within and outside the country provided varieties of contributions, including cash and labor. Eritreans in the diaspora continued to inject hard currencies in the form of remittances and aid.

In May 1993, the PGE changed its name and established a new form of government called the Transitional Government of Eritrea (TGE). But the PGE and TGE had many things in common. More important, power had been highly centralized and fell in the hands of most members of the EPLF leadership. President Isaias Afeweki continued to become the central figure of the leadership. He became the chief of state and head of government.

The TGE introduced a number of policies, such as the National Service program, a new National Charter, and Micro Policy plans. It also embarked on transforming the TGE into a constitutional and democratic government. For this purpose, it launched a massive campaign for the drafting of a new Eritrean constitution. A Constitutional Committee (under the leadership of Professor Bereket Habte Selassie) was established to draft the constitution after involving a great majority of the population. By 1997, the Constitution Commission drafted a new constitution that was approved by the government. The TGE promised that the constitution would be implemented by 1998.

Unfortunately, just before the implementation of the national constitution, the border conflict between Eritrea and Ethiopia broke out. The TGE alleged that it was too occupied by issues of national security and would postpone the establishment of the constitution for an unknown period of time. The war ended in 2000 when both countries signed agreements to end the conflict under international arbitration. The Eritrea-Ethiopia Border Commission (EEBC) was empowered to come up with a binding and final arbitration on the matter. However, while the EEBC process for the ruling was still underway, both countries continued to engage in antagonistic relations and persistent military confrontations. The EEBC passed its binding and final ruling in 2002. However, Ethiopia refused to accept the ruling, although at the same time it also stated that it accepts it but only "in principle." It requested further dialogue on the issue, which Eritrea refused. In this antagonistic manner, both countries continue their stand-off to this day (March 2010).

The internal politics of Eritrea during the postwar period went from bad to worse. The government refused to implement the constitution. In addition, it banned all private media and imprisoned most independent journalists. The government also detained most government figures—reformists commonly known as G-15. All members of the G-15 demanded the establishment of a constitutional and democratic government in the country. None of these detainees has been brought to an open court and not much is known about their condition or their whereabouts.

In general, Eritrea has been repeatedly criticized by international human rights organizations for violating the fundamental rights of its own citizens. Freedom of religion, the press, movement, and so on have been largely curtailed by government actions. As a result, there is a persistent exodus of Eritreans looking to live elsewhere in Africa, Europe, and other continents.

This book is an account of the historical, economic, political, social, and cultural aspects of the country. It is designed to serve as a handbook for all who are interested in Eritrean studies. Exceptional in its presentation on diversity and coverage of issues in Eritrea, this book presents significant academic information. Only a few handbooks have been published about Eritrea throughout the last century, which means that there has been a great lack of academic source materials about the country. This book intends to help fill this gap.

The book is organized into six main subjects. Chapter one presents detailed information on Eritrea's geography. The second chapter deals with Eritrea's history since the ancient period. Chapter three deals with Eritrea's main aspects of post-independence politics and government. Detailed analysis has been attempted to present pragmatic pictures of what has been happening in the country since 1991. The fourth chapter presents a broad overview of Eritrea's economy. A considerable effort has been made to examine historical and contemporary aspects of economic developments in the country. Chapter five deals with assorted features of Eritrean society. Some of the main subjects presented in this chapter include: Eritrea's religions and an ethnographic overview of Eritrea's ethnolinguistic groups. Chapter six focuses on rich cultural themes such as Eritrean languages, literature, arts, music, and food.

Abbreviations

AU	African Union
BMA	British Military Administration
CAF	Confederation of African Football
CCT	Central Cultural Troupe
CELU	Confederation of Ethiopian Labor Unions
EDA	Eritrean Democratic Alliance
EDF	Eritrean Defense Forces
EEBC	Eritrea-Ethiopia Border Commission
EIC	Eritrean Investment Center
EIJM	The Eritrean Islamic Jihad Movement
EIRP	The Eritrean Islamic Reconciliation Party
EISM	The Eritrean Islamic Salvation Movement
ELF	Eritrean Liberation Front
ELF-PLF	Eritrean Liberation Front-People's Liberation Front
ELM	Eritrean Liberation Movement
EMDHR	Eritrean Movement for Democracy and Human Rights
ENFT	Eritrean National Football Team
ENIL	Eritrean National Islamic Liberation Front
ENVF	Eritrean National Volleyball Federation

EPLF	Eritrean People's Liberation Front
EPRDF	Ethiopian People's Revolutionary Democratic Front
EPRP	Ethiopian People's Revolutionary Party
ERA	Eritrean Relief Association
FAO	Food and Agricultural Organization (UN)
FLN	*Front de Libération nationale*
GBZ	Green Belt Zone (also known as *semienawi bahri*)
GC	General Command
GUELS	General Union of Eritrean Labor Syndicates
GUEW	General Union of Eritrean Women
ICRC	International Committee of the Red Cross
ICSID	International Court of the Settlement of International Disputes (Hague)
IFAD	International Fund for Agricultural Development
ILO	International Labor Organization
IMF	International Monetary Fund
IPA	International Phonetic Alphabet
IRB	Islamic Reconciliation Board
IRC	International Rescue Committee
ITGLWF	Eritrean Textile, Leather and Show Workers
IUF	Food, Beverages, Hotels, Tourism, and Agriculture Workers
LWF	Lutheran World Federation
Ma.Te.A	*mahber tiyater asmera* "Asmara Theater Association"
Me.M.Ha.L	*mahber memeheyash hagerawi lemdi* "Association for the Improvement ofNational Customs"
MIGA	World Bank's Multilateral Investment Guarantee Agency
MLHW	Ministry of Labor and Human Welfare
NCEW	National Confederation of Eritrean Workers
NFC	National Fishing Corporation
NFF	National Football Federation
NUEW	National Union of Eritrean Women
NUEWO	National Union of Eritrean Workers
OAU	Organization of African Unity
ODA	Official Development Assistance
PFDJ	People's Front for Democracy and Justice
PGE	Provisional Government of Eritrea

PLF	People's Liberation Front
RC	Revolutionary Council
RICE	Research and Information Center of Eritrea
RSBCWU	Red Sea Bottlers Coca-Cola Workers Union
SICU	Somali Islamic Courts Union
SPLM	Sudan People's Liberation Movement
TFGS	Transitional Federal Government of Somalia
TGE	Transitional Government of Eritrea
TPLF	Tigrean People's Liberation Front
TSZ	Temporary Security Zone
UN	United Nations
UNGA	United Nations General Assembly
UNHCR	United Nations Higher Commission for Refugees
UNMEE	United Nations Mission in Ethiopia and Eritrea
UP	Unionist Party
WB	World Bank
WHO	World Health Organization (UN)

Geography

INTRODUCTION

Eritrea, located on the northeast coast of Africa (12° 42" and 18° 00" north latitude, and 36° 29" and 43° 20" longitude east of Greenwich), borders the Red Sea in the north and east, Djibouti in the southeast, Sudan in the west and northwest, and Ethiopia in the south. Its total area is approximately 125,320 square kilometers or 48,386.32 square miles (one of the smallest states in the continent), and its total land boundaries are about 1,630 kilometers long (1,013 miles). Eritrean boundaries with Djibouti, Ethiopia, and Sudan extend to 113 kilometers (70.2 miles), 912 kilometers (566.2 miles), and 605 kilometers (375.9 miles), respectively. Its coastline is approximately 2,200 kilometers long (1,367 miles); over 350 islands and archipelagoes (including Dahlak Kebir, Norah, Halba, Goba Baka, and Dohul) to the southern part of the Red Sea and, thereby, Eritrea borders with Yemen (Tesfagiorgis G. 2007b: 32–35). The Dahlak Archipelago is composed of a group of small, barren, and mostly uninhabited islands scattered along the Red Sea, off the port city of Massawa.

Eritrea owns a sea territory of approximately 22 kilometers (13.67 miles) from its coasts. Generally, Eritrea is located in a geopolitical position in one of the world's busiest maritime and commercial routes in the Red Sea. The strategic location of the country enables it to hold a principal position along the sea route between Bab al-Mandab (on the southern Red Sea gate from the Indian Ocean) and the

Suez Canal (an outlet to the Mediterranean Sea). The Red Sea hosts commercial ships passing to and from Europe, Asia, the Persian Gulf as well as eastern and southern Africa. The largest sea outlets and notable centers for maritime commerce in Eritrea are the ports of Massawa and Assab.

The eastern coastal parts of Eritrea also encompass parts of the great East African Rift Valley along the Red Sea. The East African Rift Valley is the world's longest rift valley. It begins in Syria and goes downward to Mozambique. The Aden or Indian Ocean Rift Valley and the Red Sea Rift Valley are the main branches of the greater rift system in Africa. The Eastern African Rift Valley extends over 7,000 kilometers (4,349.5 miles) long. The East African Rift Valley was created during the Miocene Epoch (over 23 millions of years ago) by the collision of tectonic plates that occurred in that area. The complex system of Rift Valley in eastern Africa is formed of three different rift valleys—the African Rift Valley, the Red Sea Rift Valley, and the Gulf of Aden (Indian Ocean) Rift Valley that converge at the Danakil Plains of Eritrea.

The determinant factors for the Eritrean climate, rainfall, and general ecology is its forms of physical topography. Topography is also a determinant factor in the economic activities of the country's population. The pastoral communities usually roam around areas of lower altitude where there is abundant grazing land. Farming communities are distributed throughout the highlands where there is fertile soil and mild temperature. The total arable land throughout the country accounts for only about 3 percent of the total landmass. Over 70 percent of the total Eritrean landmass is characterized by mountain ranges (used as grazing lands) and arid zones (where there are limited grazing activities). Generally, Eritrea consists of various ecological zones such as savannah, rain forests, temperate zones, and desert and semi-desert ecologies.

One of the most exciting geographical features of Eritrea is its extreme diversity in landscape; a juxtaposition of contrasting physiographical features in a small territory (Youssef 1961: 10–115). The climatic and physiographical differences can be experienced in a few hours travel across the country. For example, while traveling from Asmara (2350 meters) to Massawa (5 meters)—about 115 kilometers— one experiences cool temperature in Asmara, then mild and wet temperature along the eastern escarpments as far as Ghinda'e, and hot and arid temperature in Massawa and its vicinities. A unique feature of the annual climate in Eritrea (as summarized by the Eritrean Ministry of Tourism, Eritrea) is that one can experience "three seasons in two hours" between Asmara and Massawa. Various physiographical conditions are found in close concurrences—basalts and trachytes, granites and clays, sediments and alluviums, and others ranging from a remote geological antiquity to recent formations are distributed across the country (Youssef 1961: 10–115). Another striking feature of Eritrea is its ethnic diversity. Although small in size, Eritrea is home for a variety of peoples. The country is inhabited by nine cultural groups, and each of these ethnolinguistic groups has its own distinctive language and culture.

Eritrea is located at about 45° longitude, so local time is three hours ahead of Greenwich Mean Time.
  Sunshine hours in Eritrea vary between 11 and 13 hours.
  Working hours: 7 a.m.–12 p.m., 2 p.m.–6 p.m.

It should be noted that most of the names of the provinces provided in this text are mostly old provincial names. After the independence of Eritrea, the country has been divided into six administrative zones known as *zobatat* (ዞባታት), and 59 subzones known as *neusan zobatat* (ንኡሳን ዞባታት). Therefore, Akkele Guzay and Seraye together are renamed *Zoba Debub* (Southern Zone); Gash, parts of Barka, and Setit, are together renamed *Zoba Gash Barka* (Gash Barka Zone); the old province of Hamassien is renamed *Zoba Ma'ekel* (Central Zone); Anseba, small parts of Sahel Province, and small parts of old Barka are renamed *Zoba Anseba* (Anseba Zone); eastern parts of Sahel Province, as well as Semhar are renamed *Zoba Semienawi Qeyyih Bahri* (Northern Red Sea); and Dankalia is renamed *Zoba Debubawi Qeyyih Bahri* (Southern Red Sea Zone) (see also Tesfagiorgis G. 2007b: 23).

GEOGRAPHICAL ZONES

Eritrea comprises several contrasting geographical zones: the eastern escarpments, the eastern coastal plains, the central and northern highlands, and the western lowlands. The geographical difference of these regions lies in the difference in climate, topography, vegetation, and soil.

THE EASTERN ESCARPMENTS

The eastern escarpments (also known as the Green Belt Zone—GBZ) are the eastern edges of the central highlands facing the eastern lowlands. The altitude of this sub-tropical region varies between 700 to 2,000 meters above sea level. The climate and rainfall of the GBZ, however, varies depending on the difference in altitudes. This geographical area is mostly composed of a chain of big mountains and cliffs; it is drained by many rivers and small streams. Unlike other geographical regions of Eritrea, many areas located in the eastern escarpment enjoy two rainy seasons; therefore, it is covered by evergreen vegetation and dense forests. Areas of higher altitude in the eastern escarpments are characterized by dense forests comprising a variety of plant species such as African juniper (*Juniperus procera*) and African olive (*Olia africana*). The foothills of the mountains of the eastern escarpment (areas such as Demas and Geleb) are characterized by sparse vegetation of plant species such as varieties of *Acacia*.

Rainfall is abundant for most of the year. Annual rainfall ranges between 1,150 millimeters and 1,100 millimeters. Rainfall is intensive in the upper part (western side) of

Filfil Forests at the Eastern Escarpments. (Mahlet Abraham)

Forest Mountains at the northern parts of the GBZ. (Mahlet Abraham)

the GBZ and rapidly decreases at the eastern edges, and it disappears at the coastal plains. Moreover, this geographical area is richer in diversity of animal and plant species than other geographical zones of the country.

THE EASTERN LOWLANDS AND THE COASTAL PLAINS

The Red Sea coastal plains extend in a long tail-like prolongation from around the port of Massawa and the Gulf of Zula to Djibouti. The coastal strip of this geographical division stretches from Ras Kassar (southern tip of Eritrea) in the south to Ras Dumera (border with Sudan) in the north. Most parts of this geographical zone lie at less that 500 meters (1640.4 feet) above sea level. The coastal plains of Eritrea mainly include the administrative zones of the southern Red Sea and northern Red Sea. They constitute part of the huge Dankalia depression, which includes extensive sand and salt plains and lakes. Some parts of this arid zone sink up to 70 meters (229.6 feet) or more below sea level; and the region is characterized by hypertorrid and desert climate. In contrast, the adjacent southern parts of the eastern escarpments form steep and rugged mountains (see also Tesfagiorgis G. 2007a: 289–291).

The eastern lowlands encompass the vast plains of Semhar, Shieb, the Sahel Mountains, the eastern coastal plains, and the Dankalia Plains. The main features of most of the coastal plains to the south of Massawa include high temperature, salty plains, and volcanic (block) mountains.

The Dahlak Islands and archipelagoes are also part of this geographical zone. The Dahlak Islands comprise over 350 small islands. Few of these islands are inhabited by pastoral communities and fishermen. In addition to its rich marine resources, the area's scattered mangroves and abundant varieties of coral reefs have great potential for a tourist attraction. The sea surrounding all the islands as well as the whole Eritrean territory in the Red Sea is almost free of any sea pollution. There is also great diversity and abundance in fish and coral reefs. Most of the Eritrean islands are located in clusters with an average altitude ranging between five and six meters above sea level. For the list of the 15 largest islands, see Table C—*Some of the Larger Islands of Eritrea*, in the "Eritrea: Facts and Figures" section of this book.

Between the coastal plains and the Danakil Depression (south of the Gulf of Zula) are the Afar Alps (secluded volcanic mountains and hills). Although not covered by water, the Danakil Depression contains dense volcanic rocks distributed in some places at over 100 meters (328 feet) below sea level (at Kobar Sink). Because of its high annual temperature (over 38°C) not many plant and animal species can survive in this area. Some of the main features of the Danakil Depression include vast plains covered by volcanic rocks and fragmented salt lakes. Active volcanic steams can also be observed in some places of the Danakil Depression.

In contrast, a long strip of coastal land between the ports of Assab and Massawa (at the foothills of the eastern mountains and escarpments) is covered by sparse vegetation. This strip of land extends for about 450 kilometers (279.6 miles). A number of wild animal species such as zebras, ostriches, and varieties of antelopes also inhabit this strip of land. The main source of water in this area is the seasonal runoff of highland rivers and streams that flow toward this area.

Most of the Danakil Depression is inhabited by Afar (Cushitic-speaking) groups whose economic activities range from pastoralist actitivities to trade and fishing. The Buri Peninsula in this region hosts a number of animal species such as ostriches, baboons, varieties of bird species, and gazelles. It is also characterized by dense mangroves and vast salt plains. Small villages are distributed in the southern Dankalia (north and south of Assab). The inhabitants of these villages depend on a mixed economy of fishing, pastoralism, and salt mining for their survival.

THE HIGHLANDS

The central highlands (plateaus) are largely tablelands marked by high mountains rarely covered by vegetation; their plains are nonetheless fertile agricultural areas (see also Tesfagiorgis G. 2007a: 289–291). Its mountains consist of sedimentary, basalt, and crystalline rocks. The plateaus form a large watershed between the Red Sea (the eastern lowlands) and the western drainage basins. The three major rivers (the Mereb, the Barka, and the Anseba) rise in this region and flow west and north-westward. The central plateau mainly encompasses the administrative divisions of Zoba Debub (formerly divided into Akele Guzay and Seraye provinces) and Zoba Ma'ekel (formerly known as the Hamasien Province).

The plateaus of Eritrea provide a most favorable topography for the practice of rain-fed agriculture where farmers adjust their farming technology and cropping methods, and are favored areas of land for agriculture and settlement. This region has been the most populated area throughout history. Today, while this region represents only about 16 percent of the total landmass, nearly 65 percent of the country's population lives within this geographic zone (Murtaza 1998: 28–42; Tesfagiorgis G. 2007b: 37). Although with a considerable variation in quality, agriculturally suitable types of soils are distributed throughout this region. Most of the inhabitants of this region are highly organized sedentary farmers. However, it also suffers from erratic type of rainfall, land degradation, forest-resource depletion, and acute soil erosion.

The plateaus' physical location has been crucial for the agricultural and environmental history of the country. The Eritrean highlands have been in agricultural use for many centuries. Therefore, humans as users of the land, producers of varieties of crops, and users of the vegetation as fuel have brought about a long-term impact on the natural resources and landscape of the highlands. In addition to the dramatic change of its landscape, both massive deforestation and heavy loss of fertile soil have left this region with concurrent environmental adversities. Major agricultural plains in the plateaus include: the Hamasien plains, Tsilima (Seraye), Hazzemo, and Shimezzana plains (Akkele Guzay).

The average altitude of the plateau region is 2,250 meters (7,381.8 feet) above sea level. Mount Amba Soira, the highest altitude (3,013 meters or 9,885 feet above sea level), is located in the southeastern part of this plateau. Some of the most important towns in this geographical zone include Senafe (2,445 meters or 8,021.6 feet), Adi Keyyih (2,423 meters or 7,949.4 feet), Segeneity (2,203 meters or 7,227.6 feet), Deqemhare (2,170 meters or 7,119.4 feet), Mendefera (2,022 meters or 6,633.8 feet), and Adi Kuwala

(2,054 meters or 6,738.8 feet). Asmara (2,372 meters or 7,782 feet) is the capital city of Eritrea, and it is located almost at the center of the plateau (Ministry of Education 1995: 41–50).

The Hamasien Plateau is located opposite the eastern escarpments. It is a flat surface, although some rock hills can be seen scattered over the plains. This geographical area constitutes part of the former province of Hamasien. The flat landscape of this geographical area extends as far as Tera Imni in the south, Zager in the north, Riesi Adi and Biet Gergish in the east, and Mount Tekera in the west. Owing to its high altitude, this geographical area is characterized by mild climate throughout the year (for details see Tesfagiorgis G. 2007b: 37–38). The highest mountain in this geographical area is Mount Tekera (2,579 meters or 8,461 feet). The Hamasien Tableland encompasses vast fertile plains where a variety of crops are cultivated. Among the predominantly cultivated crops are wheat, barley, and millet. Varieties of vegetables, especially potatoes, are also widely produced in this area. Among some of the important settlement villages in this geographical area include Tse'azega, Hazega, Tsa'eda Kerestiyan, Himbirti, Adi Nefas, and Emba Derho. Other small market towns in this area include Serejeka and Adi Tekelezan.

An entirely different landscape composes the Anseba highlands, and the northwestern slopes are located on the north and northwest of the Hamasien flat terrain. This landscape extends as far as Keren and its surroundings, and in some places it is characterized by steep slopes. The western parts of this area comprise gentle slopes. This geographical area constitutes parts of the former Senhit province. Especially the northern parts of this geographical area are dissected by many rivers. The most significant river in the area is called Anseba, which originates from the Hamasien Plateau, and passes through this region to the north. This landscape is rich in drainage; and "many rivers and tributaries of the Anseba River such as Baloa, Megsas, and Tokor give it a special geographical beauty" (Tesfagiorgis G. 2007b: 37). Similar to most of the plateau landscapes, this area enjoys mild climate for most of the year. Some of the main mountains in this area include Emba Debresina (2,615 meters or 8,579 feet), Saber (2,596 meters or 8,517 feet), and Sardum (2,379 meters or 7,805 feet). Some of the main districts in this region are Halhal, Megareh, Bejuk, and Marya. Major linguistic and cultural groups who occupy this region include the Bilen, Beni Amer, and Tigre (the Marias). The main economic activity of the inhabitants of this geographical zone is agro-pastoralism.

The areas, especially the Halhal Highlands, have been dissected into steep gorges by the rivers and their tributaries. The eastern part of the former Hamasien province extends between the Anseba Valley and the edges of the eastern escarpments. Major areas of higher altitude in this zone include Mount Zager and Mount Ira with approximately 2,615 (8,579 feet) and 2,618 meters (8,589 feet) above sea level, respectively (Tesfagiorgis G. 2007b: 37). With its higher and more sufficient rainfall, this area is more favorable for settlement than the western part of this geographical zone. It includes the Mensae Plateau (east of Keren) and the Labka Valley. For a list of some of the higher altitudes of some of the major mountains in Eritrea, see Table D of the "Eritrea: Facts and Figures" section of this book.

The interior plateau receives abundant rainfall during the rainy season of June through September and is largely identified by the stripped vegetative cover. Although the *Azmera* (ኣዝመራ) rainfall (between March and May) is mostly inadequate, it allows for a limited cultivation of crops. Legumes such as peas, chickpeas, beans, lentils, and other types of crops are cultivated in the southern and western parts of the plateau during the *Azmera* season. Varieties of crops (such as barley, maize, wheat, sorghum, and various legumes) are cultivated on the plateau during the rainy season. Climatically, the plateau region is characterized by mild temperatures that hardly exceed three degrees Celsius in its annual range. The surface areas of the plateau consist of crystalline rocks and host varieties of plant and animal species.

North of the central plateau are the northern highlands. These highlands are a projection of the central plateau. They consist of the ragged and deforested mountains of Sahel, Anseba, and Habab, and they are separated from the central plateau by the Anseba River. The average elevation of the northern highlands ranges from 1,000 (3,280 feet) to 2,600 meters (8,530 feet) above sea level. Among the highest peaks of mountains in this geographical area include Hager Neus (2,770 meters or 9,088 feet) and Fengaga (2,549 meters or 8,362.8 feet). Most of the landscape in this geographical area is highly eroded. The northern highlands form higher altitude watersheds that drain toward the plains in the Barka (westward) and the coastal plains along the Red Sea (eastward).

The northern highlands are characterized by lofty mountains and arid climate, and are also characterized by impregnable and deforested mountains and cliffs (Tesfagiorgis G. 2007b: 37). The Sahel Mountains (such as Denden, Nakfa, and Himbol), where the Eritrean-Ethiopian wars took place during the Eritrean independence struggle (1961–1991), have shown dramatic landscape change in the last few decades. Most forest and wood sources of this geographical area were overused during the liberation struggle.

The Sahara Desert, which is rapidly expanding along the Sahelean Belt of Africa, is believed to have exerted a remarkable impact on parts of Sudan and the Sahel Mountains in Eritrea. Indeed, desertification has become one of the issues of concern in parts of northeast Africa. Most of the streams and seasonal rivers located in this geographical area remain dry and arid for most of the year. The erratic and inadequate nature of rainfall in this area allows no sedentary cultivation or permanent grazing. The temperature is mostly hot and dry during the day and cold during the nights, although differences in altitudes also cause differences in temperature in various locations of the highlands. The same is true of the central plateau; the rainy season of these highlands is between June and September, although the amount of rainfall has shown a dramatic decrease since the last century.

Nakfa and Afabet are some of the major market towns in these highlands. Most parts of the northern highlands are populated by pastoral communities who roam these mountains. Their grazing movements extend as far as to the border of Sudan in the west and the Red Sea coastal plains in the east.

THE WESTERN LOWLANDS

The western part of the country is characterized by gentle slopes in the east and the vast plains of Barka in the west as well as the fertile river banks of Gash-Setit. The plains of the western lowlands extend as far as Sudan. This part of the country lies

Vegetations of the Barka Lowlands, near Akordat. (S. Tesfagiorgis)

Plains of the Barka Lowlands, as seen from Akordat. (S. Tesfagiorgis)

roughly between the altitudes of 250 (820.2 feet) and 460 meters (1,509.1 feet) above sea level. The western lowlands are also characterized by temperate climate and savannah vegetation: shrubs and grasses. However, scattered forest trees (predominantly palm and various types of acacia) can be seen here and there.

Although most of the dwellers of the plains of the western lowlands are traditionally pastorals, the inhospitable climate of the region has forced many of them to adjust their systems of livelihood. Thus, the survival strategy of many rural communities in these lowlands is based on farming systems that involve a mix of crops and animal husbandry, cultivation of cash crops, and the dispersal of these economic activities over these vast plains. The traditional farming system involves growing millet for food and keeping camels, cattle, goats, and sheep for food and occasional sources of cash.

CLIMATE

The climate of Eritrea is shaped by its diverse topographical features and its location within the tropics. The diversity in landscape and topography in the highlands and lowlands of Eritrea result in the diversity of climate across the country. In general, Eritrea (especially its highlands) has a most favorable climate for human settlement and agriculture.

The highlands have temperate climate throughout the year, while the lowlands are scorched by blazing heat. The climate of most lowland zones is arid and semiarid. The distribution of rainfall and vegetation types varies markedly throughout the country. The temperature of various locations in Eritrea is usually determined by variations in altitude rather than latitude. Therefore, the temperature of all geographical zones of Eritrea varies on the basis of seasonal and altitudinal differences.

Based on variations in temperature, Eritrea can be broadly divided into three major climatic zones:

- The *dega* (ደጋ) (temperate zone comprising mainly the Eritrean plateaus): This tableland has a mild climate throughout the year. January and February are the coldest months, and the temperature drops up to 8°C or below. The altitude of this climatic zone is 2,000 meters (6,561.6 feet) above sea level. Some of the main towns located in this zone are Asmara, Adi Keyyih, Segeneity, Mendefera, and Deqemhare. The annual temperature of this climatic zone ranges between 10°C and 25°C. For example, the annual mean temperature of Asmara (2,340 meters or 7,677 feet above sea level) is 16°C.

- The *weyna dega* (ወይና ደጋ) (subtropical climatic zone that mainly comprises the eastern escarpments and western slopes as well as parts of the northern highlands): The altitude of this climatic zone varies between 700 (2,296.5 feet) and 2,000 meters (7,677 feet) above sea level. The temperature in this climatic zone varies between 16°C and 28°C. Some of the main towns in this climatic zone are Keren, Barentu, Nakfa, and Ghinda'e. During the coldest months, the temperature may drop below 10°C. For instance, the annual mean temperature of Ghinda'e is 24.6°C.

- The *quolla* (ቆላ) (tropical climatic zone that mainly comprises the eastern and western lowlands as well as the Red Sea coasts): This ecological zone consists of contrasting climatic features. The Semhar Plains (west of Massawa) have cool climate during the rainy season (November to March); during the months of June to September the area is scorched by blazing heat. During these months, the temperature around Gahtelai, Massawa, and Demas as well as the coastal plains may increase to 41°C or above. The southeastern coastal plains and the Danakil Depression are mostly arid, and it has a desert or semi-desert climate. It is very hot throughout the year. Assab, the second major Eritrean port, is located in this climatic zone, and its annual mean temperature can reach 42°C. The temperature of the Eritrean Red Sea ranges from 26°C to 29°C. This temperature is ideal for the diverse types of coral reefs along the sea. The western lowland is comprised of the greater Barka Plains and the Gash Plains. It is characterized by hot temperatures that range between 28°C and 40°C. During the coolest months of December and January the temperature may drop to 12°C to 24°C. For example, the annual mean temperature of Massawa and its neighboring (8 (26.2 feet) or more meters above sea level) territories is 28.6°C.

ERITREA

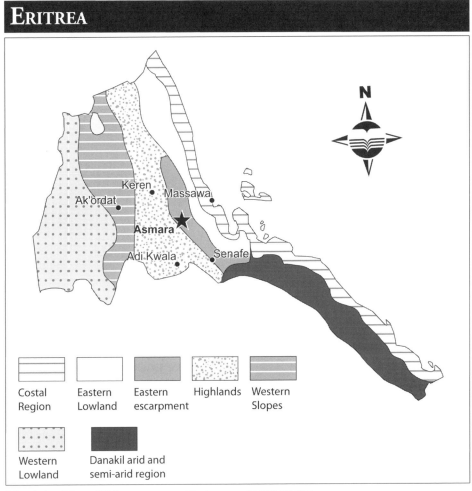

Costal Region   Eastern Lowland   Eastern escarpment   Highlands   Western Slopes

Western Lowland   Danakil arid and semi-arid region

MAP 1.1. Map of Eritrean geographical zones. (ABC-CLIO)

As noted earlier, the determining factor of environmental conditions throughout the history of the Eritrean highlands has been elevation. Elevation of the Eritrean highlands affects temperature, the distribution of rainfall, and vegetation types. There is a close connection between altitude on the one hand, and rainfall, vegetation, and climate on the other. For example, farmers of the highland differentiate which climate and temperature favors which crop; hence, different crops are cultivated at different altitudes (Tesfagiorgis G. 2007b: 38–48; 83–106). However, "much of the topsoil of the higher altitudes of Eritrea has been eroded and [washed] away to the less productive and climatically unfriendly regions of lower altitudes. This has a cumulative effect on the landscape, and thus on the agricultural productivity of the highlands. The effect of natural forces can be easily seen in the gorges, seasonal rivers, and valleys that wash away the fertile soils of the highlands every rainy season toward different directions of lower altitudes as far as the Nile River" (Tesfagiorgis G. 2007b: 36).

RAINFALL

In the Eritrean territories of such physical variety, there is also remarkable variation in rainfall amounts during two seasons. Between June and September, the *keremti* (ክረምቲ) rains, or summer rains, fall almost in all parts of the country except in the eastern lowlands and coastal plains. From October to February, the *bahri* (ባሕሪ) rains, or winter rains, fall along the eastern lowlands and coastal plains but only rarely in many parts of the Danakil Depression. Moreover, most parts of the central highlands also enjoy infrequent rainfall commonly known as the *azmera* (ኣዝመራ) rains during March to April. As noted earlier, the GBZ, because of its unique geographical position and its higher altitude, receives perennial rainfall.

Generally, the great part of the Eritrean landmass receives less than 500 millimeters annual rainfall. Although the annual average distribution of rainfall on the plateau ranges between 500 millimeters to 700 millimeters, in most parts of the lowlands annual rainfall ranges between 100 millimeters to 400 millimeters. The eastern escarpments receive an average annual rainfall of approximately 1,000 millimeters or above. For example, Filfil receives 1,150 millimeters and Mirara receives 1,050 millimeters of annual rainfall.

During normal rainy seasons, precipitation in the plateaus and highlands regularly consists of midday and afternoon thunderstorms and torrential showers. The maximum amount of rainfall in the highlands falls between the months of July and August.

DRAINAGE

The river systems originate from the plateau and northern highlands. Most of the rivers (which are important sources of water for seasonal irrigation and for human as well as livestock consumption) flow toward the Red Sea, the western lowlands, and the Danakil Desert. However, all rivers in Eritrea are not navigable.

Eritrea has four major rivers: the Setit (also known as Tekeze) River (over 600 kilometers long), the Gash (also known as the Mereb) River (over 420 kilometers or 260.9 miles long), the Anseba River (over 340 kilometers or 211.2 miles long), and the

Barka River (over 640 kilometers or 397.6 miles long). All these rivers, except the Setit River are not perennial. The Setit River originates in the central highlands of Ethiopia and flows westward into Sudan, thereby joining the Nile River. The Gash River has its tributaries in northern Ethiopia and within Eritrea (Tserona, the Hazemo Plains, and the Mai Ayni areas). One of the major tributaries of Gash is the Obel River. It originates in the Hazemo Plains and areas south of the town of Mendefera. It flows southward and merges with the Gash River at Mereb—south of the village Molqi. The Gash River also serves as a natural boundary between Eritrea and Ethiopia—especially at the Mereb, Belesa, and Muna areas. Between the rivers Gash and Setit there are fertile plains where extensive cultivation of cotton takes place. The tributaries of these rivers also contribute a great deal of seasonal water for irrigation at the Lower Barka area.

The Barka River originates from the areas located west and northwest of Asmara (in the Hamassien Plateau), and flows northward through the small town of Akordat, and it merges with the Anseba River at a confluent near the border with Sudan. The Anseba River originates in the vicinities of Asmara and flows northward into the Sudan. The Homib River is one of the major tributaries of the Barka River. It originates in areas west of Keru and flows northward.

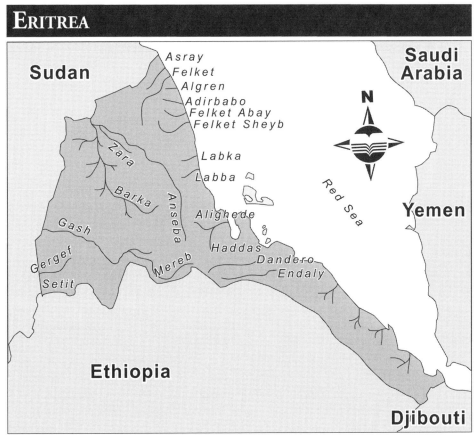

Map 1.2. Map of Eritrean Rivers. (ABC-CLIO)

Other seasonal rivers that flow toward the eastern coastal plains include the Lebka River, the Felket River, the Haddas River, the Komayle River, the Ali Ghede River, and the Siyyah Ghede River. All these rivers are seasonal, and they remain dry for most of the year. The Haddas River, the Komayle River, the Ali Ghede and Siyyah Ghede Rivers originate in the southeastern edge of the plateau and flow as far as the Red Sea. The Haddas River originates in the escarpments north of the town of Adi Keyyih and it flows northward up to the Abbahani Mountains where it turns eastward. The Ali Ghede River originates in the plains of Ala and Berazyo and flows eastward. The Siyyah Ghede River originates from the eastern side of the Halai Mountains, north of the village of Hebo and it flows eastward. The rivers Ali Ghede and Siyah Ghede merge in the southeastern foothills of the Adi-Rosso mountain ranges. These two rivers form a further confluence with the Haddas River near the town of Foro that flows to the Red Sea. The source of the Komayle River lies between the towns of Adi Keyyih and Senafe. It flows down the southeastern escarpments (south of the Haddas River) and ends at the Gulf of Zula in the Red Sea.

One of the significant rivers in the northern part of Eritrea is the Felket River. It originates in the mountains located at the northeastern part of the town of Nakfa. It flows eastward and ends at the small harbor of Marsa Teklay in the Red Sea. The River Wekiro, which originates in the eastern escarpments, flows through the Shieb coastal plains and ends at the Red Sea.

Some of the few rivers in the Danakil Desert include the Deri River and the Gola River. The Deri River originates in the interior of the Danakil plains, flows eastward, and enters the Red Sea (north of a village called Edi). The Gola River originates at the anterior of the southern Danakil (northwest of the port of Assab) and flows eastward to empty into the Red Sea—north of a small harbor called Beylul.

ENVIRONMENT

The Eritrean environment is almost entirely free of industrial and other chemical pollutants. This is mainly because the sectors of industry and modern agriculture make only a limited contribution to the national economy; hence, no significant industrial or any other chemical waste is discharged in the Eritrean terrestrial environment. Although the process of industrialization in Eritrea started early, industrial growth has not been significant. This is mainly attributed to the destructive policies implemented during the British Military Administration (BMA) as well as the prevalent military conflicts of the post-BMA decades. Most industrial plants in the country operate on outdated machinery and technology. As a result, there is low industrial production across the country.

Similarly, seawater pollution has also not been a significant environmental threat; and most parts of the Eritrean territories in the Red Sea are nonpolluted. However, there has not been safe treatment of sewage usually discharged from industrial plants and domestic wastes in most major cities and towns. Unless effective systems of discharges for toxic wastes, domestic waste, and effluents are formulated, industrial and sea pollution might be potential hazards for the future Eritrean environment.

One of the environmental concerns of Eritrea is bacteriological contamination of ground and surface sources of water. Most water source points are not protected and not chemically treated. Therefore, bacteriological contamination causes widespread types of diseases. The lack of sufficient sanitation aggravates the problems of water contamination and contributes to the prevalence of epidemic diseases such as diarrhea, malaria, and typhoid. Among many other diseases, malaria, affects almost 70 percent of the Eritrean population. It is most prevalent in the lowlands and areas with high amounts of rainfall. Yet, based on governmental sources, malaria has been one of the epidemic diseases that has been effectively combated by the Ministry of Health Eritrea. According to government reports, malaria and malaria-related diseases have been effectively controlled in a number of areas within Eritrea since the last few of years. HIV/AIDS has also emerged as one of the most dangerous endemic diseases with significant negative impact on the productive work force of the country.

Among many other forms of environmental degradation, deforestation, and land degradation have become some of the major concerns of the Eritrean public. Forests in Eritrea have been so greatly decimated that the level of coverage is less than 3 percent of the total landmass. The forest cover in Eritrea is believed to have been reduced from 30 percent of the total landmass in 1900 to 11 percent in 1950 and to less than 1 percent in the 1990s. The statistical information on the destruction of vegetative cover in Eritrea is an approximation made at various times. Although several scholars such as Boerma (1999) and Lätt (2004) consider these figures as mere exaggerations, the fact is not far from the figures presented. This is because a considerable part of the Eritrean landscape has become bare in less than two centuries. In giving credence to eyewitness accounts

Camels loaded with fuel wood on the outskirts of Asmara, a practice prevalent all over the country. (Bemnet T.)

THE ASMARA ZOO

There are not many zoos in Eritrea. The only zoo with many visitors is the Biet Ghiorgis Zoo in Asmara. It is located on the road gate toward Massawa, close to the British Cemetery. This zoo is very small, and the number and variety of wild animals on site are also few. Some of the wild animals kept in the zoo are a few lions, hyenas, ostriches and other bird varieties, baboons, and snakes.

---

of nineteenth-century travelers, the country's vegetation has dramatically declined and given way to excessive erosion and loss of fertile soil. Some of the causes of deforestation are: overgrazing, clearing forests for fuel wood and commercial use of timber, and clearing the vegetative cover in search of better farming land.

In addition to these causes, the different regimes that ruled the country, including the Italian colonial government, followed poorly studied and exploitative policies that had a cumulative negative impact on the forestry resources of the country. The forest mismanagement experienced at various times in the history of Eritrea has caused a long-term effect on the transformation of the physical landscape. For the amount of forest cover and land use, see Table E in the "Eritrea: Facts and Figures" section of this book.

Environmental damage in Eritrea was highly insolent, first during the Eritrean Liberation Struggle (1961–1991), and then during the Eritrea-Ethiopia border conflict (1998–2000). During these conflict years, the wars forced hundreds of thousands of people to be dislocated within the territories and many also left their homes seeking refuge in various countries in Africa, Europe, North America, and Australia. During the wars, a great majority of the Eritrean farming fields were abandoned by the owners, and this resulted in a reduction of productivity or no agricultural production at all. Troops occupied many parts of the country and vast territories fell under war zones. As a result, vast farming and grazing lands were planted with landmines and remained "no farming and grazing zones" for most of the years of the conflict. Together with prevalent droughts, the outcomes of these wars were misery and destitution for hundreds of thousands of people in Eritrea. Chronic starvation and death of human and livestock populations in Eritrea accompanied the years of conflict.

The flora and fauna of the country were greatly disturbed during the years of conflict (1961–1991; 1998–2000). During the war, armies exercised irresponsible consumption of ecological resources, and they inflicted irreparable damage on the Eritrean ecology. The armies of both parties massively cut all existing species of trees for use as fuel wood as well as tools of construction for trenches. The destruction of the Eritrean forests also caused enormous damage to the wildlife populations they sheltered. The Eritrean highlands are generally characterized by depleted high forest areas, shrub, and grasslands as well as bare landscapes.

Eritrea has hosted a great variety of wildlife throughout its history. Among the various wild animals that have populated the country are elephants, giraffes, hippopotamus, buffalos, gazelles, monkeys, cheetahs, leopards (commonly known by most people in the country as *nebri* (tigers)), hyenas, foxes, zebras, and a number of bird species, including ostriches. However, due to the continuous conflicts and excessive

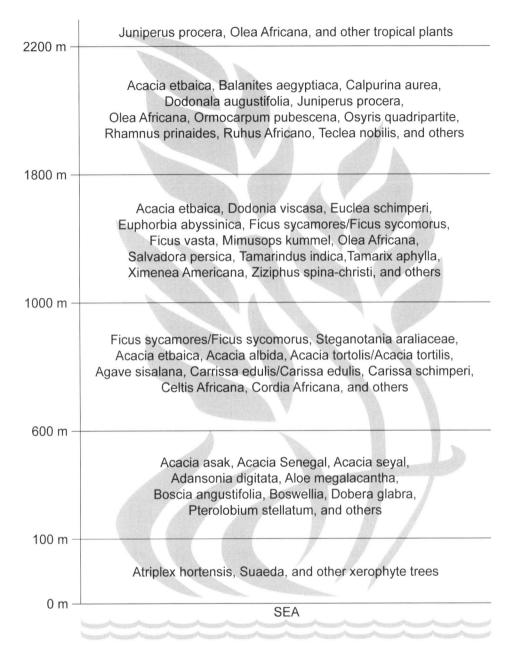

2200 m — Juniperus procera, Olea Africana, and other tropical plants

Acacia etbaica, Balanites aegyptiaca, Calpurina aurea,
Dodonala augustifolia, Juniperus procera,
Olea Africana, Ormocarpum pubescena, Osyris quadripartite,
Rhamnus prinaides, Ruhus Africano, Teclea nobilis, and others

1800 m —

Acacia etbaica, Dodonia viscasa, Euclea schimperi,
Euphorbia abyssinica, Ficus sycamores/Ficus sycomorus,
Ficus vasta, Mimusops kummel, Olea Africana,
Salvadora persica, Tamarindus indica,Tamarix aphylla,
Ximenea Americana, Ziziphus spina-christi, and others

1000 m —

Ficus sycamores/Ficus sycomorus, Steganotania araliaceae,
Acacia etbaica, Acacia albida, Acacia tortolis/Acacia tortilis,
Agave sisalana, Carrissa edulis/Carissa edulis, Carissa schimperi,
Celtis Africana, Cordia Africana, and others

600 m —

Acacia asak, Acacia Senegal, Acacia seyal,
Adansonia digitata, Aloe megalacantha,
Boscia angustifolia, Boswellia, Dobera glabra,
Pterolobium stellatum, and others

100 m —

Atriplex hortensis, Suaeda, and other xerophyte trees

0 m — SEA

Altitude and the distribution of Eritrean flora.

deforestation, the number of wild animals is highly reduced. In fact, some wild animals such as buffalo, hippopotamus, and giraffe are extinct from the country.

The biodiversity of the Eritrean marine environment is, however, sustainable, and it is one of the richest maritime ecosystems in the world. The Eritrean marine environment encompasses various ecosystems with rich natural resource reserves, including: an array type of coral reefs, evergreen mangroves, and great varieties of fishes. The

Eritrean marine and coastal environment provides a great potential for the development of fishing and tourist industrial sectors. The Red Sea in general and the Eritrean waters in particular are characterized by large number of specimens (even a considerable number of uncommon species) of fish and large shoals of fish. Among the types of fishes with significant numbers in the Eritrean Red Sea include jackfish, snappers, shrimps, crabs, mullet, milkfish, barnacles, plankton, clams, sweetlips, unicorn fish, and emperor fishes. Bumphead, parrotfish and lyretail cod are among the big fish species commonly found in this area. Although the population of sharks is believed to have been large, the number of these types of fish species has been greatly reduced for reasons that need to be studied. But presumably this can be attributed to uncontrolled and extensive commercial fishing of these particular species. Yet, dolphins, stingrays, hammerhead, nurse sharks, and more are common along the Eritrean Red Sea.

PEOPLE

As noted earlier, Eritrea is inhabited by several ethnoliguistic groups; with each of these groups having its own language and culture (see Table A.2 of the "Eritrea: Facts and Figures" section of this book). All in all, at least nine languages are spoken in Eritrea. Most inhabitants of Eritrea are either Moslem or Christian in faith. Although some of these groups, particularly the Kunama, are believed to have practiced natural African religions, today most of them have converted to either Roman Catholicism or Moslem religions. Today's ethnolinguistic diversity in the territory is the result of continuous immigrations and migrations of people to and from Eritrea throughout history. As a result, although Eritrea has a relatively small population (approximately four and half million), there is a striking human diversity in the country with an array of cultures and languages.

The eastern and western lowlands have mostly Tigre-speaking inhabitants who are almost entirely Moslem, pastoral, and agro-pastoral societies. Among the minority Christian Tigre communities are the Mensae. The Beni Amer (who are to be found mostly in the western lowlands), are members of the nomadic Beja clans and originally have heterogeneous ethnolinguistic backgrounds. Most of them speak the Tigre language, and they have been integrated into the Tigre culture. Today, the Tigre-speaking population in Eritrea constitutes about 31 percent of the total Eritrean population. The major four Tigre clans in Eritrea include the Beni Amer, Bet Asghede, the Marias, and the Mensae. The Bet Asghede is composed of four major clans: the Habab, Ad Temariam, Ad Teklies, and Bet Juk. Some smaller satellite communities such as Ad Sheikh, Ad Mualim, Bet Mela, and Ad Saura are also part of this clan and are located mostly in the northern highlands (Sahel Mountains). The area north of the Keren territories is occupied by the Maria clans. The Maria was divided into two subclans, the Maria Keyyah (the "Red Marias") and Maria Tselam (the "Black Marias"). The Bet Abrehe and Bet Shakan were the main subclans of the Tigre communities along the eastern lowlands (Semhar areas), such as in the port of Massawa and its vicinities. With an exception of small minority Tigre groups, most Tigre-speaking people are Muslims by religion.

Most parts of the plateau as far as the Halhal highlands are inhabited by Tigrinya-speaking populations. The Tigrinya language, along with Tigre and Amharic (a major

THE TALE OF MOUNT GADAM [GEDEM]

Once upon a time all the mountains held a council saying: "Let us go down to the low-lands!" And when they rose to go down, Mount Gadam was the first to set out and going onward his one end was planted in the sea without his knowing it. Now the sea was upon him so that he could not march on; and his one end was firm in the ground so that he could not return. So he shouted and said to his company: "Let every one of you stand still at his place!"

And all the mountains back of Mount Gadam stood each in its place, and they are there until this day. And for this reason Mount Gadam is ahead of all the other mountains on the sea-shore."

And they say as a proverb: "Do not make a mistake; let each one stand in its place, said Mount Gadam." And as another proverb they say: "We have been mistaken like [Mount] Gadam."

[Mount Gedem is located at the eastern coast of the country, near Massawa]

Source: Quoted from Littmann, Enno (1910). *Publications of the Princeton Expedition to Abyssinia.* Vol. II, Leyden [Leiden]: Late E. J. Brill, page 96.

language spoken in central Ethiopia), belongs to the Semitic linguistic family. The Tigrinya-speaking people whose economic activities mostly depend on sedentary agriculture and transhumant agriculture occupy the Eritrean plateau and northern Ethiopia (the province of Tigray). Mainly due to the plateau's density in population, the distribution of the Tigrinya-speaking peoples in Eritrea has been expanding to the major fertile riverine areas of the western lowland, the eastern lowlands, and the northern highlands. A majority of Tigrinya highlanders are Orthodox Christians, with a minority Muslims (Jeberti). With the expansion of European missionary activities in the regions (especially after the nineteenth century with the missionary teachings of De Jacobis and other French Lazzarist brotherhoods), minority groups also converted to Roman Catholicism and Evangelical religions. Village groups whose majority populations adhere to Catholic religion are located in the southern parts of Eritrea, especially in the subdistrict of Segeneity (including the villages Segeneity, Akrur, Hebo, Adi Qontsi, Mai Ela, Adi Fignie, Halai, etc.), the vicinities of Senafe (a few villages in Shimezana and the Irob territories such as Menokseyto), and in the north in the Bilen territories (in the vicinities of Keren, in the territory that was commonly known as Bogos). Most of these people were converted by missionaries whose activities were extended into these regions mainly in the nineteenth century. Orthodox Christianity continues to be the predominant religion throughout the highlands of Eritrea.

The mosaic of cultures in Eritrea is further diversified by the renowned Eritrean Nilotic-speaking, ethnolinguistic groups of the Kunama and Nara. These ethnolinguistic groups inhabit the southwestern parts of Eritrea along the Rivers of Gash and Setit (close to the southwest border with Ethiopia). The Kunama are believed to be among the earliest inhabitants of Eritrea. The main economic activities of the Kunama are sedentary farming and agro-pastoralism. Another Nilotic-speaking ethnolinguistic group, the Nara, is also located in the southwestern parts of Eritrea (north of the Kunama territories).

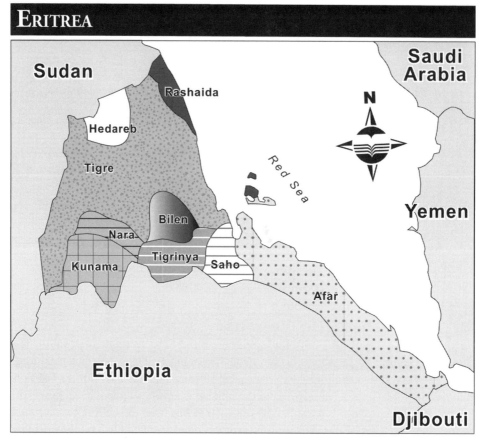

MAP 1.3. Map of Eritrean etho-linguistic groups and their geographical distribution. (ABC-CLIO)

The economic activities of the Nara are sedentary farming and agro-pastoralism. The Nara communities are believed to have followed their own faith (such as belief in ancestors), but they were massively converted to Islam during the Egyptian occupation of their territories in the nineteenth century. Today, the Nara are almost entirely Moslems.

The Saho and Afar ethnoliguistic groups are nomadic pastorals, and they occupy the southeastern escarpments and the vast Danakil Plains, respectively. The Afar who occupy climatically inhospitable territories also practice fishing and trading along the coasts of the Red Sea. The Saho are mostly located along the southeastern escarpments of the plateau. Most of the Saho are nomadic pastorals. All of the Afar and Saho (except a small minority—the Irob) are Moslems.

The Bilen, another Cushitic-speaking group, are located along the northern edges of the central plateau. Despite the long-term influences of the Tigre and Tigrinya (two major groups of people who surround the Bilen territories), the Bilen still preserve their distinctive language (also called Bilen) and culture. The main economic activities of the Bilen are sedentary farming and agro-pastoralism.

The Hedareb, a small Cushitic-speaking ethnolinguistic group, are located in the northwestern parts of the Barka plains as far as the northwestern boundaries of Eritrea and Sudan. The territories occupied by the Hedreb are arid and semiarid grazing lands, and the people are entirely agro-pastorals by economic activity and Moslems by religion.

The Rashaida, another small ethnolinguistic group in Eritrea, are recent immigrants who are believed to have arrived from the southern parts of the Arabian Peninsula in the 1840s and 1850s. The Rashaidas are also found in some parts of eastern Sudan. The Rashaida are Arabic-speaking nomadic pastorals who roam along the northern Red Sea coast of Eritrea as far as Kassala in Sudan. The Rashaida are entirely Moslems, and they are divided into several clans.

PATTERNS OF HUMAN SETTLEMENT

The Eritrean central plateau is by far the most preferred geographical area for human settlement. With its mild climate, its widely disseminated transportation network, and fertile farming soil, the Eritrean plateau has become the most densely populated of all the geographical zones in the country. Most of the inhabitants of this geographical zone are sedentary and transhumant farmers. As mentioned above, the inhabitants of this geographical zone are almost homogenous—Tigrinya ethnolinguistic societies with minority Asaworta Sahos (along the southeastern parts of the plateau). These societies exercise an ox-plough farming system that demands village settlements in which sociopolitical life of the inhabitants is based. The Tigrinya villages are mostly built on higher areas such as on top of hills or mountains. The highland villages are built on higher localities for two reasons: in order not to occupy flat areas in which farming could be convenient; and for the convenience of self-protection (during ancient times, village communities had to defend themselves from natural catastrophes such as floods as well as concurrent foreign threats and raids).

Due to the rugged nature of its mountains and widespread tropical diseases such as malaria, the GBZ as far as the Agemeda and Meskilih mountains in the south are some of the most sparsely populated parts of the country. Yet, there are a few settlement villages scattered over the GBZ. A few small villages such as Faghena, Merara, Fishey, and Filfil are populated by farming communities who cultivate various crops for subsistence and also have limited amount cash crop cultivations such as coffee. Otherwise, most of the GBZ and the Bahri-Semhar areas are populated by highly mobile pastorals whose movements range between the coastal plains and the plateaus. Among these pastorals are the Saho and Tigre ethnolinguistic groups. Some communities among these groups also exercise limited farming—cultivating crops such as maize, millet, and other crops that mature in a few months during their stay in these areas.

REFERENCES

Bein, E., Habte, B., Jaber, A., Birnie, Ann and Tengnas, Bo (1996). *Useful Trees and Shrubs in Eritrea: Identification, Propagation and Management for Agricultural and Pastoral Communities.* (Technical Handbook No 12), Nairobi, Regional Soil Conservation Unit, RSCU/SIDA.

Beyene, Teame (1993). *The Development of Eritrean Land Tenure System since the Last 100 Years*. (Unpublished paper), Asmara [Text in Tigrinya].

Boerma, Pauline A. (1999). *Seeing the Wood for the Trees: Deforestation in the Central Highlands of Eritrea since 1890*. (unpublished Ph.D. Dissertation), Environmental Change Unit, School of Geography: University of Oxford.

Dryland Coordination Group (ed.) (2002). *Sustainable Livelihoods of Farmers and Pastoralists in Eritrea: Proceedings from a Workshop Organized by DGG Eritrea* (Asmara, November 28–29, 2002).

Killion, Tom (1996). "The Eritrean Economy in Historical Perspective." In: *Eritrean Studies Review*. I, I, pp. 91–118.

Lätt, Louise (2004). *Eritrea Re-Photographed: Landscape Changes in the Eritrean Highlands 1890–2004—An Environmental-Historical Study Based on the Reconstruction of Historical Photographs*. (unpublished M.Sc. Thesis): University of Bern.

McCann, James (1995). *People of the Plow: An Agricultural History of Ethiopia, 1800–1990*. Madison: University of Wisconsin Press.

Ministry of Education (1995). *Geography for Grade 11*. Curriculum Development Division, Asmara.

Murtaza, Niaz (1998). *The Pillage of Sustainability in Eritrea, 1600s–1990s: Rural Communities and the Creeping Shadows of Hegemony*. London: Greenwood Printing Press.

Nastasi, Paolo (1994). *Notes Concerning Climatic and Floristic Regions of Eritrea*. n.p.

Naty, Alexander (2002). "Environment, Society and the State in Western Eritrea." In: *Africa: Journal of International African Institute*. 72, pp. 569–597.

Ngcheong-Lum, Roseline (2001). *Eritrea. Cultures of the World Series*. New York: Marshall

Srikanth, R. (2003). "Challenges of Environmental Management in Eritrea: A Case Study." In: *African Journal of Environmental Assessment and Management—RAGEE*, 6, pp. 62–70.

Tesfagiorgis G., Mussie (2003). *Aspects of Eritrean Environmental History: Ecological Change and Survival Strategies (ca. 1850–1900)*. (unpublished M.A. Thesis at the Institute of Asian and African Studies): University of Hamburg, Hamburg.

Tesfagiorgis G., Mussie (2007a). "Eritrea: Geography and Economy." In: *New Encyclopedia of Africa*, vol. 2, John Middleton (ed.), Detroit: Charles Scribner's Sons, pp. 289–291.

Tesfagiorgis G., Mussie (2007b). *A Fading Nature: Aspects of Environmental History of Eritrea (1800–1991)*. Felsberg: Edition Eins Verlag.

Tesfagiorgis, Gebre Hiwet (1993). *Emergent Eritrea: Challenges of Economic Development*. Trenton, NJ: Red Sea Press.

Trevaskis, Gerald Kenedy Nicholas (1960). *Eritrea: A Colony in Transition—1941–52*. Oxford: Oxford University Press.

UNDESF—United Nations Department of Economic and Social Affairs, Population Division (2007). *World Population Prospects: The 2006 Revision*, Vol 1: Comprehensive Tables. United Nations Publication.

UNICEF (1995). *Children and Women in Eritrea*. Asmara. n.p.

United Nations Conference on Desertification—UNCOD (1977). *Desertification: Its Causes and Consequences*. Oxford.

Youssef, Abdul-Haggag (1961). *A Contribution to the Physiography of Northern Ethiopia*. London.

History

KEY EVENTS IN ERITREA'S HISTORY

1832–1842	Egyptian raids toward the western lowlands of Eritrea.
1846	Egyptian occupation of Massawa.
1868	The Lord Napir Expedition against Emperor Tewodros of Ethiopia. The British expeditionary force passes through Eritrea.
1869	Italian shipping company called *Società di Navigazione Rubattino* purchases a piece of land in Assab.
1875	The Egyptian invasion of the Eritrean highlands; the Battle of Gundet between the Egyptian forces and the army of Emperor Yohannes IV of Abyssinia. The Egyptian army faces complete defeat (November).
1876	The second Egyptian invasion of the Eritrean highlands defeated by Yohannes IV of Ethiopia at the Battle of Gura'e (March).
1881–1882	Mahdist expansion from Sudan; the transfer of Assab to Italian state control.
1885	The Italians continue their expansion along the Red Sea coast, and they occupy Massawa in February. In the same year Alula defeats a Mahdist army at Kufit.
1887	Ras Alula (Commander in Chief of the Ethiopian army) defeats the Italians at the battle of Dogali.

1888–1892	A severe famine devastates Eritrea, Ethiopia, and other parts of Eastern Africa.
1889	Italians continue their expansion toward the highlands of Eritrea, and they occupy Asmara in August.
1890	Eritrea officially becomes an Italian colony (January).
1891–1894	Italians start to implement policies of agricultural colonization and massive land confiscation in the highlands of Eritrea.
1894	Italian colonialism faces a major mass-based local resistance in Eritrea led by *Degiat* Bahta Hagos (December 13–17).
1896	Italy attempts an invasion of Ethiopia, but it suffers a total military defeat by the forces of Emperor Menelik at the Battle of Adowa (March).
1897	Asmara is made the capital city of colonial Eritrea. Massawa serves as a capital city for Italian expansion until 1897. Ferdinando Martini becomes the first civil governor of Eritrea.
1911	The railroad construction connects the port city of Massawa and Asmara.
1928	The Eritrean railroad connects Asmara with major towns of Keren and eventually reaches Agordat.
1936–1941	The *Africa Orientale Italiana* (Italian East African Empire) is finally celebrated after the Italians occupied Ethiopia. But the Italian Empire in Africa ends in 1941 after the Allied Forces defeated Italy.
1941	Italy suffers a total military defeat by the Allied Forces at various battles in Eritrea, Ethiopia, and Somalia. Ethiopia reachieves its independence and Emperor Haile Selassie (who was granted refugee in Britain during World War II) comes back to his throne in Ethiopia.
1941	*Mahber Feqri Hager* (Association for the Love of Country), the first popular political organization, is founded in Asmara (on May 5).
1944–1950	Proliferation of Eritrean political parties (the Liberal Progressive Party; Moslem League; Massawa National Party; and others).
1946	The *wa'ella* Bet Giorgis (The Convention of Bet Giorgis) takes place in November, but fails to achieve its objectives.
1947	The Four Powers Commission is sent to Eritrea, but cannot come to an agreeable solution for the Eritrean question.
1949	The Bevin-Sforza Plan of partition is proposed by the British and the Italians. However, it is rejected by the UN Security Council.
1950	The UN passes Resolution 390A(V) federating Eritrea with Ethiopia.
1952	The Federal Act is implemented (September).
1955	The Chief Executive of the Eritrean government (Tedla Bairu) is replaced by Asfaha Woldemichael (an advocate of Eritrean union with Ethiopia).

1958	The Eritrean Liberation Movement (ELM) is founded in November, and starts a network of resistance against the Ethiopian violations of the principles of the federation. The Eritrean flag is lowered. Student strike in Asmara is suppressed.
1960	Eritrean nationalists found the ELF in Cairo (July 10).
1961	The first shot for Eritrean Liberation Struggle is fired by Hamid Idris Awate (September 1).
1962	Ethiopia officially annexes Eritrea as its 14th province (November 14).
1968	ELF reformist groups meet at Aredayib.
1969	The ELF leadership meets at the Adobha Conference and elects the General Command.
1973	The PLF-Dankalia and PLF-Ala Group merge and form the EPLF.
1974	The Emperor of Ethiopia is overthrown by a military junta called Dergue (September).
1977	The EPLF organizes its first congress (January).
1988	The EPLF wins a decisive battle at Afabet.
1990	The EPLF liberates most parts of Eritrea, including Massawa.
1991	Eritrea is liberated by the EPLF army (May 24).
1993	Eritrea conducts an internationally acknowledged and supervised national referendum in which an overwhelming majority of its population voted for independence from Ethiopia (99.8 %). Eritrea formally declares its independence from Ethiopia (May 24). Ethiopia also joins the international community in recognizing Eritrean sovereignty.
1998–2000	Eritrea and Ethiopia fight bloody border wars in which hundreds of thousands of lives are lost from both sides.
2000	Ethiopia and Eritrea agree to solve their border wars under internationally organized court of arbitration (December 12).
2001	The Eritrean government cracks down on some of the country's renowned political figures, collectively known as the G-15, and bans private newspapers and imprisons independent journalists (September 18).

INTRODUCTION

Eritrea's distant past and modern history is largely characterized by prolonged conflicts: for the control of its Red Sea coasts, fertile highlands, and natural resources. In addition to the prevalent movement of people and internal rivalries over the control and use of natural resources, Eritrea has also been a site of remarkable interest for several external powers, which is greatly attributed to its strategic geopolitical position along the Red Sea area. The Red Sea area in which Egypt, Sudan, Eritrea, Djibouti, Somalia, Yemen, Saudi Arabia, Israel and Jordan/Palestine are located serves as a significant sea channel for ships sailing to and from Europe and the Persian Gulf, the Indian Ocean (eastern and southern Africa), and the Far East. Whether from adjacent territories or from other continents, these external powers changed Eritrea into an endless battleground. Usually caught between crossfire, the population suffered grievously from war devastations. The conflicts created by internal and external powers affected the lives of the population for centuries. Yet the Eritrean people and their cultural values endured. They developed remarkable strategies of their own to survive all these centuries of warfare.

Eritrea has also been one of the earliest homes for Christianity and Islam (Tafla 2004: 83–84; Miran 2005). Believed to have been introduced by Byzantine missionaries, Christianity became a state religion of the Aksumite Empire in the fourth century A.D. The earlier Arab Muslims who escaped persecution in the Arabian Peninsula (in the eighth century) are believed to have crossed the Red Sea to seek asylum in the Aksumite Empire. Until the end of the tenth century, these Muslim communities expanded along the Eritrean coasts and islands, and they managed to propagate Islam among the preexisting coastal pastoralist communities. By the fifteenth century, Muslim sultanates and Islamic institutions were already well established along the coasts of the Red Sea. The Ottoman Empire, which controlled the Red Sea coasts (particularly Massawa) in the mid-sixteenth century, further facilitated the consolidation of Islam along the Red Sea area. Although the Ottoman presence in the Eritrean territory was mostly confined to the coasts, their rule had a remarkable impact on the culture, economy, religion, and art of the coastal population of Eritrea. Khedival Egypt, which replaced the Turkish administration in Massawa and the adjacent plains in the nineteenth century, also contributed its share to the prevalent turbulence in the territory.

As if the list of competitors was not big enough, Italy, France, and Great Britain also became active participants in the struggle for hegemony in the second half of the nineteenth century. Also Ethiopia, another imperial neighbor, considered itself as an important player in the area's affairs and claimed a legitimate access to the sea. Fierce competition over the control of the Eritrean territory brought Egypt, Italy, and Ethiopia into conventional warfare, which resulted in Italy and Egypt suffering some dreadful military defeats. Sudanese adherents of a new national and Islamic movement called Mahdists threatened these actors in the second half of the nineteenth century. The Ethiopian emperor was killed by the Mahdists, and Italy occupied and named its first-born colony "Eritrea" in 1890.

During World War II, the Allied Forces defeated the Italian army in Eritrea and placed the colony under their military administration until the United Nations General Assembly (UNGA) could determine its fate in 1950. The UNGA's resolution 390A(V) ended British occupation of Eritrea and the country was federated with Ethiopia in September 1952. Ethiopia's violations of the federal agreement as well as its unilateral decision to annex Eritrea in 1962 created mass discontent among the Eritrean population. The Eritrean Liberation Struggle (1961–1991), which took its momentum as an organized resistance movement against Ethiopia's occupation of Eritrea, resulted in the liberation of the country. Eritrean liberation fighters defeated the Ethiopian army and controlled the country in 1991. In 1993, Eritrea prepared a UN-monitored referendum in which great majority of Eritreans voted for independence. The country formally declared its independence on May 24, 1993.

PREHISTORY AND ANCIENT HISTORY

Archaeological findings on the Red Sea coasts indicate that Eritrea was one of the homes for the earliest hominid in Africa (McGraw-Hill 2002). Further archaeological findings on the coastal areas such as the Gulf of Zula (south of the port of Massawa) indicate that the earliest man in this area used tools for the exploitation of marine resources (Schmidt et al. 2008). Cave paintings discovered in central and northwestern Eritrea also indicate that a population of hunters and gatherers (presumably ancient Nilotic people akin to the modern Kunama and Nara) inhabited some areas in the territory during the Old Stone Age or the Epipaleolithic era (for detailed information on Eritrea's archaeology, see Schmidt et al. 2008).

The above-mentioned evidence indicates that Eritrea belongs with the African and Middle Eastern territories with the oldest history. It is also believed to have been a central part of an ancient geographical area known to the Egyptian pharaohs as the Land of Punt (located in the Horn of Africa). The Land of Punt, also known to ancient Egypt as the "The Land of gods," was believed to have been rich in various types of commercial items. Commercial contacts between ancient Egypt and the Land of Punt—starting from

Ruins at Qohayto, an ancient Eritrean city. (Dainelli, Giotto and Marinelli, Olinto (1912). Risultati scientific di un viaggio nella colonia Eritrea. Florence, Tipografia Galletti e cocci, p. 481.)

Ruins at Tekonda'e, an ancient Eritrean city. (Dainelli, Giotto and Marinelli, Olinto (1912). Risultati scientific di un viaggio nella colonia Eritrea. Florence, Tipografia Galletti e cocci, p. 503.)

ca. 2500 to 2480 B.C. (specifically starting from the 5th–6th dynasties, and frequent contacts between the Egyptians and the Land of Punt during the 17th–18th dynasties)—indicate that the region possessed rich natural resources. The exact location of the Land of Punt is yet disputed. However, it is generally agreed that Eritrea and eastern Sudan comprised an important section of this territory (see Bard and Shubert 1999: 637). For this reason, several Egyptian expeditions (ordered by Egyptian pharaohs such as Mentuhotep III and Senusret I) were dispatched to this part of Africa in search of incense, frankincense, and other valuable items. The Land of Punt's significance to the ancient commercial world was also recorded by the classical Greek historian, Herodotus. Among

ARCHAEOLOGICAL SITE

Adulis

Also known as Azuli by local people, this archaeological site is located at the Northern Red Sea Zone (about 4 kilometers west of the Gulf of Zula or some 62 kilometers south of Massawa). This site served as an ancient trading port, and its archaeological remains indicate that the port city's role as a center for trade can roughly be traced to 3500 to 1000 B.C. Today, archaeological evidence such as remains of buildings and other material remains are visible at the site.

many other items of commercial interest in the modern Horn of Africa were myrrh, various other types of incenses, gold, ivory, ebony, live animals, and ostrich feathers. These items were exported from the Horn to Egypt and later to Greece (for further information on the Land of Punt, see O'Connor 1994: 41–43; Bradbury 1988; Shaw and Nicholson 1995: 231–232).

Furthermore, historical evidence shows that Eritrea and the whole Red Sea region had commercial linkages with the ancient Greeks. The name of Eritrea is derived from the ancient Greek reference to the Red Sea (Ερυθραία). The Greek reference that came to the Italians through the Latin version—*Mare Erythraeum*—was then given as a name to Eritrea. Archaeological evidence shows that farming and stock breeding in Eritrea was already in practice at least by the first millennium B.C. (see Murtaza 1998). The development of agriculture and stock breeding led to commercial connections with ancient civilizations of the Nile Valley—Egypt and Nubia. By the second millennium B.C., evidence from archaeological sites in the western parts of Eritrea suggests that the Eritrean region had become one of the commercial sites for ancient Egypt, Nubia, and the Mediterranean world.

Evidence also shows that the southern Arabian Peninsula had developed strong trading connections with the Eritrean coasts. The legacy of these relations can be found in the old inscriptions and other archaeological evidence in south Arabia and Eritrea. It has been generally argued that these commercial linkages resulted in massive Arabian (Semitic) migration to Eritrea, which brought about major economic, political,

Ancient cave paintings at Kohayto. (Dainelli, Giotto and Marinelli, Olinto (1912). Risultati scientific di un viaggio nella colonia Eritrea. Florence, Tipografia Galletti e cocci, p. 491.)

ARCHAEOLOGICAL SITE

Metera

Located at about 135 kilometers south of Asmara, Metera is one of the ancient centers of human civilization. This pre-Aksumite site comprises various archaeological remains that can be dated back to the seventh to sixth century B.C. and after. The few standing stone monuments in the Belew Kelew are of Metera, just at the foothills of Mount Sayim.

---

and social changes over the indigenous systems. However, whether there was an African immigration to the Arabian Peninsula or vice versa is increasingly becoming a scholarly debate about the history of the Horn.

By the first millennia (1000–600) B.C., urban and rural civilizations had developed throughout the Eritrean and Tigrean highlands. The main economic foundations of these civilizations were successful agriculture and animal husbandry as well as commerce. Archaeological evidence indicates that gold mining was presumably part of the main economic foundations of the highland civilizations. Many commercial cities and towns such as the port cities of Adulis, Quhaito, Metera, and Tokondae emerged as important ancient market places, and they became favorable trading sites for regional and international sea-faring peoples.

Ancient remains. (Beccari, Camillo (1912). Il Tigre: Descritto da un missionario Gesuita del secolo XVII. 2nd edition, Rome: Casa Editore Italiana. Page 129.)

ARCHAEOLOGICAL SITE

Quohayto

Quhayto, one of the ancient city-states of Eritrea, is located about 122 kilometers south of Asmara. Based on the archaeological remains at the site, the area was flourishing starting from about 500 B.C. Quhayto was then incorporated to the Aksumite Empire and continued to serve as an important trading city.

ANTIQUITY AND MEDIEVAL HISTORY OF ERITREA

During the last few centuries of the first millennium B.C., the state of Aksum emerged in the territories of modern-day Eritrea and Tigray (northern province of Ethiopia). Among the earliest references of Aksum appears in the *Periplus Maris Erythraei* (Periplus of the Erythraean Sea), written in the first century C.E. It was a Greek periplus describing commercial circumstances and navigation patterns along Egypt, the Red Sea, and the Persian Gulf as far as India and Ceylon. Around A.D. 100, the state of Aksum rose to prominence in northeast Africa. The greater parts of modern Eritrea (especially the plateau) became an important part of this African civilization. Pre-Aksumite city-states in Eritrea such as Metera, Adulis, and Quhayto were incorporated into this new empire (see Yohannes 1991: 25; Schmidt et al. 2008). Yet these pre-Aksumite states played a crucial role for the development of the Aksumite Empire. Da'amat, another important kingdom with its capital at Yeha (Tigray), also flourished in the area since the fifth century B.C., and it was later incorporated into this new empire. Aksum reached its peak power by the seventh century A.D.

The rise and development of Aksum was closely associated with local growth such as food security (remarkable development in agriculture and stock breeding), military strength, and the development of lucrative commerce of goods such as gold, exotic animals, incense, and ivory with the outside world. The empire imported various manufactured goods such as glassware, ironware (although it also produced various local iron tools), and textiles. Among Aksum's important overseas commercial partners were merchants from Egypt and the Nile, Greece, India, and the eastern Mediterranean. The commercial partners encompassed a veritable mosaic of people, namely Cushitic, Nilotic, and Semitic speakers. The written language of Aksum was, however, Ge'ez: a written Semitic language that was in use before the emergence of Aksum and evidently in commercial and daily use in the third century A.D. (for further information on Aksum, see Phillipson 1998; Munro-Hay 1991; and Michels 2005). After the decline of Aksum, this language was dominated by other domestic languages for several centuries. Between the thirteenth and seventeenth centuries A.D., Ge'ez flourished again as a written and ecclesiastical language in modern-day Eritrea and Ethiopia. However, after the seventeenth century, Ge'ez was only passively used as a spoken language and three new languages—Tigrinya, Tigre, and Amharic—allegedly descended from this language.

Today, Ge'ez serves only as liturgical and scriptural language of the Orthodox *Tewahdo* churches of Eritrea and Ethiopia.

Aksum had many kings, and several of them are mentioned in the ancient Greek and local inscriptions in Eritrea and Yemen. One of the most important kings of Aksum was King Ezana who ruled for some decades in the fourth century A.D. He was known for his successful military expeditions to some Nubian cities such as Kush and Moroe. Many other kings ruled Aksum before Ezana. However, apart from King Sembrouthes who was referred as "the great king" in an Eritrean inscription, not much is known about these kings (Munro-Hay 1991: 73–74). King Ezana was the first Aksumite king who converted to Christianity (333 A.D.) (see Munro-Hay 1991). His conversion facilitated the expansion of Christianity across the empire, and it had a profound impact on the Aksumite culture. Little is known about the religion of the people of Aksum during the pre-Ezana period. Yet evidence shows that the people worshipped various divinities and gods such as Asthar (with symbols of crescent moon and the sun), Mahrem, Meder, and Bihrem (Appiah and Gates 2005: 146). With the introduction of Christianity, the people of Aksum abandoned the practice of worshipping gods. Christianity was also made a state religion. Another renowned king of Aksum was Kaleb who ruled Aksum in the sixth century A.D. It was during Kaleb's rule that Aksum established strong control over vast territories of the Arabian Peninsula (for further details about Aksum see Munro-Hay 1991).

The diversity in human population resulted in the emergence of a unique, sophisticated, and entirely local civilization that included complex state organizational structures, a wide commercial network, a highly structured military system, and a unique mode of economic and social life (Yohannes 1991: 24; Munro-Hay 1991: 45–49). The empire minted its own coins (made of gold, silver, and other), starting at least by the beginning of the third century A.D. Based on its wealth (accumulated through international commerce and local production) and military strength, Aksum grew as one of the greatest early civilizations in the world. During its peak power, Aksum controlled a vast stretch of territories, including the modern northern parts of Ethiopia, Eritrea, Djibouti, southern parts of Saudi Arabia, and Yemen.

By the early seventh century A.D., Arabian immigrants are believed to have crossed the Red Sea and settled along the Eritrean coasts. Aksum is believed to have offered asylum for these Arabian immigrants who escaped persecution in the Arabian Peninsula. These immigrants were the first to introduce Islam along the coastal areas of modern Eritrea. By the eighth and ninth centuries, the Eritrean coasts and the Dahlak archipelago became home for independent Muslim families who carried the religion further to the interior of the territory (see Miran 2005: 177–185).

Little is known about the political structure of the Aksumite Empire, although there are indications that the whole system was based on features of feudal systems. Most of the powers of the empire were controlled by the king who ruled the empire and other subordinate kingdoms. Almost nothing is known about the administrative systems of the empire. Similarly, not much is known about Aksumite arts and architecture. However, based on the archaeological remains of the empire, six major architectural works could be identified: huge stelae, obelisks, stone buildings and churches, royal palaces, metal statues, and stone thrones. There was a group of the seven tallest stelae. Five of them lay in fragments across the site, and one of the seven main obelisks was transported to Rome after the Italian occupation of Ethiopia in 1935. Based on agreements between the Ethiopian and Italian governments, the main obelisk was returned to Ethiopia in 2005. The tallest of these stelae was 33 meters long. The largest standing stele is that of Ezana's Stele, which is 24 meters high (Munro-Hay 1991: 17–118).

However, Aksum's powerful civilization started to decline in the seventh century. The causes for its decline were complex but some of them included internal instability and rebellions, invasions of various peoples, and presumably short-term environmental decline.

Despite Aksum's initial amiable relations with Islam and its proponents, the rise of Muslim kingdoms along the Red Sea (in the seventh century) caused serious Arab-Aksumite conflicts. During the second half of the seventh century, naval wars were fought between the Arabs and Aksumites. These conflicts weakened the naval power of the Aksumites. The Arab naval victories also resulted in the destruction of several Aksumite commercial centers and sea outlets such as Adulis and the Dahlak islands. As a result, Aksum's international commerce along the Red Sea was heavily affected.

The decline of Aksum caused a major political fragmentation in the whole region. Although greatly affected by the political fragmentation of Aksum, Eritrea hosted various ethnolinguistic and tribal groups as well as immigrants from various parts of the region. Among the significant immigrant groups were the Beja clans who expanded from the Nile Valley southward as far as the northern, northwestern, and Red Sea coasts of Eritrea. Generally, the fall of Aksum greatly affected the dominance by the Semitic-speaking peoples, and Eritrea now became home for multicultural ethnolinguistic groups.

The Beja clans (belonging to the Cushitic-speaking linguistic family) established several states across northern and northwestern parts of Eritrea. Five significant Beja kingdoms were established in Eritrea: Quata, Bazin, Baklin, Nakis, and Jarin. One of the important features of the Beja kingdoms was the intermingling of these new immigrants with the pre-existing populations. Most Beja groups established their political and military supremacy, yet mixed themselves with the pre-existing populations without causing any significant cultural transformation. Many of them converted to Christianity (the religion of the pre-existing people) and adopted the Christian culture. Although the majority of the Beja clans were nomadic pastorals (rearing herds of camels, horses, sheep, and goats), they also practiced trade and mining of gold as well as other precious stones (see Schmidt et al 2008; Yohannes 1991: 28–29; Sherman 1980: 6–7; and Tronvoll 1998: 34–35). The Beja kingdoms declined in the fourteenth century for reasons that are not clear. Beja kingdoms are, however, still remembered in many local traditions of the people of the Eritrean highlands. Among other ethnolinguistic groups whose immigration to Eritrea took place in the same era include: many clans of the Saho (Cushitic-speaking groups) and Afar (Cushitic-speaking groups).

After the decline of Aksum, two remarkable dynastic kingdoms rose in the highlands of Ethiopia. The Zagwe Dynasty was founded by Agaw-speaking Cushitic peoples in Roha and around Lasta (in the modern Amhara region). This dynasty dominated the history of the region until 1270 when it was overthrown by the Christian Solomonic Dynasty. The fall of the Zagwe Dynasty caused waves of human migration to Eritrea. Several Agaw immigrants who escaped political persecution by the Solomonic Dynasty arrived in Eritrea. Different Agaw groups arrived in the highlands but they lost their languages and culture and intermingled with the pre-existing societies and cultures. Agaw groups such as Adkeme Melgae are today assimilated in the highland Tigrinya culture. Notable of the Agaw immigrants to Eritrea were the modern-day Bilen who occupy the middle course of the Anseba Valley. The Bilen are the only unique Agaw group who kept their language and culture albeit remarkable influence of other ethnolinguistic groups in their territories (for the history of Bilen, see Ghaber 1993).

The expansion of Islam along the Red Sea coasts of Eritrea was followed by the invasion of the Ottoman Turks. The Turks under Suleiman I and Özdemir Pasha occupied Massawa (an important commercial outlet near the sea) in 1557 (for a detailed overview of the history of the Eritrean Red Sea, see Miran 2009). The Turks attempted expansion into the highlands of Eritrea but without lasting success. Their presence was limited to Massawa and Hirgigo (a nearby city), which they controlled until the 1840s. They administered Hirgigo and its adjacent territories through Beja deputes commonly known as Naibs. Although the coastal areas were controlled by the Ottomans, the highlands and the western lowlands of Eritrea took a different course of history. As the capital of the Christian empire moved further southward to Roha and later to Shoa, it was unable to establish significant and constant control over northern territories such as Eritrea and Tigray.

THE RULE OF BAHRI NEGASI

Movement of people continued all over the Eritrean highlands throughout the fourteenth and fifteenth centuries. Founded on common religion, culture, and language, the highland people established several autonomous communal units. Later, some European travelers referred to these units as "republics" with their own respective communal codes of laws and governed by elected chiefs (See Tafla 2004: 85–86). These republics continued to expand, and later jointly created a united and an autonomous kingdom and elected their own governor called Bahre Negasi (King of the Sea). Although the precise geographical positions of this kingdom are unknown, the three major old provinces of Eritrea—Akkele Guzay, Seraye, and Hamasien—were collectively referred to as *Medri Bahri* (Land of the Sea) or *Mereb Melash* (This Side of Mereb) and were ruled by the Bahri Negasi.

Medri Bahri's survival in most cases depended on its diplomatic and military maneuvers between the Turks at the coast of the Red Sea and the Ethiopians in the South. The survival of the region as a separate political entity also relied on the military and political capability of the Bahri Negasi (Yohannes 1991: 24–35). Significant diplomatic alliances existed with Ethiopia against serious military threats such as the Ahmed Gragn invasion of 1528 to 1543.

In the 1520s, numerous Muslim sultanates from Adal and other Somali territories were united under the military and religious leadership of Ahmed bin Ibrahim, a renowned Imam (nicknamed Ahmed Gragn, meaning "Left Handed"). Ahmed Gragn managed to create a strong jihad movement against Ethiopia. Until Gragn's movement, Ethiopia was considered as a "Christian Empire," and it also went into continuous confrontation with Muslim communities in Harar and the modern Somali territories. Ahmed Gragn led a jihad war that eventually broke down almost every economic, military, political, and social system of the Ethiopian Empire. Gragn led his armies to the center of the empire and he successfully occupied Shoa (the heartland of the empire) as well as the Amhara and parts of the modern Tigray territories.

Islamic expansion in the empire involved massive forced conversion of Ethiopian Christians to Islam. The emperor and his army launched fierce resistance against Muslim expansion. However, Gragn's forces engaged them in fierce warfare for over a decade and caused massive destruction on the pre-existing cultures. The Gragn wars also resulted in the creation of an international alliance—the Ethiopian emperor allied with the Portuguese, and Gragn created alliances with the Ottoman Turks. Both the Turkish and the Portuguese involvement sought the establishment of political and military hegemony in the Red Sea region (Yohannes 1991: 31–34). The Bahri Negasi of Medri Bahri also created alliances with the Ethiopian forces and attempted resistance against Muslim expansion to his kingdom. Ahmed Gragn was finally killed in battle in 1543, and his forces disintegrated. Bahri Negasi's rule declined in the eighteenth century, and the kingdom fragmented. However, the title of the governor (Bahri Negasi) continued to exist in many parts of the highlands until the nineteenth century.

MODERN HISTORY

The Funj Sultanate of Sennar expanded from the side of Sudan while the struggle for power was still underway throughout the Eritrean plateau. The Funj warriors occupied the western and northern parts of modern Eritrea (Yohannes 1991: 33–34; Longrigg 1944: 83–87). Many clans of Barka and Sahel fell under the control of the Funj. Eritrea, which suffered from the continuous military raids of Tigrean warlords (such as Wube) during the *Zemene Mesafenti* or "The Era of Princes" (1769–1855), was also under continuous economic and political turbulence throughout these years. The internal and external military conflicts continued until the nineteenth century when the situation was further exacerbated with the arrival of the Egyptians and, later, the Italians (Tesfagiorgis G. 2007: 26).

The history of the Eritrean highlands during the eighteenth and nineteenth centuries was also greatly dominated by the rise of two rival families in Hamasien—the Hazzega and Tseazzega. These two families were locked in a long power struggle. Yet these kingdoms also established strong political and military control over the Eritrean highlands. At times, they shook and confronted the Ethiopian Empire.

In the 1840s, the Funj kingdom in the Sudan collapsed and was replaced by the Egyptians who occupied the western part of Eritrea. The Egyptians were motivated by the Khedive's ambition to control the sources of the Nile River, the southern Ethiopian highlands, and the need to establish commercial and military hegemony over the Red Sea, Persian Gulf, and the Indian Ocean. By this time, the Ottoman Empire was fragmenting, and Mohammed Ali (an Albanian in the service of the Ottoman army) of Egypt and later Khedive Ismail replaced its power in northeast Africa (Yohannes 1991: 33–34). In the 1840s, the Egyptian forces advanced toward the western parts of Eritrea as far as the Bogos territories and the Anseba Valley. In the course of their military advances, they raided many clans of Eritrea including the Bilen and Kunama.

From 1852 to 1853, the Egyptians consolidated their military presence between Kassala and Anseba. They started raiding as far as the territories of Kunama in the southwestern parts of Eritrea. The Egyptians controlled the coast of Massawa in 1847. The Egyptian advancement into Eritrea threatened the Eritrean and Ethiopian political circumstances, and so Ethiopia reacted against the Egyptian military advances and confronted the Egyptians in Eritrea. Emperor Yohannes IV (a former Tigrean chief under the name of Kassa), who had already been crowned as the "King of Kings" of the Ethiopian Empire after Emperor Tewodros's death, began to mobilize his army against the Egyptian expansion in Eritrea. In the 1870s, two major battles were fought between the Egyptian and Ethiopian armies in Eritrea: the Battle of Gundet and the Battle of Gura'e. The Ethiopian army emerged victorious in both battles.

In the 1870s, the competition for the control of Eritrea was further aggravated when the British, the French, and the Italians started to intervene in the affairs of the region. The Italians, who had already established their foothold at Assab in 1869, began to expand their military hegemony, while the British and the French continued their competition over the control of the territory.

Although Italian initiatives for colonial competition emerged relatively later than that of other European powers such as the French, they already had early ambitions of having colonies in Africa. The struggle for the unification of Italy took several years, and Italy's ambitions of having colonies in Africa did not materialize until the end of the second half of the nineteenth century. Some Italian missionaries in Eritrea, such as Father Giuseppe Sapeto, served the Italian colonial interests in Eritrea. Sapeto bought a piece of land through an Italian shipping company called *Società di Navigazione Rubattino* (The Rubattino Shipping Company) in the southeastern part of the Red Sea area (around the port city of Assab). He bought this piece of land by concluding some agreements with the local chiefs in Assab. He claimed that this land would serve as a Red Sea dock for Italian ships. However, this piece of land eventually served for further Italian expansion over Eritrea.

The Egyptian Khedive (Ismail) appointed Werner Munzinger, a Swiss explorer, as the governor of Eastern Sudan (including western and northern Eritrea) in 1872. Munzinger instigated further Egyptian expansion into the highlands of Eritrea (Tafla 2004: 86). The Egyptian forces who sought further expansion toward the south appeared to be a major threat for the Ethiopian Empire. Angered by their expansionist motives, Ethiopian Emperor Yohannes IV mobilized his army and confronted the Egyptians in Eritrea. As stated earlier, two major battles—the Battle of Gundet (1875) and the Battle of Gura'e (1876)—were fought between the Ethiopian and Egyptian armies. In both battles, the Egyptian army suffered complete defeat and lost much of its expansionist ambitions in Ethiopia and other parts of the Horn of Africa. Soon after the defeat of the Egyptians, Emperor Yohannes IV appointed a trusted military commander, Ras Alula, to be the governor of the highlands of Eritrea. Alula entrenched his army at Bet Mekae (Asmara) and Adi Teklay (northwest of Asmara) and continued raids over the lowland communities of Eritrea. However, the emperor and his commander did not attempt to establish permanent military control over the western lowlands and coastal territories of Eritrea. Rather, Ethiopia resorted to negotiations with Egypt (Tafla 2004: 86). During the negotiations, the emperor demanded war indemnity, the ceding of Massawa, and the consecration of Coptic bishops by the See of Alexandria. Alula's rule in the territory also cultivated mass discontent among the inhabitants of the region.

The 1880s were also characterized by fierce competition over the control of Eritrea. The forces of Alula were trying to expand their empire toward the north. The Egyptians were trying to preserve their old positions, and the Italians were trying to dominate the region. In addition, the Great Famine caused immense environmental catastrophe in the rural economy and society of Eritrea.

THE GREAT FAMINE (1888–1892)

The Great Famine occurred in a wider geographical territory of northeast Africa, and it was one of the worst famines in the region's recorded history. It caused major ecological and demographic shock over the region. The traditional agricultural system based on fertile soil of the highlands was sufficient enough to ensure an adequate level of sustainability during the pre-famine periods. However, the famine completely interrupted local production systems. Thousands of people in the Horn of Africa died. People were unable to overcome the problem of food shortages resulting from crop failures, the ravages of locusts, and the destruction caused by war. The result was that prosperity deteriorated, leading to serious famines followed by various types of epidemic diseases such as cholera (Pankhurst 1964: 1–25).

A rinderpest epidemic (a viral disease that oral history indicates was introduced to the Eritrean coasts by infected horses from India that were used by the Italian army in the Red Sea area) accompanied the famine and it decimated cattle herds across the region. This epidemic started in Semhar and advanced toward the highlands and further south, eliminating all types of cattle. The rinderpest epidemic resulted in the loss of large numbers of livestock, which caused a major decline in the ox-plough system of agriculture. In turn, this led to the loss of human control over the natural environment (Tesfagiorgis G. 2007: 75). The lack of adequate rain from 1888 to 1889 was also accompanied by the influx of pests, locusts, and caterpillars—swarms of all types invaded the region. The combination of cattle plague and harvest failure resulted in a sudden rise in the cost of all food items (Pankhurst 1964: 1–15). There was a sharp increase of mortality rate throughout the years of famine, and it is believed that the whole region lost about one-third of its human population. In addition, about three-quarters of the livestock in the northeastern African region are believed to have perished because of the rinderpest. Anarchic political circumstances were created in which militarily superior groups, warriors, and outlaws seized and looted stored grains and other sources of food. The ecological equilibrium was highly affected, and subsistence production systems disrupted. The Great Famine affected human coping strategies. "People who had their own mechanisms of environmental control and management during the pre-famine ecology now lost everything, and their pre-famine survival strategies broke down" (Tesfagiorgis G. 2007: 76).

The years of the Great Famine were characterized by a massive exodus of people who deserted their villages and attempted to survive in other ecological zones of the region. Many highland farmers were forced to abandon their farming fields and migrated to the north and coastal areas. The Italians had established their admin-istration in Massawa and its vicinities in the 1880s. Hence, many people moved to the port city in search of jobs. On the other hand, these turbulent years created an opportunity for the Italians to expand their control over the Eritrean highlands without facing stubborn resistance. The famine circumstances also provided the Italians with an apparent justification for applying policies of land confiscation. The impact of the Great Famine continued to be felt in the entire region for over a decade. Livestock and agricultural production took many years to revive and meet subsistence food demands. Moreover, rinderpest remains to be a major threat to the stock breeding sec-tor to this day.

ITALIAN COLONIALISM IN ERITREA

As noted above, Italy purchased a piece of land around Assab in 1869 through a shipping company. This piece of land helped Italy gain its first step in creating colo-nies in northeast Africa. As many other parts of Africa were falling under the direct control of European colonizers, Italy declared Assab as its first colony in July 1882. In a few years, Italy made an expansionist attempt northward, and it successfully incorporated Massawa as part of its colony in the area. Italy attempted further coloni-zation on the coastal plains and the plateau. Its occupation of Massawa and its expansion toward the Semhar Plains was already considered a threat to the survival of Ethiopia; and its attempts of expansion into the highlands stirred the anger of Ethiopian Emperor Yohannes IV. The emperor perceived that the final destination of Italian expansion along the coasts would be the occupation of the whole Ethiopian Empire. This was considered a grave threat, and the emperor, through his military commander, Ras Alula Engeda, thwarted the Italian encroachment toward the high-lands at the Battle of Dogali in 1887. A garrison of around 500 Italians was crushed in this battle, after which Italy declared war on Ethiopia.

Meanwhile, the hegemonic power of Emperor Yohannes IV started to face serious challenges from Sudan in the 1880s. The Mahdists threatened Ethiopia from the north-west of the territory. Mahdism was an Islamic movement whose followers believed the Messiah would appear to establish a world of justice, peace, and righteousness. The Mahdi (the leader of the Mahdists) also assumed the role of Messiah. The Mahdists were based in the Anglo-Egyptian Sudan, and Mahdism proved to be one of the most damaging instruments, and the cause of bloodshed in the Horn of Africa in general and Eritrea/Ethiopia in particular during the 1880s and 1890s (Tesfagiorgis G. 2007: 28). Alula, the governor of the Eritrean territory, who had defeated the Italian army at the Battle of Dogali, was summoned by the emperor during his struggle against the Mahdists (1888–1889). The emperor attempted resistance against the Mahdist occupa-tion in the northwestern parts of today's Ethiopia. However, he was killed at the Battle of Metema. This gave the Italians a chance to advance into the highlands and western lowlands of Eritrea without facing fierce local resistance. As mentioned, the Italian advancement toward the highlands of Eritrea was facilitated by the ecological and political chaos of the time. The Italians also, in cooperation with local forces, fought fierce battles against Mahdists. The Mahdists suffered a number of defeats in the

Italo-Dervish (Mahdists) war at the battle of Akordat, 1891. (Martini, Ferdinando (1896). Nel Africa Italiana: Impressioni e ricordi. Milano, n.a. Page 277.)

western parts of Eritrea. By the 1890s, the Italians consolidated their power in the Eritrean region.

During this period, famine badly affected the whole population in the territory, and therefore, there was no substantial organized local resistance against Italian military expansion. By the end of 1889 the Italians occupied almost all of the highlands and lowlands of Eritrea. Eventually, in 1890, King Umberto II of Italy and his Prime Minister Crispi declared Eritrea an Italian colony. Yet military conflicts resumed and Eritrea was soon made a military base for the Italian ambitions (especially after 1922 when a Fascist regime under Benito Mussolini took office in Italy) of establishing its *Africa Orientale Italiana*: an "Italian East African Empire" that would include Eritrea, Ethiopia, and Italian Somaliland.

Italian colonial policies were generally inconsistent and contradictory. However, there were four principal objectives of Italian colonial policies in Eritrea. First, policies focused on extending Italian colonial administration and securing military power over Eritrea. Second, policies focused on establishing European settlement domains as well as creating opportunities for new Italian settlers in the colony. Third, the creation of an ideal sociopolitical platform for the maximum exploitation of natural resources (such as agriculture, livestock, forestry, and minerals), which they presumed would be an economic benefit for Italy. Moreover, the colonial state considered Eritrea as an important market for Italian manufactured goods. Fourth, colonial policies aimed at making Eritrea a military base for further Italian expansion and conquest in the Horn of Africa. Therefore, the Italian colonial administration in Eritrea focused on equipping the colony with the necessary infrastructure intended for military purposes (see also Negash 1987; Mesghenna 1988).

Massawa administrative office in the early 1890s, during festive event after the defeat of the Mahdists. (Schoenfeld, E. Dagobert (1904). Erythräa und der Ägyptische Sudan. Berlin: Dietrich Beimer Press.)

During the first phase of colonial rule in Eritrea (1885–1896), the Italians focused on the consolidation of their power. The Italian government considered Eritrea as part of a means to solving land shortages in southern Italy as well as unemployment problems, and so, it applied policies of agricultural colonization in many parts of the colony. Italian authorities, especially Prime Minister Crispi and Leopoldo Franchetti, considered Eritrea as a vital source of agriculture and subsistence commodities. Between 1893 and 1896, over 400,000 hectares of farming lands were confiscated in Eritrea, and landless Italian settlers were encouraged to migrate to Eritrea, where they received farming lands as well as subsidies for commercial agriculture. However, the policy of land expropriation cultivated serious local resentment among the Eritrean peasantry. In December 1894, Eritrean resistance against Italian policies in Eritrea was manifested under the leadership of *Degiat* Bahta Hagos, who had since 1889 been a trusted ally to the Italians in the expansion and consolidation of their rule in the Eritrean highlands. Note that *Degiat* was one type of the local titles given to indigenous chiefs.

Bahta Hagos was born into a peasant family in Segeneity in the 1840s. He became prominent after killing Embaye Araya in October 1875, the son of Araya Demasu, a Tigrean warlord. The soldiers of Embaye raided and looted Akkele Guzay and the locality of Bahta Hagos. Afraid of revenge from the Tigrean warlord Araya, Bahta went into the jungles of Agemeda where he lived along with his two brothers and a dozen of his armed followers until the early 1880s. He withdrew to Habab (northern Eritrea) after Ras Alula was appointed governor of the region in 1879. When the

A SHORT LIST OF ERITREAN NOTABLES IMPRISONED AND EXECUTED AT NAKURA

Located in the Dahlak archipelagoes, Nakura was one of the most brutal prisons during the Italian colonial period. The colonial administration detained many local chiefs and notables at Nakura. The following is a short list of some of the prisoners:

1. Dejazmach Hadgembes Gilwet (Adi Tekelezan, Hamassien)
2. Dejazmach Kifleyesus Gofar (Hamassien)
3. Dejazmach Negusse Gebretsadek (Areza, Seraye)
4. Dejzmach Mahray Hagos (Adi Wegera, Akkele Guzay)
5. Fitewrari Habtesiyon Mebrahtu (Himberti, Hamassien)
6. Kentiba Arey Woldu (Qushet, Hamassien)
7. Kentiba Woldegergis Teklay (Arato, Akkele Guzay)
8. Mohammed Osman Buri (Tio, Dankalia)
9. Sheikh Fekak Ali (Keren, Senhit)
10. Sheikh Osman Naib (Massawa, Semhar)
11. Yilmma Kifleyesus (Dembellas, Seraye)
12. Zeray Okbazghi (Afelba, Akkele Guzay)

Italians occupied Massawa in 1885, Bahta was requested to join the Italian army. In 1888, he joined the Italian army in Massawa, and he was soon promoted by the Italians as the chief of *banda* (native soldiers). He assisted the Italians during their expansion into the plateau, and, as a reward, he was made the chief of the Akkele Guzay province.

However, irritated by the Italian policies of land expropriation and segregation, Bahta Hagos organized a major revolt in December 1894. On December 13, 1894, he arrested Major Sanguneti (the Italian administrator of Segeneity) and cut the telegraph lines connecting the town with other Italian bases in the colony. Leading his 2,000 armed men, he marched against an Italian fortification at Halai, where he died on December 17, 1894.

Although the revolt of Bahta Hagos was crushed in few days, it shocked the Italian administration in Eritrea. Among many other impacts of the revolt, the Italian authorities in Eritrea were compelled to reconsider their land policies in the colony. This created a sense of insecurity among the Italians, and the administration started to apply policies of reconciliation by which it offered forgiveness to those who fought on the side of Bahta Hagos. Bahta Hagos became a symbol of resistance throughout the colony. To this day, Bahta Hagos is remembered as an anticolonial resistance figure, and one of his famous epigrams entered into popular memory.

"ሰንጋል ሓወይ እምብዛ ኣይትዓሹ፣	*"Sengal, my brother, do not be so silly,*
ገብረመድህን ሓወይ እምብዛ ኣይትዓሹ፣	*Gebremedhen, my brother, do not be so silly,*
ጻዕዳ ተመን እንድሕር ነኺሱ፣	*If a white snake bites you,*
ደላሊኻ ኣይርከብን'ዩ ፈውሱ።"	*You will find no cure for it."*

The first phase of Italian rule in Eritrea was also characterized by Italian ambitions of occupation of Ethiopia. Italian ambition of colonizing Ethiopia, however, ended at the Battle of Adowa in 1896, where the Italian army suffered complete defeat by the troops of Emperor Menelik of Ethiopia.

During the second phase of Italian colonialism in Eritrea (1895–1932) the colonial government focused on policies designed for the exploitation of the colony's natural resources, as well as the build-up of the colony's administrative and economic infrastructures. Studies and explorations of mineral resources such as gold, nickel, copper, iron ore, chromium, and others resumed for years. By the end of the 1930s, the colonial administration embarked on massive exploitation of minerals and precious stones across the colony. It extended its gold-mining centers in the highlands and the western lowlands with an intensive effort to exploit as much gold as possible.

Although the economic situation remained the same for most rural communities, the colonial state made remarkable investment on infrastructural development. An infrastructure of roads, railroads, ropeways, ports, telecommunications, and administrative posts were built. The development of these infrastructures had an important contribution for the integrity of the territory. The construction of roads, railroads, telegraph, telephone, and postal services connected different territories of the colony. This in turn resulted in the creation of relative stability throughout the colony. Crispi and Franchetti's plans of agricultural colonization were not fully carried out (for detailed analysis see Mesghenna 1988: 86–105; Negash 1987). Rather, Eritrea served as the main supplier of colonial soldiers who facilitated the consolidation of its rule in Libya and Somalia.

The third phase of Italian colonialism in Eritrea (1932–1941) focused on the expansion of Italian colonial rule in the Horn of Africa. During this phase, Ethiopia was targeted as the main territory to be occupied by the Italian army. The Italians, who somehow wanted to exercise revenge against their defeat at the Battle of Adowa in 1896, made preparations for the outright invasion of Ethiopia. The Italian preparations for the Ethiopian invasion involved drastic economic and military changes in Eritrea. In preparation for the war, Italy imported over 50,000 skilled Italian laborers and over

A group of Eritrean ascaris under training. (Martini, Ferdinando (1896). Nel Africa Italiana: Impressioni e ricordi. Milano, n.a. p. 113.)

300,000 troops to Eritrea. The Italians also made a massive investment in constructing/ modifying transportation and communication infrastructures. The war situation trans- formed Eritrea into one of the most powerful industrial and commercial centers in Africa. Over 60,000 Eritreans were also recruited as colonial soldiers. The short eco- nomic boom created by the war economy resulted in the emergence of a remarkable wage-labor market as well as the expansion of urban centers.

As noted, the Italian land and agricultural policies in Eritrea had not been success- ful. The colonial government attempted to expropriate vast arable lands in the high- lands and lowlands of Eritrea. However, these policies failed for reasons such as fierce local resistance, a lack of significant capital investment, and poor systems of viable land resource management. In principle, the colonial government annulled pol- icies of land expropriation by 1895; and it embarked on policies that could result in conciliatory relations with the local peasants. Nonetheless, it continued to confiscate arable lands under the pretext of *Dominale* (state-controlled land available for lease). Through decrees in 1903, 1909, and 1926 the colonial government subsequently con- fiscated vast arable lands in the highlands and lowlands of the colony. Until 1908, the colonial government had managed to expropriate over 482,000 hectares of arable land across the colony. Moreover, land lying below 350 meters above sea level was all put under *Dominale* tenure. (For further studies on the Italian land policies, see Mesghenna 1988; Negash 1987; Taddia 1986.)

The colonial state's social, educational, and employment policies were particularly designed to limit the development of an Eritrean working skill. Modern education was introduced by the colonial state, but neither generously nor consistently. Prior to the 1930s, education was in the hands of European missionaries. Yet it was also designed to be an instrument enhancing colonial rule in Eritrea. The quality of education as well

Group of local militia in Carneshim, Eritrea. (Martini, Ferdinando (1896). Nel Africa Italiana: Impressioni e ricordi. Milano, n.a., p. 89.)

as the admission of students to the Italian schools was highly controlled by the colonial administration. By the late 1930s, there were only 20 elementary schools accessible to Eritreans. Colonial policies also restricted Eritreans to only occupying positions as low-paid clerks or manual laborers (Taye 1991: 1–32).

THE CONSTRUCTION OF RAILROADS

Infrastructural development was considered by the colonial state as an essential part of its progressive expansionist ambitions. Therefore, the Italian military expansion toward the Eritrean hinterland was also accompanied by the construction of railroads. The first railroad line was constructed in 1888 between the port of Massawa on the Red Sea coast and Sa'atit (located in the Semhar Plains). However, prior to the fascist regime the process of constructing railroads was not prompt. By 1911, the single railroad line connected the port of Massawa with the capital city, Asmara. The construction of the railroad line between Asmara and Massawa was, however, a significant task. The landscape between Massawa and Asmara is characterized by rough and ragged mountains that made railroad construction very difficult. It also necessitated the construction of over 64 bridges and 35 small tunnels. A large number of Eritrean workers were also employed in the construction of railroad lines throughout the years.

The Massawa-Asmara-Akordat-Bisha railway line (ca. 337 kilometers or 209.4 miles) was accomplished between the years 1887 and 1932. It was constructed by crossing or tunneling through over 1,540 mountains and hills. It connected about 30 small stations.

In addition to its military functions, the construction of railway and roads facilitated the economic integration between the highlands and the eastern lowlands. The port of Massawa continued to develop into a commercial center and an outlet to the sea where most of the commercial resources were brought for export. Imported items were transported to the hinterland via the newly constructed infrastructures. The construction of the railroad was designed to serve as an important system for facilitating the exploitation of natural resources from all over the colony. The railroad was further extended to the western lowlands where the colonial state believed that it would also facilitate agricultural production and investment in the region. By 1928, the railroad connected Asmara and the town of Akordat. Yet, the construction of railroads was a slow development after 1928. This could be attributed to the fact that the colonial administration was occupied by plans of expansion toward Ethiopia. By the 1930s, the plan of connecting Eritrea with eastern Sudan via railroad was abandoned. For details regarding the distance and year of construction, see Table R under the "Facts and Figures" section of this book.

The construction of railroads in Eritrea made a remarkable contribution to the economic integration of the colony. Moreover, it facilitated the social interaction of populations living in different ecological zones of the territory. By the 1930s, many people used the railroad systems as a means of daily transportation. In addition, a number of small towns such as Nefasit, Embatkalla, and Ghindae emerged as important trading centers and railroad stations.

Workers at Massawa train station, early 1890s. (Martini, Ferdinando (1896). Nel Africa Italiana: Impressioni e ricordi. Milano, n.a., p. 28.)

Because of ill-considered policies during and after the British rule in Eritrea, the railway system continued to become an inefficient means of transport. Yet, this Italian-built railroad continued to function until the 1970s. Due to continuous war, however, function of the railroads continued to diminish until it was eventually damaged in 1975. Railroad transport completely stopped functioning when rail materials were disrupted and used by both parties of the war for building up fortifications and trenches. In 1994, the government initiated some new projects for the reconstruction and rehabilitation of the Eritrean railways. Therefore, the Massawa-Asmara railway line was rebuilt in 2003.

THE CONSTRUCTION OF ROADS

Another point of emphasis of the Italian colonial administration in Eritrea was the construction of road networks connecting major towns and cities throughout colony. Despite all the problems created by the nature of landscape, the Italians were able to construct a remarkable system of road network. Most of the road construction schemes involved thousands of Eritrean laborers. As stated, the bulk of the Eritrean male working force was conscripted to the colonial army, which created a reduced labor force within the colony; hence, the construction of a transport network demanded more workers from different regions. A large number of laborers were imported from Ethiopia, Yemen, and Somalia as well as from Italy and other parts of Europe. However, wages were not paid on equal bases and there were remarkable wage differences between European and African workers. The type of work that demanded skill was often reserved for European workers, while Africans served as casual or manual laborers. Moreover, African workers were kept in poor facility conditions, paid low wages, and suffered from bad treatment by Italian employers.

In addition to the road networks that were constructed for provisional purposes (such as around military headquarters), about 550 kilometers (341.7 miles) of long asphalt roads were constructed connecting Asmara to other major towns such as Deqemhare, Mendefera, Keren, and many other small towns. Although many of the road networks were constructed before the 1930s, the major road systems were modified in the 1930s; and about 1,400 kilometers (870 miles) of new roads were constructed during the 1930s.

Although the construction of road networks was intended for Italian military use, their contribution to the Eritrean economy was no less notable. Their function as transport facilities remained significant long after the Italians had left the country. The efficient transport system in Eritrea had an important role in the short-term economic boom of the 1930s and 1940s. These roads continue to be the core transport systems in today's Eritrea.

THE CONSTRUCTION OF ROPEWAY

Ropeway is a type of gondola, or aerial, lift by which goods are usually transported from one place to another. It is also known as a cableway or cable car. This system of transport is driven by an electric motor connected to a major wheel engine. Such transport systems are mostly located in areas where there is intensive exploitation of natural resources such as forests, mineral resources, or other mining areas.

Another amazing means of transport during the Italian colonial rule in Eritrea, the ropeway was the longest of its kind in the world during that time (71 kilometers or 44.1 miles long). The ropeway connected Asmara with Massawa and became an efficient means of transport for goods. The Asmara-Massawa ropeway had the capacity of transporting over 700 tons of property each day. Moreover, the colonial administration also constructed short-distance ropeways intended to facilitate the transportation of exploited natural resources such as forest resources. One example of such a ropeway was constructed in south Eritrea and connected the major forest area of Meteten and Hebo (ca. ten kilometers or 6.2 miles long) (see also Tesfagiorgis G. 2007).

URBANIZATION DURING THE COLONIAL PERIOD

The construction of various communication infrastructures was accompanied by the growth of small towns. These towns flourished in areas where, for example, railway and ropeway constructions established small stations such as in Nefasit, Embatkalla, and Ghindae. Other towns such as Mendefera, Deqemhare, Segeneity, and Adi Qeyyih emerged alongside new road construction networks and where the Italian army stationed. Policies of segregation were implemented in urban areas resulting in the subdivisions of urban centers into "European" and "African" quarters. Asmara, which was an important market town in the Hamasien plateau before the Italian occupation, was transformed into a major urban city during the colonial period. In the following paragraphs we shall see a case of rapid urbananization of the city of Asmara. Please note that part of the information contained in this section is extracted from an article published by the author in 2006 (see Tesfagiorgis 2006: 287–294).

ASMARA

Asmara (usually known by its dwellers as Asmera), the capital city of Eritrea, is located at about 115 kilometers (71.4 miles) southwest of Massawa at an altitude of about 2,360 meters above sea level. Asmara is roughly located in the center of Eritrea, in the old province of Hamasien. The city is also believed to have had a considerable significance during the Aksumite times (first century–seventh century A.D.).

According to oral traditions, the name Asmara was derived from an event when four small, rival villages in the area united. Geographically, Asmara lies midway between the ancient port of Massawa and the country's interior. There had been some trade routes that connected the town with Massawa (at the Red Sea coast) and other precolonial towns on the Eritrean plateau. Local tradition indicates that four *Gezawti* (houses, meaning family groups or clans)—*Geza Gurotom, Geza Shelele, Geza Serenser,* and *Geza Asma'e*—were located around and within the modern city of Asmara. However, these villages were rivals and also suffered from *shifta* (banditry), looting in the area. The atrocities committed by the *shifta* worsened the conflicts and tensions among these villages. In addition, the dense forests around these villages hosted great numbers of various wild animals and beasts that attacked villagers. Desperate to find solutions to these problems, the women of the four clans, or houses, eventually decided to bring the conflict to an end by convincing the men in the villages to settle their differences and face the external threats cohesively (see also Tesfagiorgis 2006: 287–294). The villagers jointly defeated the bandits, and the four villages unified. The treaty of cooperation among the four villages, which took place in November 1508, ended all rivalries and the villages agreed to unify (Yosief 1993: 11–13). The name Asmara (literally meaning—"they [fem.] unified") was given to the united four families in honor of the women of the four clans (see also Tesfagiorgis 2006: 287–294).

The political circumstances of the 1870s notably affected Asmara. In addition to the effects of military and political rivalries between the two ruling families of Hamasien—Hazzega and Tseazzega—Asmara was profoundly affected by the continuous attempts of Emperor Yohannes IV of modern Ethiopia to gain control over the city. Asmara had been a battlefield at least two times during that period—in the battles between the forces of the two Hamasien families the area suffered heavy destruction. In the early 1870s, Ra'esi Woldemichael Solomon, after consolidating his military power over Hazzega, established his control over Asmara (Tesfagiorgis 2006: 287–290).

Against the odds created by war, the population of Asmara continued to grow, and by the 1870s the total population of the city was estimated at 5,000 (Wylde 1888: I: 216). Yet during the initial period of Italian occupation, the population of the town fell to 800 in the first half of 1890s (Locatelli 2004: 89–110). Ra'esi Woldemichael Solomon's consolidation of military power over the Hamassien annoyed Emperor Yohannes and he sent one of his trusted commanders, Ras Bariau, to fight in 1878. Bariau arrived in Asmara commanding a large army and fortified in *Campo Cintato* (within the town). Battles were fought between the forces of Bariau and Woldemichael in Asmara where Bariau was defeated and lost his life in the war at the Battle of Asmara (Tesfagiorgis 2006: 287–294). Despite all the military turmoil, Asmara continued to be an important market place in the Hamasien plateau. A number of local and foreign items such as silk, wax, honey, cattle, and the like were sold and exchanged in the weekly market of Asmara. The market was also visited by merchants, peasants, soldiers, and so forth.

Desperate to establish military control over the territory, Emperor Yohannes appointed another military commander, Ras Alula Engida, to fight Ra'esi Woldemichael and the Egyptians in 1879. Alula fortified his army in a nearby village (Adi Teklay, some 40 kilometers or 24.8 miles west of Asmara). In 1884, he moved 8,000 to 12,000 armed men to Asmara. This time, Alula made his fortification at Bet Mekae, and he extended his raids to the lowlands of the territory. The occupation of Alula is believed to have had a remarkable impact on Asmara; it became more like a military camp until it was occupied by the Italians in 1889 (Tesfagiorgis 2006: 287–294).

Yet, by 1888–1889, the political circumstances of the territory changed. The Mahdists invaded the domains of Emperor Yohannes and Alula was summoned by the emperor to fight against the Mahdist advances. After Asmara was abandoned by Alula and his army, the Italians who already occupied Massawa in 1885 began to advance toward Asmara. Asmara was occupied by the Italians on August 3, 1889. In 1890, Eritrea was declared an Italian colony and Asmara was made *campo di zona* (central commanding area) for further Italian expansion in the Horn of Africa. In 1897, Ferdinando Martini was appointed as the governor of the newly created colony, Eritrea. He then made Asmara the capital of the colony the same year. Asmara was selected as the capital of the colony mainly for its location (equidistant to the mostly inhabited towns of Massawa, Keren, Adi Ugri, Deqemhare, and Segeneity), its preferable military fortifications, and for its infrastructure (Checchi 1910: 4; Tesfagiorgis 2006: 291). Prior to 1900, Asmara had only a few modern buildings: the house of Padre Bonomi, the old *commissariato*, part of the *carcceli* prison, part of the railway service, the villa of the *comandante delle Real Truppe* (Royal Army building), and a small club reserved for the Italian officials (Checchi 1910: 4–5; Tesfagiorgis 2006: 291). The few private houses were located around a *zona* called *May Bela*.

By 1900, massive construction of houses started all over the Asmara area. A remarkable number of new buildings were constructed, and the state drafted a new city plan in 1902 and began implementing it in 1908. Strikingly, the new town plan of Asmara divided the town into three "areas of settlement" (Locatelli 2004: 24–30; Tesfagiorgis 2006: 291), which were: zones reserved for people of Italian origin (mainly central parts of the town); the zone reserved for mixed descent; and the zone reserved for natives. The construction of buildings was accompanied by the construction on road networks. By 1902, at least two main roads were built within the city. The *Corso dal Re* and *Via Ilena Regina* (today's *Awet Street* and *Semaetat Street,* respectively) became the main roads of the town. Horse-driven carts and vehicles started to frequent the town for the first time along those streets (Yosief 1993: 23–30).

The city started to attract many working population groups (from the rural areas) during its massive construction period. Based on the census of 1905, the population of Asmara had reached 8,597—1,556 of which were whites (Checchi 1910: 7). However, the population of the city dramatically increased, and by 1910, it reached 36,853. The city continued to grow into a trading center. By 1907, it was characterized by a remarkable flow of capital and notable trading activities. Cattle, wax, cotton, feather, coffee, honey, silk, and textiles were some of the trading items in the markets of Asmara. At the same time, construction plans continued. By 1905 and 1906 several palaces were built: the palace of the governor; the first Italian school; and the court

Asmara in 1900. (Istituto Agricolo Coloniale (1946). Eritrea—Some Photographic Representations of Italy's actions. Firenze, n.a., p. 46.)

Asmara in 1912. (Istituto Agricolo Coloniale (1946). Eritrea—Some Photographic Representations of Italy's actions. Firenze, n.a., p. 46.)

building (Tesfagiorgis 2006: 292). A number of public institutions were also established in those years, such as the Institute of Serum Vaccination and the Asmara Electric Plant. In addition, 100 private houses were constructed between 1902 and 1905. Some remarkable public buildings were also built between 1902 and 1906; for example, the synagogue was completed in 1906. Throughout the first decade of colonial rule in Eritrea, a single military hospital treated both army and civilian patients (Tesfagiorgis 2006: 292–293).

The Italian occupation of Asmara was characterized by a significant growth in industrialization. A number of industrial plants were constructed in the city between 1901 and 1910. Some of the most important industrial plants of the time were the *Gandolfi* factory, which produced miscellaneous products such as pasta, bread, oil, and purified water; the *Stabilimento Cinerello* factory, which produced electric power; and the *Vauedetto* factory (Checchi 1910: 5–13; Tesfagiorgis 2006: 292–293). The most important event in Asmara during the early years of the 1900s was the start of its vibrant urbanization process.

The onset of new construction and industrial plants attracted thousands of indigenous workers. By 1910, manual laborers fled the city and the working class was founded. The newly established factories as well as new construction projects attracted laborers from the rural areas of the colony. Among the major construction accomplishments during the first three decades of the Italian presence in Eritrea were: the Asmara Cathedral (finished in 1922); the Asmara Theatre (finished in 1918); and the Supreme Court. These were among the noteworthy construction projects that attracted workers from the rural areas. The Italian authorities drafted the first city plan in 1902, and revised in 1908. These city plans were implemented in 1916. As stated earlier, the new decree was based on policies of segregation, but this time a new settlement zone was added: the "industrial zone" (Tesfagiorgis 2006: 293–294). Under the provisions of this decree, indigenous populations were prohibited from settling within the central parts of the city. As noted, the Italian administration in the colony, especially the Fascist Party, began drawing up plans to invade Ethiopia in the 1930s. This time, the colonial state used Asmara as an important base for its plans of a new invasion. As a result, the fascist ideology encouraged constructing a new base for the ambition of establishing an ancient Rome in Africa, which would serve as *pax*

Romana in Africa. Hence, the colonial state justified its ambitions by constructing extravagant and symbolic buildings such as the modern Ministry of Education of Eritrea. The colonial state continued to construct a number of new road networks, and it connected main towns such as Deqemhare, Adi Ugri, Massawa, Keren, and Adi Qeyyih with considerable capital and labor investments (Tesfagiorgis 2006: 294–295).

The road networks expanded and connected the colony as far as the areas bordering Ethiopia, such as Zalambessa and Adi Kwala. In addition, the colonial state established a new airport in the city of Asmara that served as the main international airport. At the same time, the colonial state imported a great number of military personnel, thus transforming the city more or less into a military base. The arrival of thousands of Italian soldiers and skilled personnel to Eritrea justified the colonial invasion of Ethiopia in the 1930s. Asmara's population increased dramatically and, by 1937 (according to the census of the *Commissariato dell'Hamasien*), it reached 101,724 inhabitants (3,236 were Europeans). The remarkable increase in migration from rural areas and the massive construction projects in the city facilitated the process of urbanization of Asmara (Checchi 1910: 5–13; Tesfagiorgis 2006: 292–293).

As part of development for the city, a progressive municipality system was established. This was partly necessitated by the rapid growth of population and urbanization of the city itself. "Municipal administrators, councils and commissioners were appointed under the decrees of 1935 and 1936. The bases for bureaucracy were founded, and Asmara expanded its commercial and industrial capacity. The fascist massive urban development of the 1930s put Asmara to hold an important position in the *Africa Orientale Italiana*. The streets were widened; the number of bars, cafés, restaurants, cinemas and theatre centers doubled" (Tesfagiorgis 2006: 294–295; see also Beyene 1964).

The city continued to become an important commercial center in the territory although the British occupation (1941–1952) did not bring about remarkable changes in the architecture and infrastructure of the city. By the 1940s Asmara had to accommodate thousands of *askaries* (native Italian ex-soldiers) who returned after serving for the Italian army in various parts of Africa, such as Libya. Asmara became an important center for nationalist movements during the post-Italian colonialism years. A number of foreign powers became interested in the strategic location of the city. For instance, since the early period of the British occupation of Eritrea, the United States wished to establish a communication base in the city. Eventually, the United States established one of the renowned military communication bases in the Horn of Africa, called Kagnew. A number of satellite military bases belonging to the United States were also established in the city, such as the Radio Marina.

The Ethiopian occupation of Eritrea resulted in adverse consequences for Asmara. The city was transformed into more of a military base, and many Ethiopian army divisions were deployed in the city. The Ethiopian army reserved several parts of the city for its use, and civilians were prohibited from entering or settling in those areas. A number of the buildings constructed during the Italian period were converted into horrific prisons. "A good example of the prisons located in Asmara was *Mariyam Gimbi*, where thousands of people were tortured and killed. The name Red Terror applied in the city during the 1980s when the Ethiopian army transformed the city from a beautiful and attractive city into an isolated military camp. However, the importance of the city as a commercial center continued to grow against all the odds of Ethiopian Red Terror" (Tesfagiorgis 2006: 295).

The Eritrean People's Liberation Front (EPLF) occupied the city in May 1991, and it soon became the heart of political and economic activities in the state. After the country's independence, new construction started along with new housing complexes such as: the *enda korya* "Korea Housing" (a city quarter where new modular housing complexes were built by Korean companies) and *Space* 2000 (another city quarter where new modular housing complexes were built by a company called Space 2000). A new international hotel, the Intercontinental Hotel, was constructed, and Asmara continued to transform into one of the most modern cities in Africa. However, Asmara's citizens are still concerned with the issue of housing although the city has shown remarkable growth since independence. Still, the construction of housing complexes has not yet satisfied the demands of Asmara inhabitants. Today (as of January 2010) the population of the city is roughly estimated at 405,000.

ADMINISTRATION

The colonial state divided Eritrea into seven administrative provinces (*commissariati*): Akkele Guzay, Seraye, Hamasien, Barka, Senhit, Sahel, Semhar, and Denkalia (Gayim 1993: 59–60). Each administrative province was also subdivided into several *residenzas* (districts). Each province had its own administration commissioner whose main task was to maintain law, order, and the execution of colonial policies. The Italian administration established municipality offices in seven provincial capital towns and cities. These municipalities were administered by the mayor (*commissare*) of the

Weekly market in Segeneity. (Mulazzani, A. (1903). Geografia della colonia Eritrea. Florence: R. Bemporad & Figlio, p. 58.)

towns whose main tasks included revenue collection. The *Commissariati* were further subdivided into *residenze* (districts) and *vice-residenze* (sub-districts).

The judiciary system was administered under four major systems: the Italian Penal Code, the Italian Civil Code, the *Sharia* Law, and the Eritrean Customary Law. The Italian Penal Code was applied to all inhabitants, while the Italian Civil Code was mostly applied to Italian settlers or cases involving Italian citizen(s). The *Sharia* was applied where both parties were Moslems. The Eritrean Customary Law was community based, and it was applied in civil cases between Eritreans. The *Sharia* and Eritrean Customary Laws were normally social guidelines and legal judiciary systems in most districts and villages. These communal laws had been used by the Eritrean communities for many centuries before the arrival of the Italians.

ERITREAN COLONIAL BOUNDARIES

As with most African countries, today's geographical shape of Eritrea is the result of an artificial creation of colonialism. The creation of Eritrea involved regional and international treaties and agreements.

The Eritrean-Ethiopian boundary was recognized on the bases of the Italo-Ethiopian agreements in 1900, 1902, and 1908. The initial Italian occupation of parts of Eritrea was recognized by Ethiopia under the Treaty of Wuchale on May 2, 1889. Under this treaty, a long border was drawn between the territories under Italian control and Ethiopia. The border runs from Irafaile via Segeneity to Halai, Adi Nefas, Asmara, and Adi Yohannes. In principle, the Treaty of Wuchale recognized the establishment of Italy's protectorate over Eritrea. Because the Italians continued to occupy more territories beyond the agreed-to line in the Treaty of Wuchale, another treaty took place in Addis Ababa on July 10, 1900. Under this agreement, a new border line, the Mereb-Belesa-Muna line, was recognized as the common border. Yet, no final delimitation of the borders of Eritrea and Ethiopia was agreed to in the southern Red Sea until May 16, 1908. The delimitation of the Eritrean-Ethiopian border line, some 60 kilometers (37.2 miles) from the Red Sea coasts along the Denkalia zone, was finally recognized by the two parties in 1908.

The delimitation of Eritrean colonial boundaries with the Anglo-Egyptian Sudan took place in 1901 and 1902. By 1901, the Italians claimed and already occupied Kassala, which was eventually ceded to Anglo-Egyptian Sudan. This part of Sudan was one of the grazing areas for several ethnolinguistic groups in Eritrea. However, the delimitation of the boundaries between Anglo-Egyptian Sudan, Italy, and Ethiopia was finally agreed to during the Treaty of Addis Ababa on May 15, 1902. Although the British were interested in annexing the Gash and parts of Barka into the Anglo-Egyptian Sudan, the areas were integrated within the Eritrean territory by the agreements of the Treaty of Addis Ababa. Similarly, the borders with the French protectorate (Djibouti) were defined in two agreements and protocols that took place in 1900 and 1901. The delimitation of all these border lines separated several ethnolinguistic groups such as the Tigrinya, Saho, Tigre, and Afar.

These borders were acknowledged until the end of the colonial era. However, border issues have become major sources of regional conflict in the Horn of Africa in the postcolonial period. In 1968, Sudan and Ethiopia claimed some territories in western parts of Eritrea. This resulted in heightened tensions between the two countries. Border issues have also become major sources of conflict after Eritrean independence. The Hanish Islands along the Red Sea were claimed by Eritrea and Yemen in 1995. The dispute over these islands resulted in military clashes between the two countries. The conflict was eventually resolved by the verdict of the International Court. Moreover, territories along the Eritrea-Ethiopian borders, such as Bademe, Zalambessa, and Bada, were claimed by both countries in the late 1990s. Military conflicts erupted in 1998, resulting in offensive military clashes between the two countries in which both sides lost hundreds of thousands of people. The military clashes came to an end with the Algiers Peace Agreement in 2000. Despite the final adjudication given by the Eritrea-Ethiopia Boundary Commission (EEBC) under The Hague Permanent Court of Arbitration, border tensions between the two countries remain to this day.

THE IMPACT OF ITALIAN COLONIALISM IN ERITREA

Italy ruled Eritrea for 51 years, during which time fundamental changes also occurred in the Eritrean political, social, and economic structures. As we have seen, the opening of the Suez Canal in 1869 sparked a growing colonial interest from European powers in the Red Sea area. In the same year of the opening of the canal, Italy got its first foothold in Eritrea in particular and in Africa in general. The Italian occupation of Assab and its expansion into the whole territory was encouraged by the British. The British believed that Italy was less aggressive and less dangerous in their competition for Africa than France.

Throughout the colonial period, the state's policies were entirely shaped and designed on the basis of colonial attitudes that had long-term impact on the local systems of justice and natural resources management—such as land—as well as institutions of education and health. The colonial state established various mechanisms of segregation run by its own institutions.

The colonial government concentrated its economic activities on the highlands throughout its rule in the colony. It preserved ethnolinguistic diversity in the colony; and it let most of the ethnolinguistic groups be locally administered under their customary laws. Yet the colonial government exploited ethnolinguistic differences in many ways. Moreover, the colony was simply considered as a supplier of raw materials and as a source of colonial soldiers. Eritrea continued to serve Italian interests: as a source of manpower; as a means of generating economic benefits such as maritime commerce; and as a source of raw materials for Italian industries. Italy conscripted tens of thousands of Eritrean soldiers, and about 4,000 of these soldiers were stationed (on permanent bases) in various localities in Libya. By 1939, Italy had conscripted over 60,000 Eritreans.

Most rural areas in Eritrea were affected by the massive conscriptions. Villages lost most of their productive manpower, who served as the backbone of their farming and herding economic systems. In turn, this created an upheaval in the economic system of rural Eritrea. Many people abandoned their farming or herding occupations and became wage laborers on the Italian plantations, gardens, construction projects, or industrial centers. The Eritrean soldiers contributed substantially to the preservation of the Italian colonial needs in Africa. However, after the defeat of Italy by the Allied

Forces in 1941, most of these soldiers were left to find their own ways of making a living. Most of them returned to their villages angered and disillusioned, which increased the threat of social disorder across the country.

The colonial state also created an administration system based on policies of segregation. For example, cities and towns such as Asmara were divided between native and Italian quarters. It created separate judicial and institutional systems in which colonial subjects were put at the periphery. Institutional policies of segregation were designed to preserve its ruling power and to keep subjects in inferior positions. The religious and ethnolinguistic diversity of the territory provided the colonial government a unique opportunity for establishing hegemonic political control over the subjects. The colonial state was able to manipulate ethnolinguistic conflicts usually caused by competitions over the control of natural resources such as grass- and farming-lands, and water. Yet it created administrative and economic integrity of the territory, and this laid the foundations of the modern Eritrean nation.

As part of a strategy of colonial consolidation, many local popular authorities were transformed into salaried chiefs. The colonial state applied brutal policies and ruthless treatments against local chiefs who attempted resistance to any colonial policies. Many such leaders were brutally murdered, hundreds were placed in lifelong imprisonment at Nakura, located at the Dahlak archipelago, and many more fled into exile in the neighboring regions. The colonial administration also transferred chieftainships from popular and charismatic local families to other loyal families and individuals, which created dissatisfactions and tensions among rural communities.

As part of its policies of subjugation, the colonial state established territorial boundaries within the colony, and its subjects (especially rural communities) were fraught with heavy taxation. Free movements of pastorals were curtailed. The expropriation and granting of pasturelands for Italian concessions weakened the traditional patterns and strategies of pastoralist communities. Nomadic pastorals were required to pay taxes when they had to trespass these boundaries where they once had free access in the pre-Italian periods. Many former grazing lands were also transformed into gardens, plantations, or mining areas.

The Italians founded industrial and communication infrastructures that played an important role in creating relative harmony and integration across the colony. These infrastructures are also believed to have facilitated the creation of an "Eritrean" consciousness and identity. In the urban centers, the Eritrean white collar and urban elite was founded, which eventually served as an important catalyst for Eritrean identity and national consciousness.

ERITREA UNDER THE BRITISH MILITARY ADMINISTRATION (BMA)

Great Britain had long-standing commercial and political interests in Eritrea. However, British interests in the Eritrean region increased with the opening of the Suez Canal in 1869. Britain considered Eritrea as one of the strategic territories in the Red Sea. To preserve its interests in the region, Britain sent explorers and

THE BEVIN-SFORZA PLAN (1949)

Bevin Ernst, the British Foreign Secretary, and Consul Sforza of Italy drafted a secret plan in 1949 regarding the settlement of questions related to the former Italian colonies in Africa, including Eritrea. This plan involved the partitioning of Eritrea between Ethiopia and the Anglo-Egyptian Sudan. Based on the plan, the Eritrean plateaus were to be incorporated with the Ethiopian Empire while the Western Lowlands and Northern Highlands were to be annexed by Anglo-Egyptian Sudan. In May of the same year, Mr. Bevin and Mr. Sforza presented their "new" political plan to the United Nations during which the plan was rejected by majority vote.

missionaries such as James Bruce (1769) and Henry Salt (1805–1809). However, increasing French interests in the territory also caused confrontation with the British in the area. Britain attempted several ways to withstand such French influence. For instance, the British appointed consuls at Massawa such as Walter C. Plowden (1848), Charles Duncan Cameron (1861), and Hormuzd Rassam (1866). The British consuls defended British interests in the territory.

In the 1860s, diplomatic conflicts between Emperor Tewodros of Ethiopia and the British caused serious frictions between the two governments. The Ethiopian emperor imprisoned Cameron and one of his colleagues as well as several British Protestant missionaries. As a result, hostilities escalated between the two countries. Under the pretext of freeing the prisoners, the British dispatched a major military expedition (commonly known as the Lord Napier Expedition) led by Sir Robert Napier against Emperor Tewodros in 1868. The British expedition of over 42,000 men arrived at the Eritrean coasts in 1867. The expedition continued to Magdala (the imperial capital in Ethiopia), and it involved the construction of short-distance railroad and roads between the coasts and highlands of Eritrea to be used by the British expeditionary army. Despite Tewodros's attempted negotiations, the British army attacked and defeated the army of the Ethiopian emperor. After losing hope for diplomatic negotiations with Napier, and when the British army controlled Magdala in April 1868, Tewodros is believed to have committed suicide.

Increased French interests in the region as well as unstable political circumstances in the territory compelled the British to give up their desires of direct control of Eritrea. In 1884, considering that Italy would be less influential than the French, the British secretly encouraged Italy to occupy Eritrean territories. After Italy formed its *colonia* Eritrea, the Anglo-Egyptian Sudan was among the first states to recognize Eritrea as an Italian colony. No major military confrontations were recorded between the British in the Sudan and the Italians in Eritrea up through the Italian alliance with the Axis Powers during World War II.

In 1940, in relation to events of World War II, military confrontations were instigated between the British and Italian forces on the border between Eritrea and Sudan. In 1941, the British launched a major military attack against the Italian forces in Eritrea. They defeated the Italians in several battles in western Eritrea. Keren, one of the most strategic fortifications of the Italian army, was attacked and occupied by the

British army, and Asmara, the capital of the colony, was occupied by the British on April 1, 1941. On April 8, 1941, Massawa fell under the hands of the British forces. The occupation of Massawa marked the end of Italian colonialism in Eritrea.

The British occupation of Eritrea was followed by the establishment of the British Military Administration (BMA), which lasted until 1952. Eritrea was then administered by several military officers of the BMA. Initially, the Eritrean population welcomed British occupation of their country, hoping that Italian colonialism, which had deprived them of their rights and marginalized their status, would be replaced by self-determination and the restoration of their rights. The aftermath and result of British administration, however, caused frustration for the majority of the Eritrean people.

The British, who presented themselves as "caretakers" on a "transitional" basis under the rules of the Hague Convention of 1907, brought about almost no change to the economic and political systems of the rural populations. The administrative and economic arteries of the country were still controlled by the Italians. The territorial structure of the former Italian administration remained without any substantial change. Italian codes of law were maintained and Italian judges were reappointed, Italian officers were put on duty to continue their colonial practice over the natives, and so forth. Most of the Italian systems of civil service were retained. The BMA targeted and disbanded only the Italian fascist elements and extreme members of the Fascist Party in the colony. All else, including Italian civil laws in this former Italian colony, was retained. This cultivated increased dissatisfaction among the Eritrean people. As a manifestation of their dissatisfaction, a considerable number of Eritreans attempted resistance. Many turned to being *shiftas* (bandits) and challenged the Italian and British presence in Eritrea. Whether fueled by Ethiopia (which wanted Eritrea as part of its empire) or driven by their own motives, *shiftas* such as the sons of Mosazghi and Gebre Tesfatsion also threatened the BMA and the Italian communities in Eritrea.

The BMA prioritized the utilization of Eritrea's natural resources. The British policies in Eritrea were directed to contributing to the military achievements in the region and the Middle East. Therefore, the Eritrean economy was fully dependent on military events of the Middle East and the Horn of Africa. During the first four years of British occupation, Eritrea experienced a great economic boom and became the strongest industrial power in the region. Eritrean industrial products such as metalwork, ceramics, textile, and foodstuffs dominated the markets of East Africa and the Middle East. Moreover, various types of construction such as garages and stores were installed in the country. The United States, which showed great interest in Eritrea starting from the early 1940s, constructed an aircraft-assembly plant and an airport at Gura'e, opened workshops and repair bases in Asmara as well as an ammunition warehouse at Gindae, and a Naval Base at Massawa. The United States used Eritrea as a depot for military supplies as well as a docking ground for U.S. ships passing to and from the Indian Ocean and the Persian Gulf. The overall economic boom created by the war provided jobs for many formerly unemployed Eritreans, and it led to the development of an industrial economy.

However, the postwar industrial economy of Eritrea suffered from severe economic recession. Eritrean industrial goods lost value in the markets of the Middle East and north Africa. Moreover, the BMA dismantled large parts of the Eritrean port infrastructures and industrial plants and either exported them to other British colonies or

Demolition of buildings and warehouses by the British Military Administration in Eritrea. (Pankhurst, Sylvia (1952). Eritrea on the Eve: The Past and Future of Italy's "First Born" Colony, Ethiopia's Ancient Sea Province. London: Woodward Green, p. 49.)

Building under a process of destruction by the British Military Administration in Eritrea. (Pankhurst, Sylvia (1952). Eritrea on the Eve: The Past and Future of Italy's "First Born" Colony, Ethiopia's Ancient Sea Province. London: Woodward Green, p. 19.)

sold them. The Asmara-Massawa ropeway was also dismantled (for further informa-tion of British actions of economic devitalization in Eritrea, see Pankhurst 1952).

One of the most important changes introduced by the British in Eritrea was in the education sector. Educational institutions, such as various schools and a teacher's training institute, were opened and Eritreans were admitted to these schools. The BMA educational policies facilitated national consciousness and educational capabil-ities of Eritreans. The BMA dramatically increased the number of schools, and the number of students also increased dramatically. By 1952, there were 100 primary schools with 13,500 pupils, 14 junior schools with 1,200 pupils, and two secondary schools with 167 pupils. In addition, 30 students were sent abroad for further educa-tion (see Trevaskis 1960: 33–34). During the Italian period education was highly restricted, and there were only a few schools throughout the country.

THE YEARS OF POLITICAL TURMOIL AND THE PROLIFERATION OF ERITREAN POLITICAL PARTIES (1941–1949)

The expansion of educational opportunities and the emergence of the Eritrean intel-ligentsia and a working class significantly contributed to the further development of "Eritrean nationalism." Eritrean nationalism, which had its roots many years before, was fueled by events during British rule in Eritrea, and it became one of the most important aspects of modern Eritrean history. The development of Eritrean national-ism served as a catalyst for the prolonged armed struggle for independence. The strug-gle, which followed British rule in Eritrea, also affected every fabric of social, political, and environmental life of the Eritrean people throughout the second half of the twentieth century. In the 1940s, many pro-independence political parties had emerged. At the same time, the Unionist Party (UP), which advocated for the uncondi-tional union of Eritrea with Ethiopia, actively participated and was involved in the political upheaval of the 1940s.

On May 5, 1941, a national political organization commonly known as *Mahber Feqri Hager* (Association for Love of Country) was founded by a group of leading nationalist figures such as Abdulkader M. S. Kebire (vice-president), Gebremeskel Woldu (president), Hassan Ali, Demssas Woldemichael, Woldeab Woldemariam, and Berhanu Ahmedin in Asmara (for details see Tesfai 2001; Trevaskis 1960: 46–80). Ini-tially, this popular political organization intended to protest against Italian domina-tion, to call upon the BMA to fulfill its wartime promises, and to demand Eritrea's self-determination. However, not all of its members continued to have a united voice for independence. Moreover, the continuous intervention of Ethiopia affected *Mahber Feqri Hager*. Hence, some founding members left the party and founded new parties of their own. By 1944, the proponents of the UP also dominated the Union and many of its founders (advocates of Eritrean independence) abandoned it.

The UP had been supported by Emperor Haile Selassie I. The emperor's intention was to gain as much support as possible from the Christian section of the Eritrean pop-ulation to legitimize his intended annexation of Eritrea. The Ethiopian claims over

Eritrea appealed to alleged sociocultural and historical links between these two territories. The members of the UP helped in implementing the emperor's policies and political involvement in Eritrea. Through its newspaper *Etiopia* (Ethiopia), the UP distributed its propagandas for the Eritrean unification with Ethiopia, and subsequently it cultivated significant supporters from among the Tigrinya-speaking highland population. Moreover, the UP claimed loyalty of Eritreans through acts of terrorism and coercion. By 1947, the UP had grown stronger, and it claimed that it had the support of about 40 percent of the Eritrean population (for details regarding the UP and other political parties, see Negash 1997: 44–60; Tesfai 2001; Bereketeab 2000). In addition to using the UP as a tool for his objectives in Eritrea, the Ethiopian emperor also applied diplomatic efforts to win the support of the BMA and the United States during his claims of control over Eritrea.

In 1944, prominent nationalist figures such as Ibrahim Sultan Ali, Woldeab Woldemariam, Tessema Asmerom, and Berhanu Ahmedin founded a new political organization called *Ertra N'ertrawyan* (Eritrea for the Eritreans). This party served as an umbrella for pro-independence figures until it fragmented and was substituted by many other political parties. But the UP launched numerous treasonable and violent actions against the leaders of the pro-independence parties. Woldeab Woldemariam, whose popularity was growing among the pro-independents, was targeted by members of the UP; by 1953, he had survived several assassination attempts. Abdel Kader Kebire, another pro-independence figure was assassinated on March 30, 1949 (see Diagram 1 in the "Facts and Figures" section of this book for the overview of political parties' propagation in Eritrea).

Concerned by the continuous frictions and fragmentations of pro-independence parties, worsening security problems, religious and regional turmoil, Woldeab Woldemariam, a renowned advocate for Eritrean independence, pushed for creating a platform for dialogue among all political parties. After discussing his concerns with leaders of other political parties, he helped organize a convention commonly known as the *wa'ella* Bet Giorgis in November, 1946. However, due to the UP's (especially Tedla Bairu's—the head of the UP) conspiracies, the *wa'ela* ended without any significant dialogues or agreements. Woldeab Woldemariam was also threatened by the supporters of the UP.

In addition, the British implemented controversial policies during the post-war period: recurrent confiscation of land, maintaining Italian administration and personnel intact, devitalization of the industrial and agrarian economy, and dismantling rural power structures. As a result, massive rural and urban discontent and upheaval, mostly expressed in the form of *shiftnet* (banditry), continued to affect every section of the Eritrean population; and it reached the point that the BMA found it difficult to govern Eritrea. In addition, Ethiopia, under Emperor Haile-Selassie I, continuously made claims for the union of Eritrea with Ethiopia. The objective of the Ethiopian claim was to secure an outlet to the sea. For this purpose, the Ethiopian emperor made various diplomatic efforts. At the same time, the British had long-term interests in the whole region; and they established a sphere of influence in the Horn of Africa of which Ethiopia comprised the main body. The United States also had considerable interests in the territory. It considered Eritrea as a strategic place for its communication facilities. Hence, it exerted continuous pressure to have Eritrea incorporated into Ethiopia and be administered by the imperial government.

Soon after the end of the World War II, the issue of the former Italian colonies was raised by the allied powers, and the Eritrean question was internationalized. However, owing to internal and external factors, the Eritrean question became a complicated matter. The proposals and decisions of the allied powers were highly influenced by their respective national interests and did not reflect the main principles of the Atlantic Charter. The allied forces agreed to send a Four Power Commission of Britain, France, the United States, and the Soviet Union (USSR) to inquire about political circumstances in Eritrea and come up with proposals on how to dispose the territory. Yet the delegates in the Commission could not readily agree on the best choice regarding Eritrea's future. Eventually the Commission came up with four different proposals: The United States proposed a complete union of Eritrea with Ethiopia; Britain suggested the partition of the territory (the western parts to be incorporated into Sudan and the highlands and coast to be annexed with Ethiopia); the USSR proposed a trusteeship under a body of international administration; and France suggested an Italian trusteeship. Unable to agree on a single proposal, the Four Powers referred the Eritrean case to the UN General Assembly (UNGA). The UN set up a new Commission composed of five countries (Pakistan, Guatemala, Burma, South Africa, and Norway). The main task of this Commission was to study the problem and propose a solution. In 1949, the Italian Minister of Foreign Affairs—Mr. Count Sforza and the British Foreign Secretary—Ernest Bevin—also presented what they claimed was a "new plan" commonly known as the Bevin-Sforza Plan. According to this plan, Eritrea was to be partitioned between Ethiopia and Sudan, which was rejected by majority vote at the UNGA.

Meanwhile, the UN Commission of Enquiry presented its report, but again without an agreeable solution to the problem. The South African delegate proposed an Eritrea-Ethiopia federation with defined autonomy for Eritrea while the Norwegian delegate proposed a full union of Eritrea with Ethiopia. Guatemala and Pakistan proposed a trusteeship of the territory under the administration and arrangements of the UN. Owing to Ethiopian and U.S. diplomatic pressure, and the disagreement of the international community on a possible solution regarding the fate of Eritrea, the UNGA could not come to a reasonable decision until 1950. Finally, the UN passed Resolution 390A(V) on December 2, 1950, making Eritrea an autonomous country federated with Ethiopia.

THE ERITREAN-ETHIOPIAN FEDERATION (1952–1962)

Resolution 390A(V), commonly known as "The Federal Act," was to be implemented under the principles that defined the status of Eritrea and Ethiopia. Hence, the UN elected Mr. Anze Matienzo (Bolivian diplomat) to serve as the UN Commissioner to Eritrea and to lay a foundation for the implementation of the resolution and to supervise its implementation. Among Matienzo's main tasks were: drafting an Eritrean constitution, the election of a Constituent Assembly, the definition of the divisions of powers between Eritrea and Ethiopia, and the creation of a government based on the new constitution. Matienzo and his team of experts worked on the above-mentioned tasks until 1952; and the Eritrean-Ethiopian Federation was finally implemented on September 15, 1952.

The federal constitution permitted Eritrea to have its autonomy and government. The Eritrean government was entitled to exercise complete authority over internal affairs such as taxation, education, health, agriculture, and commerce. However, the constitution made Ethiopia responsible for issues related to foreign affairs such as communication with the outside world, financial affairs, and defense. Although the constitution maintained serious set-backs, it principally defined the powers and spheres of both governments.

However, due to Ethiopian interventions in the internal affairs of the Eritrean government, frictions and tensions started to mount from the early periods of the federation. For example, the Eritrean General Union of Labor Syndicates (the biggest labor union in Africa at that time) was founded by Woldeab Woldemariam in December 1952. However, it was soon banned by the federal government. This resulted in armed clashes between the Eritrean police, the Eritrean workers at the ports of Massawa and Assab (who went on strike in response to the ban) and the Ethiopian army (see Tesfai 2001).

The Eritrean Assembly repeatedly complained and presented petitions to the UN, but without avail. Within the first three years of the federation, it became clear that Ethiopia was ready to defy the federal agreements and incorporate Eritrea as part of its territory. The emperor and his representatives in Eritrea continued to campaign for the incorporation of Eritrea with Ethiopia. As far as Eritrean politicians were concerned, they continued to demonstrate that Ethiopia was violating the principles of the federation, and that it intended to annex the country. Although Ethiopia continued to target most of the Eritrean nationalists who demanded autonomy for Eritrea, it also continued to infiltrate the core organs of the Eritrean government.

Ethiopia's eventual aims were also demonstrated in its economic policies toward Eritrea. The economic situation of the majority of rural and urban populations started to deteriorate. Prices of all goods, services, and taxes continued to rise, causing serious problems for the majority of the rural people. As part of its policies of weakening the Eritrean economy and making it dependent on Ethiopian production, Ethiopian officials discouraged foreign investments and threatened foreign investors with expulsion if there was any commercial engagement in Eritrea. As part of this policy, the Ethiopian government unilaterally abrogated agreements between investors and the Eritrean government. For example, Fiat (an Italian Automotive Company) made agreements with the Eritrean government to set up a factory in Deqemhare. However, the Ethiopian government annulled this agreement.

Many factories were either shut down or replanted in Ethiopia. The deliberate relocation or shutting down of Eritrean factories resulted in a dramatic decrease in the total number of industrial plants in Eritrea—from 165 factories in 1958 to 83 factories in 1961. On the other side, the number of industrial plants in Ethiopia increased—from 55 plants in 1958 to 95 plants in 1961 (Murtaza 1998: 76). The systematic policy of economic devitalization negatively impacted the Eritrean working class. Higher rates of unemployment resulted in massive migration of Eritrean workers to Sudan, the Middle East, and Ethiopia in search of jobs.

The power of Eritrean executive and legislative government bodies was reduced and controlled by the representatives of the emperor. Tedla Bairu, the chief executive of the Eritrean government, was replaced by Asfaha Woldemichael (unionist) who exercised coercive methods over the Eritrean Assembly to vote for the unconditional union between Eritrea with Ethiopia and the end of the federation. In 1956, the federal government banned the legal Eritrean official languages (Tigrinya and Arabic allowed under the federal constitution), and Amharic (a major language in Ethiopia) was made the only official language in Eritrea. Ethiopia soon banned Eritrean official seals and its coat of arms. In December 1958, the Eritrean flag was lowered.

In general, the federation did not bring any lasting solution to the Eritrean problem, and it failed to create integrity and harmony between the two countries. The continuous overt and covert intervention of Ethiopia in the internal affairs of the Eritrean government resulted in massive peaceful protest by Eritreans. One of the Eritrean protest demonstrations in 1958 was by 300 to 450 students who went on strike in the streets of Asmara demanding the restoration of the Eritrean flag, seal, and coat of arms. The Ethiopian government reacted to the protest by imprisoning many of the students. The general peaceful trade union strike in Asmara was also brutally crushed by the troops of the federal government in February 1958 (for details regarding developments of the Eritrea-Ethiopia federation, see Iyob 1995; Tesfai 2005; and Negash 1997).

On November 15, 1962, allegedly by the majority vote of the Eritrean Assembly, Ethiopia formally declared that the Eritrea-Ethiopia federation had been terminated, and Eritrea was annexed as the fourteenth province of Ethiopia. The annexation of Eritrea marked the escalation of Eritrean resistance.

THE ERITREAN STRUGGLE
FOR INDEPENDENCE (1961–1991)
Eritrean Liberation Movement (ELM)

The ELM, which was commonly known as *harekat al-tahrir Eritrea* or simply *harekat,* was founded in Port Sudan in 1958 and demonstrated against the Ethiopian violations of the principles of the federation. The ELM enjoyed wide popular support of Eritreans in the Sudan and within Eritrea. Although the ELM was founded mostly by Muslim communities in Port Sudan, it also achieved wide support in the Christian populations in the highlands of Eritrea. Among the Christian supporters, ELM was known as *Mahber Show'ate* (ማሕበር ሸውዓተ) "the Association of Seven." Members of *Mahber Show'ate* swore an oath of support for the ELM and attended clandestine political education and meetings organized by the movement (Markakis 1987: 104–109). The ELM was successful in recruiting many members across the country as well as in some towns in Ethiopia.

Generally, the initial goal of the ELM was to defend against Ethiopian intervention. Later the goal of the ELM resorted to achieving Eritrean independence. However, the leadership of the ELM was unable to set feasible strategies for the achievement of its goals for the following few years. In September 1960, the leadership of the ELM embarked on a strategy of infiltration into the governmental administrative structures so that the administration in Eritrea could eventually be overthrown by a *coup d'etat*. They intended to spread their political education and organizational structures into the basic fabric of the Eritrean police and army, which they considered could be a good source for weapons.

The Eritrean Liberation Front (ELF) was founded in July 10, 1960, and it began its campaigns across the western lowlands of Eritrea. Considering ELM as a potential rival, the ELF distributed anti-ELM propaganda, and it accused the leaders of the movement as Communists with anti-Muslim agendas. This created continuous tensions between the two movements. The ELM, trapped by the threats of the new antagonist front and the Ethiopian army, suffered great losses of membership in the 1960s, and many of its members joined the newly created ELF. Finally, the movement disbanded in 1970.

The ELF

The ELF (usually known as *Jebha*) started the liberation struggle in September 1961 (a year before Eritrea was annexed by Ethiopia). Founded in Cairo by a group of exiled Eritrean nationalists (such as Idris Mohammed Adem, Idris Osman Geladewos, and Mohammed Saleh Hamid) and Eritrean students, the ELF dispatched a small group of fighters who gathered in the western lowlands of Eritrea. These fighters were composed of newly recruited conscripts, Eritrean soldiers formerly in the service of the Sudanese army, and ex-*ascaris* who served in the colonial army such as Hamid Idris Awate (who fired the first shot of the liberation struggle). By 1962, they formed the armed nub of the ELF. They operated in small squads across the Gash and Barka territories. Most of their operations applied guerilla tactics (see Killion 1998: 186–192).

Based in Cairo and later also in Kassala, the ELF leadership attempted to raise support from various countries in the Arab world. Saleh Sabbe, a renowned politician, joined the ELF in 1961 and cultivated remarkable support for the front through his personal diplomatic capabilities and networks in the Middle East. Logistical supports, arms, and ammunition started to enter Eritrea through Sudan, and some fighters were also trained in Syria.

As far as the Ethiopian government was concerned, Arab support for the ELF implied a conspiracy of the Arab countries against Ethiopia. It depicted the ELF as a communist insurgency backed by hostile Arab countries. Hence, it continued attempts to legitimize its military offensives across the western lowlands of Eritrea.

However, from the very beginning, the ELF failed to create a well-defined organizational structure. Idris Mohammed Adem and Idris Geladewos served as president and secretary respectively. When Saleh Sabbe joined the front, three of them constituted the Supreme Council (SC) of the ELF, which was aided by its central branch, the Revolutionary Council (RC), founded in May 1965 (for further details, see Markakis 1987).

The organizational structure of the ELF army was, however, based on a model somehow resembling that of the Algerian FLN (*Front de Libération Nationale*). The ELF army was divided into five zones of commands each with its own hierarchical command, logistics, and other supplies. This created a remarkable drift of power among the commands of the five zones as well as their attachment with the central commands in Sudan and Cairo. Each command grew somehow like an autonomous military unit and levied its own taxes on the population and recruited its own soldiers. Over time, the central command in Kassala and the SC in Cairo reached the point they could no longer exercise full control over the five zonal commands. The absence of a strong centralized command resulted in a long-term power struggle among the zonal commands and within the RC. In addition to the power struggle among the commands, their leaderships suffered from conservatism and parochial sentiments that continued to affect the composition and structure of each zonal command. Consequently, rural resentment against the ELF also continued to mount throughout the 1960s. Yet the ELF zonal commands continued to effectively confront the Ethiopian army through guerilla tactics and offensives.

Without a formal consent of loyalty to the RC, a group of concerned reformists of the ELF, also known as Eslah and others (some of them former students at the University of Addis Ababa, including Abraham Tewolde, Romodan Mohammed Nur, Isaias Afeweki, and Mohammed Ali Omero), called for a meeting in June 1968. All zonal commands were invited to attend the meeting held at a place called Aredayib. They jointly demanded unity of the ELF army, the establishment of centralized leadership within Eritrea, the strengthening of relationship between the army and the civilian population, and the protection of civilian rights.

The Aredayib meeting was followed by the Adobha Conference in which the ELF leadership elected a new organ called General Command (GC), also known as the *qiyad al-'ama,* in August 1969. In principle, the GC replaced the SC and RC but failed to consider the demands raised during the Aredayib meeting. Instead, threatened of losing its power, the GC applied violent tactics to suppress the reformists and splinters. Consequently, the ELF started to fragment resulting in the formation of several splinter groups. By 1971, at least three new groups, the Eritrean Liberation Front—Obel Movement, the People's Liberation Front (PLF), and the Eritrean Liberation Front-People's Liberation Front (ELF-PLF), had emerged from the ELF. In 1973, while the other splinter groups continued to disintegrate, the PLF-Denkalia led by Saleh Sabbe and PLF-Ala Group led by Isaias Afeweki merged their forces and became the Eritrean People's Liberation Front (EPLF). The fragmentation of the ELF marked the beginning of military turmoil within the Eritrean field, and each group's struggle for its own survival. Unable to unite, these splinter groups confronted each other resulting in the outbreak of a bitter civil war (1972–1974; 1978–1981).

The EPLF

The EPLF (formerly ELF-PLF) emerged as a splinter group from the ELF in 1970, but its formation was formally acknowledged in the First EPLF Congress in January 1977. Amidst the civil war, the EPLF rose as the strongest organization under the initial leadership of Romodan Mohammed Nur (Secretary) and Isaias Afeweki (military commander). Several members of its leadership had studied Marxism and Maoist tactics of guerrilla warfare in China. The EPLF embarked on programs of secular nationalism and mass-based political mobilizations. Its rural social policies were also based on Marxist orientations. However, soon after its emergence, the EPLF also faced a major internal crisis during the turbulent years of civil war in the Eritrean fields. The internal crisis emanated mainly from ideological differences among its members, especially by a leftist group of people organized under a new movement called *Menka'e*. Among the main demands of the *Menka'e* movement included radical reforms in the structures of the EPLF leadership and the introduction of democratic principles of leadership within the organization; demands that were considered as a great threat by the EPLF leadership. The EPLF leadership denounced members of *Menka'e* and accused them of becoming "anarchists." As a result, the EPLF sentenced most members of *Menka'e* to death, including Mussie Tesfamichael and Tewolde Iyob, two of the most significant ringleaders of the movement (Markakis 1987: 135–138).

Once the civil war came to an end, the EPLF started to actively implement its political campaign in rural Eritrea. By 1975, the EPLF managed to distribute its forces across the plateau and the eastern escarpments, and thousands of new conscripts started to join the organization. The organization's policy toward the status of women (which appeared to be moderate) also stimulated great support in the Eritrean rural populations. The EPLF encouraged women to join the organization, and thousands of women joined the front starting in 1973. At the end of the liberation struggle (1991), women constituted one-third of the EPLF army.

On the war front, the EPLF launched remarkable offensives against Ethiopian troops throughout Eritrea. By 1977, the EPLF and other groups of the ELF managed to liberate the whole country except for a few cities such as Asmara and Assab. On the regional level, the EPLF also managed to establish mutual military and political alliances, first with the Ethiopian People's Revolutionary Party (EPRP) and later with the Tigrean People's Liberation Front (TPLF). The cooperation between the EPLF and the TPLF played a pivotal role in defeating the Ethiopian army.

The secret of military success for the EPLF is usually attributed to the Front's effective military strategies. However, EPLF's very survival was dependent on the broad support of Eritrean rural populations. The Eritrean masses (including the Eritrean diaspora) that were bitter about Ethiopian rule provided massive support in various forms: material, morale, labor, and food for the fighters. The EPLF involved civilians during military offensives. Civilians carried and transported wounded fighters, provided food and ammunitions for the EPLF fighters in the battles, facilitated exchange of information among the fighting units, and gathered intelligence information for the Front. Basically, the Eritrean rural populations served as the arteries of the Front, and without these arteries the EPLF would not have survived the Ethiopian military offensives, which threatened its very survival in the mountains of Sahel, highlands and in the Barka Lowlands.

THE ETHIOPIAN REVOLUTION AND THE ERITREAN LIBERATION STRUGGLE

In the mid-1970s, several events took place in Ethiopia that also markedly changed the magnitude of success for the EPLF. A military junta called *Dergue* led opposition against the imperial government. Subsequently, the Ethiopian emperor was overthrown and replaced by a Provisional Military Advisory Committee in September 1974. In 1977, Colonel Mengistu Haile Mariam, a member of the revolutionaries who toppled the emperor, rose through the ranks of the *Dergue* by eradicating his opponents within the movement such as General Tefferi Bante, Atnafu Abate and General Aman Andom (who served as the first post-imperial acting leader of Ethiopia).

Within the country, the *Dergue*, led by Colonel Mengistu, applied coercive and militant tactics against its opponents. It created a state of terror in which thousands of people were killed in Ethiopia and Eritrea, and hundreds of thousands left their homes seeking refuge in neighboring countries such as Sudan.

Ethiopia under Colonel Mengistu adhered to Marxist policies. Its Marxist policies made it the most popular African communist regime with the communist bloc of members of the Warsaw Pact during the cold war. The *Dergue* refuted the traditional Ethiopian-American bilateral relations and established a new relationship with the Soviet Union (USSR). The USSR, which already had a wish of this kind of relationship with Ethiopia (which mainly aimed at defending and expanding its communist interests in the Horn of Africa), supported the *Dergue* rule with hundreds of varieties of arms, military personnel, various military equipment, tanks, warplanes, varieties of artilleries, and more. The direct involvement of the USSR threatened the Eritrean liberation fighters, and they were forced to withdraw in 1978. The EPLF fighters fled to the mountains of Sahel from where they started their offensive wars in the late 1980s.

Within the Eritrean fields civil wars also resumed between the ELF and its factions on the one hand, and the EPLF on the other. Consequently, the ELF (which initially led and later actively participated in the Eritrean liberation struggle for two decades) was expelled from Eritrea by the EPLF forces in 1981.

The EPLF continued to cultivate support from the Eritrean masses and managed to effectively mobilize the Eritreans against the *Dergue* rule. It survived massive *Dergue* military expeditions in the 1980s and started to launch counteroffensives. By 1988, the EPLF won major battles such as the Battle of Afabet/Nadow. The defeat of the Ethiopian army at the Battle of Afabet (which the renowned BBC correspondent of the time, Basil Davidson, compared to the Battle of Dien Bien Phu of Indochina in 1954) was an immeasurable military loss for Ethiopia, but it remarkably boosted the fighting morale of the liberation army. By 1990, the EPLF liberated the main Eritrean port of Massawa, followed by the liberation of all major towns of Eritrea, including the capital city of Asmara on May 24, 1991.

In 1993, the United Nations' supervised referendum was conducted in which a great majority of the Eritrean people voted for their independence from Ethiopia. On May 24, 1993, Eritrea officially became an independent state. Soon, the country was also admitted for membership in some major international organizations such as the UN and the Organization of African Unity (OAU). Ethiopia was also among the first nations to acknowledge the independence of Eritrea. Both countries also established good diplomatic relations and opened their respective new embassies.

However, the impact of the war was immense. Eritrea was left in a state of complete ruins. The infrastructural and communication infrastructures were disrupted. The war virtually consumed every resource of the country. More than 60,000 Eritrean fighters and over 50,000 civilians were lost in the war while over 700,000 people were forced to flee the country.

After seven peaceful years, a new war known as a "border conflict" broke out between Eritrea and Ethiopia. The exact reasons of the war are not yet known, although many scholars and commentators have speculated on various possible causes. Broadly, the speculations can be categorized into three factors: economic, political, and personal rivalry between the two heads of state. However, none of the speculations have been well established and documented.

The war was fought in many battles along the border between the two countries in which over a hundred thousand lives have been lost, and over half a million people displaced on both sides. The border conflict came to an end when both parties signed an agreement commonly known "The Algiers Peace Agreement" in December 2000. Among other provisions, the two parties agreed to establish a buffer zone within the Eritrean territory in which UN peacekeeping forces were to be stationed, the formation of an international committee to examine the causes and assesses the damages of the war, and settlement of the border issue by the rulings of the International Court at the Hague. Over 4,000 UN peacekeeping forces (known as UNMEE) were stationed in the buffer zone. In the meantime, UNMEE was expelled from Eritrea. Despite the court's verdict in 2002, the border between the countries has not yet been demarcated on the ground. Border tensions continue to this day. Both parties continue to spread hostile propaganda against each other.

REFERENCES

Anfray, Francis (1991). *Les anciens ethiopiens.* Paris: Armand Colin.

Appiah, Anthony & Gates, Henry Louis (2005). *Africana: The Encyclopedia of the African and African American experience.* (Vol. 1), University of California: Oxford University Press.

Bard, Kathryn A. and Shubert, Steven Blake (eds.) (1999). *Encyclopedia of the Archaeology of Ancient Egypt.* London/New York: Routledge.

Beccari, Camillo (1912). *Il Tigre: Descritto da un missionario Gesuita del secolo XVII.* 2nd edition, Rome: Casa Editore Italiana.

Bereketeab, Redie (2000). *Eritrea: The Making of a Nation, 1890–1991.* Uppsala: Uppsala University Press.

Beyene, Asmelash (1964). *Municipal Administration of Asmara: A Profile of Bureaucracy.* Addis Ababa.

Bradbury, Louise (1988). "Reflections on Travelling to 'God's Land' and Punt in the Middle Kingdom." In: *Journal of the American Research Center in Egypt*, Vol. 25, pp. 127–156.

Checchi, Michele (1910). *Asmara: Estrato della Coloniale.* Roma.

Chelati Dirar, Uoldelul (2007). "Colonialism and the Construction of National Identities: The Case of Eritrea" in: *Journal of East African Studies*, 1 (2), pp. 256–276.

Cliffe, Lionel & Basil Davidson (eds.) (1988). *The long struggle of Eritrea.* Nottingham: Spokesman.

Connel, Dan (1993). *Against All Odds: A Chronicle of the Eritrean Revolution.* Philadelphia: Red Sea Press.

Dahlgren, Skip: http://hometown.aol.com

Davidson, Basil (2001). *African in History.* London (revised edition): Phoenix Press.

Doornbos, Martin and Tesfai, Alemseged (ed.) (1999). *Eritrea: Prospects for Reconstruction and Development*. Lawrenceville: Red Sea Press.

Ellingson, Lloyd Shettler (1986). *Eritrea: Separatism and Irredentism (1945–1985)*. Michigan (Ph.D. Dissertation): Michigan State University.

Erlich, Haggai (1996). *Ras Alula and the Scramble for Africa. A Political Biography: Ethiopia and Eritrea 1875–1897*. NJ: Red Sea Press.

Fattovich, Rodolfo (1990). "Remarks on the pre-Aksumite period in northern Ethiopia." In: *Journal of Ethiopian Studies*. 23, pp. 1–33.

Fattovich, Rodolfo (1991). "The Problem of Punt in the Light of the Recent Field Work in the Eastern Sudan." In: Schoske, Sylvia (ed.). *Akten des vierten internationalen Ägyptologen Kongresses, München 1985* (Vol. 4), Hamburg: Helmut Buske Verlag, pp. 257–272.

Foreign Office (USA). *Handbook—Eritrea* (prepared under the direction of the Historical Section of the Foreign Office for use during the 1919 Peace Conferences, No. 121, May, 1919).

Ghaber, Michael (1993). *The Blin of Bogos*. Bagdad, Iraq.

Gayim, Eyassu (1993). *The Eritrean Question: The Conflict Between the Right of Self-determination and the Interests of States*. Uppsala: Uppsala University.

Gebre-Medhin, Jordan (1989). *Peasants and Nationalism in Eritrea: A Critique of Ethiopian Studies*. Trenton, NJ: Red Sea Press.

Great Britain—Information Service (1944). *Eritrea: A Handbook*. London: British Ministry of Information.

Habte Selassie, Bereket (1989). *Eritrea and the United Nations and Other Essays*. Trenton, NJ: Red Sea Press.

Hagai, Erlikh (1983). *The Struggle over Eritrea, 1962–1978: War and Revolution in the Horn of Africa*. Stanford, California: Hoover Institution Press.

Hepner, Tricia Redeker (2009). *Soldiers, Martyrs, Traitors and Exiles: Political Conflict in Eritrea and the Diaspora*. Ethnography of Political Violence Series. Philadelphia: University of Pennsylvania Press.

Istituto Agricolo Coloniale (1946). *Eritrea—Some Photographic Representations of Italy's actions*. Firenze, n.a., p. 46.

Iyob, Ruth (1995). *The Eritrean Struggle for Independence: Domination, Resistance, Nationalism (1941–1993)*. Cambridge: Cambridge University Press.

Killion, Tom (1998). *Historical Dictionary of Eritrea*. London: The Scarecrow Press.

Locatelli, Francesca (2003). "Colonial Justice, Crime, and Social Stratification in the 'Native Quarters' of Colonial Asmara, 1890–1941." In: *Northeast African Studies, 10 (3)*, pp. 101–115

Locatelli, Francesca (2004). *Asmara During the Italian Period: Order, Disorder and Urban Identities—1890–1941*. (Ph.D. Dissertation), SOAS, University of London.

Longrigg, Stephen H. (1945). *A Short History of Eritrea*. Oxford: Clarendon Press.

Markakis, John (1987). *National and Class Conflict in the Horn of Africa*. Cambridge: Cambridge University Press.

Martini, Ferdinando (1896). *Nel Africa Italiana: Impressioni e ricordi*. Milano, n.a.

McCann, James (1995). *People of the Plow: An Agricultural History of Ethiopia, 1800–1990*. Madison: University of Wisconsin Press.

McGraw-Hill Encyclopedia of Science and Technology (2002). The McGraw Hill Companies Inc. (9th edition).

Mesghenna, Yemane (1988). *Italian Colonialism: A Case Study of Eritrea, 1869–1934—Motive, Praxis and Result*. Lund: Lund University Press.

Michels, Joseph W. (2005). *Changing Settlement Patterns in the Aksum-Yeha Region of Ethiopia: 700 BC–AD 850*. Oxford: Archaeopress.

Ministry of Information, Eritrea (2002). *Eritrea: A Country Handbook*. Asmara: Ministry of Information.

Miran, Jonathan (2005). "A Historical Overview of Islam in Eritrea." In: *Die Welt des Islams* 45(2), pp. 177–215.

Miran, Jonathan (2009). *Red Sea Citizens: Cosmopolitan Society and Cultural Change in Massawa*. Bloomington: Indiana University Press.

Mukhtar, Muhammad Jamal al-Din (1981). *Ancient civilizations of Africa*. General History of Africa, 2. London: Heinemann Educational Books.

Mulazzani, A. (1903). *Geografia della colonia Eritrea*. Florence: R. Bemporad & Figlio.

Munro-Hay, Stuart (1991). *Aksum: An African Civilisation of Late Antiquity*. Edinburgh: Edinburgh University Press.

Munzinger, Werner (1883). *Ostafrikanisce Studien: Mit einer Karte von Nord-Abyssinien und den Ländern am Mareb, Barka und Anseba*. Basel.

Murtaza, Niaz (1998). *The Pillage of Sustainability in Eritrea, 1600s–1990s: Rural Communities and the Creeping Shadows of Hegemony*. London: Greenwood Press.

Nastasi, Paolo (1994). *Notes Concerning Climatic and Floristic Regions of Eritrea*. Rome.

Negash, Tekeste (1987). *Italian Colonialism in Eritrea—1882–1941: Policies, Praxis and Impact*. Uppsala: University of Uppsala.

Negash, Tekeste (1987). *No Medicine for the Bite of a White Snake*. Uppsala: University of Uppsala.

Negash, Tekeste (1997). *Eritrea and Ethiopia: The Federal Experience*. Uppsala: Nordiska Afrikainstitutet.

O'Connor, David (1994). *Ancient Nubia: Egypt's Rival in Africa*. Philadelphia: University of Pennsylvania Press.

Odorizzi, Dante (1911). *Colonia Eritrea: Il Commissariato Regionale di Massaua al 1° Gennaio 1910*. Asmara.

Oriolo, Leonardo (1998). *Asmara Style*. Asmara: Italian School.

Pankhurst, Richard (1964). *The Great Ethiopian Famine, 1888–92: A New Assessment*. Addis Ababa.

Pankhurst, Richard (1982). *History of Ethiopian Towns from the Mid-Nineteenth Century to 1935*. Wiesbaden: Harrassowitz Press.

Pankhurst, Sylvia (1952). *Eritrea on the Eve: The Past and Future of Italy's "First Born" Colony, Ethiopia's Ancient Sea Province*. London: Woodward Green.

Pateman, Roy (1989). "Eritrean Resistance During the Italian Occupation." In: *Journal of Eritrean Studies*, 3/2 (1989) 13–24.

Pateman, Roy (1990). *Eritrea: Even the Stones are Burning*. Trenton: Red Sea Press.

Pateman, Roy (1991). "Eritrea and Ethiopia: Strategies for Reconciliation in the Horn." In: *Africa Today*, 38 (2), pp. 43–54.

Pateman, Roy (1991). "The War in Eritrea: Drawing to an End." In: *The Horn Review*, 1 (1), pp. 1–13.

Phillipson, David W. (1998). *Ancient Ethiopia, Aksum: Its Antecedents and Successors*. London: British Museum Press.

Phillipson, David W. (2000). *Archaeology at Aksum, Ethiopia, 1993–97*. London: British Institute in Eastern Africa.

Pollera, Alberto (1935). *Le populazioni indigine dell'Eritrea*. Bologna.

Rassam, Hormuzd (1869). *Narrative of the British Mission to Theodore, King of Abyssinia: With Notices of the Countries Traversed from Massowah—Through the Soodân, the Amhâra, and Back to Annesley Bay, from Mágdala*. London.

Reid, Richard (2001). "The Challenge of the Past: The Quest for Historical Legitimacy in Endependent Eritrea." In: *History in Africa*, 28, pp. 239–272.

Saulsberry, Nicole Denise (2001). *The Life and Times of Woldeab Woldemariam (1905–1995)*. (Ph.D. Dissertation): Stanford University.

Schmidt, Peter, Curtis, Matthew C., et al. (2008). *The Archaeology of Ancient Eritrea*. Trenton, NJ: Red Sea Press.

Schoenfeld, E. Dagobert (1904). *Erythräa und der Ägyptische Sudan*. Berlin: Dietrich Beimer Press.

Shaw, Ian and Nicholson, Paul (1995). *The Dictionary of Ancient Egypt*. London: British Museum Press, pp. 231–232.

Sherman, Richard (1980). *Eritrea: The Unfinished Revolution*. New York: Praeger Publishers.

Stansfield, Gareth R. V. (2001). *The 1995–96 Yemen-Eritrea Conflict over the Islands of Hanish and Jabal Zuquar: A Geopolitical Analysis*. University of Durham: Centre for Middle Eastern and Islamic Studies.

Taddia, Irma (1986). *L'Eritrea colonia (1890–1952): paesaggi, strutture uomini del colonialismo* [Colonial Eritrea—1890–1952: Landscape, Structure and the People of Colonialism]. Milan: Franco Angeli Press.

Tafla, Bairu (1994). "Interdependence Through Independence: The Challenges of Eritrean Historiography." In: Harold G. Marcus (ed.). *New Trends in Ethiopian Studies*, 1, pp. 497–514.

Tafla, Bairu (2004). "Eritrea: Remote Past and Present." In: *Journal of Eritrean Studies*, 3 (1), pp. 82–98.

Tafla, Bairu (2007). *Troubles and Travels of an Eritrean Aristocrat: A Presentation of Kantiba Gilamika'el's Memoirs*. Shaker Verlag GmbH.

Taye, Adane (1991). *A Historical Survey of State Education in Eritrea*. Asmara: EMPDA.

Tesfagiorgis G., Mussie (2007). *A Fading Nature: Aspects of Environmental History of Eritrea*. Felsberg: Edition Eins Verlag.

Tesfagiorgis, Mussie (2006). "A Brief History of Asmara." In: Steffen Wenig (ed.), *In Kaiserlichem Auftrag: Die Deutsche-Aksum Expedition 1906 unter Enno Littmann*. Deutsches Archäologisches Institut, Leiden Soft Verlag, Bielefeld, pp. 287–94.

Tesfai, Alemseged (2001). *Aynefelale: ertra 1941–1950*: [Let Us Stay United: Eritrea from 1941 to 1950]. Asmara: Hidri Publishers.

Tesfai, Alemseged (2005). *Federeshin ertra mis ityopiya: kab matiyenzo kesab tedla (1952–1955)* [The Federation of Eritrea with Ethiopia: From Matienzo to the reign of Tedla (1951–1954)]. Asmara: Hidri Publishers.

Trevaskis, Gerald Kenedy Nicholas (1960). *Eritrea: A Colony in Transition—1941–52*. London: Oxford University Press.

Tronvoll, Kjetil (1998). *Mai Weini: A Highland Village in Eritrea*. Lawrenceville, NJ: Red Sea Press.

Wrong, Michela (2005). *I Didn't Do It For You: How the World Used and Abused a Small African Nation*. London: Fourth Estate.

Wylde, Augustus B. (1888, repr. 1969). *'83-'87 in The Soudan: With an Account of Sir William Hewett's Mission to King John*. Vol. I, New York: Negro Universities Press.

Yohannes, Okubazghi (1991). *Eritrea: A Pawn in World Politics*. Gainesville: University of Florida Press.

Yosief, Yisaak (1993). *Zanta ketema asmera*: [History of the City of Asmara]. Addis Ababa, n.p.

CHAPTER 3

Government and Politics

INTRODUCTION

Eritrea has experienced different systems of government throughout its history. The Italians established a colonial government that established the modern form of state. This modern state also introduced modern sectors of the economy—the industrial system, agricultural production systems, social services, and medicine. The government created by the European colonizers was designed to protect the rights and privileges of European settlers and government personnel. On the basis of the colonial system, Africans were reduced to holding a marginal status. During the Italian administration, minority Eritreans had access only to junior posts in the administration.

The governmental system established during the British rule in Eritrea neither provided chances for Eritreans to hold key positions in the administration nor allowed them to participate in major policymaking issues. Yet British rule in Eritrea is credited with introducing an expanded and better system of modern education. The British administration also allowed Eritreans to express their political wishes and demonstrate those wishes through a number of political parties.

The federal period was the first time Eritreans saw a more liberal system of governmental rule. The constitution provided by the UN offered them more liberties and rights than ever before. However, continuous Ethiopian intervention frustrated their desires to live under the constitutional and democratic rule of law. The annexation of Eritrea by Ethiopia (1962) dismissed the democratic federal system, and Eritreans were brought back to an authoritarian system of government. The Ethiopian occupation (1962–1991) was characterized by a state of warfare and emergency. The Ethiopian government, especially under the *Dergue* rule, violated most of the Eritreans' rights.

In 1991, the Eritrean People's Liberation Front (EPLF), which had liberated the country from Ethiopian occupation, established a provisional government that lasted until 1993. Just after the Eritrean referendum in 1993, the provisional government changed its name and became a transitional government and it embarked on establishing a constitutional and democratic government. For this purpose, a new constitution was drafted and ratified in 1997. Although the government was expected to allow democratic elections after the ratification of the constitution, it has not yet done so.

THE PROVISIONAL GOVERNMENT OF ERITREA (MAY 1991–MAY 1993)

The post-independence period in Eritrea was characterized by a number of changes. These changes dealt mainly with the process of transformation intended to replace the structures of Ethiopian military dictatorship, which devastated the sociopolitical infrastructures of the country, with a democratic and constitutional government. The period was also characterized by the transformation of the ruined economy of the country into a progressive model by a process of rehabilitation and reconstruction programs. Therefore, the administrative structure of the Ethiopian occupation was abandoned and replaced by a new political and administrative structure.

Immediately after the military victory on May 24, 1991, the EPLF established the so called *giziyawi mengesti ertra* (ግዝያዊ መንግስቲ ኤርትራ)—Provisional Government of Eritrea (PGE) under Proclamation 1/1991, which was further articulated by Proclamation 23/1992. Hence, it established a *de facto* sovereign state. The law under Proclamation 1/1991 provided for three main organs of the new government: legislative, executive, and judiciary. These proper governmental organs were established by transforming the EPLF organizational branches founded during the pre-liberation periods. Under this arrangement, the chief executive of the government was given the title Secretary General, while the governmental departments were administered under their respective Secretaries.

The PGE implemented various other provisional laws as well. It issued a number of proclamations and enacted transitional codes. Among the most important proclamations issued by the PGE included Proclamation 26/1992. The government introduced new territorial divisions of the country and established *zobawi memehedarat* (ዞባዊ ምምሕዳራት) "regional administrations," ratified in 1996 by the Assembly—commonly known as *hagerawi bayto* (ሃገራዊ ባይቶ). It defined their relationships with the central government; and it also enacted guidelines regarding the extent of power-sharing between the central government and its regional administrations. Although the executive and legislative branches were considered as important functioning appendages in this arrangement, the judiciary branch was made an independent body at all levels of the new administrative structure. The Ministry of Local Government was established to coordinate the regional administrations.

The executive branch of the government consisted of the Secretary General at the top and 13 different secretariats, including commanders of the terrestrial and naval army, as well as regional administrators who were under the State Council of the PGE. Therefore, as had been the tradition of leadership in the EPLF, the PGE established a highly centralized political leadership. For example, the Secretary General of EPLF had direct control over the Politburo and Central Committee of the organization, a structure that was adopted for the PGE. The Central Committee and the Politburo combined legislative and executive powers, leaving no room for further sharing of substantial political powers among other institutions of the organization. In simple terms, the highly centralized and strong executive power structures of the EPLF leadership (as also later reflected in the National Charter for Eritrea of 1994) were considered as a model for the PGE. The EPLF Secretary General, Mr. Isaias Afeweki, was made chairman of the new government's State Council and the head of the Central Committee and, thereby, the head of state.

Other important proclamations issued by the PGE were related to providing transitional laws. A number of amended versions of the Ethiopian Civil and Penal Codes that had been in use for several decades were introduced by the PGE as transitional laws. The PGE amended or modified some of these codes in a way so that the laws became consistent with the principles and values of the Front (now PGE), and implemented them as transitional laws with the intention of substituting them after the ratification of the new Eritrean constitution. Among many other legal decrees, the PGE issued Proclamation 2/1991, which provided the Transitional Civil Code of Eritrea (an amended version of the Ethiopian Civil Code of 1960). In the same year, the PGE also issued Proclamation 3/1991, implementing the Transitional Code of Civil Procedure of Eritrea (an amended version of the Ethiopian Civil Procedure of 1965); Proclamation 4/1991, enacting the Transitional Penal Law of Eritrea (an amended version of the Ethiopian Penal Code of 1957); and Proclamation 5/1991, providing the Transitional Code of Penal Procedure of Eritrea (an amended version of the Ethiopian Code of Penal Procedure of 1957). The PGE also issued further legal proclamations such as Proclamation 6/1991, which introduced the Transitional Commercial Code of Eritrea (an amended version of the Ethiopian Commercial Code of 1960); Proclamation 9/1991, which established The Gazette of Eritrean Law; and Proclamation 22/1992, which set the criteria and procedures for the Eritrean Referendum (for further information, see Iyob 1995: 108–179).

The PGE effectively lasted for two years, during which time remarkable changes occurred for the Eritrean society. The PGE expanded civic education, drafted new rehabilitation and reconstruction programs, and established the rule of law. Moreover, it issued the Eritrean Nationality Proclamation 21/1992, which introduced new laws of citizenship. Under this proclamation, all persons born to a father and/or a mother of Eritrean origin were entitled to the right of Eritrean citizenship. Moreover, all persons who were not Eritreans by birth but who lived in Eritrea for over ten years from the 1930s onward had the right to claim Eritrean citizenship—citizenship by *naturalization* (Iyob 1995: 138–141).

The first few years after independence were also characterized by a number of serious problems. Lack of a skilled work force caused a series of obstacles in the fields of administration, education, and economy. For example, most courts in the country suffered from a lack of trained personnel. Most of these courts did not have enough qualified judges. Considering most of the judges who served under the *Dergue* to be incapable and corrupt, the PGE suspended them from their posts. This aggravated the problems in the administration of justice in urban centers. Even at the village level, many of the village judges elected in 1991 were illiterate and incapable of performing the duties assigned to them. Almost all the courts continued to be flooded by new cases, and unfinished cases while they were crippled by lack of personnel.

As regard to the Eritrean masses, the first few years of independence were years of higher expectations, renewed hope, and general happiness. The government also enjoyed the full support, tolerance, and understanding of the population. The Eritrean people, who had suffered from colonial oppression and decades of postcolonial warfare, considered the new government as a representative of their own interests and wishes; and they had higher expectations for peace and prosperity. The people fully cooperated with the government in all matters; and they even willingly sent their children to take part in the National Service Program, which was introduced by the PGE. The government (which claimed that the country had no capital) was continuously rewarded with immense amounts of cash and material contributions by citizens living inside and outside the country.

THE ERITREAN REFERENDUM

The EPLF did not opt to declare Eritrean independence immediately after the military victory on May 24, 1991. Instead, it preferred to hold a referendum in 1993 by which Eritreans were to be given the chance to cast their votes (for determining the future of their country). The EPLF's decision for a referendum was intended to gain international recognition, appreciation, and to prove that the Eritrean liberation struggle was a popular movement in which most Eritreans participated. Meanwhile, as stated above, the EPLF established a *de facto* independent state that replaced the Ethiopian administrative and governmental structures.

The EPLF had already considered settlement of the Eritrean question through a referendum in the 1980s. When the PGE was established in 1991, the idea of referendum was introduced to the public and it was widely accepted. In April 1993, the PGE arranged for the Eritrean referendum in which many international observers, including the UN special representative, Mr. Samir Sanbar, the UN Technical Team, U.S. delegates, Organization of African Unity (OAU) observers, as well as representatives from the Arab League, the United Kingdom, Egypt, and a number of other countries, participated.

The Eritrean referendum was scheduled for April 23–25, 1993. Starting in 1992, the PGE launched local campaigns and provided civic education about voting procedures. The Eritrean Referendum Commission, established by the PGE, made remarkable efforts to provide equitable distribution of civic education in rural and urban Eritrea. It organized public meetings and seminars through which the government presented its ideals about the importance of the referendum for the country's legitimate independence and sovereignty. It extended its campaigns across the country, and citizens were encouraged to cast their votes as provided under Proclamation 22/1992. The Eritrean media also continued to broadcast information about various issues related to the scheduled referendum. Seminars and meeting, intended to involve the Eritrean diaspora in the referendum were also held in other continents, including North America and Europe. The PGE characterized the vote for independence in a simple "yes" or "no" manner, and the ballots presented a simple question: "Do you approve Eritrea to become independent and sovereign state?" "Yes" (blue card) or "No" (red card) (see also Iyob 1995: 139).

Voters for the referendum were required to be registered, and registration to vote was dependent on proof of Eritrean citizenship as provided under Proclamation 21/1992. Eligible voters were required to be Eritrean citizens, and all Eritreans who lived within and outside the country were eligible to register and to vote. However, those who applied for voting were required to be over eighteen-years old, free of any previous criminal conviction, and to present an *ertrawi wereqet meninet* (ኤርትራዊ ወረቐት መንነት), usually called *meninet* (Eritrean identification). All citizens were required to get an Eritrean identification through a procedure that involved filling out forms (commonly known as *ornik*) in which detailed information, including the person's religious affiliation, residence address, genealogical/kinship details, and statement on his/her basis of citizenship claims, was to be provided. The person claiming to be entitled to vote in the referendum and have an Eritrean ID was required to present three (usually elderly) citizens who would be able to provide their testimony to the government officials that the statements made by the person claiming citizenship were all true; and that they had to sign in front of the officials. Registration forms and legal procedures for registration were also distributed in various localities abroad where Eritreans were registered for voting.

In early April 1993, over 1.17 million Eritreans (out of approximately 3.5 million of the total population) were registered to vote, and 1,007 polling stations were established across the country. The Referendum Commission trained over 5,000 people (including teachers and students) to offer their help during registration (for more details, see "The Government of Eritrea 1993": 1–28). As discussed in chapter two, the Eritrean people had never participated in an electoral process of any kind, and the referendum was to be the first exercise (after the Federation) in a voting process. Hence, the Commission undertook extensive public education designed to increase voter awareness and explain the voting process to rural and urban populations throughout the country.

As scheduled, the Eritrean referendum took place on April 23–25, and over 1.15 million voters participated within the country. Of total voters, 99.8 percent voted in support of Eritrean independence and sovereignty. In Ethiopia alone, over 57,000 Eritreans were registered to cast their votes and over 99.5 percent voted "yes" for Eritrean independence. In Sudan, over 150,000 Eritreans were registered to vote, and an overwhelming majority voted for Eritrean independence.

Votes for the Eritrean referendum were counted in April 1993 under the observation of the UN and many other national and international observers. On April 27, 1993, Eritrea officially declared that the referendum was concluded with 99.8 percent of yes votes for Eritrean independence. The country also officially declared its independence on May 24, 1993. The UN delegate and most other international observers also

Eriitrean flag. (Dreamstime.com)

provided their testimony, saying that the referendum was free and fair at all standard measures.

Most Eritreans who were eligible to vote participated in the Eritrean referendum. Among the extreme minority sections of the population who did not take part in the referendum were the Eritrean followers of Jehovah's Witnesses. Followers of this religion are less that 1 percent in the country's population. Most followers of this religious sect refused to participate in the referendum not on political grounds, but on the basis of their own religious principles. Nevertheless, it caused them serious political consequences during the post-referendum periods.

THE TRANSITIONAL GOVERNMENT OF ERITREA (MAY 1993–PRESENT)

Following the legitimate and successful referendum, and after the declaration of Eritrea's formal independence, the PGE started a new process designed to transform itself into a more institutionally structured government. The EPLF leadership met on May 11–12, 1993, to set up procedures for the formation of a new formal government. Just after the meeting, the PGE issued Proclamation 37/1993 on May 19, 1993, in which it established the *De Jure* Transitional Government of Eritrea (TGE) (መስጋገሪ መንግስቲ ኤርትራ). As provided under the proclamation, the TGE was to serve for only the following four years, after which time democratic elections would take place replacing the TGE by an elected and democratic government. Mr. Isaias Afeweki, the Secretary General of the PGE, continued to hold his position as the chief of state and head of government, but now his title was changed from Secretary General to President. However, the TGE has not yet been replaced by an elected government, and elections have been repeatedly postponed. The Eritrean constitution, which was ratified on May 23, 1997, has not been implemented to this day.

The transformation of PGE to TGE did not involve major changes in the political structure of the existing governmental system and organization. Yet the EPLF reformed itself as a Liberation Front and changed its structure as a national party by naming itself the People's Front for Democracy and Justice (PFDJ). The EPLF renamed itself the PFDJ during its Third Congress in Nakfa in February 1994. At the same congress, the PFDJ drafted its political visions and approved a document that it called "A National Charter for Eritrea."

THE ADMINISTRATIVE DIVISIONS OF ERITREA

The Eritrean government divided the country into six new administrative zones (*zobas*). According to the current government's rationale for the new administrative set-up, the previous administrative division had been a structure that the European colonial and post-European governments used as a means for their "divide and rule" policies. As a result, the old administrative structures and the colonial policies sowed seeds of regional parochial sentiments. To reform these sentiments and politics of division, the government established a new administrative set-up. Hence, it dispensed with the old administrative structure and established six new divisions, in some cases by merging two old administrative zones—Akkele Guzay and Seraye, for example. Although this new plan was not welcomed by several sections of the Eritrean population, the government implemented its new policies of administrative structure and division. The current (December 2008) administrative divisions are shown in Table G of the "Facts and Figures" section of this book.

The new administrative set-up also created some shifts of the former provincial capitals. For example, Adi Keyyih, the former capital of Akkele Guzay Province lost its position due to the newly introduced administrative structure, and Mendefera was made the capital of the new zone. Several other towns that used to be central administrative zones for many years lost their political importance during the new government. For the list of Eritrean Ministries, see Table H in the "Facts and Figures" section of this book.

THE PFDJ'S NATIONAL CHARTER FOR ERITREA (FEBRUARY 1994)

The Charter expressed the PFDJ's political visions for the future of Eritrea, and it starts by expressing its wishes and ambitions for "building a peaceful, just and prosperous society." Furthermore, it states that the generation that fought for the independence of Eritrea has the "responsibility to pass on to future generations the basic elements for modern and just society." The PFDJ's document enumerates six basic goals and six basic principles as comprising the PFDJ's visions for future Eritrea. The basic goals listed in the document are:

1. National harmony—to facilitate the prevalence of peace and stability that would allow the Eritrean people to live in harmony and without religious, regional, ethnolinguistic class, and gender distinctions.

2. Political democracy—for the Eritrean people to participate in decision-making and have their rights guaranteed by law and practice.

3. Economic and social development—to achieve social and economic progress in education, technology, and the standard of living.

4. Social justice (economic and social democracy)—to secure equitable distribution of wealth, services, and opportunities, and also give attention to the disadvantaged sections of the society.

5. Cultural revival—to attain the revival of Eritrean culture characterized by love of country, respect for humanity, solidarity between men and women, love of truth and justice, respect for law, hard work, self-confidence, self-reliance, open mindedness, and inventiveness.

6. Regional and international cooperation—For the country to become a respected member of the international community, by coexisting in harmony and co-operation with its neighbors, and by contributing to regional and global peace and development.

The above-stated goals of the PFDJ were also the dreams and wishes of all Eritreans. Therefore, the Eritrean people also welcomed these goals. To achieve these goals, the PFDJ articulated six basic principles that it emphasized were among the underlining reasons of success for the liberation struggle and would continue to be policy guidelines for the TGE. These are:

1. National unity—The preservation of national unity based on the participation of all sections of the Eritrean society; by creating a national government that ensures unity and equality of all Eritrean people, rejects all divisive attitudes and activities, places national interests above anything else, and enables the participation of all sectors of the Eritrean society.

2. Active participation of the people—Demand for the active participation of the people based on political consciousness in all aspects of decision-making.

3. Decisive role of human factor—The acknowledgment of human factor as decisive for the success of the liberation struggle and for the reconstruction of the country.

4. The relationship between national and social struggles (struggle for social justice)—The need for active participation of the people by keeping promises and stimulating their enthusiasm through various progressive programs. The PFDJ stated its ideals about social justice: "for us, based on our actual experience, social justice means narrowing the gap between the haves and have-nots, ensuring that all people have their fair share of the national wealth and can participate in the political, social and cultural life of the country, to creating balanced development, respecting human rights and advancing democracy."

5. Self-reliance—To apply economic, political, and cultural self-reliant strategies by following independent political aims and giving priority to internal conditions, as well as by relying on internal economic capabilities.

6. A strong relationship between people and leadership—Creating a strong relationship between the leadership (as defined by the PFDJ: "the organized broad political force that provides leadership") and the people through a transparent and corruption-free system of administration.

GOVERNMENTAL BODIES OF THE TGE

As stated earlier, the Eritrean government includes three main bodies: the executive, the legislative, and the judiciary. As part of the legislative body, the Central Committee of the PGE was retained and became a central part of the newly created *hagerawi bayto* (National Assembly) of the TGE.

The Legislative Body

The main legislative body of the Eritrean government is the National Assembly. In addition to the members of the Central Committee of the PFDJ, the National Assembly was established by newly elected representatives from the provinces and new members directly elected by the Central Committee itself. All in all, the National Assembly is composed of 150 members, 75 of whom also belong to the Central Committee of the PFDJ, and the remaining 75 members who are elected by the general population as their representatives to the parliament. Included among the members of the National Assembly are 10 women.

The rationale behind the National Assembly was for it to serve as the highest legal power of the TGE until and after the establishment of a constitutional and democratically elected government. In theory, the National Assembly would also become one of the most important branches of the Eritrean government. In practice, there have not been further elections to renew the composition and nature of the Assembly membership through democratic national elections since its establishment. Hence, the Assembly has not functioned effectively on its founding principles, especially since 1998. It has not called a formal assembly meeting since 2002.

Among the main tasks of the National Assembly are: the approval and execution of the government's foreign and domestic policies; the election of the country's president (who would have the power to chair the TGE State Council and the National Assembly); and the power to approve the national budget.

Apart from the National Assembly, regional administrations also possess Regional Assemblies. Based on the administrative divisions introduced after independence, Eritrea has six administrative zones (set up under Proclamation 86/1996). Each of these zones has its own Assembly. The members of the Regional Assemblies are directly elected by the people through popular regional elections. Unlike the national level, elections on the regional administration level have been conducted on a relatively regular basis, and popular elections for the membership of Regional Assembly have taken place at least twice since 2000. The main task of Regional Assemblies is to set local (regional) political and policy agendas as well as to protect local administration from overrules from the top. However, the Regional Assemblies do not have the power to elect their respective local administrators. Rather, the president himself directly appoints local administrators.

The Executive Body

The executive body of the TGE is the *cabine ministerat* (ካቢነ ሚኒስተራት) (Cabinet of Ministers or State Council) composed of all ministers entitled with executive authorities and directly chaired by the president of the country. The minister of each ministry becomes a member of the Cabinet of Ministers. The president is the highest authority in the executive body. In principle, the election of each member of the Cabinet is approved by the General Assembly, although this has not been a regular exercise. In practice, each minister is directly appointed by the president himself. Most of the positions in the Executive Branch are held by former members of the EPLF Political Bureau. As the appointment of ministers has not been based on certain defined criteria, it is possible that the same minister might hold different ministry or administrative positions at different times. It has also been observed that, in some instances, the personal and professional qualifications of the appointee might not necessarily be taken into consideration when making an appointment. The duration and position of each minister is also defined by the president himself. The main task of the Cabinet of Ministers is to execute the day-to-day activities of the TGE. Table H in the "Facts and Figures" section of the book shows the current (as of December 2008) ministries and ministers in Eritrea.

The Judicial Body

As stated earlier, the judicial division is an independent body with its court systems distributed at the national, regional, and village levels. In general, the judicial body has three types of courts: the military court, civil court, and special court (*filuy bet ferdi*— ፍሉይ ቤት ፍርዲ). All the courts are administered under the Ministry of Justice. At the national level, justice is administered under the Supreme Court, which has not yet been enforced. Rather, the High Court also plays the role of the Supreme Court. The highest level of civil court is the High Court. At the regional level, justice is administered under the *bet ferdi zoba* (Regional Court). Similar to the High Court, the Regional Court also has various branches.

The Special Court was established by the government to provide jurisdictions that involved corruption. The Eritrean government embarked on combating corruption, and it considered the need to establish a special court in which cases related to corruption would be treated. However, the Special Court's judges have been appointed directly by the President, and a number of them belong to high-ranking military officials; but they do not have formal higher educational opportunities or training to pursue their jobs.

The Communal Laws

Eritrean societies have a long tradition of community-based legal systems and legal institutions, and they have very rich communal laws (customary laws). The Eritrean communal laws have been in effective use since the fifteenth century, and they have been orally passed down from generation to generation. There have been about fourteen recorded communal laws across Eritrea. The laws dealt with all issues that guided the cultural, economic, social, ecological, and political aspects of rural communities. In many cases, the communal laws have been passed on orally, but few have been documented in writing for a number of centuries. The documented codes and bylaws were preserved in villages and monasteries where they functioned as central guidelines for the overall livelihood of the communities. Because of the unstable political situation in the country throughout the last centuries, many of the written codes were destroyed or lost.

Ecological differences among the various regions of Eritrea caused variations in economic activities. Hence, different regions had different communal laws. All the laws and bylaws, however, clearly defined their natural resources and adopted legal procedures on mechanisms of appropriate natural resource exploitation, mechanisms of conflict resolution, and guidelines to their social and political livelihoods. The difference in the communal laws largely concerned geographical, economic, and religious issues. For instance, as the highland population consisted of sedentary farmers (and also the majority of the population were Christians), their local laws reflected their beliefs and their economic situations. On the other hand, the lowlanders were pastoral communities (the majority being Moslems), and their local laws reflected their beliefs and their economic circumstances. Although the geography of the regions played a dominant role in solidifying their laws, religious factors also played their important part in the composition of those local laws.

During the Italian colonial rule, some Italian scholars collected and compiled several of these laws. There was a local wish that the colonial government would include communal laws in the new colonial legislation; but it did not materialize. On the contrary, the colonial government considered these old laws simply as social norms of little value for its governmental function.

Although the colonial administration formally allowed the presumption of function of these communal laws, there was little effort to encourage further improvement. Therefore, they were not effective after the establishment of the colonial government (apart from serving as partly written and otherwise orally transmitted guidelines of social norms and guiding principles for jurisdiction in the villages).

Similarly, governments during the post-Italian colonial period also followed the Italian colonial policies, and the communal laws have not been incorporated into the state-run systems of justice. However, communal laws are by no means extinct, and they still serve as central judicial systems of rural conflict resolution mechanisms as well as guiding principles in village courts. For most rural communities, it has been highly bureaucratic and costly to appeal in state courts, and, so, they continue to apply their traditional legal systems in their respective villages. They use these laws to resolve disputes, preserve their cultural traditions such as marriage arrangements and to attain fair consumption of natural resources.

The post-independence Eritrean government does not recognize communal laws as an official part and source of justice in the country. However, it acknowledges the importance of these laws as complementary sources of law for the judicial body of the government. The government also allows for the practice of customary laws at the village courts whenever applicable.

THE ERITREAN CONSTITUTION

The TGE National Assembly set up the Constitutional Commission under Proclamation 55/1994 of March 1994. The commission consisted of about fifty team members. The main task of this commission was to draft a democratic constitution for the country. The commission established further internal committees that were assigned various tasks in the process of constitution making. The Constitutional Commission started its work in April of the same year and launched an extensive campaign aimed at cultivating popular participation in the constitution making. It also delivered public seminars and lectures regarding the process of constitution-making throughout the country. Similar to the campaigns for the Eritrean referendum, the constitution making process also involved remarkable activities intended to increase public awareness: through media campaigning, formal public meetings, civic education, and public debates in towns and villages across the country. It also held preliminary public meetings inside and outside the country.

Bereket Habte Selassie, professor at the University of North Carolina at Chapel Hill and the chair of the Constitutional Commission, played a significant role in the process of constitution making. After three years of intensive public debates and meetings, the National Assembly approved the final draft of the constitution in May 1997. The draft of the constitution was also published and distributed to the public in the major Eritrean languages of Tigrinya and Arabic.

The "domestically generated" constitution of Eritrea was the result of wider public participation, and it provides ultimate guidelines of all types of laws in the country. The Constitution is divided into seven major chapters, containing 58 articles and around 190 subarticles. Providing detailed analysis of the constitution is out of the scope of this study, although Bereket Habte Selassie (2003) provides detailed analysis on the subject. However, brief descriptions of the chapters contained in the constitution follow.

- **Chapter I: General Provisions**. Under this chapter, the constitution defines the State of Eritrea and its territory (Art. 1). It elaborates that the country is "a sovereign and independent state founded on the principles of democracy, social justice and rule of law." This chapter also provides articles related to legal guidelines for the "supremacy of the constitution" (Art. 2), "Citizenship" (Art. 3), "National Symbols and Languages" (Art. 4) and "Gender Reference" (Art. 5).

- **Chapter II: National Objectives and Directive Principles**. This chapter of the constitution provides legal guidelines for the "national unity and stability" (Art. 6); the State's "democratic principles" (Art. 7); "competent justice system" (Art. 8); the establishment of "competent public administration" (Art. 9); securing "economic and social development" (Art. 10); preserving and developing "national culture" (Art. 11); laws related to "national defense and security" (Art. 12); and guidelines for "foreign policy" (Art. 13).

- **Chapter III: Fundamental Rights, Freedoms, and Duties**. This chapter of the constitution provides detailed guidelines for collective and individual rights, liberties, and duties. It includes articles and subarticles on: "equality under the law" (Art. 14); "right to life and liberty" (Art. 15); "right to human dignity" (Art. 16); "arrest, detention, and fair trial" (Art. 17); "right to privacy" (Art. 18); "freedom of conscience, religion, expression of opinion, movement, assembly and organization" (Art. 19); "rights to vote and to be candidate to an executive office" (Art. 20); "economic, social and cultural rights and responsibilities" (Art. 21); "family" (Art. 22); "rights to property" (Art. 23); "administrative justice" (Art. 24); "duties of citizens" (Art. 25); "limitation upon fundamental rights and freedoms" (Art. 26); "state of emergency" (Art. 27); "enforcement of fundamental rights and freedoms" (Art. 28); and "residual rights" (Art. 29).

- **Chapter IV: The National Assembly**. This chapter of the constitution provides detailed guiding laws regarding the legislative body of the constitutional government. It establishes the National Assembly as the highest legislative division of the government. Hence, it provides articles and subarticles on the "representation of the people" in the Assembly (Art. 30); "establishment and duration of the National Assembly" (Art. 31); "powers and duties of the National Assembly" (Art. 32); "approval of draft legislation" (Art. 33); "Chairman of the National Assembly" (Art. 34); "oath" (Art. 35); "rules of procedure in the National Assembly" (Art. 36); "office and Committee of the National Assembly" (Art. 37); and "duties, immunities and privileges of members of the National Assembly" (Art. 38).

- **Chapter V: The Executive**. Chapter five of the constitution provides detailed legal guidelines for the executive branch of the government. It provides articles and subarticles on the "President: head of state and government" (Art. 39); "qualifications to be a candidate to the Office of the President" (Art. 40); "elections and term of office of the President" (Art. 41); "powers and duties of the President" (Art. 42); "immunity from civil and criminal proceedings" (Art. 43); "privileges to be given to former presidents" (Art. 44); "oath" (Art. 45); "the Cabinet" (Art. 46); and "ministerial accountability" (Art. 47).

- **Chapter VI: The Administration of Justice**. The constitution also presents detailed legal provisions regarding the administration of justice in the country. Under this chapter of the constitution, the following articles are provided: guidelines regarding "the Judiciary" (Art. 48); "the Supreme Court" (Art. 49); "lower courts" (Art. 50); an "oath" for all newly appointed judges (Art. 51); procedures about "removal of judges from office" (Art. 52); and procedures and rules of "the Judicial Service Commission" (Art. 53).

- **Chapter VII: Miscellaneous Provisions**. The constitution also provides legal guidelines for the "Auditor General" (Art. 54); "National Bank" (Art. 55); "public service administration" (Art. 56); "Electoral Commission" (Art. 57); and legal procedures for the "amendment of the constitution" (Art. 58).

The Eritrean constitution was drafted and ratified by majority support of the government and the people of the country. But even though an overwhelming majority of Eritreans expected an immediate implementation of the constitution after its ratification, the government still has not done so. The implementation of the constitution was expected in 1997–1998. However, due to the Ethiopia-Eritrea border conflict that broke out in 1998, the government postponed the implementation of the constitution for an open date. Therefore, the issue of the Eritrean constitution has been one of the sources of hot debate in Eritrean politics, especially since 2000. In fact, for many observers and citizens, the behavior of the government regarding the constitution has been paradoxical. Many ask: Why is the Eritrean government, which fully supported and ratified the constitution, not ready to implement it? Apart from formal and informal excuses, such as the issue of the border conflict and the question of "national security," the Eritrean government has not made any public announcement as to why it does not really want to implement the constitution. However, speculations about the issue can be broadly classified in the following points:

- The TGE leadership's fear of losing power
- The TGE leadership does not want to keep its promises for establishing a constitutional democracy in the country
- The PFDJ's wish to remain as a single national party, and more

INDEPENDENT ERITREA AND ITS NEIGHBORS

Eritrea's independence was followed by regional and international recognition of the country as a sovereign and independent state. All neighbors of Eritrea—Djibouti, Sudan, Yemen, and Ethiopia—also officially recognized the country as an independent and sovereign state; and they established their respective bilateral relations with the State of Eritrea. Their diplomatic relations were facilitated through their respective embassies in Asmara and Eritrea's embassies in these countries.

ERITREA-SUDAN RELATIONS

Sudan, one of the few countries that played a crucial role during the Eritrean liberation struggle, was also one of the first countries to acknowledge Eritrean independence. Based on the longstanding relations between the Eritrean Fronts and successive Sudanese governments, both countries signed a Defense and Security Pact in 1991. With this pact, they agreed to continue their cooperation and share security information that concerned both parties. However, it took only a year or so until the cordial relations between Sudan and Eritrea started to deteriorate, leading to conventional tensions in 1994.

Eritrea accused Sudan of facilitating Islamist jihad activities on Eritrean soil. Hassan al-Turabi, a key figure in Sudanese politics during the Al-Bashir government, stimulated ambitious attempts to extend Islamist radicalization in the Horn of Africa. This resulted in a series of conflict with the neighbors of Sudan, including Eritrea.

For Sudan and its Arab allies, Eritrea's strong diplomatic relations with the United States, Israel, and Ethiopia was also seen as a potential danger in the region. Moreover, Sudan accused Eritrea of supporting Sudanese rebels such as the Sudan People's Liberation Movement (SPLM). Eritrea's diplomatic stand was questioned by several Middle East nations, especially after the Eritrean president's speech at the Qatar press conference in May 1992 in which he declared that "the Arab League does not represent anything in the world and is ineffectual . . . The Arab League does not have a role or a presence" (quoted in Mengisteab and Yohannes 2005: 203). The president's speech caused diplomatic tensions with several Arab countries.

Sudan, which felt insecure because of the changing political environment in the region, started to be bitter toward the Eritrean government. As tensions continued to mount, Eritrea expelled the Sudanese consuls from Asmara after claiming to have identified them as being involved in promoting Islamic fundamentalism in Eritrea. By December 1993, several jihad insurgencies occurred in Eritrea. The Eritrean government identified Sudan as the main source of these insurgencies, and it made public announcements regarding the issue. After several months of tensions between the two countries, they eventually agreed on principles of nonintervention in August 1994. However, since then, the Eritrea-Sudan relationship has been erratic and unpredictable. Their relations are characterized sometimes by tensions while at other times they establish cordial relations. Recently, Eritrea has played a prominent role in the Sudanese civil war settlement and reconciliation efforts.

THE ERITREA-YEMEN DISPUTE (1995–1996)

After a series of disputes over the Hannish Islands, which are located in the Red Sea, Eritrea and Yemen fought a brief border war on December 15, 1995. Yemeni and Eritrean forces also clashed over the Hannish Islands. On December 16, 1995, the Eritrean forces defeated the Yemeni garrisons on these islands and captured over 150 Yemeni soldiers.

The Hannish Islands are located about 160 kilometres (99.4 miles) north of Bab al-Mandab (the southern gate of the Red Sea) at an almost equidistant position between the two countries. Therefore, these islands are located at a geopolitically strategic part of the Red Sea. Most trade ships coming and going through the Suez Canal pass through these islands. The Hannish Islands are also considered by both parties as possible sites for great oil reserves.

The two countries agreed to a ceasefire on December 17, 1995. Yet tensions between the two countries continued until the next year. On May 26, 1996, Eritrea and Yemen agreed to settle the dispute peacefully. Based on this agreement, they referred the case to the Permanent Court of Arbitration at Hague. The Permanent Court of Arbitration passed its unanimous ruling on October 9, 1996. On the basis of the Court's unanimous ruling, Yemen was awarded sovereignty over the group of bigger islands commonly known as the Hannish-Zuqar archipelago, and the Zubayr islands. Eritrea was awarded sovereignty over the smaller islands located to the southwest. The ruling also stated that Eritrean and Yemeni fishermen would have free access to all the disputed islands.

THE ERITREA-ETHIOPIA BORDER CONFLICT (1998–2000)

In 1991, the joint military operations of the EPLF (on the Eritrean side) and the Tigrean People's Liberation Front (TPLF) (on the Ethiopian side) resulted in the overthrow of the dictatorial communist regime that devastated Ethiopia and Eritrea for almost two decades. In Ethiopia, the TPLF along with other political organizations formed the Ethiopian People's Revolutionary Democratic Front (EPRDF) and established a new government. However, among all the political units represented in the EPRDF, the TPLF became and still is the dominant political unit. In Eritrea, the EPLF alone formed the PGE and later TGE.

Starting in 1991, the two governments set up cordial relations. Their friendly relations were demonstrated on several occasions between their respective leaders. For instance, during his official visit to Eritrea following the Eritrean Referendum in 1993, Ethiopian Prime Minister Meles Zenawi advised the Eritrean people not to scratch their wounds that were caused by decades of conflict with Ethiopia. Similarly, the PGE also demonstrated on many public occasions that good relations with Ethiopia would be the only way to heal the wounds and eliminate the scars sustained during all the years of conflict between the two countries.

ERITREA'S NATIONAL ANTHEM

Tigrinya	English version
ኤርትራ ኤርትራ ኤርትራ	Eritrea, Eritrea, Eritrea,
በዓል ደማ እናልቀስ ተደምሲሱ፡	The barbarian enemy humiliatingly defeated
መስዋእታ ብሓርነት ተደቢሱ።	And martyrdom has paid for freedom
መዋእል ነኺሳ ኣብ ዕላማ	Decades of devotion for purpose
ትእምርቲ ጽንዓት ኮይኑ ስማ፡	Your name became challenger, miraculous
ኤርትራ እዛ ሓበን ውጹዓት	Ertra, comfort for the oppressed
ኣመስኪራ ሓቂ ክምትዕወት።	Proved that truth can win after all
ኤርትራ ኤርትራ	Eritrea, Eritrea, Eritrea
ኣብ ዓለም ጨቢጣቶ ግቡእ ክብራ።	A sovereign state on earth after all
ናጽነት ዘምጽአ ልዑል ኒሕ	Dedication that led to liberation
ንህንጻን ልምዓትን ክስርሕ፡	Will build-up and make her green
ስልጣነ ክነልብሳ ግርማ	We shall honour her with progress
ሕድሪ ኣለና ግምጃ ክንስልማ።	We have a word to her to embellish
ኤርትራ ኤርትራ	Eritrea, Eritrea, Eritrea
ኣብ ዓለም ጨቢጣቶ ግቡእ ክብራ።	A sovereign state on earth after all

The two governments embarked on a number of joint economic, security, and other cooperative programs. In July 1993, they signed an agreement on "Friendship and Cooperation." The Friendship and Cooperation agreement provided, among many things, free movement of people between the two countries and free flow of commercial goods and capital. Moreover, the agreement allowed Ethiopia to have free access to the sea, although it was required to pay for port services. The cordial and progressive relations between the two countries continued for some years. Their cooperation was considered by the people of the Horn at large as a great step forward in achieving peace and stability in the region, which had suffered from long-term conflicts.

Unfortunately, the cordial relations between the two governments deteriorated in early 1998. Although not publicly addressed by the two governments, border tensions between the countries had started in 1997. In 1998, the Eritrean government publicized that both heads of state had already exchanged letters regarding the border tensions. According to the Eritrean government, the Eritrean president wrote to Prime Minister Meles Zenawi on issues related to the growing tensions along the borders. In his alleged letter (written August 16, 1997), the president stated that Ethiopian forces had occupied Adi Murug, and he requested the prime minister to take necessary measures to help avoid pointless conflicts. He further stated in his letter that the border issue would not be otherwise difficult to solve affably. Although the prime minister did not reply (or at least it has not been publicly known if he replied to the first letter of the president), the Eritrean president is alleged to have written a second letter on August 26, 1997.

Through this letter, the president reminded the prime minister that Adi Murug was located inside Eritrean territory, and he informed him that the Ethiopian forces had also recently dismantled the Eritrean administration in the area and expelled Eritrean officials from the territory. The president also indicated that similar actions had occurred at a place called Badme. Replying to the second letter of the president, the prime minister is believed to have stated that the Ethiopian forces did not occupy any of the disputed areas and that both parties had to respect the earlier agreements made between the two countries. Although the prime minister's letter indicated that some agreements were reached between the two governments regarding border issues before 1997, no solid information regarding these agreements has been made available during this work. Without making it known to the public, the two governments had established a bilateral commission to deal with the border issue sometime before the tensions escalated. However, little is known about either this commission's tasks or its findings regarding the issue.

On May 12, 1998, the border tensions between these countries changed into conventional warfare. The outbreak of the war surprised most people in Eritrea and Ethiopia. The immediate cause of the war is not yet clear, and, both parties provide different accounts as to how the war started. According to the Eritrean government, on May 12, the Eritrean army gained control of Badme (a village located near the border and claimed by both parties) by driving out the Ethiopian militia who had controlled the area on May 6, 1998 (after attacking the Eritrean patrol units in the same territory). The Eritrean government also alleged that some Eritrean farming communities had been expelled from the border area (especially Badme) in July 1997.

To the contrary, the Ethiopian government alleged that the Eritrean army invaded its territories around Badme, and the Tigrean militias engaged in fighting against the Eritrean invasion. Needless to say, the Ethiopian government also claimed Badme as part of its territory, and the Eritrean occupation of the area (on May 12) was considered as an outright invasion of an Ethiopian territory.

Until June 1998, the war changed its course and magnitude and involved many military garrisons from both sides. Tensions continued to escalate and on June 5, 1998, Ethiopia launched air raids and bombed the Eritrean International Airport located at Asmara. In retaliation, the Eritrean Defense Forces (EDF) bombed Mekele, the capital of the Tigray province in Ethiopia. Soon, the border war at Badme changed into full-fledged warfare throughout the border areas between the two countries. Battles were fought at Badme, in the Mereb-Setit territories, Tsorona, Zalambesa, and Bure.

In Eritrea, the government did not publicize the tensions or the threat of war with Ethiopia until the Ethiopian government officially issued an ultimatum against Eritrea on May 13, 1998. Even during the initial stages of the war, the Eritrean government remained almost silent, while the Ethiopian government broadcasted war propaganda through its radio station in Tigray and Addis Ababa. Generally, the war was a great shock for most people in Eritrea. Owing to the lack of information about the tensions, the war became a mystery for most Eritreans. The government refused to be transparent on the issue until the Ethiopians bombed Asmara, and the issue became outrageous for most people.

Both sides mobilized hundreds of thousands of men as ground forces along their common borders, dug trenches that extended for hundreds of kilometers, and purchased new war planes and other weapons. The war continued throughout 1998 and 1999 in a terrifying magnitude. Both sides sustained immense human and capital losses in the warfare. Needless to say, these countries also missed significant diplomatic opportunities that otherwise would have led to a peaceful resolution of the conflict.

The U.S.-Rwanda initiative for a peaceful resolution of the conflict was one of the opportunities. Through this initiative mediators proposed the redeployment of troops to their positions during the pre-May 6, 1998 period and the demarcation of the borders on the bases of colonial treaties and agreements. Eritrea refused this initiative on February 22, 1999, and demanded an immediate demilitarization of all the disputed areas and the start of direct talks. Another opportunity for a peaceful resolution of the conflict was presented to both sides by the OAU. Similar to the U.S.-Rwanda initiative, the OAU initiative, which came to be known as "Framework, Modalities, and Technical Arrangements," proposed an immediate ceasefire, a withdrawal of troops from the conflict areas, the deployment of peacekeeping forces along the borders, and the demarcation of the borders on the bases of the treaties and agreements during the colonial era. Eritrea accepted this initiative in February 1999; however, Ethiopia was reluctant to accept the initiative and continued its military advances on the pretext that Eritrea should withdraw its forces from the disputed areas.

The war continued the length of the border, while both sides also distributed their war propaganda and campaigns among their respective populations. In May 2000, Ethiopia launched massive military attacks throughout the Ethiopia-Eritrea border and occupied a sizable amount of Eritrean territory. Eritrea also launched counterof-fensives across the Gash-Barka areas and other war fronts. In the meantime, Algerian mediators initiated a new proposal for a peaceful resolution to the conflict to which both countries complied. Some of the Algerian peace initiative proposals were the establishment of a Temporary Security Zone (TSZ); the establishment of a neutral commission with the main task of demarcating the Eritrean-Ethiopian border on the basis of colonial treaties and applicable international laws; the establishment of a Boundary Commission; and the deployment of UN peacekeeping forces along the TSZ. On December 12, 2000, both countries signed the Algerian peace initiative, which came to be known as the Algiers Peace Agreement. Through the Algiers Peace Agreement, both sides agreed to commit themselves to binding arbitration. On the basis of the agreement, the Eritrea-Ethiopia Boundary Commission (EEBC) was established. The Commission was located at The Hague, and was composed of five members. Soon after the Algiers Peace Agreement, TSZ (25 kilometers in width) was established within the Eritrean territories, and the UN-deployed peacekeeping forces (known as United Nations Peacekeeping Mission to Ethiopia and Eritrea—UNMEE) along the TSZ.

In cooperation with the Permanent Court of Arbitration at The Hague, the EEBC passed its final and binding verdict on April 13, 2002. Based on this verdict, Badme, the catalyst of the conflict, was awarded to Eritrea, while each party lost territories in some parts and gained some in other parts of their common border territories. Initially, both governments stated that they accepted the ruling provided by the EEBC. To the surprise of most observers, only a few months after accepting the ruling, Ethiopia showed dissatisfaction with the verdict and asked for more clarifications. Eritrea con-tinued to request for more pressure on Ethiopia from the international community to accept the ruling issued by the EEBC. However, the Eritrean request for the UN and other international organizations to exercise pressure on Ethiopia was to no avail. Ethiopia refused to accept the verdict until 2004 when it again stated that it accepted the ruling, but this time only "in principle." The Eritrea-UNMEE relations also contin-ued to deteriorate, and by 2007 the UN withdrew most of its peacekeeping forces from the Eritrean side. Key members of the UNMEE were also expelled by the Eritrean government.

As of 2008, the border between the two countries has not been demarcated on the ground, and the EEBC ruling has not been implemented. Despite the Algiers Peace Agreement and the EEBC binding arbitration, border tensions resumed between the two countries. They continue to exercise hostile relations, and their hostile relations have become sources of instability, security problems, and economic hardships in Eritrea and Ethiopia.

The impacts of the war have been enormous. Casualities on both sides are estimated at 100,000. In addition, over 600,000 Eritrean civilians have been displaced. Needless to say, the war has also been characterized by gross human rights violations, and thou-sands of civilians became victims of ground and air raids, killings, rapes, and more. In addition, thousands of Eritreans living in Ethiopia have been inhumanely deported by the Ethiopian government.

ERITREA-DJIBOUTI RELATIONS

Eritrea and Djibouti share a border of about 113 kilometers (70.2 miles) along the southern Red Sea area. After Eritrean independence, the two countries established cordial bilateral relations. However, the relations between these countries became more volatile in the following years, and they nearly had a border conflict in 1996. In April 1996, Djibouti alleged that Eritrea bombed Ras Dumeira, which it claims is part of its territory. Eritrea rejected the accusation, and it withdrew its forces from the area in May 1996. The two countries neutralized their relations in May 1996.

However, relations between Eritrea and Djibouti started to deteriorate again in 1998. Eritrea accused Djibouti of deploying military forces along the common border. Tensions further escalated when Djibouti exploited the war situation between Eritrea and Ethiopia by making its ports available for Ethiopian use. Ethiopia transacted its outside commercial activities as well as its imports of arms through the Port of Djibouti. This alliance created mounting tensions between Eritrea and Djibouti; in November 1998, Eritrea rejected Djiboutian President Hasan Gouled Aptidon, who was considered a potentially key member of the OAU mediation team. The following year, the two countries exchanged accusations—Djibouti accused Eritrea of supporting Djibouti rebels, while Eritrea accused Djibouti of siding with Ethiopia. Tensions between the two countries continued to rise until 2000. In 2000, the two countries again renewed their relations through the mediation efforts of Libya. In 2001, the presidents of the countries made reciprocal official visits. After the visits, the presidents also agreed to establish cooperative program. In 2004, they signed agreements designed to create cooperative program on political, economic, and social matters.

To the surprise of most observers, the two countries started tensions anew in 2008. On June 10, 2008, they fought a brief border war in which reports show that some nine Djiboutian soldiers were killed and over fifty wounded. Although the war was quite brief, it resulted in tensions being resumed between the two countries. Djibouti has been appealing to the UN and Eritrea has demonstrated that it does not wish to take any territory that belongs to Djibouti.

POST-CONFLICT INTERNAL POLITICAL DEVELOPMENTS

Despite popular expectations and hope for democratic rule of law, the political development in Eritrea took a different path after the Eritrea-Ethiopia border conflict. The Eritrean government has been repeatedly accused by national and other international organizations of violating human rights. The root cause of human rights violations in Eritrea is the absence of a constitutional government. The Eritrean constitution (which was ratified in 1997) allows for the creation of a multiparty political system. As the constitution has not yet been implemented since its ratification, the TGE banned all political parties other than the PFDJ. Therefore, the current political system is a single-party system.

In 2000, a group of key members of the PFDJ and TGE leadership demanded a reform in the governmental structure as well as the political system of the country. The group of reformers commonly known as the G-15 called on the PFDJ and the TGE to implement the ratified constitution and to establish a constitutional political system. Most members of G-15 were high-ranking government officials composed of 14 men and one woman. They published their demands in a letter entitled "An Open Letter to the PFDJ" in May 2001, in which they also exposed to the public that the current government lacks accountability and transparency. However, the government responded by detaining 11 members of the G-15. The detainees have not yet been charged or brought to court. For the list of members of the G15 and their former positions in the government, see Table I of the "Facts and Figures" section of this book.

Among many other demands for reforms, members of the G-15 called for:

- implementing the ratified constitution
- amending laws governing the national economy
- establishing a democratic and pluralist governmental system
- defending the rights of minorities and women
- establishing a civil service system based on merit and equality

Starting in 1997, a number of private newspapers emerged in Eritrea such as Setit, Zemen, Mekalih, and Keste Debena. These newspapers played pivotal roles in distributing information in the country. In fact, several members of the G-15 were interviewed by these private newspapers, and some of these newspapers published the interviews they conducted.

Irritated by the publicity that the G-15 achieved through these newspapers, the government announced that all private newspapers were banned starting September 18, 2001. The government also detained a number of journalists including Dawit Isaak, Amanuel Asrat, Temesgen Gebreyesus, Mattewos Habteab, and Dawit Habtemichael. Although not formally grounded on a legal procedure, the government accuses these journalists and members of the G-15 of creating political instability and planning conspiracy (in cooperation with Ethiopia and the American CIA) against the government.

The government also followed a strict line regarding religious freedom in the country. International organizations have repeatedly accused the government of exercising religious persecution. Religious faiths and groups, particularly the Jehovah's Witness and Pentecost have been banned. A number of their churches and places of worships have been shut down, and religious gatherings have been prohibited. Reports indicate that a number of followers of these faiths have also been detained in many places across the country. Based on their religious principles, members of the Jehovah's Witness were not willing to take part in various national activities such as military service. Yet, they have been willing to provide their service in various civil administrations. However, members of the Pentecostal faith have been participating in national programs such as the military service, and there are no formal governmental accusations against followers of the Pentecostal faith.

The government formally acknowledges four religions in the country—Islam, Catholic Christianity, Orthodox *Tewahdo* Christianity, and the Lutheran faith. Yet, religious institutions also accuse the government of intervening in the affairs of the Orthodox *Tewahdo* Church. In 2005, the government stripped the powers of the Patriarch of the Orthodox Church, Patriarch Antonios, and appointed another loyal patriarch. Since then, His Holiness Patriarch Antonios has been held under house arrest. Reports also show that a number of other priests in the same church have been detained.

Another popular dissatisfaction arises from the government's policy of National Service. The National Service Program was launched by the PGE, and it was further enforced by Proclamation 82/1995. Based on the National Service Proclamation, every Eritrean (physically fit man and woman) between ages ranging from 18 to 45 was required to deliver service for 18 months. All members of the National Service are required to accomplish military training at the Sawa Military Training Camp for six months. After the military training, most members are deported to the EDF while a few may deliver their services at various ministries and governmental institutions. The main objectives of the National Service Program were to cultivate a hard-working and capable society and to contribute to the intended goals of achieving a domestically generated national rehabilitation and development program.

However, in practice, the National Service Program has become an endless service for most of its members. Owing to the unstable military situation in the region, Eritrea does not often demobilize members of the National Service. Members of the Eritrean National Service Program, usually known as *warsay* (ዋርሳይ), have been providing unpaid services in the army and many other institutions for many years.

In general, a lack of internal political stability and the post-conflict economic crisis have created a great concern for most people of the country. Thousands of Eritrean youth have been leaving the country. There have been a number of reports that many members of the National Service Program have been deserting their units. Many crossed the borders to Ethiopia and Sudan and made their way to Europe and North America. As of 2007, there were about 15,000 Eritrean refugees living at the Shimelba Refugee Camp in Ethiopia. Thousands more lived in various refugee camps in Sudan. Others traveled the whole way via the Sahara Desert to Libya and then (by crossing the Mediterranean Sea with ships and boats) to Italy. These refugees allege that they were victims of serious life-threatening situations in Eritrea. Generally, they assert that they suffered from gross violations of their fundamental rights when they were members of the EDF.

THE PROLIFERATION OF OPPOSITION GROUPS IN THE DIASPORA

As stated earlier, the Eritrean government does not allow any opposition group to actively function within Eritrea. Therefore, most Eritrean opposition groups are based in the diaspora. Most of these groups have been suffering from internal crises and splits; and they have not been successful in creating a united and strong opposition organization. Interestingly, a number of these opposition movements have their roots in the ELF and EPLF; splits that have been active since the 1970s. Therefore, many of the contemporary opposition groups are offshoots of the major liberation fronts in Eritrea—the ELF and EPLF.

Since 2002, there has been a remarkable proliferation of opposition groups across Europe and North America. Moreover, a number of human rights activists have also founded their own groups and are involved in Eritrean politics in many ways. Table J of "Facts and Figures" section of this book shows a list of political movements and parties. However, the list shows only some of the opposing groups, and it should be noted that there are many more groups not included on this list.

In February 2007, 13 opposition Eritrean groups met in Addis Ababa, Ethiopia. On the bases of agreements reached during the Addis Ababa meeting, these opposition movements formed an umbrella alliance—the Eritrean Democratic Alliance (EDA). Based on the Addis Ababa agreement, the main goals of the EDA are to facilitate strategies and ways for the creation of a democratic government in Eritrea. How successful this alliance will be is a matter to be seen in the future.

REFERENCES

Amnesty International: http://www.amnestyusa.org

Byrne, Hugh (2002). "Question and Answer Series—Eritrea and Ethiopia: Large-Scale Expulsions of Population Groups and Other Human Rights Violations in Connection with the Ethiopian-Eritrean Conflict (1998–2000)." Unpublished Research Paper: Washington DC.

Connell, Dan (2003). *Taking on the Superpowers: Collected Articles on the Eritrean Revolution (1976–1982)*. Vol. I, Trenton, NJ: Red Sea Press.

Connell, Dan (2004). *Building a New Nation: Collected Articles on the Eritrean Revolution (1983–2002)*. Vol. II, Trenton, NJ: Red Sea Press.

Doornbos, Martin and Alemseged Tesfai (1999). *Post-Conflict Eritrea: Prospects for Reconstruction and Development*. Lawrenceville, NJ: Red Sea Press.

Favali, Lyda and Pateman, Roy (2003). *Blood, Land and Sex: Legal and Political Pluralism in Eritrea*. Bloomington, IN: Indiana University Press.

Gebremedhin, Tesfa G. (1996). *Beyond Survival: The Economic Challenges of Agriculture and Development in Post-Independence Eritrea*. Lawrenceville, NJ: Red Sea Press.

Gebremedhin, Yohannes (2008). *The Challenges of a Society in Transition: Legal Development in Eritrea*. Lawrenceville, NJ: Red Sea Press.

Habte Selassie, Bereket (2003). *The Making of the Eritrean Constitution: The Dialectic of Process and Substance*. Lawrenceville, NJ: Red Sea Press.

Hirt, Nicole (2001). *Eritrea zwischen Krieg und Frieden: die Entwicklung seit der Unabhängigkeit*. Hamburg: Institut für Afrika-Kunde.

Institute for Security Studies (ISS): http://www.iss.co.za

Iyob, Ruth (1995). *The Eritrean Struggle for Independence: Domination, Resistance, Nationalism (1941–1993)*. Cambridge: Cambridge University Press.

Kibreab, Gaim (2008). *Critical Reflections on the Eritrean War of Independence: Social Cpital, Associational Life, Religion, Ethnicity and Sowing Seeds of Dictatorship*. Trenton, NJ: Red Sea Press.

Killion, Tom (1998). *Historical Dictionary of Eritrea*. London: The Scarecrow Press.

Mengisteab, Kidane & Yohannes, Okbazghi (2005). *Anatomy of an African Tragedy: Political, Economic and Foreign Policy Crisis in Post-Independence Eritrea*. Trenton, NJ: Red Sea Press.

Mesfin, Berouk (2008). "The Eritrea-Djibouti Border Dispute." In: *Situation Report,* Institute for Security Studies (Issue September 2008).

Murtaza, Niaz (1998). *The Pillage of Sustainability in Eritrea (1600s–1990s): Rural Communities and the Creeping Shadows of Hegemony.* London: Greenwood Press.

PFDJ (1994). *National Charter for Eritrea.* Nakfa.

Pool, David (2001). *From Guerrillas to Government: The Eritrean People's Liberation Front.* Athens: Ohio University Press.

Reid, Richard (2003). "Old Problems in New Conflicts: Some Observations on Eritrea and its Relations with Tigray, from Liberation Struggle to Inter-State War." In: *Africa,* 73 (3), pp. 369–401.

Reid, Richard (2007). "The Trans-Mereb Experience: Perceptions of the Historical Relationship Between Eritrea and Ethiopia." In: *Journal of Eastern African Studies,* 1 (2), pp. 238–255.

Stansfield, Gareth R. V. (2001). *The 1995–96 Yemen-Eritrea Conflict over the Islands of Hanish and Jabal Zuquar: A Geopolitical Analysis.* University of Durham: Centre for Middle Eastern and Islamic Studies.

Tesfagiorgis G., Mussie (2007). *A Fading Nature: Aspects of Environmental History of Eritrea.* Felsberg: Edition Eins.

The Government of Eritrea (1993). *Eritrea: Birth of a Nation.* Occasional Journal: Department of External Affairs.

Volker-Saad, Kerstin (2004). *Zivilistinnen und Kämpferinnen in Eritrea.* Berlin: Weißensee-Verlag.

CHAPTER 4

Economy

INTRODUCTION

Over three decades of warfare, ecological volatility, and resource mismanagement have presented enormous obstacles to Eritrean economic growth. The liberation war (1961–1991) shattered all economic sectors; and Eritrea, on gaining independence, inherited a devastated economy. Most parts of her industrial sector were in ruins because of a lack of spare parts and raw materials. In 1991, the industrial sector of the country consisted of less than 50 public factories and enterprises, a small number of workshops, and some 600 small-scale private enterprises. Making matters worse, most of these enterprises and workshops were in states of disrepair and almost nonproductive. By 1991, the agricultural sector that had been the backbone of the Eritrean economy prior to the conflict was on the verge of collapse. Although a major economic component in Eritrea, agriculture contributes poorly to the national economy, and the country's domestic grain cultivation fails to meet the minimum national consumption requirements.

Eritrea's economy showed a sharp decline after 1998, which can be attributed to the destructive effects of the renewed Eritrea-Ethiopia conflict that broke out in 1998. The war (1998–2000) and the continuing, unsolved border tensions have crippled the general economy. Moreover, the country's erratic relations with neighboring countries such as Djibouti, Yemen, and Sudan negatively affect its regional trade. Today, Eritrea is one of the poorest countries in the world. Over a million of its people are said to be in need of foreign aid. Yet the Eritrean government continues to reject aid on the

---

LOCAL CONCEPTS OF MEASUREMENTS FOR GRAINS

enqe'a (እንቀዓ): two full of *melelikh* (መለሊኽ) (also local container for *suwa*—local beer)—roughly weigh a kilogram.

me'ero (ምዕሮ): double weight of *enqe'a* (four *melelikh*)

ka'bbo (ካቦ): double weight of *me'ero* (eight *melelikh*)

ka'bbo me'ero (ካቦ ምዕሮ): 12 full of *melelikh*

nefqi (ነፍቲ): double weight of *ka'bbo* (sixteen *melelikh*)

mesles (መስለስ): twenty-four full of *melelikh*

gebeta (ገበታ): double weight of *nefqi* (thirty-two *melelikh*)

enfeqti (እንፍቅቲ): double weight of *gebeta* (sixty-four *melelikh*)

yahit (ያሒት): double weight of *enfeqti* (128 full of *melelikh*)

Note that the basic unit of measurement for grain is *melelikh*. Other measurements can also be employed'such as *tenno,* also known as *'essi* (which is roughly equivalent to two-and-half of *melelikh*). Also note that the weight of grains can greatly vary. For example, a *melelikh* of *taff* (ጣፍ) may not be equivalent to a *melelikh* of barley or maize or sorghum, etc.

---

pretext of its "self-reliance" policies. Among the main trading partners of Eritrea include China, Italy, South Korea, South Africa, and recently Iran.

Eritrea's industrial sector contributes only about 53 percent of the country's GDP. Among the main products in this sector are leather, textiles, marble, as well as food and beverages. Eritrea is believed to be rich in various minerals, particularly gold. However, no substantial mineral exploitation has yet taken place. Agriculture constitutes about 16 percent of the nation's GDP. Among the main farming crops include sorghum, millet, maize, barley, and more. Although there is no reliable source of information about Eritrea's fishing industry, it exports fish and other sea products to Asia and Europe. Eritrea's tourism industry does not yet generate significant income. This can be mainly attributed to the country's poor tourism infrastructure, military instability (especially tensions with Ethiopia), and limitations of movement for tourists.

In 1997, Eritrea introduced its own currency called Nakfa. Nakfa is also the name of a town located in the Sahel Mountains. This town was a highly strategic site for the EPLF army during the liberation war. The nation's currency is, therefore, named in honor of the strategic importance of the town during the liberation struggle, as well as in memory of the national heroes who fell at the Battles of Nakfa. Owing to its need for hard currency reserves, the Eritrean government decreed in 2005 that all transactions within Eritrea shall be conducted in the local currency. Since then, private holding and private hard currency exchange in the country has become illegal. As set by the government, the exchange rate of Nakfa to the U.S. dollar is 15 to 1.

The country's economy also continues to suffer from a high rate of inflation. Although the national media repeatedly broadcasts about the "great economic

One Nakfa. (Scan courtesy of M. Tesfagiorgis)

Five Nakfa. (Scan courtesy of M. Tesfagiorgis)

One hundred Nakfa. (Scan courtesy of M. Tesfagiorgis)

achievements" the country is allegedly making in various areas of development, they do not reflect reality (Denison and Paice 2007: 35–36). By 2008, the economic situation of the country in general and of ordinary Eritreans in particular was, in some places, worse than during the decades of war. Prices of all basic goods and services have increased so dramatically that they are beyond the means of most ordinary Eritreans.

BRIEF HISTORICAL OVERVIEW OF ERITREA'S ECONOMY

Since ancient times, most Eritreans have been dependent on subsistence farming and animal herding for a living. The abundance in natural resources and farm land enabled them to produce adequate subsistence production. Farming is well practiced as is the local ox-plow system, which is well adapted to the physical landscape of the cool and temperate highlands of Eritrea where over half of the country's population live.

Although agriculture was practiced in the Horn of Africa long before the Christian era, its major achievements in the region were recorded during the rise of the Aksumite Empire (A.D. first century). Domestication of plants and animals started many centuries before the rise of Aksum. The rock art drawings showing humpless cattle, discovered in northern Eritrea, were depicted around 8000 B.C., and this pictorial evidence suggests that pastoralism was also an important part of the economy of the region. As compared to other regions of northeast Africa, Eritrea is among the earliest sites for the domestication of crops such as barley, sorghum, and millet (Murtaza 1998: 45–47).

The ox-plow system of farming was already in practice by the first millennium B.C. (Fattovich 1990; Schmidt, Curtis et al. 2008). In addition to its sophisticated military power and commerce, the Aksumite Empire achieved domestic food security through agriculture and developed a "sophisticated management of environmental resources" (McCann 1999). The ox-plow system of farming is one of the most labor-demanding techniques of plowing. Yet farmers of the region adjusted the system in a way to fit the climatic and physiographic features of the farming areas. Interestingly, the same system of farming that evolved thousands of years ago is still in practice today, and the farming system has not shown remarkable changes.

The country's economy during the Italian colonial occupation (1890–1941) was characterized by industrialization, infrastructural development, and limited mechanized farming. However, the colonial economy was governed by policies of segregation, and racial discrimination marginalized the majority of people. The colonial government's policies that were intended to establish a successful agricultural colonization neither succeeded nor stimulated major changes in the traditional means of agricultural production.

The post-Italian economy showed a short-term boom fueled by the ongoing wars in the Middle East and the Horn of Africa during the British Military Administration (BMA) (1941–1952). The short-term boom that showed sharp fluctuations during the post-war period (1945–1952) almost collapsed at the end of the Federal Period (1952–1962). In spite of the post–World War II economic devitalization, Eritrea possessed a stronger industrial economic infrastructure than its neighbor, Ethiopia. During the years of federation and Ethiopian occupation, the industrial infrastructure of the country was dismantled and many of its factories were either sold to other countries or replanted in Ethiopia.

The Eritrean economy during the liberation struggle and the Ethiopian occupation period (1961–1991) was characterized by ferocious warfare, and the destruction of economic resources, massive human displacement, repetitive cycles of famine and drought, and significant loss of the work force. The years of conflict were characterized by environmental degradation such as massive deforestation, soil erosion, and depletion of water resources. The *Dergue* (communist regime in Ethiopia—1974–1991) introduced a socialist-oriented economic system in which most private enterprises were nationalized.

When Eritrea was liberated by the Eritrean People's Liberation Front (EPLF) army in 1991, it was devastated by the ravages of war and wracked by consecutive droughts and famines. A majority of the country's population was almost entirely dependent on international food aid, most of its economic infrastructure was seriously damaged, and the bulk of its manpower was displaced. Observing the whole post-war situation of Eritrea, Cliffe (1996) notes:

> The consequences of the war were not restricted to the many thousands of deaths in combat, the killing, imprisonment and torture of civilians, the general repression or the flight of refugees or internal displacement, but extended to the basic fabric of the economy and of everyday life (Cliffe 1996: 21).

Thanks to its citizens living inside the country and abroad who injected hard currency and annual remittances, the country started a determined economic rehabilitation and massive reconstruction programs. Unfortunately, Eritrea's post-independence economic rehabilitation and reconstruction programs were dealt serious setbacks by the Eritrea-Ethiopia border conflict (1998–2000), and the postwar—"no peace no war years" (2000–presently, 2009). In the following sections we shall examine Eritrea's various economic systems, especially farming, animal husbandry, manufacturing, and trade.

ECONOMIC SYSTEMS

As stated earlier, the main economic sector of Eritrea is agriculture. However, Eritrea's agricultural economy was devastated by the thirty-year war of liberation (1961–1991) and the renewed Eritrea-Ethiopia conflict (1998–2000). Generally, about 80 percent of Eritreans are involved in subsistence farming and herding. Farming is largely practiced along the highlands where over 65 percent of the total Eritrean population live (which constitutes only about 16% of the total landmass), while herding is practiced in the lowlands (FAO-FOSA 2003: 1). Herding involves seasonal movement of people between various ecological zones. Some highland farmers and agro-pastoralists move to the lowlands during the rainy season and retreat to the highlands during the dry

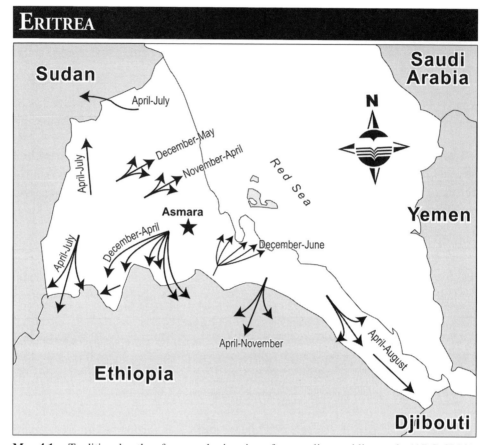

ERITREA

MAP 4.1. Traditional paths of seasonal migration of pastoralists and livestock. (ABC-CLIO)

season in the lowlands. Some highland sedentary farmers also practice transhumance farming (a way of economic activity that involves the movement of farming and pastoral communities from one place to another), where they cultivate in the highlands and the escarpments during rainy seasons of these respective ecological zones. A large percentage of the population also practices pastoralism (raising of animals), where they raise certain types of animals such as cattle, camels, goats, and sheep. Eritrean farmers and agro-pastoralists as a whole also possess deep knowledge about subsistence agriculture and their physical environment.

Although agriculture comprises the largest economic sector of Eritrea, it usually provides less than 20 percent of the country's GDP. This is mainly attributed to the fact that farming has largely been based on a subsistence level, and mechanized farming has not been well practiced. Other factors limiting agricultural development in Eritrea include devastating warfare, consecutive droughts, locust infestation, and erratic rains. Among the main agricultural products of Eritrea include sorghum, millet, wheat, cotton, legumes, and various types of vegetables. Annual production is, however, estimated usually at less than half of the overall annual cereal and other food requirements (Horizon Business Group 2007).

Typical livestock market. (S. Tesfagiorgis)

Because of low agricultural productivity, poverty severely affects rural communities (farmers and pastoralists) and jeopardizes their survival. Moreover, a large segment of Eritrea's productive manpower is kept in compulsory military service for over a decade. This in turn has severely affected farming and other means of food production across the country (Horn of Africa Group 2008: 7–10). Today, Eritrea faces substantial challenges caused by food shortages, resource mismanagement, and poverty.

The industrial economy of Eritrea is mainly composed of light industries such as salt, cement, textiles, tanneries, and salt mining. The mining industry has not been well established and Eritrea's mineral deposits are largely unexplored. Yet the country possesses rich natural mineral resources such as copper, gold, zinc, silver, iron ore, and other non-metallic resources.

Another industrial sector with favorable potential for progress is the fishing industry. If adequate investment would be used in developing this industry's infrastructure, Eritrea could benefit greatly from the diverse fish resources of the Red Sea. Similarly, tourism is another economic sector with a great potential for growth. The diversity of attractive coastal and sea environment, the healthy climate of the highlands, diverse archaeological and historical sites, and diverse geographical topography may well contribute to the development of this sector.

Generally, Eritrea's value of imports and exports are usually not proportional. The value of the country's imports greatly exceeds the value of her exports. Among the main trading items exported by Eritrea include textiles, cereals, livestock, and hides while its imports include various types of machinery, foodstuffs, fuel, and more.

Typical market in Akordat. (S. Tesfagiorgis)

The first years of post-independent Eritrea (1991–1997) were characterized by major economic achievements: It showed a steady economic growth, and by 1997 the GDP was estimated at eight percent growth. Following the promising economic growth of Eritrea prior to 1997, the renewed conflict between Eritrea and Ethiopia (1998–2000) greatly altered the country's economic capability. Eritrea sustained heavy war damage: property damage can be roughly estimated at over U.S.$500 million, about a million displaced people and deportees from Ethiopia, and great losses of productive manpower. Since 2000, the country's GDP has sharply declined, while inflation has continued to rise from time to time, leading to a continuous depletion of foreign exchange reserves.

It should be noted that the economic performance of the country has been usually mixed and unclear since 2000, and there is no clearly recorded and measured growth. Although governmental sources claim that the real GDP of the country grew by five percent in 2007, the agricultural performance (the backbone of the country's economy) has shown major decline as compared to the prewar periods. In general, by all international standards, the country's GDP per capita remains at the lowest level and has not shown any measured growth. The country's poor economic performance has led to serious food shortages and widespread poverty. The gap between the rich and the poor has been widening steadily. In addition, there has not been an even economic distribution between the country's regions. Generally, the country's economic outlook is poor. Official records show that the country's GDP growth between the years 2001 and 2005 was 3.1 percent, while its per capita GDP showed remarkable decline in the same period (Horn of Africa Group 2008:10).

RESOURCES

Eritrean agriculture is mostly rainfed and production is seasonal. The lowland areas comprise the largest proportion of the country's landmass. Most of the Eritrean lowlands are inhabited by communities whose economic activities can be largely classified as pastoralism or/and agro-pastoralism. Agro-pastoralism is a way of living that combines farming and animal herding. Owing to their hot climate and fragile ecosystems, the eastern and western lowlands of Eritrea are usually inconvenient for rainfed agriculture. In addition, the topography of the highlands is mainly characterized by rugged mountains and hills. Therefore, due to the rugged nature of topography of the highlands and the inconvenient climate of the lowlands, only 12 percent of the total Eritrean landmass is suitable for rain-fed agriculture, yet only about 3.5 percent of the total arable land is contemporarily under use (FAO-FOSA 2004).

Altitude, rainfall, and climate are the most important factors for crop production in Eritrea. Various types of grains are produced at various altitudes and ecological zones of the country. For example, although the highland's altitude and climate are favorable for grains such as barley, wheat, and *taff* (*Eragrostis tef*), drought-resistant grains such as sorghum and millet are grown in lower altitudes. Pulses such as beans and peas are grown in some parts of the highlands, while various types of oilseeds are grown in the lowlands. Subsistence cultivation involves almost no improved varieties of crops or the use of pesticides. Use of fertilizers is also quite limited across the country, and only about 10 percent of subsistence farmers use limited amount of inorganic fertilizers. Most farmers depend on organic fertilizers (especially animal dung). As stated earlier, crop yields in Eritrea have been considerably less than the annual food-consumption requirements.

Among many other challenges, the agricultural sector suffers from erratic and inadequate annual rainfall. Rainfall distribution is also usually uneven in almost all the ecological zones of the country. Usually, annual rainfall decreases from south to north ranging between 700 and 500 mm in the southern parts, and 200 mm or less in the northern parts of the country. There are mainly two classifications of rainy seasons in the country: the *keremti* (ክረምቲ), "rainy season," rainfall usually occurs between May and August; and the *hagay* (ሓጋይ), "dry season," rainfall occurs between November and February. The highlands and western lowlands receive the *kremti* rainfall, while the eastern lowlands and coastal plains receive the *hagay* rainfall. Due to its strategic location and high altitude, the eastern escarpment (commonly known as the Green Belt Zone—GBZ) enjoys rainfall during both seasons, and parts of this zone are convenient for crop production throughout the year.

Irrigation, although in small scale, is also practiced in some highland and lowland areas. In most cases, irrigation is practiced by diverting streams. Along nonperennial streams irrigation agriculture may also depend on sources of water such as dams, ponds, and wells. Various types of vegetables and fruits such as potatoes, tomatoes,

---

BELES (OPUNTIA FICUS-INDICA)

Beles is one of the most popular wild fruit in Eritrea. It is gathered during the rainy season in the Eritrean highlands. It provides remarkable nourishment for many highland communities. Beles are gathered for local consumption and also to sell in urban markets in the country. Based on local classifications, there are a at least three varieties of beles: chincha or tsetse "wild beles fruits" (also most favored by local communities), tsaeda beles or "white beles" (less favored variety), and beles duk'l or "the dung beles" (least favored variety).

---

papayas, oranges and more are produced in various parts of the country by means of irrigation.

One of the main concerns of the majority of Eritrea's population is food security. Even during good rainy seasons, most of the rural communities cannot manage to produce enough food to meet their subsistence-consumption requirements. As stated above, this can be attributed to many factors such as consecutive droughts, land degradation, and the country's persistent compulsory national service that inflicts remarkable disorder on the rural economy. Tens of thousands of young men and women were also lost in the Eritrean-Ethiopian conflict (1998–2000). Moreover, the compulsory Eritrean national service (theoretically 18 months service, but in practice lasting for unlimited periods) also monopolizes the bulk of Eritrea's productive manpower, which cripples a labor-intensive sector like farming. Therefore, the majority of the rural households are usually vulnerable to endemic hunger, poverty, and occasional famines. Amid consecutive droughts, war, and other natural calamities, rural households run out of options and their survival strategies have been left highly vulnerable.

Repeated droughts that occurred between 2002 and 2006 further diminished agricultural productivity. By 2004, crop production fell to almost less than one-third of the pre-2000 production scale, and a large number of livestock also perished during the drought years. Prices of all types of food items have dramatically risen beyond the means of most poor farming and pastoral communities. As part of their struggle for survival, rural communities are usually forced to sell their assets (such as livestock) and deplete all of their food stores. However, these strategies of survival could not sustain rural communities amid consecutive ecological and manmade hazards. Therefore, most contemporary rural communities are highly vulnerable to hunger and other ecological adversities.

Currently, Eritrea's annual agricultural production can be roughly estimated less than 35 percent of its basic food requirements. In general, agricultural production at the moment is at its lowest level (constituting less than 16% of the nation's GDP), and Eritrea needs approximately over 700,000 metric tons of additional grain annually to meet its basic food requirements. A great majority of the population is in need of food aid. However, the government's stubborn "self-reliance policy" has resulted in a continuous confrontation with global aid agencies. Most aid agencies have been deactivated from the country, so Eritrea receives almost no food in the form of international aid.

Young man tilling farmland. (J. Miran)

Eritrea's rainfed agriculture is largely based on a simplified ox-plow system in which oxen play a dominant role as farming tools. Other major components of the farming tools are the *naweti mahres* (ናውቲ ማሕረስ) "plowshare tools" mainly consisting of *mahresha* (ማሕረሻ) "plowshare," *'erfi* (ዕርፊ) "the stilt," *newit* (ነዊት) "the beam," *'ar'ut* (ኣርዑት) "the yoke," *meran kerfes* (ምራን ከርፈስ) the leather strap, *kerfes* (ከርፈስ) "the sheath," and *'adagur* (ኣዳጉር) "wooden plow-ears." All of these tools are locally designed and easily replaceable. Farmers adjust the farming tools depending on the specific needs of their farming fields. They also adjust the plowshare's angle to achieve the desired plowing depth (for further details of farming techniques, see Goe 1989; McCann: 45–55).

Land constitutes the most important asset of the country's agricultural economy. It is the main source of wealth, and all economic, social, and political power emanated from possessing it or fully controlling the arable and grazing lands. Human beings (especially sedentary peasants, meaning settled farmers) are directly attached to the land; hence, they consider the land as the foundation of their survival. These communities developed various types of land-tenure systems that were usually regulated by their communal laws.

Traditional land tenure is interwoven with the history, cultures, and customs of the communities (Zekarias 1966: 1–33). However, the highland tenure systems were complex, and dealing with all land tenure systems in Eritrea is out of the scope of this study. Generally, they can be categorized as private ownership, *resti tsilmi* (ርስቲ ጽልሚ), and communal ownership, *desa* (ዴሳ). Private ownership of land includes absolute ownership, charter land holdings, *resti gulti* (ርስቲ ጉልቲ), and church lands (Zekarias 1966). In the *resti tsilmi* type of land ownership members of the *enda* (families that claim a common ancestry) had the right to individually own plots of land. The owners or inheritors of land in *resti tsilmi,* known as *restegnatat* (ርስተኛታት) had an absolute right of ownership of farming and residential plots. They had the right to dispose of their land possessions. The inherited land was also passed on from generation to generation. Sometimes, the absolute nature of ownership in this type of tenure caused conflicts between individuals and villages. Even today, a shortage of farming land in the highlands aggravates social conflicts and land degradation.

In *resti gulti*, absolute ownership of the land was in the hands of the absolute rulers or governors. In this tenure type, land was allotted in various ways, mainly as *gulti seb* (charter land holdings assigned to ordinary individuals), *gulti chewa* (ጉልቲ ጭዋ—charter land allocated to noblemen) and *gulti tsadkan* ((ጉልቲ ጻድቃን—charter lands allocated to monasteries and convents). Under these headings, charter lands could be given to officials and noblemen, to *liqawnti* (ሊቃውንቲ) or *debteras* (ደብተራታት—religious figures), to heroes, to traditional doctors, and the like (Zekarias 1966). The absolute ownership of land also included systems of *medri worki* (መሬት ወርቂ—sale of land on a conditional basis), *medri sedby* (ምድሪ ሰድቢ—leasing of land on a legal basis), *grat kahnat* (ግራት ካህናት—donation of land to churches and priests by the absolute owners of land) and *grat shum* (ግራት ሹም—land allocated to chiefs—where in the old times each *shum* had estates of land worked by the peasants or tenants) (Tesfagiorgis 2007: 211–258).

Farming land is also locally classified according to its fertility. Therefore, six major types of farming lands could be recognized in the highlands: the *bodu* (ቦዱ—local classification for fertile soils with better nutrient content and higher production capacity: type of plots usually found in a newly cleared forest or bush areas); the *duka* (ዱካ—local classification for one of the most fertile plots; usually with high content of soil nutrients); the *walakha* (ዋላኻ—local classification for clay type of soils and plots with high capacity of water storage and fertile and loamy features); the *jerif* (ጀሪፍ—local term for highly fertile plots of land usually irrigated from gorges or seasonal streams); the *wotsel* (ወጸል—local classification for highly degraded plots; soils with very low nutrient contents); and the *ba'kel* (ባዕከል—local classification for degraded types of soils with less water absorption capacity; plots less fertile than *wotsel*). All these tenure systems were subject to the highlands' respective communal laws (for further details regarding land tenure in the highlands of Eritrea, see Okbasillassie Tikabo 2003 and Zekarias 1966; Tesfagiorgis 2007).

In 1994, as part of its new policies and programs, the Eritrean government introduced new regulations regarding land ownership, allocations, and registration of all allotted lands across the country. The Eritrean government issued Proclamation 58/1994 creating new procedures for land ownership and rights. Under Proclamation 58/1994, the government nationalized all types of land and vested ownership and land rights entirely in the State. The government created a new body called "The Land Commission" that had the sole task of land allocation and land usufruct. The proclamation entitles every Eritrean citizen to own a residential plot in his/her village of origin. All members of a village whose livelihood depends entirely on farming are also entitled to possess a plot of farming land (theoretically a lifelong usufruct). All forms of land allocations, according to the proclamation, are nondiscriminatory with respect to gender, marital status, origin, and religion. Although the nationalization of land, allocation inefficiencies, administrative restructuring caused a series of discontent in many rural areas of Eritrea, the government fully implemented Proclamation 58/1994, and now the State enjoys unlimited rights of land ownership and usufruct.

The agricultural economy also greatly comprises livestock husbandry. Many rural communities in the lowlands are purely pastoralists or agro-pastoralists. They raise various types of animal herds such as goats, sheep, cattle, and camels. Livestock production in the lowlands aims mainly at meeting basic consumption requirements such as milk and meat as well as for sale. In the highlands, livestock raising comprises mainly cattle. As the ox-plow system of farming also requires animal power, most households usually keep a limited number of oxen. Pastoralism usually involves a seasonal migration of livestock in search of pasturelands. Sometimes, seasonal migration of cattle took place across national borders (such as across the borders with Ethiopia and Sudan).

However, production related to the pastoral economy is usually low. This is attributed to various factors such as consecutive droughts and lack of enough animal nutrition, fragility of lowland ecosystems where pastoralism usually takes place, lack of adequate veterinary services and facilities, and poor quality of herds. Forage production is very low in Eritrea, and grazing mostly depends on common seasonal grazing and range lands. In the highlands, lack of vast grazing lands continues to result in a phenomenon commonly called overgrazing. This in turn results in extensive deforestation and land degradation.

INDUSTRY
Historical Overview of Industrialization in Eritrea

Eritrea's modern industrial development can be largely associated with Italian colonialism of the territory (1890–1941). Italian colonialism in Eritrea was characterized by a marked growth of urban centers, some of which grew as main industrial bases. The most notable industrial towns that emerged during the Italian colonial period include Asmara, Deqemhare, Massawa, and Assab. To achieve maximum revenues, the colonial state established various industries in many parts of Eritrea such as mining industries at Karora, Debarewa, and Augaro as well as agro-industries at Elabered, Sabur, Halhale, and Ghinda'e. Many other temporary and small-scale manufacturing plants were based in towns where Italian garrisons were stationed such as Mendefera, Segeneity, and Adi Keyyih. The industrial sector that emerged as an important and strong economic segment during the Italian colonial period was mainly based on light industries. The Eritrean industries included pasta factories, bakeries, meat-processing factories, tanneries, salt mining factories, beverage factories, soap factory, cement factory, button factory, and edible oil factory. By the 1950s, there were over 620 industrial plants in Eritrea. The following are some of the most notable industries that emerged during the Italian colonial period in Eritrea.

THE MINING INDUSTRY

The mining industry consists of such mining concessions as:

- The Massawa Salt Mining Plant: Established in 1905 by a society called *Saline di Massawa*, this plant produced about 1,000 tons of salt a day. It exported salt to Ethiopia and countries such as Kenya, Tanganyka (Tanzania), and Uganda. It also employed over 300 African and European workers. Other small salt-mining firms were also established in the Danakil Depression, in areas such as Assale.

- The Mining Company of Eritrea: Established by an Italian mining society, this plant focused on the exploitation of mineral resources such as gold. Its principal mining sites were located in the lowlands, mainly at a place called Augaro. The plant exploited and processed mineral ores; by the 1950s, it was able to produce a remarkable amount of gold and silver. It also employed over 200 Eritreans who worked as miners and laborers as well as skilled Europeans (managers, clerks, and technicians).

- The Tocumbia Mining Factory: Founded by an Italian mining society, this plant was located in Tokombia (southwestern part of Eritrea). It exploited mineral resources, mainly gold, and employed over 100 Eritrean workers in the mining fields.

- The Dallol Mining Grants: The colonial government provided companies and mining enterprises with mining concessions in the Dalul area of the Dankalia Depression. The primary mining activities of these plants included the exploitation of minerals such as magnesium, beryllium, and sodium chloride.

THE AGRO-INDUSTRY

A number of agro-industrial plants were also established in many parts of the country. Several of these industries achieved remarkable success. The agro-industrial plants comprised, among many others, the following factories:

- The Dum Palm Industry: This industry was established in 1912. Two main branches of this industry were situated in Keren and Akordat. This industry specialized in the exploitation and processing of doom palm (*Hyphaene thebaica*) byproducts. It gathered and processed ripe fruits of doom palm trees from the Barka lowlands. The nuts of doom palm fruit were in high demand for button making in various parts of Africa and Europe. This industry also supplied necessary raw materials for the button factory in Eritrea, and it exported a remarkable amount of these raw materials to the manufacturers in the United Kingdom. This industry employed about 1,500 Eritrean workers.

- The *Ditta de Nadai* (Elabered Factory): Established by an Italian entrepreneur, this factory processed and exported vegetable (especially tomato) products. The factory processed vegetable products cultivated on the Elabered farming estate and the gardens in the area. It had the capacity of producing over 2,000 concentrated and canned tomato paste per hour. The Ditta de Nadai industry exported its processed vegetable products to Sudan and Ethiopia as well as to the Middle East (such as to Saudi Arabia).

- The Barattolo Cotton and Textile Factory: Based in Asmara, this factory manufactured various types of textiles. Its cotton came mostly from the Alighider cotton plantation. This factory is one of the few significant remaining Italian industries in Eritrea.

THE BEVERAGE AND LIQUOR INDUSTRY

The beverage and liquor industry also flourished in Eritrea during the Italian colonial period. Among the notable beverage and liquor factories in Eritrea were:

- The Melotti Brewery Factory: This industrial plant was established in 1939 in Asmara by an Italian engineer and entrepreneur (Luigi Melotti). This factory produced beer that mostly focused at satisfying the local market. It also produced various types of liquor such as cognac and gin. It employed over 150 local workers.

- The Fenili Liquor Factory: Established in 1936, this factory produced varieties of liquors and wines. The markets for the products of this factory were mainly within Eritrea. It also exported some of its products to Ethiopia.

- Other significant brewery and liquor factories included: Emiliano Liquor (*Liquorifico Emiliano Asmara*) and the Mineral Water Factory (*Vendite Aque Minerali Sorgive*).

THE MILLING INDUSTRY

This industry included a number of factories and enterprises such as the ALFA Milling Factory and the Vaudetto Pasta Factory.

Many other industries also flourished in Eritrea during the Italian period, including wood, paper, cement, marble, and metal industries; electromechanical industries; the hotel industry; tannery industries; and jewelry industries.

As mentioned above, the Eritrean industrial sector has shown a major decline since the 1940s. Prior to the 1970s, Eritrea also possessed a flourishing private industrial sector that constituted a remarkable part of Ethiopian industrial output. However, the Ethiopian government's command economic system (adopted by the Marxist regime in 1975) led to the nationalization of most Eritrean private industries. Yet, the government failed to provide inputs deemed necessary for the manufacturing industries; and these enterprises were neglected for over two decades. Affected by policies of neglect and lack of supplies, most of the private enterprises went out of business.

By the end of the liberation war (1991), a number of the remaining industries were on the verge of closing down. Most industrial plants in the country were generally inefficient and required significant repair. Eritrea inherited the remaining 42 large-scale factories in the public sector and about 650 small-scale enterprises in the private sector. A number of these light manufacturing industries were quite old, and their equipment and facilities were in a state of disrepair. Getting the necessary spare parts for these outdated factories was also a great challenge.

Eritrean heavy industry consists of the oil refinery plant in Assab and the cement and salt plants in Massawa. The oil refinery in Assab was built by the former Soviet Union on the basis of its cooperation agreements with the regime in Ethiopia.

According to World Bank estimates, industry constituted about 23.5 percent of Eritrea's GDP in 2007. The economic recession after the border conflict with Ethiopia has severely affected most of the private industrial firms. A large number of private enterprises, except those owned by the People's Front for Democracy and Justice (PFDJ), were handicapped by a lack of supplies and skilled workers and went bankrupt. Even the Assab oil refinery plant, which had the capacity of processing and refining over 18,000 barrels of crude oil a day, was closed—according to government sources—because of high operating costs. The products of most manufacturing industries in Eritrea are consumer goods.

The only industry with a considerable record of growth is the construction industry. This industry includes plants ranging from road and rail construction to the expansion of power plants, such as: railway reconstruction; dam construction; and the construction of educational and health centers. However, not many private construction companies or industries are taking part in the growth of national construction. Owing to the lack of construction materials, a skilled work force, and the government's interventionist policies, most privately owned construction companies have gone bankrupt. Many highly qualified Eritrean engineers and contractors have also left the country. Although there is no feasible available statistical information regarding the current construction industry and its achievements, the government in Eritrea presents this industry as a key success in its national reconstruction programs. However, evidence demonstrates that the major construction achievements that the government in Eritrea claims to have made are the result of unpaid Eritrean labor (Kibreab 2009). The notable construction industries and companies that are owned by the government and are currently active include the Segen Construction Company, Gedem Construction Company, Homib Construction Company, and the Horn Corporation.

During the post-independence years, the Eritrean government has made every effort to establish and strengthen the economic institutions of the country, and it has issued and implemented policies intended to encourage economic development. In 1994, the government issued the national macroeconomic policy. The objectives of this policy focused on the establishment of an efficient market economy with the government playing a pivotal role in enhancing and stimulating a competitive private economic sector. As set up in the macropolicy of 1994, the government embarked on laying basic foundations and guiding principles for the overall Eritrean economy. Some of the goals in the Eritrean macropolicy include:

- *The investment polic*y: Under Investment Proclamation 59/1994, which replaced Investment Proclamation 18/1991, the government announced that it had adopted a liberal investment policy. The proclamation further describes that the government's policy was to create an attractive and supportive atmosphere for local and foreign investment. Through this proclamation, the government introduced a new tax system aimed at attracting and encouraging investors. It also established a new autonomous investment center known as the Eritrean Investment Center (EIC). The EIC's main objective was to facilitate and create an appealing environment for investors. Through its macropolicy, the Eritrean government also guaranteed investors full ownership of their firms and that it would not nationalize their enterprises. Based on this principle, Eritrea also became a member of the Hague International Court of the Settlement of International Disputes (ICSID). It also attained membership in the World Bank's

Multilateral Investment Guarantee Agency (MIGA). However, owing to various problems such as the limited capacity of Eritrean markets, the lack of hard currency reserves, and an unskilled labor force, there has not been significant foreign and local investment in the country. Due to the border conflict and the post-conflict economic and political instability of the country, no significant number of local or foreign investors has yet been attracted to the Eritrean investment policy.

- *The industrial policy*: The government also set up guidelines aimed at promoting industrial development in Eritrea. As stated in the macropolicy, one of the main objectives was to "develop light manufacture based on agro-industry as a start and promote high-tech industries" (Government of Eritrea 1994: 17). Moreover, the government aimed at promoting an attractive environment for specific industries that focused on export production. In its macropolicy, the government stated, "Even though the general policy is to allow market forces to guide decisions with respect to investments, strong promotional support will be given to export industries that indicate clear competitive advantage in international markets and to specific projects designed to exploit the special factor endowments of the country (like tourism, entreport services, marine transport, etc." (Government of Eritrea 1994: 19). Through its policy directions, the government showed interest in developing local industries. In its macropolicy, the government stated, "Handicrafts and cottage industries will be provided with the know-how and other required inputs to help boost productivity. Those investors who initiate training and retraining and promote greater participation of Eritreans will be entitled to special support." (Government of Eritrea 1994: 19–20). The judgment about 14 years after the above-mentioned policies were drafted and implemented is that the state has not yet achieved much of its desired goals. The private industrial sector is still in its fragmented state, and private enterprises have not yet been competitive in the government-controlled market. Also, the special support promised for investors in local industries has not yet come through.

Based on the industrial policies adopted by the government in 1994, Eritrea has focused on regulating measures that affect production and competition, ownership and technology choices. The state's industrial policies also aimed at creating an environment that would create and maintain a convenient environment for the expansion of manufacturing industries. However, most of the manufacturing (public and private) enterprises have not yet been able to achieve the desired goals. Most of them are crippled by a list of obstacles. As we shall see in the following sections, most manufacturing industries in Eritrea have not been able to satisfy the local markets let alone make sufficient production for export.

THE MANUFACTURING INDUSTRY

As stated earlier, the modern manufacturing industry began with the advent of Italian colonialism, and a significant number of manufacturing industries were established during the Italian colonial rule in Eritrea. Indeed, the manufacturing industry made

A local recycling and production center in Asmara. (S. Tesfagiorgis)

the Italian colony of Eritrea one of the most economically developed countries on the continent. However, the Eritrean manufacturing industry went through a remarkable process of transformation during the post-Italian colonial period. First, it was negatively affected by the British policies of economic devitalization during the post–World War II period, and then it suffered from the Ethiopian occupation period. Exacerbating the effects of destructive warfare, the *Dergue* regime of Eritrea nationalized most of the manufacturing factories. By the 1990s, most of the factories were in a state of ruins. Among other factors, this could be attributed to the regime's policies of neglect. Independent Eritrea started a significant process of reconstruction and revival of the manufacturing sector. Yet, despite all the primary efforts made to revive the manufacturing industry, production has remained low throughout the post-independence period. The following are some of the manufacturing industries in Eritrea.

THE FOOD INDUSTRY

The food industry is an important part of the Eritrean manufacturing industry. Among the most significant factories in this sector include the edible oil factory and the canned food processing factory. However, the market contribution of this industry has been considerably limited throughout the years after independence, and the local markets have not been main beneficiaries from this sector.

The National Edible Oil Factory: The oil factory, which has a long recorded history, is one of Eritrea's most important enterprises. Its main products include edible oil, salad oil, and limited amounts of processed butter. Most of its raw material supply (oil-seeds) comes from the farming plantations on the Barka Plains.

The Barka Canneries: This factory is the only significant enterprise handling canned food in Eritrea. The factory was nationalized by the Ethiopian government in 1975, and most of its production has been directed toward army supplies. It produces canned foodstuffs such as meat and vegetables. Because of its strategic importance, the Eritrean government renationalized the factory and assigned it to the Eritrean Ministry of Defense. However, almost none of the products of the cannery appear in Eritrean markets; instead, they are usually consumed by the army.

THE BEVERAGE INDUSTRY

Starting from the Italian period, the beverage industry has been an important part of the manufacturing sector. As mentioned earlier, a number of beverage enterprises were established by Italian colonial rule in Eritrea. Although the beverage industry suffered from the effects of war and policies of neglect throughout the Ethiopian occupation period, most continued to be a vital part of the Eritrean industrial sector. Among the notable enterprises in this sector are:

The Melotti Brewery Factory: Established in 1939 (in Asmara), the Melotti Brewery Factory is the only notable producer of commercial beer in Eritrea. It was nationalized by the Ethiopian government in the 1970s. After independence, the factory continued to be a state-owned enterprise, and employed over 400 workers. Since 2000, this factory has suffered greatly from a lack of both skilled workers and raw material supplies. Therefore, its production has sharply diminished. Currently (February 2009), there is almost no sufficient supply of Melotti Beer in the local markets.

The Fenili Liquor Factory: Based in Asmara, this factory is also of Italian heritage. It produces various types of liquor such as gin and ouzo (*areki*). However, the factory's production has been steadily decreasing since 2000.

The Coca Cola and the Red Sea Soft Drink Factories: Based in Asmara, these two bottling factories are the only significant producers of soft drinks in Eritrea. The factories are share companies in which the Eritrean government owns over 50 percent of the shares. These factories have the capacity of producing over 7,000 cases of various types of soft drinks a day. Although remarkably successful, these factories have not yet been able to satisfy the local markets.

THE TEXTILE INDUSTRY

The textile industry is one of the most significant production enterprises in Eritrea. Although affected by mismanagement and policies of neglect during the Ethiopian occupation period, the Eritrean textile industry has continued to be an important part of the manufacturing industry. This industry comprises a number of private enterprises and state-owned factories such as the Lalemba Sack Factory and the Asmara Sweater Factory. Among the significant public factories in this industry are:

The Baratollo/Asmara Textile Factory: Established by an Italian investor, this factory has become one of the largest and most significant textile-producing enterprises in Eritrea. It produces cotton yarn as well as performing other textile activities such as spinning, winding, knitting, and dyeing. Most of the cotton supplies for this factory come from cotton plantations in the western lowlands. As with most other factories in Eritrea, the Baratollo also fell into the hands of the government in 1991. After independence, the factory employed over 2,000 workers, whose activities ranged from making various types of cotton fabrics to producing blankets and sanitary towels. The factory also provided enough production for exports to Ethiopia and other regions. After 1998, owing to the war and the border tensions, this factory lost all its markets in Ethiopia.

The Eritrea Textile Factory: Although of smaller scale, this factory produces similar items to that of the Asmara Textile Factory. It was established in 1964 through a merger of two smaller factories (the Ethiofile and the Ethiopian Textile Industry). It produces various types of textiles such as cotton yarns, knitted fabrics, and cotton wool. The factory is state-owned and employs over 420 workers. As with most other factories in the country, the Eritrea Textile Factory also suffers from insufficient raw material supplies, a lack of skilled workers, and an inadequate supply of markets.

THE FISHING INDUSTRY

Eritrea is located at the widest part of the Red Sea and is strategically located on the most highly productive part of the sea. Eritrea possesses over 1,200 kilometers (about 625 miles) of coastline and large territorial waters along the Red Sea. It has a continental shelf of about 52,000 square kilometers (20,077.3 square miles). Eritrea's coastline is divided into two administrative zones: the Northern Red Sea Zone that includes Massawa (the major port city in this administrative unit) as well as the Dahlak Archipelagoes; and the Southern Red Sea Zone that includes Assab (the major port city in this administrative unit), Tio, and Eddi. Based on the report by the Food and Agricultural Organization (FAO) (2002), the population of these administrative units was estimated at 302,000 and 120,000, respectively. The total fishers' population in both administrative units was estimated at one percent of the total population, and fishers are sparsely distributed along the coastline and the islands (FAO 2002).

According to the FAO, the allochthonous (physical formations such as rocks originated not in the place(s) where they are located) advection of monsoon brought to the Red Sea via Bab El Mandab rewards this part of the sea with nutrient-rich waters (FAO 2002). These features, as well as the unpolluted nature of the sea, support significant fish and coral populations. Therefore, as in most parts of the Red Sea, the Eritrean territorial waters are characterized by rich and diverse marine resources that include over 1,000 species of fish and over 220 varieties of coral species (FAO 2002; Teweldemedhin Y. 2008: 327). Some of the abundant fish varieties include reef dwelling such as groupers, snappers, and emperors; demersal such as breams; pelagic such as tunas, sharks, sardines, and jacks as well as other varieties such as cuttlefish, crabs, oysters, and parrotfish (FAO 2002). All these diverse resources are commercially valuable, and Eritrea could make great commercial use of the diversity of marine resources.

The Eritrean coastline has several harbors, including the major ones at Massawa and Assab. Smaller harbors are also found at Tio, Wokiro, Eddi, and Barasole. Several other small harbors such as Marsa Gulbub, Marsa Ibrahim, and Marsa Kubba, are located north of Massawa and are usually used by small-scale local fishermen. However, owing to lack of efficient infrastructure, most of these harbors have not been able to meet standard services for either artisanal fishermen or industrial fishing companies. If adequate investment was committed to developing efficient infrastructure, competitive distribution systems, improved facilities and services, fishing would be one of the few Eritrean industries with a great potential for development.

Commercial fishing has not been intensive, and the Eritrean fishery sector has not been able to make significant use of the marine resources. Only a few hundred traditional fishermen (whose movement is greatly limited along the ports of Massawa and Assab) are engaged in artisanal or subsistence fishing (NgCheong-Lum 2005: 42). Although the Eritrean Ministry of Marine Resources/Ministry of Fisheries was established to maximize revenue through offshore fishing and other marine resource exploitation, not much is known of its achievements. Industrial fishing is still in its preliminary stages. Eritrea has the potential of achieving the Maximum Sustainable Yield (MSY) ranging between 36,000 and 79,000 tons per year (Teweldemedhin Y. 2008: 327). Yet, its current level of production ranges only between 4,000 and 12,000 tons per year, and fish has not yet become one of the major food/protein resources for most Eritreans. About three-fourths of the current fish production in Eritrea is conducted by the government owned company—the National Fishing Corporation (NFC). The remaining one-fourth of the fish production is produced by local fishermen whose fishing techniques depend on traditional knowledge and experience. Currently (as of February 2009), fish production scale in Eritrea can be estimated at a much lower scale than in the 1950s and 1960s. In the 1950s, there were about 20,000 artisanal or traditional fishermen who produced a significant amount of fish (example, ca. 25,000 tons in 1954), a bulk of which was exported (Government of Eritrea 1994: 5). Most of the current Eritrean fishermen also suffer from lack of various supplies and preserving materials necessary for their fishing activities, including ice, chillers, and blast freezers. Founded in 2004, the NFC has established and reopened at least five fish-processing plants in Massawa, Assab, Asmara, and Tio. It has also imported new fishing boats that are expected to increase the company's fish production.

Various types of fishes are exported to Europe and neighboring countries such as Saudi Arabia and Yemen. Exports of fish include fresh whole fishes, semi-processed as well as salted, and sundried fish products (FAO 2002). Local markets such as Asmara and other towns of Eritrea, however, do not get enough fish supply. Therefore, fish prices across the country have been high; usually unaffordable for the great majority of ordinary Eritreans.

THE TOURISM INDUSTRY

Due to its strategic location along the Red Sea, Eritrea is endowed with a remarkable terrestrial and marine ecological diversity. As mentioned in chapter one, the landscape diversity and climatic contrast is significant—ranging from the blazing heat of the Danakil Depression to the cool highland mountains. Despite its small size, the country possesses diverse natural resources—botanical and zoological resources. Above all, Eritrea possesses diverse people with great values of hospitality for visitors. Observing the physical and ethnographic diversity of the territory Dr. Georg Schweinfurth, a German botanist, noted in 1893:

> The regions occupied by the Italians in Northern Abyssinia and in the northern extremity of the Ethiopian highlands are distinct for an extraordinary variety of physical and ethnographic conditions; they, hence, have a particular charm in our study of Africa, the contrasts which present themselves—often in surprisingly short distances—being there easily observed, and new stimuli to the investigation of as yet unsolved problems being everywhere offered. (Schweinfurth 1894: 379).

The truth of the above statement is still acknowledged in today's Eritrean ecology. Moreover, the country comprises a number of archaeological and historical sites that demonstrate its remarkable cultural heritage. Some of the already excavated archaeological evidence contributes a significant part to the universal human history (Schmidt, Curtis et al. 2008).

Apart from ecological diversity, Eritrea is also characterized by human diversity. Nine different ethnolinguistic groups, each with a distinctive language and culture, occupy different parts of the country. In addition to its proximity to tourism markets in Europe and the Middle East, the diverse natural resources give the country a remarkable potential to develop a strong tourism industry. Recognizing the outstanding potential of this industry, the TGE established the Ministry of Tourism in 1993. It opened tourism offices in almost all of the administrative zones of the country. Among the main objectives of this ministry include facilitating the conservation and enhancement of the country's cultural and environmental heritages. Through this ministry, the government also developed its National Tourism Development Plan (a twenty-year plan) aimed at enhancing cultural and natural resources for tourism and making the resources available for generating economic benefits.

Yet, the Eritrean tourism industry is facing major challenges and has not been able to provide significant financial input into the national economy. In addition to the lack of a skilled professional work force deemed necessary for the industry's success, the available communication infrastructure is not sufficient for the growth of modern tourism. Effective tourist information channels such as the Internet and magazines have been limited, and the few available tourist information publications (mostly from the Ministry of Tourism) have been almost inaccessible. Despite these challenges, Eritrea hosted a significant number of tourists between 1991 and 1998. Most of the tourists were Eritreans living abroad. A remarkable number of tourists from different corners of the globe also visited the country. However, the number of tourist visitors has shown a sharp decline since 2000, which can be attributed to the effects of the border conflict with Ethiopia. Moreover, the government's recent travel restrictions imposed on visitors have further affected the development of tourism in the country (Denison 2007: 45).

PRIVATIZATION OF INDUSTRIAL PLANTS IN ERITREA

After independence, the Eritrean government embarked on a large-scale privatization process of various public enterprises. By 1993, the government started to implement policies aimed at improving the frameworks and production systems of public enterprises. It disbanded a number of centralized marketing institutions with an objective of providing enterprises significant liberty to freely decide on their respective systems of production and quality of their products. It also attempted a vigorous process of returning housing complexes and private buildings that had been nationalized under the *Dergue* regime to their owners. Moreover, the government also engaged itself in returning large numbers of small-scale enterprises to their private owners.

On different occasions, the government also demonstrated its belief that private enterprises would be much more likely to accelerate economic growth than public enterprises. Based on this belief, the government opted for an open-market economy dominated by the private sector. Through its macropolicy, the government also announced that "the private sector is the lead actor in the economic activities of Eritrea ... The government will take all necessary policy and other supportive measures to promote, encourage and develop the private sector and protect its interests" (Government of Eritrea 1994: 15–16). The government also issued Proclamation 83/1995 which established an agency known as the National Agency for the Supervision and Privatization of Public Enterprises. Some of the main objectives of this agency were to facilitate the process of privatization and the reduction of public enterprises. The agency was entitled with considerable powers such as implementing appropriate management policies, functions, optimization and transformation of productivity, and the establishment of a competitive and conductive economic climate in all public enterprises and the enhancement of their privatization.

However, since the day of its establishment, this agency has not been transparent, and its achievements have not been well elaborated for the public. All members of the Board of Directors, the main organ of this agency, were members of the EPLF who were directly appointed by the president. Therefore, most of the appointees seem not to have had accumulated knowledge and experience in managerial tasks of a free-market economy. Moreover, the agency's privatization scheme did not include all public enterprises in its direct-sale agenda. Apart from some of the enterprises that were offered for foreign and domestic buyers, the agency also reserved a number of large-scale enterprises for the ruling party (PFDJ) and other enterprises that the state considered were strategic and then retained them (examples: the Barka Canneries Factory and the Dekemhare Flourmills Factory). Some of the state-owned factories are run by the Ministry of Defense. The PFDJ, the only ruling party in the country, runs a number of manufacturing and printing enterprises.

In general, the privatization policy that rolled out in 1993 has yet to achieve its desired goals. By 2005, only a few large-scale enterprises and about 33 small-scale enterprises had been privatized. Most of the large-scale enterprises are still owned by the state, and about 80 percent of employees in manufacturing enterprises are still involved in the enterprises run by the state. However, due to an increasing lack of material supplies, and skilled work force, most private enterprises have not been productive.

LABOR

As mentioned earlier, the main economic activity for over 80 percent of the Eritrean working population is agriculture. Subsistence farming and animal herding are the main sources of livelihood for most Eritrean households. About 20 percent of the total population is employed in various sectors such as the manufacturing industry, trade, and services. However, massive mobilization of the population since the 1990s, particularly since the Eritrea-Ethiopia border conflict in 1998, has resulted in critical shortages of all types of workers in all economic sectors of the country. The government's National Service Program (which constantly demands the mobilization of people between the ages of 18 and 40) has adversely affected all private sectors. A large number of private enterprises have gone bankrupt, among other factors, because of a lack of professional and skilled workers. Even the local agricultural sector has suffered immensely because of a lack of manpower. The Eritrean traditional agricultural system demands intensive labor that most villages cannot afford to supply. Most rural households are, therefore, unable to achieve sustainable subsistence production because their productive manpower is kept in the army.

Gender plays an important role in the pattern of labor of the rural economy. The traditional pastoral and farming economies are characterized by division of labor usually based on gender and age. The gender- and age-based system of labor division is deeply rooted in the cultural values and norms of the Eritrean societies. Social norms and values regulate the participation of different sections of the society in a collective as well as in household-based farming and other income-generating activities. In rural farming households, the woman's role is vital. Although certain types of tasks such as plowing, sowing, and threshing are conducted by men, most other activities such as taking care of children, cooking, and fetching firewood and water are carried out by women (see chapter five). Children also contribute appreciably part to a household's labor. Among the main activities of children in the rural households are herding animals and assisting parents in their farming and household tasks. However, gender disparity continues to be one of the concerns in the labor systems of the country. Apart from a household-based labor system, rural villages also organize collective labor (commonly known as *wofera* (ወፈራ)) on occasional bases. *Wofera* is usually a system of voluntary labor organized in the form of mutual cooperation among members of a village. It usually takes place during particular occasions such as construction of houses, preparation for a wedding, and other cultural ceremonies. Moreover, labor can also be exchanged between members of a village in the form of *wofera* during farming and other economic and social activities.

HISTORICAL OVERVIEW OF LABOR UNIONS

Although the Eritrean working class emerged during the Italian colonial period, no significant labor unions appeared until the 1940s. Unlike most parts of colonial Africa, the development of labor unions in Eritrea did not evolve through a typical pattern of formation during Italian colonial rule. Italian labor policies in Eritrea were based on principles of racial segregation. Eritrean workers were simply considered as sources of cheap labor and usually suffered from low wages and discriminatory treatments by employers. The colonial state did not provide rights for Eritrean workers' collective action, so the formation of an organized Eritrean labor force was out of question (Tesfagiorgis 1993: 65). One of the main sectors that employed a large number of Eritreans was the colonial army. The Italian colonial army, which totaled (in the late 1930s) about 60,000 Eritreans, was based on discriminatory policies. No significant promotions were given to Eritreans serving in the colonial army. Most of the higher military ranks were also occupied by Italians. Even in the civil service, Eritreans did not have the right to form an organized body of labor within the overall colonial system.

Post-Italian colonialism in Eritrea was characterized by the proliferation of political movements. The expansion of secular education as well as the rise of political consciousness also further stimulated the creation of worker groups. Worker groups intended to defend workers' rights and to facilitate conditions for economic improvements and political freedom. The formation of labor organizations was, however, a slow process. As mentioned earlier, this was attributed to repressive employment policies. Even until the end of 1940s, the British Military Administration (BMA) exercised restrictive policies against the formation of labor organizations. The BMA favored Italian employees, and "upheld racially-defined labor codes that gave Italian workers wages and benefits far superior to those of Eritreans" (Killion 1998: 288).

The formation of political movements and parties in the 1940s created a platform for worker groups to share common concerns and create collective labor bodies. Included among the agendas of some political movements were the promotion of equality and workers' benefits of Eritrean employees (see Killion 1998: 288). The BMA's post-war economic policies involved the dismantling of several key industries in the country. As a result, a large number of Eritrean workers were adversely affected. Coupled with the fermentation of Eritrean political movements, the economic recession of the late 1940s led to the proliferation upheaval reaching the point where the British found it difficult to govern the territory. By 1948, the economic recession, aggravated by British policies of economic devitilization, continued to affect the working class (Tesfai 2005: 112–129; Connell 2001: 204–209; Pankhurst 1952). In the same year, about 637 workshops and small-scale enterprises were closed down because of a lack of raw material supplies and the draining of hard currency reserves. As a result, about 10,000 Eritrean and 4,000 Italian workers became unemployed (Tesfai 2005: 112). By 1952, unemployment reached its peak with over 30 percent of the work force unemployed. Since the late 1940s, formal labor organizations have started to emerge. Until 1958, thousands of skilled workers left the country in search of jobs in neighboring countries. Tens of thousands of Italian skilled workers also returned to their home country.

Amid critical political frictions and economic recession, Eritrean workers' groups also organized strikes against inequality and discrimination at their work places. Affected by the rocketing prices of goods and services, low wages, discrimination, and widespread job loss, dockworkers in the port city of Massawa organized themselves and went strike in 1949. Eritrean Railway workers organized another major strike the same year. Their demands included equal pay and the promotion of Eritrean workers. This strike, which involved over 1,325 workers, continued for six weeks in February and March of 1949 (Tesfai 2005: 114). The strike had also far-reaching political implications in the BMA. Recognizing the scale and magnitude of the workers' strikes, the BMA established a formal body known as the Native Employment Advisory Committee in 1949. Among the main tasks of this committee included creating nondiscriminatory procedures of employment for Eritreans.

Immediately before the Eritrea-Ethiopian federation in 1952, the BMA also attempted to liberalize labor laws. This increased the momentum for the formation of labor organizations and trade unions throughout the country. A number of small labor groups such as traders' associations and shop owners' associations also emerged. Most importantly, the General Union of Eritrean Labor Syndicates (GUELS) was founded in 1952.

THE GUELS

According to Alemseged Tesfai, the formation of GUELS was initiated by a couple of Eritrean workers who found it difficult and offensive to work in a discriminatory work environment (Tesfai 2005: 112–129). Based on first-hand accounts gathered and presented by Tesfai (2005): in 1951, a certain American fuel company in Eritrea named Aramco was employing Eritreans to work in Saudi Arabia. As many other members of the Eritrean working class, Mr. Tsegai Kahsay, Mr. Kefela Beraki, and Mr. Tesfai Zerakerestos wanted to apply for the work positions offered by Aramco. However, considering that all three of these people were Christians, the company refused to offer them a job. Instead, it preferred Eritrean Muslim workers whom various positions were offered in the company's employment positions in Saudi Arabia. The preference of Muslims to Christians was also openly told to these applicants (Tesfai 2005: 115-120).

These workers appealed to Aramco office in Asmara, the American Consul in Eritrea and the Arab Communities in Asmara, but to no avail. Concerned by the outright labor discrimination on the bases of religion, these individuals published their grievances in two of the Eritrean newspapers on July 7, 1951. Their article in the newspapers appeared under the title "Labor situations which the public have to know" (title translated from Tigrinya). Part of the content of the article was as follows:

> When we say that such a situation has annoyed Eritrean workers, we would like to state that it has, indeed, broken the heart of all Eritrean Muslim and Christian workers and non-workers. Indeed, any Eritrean—Muslim by religion would not be happy to see another Eritrean brother—Christian by religion who is suffering and feeling anger. Similarly, a Christian Eritrean shares the same feeling of anger or

happiness with another Eritrean brother who is Muslim by religion. We are writing this not because we are jealous of our Muslim brothers, rather we just want to aware the public. As long as they are Eritrean brothers, their happiness is ours and their joy is also ours. However, we are annoyed and surprised, because in spite of the fact that the Arabs are geographically our neighbors, they come to our land and live in peace, liberty and accumulate wealth, they are said to have ordered this company not to let any Eritrean Christians to step in their land?! (quoted in Tesfai 2005: 119, translation from Tigrinya by author).

This became a significant issue of discussion and concern among Eritrean workers for several weeks. A number of correspondences were published in the local newspapers. Perhaps concerned by the magnitude of discussions, the American Consul in Eritrea, Mr. Edward Malkehi, responded to Mr. Tsegai Kahsay's letter on October 28, 1951. The following is an excerpt of his letter:

This American company which has become a theme of discussion did not discriminate Eritrean Christians neither did it refuse to offer them jobs. However, because it is located in Saudi Arabia, it is obliged to obey the rules and regulations prevailing in that area. The Saudi Arabian government rejects to let any non-Muslim foreigner to come into her soil . . . Therefore this American company and the government of the United States do not have the right to improve the laws prevalent in Saudi Arabia (quoted in Tesfai 2005: 120, translation from Tigrinya by author).

Discussions on labor and workers' rights continued for some time and it involved politicians and intellectuals such as Tsegai Teferi, Woldeab Woldemariam, Tesfamichael Worke, and many others. As a result of workers' efforts, the GUELS was eventually founded in 1952 on the basis of legal procedures as provided under the labor code of the BMA. Woldeab Woldemariam, one of the veteran leaders of the Eritrean independence movement, was elected the first president of GUELS (Tesfai 2005: 120–123). Until the end of 1953, the GUELS had about 4,000 employed, and about 6,000 associate members (see also Killion 1998: 289). In general, the GUELS was one of the biggest labor organizations of the kind in Sub-Saharan Africa.

Although the federal constitution provided Eritrea with the right to form trade unions, Ethiopia started to attack trade unions in Eritrea starting from year one of the federation. It also banned GUELS in 1954 and Woldeab Woldemariam, who served as the first president of the labor organization, left the country after he survived several assassination attempts. When Ethiopia took over port facilities and other industrial sectors starting in 1954, it started to brutally suppress labor unions. As part of its policies of control, Ethiopia relocated several industries to Addis Ababa. This also resulted in the loss of two-thirds of the Eritrean employment positions (Connell 2001: 206).

Eritrean labor movements continued to confront Ethiopian labor polices in Eritrea throughout the 1950s. For instance, a general labor strike was organized in some Eritrean towns in March 1958. The strike was organized against the new Ethiopian labor code that threatened further curtailing of Eritrean workers' rights. Again, Ethiopia brutally suppressed these strikes. In Asmara alone, a large number of workers went on strike in the streets of the city. However, the Ethiopian police opened fire on the strikers as well as on about the 80,000 dwellers of the city who gathered for a rally to support the strikers—about nine people were killed and about 535 were injured (Connell 2001: 206; Killion 1998: 289).

Ethiopia continued to oppose any organized labor movement or strikes and made it extremely difficult for Eritrean workers to form an organized way of defending their rights. As the unemployment rate increased, working conditions for the Eritrean working class continued to worsen. As a result, nonviolent labor organizations faded away and many urban workers started to join clandestine political movements and later Eritrean armed liberation fronts. On the other hand, over 10,000 remnants of Eritrean labor organizations were absorbed by the government-sponsored Confederation of Ethiopian Labor Unions (CELU) (Connell 2001: 206). The CELU was an umbrella organization of many Ethiopian labor unions, and among the people who played a pivotal role in the formation labor unions in Ethiopia were Eritrean workers who migrated to Ethiopia (Tesfagiorgis 1993: 65). The few remaining labor unions in Eritrea were also made subordinate to CELU. In 1977, the Marxist regime in Ethiopia banned CELU and replaced it with another organization called All-Ethiopia Trade Union. However, these government-sponsored organizations were mostly influenced by government political agendas—they aimed at controlling the working class and cultivating support for governmental policies.

Similarly, the Marxist regime in Ethiopia introduced a new land allocation policy under the slogan of "land to the tiller." Under this policy the government confiscated large tracts of farming land and redistributed them to landless farmers. However, this policy was futile in Eritrea because the regime had neither full control of the territory nor acceptance and recognition by the rural communities. As a means of controlling the farming communities, it established various forms of workers associations, including farmers' associations commonly known as *yägäberiewotch mahber* (የገበሬዎች ማህበር), "Farmers' Association," in several Eritrean towns and villages. Farmers' Associations were formed along Marxist political lines. Included among the main tasks of these associations were the implementation of governmental land policies and the establishment of marketing and credit initiatives for farmers.

WORKERS IN THE LIBERATION ARMY

Ethiopian control and suppression of autonomous labor unions resulted in a steady exodus of skilled workers to the Eritrean liberation fronts (Killion 1998: 289). This, in turn, clearly benefited the liberation fronts. In the late 1970s and 1980s, a considerable number of Eritrean workers joined the EPLF. Among other professionals and skilled workers, the EPLF army had in its ranks medical doctors, nurses, practitioners, teachers, journalists, mechanics, electricians, and more. Based in the Sahel Mountains, the EPLF opened a number of underground factories, workshops, construction operations, and small-scale, sophisticated enterprises where skilled members of the army worked for free. It should be noted that all members of the EPLF army were not paid, and they worked for the liberation front on a voluntary basis. All members of the army (professionals or non-professionals) also worked in strict, centralized military methods—some of them for over twenty years. Recognizing the significance of workers within the front as well as members of the front in the diaspora, the EPLF founded the National Union of Eritrean Workers (NUEWO) in November 1979.

The NUEWO created effective clandestine workers' cells within towns that were occupied by Ethiopia. Through these cells, it enacted various operations within Eritrean towns and cities. Moreover, the NUEWO also managed to organize Eritrean workers in the diaspora who not only injected financial support for the EPLF but also supplied the organization with professional and skilled expertise. In the 1980s, the NUEWO had successfully managed to organize construction workers in the Sudan. Among the most important institutions run by the Eritrean professional and skilled members of the EPLF in diaspora included the Eritrean Relief Association (ERA), the Research and Information Center of Eritrea (RICE), and several youth and student unions in North America and Europe.

LABOR ORGANIZATIONS SINCE INDEPENDENCE

The EPLF retained NUEWO after its military victory in 1991. By the early 1990s, the NUEWO, which was still run by its wartime leadership, focused on organizing workers into trade unions and on the mobilization of the working class for national reconstruction programs (Connell 2001: 208–209). As summarized in the NUEWO's programs, it embarked on providing Eritrean workers an atmosphere in which they become "proud actors of progress and development in the building of Eritrea as a nation full of human rights, human dignity, and socio-economic well-being" (quoted in Connell 2001: 209). Yet, although the government enacted a new Labor Code in December 1991 (Labor Proclamation 8/1991—allowing workers to form organizations and defend their rights), the NUEWO remained as the only significant labor organization on the national level. This union also played a leading role in organizing Eritrean workers in the early 1990s. By 1994, the NUEWO had already managed to bring together "thirty-three locals to launch the Federation of Mining, Chemical and General Workers. The largest was that at Assab Oil Refinery with 1,000 workers. The smallest was the Kokebe Tzeba Printing Press with seventeen" (Connell 2001: 209–210). Included among its major activities were fostering industrial relations and assessing of working conditions in public and private enterprises. It is also believed that the government decreed a 50 percent salary increase in 1992 on the bases of NUEWO's counsel (Killion 1998: 290).

The NUEWO organized a major labor congress in 1993, at which it elected new leadership (although most members of the new leadership were still wartime personnel). It also attained membership in the International Labor Organization (ILO) in the same year. In 1994, NUEWO was transformed into the National Confederation of Eritrean Workers (NCEW).

However, a great number of Eritrean workers lost their jobs in 1994/1995 due to the government's privatization policy as well as its human resource management strategies. Many of the privatized small-scale enterprises cut their human resources by laying off many workers. Moreover, on the basis of its human resource management strategy, the government alleged that many workers in various sectors were unskilled, and they were immediately laid off from their work posts. *Metseltsal* (ምጽላጽል—literally meaning, "to get rid of"), a term coined by the government to signify that unskilled workers should be laid off, was implemented and it affected thousand of Eritrean workers. This increased the momentum toward layoffs across the country—especially since 1994. Although faced with both a shortage of resources and personnel, the NCEW was flooded with new issues: addressing fresh jobseekers who flooded the market; tens of thousands of ex-soldiers who were demobilized from the army but were not resettled and looking for a job; and hundreds of thousands of refugees who returned from Sudan and other parts of the world. As noted by Connell (2001), Tsegai Mogos, then (shortly after the launch of NCEW) the vice general secretary of NCEW, was quoted as saying:

> We have a huge number of unemployed already, and we have 50,000 or 60,000 ex-fighters who will soon be demobilized and go to the job market. We are also waiting for about 750,000 refugees who are supposed to come from Sudan, and of these 250,000 are potential workers. And we have the problem of war-disabled—they should be involved in productive work. If you take all these figures and you compare them with the 20,000 members we have in NCEW, the situation is not encouraging (quoted in Connell 2001: 212).

As stated earlier, the PFDJ, which has been the biggest employer in the country, controls some of the biggest enterprises. In spite of the fact that the government provided relative autonomy for labor unions in its labor proclamations, it still exercises strict control over free unions and associations. The government also does not allow the formation of unions within the police and related service-providing institutions. Although the government does not formally oppose the formation of civil unions and associations, in practice, new unions of more than twenty members must be approved by the Ministry of Labor and Human Welfare (MLHW) to be registered and acknowledged by the state. The NCEW and MLHW are closely monitored by the government, which makes the process of their approval for the formation of a trade or workers union rather slow and bureaucratic. Moreover, the government repeatedly gets involved in the matters of legally autonomous labor and trade unions. As a result, human rights' reports indicate that a number of figures in labor unions such as Minase Andetsion (secretary of the affiliated federation of Eritrean Textile, Leather and Shoe Workers' (ITGLWF)), Tewolde Gebremedhin (chair of the affiliated federation for Food, Beverages, Hotels, Tourism and Agriculture Workers [IUF]), and Habtom Woldemichael (head of the Red Sea Bottlers Coca-Cola Workers Union (RSBCWU)) were arrested and held incommunicado in 2005.

According to the country's Labor Code workers have the right to form unions, and organize strikes and collective bargains. As a result, many labor unions have been formed on various levels. Most of the existing labor unions, however, do not have a significant number of members and are usually based on the type of occupation. Hence, workers are usually organized or grouped by the companies, enterprises, or industries for which they work. Included among the few autonomous and significant labor unions is the Eritrean Teachers' Association. Since 1994, the NCEW has attempted to institutionalize worker unions into federations of various institutions, including mining, hides and shoes, transport and communication, and textile. The NCEW also cooperates with and is supported by a number of foreign labor unions such as the Italian and Norwegian trade unions. Currently (as of February 2009) there are five major NCEW labor federations and over 230 small unions in Eritrea. The federations are for:

1. textile, leather, and shoes
2. transport and communication
3. mining, chemicals, metalwork, and other manufacturing
4. food, drink, hotels, tourism, and agriculture
5. service industries

The government also established the Ministry of Labor and Human Welfare (MLHW) as one of its oversight authorities, with its main tasks, among others, of facilitating and supervising labor and human welfare conditions in the country. Since its establishment, this ministry has been actively running various programs such as HIV awareness campaigns, assessments related to child labor, assistance to orphans and the disabled, human development programs and training, and more. However, the MLHW has not been able to provide significant published information related to its activities and achievements. Therefore, there is little public information on its overall roles, activities, and accomplishments. The ministry and the government as a whole have, however, refused to comply with the rules and regulations of the International Monetary Fund (IMF) and the World Bank (WB). Hence, these international institutions do not provide substantial financial assistance deemed necessary for the development of labor unions in Eritrea.

CHILD LABOR IN ERITREA

There is no child slavery in Eritrea. Based on the Eritrean Labor Code 8/1991 (also Labor Proclamation 118/2001), the minimum age for workers in Eritrea is set at 18-years old, although novices can start working at an earlier age (Government of Eritrea 1991). The Eritrean Transitional Penal Code (art. 276 and 278) and the Eritrean Civil Code also strongly prohibits sexual abuse and forced labor against children.

Based on fragmented sources, many children are involved in commercial sex. Prior to 2000, it was assumed that about five percent of the country's prostitutes were children aging between 12 and 17 years old. The composition of children in the "commercial sex business" is believed to have markedly increased since 2000. Yet, issues related to child sexual exploitation, such as through child pornography, are culturally immoral and are not practiced across the country, and the government considers any practice of child pornography as illegal and a highly punishable offense.

Also, the formal employment procedure in Eritrea does not allow child labor. But it is common to see children from rural areas who do not attend school to take part in various household and farming activities—such as livestock herding, fetching fire-wood and water. In big cities and towns, some children also work as hawkers of small items such as cigarettes, chewing gums, boiled eggs, nuts, and so on. However, it should be noted that there is a great difference between child labor contribution in one's household work and child labor aimed at generating wages (as practiced in some countries). There are no exhaustive sources that indicate the practice of wage-generating child labor in the country.

The Eritrean government launched a series of controls against street vendors in the 1990s. Using agents from the MLHW, city municipalities, and the police departments, the government used trucks (which were ironically known by the street vendors as *lemlem* [ለምለም—a Tigrinya term for "fertile"; "evergreen"]) to load up street vendors (including children) and take them to temporary camps (such as *Enda Se'al*, Asmara). The government claimed that this action was part of its policy of fighting poverty.

TRADE AND FINANCE

Brief Historical Overview of Trade and Finance in Eritrea

It is generally believed that the ancient trade system in the Eritrean region was based on a simple system commonly known as barter trade (a system in which there is usu-ally a perfectly balanced terms of trade; and trading items were directly exchanged among consumers). Archaeological evidence shows that trade was one of the most important factors in the territory's ancient regional and international relations. Ancient regional civilizations, including ancient Egypt, developed remarkable commercial and trading networks with the territory commonly known as the Land of Punt (to which—although no defined geographical information is available—Eritrea is believed to have been one of the main territories). Among other trading items, the Land of Punt is believed to have been rich in incense (a highly valued item during that time, and still used as a hallowed item during holy masses in traditional churches). Egyptian pha-raohs sent expeditions to the region to gather incense for its domestic and commercial use. The ancient people of the western lowlands also practiced trade with various regional communities. Generally, the history of the Eritrean region has been character-ized by the continuous movement of people. Among other economic activities, trade is believed to have been practiced by those ancient people. Yet, not much recorded his-tory is available about the extent and content of trade during the pre-Aksumite Empire. Commercial ports continued to grow along the coastal areas of Eritrea, particularly at places in the Gulf of Zula. Some ancient cities such as Quohaito and Metera as well as the port of Adulis became important sites of regional and international trade and com-merce. Various networks of trade routes were also used between the coast and the hinterland.

As mentioned in chapter two, the ancient Aksumite Empire rose to prominence during the first century of the Christian era. The rise of the Aksumite Empire emanated from its political development and wealth, which were generated through its trade and economic activities. Aksum developed widespread trading networks with the Mediter-ranean world, Egypt, and the Persian Gulf, which further rewarded the empire with wealth and power. Its military expansion into regional territories such as Moroe and Nubia are also believed to have diversified its wealth.

The Aksumite Empire introduced its own currency system, and it minted its own coins (from silver, gold, and other), which facilitated its foreign trade and commerce (see Munro-Hay 1991). Some of the most important export items of the Aksumite Empire were gold, silver, iron ore, lead, beads, animals and animal products such as skins and hides, and other items that Aksum gathered from its area of hegemony (see Munro-Hay 1991: 130–145). Salt and iron were some of its domestic trading items.

For several centuries of the post-Aksumite period, regional and international commerce slowed, and there are not many available sources about the extent and type of trade in the region during this time. The distribution and value of the Aksumite currency also disappeared after the downfall of the empire. Although domestic and regional trade remained part of the overall economy of the people of the Eritrean region, the absence of a widely accepted currency might have fostered the practice of a barter system (at least until the introduction of Maria Theresa *Thaler*, an Austrian coin minted in the late eighteenth century, and that was widely distributed and used in northeast Africa). The Austrian Thaler was widely used as an ornament as well as a purchasing currency for imported goods (see also Negash 1987: 38 and Rena 2007: 135–153).

Sketchy sources indicate that trade remained an important economic activity in the region until the Italian occupation. Foreign trade during the post-Aksumite period was first centered on the coastal areas (Dahlak Islands, Massawa, and Hergigo), where commerce continued between the Eritrean region and the Arabian Peninsula. By the fifteenth century, foreign trade again expanded as far as the highland political center of Debarewa (see also Killion 1996: 94–97). According to Negash, in 1879 (eleven years before Eritrea formally became an Italian colony), the value of goods imported through Massawa (to Eritrea and Ethiopia) was estimated at two million *lire* (also written as *lira*—Italian currency) as opposed to two and half million lire worth in exports (Negash 1987: 38).

In Eritrea, the modern systems of trade and finance started with Italian colonialism. In the 1890s, the Italians introduced their own currency (lire, also known as the Thalero Eritreo) and modern forms of financial institutions. The Italians, who found Eritrea a strategic territory for the development of commerce, embarked on large-scale trade with surrounding regions, including southern Arabia and as far as the Indian subcontinent during the first years of their occupation of the territory. According to Negash, the Italian colonization of Eritrea created an economic boom for countries such as Austria and India, who increased their trade with Eritrea more than fivefold (Negash 1987: 38). Soon, however, the colonial state applied a sort of protectionist policy of "placing Italy in a dominant position vis-à-vis the import/export trade of the colony" (Negash 1987: 38). Therefore, by 1910, most of the colony's trade was mandated to be with Italy.

Italy also provided financial institutions that became important catalysts for regional and foreign trade. By 1941, four major banks—Banca d'Italia (the Bank of Italy), Banco di Roma (the Bank of Rome), Banco di Napoli (the Bank of Napoli), and Banca Cooperativa Populare Eritrea (the Cooperative Bank of Eritrea)—were serving as the main financial institutions in the colony. Bank of Italy, the first modern bank in Eritrea, established its branches in Massawa and Asmara, and it became the most important financial institution in the colony; by 1921, the total virtual circulation of lire notes in the colony reached nearly thirty million (Rena 2007: 138–145). A couple of more credit institutions were also established in Asmara.

During the 1930s, when Italy was preparing for the invasion of neighboring Ethiopia, the economy showed a short-term dramatic boom in trade and commerce. Once the war was over, there was a steep fall off in both exports and prices of raw materials—such as agricultural products—that were significant prewar trading items. Most of the commercial production sectors were hit by the postwar crisis, which led to the fall of prices of market items such as silver (Rena 2007: 140–41).

According to Trevaskis, when the British occupied Eritrea in 1941, "the currency resources of the four banks had been reduced to fifteen percent of their deposit values, largely as a consequence of the Italian Government ordering them to destroy their stocks on the eve of Asmara's occupation" (Trevaskis 1960: 43). Furthermore, the British restricted the activities of the Italian financial institutions and passed orders against their dealing with matters that involved foreign exchange (Trevaskis 1960: 43). At the same time, the British introduced their own financial institutions that aimed at monopolizing trade in this former Italian colony. Barclays Bank, the only significant British financial institution in the territory, assumed privileged financial status that was protected by the BMA. To make matters worse, the BMA also increased direct taxes that they called "native tribute" (that included income, property, and municipal taxes). Every Eritrean village was required to pay various forms of taxes through their administrators and village chiefs. Yet, the BMA extended banking services to local populations, a practice that was not prevalent throughout the Italian colonial period.

During the period of federation, the Ethiopian State Bank extended its services to Eritrea, and the Ethiopian currency (*birr*) was introduced in the country. The Ethiopian birr remained the currency of the country until 1997, when a new national currency (Nakfa) was introduced. The Ethiopian State Bank remained as one of the most influential financial institutions in the country until the end of the federation between the two countries. After 1963, Ethiopia diversified its financial institutions, and some of its banks also opened branches in Eritrea. By 1970, in addition to the old Italian banks that were still functioning, Eritrea had several Ethiopian branches of financial institutions. After 1974, the communist regime (*Dergue*) in Ethiopia nationalized most of the major financial institutions of the country, and most of these institutions were purposely made to be major financial instruments of the regime. All of the former Italian banks which were still functioning under the imperial regime in Ethiopia were also nationalized under the communist regime.

TRADE AND FINANCE SINCE INDEPENDENCE

As mentioned in the previous sections, Eritrea inherited a ruined economy in 1991. Most of the financial institutions were also in a bad state. The destructive effects of war (the course of which dramatically increased after the Battle of Afabet in 1988) also wreaked havoc on the whole trading and financial activities in the territory. The EPLF, which established the PGE in 1991, inherited a collapsing economy. Most of the state-owned branches of banks lacked the minimum reserves necessary for their financial activities. Among the few institutions in the financial sector included the Ethiopian Insurance Corporation (commonly known as *Medhin Derejet*) and the Commercial Bank of Ethiopia.

Immediately after the independence of the country, the government renounced all sorts of debts belonging to governments that previously ruled Eritrea. It also immediately nationalized all financial institutions (especially the Ethiopian banks) and formed two major banks: the National Bank of Eritrea and the Commercial Bank of Eritrea (Killion 1998: 218–219). Later, one large-scale and two small-scale (all state-owned) financial institutions were established: the Housing and Commerce Bank of Eritrea, the National Insurance Corporation of Eritrea, and the Eritrean Development and Investment Bank.

Until 1993, the financial sector of the country received financial support in the form of foreign aid (for reconstruction programs) from various NGOs such as institutions led by the Catholic Church and other forms of loans generated from bilateral agreements—about U.S.$32 million in the form of foreign aid and about U.S.$72 million in the form of loans (Killion 1998: 219). World financial institutions such as the World Bank also extended their financial credits to the new nation—by 1993, the World Bank extended Eritrea U.S.$525 million in credit; by 1994, Eritrea was also granted membership in the World Bank Organization, which further rewarded her with about U.S.$50 million credit for recovering its educational, port, and energy facilities (Killion 1998: 219). However, Eritrea's contemporary confrontation with international financial institutions has resulted in the interruption of formal foreign aid from the IMF and WB.

The 1994 macropolicy of the country introduced clearly defined trade and financial regulations. Based on the macropolicy, the government introduced general rules of the country's monetary, fiscal, and trade policies. Regarding issues of credit, the government adopted a policy in which "access to credit and credit conditions to various institutions and sectors of the economy would be largely left to be determined by the market demand and supply in monetary and capital markets" (Government of Eritrea 1994: 23). The governmental policies also clearly defined types of taxes and custom duties. As stated in the macropolicy, the government stated that Eritrea's monetary policy would aim at:

> Stimulation of growth through the mobilization of savings and their optimal allocation to competing investment demands, the control of inflation and insurance of price exchange rate and overall macro-stability and the maintenance of a healthy and sustainable balance of payments position (Government of Eritrea 1994: 21).

Financial institutions set their policies in accordance with the international financial tenets—on the basis of free-market principles. However, the country's post-independence financial institutions faced a series of challenges such as a lack of professional and skilled staff as well as inadequate financial facilities. Crippled by these various obstacles, the institutions have been unable to provide widespread services, and the financial sector is still state-owned and underdeveloped. Banking services lag way behind modern financial development—with an outdated organizational structure, manual services, and unskilled bankers. Moreover, a great majority of Eritreans do not have access to banks or any other forms of financial or credit institutions. Rural populations do not have easy access to most contemporary financial institutions, which are based in urban areas; neither do they have any recorded credit history in the government-run financial bodies (Rena 2007: 141–48).

As stated earlier, post-independent Eritrea also has a negative balance of trade. Owing to various challenges, especially the impact of the Eritrean-Ethiopian border conflict (1998–2000) and decline of the manufacturing and industrial sectors, the country imports significantly more than she exports. The fact that Eritrea's limited items of exports are usually primary and low-value goods increases its deficit in trade. It usually imports manufactured and high-tech products, but it exports a limited amount of agricultural products such as live animals, skins, and hides. For example, in 1996, Eritrea's exports (primary goods such as livestock, grains, and salt) were estimated at U.S.$95 million, and its imports in the same year (machinery, manufactured foodstuffs, and goods) were estimated at U.S.$514 million (NgCheong-Lum 2005: 45). Prior to the border war, Ethiopia was Eritrea's largest regional market. Since the conflict in 1998, Eritrea has lost its markets in Ethiopia which also remarkably affected its trade and revenues.

ERITREAN REMITTANCES AND ECONOMY

"Remittances" in this context shall be understood as any "officially required" or informally channeled cash contributed by Eritrean diaspora from their country of employment to Eritrea. Based on the estimates made by the Eritrean government, the Eritrean worldwide diaspora is about 530,000 (Fessehatzion 2005: 166). Although there are no precise data, hundreds of thousands of Eritrean diaspora live in Europe and North America—in Germany alone there are over 25,000 Eritreans. Greater numbers of Eritreans also live in Sweden, Italy, and the United Kingdom. In addition to the contemporary incessant and massive numbers of Eritrean refugees, Sudan also hosts a great number of Eritrean refugees (over 350,000). Other Eritrean refugees are distributed in Ethiopia, Libya, Egypt, Uganda, and Israel.

As most people of Africa, the Eritreans are highly attached to their country of origin. Events in Eritrea deeply affect the Eritrean diaspora wherever they live. The diaspora carry the burden of providing financial support to their parents and members of their extended families who live in Eritrea. Amid economic crisis and instability in the country, a majority of households are dependent on financial support provided by family members and relatives in the diaspora. The motives behind remittances are diverse but usually differ on the bases of individuals' personal interests.

Remittances have played a significant role since the liberation struggle. Eritreans in the diaspora supported the country's liberation struggle by injecting immense amounts of financial and material support to the country. During the post-independence years, the Eritrean government also enjoyed a great amount of financial support from

Eritreans living abroad. Whether the value of remittances that the TGE collected have achieved the desired goals of contributors is a debate that is out of the scope of this work. But it is worth mentioning that the greatest part of the Eritrean diaspora bitterly complain that their contributions have not yet been used to achieve the intended development goals.

As with many African countries, remittances still remain an important part of Eritrean financial sources, especially for the private sector. According to Fessehatzion, the Eritrean remittances (in 2002) were estimated at 30 percent of the country's GDP per capita—comprising about U.S.$206 million; "and Eritrea by far depends on remittances compared to the rest of Africa" (Fessehatzion 2005: 168). According to Fessehatzion, remittances and Official Development Assistance (ODA) provide two-thirds of the country's GDP. For statistics related to remittances and development assistance in Eritrea (1993–2002), see Table P of the "Facts and Figures" section of this book.

Remittances are critical to Eritrea's economic performance and constitute an annual input of about U.S.$226 million (Fessehatzion 2005: 170). Since the country's independence, the government has introduced a new remittance policy called "the diaspora tax." Under this policy, all Eritreans living in the diaspora are in principle required to pay a two-percent tax from their income in their employment country. Also in principle, those who pay two-percent tax from their income have the privilege to own property in the country. Since 2001, the two-percent income tax has also become an absolute prerequisite for any Eritrean living abroad who would like to claim any service from the government. Therefore, most Eritreans living abroad who would wish to keep their socioeconomic contacts or properties in Eritrea must pay the two-percent income tax. In other terms, Eritrean diaspora are required to pay income tax to the country of their employment and two-percent of their overall income for their home country. In this way, the Eritrean government has collected large sums of money throughout the years after independence. In 1997, remittances collected in the form of two-percent taxes averaged U.S.$5.9 million; during the border war between Eritrea and Ethiopia (1998–2000), remittances collected in the form of contribution or in the form of purchased bonds reached U.S.$142.9 million (Fessehatzion 2005: 173). These figures do not include remittances sent to Eritrea through informal channels.

REFERENCES

Bereketeab, Redie (2000). *Eritrea: The Making of a Nation, 1890–1991*. Uppsala: Uppsala University Press.

Cliffe, Lionel (1996). "The Indirect Effects of the War and the Distribution of the Overall Economy." In: Resoum Kidane, Lionel Cliffe, June Rock and Philip White (eds.). *The Patterns and Socioeconomic and Environmental Impacts of Conflict in Eritrea—Occasional Papers Series on Environment and Development in an Age of Transition*, Centre of Development Studies, University of Leeds, 14, pp. 21–43.

Connell, Dan (2001). *Rethinking Revolution: New Strategies for Democracy & Social Justice: The Experiences of Eritrea, South Africa, Palestine& Nicaragua.* Lawrenceville, NJ: Red Sea Press.

Denison, Edward and Paice, Edward (2007). *Eritrea*. Chalfont St. Peter: Brandt Travel Guides.

Doornbos, Martin and Tesfa, Alemseged (eds.) (1999). *Eritrea: Prospects for Reconstruction and Development*. Lawrenceville, NJ: Red Sea Press.

FAO (2002). *Fishery and Aquaculture Country Profile: Eritrea*. Online Report: (http://www.fao.org/fishery/countrysector/FI-CP_ER/en). Accessed March 16, 2009.

Fattovich, Rodolfo (1990). "Remarks on the Pre-Aksumite Period in Northern Ethiopia." *Journal of Ethiopian Studies* 23: 1–33.

Fessehatzion, Tekie (2005). "Eritrea's Remittance-Based Economy: Conjunctures and Musings." *Eritrean Studies Review*, 4(2): 165–184.

Gebremedhin G., Tesfa (1996). *Beyond Survival: The Economic Challenges of Agriculture & Development in Post-Independence Eritrea*. Lawrenceville, NJ: The Red Sea Press.

Goe, Michael R. (1989). "The Ethiopian Maresha: Clarifying Design and Development." In: Marcus, Harold G. (ed.). *Northeast African Studies*, 11 (3), pp. 71–112.

Government of Eritrea (1991). *Transitional Labour Law No. 8/91*. Asmara, The Government of Eritrea.

Government of Eritrea (1994). *Macro Policy*. Asmara, Department of Macro Policy.

Hansson, G. (2001). "Building New States: Lessons from Eritrea." *World Institute for Development Economics Research*, United Nations University. Wider Discussion Paper No. WDP 2001/66, pp. 1–19.

Horizon Business Group, P. L. C. (2007). *Country Environmental Profile: The State of Eritrea*. Asmara: Horizon Business Group, P.L.C.

Horn of Africa Group—Chatham House (2008). *Eritrea's Regional Role and Foreign Policy: Past, Present and Future Perspectives*. The Rift Valley Institute and Centre for African Studies at London University, (file posted at: http://www.aigaforum.com/11455_171207 eritrea.pdf accessed on May 12, 2009).

IFAD (November 2006). *Enabling the rural poor to overcome poverty in Eritrea*. Rome: International Fund for Agricultural Development (IFAD).

ILO—Working paper, 1997 (http://www.globalmarch.org/resourcecentre/world/eritrea.pdf. Accessed March 29, 2009.

Istituto Agricolo Coloniale Italiano—IACI (1932). *Nel cinquantennio dell'occupazione di Assab: 1882–1932—L'economia Eritrea*. Firenze.

Kibreab, Gaim (2001). "Displaced Communities and the Reconstruction of Livelihoods in Eritrea." In: *World Institute for Development Economics Research*, United Nations University. Wider Discussion Paper No. WDP 2001/23, pp. 1–15.

Kibreab, Gaim (2009). "Forced labor in Eritrea." *Journal of Modern African Studies*. 47(1): 41–72.

Killion, Tom (1996). "The Eritrean economy in historical perspective." In: *Eritrean Studies Review*, 1(1): 91–118.

Killion, Tom (1998). *Historical Dictionary of Eritrea*. Lanham, MD: Scarecrow Press.

McCann, J. C. (1999). *Green Land, Brown Land, Black Land: An Environmental History of Africa*. Portsmouth: James Currey.

Mesghenna, Yemane (1988). *Italian Colonialism: A Case Study of Eritrea, 1869–1934: Motive, Praxis, and Result*. Lund: University of Lund Press.

Munro-Hay, Stuart (1991). *Aksum: An African Civilisation of Late Antiquity*. Edinburgh: British Library Cataloguing in Publication Data.

Murtaza, Niaz (1998). *The Pillage of Sustainability in Eritrea, 1600s–1990s: Rural Communities and the Creeping Shadows of Hegemony*. London: Greenwood Press.

Negash, Tekeste (1987). *Italian Colonialism in Eritrea, 1882–1941: Policies, Praxis, and Impact*. Uppsala: Uppsala University.

NgCheong-Lum, Roseline (2005). *Eritrea*. New York, Marshall Cavendish.

Okbasillassie Tikabo, Mehari (2003). "Land Tenure in the Highlands of Eritrea: Economic Theory and Empirical Evidence." Unpublished Ph.D. Dissertation: Agricultural University of Norway.

Pankhurst, E. Sylvia (1952). *Why Are We Destroying the Ethiopian Ports*? Woodford Green, Essex, UK: New Times and Ethiopia News Books.

Rena, Ravinder (2007). "Historical Development of Money and Banking in Eritrea from the Axumite Kingdom to the Present." In: *African and Asian Studies*, 6(1&2): 135–153.

Schmidt, P. R., M. C. Curtis, et al. (2008). *The Archaeology of Ancient Eritrea*. Trenton, NJ: Red Sea Press.

Schweinfurth, Georg (1894). "Dr. G. Schweinfurth über seine letzte Reise mit Dr. Max schoeler im der italienischen Kolonie Erythrää." In: *Verhandlungen der Gesellschaft für Erdkunde zu Berlin*. 21 pp. 379–431.

Tesfagiorgis, Gebre Hiwet (eds.) (1993). *Emergent Eritrea: Challenges of Economic Development*. Trenton, NJ: Red Sea Press.

Tesfagiorgis, Mussie (2007)"Some Aspects of Environmental History of Eritrea: An Appraisal of the Historiographical Sources" In: *Eritrean Studies Review*, Vol. 5, No. 1, pp. 211–258.

Tesfai, Alemseged (2005). *Federashin ertra mes ityopia: kan matiyenzo kesab tedla (1952–1955)* [The Federation of Eritrea with Ethiopia: From Matienzo to the reign of Tedla (1951–1954)]. Asmara: Hidri Publishers (text in Tigrinya language).

Teweldemedhin Y., Mogos (2008). "The Fish Industry in Eritrea: From Comparative to Competitive Advantage." *African Journal of Agricultural Research*. 3 (5), pp. 327–333.

The World Bank Group (http://devdata.worldbank.org/AAG/eri_aag.pdf) accessed May 5, 2009).

Trevaskis, G. K. N. (1960). *Eritrea: A Colony in Transition—1941–52*. London: Oxford University Press.

Tseggai, Araia (1991). "Eritrea: The Socio-economic Challenges of Independence." In: *Africa Today* 38(2), pp. 15–30.

Zekarias, Ambaye (1966). *Land Tenure in Eritrea (Ethiopia)*. Addis Ababa, N.A.

CHAPTER 5

Society

INTRODUCTION

According to the 2005 census estimates, the Eritrean population reached over 4.5 million (UNDESF 2007: 220). About a million Eritreans live abroad as refugees and immigrants. The annual population growth was also estimated at 2.6 percent. Based on these estimates, the average population density is about 36.5 people per square kilometers. However, population density is not spread evenly across the Eritrean territory. The highest concentration of population is in the highlands and the lowest population concentration is on the coast of the Red Sea.

Eritrea's geographical location along the crossroads between the Nile Valley, the Red Sea, and the Ethiopian plateau made it an important site for migration and population movement for many centuries. As a result, the population of Eritrea today is relatively small but reflects a great human diversity of linguistic and cultural groups. The Eritrean society is composed of nine ethnolinguistic groups, each with its own language and culture. Patterns of settlement differ largely based on geographical and ethnographic factors. Most parts of Eritrea's plateaus are inhabited by the Tigrinya ethnolinguistic group, while the lowlands and coastal areas are inhabited by heterogonous ethnolinguistic groups.

The Afar ethnolinguistic group inhabits the southeastern coastal plains, usually known as Dankalia. The Saho ethnolinguistic group is distributed along the eastern plains, foothills, and escarpments as far as the southern plateau. The Rashaida, another ethnolinguistic group in Eritrea, inhabit the northern coastal areas as far as the borders with Sudan. The Nara and Kunama ethnolinguistic groups inhabit southwestern parts of Eritrea along the Gash areas. The Tigre, another major ethnolinguistic group in Eritrea, is distributed along the eastern and western lowlands and northern highlands. While the Bilen ethnolinguistic group inhabit areas north of the central plateau (along a geographical area that is commonly known as Bogos), the Hedareb occupy the northwestern parts of the country. All of the lowland ethnolinguistic groups, except the Tigre, are small in number. The Rashaida, Nara, Kunama, Saho, Bilen, Hedareb, and the Afar each constitute less than 7 percent of the overall population, and the Tigre comprise over 31 percent of the Eritrean population. Some of the Eritrean ethnolinguistic groups are also divided between neighboring countries. The Afars are divided among Eritrea, Djibouti, and Ethiopia. The Tigrinyas are divided between Ethiopia and Eritrea, and pockets of Tigre speakers are also found in Sudan. Ethnolinguistic divisions between different countries of the Horn of Africa are the result of colonial scramble. Contemporarily, although not on a large-scale, ethnolinguistic alliances along border lands remain real threats to national political unity and identity.

Over 80 percent of the population belongs to the Tigrinya and Tigre (Semitic linguistic groups) ethnicities. The rest of the population is composed of other ethnolinguistic groups (mainly Cushitic and Nilotic linguistic groups). As we shall see in Chapter 6, many of these ethnolinguistic groups are at least bilingual. All ethnolinguistic groups developed understanding and tolerance of each others' cultures and languages through continuous economic interactions across the ecological zones of the country. Moreover, the colonial and postcolonial history of oppression and degradation shared by all the ethnolinguistic groups of Eritrea has resulted in the development of a strong sense of attachment and common identity.

Regarding the religious profile of the population, Islam and Christianity are the most important religions in the country. The population of Eritrea is almost equally divided between Christians and Muslims. These two world religions have a long historical tradition in the territory. In fact, Eritrea is one of the territories in the region that was exposed to earliest Islam and Christianity.

Christianity was introduced to the territory during the early centuries of its surfacing; by the fourth century, Christianity already had become the state religion for the Aksumite Empire. Today, a great majority of the populations in the plateau are followers of Orthodox *Tewahdo* (Coptic) Christianity, yet Catholicism and Protestantism are also important religions for small sections of the highland society. Among the Tigrinya linguistic group, there are also Muslim minorities—the *Jeberti*. The Jeberti are Tigrinya by language and culture but Muslims by religion. Although some members of the Jeberti have been advocating for a separate ethnolinguistic formation, the government has not yet recognized the Jeberti as a separate ethnolinguistic group.

Religion and Thought

RELIGION AND THOUGHT

As stated earlier, Eritreans are almost equally divided between Muslims and Christians. Religion is an important component of a daily life and activity for the majority of people in Eritrea. Most daily activities of the people of Eritrea reflect each respective group's religious and cultural affiliation. For example, most Tigrinya holidays acknowledge Christian traditions, and Christian holidays include the Christmas (*ledet*), epiphany usually known as baptism (*timket*), and Easter. Muslim holidays usually follow the lunar calendar and change each year. Among the most important Muslim holidays include Id el-Fetir (which is celebrated in the spring), Id el-Adha (which is celebrated in summer), and Id el-Nebi (which is celebrated in autumn).

In general, the two religions—Islam and Christianity—play vital roles in the ways of thoughts, identities, and even relations among individuals and groups. Interestingly, both religions are well integrated in the local cultures and customs. Most religious communities in Eritrea are culturally separated, and intermarriages among various cultural and religious groups are uncommon (Woldemikael 2005: 343). The Tigre, Afar, Saho, Rashaida, Hedareb, and Nara ethnolinguistic groups are predominantly Muslims. The Tigrinyas are predominantly Christians, and the Bilen and Kunama ethnolinguistic groups are almost equally divided between Islam and Christianity. Few members of the Nara and Kunama ethnolinguistic groups are followers of indigenous African religions.

BRIEF HISTORICAL OVERVIEW OF ISLAM IN ERITREA

The history of Islam in Eritrea dates back to the seventh century, and, therefore, Islam has been historically associated with the Eritrean region since the time of its first emergence in Hjaz (for in-depth study of the history of Islam in Eritrea, recommended readings include Jonathan Miran's article [2005], "A Historical Overview of Islam in Eritrea," and J. S. Trimingham's book [1965], *Islam in Ethiopia*). Early Islamic relations are also reflected in the oral and written traditions of Muslims in the region,

COMMUNITY FESTIVALS

Eritrean communities also celebrate various annual festivals. Among such festivals is Mariyam De'arit (at a place also known with the same name, located near the town of Keren). It takes place during the month of May. During this religious and cultural festival pilgrims come from all over the country for at least three days of festivities, usually accompanied by prayers, dancing, and singing contests.

View of Akordat Mosque. (S. Tesfagiorgis)

and so "Muslims in Eritrea and northern Ethiopia attach unique symbolic importance to what is known in early Islamic history as the *hijira al-ʿUla* (first emigration), perceived by them as the cornerstone of a unique cross-Red Sea Islamic relationship" (Miran 2005: 180). Only a few years after the Prophet Mohammed started to preach his Devine Revelations (the Qur'an began in 610 A.D.), a number of followers of the Prophet are believed to have crossed the Red Sea and arrived at Massawa in 615 A.D. The Prophet Mohammed is believed to have personally advised these adherents to escape and save their lives from local enemies (the nobility—the Meccan Qurayyshi) and seek refuge in the Eritrean region (at that time under the Aksumite Empire).

Many followers of the Prophet arrived at the coast of Eritrea where they settled for many years. The early emigrants built their dwellings and also small hut-like mosques designed for their worship. As proponents of the religion started to grow in number, various such mosques were constructed in many places along the coast. According to oral sources, the mosque of Sheikh Hamal was among the earliest of such places of worship in Massawa (which survived at least three catastrophic earthquakes). In addition to its remarkably interesting ancient decorations, the mosque of Sheikh Hamal contains significant ancient scripts engraved on its walls. These scripts are believed to have been engraved by the early proponents of Islam. The mosque of Sheikh Hamal was named after one of the renowned member of the early Meccan immigrants (Omar el-Sherif), who is believed to have founded this mosque.

Hanfi Mosque in Massawa. (J. Miran)

However, the religious influence of these immigrants was not felt much until the beginning of the eighth century when massive Islamic conversion took place in South Arabia under the Umayyad Caliphate (661–750 A.D.), and many Islamized Arabs occupied the Eritrean coast (Miran 2005: 180). By the late seventh and the beginning of the eighth centuries, Islamic sultanates along the Eritrean Red Sea coast and Southern Arabian Peninsula became major challengers to the Aksumite Empire. Aksum, which is believed to have welcomed and secured safety for the early Islamic holy men and tolerated the religion, was now confronted by major Islamic forces along the coast. Although Aksum engaged in warfare against Islamic forces in the Red Sea, it lost some significant battles, which contributed to Aksum's loss of commerce along the Red Sea.

By the ninth century, Islam had expanded to the eastern coast of Eritrea and was introduced to some of the Eritrean clans, particularly the Beja who lived in areas stretching between the eastern plains of Eritrea and the Nile. By the twelfth and thirteenth centuries, the Dahlak archipelagoes became the "seat of an independent emirate ruled by a line of sultans, and served as a lucrative transit station in the trade between Egypt and India, but also in the cross-Red Sea trade between Abyssinia and Yemen" (Miran 2005: 181).

Through an expanding lucrative trade along the Red Sea coast, Islam came into contact with many pre-Islamic societies along the eastern parts of Eritrea and other

People praying during an Islamic holy day in Asmara. (J. Miran)

parts of the Horn of Africa. By the thirteenth century, a number of nomadic groups in the region, including the Saho and Afar ethnolinguistic groups, became adherents of this religion. It did not take long for Islam to expand among most members of these ethnolinguistic groups who further propagated the religion southward. Islam also became an important factor in clan relations within and among ethnolinguistic groups of the Eritrean region. As is usually stated in their oral traditions, many Muslim communities in the region claim common ancestry with early adherents of Islam who originated from Hijaz. For many ethnolinguistic groups, Islam became an important factor for the formation of wider social organizations as well as the emergence of clans and the confederation of clans. By the fifteenth century, Islam was well integrated in the daily life of large populations of the Horn of Africa.

As discussed in Chapter 1, Islam became a major political instrument in the sixteenth century and unified considerable parts of the Horn. In the same century, the sultanate of Adal under Ahmed Gragn managed to bring numerous Muslim clans under Islamic thought and launched a major *jihad* war against "Christian" Abyssinia (former reference for Ethiopia). The forces of Ahmed Gragn achieved a remarkable military victory, and "one result of the Muslim victories over 'Christian' Ethiopia between 1527 and 1543 was to foster the diffusion of Islam in the Ethio-Eritrean region,

Gathering during a Muslim holy day prayer in Asmara. (J. Miran)

prompting a more elaborate formation of Jabarti [Jeberti] communities in the high-lands" (Miran 2005: 182). Moreover, the war was soon internationalized with Ottoman Turks and Portugal involved on the side of the jihadists and Abyssinia, respectively. Although the war eventually ended in Abyssinian victory, its Islamic impacts were felt over the whole region for many centuries to come. Massawa and neighboring territories were occupied by the Ottomans in 1557 and remained under their influence until 1865. The Ottoman occupation of Massawa and the coastal territories (1557–1865) further strengthened the prosperity of Islam in Eritrea. Under the Ottomans, Massawa became home for various Arab immigrants from the Arabian Peninsula who somehow transformed the city and neighboring territories into important commercial and Islamic centers. A number of mosques and tombs were constructed during the Ottoman occupation of Massawa (a legacy that can still be seen in this port city). Some of the buildings in Massawa display the influence of Ottoman architecture.

As in most territories, including northeast Africa, Islamic expansion and revival in Eritrea continued throughout the nineteenth century. In addition to a widespread movement of Muslim Sufi brotherhoods who carried out missionary activities aimed at the revival and expansion of Islam in the region, the political shift that occurred in wider northeast Africa also changed the magnitude of Islamic expansion in Eritrea. The impact of the activities of Islamic brotherhoods continued to be an important catalyst for religious expansion and dynamism, and the *turug* (singular *tariqa*) brotherhoods of the Sufi order became active in the region, aiming at the revitalization of Eritrean older Islamic orders such as the Quadiriyya and the Shadhihiliyya (Miran 2005: 184).

Egypt under Mohammed Ali started a long-term Islamic and political expansion toward northeast Africa, followed by Khedive Ismail's ambitious expansion to the region, which aimed at controlling the sources of the Nile and Islamic expansion to the greater Horn of Africa. As a result, by the late 1850s, greater parts of western and northern Eritrea had fallen under direct Egyptian control. Egyptian expansion to the Eritrean territory was accompanied by massive Islamic conversion. Among other Eritrean ethnolinguistic groups, the Kunama, Nara, and Bilen were remarkably affected by Egyptian occupation of their territories. By the 1880s all Eritrean lowland ethnolinguistic groups except part of the Kunama and Bilen were converted to Islam (Miran 2005: 184).

The years in the first half of the nineteenth century were accompanied by massive political instability that usually resulted in ethnolinguistic conflicts and military raids. In addition to internal conflicts, the lowland communities of Eritrea also suffered from continuous military raids by warlords from Tigray (within the modern territory of Ethiopia). Such military raids usually resulted in catastrophic loss of human and material power in these communities (for such events in the case of Bilen, see Ghaber 1993). Therefore, for many lowland groups, Islam and Egypt served as alternative allies that they believed would help defend themselves from such raids. For some clans such as the Tigre-speaking (the largest ethnolinguistic group in the lowlands) groups, "conversion to Islam in this context vested ... with a new identity and a powerful counter-hegemonic force and ideology, endowing them with a source of authority and political legitimacy" (Miran 2005: 185). Several clans such as the 'Ad Sheykh in the Barka areas of Eritrea associated (based on claims of common descent) themselves with Islamic holy families in the eastern lowlands and elsewhere and facilitated further propagation of the religion among the communities of the northern highlands. By the second half of the nineteenth century, most groups in the northern highlands, especially the Tigre clans and their subclans such as the Mensae and Bet Asghede, were converted to Islam.

Expansion of Islam in the region was further facilitated through missionary activities by the Katmiyya *tariqa* (another brotherhood under Sufi order). Katmiyya became a well-established *tariqa* in Sudan under the Turco-Egyptian occupation of the territory (1820/21–1885), and it further spread toward the Red Sea, including the Eritrean region. This Islamic brotherhood attracted great numbers of Muslim groups in the region mainly because it relied on local religious leaders (who preserved their previous local religious roles and managed easy introduction of Katmiyya practices among local fellow Muslims) and offered larger sociopolitical structures for adherents of the religion. Its rising popularity in the region was attributed to its efficient expansion methods that were characterized by an amalgamation of pre-existing Islamic religious formations, including holy families and lineages, religious figures and notables "into a new supra-community *tariqa* network" (quoted in Miran 2005: 187). It soon became one of the largest Sufi brotherhoods in the Horn of Africa. The methods applied by Katmiyya provided preferences for followers to preserve their old social and political structures, and so it secured relative local stability and continuity among Islamic holy families as well as for the majority of adherents of the religion in the Horn of Africa. In the nineteenth century Islam continued to flourish in the eastern coastal areas of Eritrea where Massawa became an economic hub. Owing to its strategic location on the Red Sea, the port city continued to attract Muslim merchants, missionaries, and Arabian immigrants.

Islam was again politicized in the 1880s when a new Islamic movement commonly known as Mahdiyya emerged in Sudan. Mahdiyya was an Islamic messianic

Members of Muslim communities in Asmara. (J. Miran)

movement/rebellion in Sudan that took its momentum from the spirit of resistance against Egyptian and European occupation and suppression. Mohammed Ahmed, who proclaimed himself as Mahdi (literally meaning "the expected holy messiah"; a divine leader who is expected to come for the restoration of justice in the future and whose rule is guided by divinely powers), led the Mahdist revolt and achieved remarkable success in the region. In the Mahdi's view, the preexisting Islamic practices (under the Ottomans and Egyptians) in the region were not based on ideal Islamic

The main mosque in Asmara. (J. Miran)

principles of religious purity and God's just rule on earth. In addition to European competition over the occupation of the Eritrean region as well as Ethiopia's reaction against European expansion, the Mahdist movement had a remarkable impact on the history of Islam in Eritrea in general and on the religious communities of Eritrea in particular. External powers (the Mahdists, the Egyptians, the Italians, the British, and the French) fiercely competed for control of the Eritrean region, "ultimately leading to the politicization of the religion in the area [lowlands] and to deep internal divisions within these societies" (Miran 2005: 193).

The political and military competition among these powers resulted in major divisions of Eritrean lowland Muslim communities—major rifts started to occur between pro-Mahdists and anti-Mahdists. Moreover, Ethiopia under Emperor Yohannes IV attempted ambitious expansion toward Eritrea. Ethiopia's expansion into the territory was at times accompanied by the conversion of Muslim and pagan groups into Christianity.

Italian occupation of Eritrea brought the Islamic and Christian communities of Eritrea together. On a broad level, colonial rule imposed laws and created institutions that both Muslim and Christian communities had to share. In addition, other developments under colonial rule (such as the expansion of communication infrastructure, massive conscription to the army, and more) contributed to the development of a common feeling of oppression and sharing actual historical developments. Colonial rule appeared to be a common challenge for both Christian and Muslim communities who shared experiences under a foreign rule, which eventually resulted in the development of a common identity. The colonial government applied ethnolinguistic and religious policies that were usually contradictory and not consistent. Although the colonial rule in Eritrea was oppressive, discriminatory (racially), and exploitative, the colonial state somehow adopted a tolerant approach toward Muslim communities

Young boy (member of the Muslim community in Asmara). (J. Miran)

in the territory. Italian religious policies in Eritrea were influenced by political developments in which the colonial state usually pretended to be a devotee of the development of Islam in the region.

According to Miran, we can distinguish three chronological phases of history of Islam in Eritrea under colonial rule. The first phase was characterized by fierce competition for the conquest of the region and the expansion and threat of Mahdists (1885-c.–1910-c). The second phase was highlighted by the Italian conquest of Libya and the process and development of colonial understanding and attitudes toward Islam in general (1910s–1920s). The third phase was characterized by "the period of overt pro-Muslim policies under the fascists and the more pronounced propagandistic articulation of Italy as a 'Muslim power' (1920s–1941)" (Miran 2005: 195).

From the time of their expansion toward Massawa and the highlands, the Italians (hampered by Mahdist threats and possible local resistance from Islamic communities) claimed that they would respect local religions and cultures. Although the colonizers played tricks with religious and community figures in the territory, they did not use Islam as a main instrument for local cleansing. In fact, in the initial phase of its rule, the colonial government applied tendencies of "tolerance" toward Islam, and so Christian missionary activities were prohibited in some areas dominated by Muslims (Miran 2005: 196). This policy was designed to keep stability within Muslim territories and also cultivate local support against Mahdist threats. Fearing further influences, the colonial government launched campaigns against some holy families who took stands either as pro-Mahdist or anti-Italian conquest. The colonial government attempted the formation of a single administrative and religious block that included many Muslim communities in the Sahel and Barka territories. Moreover, it encouraged the expansion of Khatmiyya *tariqas* in the territories inhabited by Muslim communities.

After the 1920s, Italian policies focused on the cultivation of support from Islamic communities within the colony and elsewhere in the Arab world. Their propaganda also reflected their objectives of achieving maximum support of local Muslim societies in the region. Even under Fascist rule (1935–1941), the colonial state continued to pretend that it respected and defended the rights and practices of Islamic communities in the Horn of Africa.

In general, development of Islam in Eritrea was remarkably shaped by various factors under the consecutive colonial and post-colonial rules in the country. Colonial conquest applied tactics and policies that contributed to shaping the history of lowland Islamic communities in the country. As stated by Miran, "Italian policies and practice towards Islam, the establishment of Islamic institutions, and the shared experiences of Eritrean Muslims under colonial rule, all worked towards the genesis and formation of an 'Eritrean' Muslim consciousness, at least among the growing urban elite" (Miran 2005: 203).

Amid a turbulent political environment under the British Military Administration (BMA) Islam continued to flourish in the country. Although "common identity" and "political consciousness," which started long before the BMA became a dynamic force for most nationalist movements of the 1940s, few political parties in the country also considered religious issues as factors for mobilization. Islamic religious and educational institutions also continued to flourish in the country under the BMA. Moreover, Arabic (the main religious language for Islamic communities of Eritrea) became one of the major languages in the country. The state's media (especially newspapers) published issues in Arabic that further facilitated the growth of Arabic in the country. Yet, BMA's paradoxical and inconsistent policies usually resulted in serious tensions and clashes between Muslim and Christian communities. For example, the Tora-Tsinaadcgle conflict that was originally based on disputes over rights to natural resource use now took on a religious tint (1912–1914; 1946–1949; 1990–1995).

The federal period (1952–1961) was characterized by continuous Ethiopian involvement in matters of the country. Ethiopia under Haile Selassie usually identified Muslim communities in Eritrea as anti-"Christian" Ethiopia. The Ethiopian government started to limit Muslim legal and educational practices in the country and targeted Muslim communities, especially in the lowlands. Some Muslim independence parties, such as the Muslim League, were also purposely targeted.

After the annexation of Eritrea by Ethiopia (1962), the Ethiopian government continued not only targeting nationalist figures, but it also replaced Arabic and

The Eritrean Mufti during religious festivity in Asmara. (J. Miran)

Muslim communities gathered for prayer during religious holiday in Asmara. (J. Miran)

Tigrinya (previously official languages of the country) with Amharic. Anti-Muslim sentiments continued to grow throughout Haile Selassie's rule. This in turn resulted in a steady erosion of the autonomy of many Islamic institutions (such as local Muslim courts) in the country, and members of Muslim communities in Eritrea were brutally oppressed. Many Muslim rural communities became victims of ruthless government massacres. This resulted in an exodus of Eritrean rural refugees, mainly to Sudan (Kibreab 1987). As also reflected in its policies, the imperial government took anti-Arab and anti-Muslim stances. The religious tasks of Muslim figures (such as *qadis* and *muftis*) were highly limited because of government interventions imposed on them.

The *Dergue* rule (1974–1991) was characterized by massive aggression against all societies of Eritrea, who, the regime considered, should accept unconditional union of Eritrea with Ethiopia. The *Dergue* under Mengistu Haile Mariam (communist dictator in Ethiopia) dispatched continuous propaganda accusing Arab nations of supporting Eritrean liberation fronts. Military conflicts in Eritrea, which Mengistu was unable to bring to an end, fueled further aggression by Ethiopian army in the country.

Residents of rural areas, especially those who lived around areas where fierce battles were fought (Barka, Gash, and Sahel), continued to be victims of massive suppression, lootings, and massacres of the Ethiopian army. Most of the formerly active Muslim brotherhoods were crippled by the unstable military and political situations of the region. On the other side, the Eritrean liberation struggle (1961–1991) involved a great majority of Muslim and Christian communities in the country. The Eritrean Liberation Front (ELF) and later the Eritrean People's Liberation Front (EPLF), which had been successful in distributing their wartime propaganda, convinced all Eritrean communities to unite under the umbrella of nationalism, no matter their religious affiliations. Muslims and Christians fought side by side throughout the years of liberation struggle.

SOME ISLAMIST POLITICAL ORGANIZATIONS

During the early phases of the Eritrean liberation struggle, Islamist sentiments and anti-Christian attitudes started to emerge among a group of members of the liberation struggle. These sentiments were reactionary to the newly emerging EPLF group that was dominated by Christian elements (Killion 1998: 267). Radicalism among Islamic groups also intensified in response to the widespread discrimination and oppression of the Ethiopian army over lowland Muslim communities of Eritrea. Islamism was further fueled during and after the civil war in which the ELF was pushed out of Eritrea by the EPLF.

The ELF (which had been the strongest liberation front in Eritrea prior to the emergence of the EPLF; and which had involved a great number of Muslims in its struggle) now fragmented and a great number of its fighters entered Sudan where they lived as refugees. In the 1980s, Islam, influenced by the rise of widespread Islamic movements in the Muslim world, started to become an important tool for some Eritrean groups in the Sudan. Some of these Islamic groups also attained foreign support, especially from Saudi Arabia (Killion 1998: 267). By the 1980s, few of these Islamic groups continued to exercise radical stances, mainly against the EPLF. Even during post-independence years of the 1990s, the Eritrean government continued to accuse Islamist groups who were based in Sudan of exercising militant insurgencies against the government's army. Several times, the Eritrean government also alleged that Sudan was the main force behind Islamist (jihadist) actions within Eritrea. Since 1993, this belief has continued to be a source of diplomatic trouble between Eritrea and Sudan. Some of the main Eritrean Islamic political movements follow.

The Eritrean Islamic Jihad Movement (EIJM): Several Islamic groups (which had their origins in the 1970s and 1980s) formally founded the EIJM in 1988. Among the groups that merged and founded the EIJM included the Eritrean National Islamic Liberation Front (ENIL) and the Islamic Reconciliation Board (IRB). The ENIL was founded and led by some ex-members and cadres of the ELF such as Omer Haj Idris, Ibrahim Malik, and Arafa A. Mohammed. Most members of the EIJM were ELF ex-fighters who were living in Sudan as refugees. Members of the EIJM were considered by the ELF organization as "rightists" or "conservatives," and many of them were formally expelled from the organization. Some of the early objectives of these groups were the launching of a *jihad* war against forces in Eritrea and the establishment of an "Eritrean Islamic Republic." The EIJM established sophisticated organizational structures, including an armed wing that aimed at launching a "Muslim oriented" armed struggle within Eritrea. The EIJM is also believed to have fought a number of battles not only against the EPLF but also against the ELF—to which most of its members belonged. Although it suffered repeated defeats at the hands of the Eritrean liberation fronts, the EIJM continued to achieve support from some sympathizers in the Arab world. Owing to internal crisis and also as a result of continuous loss in its military operations, some members of the EIJM showed grievances against their leadership.

By 1993, a great number of its members in the armed wing splintered and formed another movement with the same name—EIJM. The new EIJM achieved substantial support from Sudan and continued its military insurgencies within Eritrea throughout the 1990s. Although the EIJM usually suffered from both repeated defeats during its operations against the Eritrean army and continuous splints within its organizational structures, it still remains a strong potential Islamic movement in the region. Throughout the 1990s, these movements' activities in Eritrea resulted in a series of diplomatic confrontations between the governments of Eritrea and Sudan.

The Eritrean Islamic Salvation Movement (EISM): The EISM is an offshoot of the EIJM that became active in the 1990s. Among the main objectives of the EISM are the removal of the current Eritrean regime and the establishment of an Islamic government. The EIJM and EISM rally local and regional support on the basis of an Islamist ideology. Some sources indicate that the EISM is still active in Islamist measures in the area.

The Eritrean Islamic Reconciliation Party (EIRP): The roots of the EIRP can be traced back to the late 1970s and the 1980s. Some of its founding members (such as Adem Mejawiriyay) were veteran fighters in the liberation struggle. Although the EIRP is believed to have been a part or coalition of the EIJM, it became a separately active movement after 1998. However, because of lack of source materials, not much is known about the objectives and achievements of this movement.

The EIJM's movement resulted in the formation of several small Islamist organizations in the late 1980s and 1990s. Many of the splinters from the EIJM and other similar organizations rallied support from sections of the Eritrean, Sudanese, and other communities; their strategies and goals were somewhat based on Islamist ideologies. However, because of lack of source materials, not much detail related to these organizations can be presented in this work. Yet, as stated earlier, most of the Eritrean Islamist organizations originated as reactionary groups, first against the EPLF (which was dominated by Christian members) and later against the political regime in Eritrea that many of them considered as oppressive to the Muslim communities in the country. Moreover, most of the early Islamist organizations were also reactionary against the "Christian" Ethiopian army that brutally oppressed Eritrean lowland Muslim communities. Therefore, most Islamic jihad movements in the area were local in nature. Although some of these organizations achieved few foreign sympathizers, no credible source has been available during this study that shows an association of Eritrean Islamists with global terrorist networks.

ISLAM SINCE INDEPENDENCE (1991–2008)

The policies of the post-independent Eritrean government also reflected secular principles. Muslim communities in Eritrea were allowed to practice their religion and reopen their religious institutions, including *Shari'a* courts and religious schools. The government also considers Arabic as a second major working language.

The government's media (radio, television, newspaper, and official decrees) usually contain versions in Arabic.

Although post-independence Islamic institutions started to show quick revival, the country's continuous political instability and contemporary lack of maximum protection of human rights, including religious freedom, negatively affect the revival of Christian and Islamic institutions. The government has been repeatedly criticized by national and international human rights activists of violating human and religious rights and freedoms.

CHRISTIANITY IN ERITREA

As stated earlier, Christianity is one of the two principal religions in Eritrea. A majority of Eritrean Christians belong to the Eritrean Orthodox *Tewahdo* Church. Small groups of Roman Catholics, Protestants, Jehovah's Witnesses, and others are

---

EARLY TRANSLATION OF THE HOLY BIBLE INTO TIGRINYA LANGUAGE

The first translation of the Holy Bible (specifically, the Gospel according to John) into Tigrinya was conducted by Samuel Gobat (1799–1879). However, there has not been a complete translation of Gobat's translation of the Bible into Tigrinya. Gobat, an Evangelist missionary, was born in Bern, Switzerland. He served in Basel, Switzerland as a missionary (1823–1826). Interested in Ge'ez language and religions of the Horn of Africa, Gobat travelled to Ethiopia in 1830 and stayed in the country for almost two years. Impressed by the diversity in language, culture, and religion of the peoples of the Horn, he returned to Ethiopia in 1835 where he stayed for one more year. Owing to bad health conditions, Gobat left Ethiopia in 1836 for Europe where he published books about his travel experiences in the region. Consecrated to be the bishop of the Protestant Church in Jerusalem, Gobat left for Jerusalem in 1846 where he served for most of the rest of his life.

In 1866, four sections of the Bible were translated into Tigrinya with the help of missionaries in the country. In 1909, some parts of the Bible were translated into Tigrinya by Haleqa Teweldemedhen.

The major publication of the Holy Book appeared in 1956. The translations were conducted by Eritrean evangelists. The Old Testament of the Bible was published in Tigrinya by the Petros Silla Printing Press in Asmara, while the New Testament was published by the Government Press.

A complete translation of the Bible appeared in Tigrinya in 1967. The translator and publisher was a Catholic priest, Abba Adhanom Se'ellu. Two years later, Abba Fesehatsiyon Okbagaber also published the "Psalms of David" section of the Tigrinya version of the Bible. In 1985, a revised version of the New Testament was published by the Catholic Church of Eritrea, Eparchy Asmara. In 1985, The Holy Book Association (comprising a number of Christian groups) was founded. This association published a revised Tigrinya version of the New Testament of the Holy Bible in 1991 (see also Tewolde 2009: 44–46).

also distributed mostly among the highland population of the country. Adherents of Roman Catholicism are mainly located in small groups in the southern part of the country (in places such as Tsinaadegle and as far as the Eritrean Irob areas) as well as in the northern part, particularly in the Keren area (in the Bilen territories) and among the Kunama territories in the western lowlands. Adherents of Protestantism are distributed in small pockets among the highland population.

BRIEF HISTORICAL OVERVIEW OF CHRISTIANITY IN ERITREA

As in the case of Islam, the Eritrean region is also associated with early Christianity. Although the Biblical monotheistic belief was already in practice long before the Christian era, Christian tradition in the region stretches back to the early periods of the Aksumite Empire. By the fourth century A.D. Christianity had already become the state religion of the Aksumites. Since then, the religion has had a deep impact on the overall societies and cultures of Eritrea.

According to the Christian tradition in Eritrea and Ethiopia, Christianity was brought to the state of Aksum by two Syrian Christians traveling home from the Indian subcontinent. On their way back home, these Syrians (whose names appear as Frumentius and Aedisius) were shipwrecked on the Red Sea coast where they then took refuge in the Aksumite Empire. These two persons are believed to have carried the religion deep into the state palace, and at around 340 A.D., King Ezana, then the Emperor of Aksum, is believed to have converted himself to Christianity. Ezana's conversion to Christianity is believed to have facilitated the religion's spread across the empire. Soon after Ezana's conversion to Christianity, *Maryam Tsiyon* (St. Mary of Zion), believed to be the first Christian church in the whole region, was built. By the mid-fourth century, it is believed that Christianity had already started to flourish in the highlands of Eritrea—churches were built and Christian teachings and the gospel spread. The Eritrean/Ethiopian Orthodox *Tewahdo* Church developed strong relations with the Coptic Church in Alexandria. As a sign of the harmonious tradition between these two churches, the Alexandrian Coptic Pope assigned or named the *Abuna* (Archbishop) for the Ethiopian Orthodox *Tewahdo* Church, a tradition that started in the Aksumite period and continued until the 1950s. Other Christian church traditions in the region claim that Christianity was already accepted during the life and teachings of Jesus. Although not well supported by evidences they assert that few of the followers and disciples of Jesus were citizens from northeast Africa. Whatever its origins in the region, Christianity became an important factor in shaping the traditions, beliefs, and customs of the societies of the Eritrean region.

As mentioned, Christianity and Islam came into coexistence in the region in the seventh century. Initially, both religions were friendly to each other. Christian Aksum welcomed, tolerated, and protected Islam and its adherents. However, the harmonious coexistence between the two religions deteriorated in the eighth century, and Islam started to grow as the principal religion for a considerable part of the population in

The Orthodox Tewahdo Church Clergy and the Eritrean Patriarch at Bahti Meskerem Square during the feast of Meskel. (J. Miran)

the region. Muslim sultanates in the Red Sea coasts confronted the Aksumites and contributed to the decline of the empire.

In addition to the political instability created after the fall of Aksum, religious confrontations continued to cause disorders in the region at least until the thirteenth century. Despite the political and religious unrest, Christianity continued to be the principal religion for the Eritrean highlanders. By the sixteenth century, a number of monasteries and churches existed across the highlands of Eritrea. Throughout the centuries, greater parts of Africa remained pagan or accepted Islam, while the Eritrean and Ethiopian populations developed strong ties to Christianity in their own fashion (Davidson 2001: 34–49). Although wars in the region caused by political and economic rivalries usually took on religious orientations, Christianity in Eritrea continued to become an important part of the people's lives, and the Christian population fashioned its own distinctive indigenous traditions of religious culture and art

EARLY TRANSLATIONS OF THE HOLY BIBLE INTO THE TIGRE LANGUAGE

The first translation of the Holy Bible into the Tigre language appeared in 1889 by the Swedish Missionary Institution in Mokulu, Massawa. In 1902, the New Testament of the Holy Bible was published in the Tigre language. The publishers were again Swedish missionaries in Eritrea, but the translators were the Eritreans Ato Teweldemedhen and Ato Amanuel (Abba Teclemicael 2009: 49). In 1988, a complete version of the Holy Bible was translated into the Tigre language, although it is not known much about who, by whom, or how it was published (see also Tewolde 2009: 49).

EARLY TRANSLATION OF THE HOLY BIBLE INTO KUNAMA LANGUAGE

In 1927, the Evangelical Church in Eritrea prepared a translation of the New Testament of the Holy Bible. The revised version of the translation was published in 2008 and is still serving as the main document of the Bible among the Kunama (Tewolde 2009: 49).

(Davidson 2001: 48). As a result of the introduction of European missionaries in Africa, religions such as Roman Catholicism and Protestantism started to spread across the country. Among Protestant churches, the Evangelical/Lutheran Church of Eritrea was founded by Swedish Evangelical missionaries in 1926. Although associated with the Lutheran World Federation (LWF), the Evangelical/Lutheran Church is the oldest autonomous Lutheran church in Africa (Tesfay 2001: 121). As of 2000, there were about 12,000 members of the Eritrean Evangelical Church (Tesfay 2001: 121). In the following sections brief descriptions of the Eritrean Orthodox *Tewahdo* Church and the Eritrean Catholic churches are presented.

THE ERITREAN ORTHODOX *TEWAHDO* CHURCH

The Orthodox *Tewahdo* Church in the region is an Oriental Orthodox Church, and its origin can be traced back to the Aksumite period. *Tewahdo* is a term derived from Ge'ez (classical language in the region) and it literally means "absolute unity; unification." The term has deep spiritual meaning, which signifies the fundamental principles of the Orthodox Church of the Eritrean-Ethiopian region. It implies that the belief in Christ's unique unity between the divine and the human is designed for the salvation of human beings. Therefore, the Eritrean/Ethiopian Orthodox *Tewahdo* Church's belief and liturgy as taught are slightly different from the so-called Eastern Orthodox churches that adhere to the belief in the hypostatic union of Christ's nature (Christ as demonstrating two separate natures—the divine and the human). The hypostatic union (or the two separate natures of Christ) was a type of Christology introduced by King Chalcedon of the Byzantine Empire in the fifth century A.D.

As with several other Orthodox Churches who refused to accept the religious decree of King Chalcedon, including the Coptic Orthodox Church and the Eritrea/Ethiopia Orthodox, the *Tewahdo* Church somehow separated from the Eastern Orthodox Church (Chalcedonian churches) and developed its own respective method of interpreting Orthodox Christian ways of belief. The Eritrean Orthodox *Tewahdo* Church (which is also known as the Autocephalous Eritrean Orthodox Church), in the same manner as that of the Ethiopian Orthodox *Tewahdo* Church, adheres to the Miaphysite liturgy in Christology. Miaphysitism is a type of Christology for many Oriental Orthodox churches in which Jesus Christ is represented as the absolute unity between the divine (spiritual) and human (worldly) natures. Since the time of their foundations, the Alexandrian Coptic Orthodox Church and the Ethiopian/Eritrean Orthodox *Tewahdo* Church—both of them Oriental and non-Chalcedonian churches—developed a strong relationship that

The Enda Mariam Church in Asmara. (S. Tesfagiorgis)

continued for over fifteen centuries. For the list of monasteries in Eritrea, see Table T in the "Facts and Figures" section of this book.

In Eritrea, the foundation and expansion of strong Orthodox churches were demonstrated by the emergence of well-established monasteries such as the Monastery of Debre Bizen, the Monastery of Debre Libanos, and the Monastery of Debre Sina. (Tesfay 2001: 120–121).

Unlike Catholic church practices in the region, members of the Orthodox *Tewahdo* clergy can marry during or before the period of their religious services. The wedding ceremonies of the clergy are slightly different than the non-clergy followers. The church celebrates occasions of clergy weddings in traditional church custom, with singing and dancing that demonstrate the groom remains part of the church.

Church services among the clergy are absolutely reserved for men. Interchurch marriages of members of the church are usually discouraged, and divorce is also not encouraged unless the parties decide to get divorced on the basis of adultery (a practice that the church fully condemns). Although women can become nuns in the church monasteries, they are not supposed to lead holy masses and other important services of the church. Therefore, all priests in the Eritrean Orthodox *Tewahdo* Church are males whose age can range roughly between 25 and above. Followers of the Eritrean Orthodox *Tewahdo* Church are usually deeply religious and claim services from the church on a regular basis. Each member of the church can also claim a personal *abbat nefsi* (አባት ነፍሲ) (a priest—confessor for reconciliation practices in the

A group of Orthodox Tewahdo Priests in Bahti Meskerem Square, Asmara celebrating Meskel festivity. (J. Miran)

sacrament). The *abbat nefsi* attends to the personal spiritual advice of each member for whom he becomes the confessor.

The main language of the Eritrean Orthodox *Tewahdo* Church is Ge'ez—the classical language of the Aksumite Christian people in the region. Although Ge'ez has no more mother tongue speakers, all church masses and festivities are conducted in this language. *Sibket,* or sermons, are, however, usually delivered in the Tigrinya language. It is said that the Eritrean Orthodox *Tewahdo* Church is also considering Tigrinya as its main medium of communication and instruction.

The Eritrean Orthodox *Tewahdo* Church was part of the Ethiopian Orthodox *Tewahdo* Church until the independence of Eritrea. Based on the request of the Eritrean government, the Pope of Coptic Orthodox Church in Alexandria recognized the autocephaly of the Eritrean Orthodox *Tewahdo* Church in 1993. Despite its expressed objections against the Eritrean Orthodox *Tewahdo* Church's need for auto-cephaly, the Ethiopian Orthodox *Tewahdo* Church also recognized the decision and accepted the formation of the Eritrean Orthodox *Tewahdo* Church. Patriarch Paulos of the Ethiopian Orthodox *Tewahdo* Church side and Archbishop Filipos of the Eritrean Orthodox *Tewahdo* Church approved the separation or the autocephalous for-mation of their respective churches in September 1993. In early 1994, both churches formally reaffirmed their respective autocephalous status.

The Eritrean Orthodox *Tewahdo* Church launched an intensive prayer and fasting period during late 1997 and early 1998. After repeated gatherings and discussions among the leaders of the church, Archbishop Filipos was elected the first Patriarch of the Eritrean Orthodox *Tewahdo* Church in April 1998. The Coptic Orthodox Church in Alexandria under Pope Shenouda III immediately recognized the new Eritrean Orthodox *Tewahdo* patriarch. After a few years of reign in the Eritrean Orthodox *Tewahdo* Church, Patriarch Filipos passed away of illness in 2002 at age

Priests gathered for service during Meskel ceremony at Bahri Meskerem Square in Asmara. (J. Miran)

of around 100 years old. The Eritrean Orthodox *Tewahdo* Church then elected the second patriarch, Patriarch Yakob, at the end of 2002. However, the reign of Patriarch Yakob also did not last long, and he died of illness in 2003. After the death of Patriarch Yakob, the Eritrean Orthodox *Tewahdo* Church had to elect their third patriarch, and Patriarch Antonios was elected and enthroned as the third patriarch of the church in March 2004. The election of Patriarch Antonios was recognized by the Coptic Orthodox Church of Alexandria and the Holy Synods of Eritrea and Alexandria.

However, the Eritrean Orthodox *Tewahdo* Church entered into a new phase of crisis in 2005 when the Eritrean government was believed to have intervened in the affairs of the church. The Holy Synod of Eritrea repeatedly excluded the patriarch from attending necessary meetings and ceremonial occasions for reasons that are not yet clear. Based on sketchy sources, the patriarch viewed the church as having only spiritual obligations to its followers and would not confuse its power with political ambitions, as he repeatedly warned government agents who interfered in the affairs of the church. As a result, government bodies developed their grievances against Patriarch Antonios and, through its agents in the Holy Synod, the Patriarch was repeatedly excommunicated from his ceremonial roles in the church. Finally, the Holy Synod of the Eritrean Orthodox *Tewahdo* Church officially toppled the Patriarch for reasons that are not yet clear. In Patriarch Antonios's view, which has also been shared by a great majority of the followers of the church, some members of the Holy Synod, for instance, Yiftahe Dimetros (the son of Keshi Dimetros (*Melake Selam*)—a key Orthodox *Tewahdo* Church figure in Eritrea in the 1950s—who supported the unconditional unity of Eritrea with Ethiopia) and several other members of the Holy Synod were responsible for the internal crisis of the Eritrean Orthodox *Tewahdo* Church. According to many observers, the disposal of the patriarch by the Holy Synod was done under

Women gathered at Meskel feast in Asmara. (J. Miran)

governmental pressure. Since 2005, the Eritrean government has put Patriarch Antonios under house arrest and not much information is available regarding his overall condition.

In 2007, the Eritrean Orthodox *Tewahdo* Church (according to some observers, in cooperation with the Eritrean government) elected Abune Dioskoros (the former bishop of the Seraye part of Zoba Debub) as its patriarch. His patriarchate is, however, not yet recognized by the Coptic Orthodox Church of Alexandria. Because Patriarch Antonios is under house arrest, the Orthodox *Tewahdo* Church is suffering from internal strife, and followers of the church (including in the diaspora) are demonstrating their grievances in many ways.

BRIEF OVERVIEW OF THE ERITREAN CATHOLIC CHURCH

Starting in the nineteenth century, many Roman Catholic missionaries became active in Eritrea and Ethiopia. Despite political instability and continuous rejection by followers of the indigenous Orthodox *Tewahdo* Church, initial Catholic missionaries such as Justin de Jacobis and Giuseppe Sapeto penetrated deep into Eritrean territory and started to spread religion among the local populations. By the mid-nineteenth century, the Catholic Church was established in Eritrea, and various eparchies such as those at Keren and Hebo were founded. Justin de Jacobis, who became a dedicated Apostolic Vicar of Abyssinia, had appointed several Vicars in Eritrea (see O'Mahoney 2001). Among the main tasks of these Vicars was to assure the spread of Catholicism among various communities of Eritrea. Through the efforts of Monsignor Bianchieri, who was appointed by de Jacobis as the Vicar of Keren in 1860, the Catholic Church in Keren became the center of ecclesiastical circumscription.

St. Michael Catholic Church in Segeneity, built in 1937. (S. Tesfagiorgis)

The Vicar of Keren was led by the Vincentian-Lazarist missionaries. However, the political circumstances that followed after the 1860s forced the Lazarists to leave the area. Lazarist missionaries in Keren were substituted by the Capuchins (the Sons of St. Francis) who continued Catholic missionary activities in the area. In the meantime the religion spread among considerable part of the population in the area, principally among the Bilen ethnolinguistic group.

The establishment of the Italian colonial government in Eritrea (1890) further facilitated the spread of Catholicism in the country. By 1911, the Catholic Church in Eritrea established its own Catholic Apostolic Vicariate. Monsignor C. Carrara, a Capuchin missionary, became the first Apostolic Vicar of Eritrea. Carrara managed to embark on a large-scale conversion of various ethnolinguistic groups such as the Bilen, Tigre, and the Kunama. By the 1920s, the Catholic Church was well established in the areas of Bogos, Gash, and Akkele Guzay, and considerable seminary activities took place through the church. However, it was only in the 1930s that the Catholic Church in Eritrea attempted to consider local hierarchy.

Yet the Catholic Church started to consider indigenous rites, and local priests began to take notable positions in the church only in the 1930s. Abune Kidanemariam Kasa, an Eritrean Catholic bishop, was promoted to the title of Pro-Vicar and Ordinary. Other local priests also started to take other positions, for example, as church parishes and administrators. Abune Kidanemariam, who served in the position until 1951, was replaced by Gebreyesus Yakob, local cardinal of the Eritrean Catholic Church.

St. Francisco Catholic Church at Gejeret, Asmara. (S. Tesfagiorgis)

Cardinal Gebreyesus served in the position until 1958 and resigned from his position for unknown reasons. During the following three years, Abune Asratemariam Yimru took over the position of cardinal for the Eritrean Catholic Church. Abune Francois Abraha succeeded Abune Asratemariam and served as the cardinal of the Eritrean Catholic Church until 1984. Abune Zekarias Yohannes was elected the fifth local cardinal of the Eritrean Catholic Church and served in the position until 2001. Since 2001, Abune Mengesteab Kidane has served as the cardinal of the Eritrean Catholic Church. All of the above-mentioned cardinals served in the Eritrean Catholic Church as bishops before their appointment for the position of cardinal. Today (as of 2009), there are over 35 parishes in the Keren Eparchy alone, over 10 parishes in the Hebo (Akkele Guzay) Eparchy, and several parishes in the Barentu Eparchy.

Catholic churches and parishes were built in most parts of the country. Among the notable Roman Catholic churches were the Asmara Cathedral (built in 1922, Asmara), St. Joseph's Cathedral (the Episcopal church in the Asmara Eparchy), the Kidane Mihret Church (Asmara), the St. Francesco Church (Asmara), St. Michael Church (Segeneity), St. Mary Church (Hebo), and many others across the country. Missionary activities and seminary schools were also diversified throughout the country. Moreover, several Catholic orphanages and colleges were opened in Asmara and other parts of the country.

During the years of famine in the 1970s and throughout the 1980s, the Catholic Church in Eritrea played a prominent role in distributing food aid to the needy.

The Asmara Cathedral. (S. Tesfagiorgis)

The Caritas International and the Red Cross in cooperation with the Eritrean Catholic Church and other institutions managed to deliver food aid to the rural and urban population of the country, which saved the lives of over one million people who were severely hit by the famines, drought, and consequences of war. Among the areas where greater concentration of Catholic population is found are Keren, Barentu, and Tsinaadegle, where the total number of Catholic followers can be roughly estimated at eleven, five, and over fifty percent of the total local population, respectively.

The main language of the Eritrean Catholic Church is Ge'ez—the classical language of the Aksumite Christian people in the region. All church masses and festivities are usually held in this language. *Sibkets,* or sermons, and *timherti kerestos* ("Christ's Teachings"—basic religious teachings of the church) are usually delivered, however, in local languages. In more recent times, church masses and prayers are also being conducted in local languages. The Eritrean Catholic church continues to consider local languages as the main mediums of instruction, although its traditions are based on the Ge'ez and Latin liturgical languages.

THE ISLAM-CHRISTIAN COEXISTENCE IN ERITREA

As we discussed earlier, Islam and Christianity have a long common history in the Eritrean region. Although these religions were at times used as political tools for local and regional conflicts, they coexisted for almost fourteen centuries. Their coexistence is usually based on mutual economic, political, and social interactions as well as cultural understandings and tolerances among various ethnolinguistic societies and religious groups. Islam is usually a common religion in the lowlands of Eritrea, while most highlanders are traditionally Christians. Yet owing to their economic necessities, highlanders and lowlanders developed mutual interactions. The lowland Muslim communities are usually pastorals who roam around the grazing lands. The highlanders are sedentary farmers and agro-pastoralists. Yet, the economic activities of the Muslim and Christian communities are not confined only to their respective ecological domains. The lowlanders keep moving from place to place and from season to season in search of pasturelands. Similarly, parts of the highland communities also practice transhumance farming along the eastern escarpments and parts of the lowlands. In addition to the experience of common history, especially since the Italian colonial period, the economic movement of religious and ethnolinguistic groups resulted in the development of understanding, tolerance, and appreciation of each other's religion, culture, and sociopolitical livelihoods. Therefore, most Eritrean ethnolinguistic groups (especially lowlanders) are at least bilingual, which they developed through economic interactions, and their relationships are based on mutual understanding and respect. During recent decades, the harmonious coexistence of both religions was also further strengthened through the EPLF's secular movement. The EPLF followed a secular line and involved Muslim and Christian communities alike.

On the social level, it is common to see Christian and Muslim communities and individuals close to each other as friends, neighbors, and colleagues. They pay visits to each other during their respective festivities—religious and social. During such celebrations, everyone shares whatever food is presented on together, unless dishes of meat are served. For Muslims, meat must be *halal*—meat of an animal that is slaughtered by a Muslim—while for Christians it is also a sort of taboo to consume meat of an animal slaughtered by a Muslim. Although concerned Muslim and Christian community elders tried to avoid this habit in previous times, it is still common to see Muslims and Christians prepare their respective meat dishes during festivities and special occasions. This practice is fading, however, because new generations who are exposed to much more secular experiences—during national services and other organized work campaigns—are routinely ignoring it.

REFERENCES

Chelati Dirar, Uoldelul (2003). "Church-state Relations in Colonial Eritrea: Missionaries and the Development of Colonial Strategies (1869–1911)." In: *Journal of Modern Italian Studies*, 8 (3), pp. 391–310.

Davidson, Basil (2001). *African in History*. London (revised edition): Phoenix Press.

Kibreab, Gaim (2008). "Gender Relations in the Eritrean Society." In: Tesfa G. Gebremedhin and Gebre H. Tesfagiorgis (eds.), *Traditions of Eritrea: Linking the Past to the Future*. Trenton, NJ: Red Sea Press, pp. 229–262.

Killion, Tom (1998). *Historical Dictionary of Eritrea*. Lanham, MD: Scarecrow Press.

Miran, Jonathan (2005). "A Historical Overview of Islam in Eritrea." In: *Die Welt des Islams* 45(2), 176–215.

Nadel, Siegfried Frederick (1944). *Races and Tribes of Eritrea*. Asmara: British Military Administration—Eritrea.

O'Mahoney, Kevin (1982). *"The Ebullient Phoenix". A History of the Vicariate of Abyssinia*, (vol. I). Asmara: Ethiopian Studies Centre.

O'Mahoney, Kevin (1987). *"The Ebullient Phoenix". A History of the Vicariate of Abyssinia*, (vol. II). Asmara: Ethiopian Studies Centre.

O'Mahoney, Kevin (1992). *"The Ebullient Phoenix". A History of the Vicariate of Abyssinia*, (vol. III). Adis Ababa: United Press.

Tesfay, Yakob (2001). "Eritrea." In: Fahlbusch, Erwin and Bromiley, Barrett, David B., and Geoffrey William (eds.). *The Encyclopedia of Christianity*. Evangelisches Kirchenlexikon, Vol. 2, pp. 120–121.

Tewolde, Teclemicael (2009). *Meseretawi temherti qedus metshaf: negebue aredadean ateqaqeman qal egziabeher [Basic Teachings of the Holy Bible: For Better Understanding and Usage of the Word of God]*. Asmara: Francescana Printing Press.

Trimingham, John Spencer (1965). *Islam in Ethiopia*. London: Frank Cass & Co. Ltd.

Trimingham, John Spencer (1949). *Islam in the Sudan*. London: Frank Cass & Co. Ltd.

Woldemikael, Tekle M. (2005). "Eritrea's Identity as a Cultural Crossroads." In: Spickard, Paul R. (ed.), *Race and Nation: Ethnic Systems in the Modern World*. New York: Routledge Publishers, pp. 337–354.

Social Classes and Ethnicity

Eritrea comprises an ethnically heterogeneous society. The Tigrinya ethnolinguistic group makes up roughly over 50 percent of the total population. The Tigre, the second biggest ethnolinguistic group in the country, comprise over 31 percent of the total population. Other ethnolinguistic groups are distributed in the lowlands of the country in smaller groups. As mentioned, there are nine ethnolinguistic groups in Eritrea: the Tigrinya, Tigre, Saho, Afar, Bilen, Hedareb, Nara, Kunama, and Rashaida. Each ethnolinguistic group has its own language and culture. These ethnolinguistic groups are distributed all over the highlands and lowlands of the country. Their patterns of settlement differ according to the climatic and physical characteristics of different ecological zones in Eritrea. Modes of production have also depended on climatic differences in the regions (Tesfagiorgis G. 2007). The majority of the inhabitants of Eritrea are of Semitic stock, representing about 81 percent of the total population. The classification of today's Eritrean ethnolinguistic categories could largely fall into three major groups on the basis of linguistic factors: Semitic, Hamitic (Cushitic), and Nilotic. The ethnolinguistic groups, which fall under the classification of the Semilitc family, are the Tigrinya, Tigre, and Rashaida. The Cushitic, family is divided into four major linguistic groups: Saho, Afar, Bilen, and Beja (mainly known as Hedareb). The Nilotic family is composed of the Kunama and Nara ethnolinguistic groups. The Nara ethnolinguistic group has also been known by neighboring clans, such as the

Beni Amer, as *baza* or *baria*, which is perhaps a derogatory reference. In the Tigrinya language, *baria* means "slave" or "servant." It is not clear, even from references in oral sources, if "Baria" indicates any social status of the Nara people. Also no concrete evidence has been found to trace the name and associate it with possible activities of slavery in the region. The process of settlement and resettlement was directly related to economic activities of the respective linguistic groups vis-à-vis the climatic conditions of the different zones.

Starting from early times, most of the human settlements in Eritrea were affected by the availability of fresh water, grazing, agricultural fields, and primarily by climate. In most cases, malfunction of one or more of the above-mentioned factors resulted in massive movement of people to and from ecological zones. Moreover, amid changing landscapes and ecology, rural people constantly struggled to develop mechanisms of survival (such as crop selection, adopting irrigation agriculture, and adjusting pastoral movement strategies). In the course of movement of people, mutual interdependence evolved among ethnolinguistic groups living in different ecological zones regardless of their respective religious affiliations. Pastoralist communities created sophisticated mutual alliances with agro-pastoral and agrarian communities by which they secured informal insurance against livestock losses caused by drought or animal epidemic diseases. Similarly, agrarian societies also developed cosurvival strategies by adopting mechanisms of agro-pastoral movements between the highlands and lowlands (Tesfagiorgis G. 2007). The establishment of colonialism also facilitated the interaction of people from different ecological zones.

Yet new administrative boundaries were created by the colonial state that limited free transnational and transclimatic pastoral movements. The colonial state established new plantations and gardens on vast areas of land that had historically been used by pastoral communities as grazing lands. Their interdependency was based on economic and socioeconomic factors. In cases of severe droughts or other forms of ecological problems people of different climatic regions had to temporarily abandon their lands and move to areas of better sustainability. The movement of people from one area to another has become an important feature of the adverse environmental situation of the country. As a consequence of their socioeconomic interaction and interdependency, Eritrean agro-pastoralists often speak more than one language (in all cases, they learn each other's languages not in schools, but through frequent and mutual interactions) and extend their economic activities over several climatic zones. Their relationship with others, for example, the highlanders with the lowlanders, is usually cordial and mutual. Hence, the respect and tolerance of their respective cultural, linguistic, and religious traditions has been the cumulative result of their common history and experience over the last centuries (Tesfagiorgis G. 2007).

As noted earlier, the diversity in human ecology across Eritrea is the result of the continuous movement of people from different parts of northeast Africa toward this area. One of the important factors of such movement of people to the area was its proximity to the Red Sea. The Nilotic migrants to the region, who are considered to

Eritrean children at a festive event in Asmara. (J. Miran)

be original inhabitants of the area, were followed by waves of migration of other eth-nolinguistic groups, such as the Semitic and Cushitic groups. In fact, the last millennia have been characterized by waves of migration to and from modern Eritrea. This resulted in the creation of today's mosaic of cultures and languages as well as new

A young man working at Medeber Workshop in Asmara. (S. Tesfagiorgis)

settlement patterns all over the ecological zones of the country. Raids and conquests of superior communities, mostly aimed at controlling resources, also accompanied the movement of people. As can be seen today, the Semitic groups (particularly the Tigrinya) occupied the fertile highlands while the groups who were pushed in the process, such as the Kunama, occupied the lowlands.

Throughout the process of migration and emigration, various ethnolinguistic groups intermingled. Therefore, in today's Eritrean societies it is usually difficult to find a pure descendant of the original groups, and their classification is rather based on cultural and linguistic differences (Murtaza 1998: 45; Bereketab 2000: 62–74; Tesfagiorgis G. 2007). Intermixture and continuous migrations make it difficult to clearly set a classification line among the nine different ethnolinguistic groups and their kinship genealogies. But it is generally believed that the Nilotic groups migrated from south Sudan, mostly from the Nile, and settled in the Gash Setit area. The Cushitic nomadic migrants are believed to have migrated from the south. The Semitic groups are believed to have migrated from south Arabia. Domestication of animals and grains took place several centuries before the Semitic migration to the Horn of Africa. Many scholars argue that the Semitic migrants, also referred to as Sabeans, crossed the Red Sea and brought about a fundamental change in farming techniques to highland settlers.

PEOPLES OF ERITREA

As stated earlier, geographical diversity has been a decisive factor in difference of lifestyle between highlanders and lowlanders. While sedentary farming has been the main economic mode of livelihood in the Eritrean highlands, nomadic and semi-nomadic pastoralism forms of life have prevailed both in the east and west lowlands and the north highlands. The main characteristic of highland communities has been their strong attachment to the land as their main source of livelihood. Possession of land has played an important role in the social, political, and economic organization of the highland communities.

For pastoralist communities, livestock has been the main source of livelihood; their attachment to the land was relatively weak, and their social, political, and economic organization has not been based on the possession of land (Bereketeab 2000: 66–80). The social, economic, and political organizations of those communities also directly relate to their modes of life. According to Bereketeab, the variation in economic organization of the highland and lowland communities influenced the sociopolitical organization of the communities. So, while sedentary farming communities developed cohesive social and political organization, the nomadic communities lacked social and political cohesions (Bereketab 200: 68). However, cohesive relationships have been highly dependent on clan and kinship lineages.

In the following section, we will look briefly at each ethnolinguistic group in Eritrea. This can help us understand distinctive features of each group's social, political, economic organization, and resource-management system.

THE TIGRINYA

The Tigrinya communities occupy almost all parts of the central highlands of Eritrea—especially the old territorial boundaries of Hamassien, Akkele Guzay, and Seraye that were collectively referred to as *Mereb-Mellash* or *Medri Bahri*. These highland areas are also known as *kebessa*. The lowland regions of Eritrea are inhabited by a number of other ethnolinguistic groups. Owing to the common environmental situation of the highland region, the communities of these old provinces formed a common religion, culture, and way of life. The majority of Tigrinya highlanders are Christians, with a minority Muslim group. Although members of this community claim to be a separate ethnicity, they are still widely accepted as part of the Tigrinya cultural and ethnolinguistic group. Minority members of the Tigrinya ethnolinguistic group were also converted into Roman Catholicism and Evangelical religions with the expansion of European missionary activities in the regions (especially during the nineteenth century).

Settlement patterns of the highland Tigrinya were based on *'adi* (ዓዲ)—village. Numerous *enda* (እንዳ), families that claimed common ancestry, formed villages. The size of villages differs from place to place. Based on travellers' observations, a majority of villages in the Eritrean highlands were small in size. For instance, Markham, describing the geographical situation in the southern plateau, noted that they had few inhabitants. He states that Senafe, one of the significant towns in modern Eritrea, had a population of approximately 240 inhabitants in the 1860s (Markham 1868: 20–21). The size of most villages increased with the increase of the country's population. Observing the type and distribution of Eritrean highland villages in the nineteenth century, Wylde notes as follows:

> Here are reached the first villages in Abyssinia that are different to those in the North Hamasen and Bogos country. They are always situated on the top of the hills, and either one or two sides are formed by the rocks against which the houses are built. They look very curious, and are not visible at any great distance, and if trees were planted in the front of the collection of huts they could not be seen at all. The tendency of the natives in Abyssinia is to build their houses and villages as far as possible from the usual and most frequented roads (Wylde 1888: I: 236).

As observed by Wylde, the highland villages were often located on hills and not located on frequently used roads. This is simply because communities considered a number of factors before they established their villages: the availability of water, wood, farming and grazing lands, and more. In the nineteenth century when Wylde visited the area, the site of a village was determined by such factors as not being easily accessible by wild beasts, irregular armies, or outlaws. The formation of many villages in a locality resulted in the creation of districts and later provinces. At the village level of settlements, communal, social, economic, and political organizations were important for the communities, especially to members of an *enda*. In other words, the *enda* became the fundamental social organizational unit throughout the highlands that were predominantly occupied by the Tigrinya. The *enda* units were named after the common ancestor, or founder, of the lineage. Labor and resource management depended on communal systems (village communities), which collectively possessed the grazing, agricultural, and forestry lands communally. The land tenure differed from region to region and from community to community. But mostly the land possession among the Tigrinya was generally classified into individual, family, communal, or village ownership.

The style of highland dwellings or houses was *hidmos* (ሂድሞ). These types of houses were made of earth, wood, and stones; and usually comprised of fences made of branches of acacia, euphorbia, or stone. Under continuous renovation, *hidmo* types of houses may stay and serve as housing for several decades. Today, these types of dwellings are becoming uncommon, which is attributed to the fact that most parts of the Tigrinya highlands have been deforested. Construction of *hidmo* houses requires a great number of trees and tree branches. The pillars used for the construction of *hidmo* houses are especially not easy to find. Trees such as African olive (*Olia africana*) and African juniper (*Juniperus procera*), which are important for hidmo construction, are almost extinct from many places of the highlands. Instead, *merebae* (rectangular dwellings made of stones, corrugated iron sheets, cement, and wood) are increasingly becoming popular dwellings among the Tigrinya communities.

The social organization of the Tigrinya village communities was largely based on kinship. Kinship groups served as a fundamental unit for social relations and systems of resource management. This type of social organization bypassed the territorial considerations of social cohesion and village formations. Many families who were attached by kinship also had strong attachments to the lands of their village. Although marriages and blood relations were common connections between neighboring villages, families of respective villages had to defend natural resources that were under their domain. Newcomers, known as *ma'ekelai alet* (ማእከላይ ዓሊት), were not allowed to share equal status with the *enda* families of the villages. Some villages admitted newcomers to settle and to eventually have access to the village lands after a long period of residence and a record of service in that particular village (Tesfagiorgis G. 2007: 133).

The livelihood of the Tigrinya-speaking people was based on social cohesion and communal life. Labor was organized in a communal form; for example, in the form of *wofera* (ወፈራ—a form of communal and voluntary work in which people of the same village gathered and worked for a member of the village). Members of the same *enda* or village shared labor during various social occasions such as weddings, funerals, and other community ceremonies. Even during major ecological adversities *wofera* was organized and productions were shared. In addition to *wofera,* village communities formed religious and other associations that served as social platforms for discussing issues of common concern.

The associations were organized in the form of *mahber qudusan* (ማሕበር ቅዱሳን—in remembrance of Saints). Although *mahber qudusan* were religious associations, these occasions were also kind of "get together" events for members of the communities. These events were considered as important social interactions where villagers gathered for celebrating their achievements and discussing various issues that concerned them. Similarly, *equb* (ዕቑብ—a form of association in which members contribute specified amounts of cash as savings) has become a form of social occasion (especially for women) during which various issues of common concern could be raised and discussed.

As stated earlier, *mahber qudusan* was a common form of association throughout the Christian Tigrinya domain. These forms of associations could take various names and forms, depending on the number of saints a village community wants to remember. The following are some of the common ones: *mahber maryam, mahber michael, mahber gebriel,* and *mahber abune aregawi.* These were usually celebrated every year, but in some cases, villages could also celebrate *mahbers* every month—on a cyclical form among the village households. Members of a village may belong to various *mahbers.* During such events, community figures such as priests and the elders play decisive roles in creating harmonious social relations among members of the village. In case there is any group or individual conflict among members of the community, the priests and elders help them settle their differences and ask both parties to offer forgiveness for each other. In such a way, priests and elders help individuals, couples, neighbors, and so on to improve their relations.

Although more of an economic association, an *equb* more or less serves the functions of a *mahber.* There are significant differences between a *mahber* and an *equb.* A *mahber* is more religious in formation, and all members of the community can be admitted as members of a particular *mahber.* On the other hand, an *equb* is nonreligious in scope, and usually women are the members of such an association. In an *equb,* members contribute certain amounts of cash during every regular meeting. The amount of cash contributed is gathered and given to one member this term and to another member the next term. In such a way, all members receive collected sums of contributions once during the number of meetings (depending on the number of members of the *equb*). For example, if there are three members of an *equb,* one of the members (usually the one who hosts the meeting of that particular term) would get the collected sum for the term, the second person would get the same sum the next term, and the last person would get the same sum the following term. Therefore, the money contributed for the *equb* takes the form of cash savings for members of the association.

Another important factor of social cohesion, which bypassed the village community level, was the monthly or annual pilgrimage organized by respective villages collectively. This form of social and religious occasion is called *negdet* (ንግደት). Similar to *mahber,* a *negdet* may be named after a particular saint, say Saint Michael. This is celebrated once a year and pilgrims attend the feast from various neighboring villages as well as from distant places. In many cases, *negdet* feasts are also celebrated in churches where religious prayers take place. The village may prepare a special place where attendants of the ceremony can get food and drink after prayers. Usually, the village elects a special committee of three or more individuals for this occasion. The committee is responsible for gathering food and drink for the attendants. All members of the village contribute a specified amount of food and drink for the occasion. Yet, every household also provides food, drink, and places to stay overnight for its own guests. These events are important for the fact that many people from various villages gather and closely discuss their past, current, and future concerns (Tesfagiorgis G. 2007: 133–134).

THE SAHO

Following different paths of migration, the Saho settled along the eastern foothills of the southeastern escarpments, southern plateau, and parts of the Semhar Plains, as far as the Gulf of Zula and Gedem. Some pockets of the Saho can also be found in different parts of the country such as in the highlands and the Gash-Barka areas. Some Saho groups, such as the clans of Hazo and Irob, are also found in the northern parts of Ethiopia (particularly in the Tigray Province) (for more information on Saho see Saleh Mohammad 1984; Conti Rossini 1913; Favali and Pateman 2003: 27).

The social organization of the Saho clans and subclans is based on genealogical branches that claim common ancestry. The main genealogical branches are the *Are*, *Kisho,* and *Mehla* (Saleh Mohammad 2009: 13). The subclans are further subdivided into kinship groups called House or *Are*, *Dik*, or *Qaisha*. These kinship groups are named after the individuals who are considered as founders of the genealogies (Saleh Mohammad 2009: 13). Organized in agnatic lineage structures, the Saho are highly organized pastoralists. Some members of the Saho also practice mixed farming, especially those who live in the southern plateau. Other Saho groups, such as the Tora clans, practice pastoral activities by migrating between the escarpments and the Semhar Plains seasonally. They move between the eastern foothills as far as the southwest parts of the plateau (Hazemo) and the Dankalia Plains. They raise large herds of cattle, goats, and sheep. Among the few Saho clans who practice sedentary farming are the Menifere (Favali and Pateman 2003: 27). The Saho kinship groups comprise patriarchal and egalitarian social structures. All Saho clans speak the same language—Saho. However, there are some remarkable Saho dialects among Saho clans, depending where they are found. For example, notable dialectical differences can be observed between the Saho language spoken by the Irob and Tora clans. Most Saho are also multilingual. Depending where they are found, Saho communities may speak Tigrinya, Tigre, or Arabic as their second language. Except the Irob and part of the Debri Mela clans, who adopted Roman Catholic religion with the expansion of European missionary activities in the area during the nineteenth century, by religion, all Saho are Muslims (for further details, see Saleh Mohammad 1984: 37–68).

According to Saleh Mohammad, there are ten semiautonomous Saho clans. Seven of these clans comprise big numbers and subclans (Saleh Mohammad 2009: 13). The following are the main Saho clans and subclans that are distributed across the territory.

Asaworta—This clan consists of five subclans: Assa-Kare, Assa-Leesan, Foqreti-Are, Foqrota-Are, and Lelish Are. The Asworta are pastoralists (with some agro-pastoralists) who migrate between the mountains of Soira to the Semhar Plains in the east, and as far as the Hazomo plains in the west. Their migration paths depend on seasonality as well as availability of grazing lands.

Baradotta—Members of this clan are distributed in small groups along the Semhar Plains, Dankalia Plains, and the Gash-Setit areas.

Debri Mehla—This clan comprises the Ala Des-Are and Labhalet-Are subclans. These subclans are agro-pastoralists who are distributed in pockets in the southern plateau, such as the mountains of Mola (see Saleh Mohammad 2009: 14).

Hassabat-Are—Divided into small subclans, these communities are found near the town of Senafe and Adi Keyyih.

Hazo—This clan is divided into ten subclans: Comarta, Mussa-Ebbago, Hamadi-Qaisha, Asa Ali-Geisha, Konsubi-fere, Asa Alila, Kaiwana, Enda Omarto, Bukarte, and Hakaibe-Qaisha. These are pastoral clans that live and move around the foothills of the southeastern escarpment, such as Zula, Foro, and River Endali (see also Saleh Mohammad 2009: 14).

Idda—This clan comprises the oldest Saho-speaking communities in the country. They are distributed in small pockets in the Akkele Guzay and Barka Plains.

Iddefer—This clan comprises a number of subclans. They are found in the Semhar Plains and the northern parts of Dankalia.

Irob—The Irob is divided into five subclans, including Haseballa, Bouknaitee, and Adgadee; their Saho dialects slightly differ from the Tora and Asawerta clans. Great numbers of these clans adhere to Christianity. They occupy areas such as Shimezana, southward to Monekseyto and as far as Adi Grat in Tigray (Ethiopia).

Minifere—Comprised of subclans, including Gaaso, Silaita, Ellas, Faqih-harak, Senafe, Dasamo, and a number of other subclans

The Melhina-Me'embara (The Seven Holy Subclans)—These subclans are: Haji-Abkur, Intile Sheikh-Are, Dembagog, Sheikh Lalaha, Akhader-Abusa, Imbarak-Abusa, and Iryo Naba.

Tora—This clan is divided into two "Ares" (houses): the Sarrah-Are and the Mussa-Are. These subclans are pastoralists raising varieties of livestock such as cattle, goats, and sheep. They are located along the Haddas River and Degaa Mountains. Their main market towns are Gindae, Hergigo (Dekhono), and Segeneity.

The Saho communities have a decentralized and egalitarian or democratic type of internal administration. Each clan or subclan elects its own shum (chief) whose authority is nonhereditary. As stated earlier, most Saho clans are pastoralists who raise large herds of livestock and depend on livestock products for their living. But some clans also practice mixed farming in which they also cultivate grains such as maize, sorghum, and millet. Most Saho territories are owned by communities who claim common clans. Therefore, all Saho members who share the same territorial boundaries have equal rights for use of grazing lands. Unlike the highland farming communities, Saho clans share their grazing resources equally.

THE TIGRE

Tigre-speaking communities are scattered along the eastern and western lowlands of Eritrea. They occupy the coastal areas starting from the southern Semhar (north of the Bay of Zula and around the Hergigo) to the borders with Sudan in the north. They spread toward the interior up to the foothills of the eastern escarpments, over most parts of the Barka and Anseba in the western lowlands, and the northern mountains such as the Roras in the Sahel Mountains. The Tigre communities are also divided into various clan groups in which kinship affiliation is an important element of social organization.

A number of Tigre clans are found in the region between the Anseba River (territories that were known as Bogos) in the south and the Eritrea-Sudanese border in the north. These clans are: the Bet Asghede, Beni Amer, Mensae, and Maria. The Bet Asghede comprises four major clans: the Habab, Ad Temariam, Ad Teklies, and Bet Juk. Some smaller communities such as Ad Sheikh, Ad Mualim, Bet Mela, and Ad Tsaura are also part of this clan and are found mostly in the northern highlands (Sahel Mountains). One clan found north of the Bogos territories is commonly known as the Maria. The Maria clan is divided into two major subclans: the Maria Qeyyah (the "Red Marias") and Maria Tselam (the "Black Marias"). In the eastern lowlands, the main Tigre clans are: the Bet Abrehe and Bet Shakan. They occupy areas along the Semhar Plains such as in the port of Massawa and its vicinities as well as Hergigo.

Most Tigre clans trace their origins back to early notable Arab families in the Middle East. For example, the Mensae clans trace their origins to Mohammad's ancestors of the Meccan Koraish of the Zed clan (Pollera 1935: 156). Similarly, the Ad Sheikh who inhabit areas south of Habab territories (in areas such as Afabet), attempt to justify their blood relations with the Prophet Mohammad by claiming their descent to a holy family in Mecca. The Ad Sheikh are pastoralists who raise mostly camels and goats (Tesfagiorgis G. 2007: 136–137).

Like the Saho, most Tigre clans are pastoralists. They raise large herds of livestock such as cattle, sheep, goats, and camels. Owing to their constant movement in search of grazing territories, most Tigre clans have mobile settlement environments. They roam the lowland areas in search of grazing lands, although some Tigre communities have also adapted farming in riverine areas and the Shieb plains. In some areas, such as in Shieb, Tigre communities practice agriculture using irrigation. Tigre farmers cultivate mostly durra, sorghum, and millet. Most Tigre communities in Eritrea adhere to Sunni Islam. Small sections of the Tigre are also Christian (especially sections of the Mensae).

One of the unique types of social organizations of some Tigre clans was based on the master-serf social relationship. According to oral sources, the origin of the master-serf social relationship can be traced to as early as the sixteenth century when the Bet Asghede migrated from the Tsinadegle area in the highlands to Sahel (Rora Habab) for reasons that are still unclear. Oral sources indicate that the Bet Asghede clans were Tigrinya speakers, and originally adherents of the Orthodox *Tewahdo* Church, who migrated to the Roras and Sahel from the Tsinadegle areas in the Eritrean plateau. Prior to their migration to the area, they practiced agro-pastoralism and owned large herds of cattle. Although newcomers to the Habab and Mensa region, they adopted Islam as well as the Tigre language of the preexisting communities and were able to transform those small communities into their serfdom (see also Nadel 1944: 40–42).

The master-serf relationship of the aristocratic families, or *Shumageles*, and the Tigre serfs was inherent. The serf rendered various dues and services to the aristocratic household, and his dues and social status were also inherited by his sons (Pollera 1935: 192). The master or landlord had obligations to his serfs, such as providing them protection as well as allocating farming and/or grazing fields. On the other hand, the serfs provided all of their labor and services to their masters. These types of relationships were discontinued in the twentieth century, especially during the British colonial rule and occupation of the country. The *shums* (hereditary chiefs) used to lead the affairs of respective kinship groups and were subordinate to the leadership of the overall chief called *kentibay* (ከንቲባይ) (for further details, see Tesfagiorgis G. 2007: 137; Nadel 1944: 40–44; Trevaskis 1960; Longrigg 1945; Pollera 1935).

The economic activities of the Tigre pastoralists demand periodic movement. As with most communities in dryland ecosystems, the settlements or dwellings of many Tigre clans are temporary and mobile. In most cases, the house styles of the Tigre ethnolinguistic group are *agudos* (ኣጉዶ—a thatch roofed house made up of grasses and tree trunks; or *Agnet* (ኣግነት)—a kind of tent that in most cases is mobile and simple).

Although a number of Tigre communities have adopted agro-pastoralist systems of economic activities where they have established sedentary settlements, other Tigre clans roam around the lowlands on a seasonal basis. This is because the dryland ecological zones where the Tigre communities live demand constant and seasonal migrations in search of grazing lands. Based on the observation of nineteenth-century travelers, most of the lowland settlers had only temporary villages; they possessed numerous animals and most of their food supplies depended on the products and/or byproducts of these animals. Also according to travellers' observations during and before the nineteenth century, many Tigre clans possessed a great variety of livestock, and their households often managed to get abundant resources.

THE BILEN

The Bilen, who call themselves *Blin* or *Blean,* are Cushitic-speaking clans who migrated to the northern parts of the highlands, particularly the Bogos territories during or after the fall of the Zagwe Dynasty in the thirteenth century. They are small but unique pockets of communities in the Keren area. According to their tradition, the Bilen are Agaws who migrated from Lasta, Ethiopia. The Zagwe Dynasty (comprising Cushitic or Agau peoples) was a mighty dynasty that was established after the fall of the Aksumite Empire. Although the exact cause of the Bilen migration is yet speculated and not evidently known, they are believed to have escaped persecution by the newly founded Solomonic Dynasty. Some scholars suggest that the Bilen were probably sent toward the north (Eritrea) for military expeditions, and that their migration must have taken place around the tenth century (Mengeste-ab 1984: 747). The Zagwe Dynasty fell in 1270. This was followed by waves of migration toward the north. The Agau migrations toward the north might have also taken place because of prolonged environmental adversities such as famine (Pollera 1935: 23–45).

The Agau migration to Eritrea followed in the paths of a number of Agau communities such as the Adkeme Melgae, who settled in the highlands where they lost their language and culture. Most of these Agau groups were integrated into the highland communities. Therefore, it is difficult to identify Agau migrants who integrated themselves within the highland communities, particularly within Tigrinya-speaking communities.

The most renowned Bilen clans are the Tarqe and Tawqe. Other Bilen subclans are the Jengeren and Bet Mussi. Originally, most of the Bilen clans were entirely pastoralists who raised large herds of livestock. However, the continuous migration of other peoples into the Bilen territories left these clans surrounded by other ethnolinguistic groups such as the Tigre. Perhaps owing to the lack of vast grazing lands in their former territories, the Bilen seem to have been forced to diversify their economic activities to include sedentary farming. Today, the majority of Bilen clans are settled farmers and animal herders. Some of the main grains cultivated by the Bilen are millet, maize, barley, and durra. Crop productions are adopted on the bases of topography and climate variation of the region. The agricultural system of the Bilen is based on rainfed crop production. Land possessions were administered by local laws (known as *Fetha Megareh*). Yet, population increase has resulted in a shortage of farming land throughout the Bilen territories. Low and erratic rainfall has also resulted in a continuous deterioration of agricultural production in recent years (Tesfagiorgis G. 2007: 140). The occupation of the territories by various groups, as well as the establishment of plantations and gardens by colonialists, made it difficult for the majority of the Bilen to keep large herds of livestock that they had formerly possessed (Tesfagiorgis G. 2007: 139).

Interestingly, the Bilen clans are one of the unique ethnolinguistic groups in the country, because they have preserved their language and culture despite persistent external influences from neighboring ethnolinguistic groups such as the Tigre and Tigrinya. The attempted influence of other clans over the Bilen was accompanied by continuous forms of raids (see Ghaber 1993: 12–22). The fertile lands of the Bogos coupled with good grazing lands offered opportunities for the Bilen to adopt a settled agro-pastoralist economy. European travellers who visited the Bilen territories of Bogos in the nineteenth century described the territories as rich in land resources. For example, observing the natural richness of the area amid continuous military or tribal raids on the region, Plowden states the following:

> Being plains, and richly cultivated with Indian corn, they are the favorite field for the incursion of [Wube's] troops affording the most spoil with the least fighting. (Plowden 1868: 15)

As observed by Plowden, the Bilen population suffered from destructive intertribal conflicts and from raids by Tigrean warlords such as the nineteenth-century Wubie. In the 1860s, the Bilen also suffered from various tribal attacks, mainly led by the Beni Amer. For instance, the Beni Amer warriors invaded Bogos on October 25, 1864. They killed many men, women, and children; plundered several herds of cattle; and took 120 boys and girls as slaves (Rassam 1869: 44). Egyptian expansion to the region (nineteenth century) was also accompanied by massive religious conversion of Christian Bilen to Islam. The European missionary expansion in the region facilitated the conversion of a significant number of the Bilen to Christianity, particularly Roman Catholicism. Today, the Bilen are half Christians and half Muslims. The Bilen speak a distinct Agau (Cushitic) language also called Bilen. Most members of the Bilen are able to speak at least two languages—Bilen and Tigrinya or Bilen and Tigre.

Each clan of the Bilen had its own chief whose authority was nonhereditary (see also Ghaber 1993). Therefore, internal administration was highly decentralized among the various Bilen subclans. The Italian colonial administration in Eritrea attempted to centralize the internal administration system of the Bilen by appointing new chiefs in 1932. However, local resistance to this form of administration discouraged the Italian administrative policy in the area (Ghaber 1993: 59).

THE KUNAMA

The Kunama are the Nilo-Saharan ethnolinguistic groups who occupy the southwestern parts of Eritrea. Small numbers of Kunama groups may also be found in Ethiopia. In Eritrea, the Kunama population is located in the southwest part of the country—along the Rivers of Gash and Setit (close to the southwest border with Ethiopia). They constitute about 2 percent of the total population. The Kunama are believed to be among the earliest inhabitants of Eritrea. They used to live in parts of the highlands, until they were eventually pushed by new migrants such as the Tigrinya and Bilen to the areas where they live today (Naty 2002: 569–97).

Similar to the Bilen and other lowland ethnolinguistic groups of Eritrea, the Kunama were victims of various forms of internal and external raids. Tigrean warlords during the nineteenth century frequently raided the Kunama lands. In addition to the continuous friction with the neighboring Beni Amer, the Egyptians and Abyssinian troops continuously raided the Kunama. Be it raids from the Adiyabo areas, other parts of Tigray, or from territories within the Eritrean lowlands, the Kunama and Nara people were routinely exposed to various forms of atrocities.

The Kunama were predominantly hunters and gatherers. They also practiced subsistence farming using simple techniques of farming—commonly called "hoe-farming." As agricultural land became increasingly scarce, the Kunama adopted a more pastoral way of life. Today, the Kunama are sedentary agro-pastoralists settled along the Gash Barka area where Barentu has become the central town in the region. Today, the Kunama cultivate lands along the rivers Gash and Setit where they produce sorghum, millet, maize, beans, and a variety of fruits and vegetables. Moreover, considerable segments of the Kunama are also cattle herders whose grazing land is distributed along the Gash and Setit areas (Tesfagiorgis G. 2007: 140).

The social organization of the Kunama is somewhat different than most other ethnolinguistic groups in the country. Their kinship social structures are based on matrilineal lineages. As with most ethnolinguistic groups in Eritrea, the Kunama are divided into clans and subclans. Some of the notable Kunama clans are the *Alaka*, *Kara*, *Nataka*, *Serma*, and *Lakka*.

Traditionally, the Kunama have followed their own faith (also known as the *Kunama Beliefs*), which was centered on the belief and worship of their creator called *Anna* and also on reverence of heroic ancestors. With the expansion of Islam and Christianity into the region, the majority of the Kunama clans converted either to Islam or Roman Catholicism. The Kunama sociopolitical organization is egalitarian, that is, clan members become loyal to village elders and elected assemblies (see also Tesfagiorgis G. 2007: 140–141).

The internal and external raids were brought to an end after the establishment of Italian colonialism in Eritrea. Yet, the Italian colonial rule in Eritrea also confiscated vast agricultural lands in the Gash and Setit rivers and established commercial plantations such as Alighider (in 1928). Since the colonial era, the Kunama have cultivated their land freely. However, divisive tribal policies during the post-Italian periods have also affected the livelihood of most Kunamas. The ecology of the Kunama lands is believed to have been affected by the establishment of colonial plantations and gardens as well as consecutive migration of other peoples to the traditionally Kunama territories. Increased use of natural resources, as well as landscape changes, has caused considerable environmental degradation in the area. The prolonged wars of liberation as well as the renewed Eritrean-Ethiopian conflict have also contributed to undeniable ecological changes in the region (see Naty 2002: 569–597).

Land was owned on a tribal basis in which every member of the clan had access to grazing and farming land. The establishment of these plantations not only exacerbated the scarcity of farming lands in the region, but it also transformed the whole landscape. Vast forest lands were cleared and converted into farming lands. Ecological change in the area was further aggravated by the influx of people from different regions in search of jobs on the plantations (Tesfagiorgis G. 2007: 141).

THE NARA

The second Nilo-Saharan people in Eritrea are the Nara. Located north of the Kunama, in the western parts of Barka Plains, the Nara constitute about 1.5 percent of the total population of Eritrean. Although the Nara and Kunama share some customs, their languages as well as social organizations are not the same. Unlike the Kunama, the social organization (lineage system) of the Nara is patrilineal. The Nara speak the Nara language. Owing to interaction with other neighboring ethnolinguistic groups, the Nara are also at least bilingual. They speak Tigre and/or Arabic as their second language. In fact, the few available written pieces of Nara literature are recorded either in Tigre or Arabic. There had not been a Nara writing tradition until recently.

Today, the Nara communities are sedentary farmers with small-scale pastoral activities. These subsistence farmers produce a variety of crops, legumes, and vegetables. The Nara people are believed to have followed their own faith until the nineteenth century when the Egyptian occupation brought about a massive conversion to Islam. Today, most of the Nara people are Muslims (Tesfagiorgis G. 2007: 141).

The sociocultural organization of the Nara is based on clan and subclan divisions. Nara communities live in organized settlement hamlets and villages. Their livelihood is mainly based on sedentary farming and animal husbandry. The Nara have highly organized traditional systems of resource management, tenure systems, and communal conflict resolution strategies. The dominant systems of land tenure among the Nara are the *dar* and *qowshi*. In the *dar* land tenure system, each clan has its own land. Land is distributed to each family belonging to the same clan. Households have the right to use, lease, and inherit land. Unlike the *meriet worqi* of the highland tenure system, land cannot be sold or purchased in the *dar* system. In the *qowish* (communal) land tenure system, land is owned by the whole clan. The types of communal land owned

by the clans include forest lands (where the people seek shelter during raids and conflicts), grazing lands, and common water sources (Tesfagiorgis G. 2007: 241–242).
Any Nara clan, family, or individual has the right to use lands under the classification
of *qowish*. Lands under the *qowish* tenure system are highly protected by all Nara
communities. Similar to the Kunama, the Nara people also suffer from the effects of
poor environmental management caused by combined factors such as deforestation
and land degradation. Today, Nara lands are remarkably degraded due to the effects
of overpopulation, soil erosion, and more. As in all regions of Eritrea, the scars of prolonged military conflicts can be seen everywhere in the Nara territories (Tesfagiorgis G.
2007: 141).

THE HEDAREB

The Hedareb (also known as the T'bdawe) people are located in the northwest parts of
Barka as far as the borders with east Sudan. With their associated clans (the Beni
Amer and the Beja), the Hedareb constitute about 2.5 percent of the total Eritrean pop-
ulation. Most members of the Hedareb speak Tigre as their first or second language.
Most Hedareb people are pastoralists who move from place to place on a seasonal
basis, and they predominantly keep large herds of camels, goats, and sheep. The Beni
Amer, who are organized in a hierarchical social structure, are known for their pastoral
skills, especially in raising camels (Tesfagiorgis G. 2007: 142).

The Hedareb territories are mostly arid and semiarid. These highly organized pastoral communities practice animal husbandry as their main economic activity in the
fragile ecosystems of the northwestern parts of Eritrea and as far as the areas bordering
Sudan. The Hedareb are mostly Muslims by religion. Their social structures are based
on clan and subclan organizations. Similar to the Saho, Afar, and Bilen, grazing lands
were owned by the clans.

THE RASHAIDA

The Rashaida are believed to have migrated from south Arabia to Eritrea in the 1840s
and are by ethnicity Arabs. They are exclusively Muslim communities whose predominant economic activities are trading and nomadic pastoralism. They constitute
about 0.5 percent of the Eritrean population—the smallest ethnolinguistic group in
the country. Their economic movements include the northeastern parts of Eritrea and
as far as the Sudan. According to their tradition, they migrated from Hijaz, Yemen to
escape political persecution in the nineteenth century.

The Rashaida are composed of approximately 13 clans. Kinship relationship is the
dominant system of family structures among the Rashaida (Tesfagiorgis G. 2007: 142).
They are predominantly nomadic pastoralists and raise large herds of camels and
goats. Camels are an important means of transport as well as a source of wealth for
the Rashaida. Apart from limited cultivation and the production of millet, they are
entirely dependent on their herds and trade for a living. Similar to the Hedareb and
Afar, there have not been detailed studies dealing with this ethnolinguistic group
(Tesfagiorgis G. 2007: 142).

THE AFAR

Like the Hedareb, Bilen, and Saho, the Afar are members of the Cushitic-speaking groups. They are located in several countries of the Horn of Africa—Eritrea, Ethiopia, and Djibouti. In language and customs, the Afar are similar to the Saho. The Eritrean Afar have been commonly referred to by various sources as "Danakils." They are found along the southeast coast of the Red Sea, in the huge desert zone known as Dankaila and have adapted to the inhospitable desert environment. They constitute about 5 percent of the entire population of Eritrea.

Many of the Afars are pastoralists who raise large herds of goats and camels. Part of the Afar population also depends on trading (salt is their main trading item) and fishing. Although most of the Afar people live in specific grazing areas along the Dankalia Plains, some migrate short distances with their goats and camels in search of grazing lands. In a few areas along the oasis, some Afar people also practice subsistence farming. They cultivate maize, tobacco, and durra. The Afar are entirely Muslim by religion (Tesfagiorgis G. 2007: 142; Saleh Mohammad 1984).

Similar to the Saho, the social organization of the Afar is founded on clan divisions and subdivisions. The Afar can be divided into two main groups of social classes: the *assoymara* (the "red") and the *addoymara* (the "white") (see Saleh Mohammad 1984). Based on the Afar oral traditions, the *addoymara* were the earlier inhabitants of the Dankalia region. Later, the *assoymara* migrated to the area and dominated the pre-existing Afar clans. The newcomers also seem to have dominated the main economic activities—fishing and trading along the coastal areas of the Red Sea. The preexisting clans seem to have been pushed to the rugged mountains and the Danakalia Desert where they practice pastoralism. Their political and sociocultural organization is based on clans composed of many extended families. They trace their lineages through patrilineal lines. The pastorals normally have temporary settlements and their huts, known as *aris*, are simple and mobile.

REFERENCES

Baden Kunama: http://www.baden-kunama.com

Bereketeab, Redie (2000). *Eritrea. The Making of a Nation 1890–1991*. Uppsala: Uppsala University Press.

Beyene, Teame (1990). *The Development of the Eritrean Land Tenure in the last 100 Years* [text in Tigrinya]. Asmara: unpublished paper.

Conti Rossini, Carlo (1913). *Schizzo del dialetto saho dell'alta assaorta in Eritrea*. Rome: Accademia dei Lincei.

Conti Rossini, Carlo (1916). *Principi di diritto consuetudinario dell' Eritrea: (Manuali coloniali pubbl. a cura del Ministero delle colonie)*. Roma: Tipografia dell'Unione editrice.

Favali, L. and Pateman, Roy (2003). *Blood, Land, and Sex: Legal and Political Pluralism in Eritrea*. Bloomington: Indiana University Press.

Gebre-Medhin Jordan (1989). Peasants and Nationalism in Eritrea: *A Critique of Ethiopian Studies*. Trenton, NJ: Red Sea Press.

Ghaber, Michael (1993). *The Blin of Bogos*. Bagdad, Iraq.

Killion, Tom (1998). *Historical Dictionary of Eritrea*. Lanham, MD: Scarecrow Press.

Longrigg, Stephen Hemsley (1944). *A Short History of Eritrea.* Oxford: Clarendon Press.

Markham, Clements (1868). "Geographical Results of the Abyssinian Expedition." In: *Journal of Royal Geographical Society.* 38 (1868), pp. 12–49.

Mengeste-ab, Adhana (1984). "Ancestor Veneration in Blean Culture." In: Beyene, Taddese (ed.) *Proceedings of the Eighth International Conference of Ethiopian Studies*, Vol 1, 8 (1984) University of Addis Ababa.

Munzinger, Werner (1883). *Ostafrikanische Studien: Mit einer Karte von Nord-Abyssinien und den Ländern am Mareb, Barka und Anseba.* Bassel: Schaffhausen.

Nadel, Siegfried Frederick (1944). *Races and Tribes of Eritrea.* Asmara: British Military Administration—Eritrea.

Naty, Alexander (2002). "Environment, Society and the State in Western Eritrea." In: *Africa: Journal of International African Institute.* Vol. 72, pp. 569–97.

Plowden, Walter (1868). *Travels in Abyssinia and the Galla Country: With an Account of a Mission to Ras Ali in 1848.* London.

Pollera, Alberto (1935). *Le poplazioni indigene dell'Eritrea.* Bologna: Cappelli Ed.

Rassam, Hormuzd (1869). *Narrative of the British Mission to Theodore, King of Abyssinia: With Notices of the Countries Traversed from Massowah—Through the Soodân, the Amhâra, and Back to Annesley Bay, from Mágdala.* London: Murray.

Saleh Mohammad, Abdulkader(translator and editor) (2009). *The Customary Law of the Akkele Guzai Muslims [the Saho].* British Military Administration (1943). Berlin: Lit Verlag.

Saleh Mohammad, Abdulkader (1984). *Die Afar-Saho-Nomaden in Nordost-Afrika.* (Ph.D. Dissertation): University of Bayreuth.

Tesfagiorgis G., Mussie (2007). *A Fading Nature: Aspects of Environmental History of Eritrea (1980–1991).* Felsberg: Edition Eins.

Tesfagiorgis, Gebre Hiwet (1993). *Emergent Eritrea: Challenges of Economic Development.* Trenton, NJ: Red Sea Press.

Trevaskis, Gerald Kenedy Nicholas (1960). *Eritrea: A Colony in Transition—1941–52.* London.

UNDESF—United Nations Department of Economic and Social Affairs, Population Division (2007). *World Population Prospects: The 2006 Revision.* Vol 1: Comprehensive Tables. United Nations Publication.

Wylde, Augustus. B. (1888). *'83 to '87 in the Soudan, with an account of Sir William Hewett's mission to King John of Abyssinia* (2 Vols.). New York: Negro Universities Press.

Women and Marriage

In general, Eritrean societies (perhaps with the exclusion of the Kunama ethnolinguistic group) are highly patriarchal. Yet women in Eritrea play a vital role in society. In patriarchal societies such as Eritrea, women usually occupy marginal social and cultural status. The patriarchal and "men-dominated" structure of Eritrean societies is deeply rooted in traditions that are widely accepted as the cultural norms, values, and guidelines that control the social interactions and relations between the two genders (Kibreab 2008: 229–262). These patriarchal social norms are formally or

informally institutionalized and "are transmitted culturally from generation to generation" (Kibreab 2008: 230). Among the multicultural societies of Eritrea, the nature and
extent of patriarchal norms and values vary from culture to culture. The patriarchal
nature of social interactions in Eritrea is also usually demonstrated in the communal
guidelines and codes of conduct of respective cultures. For example, communal laws
(which have been in use for many centuries) of the Tigrinya and Tigre clearly demonstrate gender roles and positions of their respective societies.

Based on the cultural norms that are formally or informally passed on from generation to generation, Eritrean cultural groups assign different roles to men and women
in which most groups consider the roles (social, cultural, or economic) played by
men as more highly valued. Men's roles in an Eritrean household are also usually considered as the most important factors for the survival, prosperity, and continuity of the
household and its members. Although it is generally understood that the roles of
women in a household's survival and continuity are not without value, the social
biases and perceptions usually put women in lower positions. Therefore, women are
usually considered as a necessary part of the household only in terms of reproduction
and their involvement in tasks of household management. Vital decision-making
powers of Eritrean households are usually vested in the hands of the men. Division
of labor and women's social or communal interactions within a society are also regulated by the patriarchal cultural values. Therefore, there are informally transmitted but
culturally accepted types of labor that women are expected to assume: household
duties such as cooking, cleaning, washing clothes; fetching water; and taking care of
children. Included among the types of labor usually reserved for men are cultivating
the land and allocation of resources in the household. Women are also expected to provide help related to work on the land and certain types of labor such as weeding are
reserved for women. As rightly stated by Kibreab, even the way the patriarchal communities in Eritrea welcome their newly born babies reflect their gender relations: In
the Tigrinya culture, women ululate (an expression of happiness with wordless lamentation) seven times to celebrate the birth of a boy, but only three times if the newly
born baby is a girl; a baby boy is christened on the fortieth day after his birth and a girl
on the eightieth day after her birth (Kibreab 2008: 233). Therefore, cultural gender
prejudices start from childhood and accompany individuals throughout their lives.

Males are usually raised with clear orientations toward fulfilling their future duties
as respected husbands and heads of their families with the responsibility of exercising
power in their households. On the other hand, females are raised to become "good
daughters, wives, and mothers," and usually occupy a subservient status in the distribution of power and decision-making processes within their households (see also
Gebremedhin 1996; Gebremedhin 2002; and Kibreab 2008). Men are trained from
their childhood with basic skills that are deemed important for their future positions
as husbands, heads of their families, and as responsible "good men" in their respective
communities; women, meanwhile, receive household training from their youth that
includes basic domestic skills such as cooking and cleaning as well as social norms
related to gender and age relations.

Among the informal cultural institutions that deprive women of equal legal status
with men are their rights related to marriage, divorce, and inheritance (see also Killion

Tigrinya woman in typical traditional dress.
(M. Tesfagiorgis)

1998: 436; Kibreab 2008). Traditional cultural and legal systems of almost all societies in Eritrea deny women's rights to choose their partners, and the equal right of all unmarried and divorced women to own property.

In addition to pervasive cultural rites that suppress women's physical and psychological freedom, practices such as genital mutilation (female circumcision) reinforce the deprivation of women's rights (Asefaw 2008: 50–122). Female circumcision is a widely practiced cultural ritual in the country. Some of the main regions with the accepted practice of female circumcision or genital mutilation are societies in sub-Saharan Africa. This practice involves the removal of partial or total parts of a woman's external genitalia (including the clitoris and labia) (For further details, see below, and Fana 2008 and NSEO and ORC Marco 2002: 197–216).

Women (also young girls) take greater household responsibilities and spend many hours a day working in the household instead of going to school. As we shall see in Chapter 6, another factor for the illiteracy and constraint of women in the Eritrean societies is early marriage. Traditionally, marriage among most Eritrean societies is arranged. Women at an early age (usually starting from ages 12 to 13) are required to respect and obey the decisions of their parents and relatives who organize arranged marriages. Once arranged, marriage usually takes place in a short period of time after the arrangement (usually between three months to one year). Once married, women carry out their tasks and responsibilities as mothers in their new households. Family marriage arrangements depend on many factors, including the amount and type of dowry and the type of relationships between the families of the groom and bride (Gebremedhin 1996; Kibreab 2008). An arranged and early marriage is still practiced, especially in rural Eritrea. Cultural practices such as the issue of virginity among the Tigrinya also have humiliating consequences for brides. Virginity of the woman is usually confirmed by traditionally acknowledged practitioners.

Brides among the Tigrinya are expected to be virgins, and so wedding rituals are well celebrated if the bride is virgin, and if not the bride is rejected. Being non-virgin has serious consequences for the bride and her family—she is rejected and sent back to her village of origin with a great sense of shame. In addition to the social exclusion she might encounter in her home village, the psychological scars she may sustain as a result of her canceled marriage can be fatal (Kibreab 2008: 235).

As well elaborated by Kibreab, the disadvantages of women who fall into arranged marriages are aggravated by customary practices of patrilocality—"marriage arrangements that reinforces men's dominance and women's subordination" (Kibreab 2008: 234). As part of the patrilocal practices brides are required to be relocated to the village of their husbands and in-laws'. Patrilocal practices may involve the relocation of brides to husbands' villages, sometimes far away from their villages of origin. Observing the disadvantages of patrilocal practices over women, Kibreab notes as follows:

> When a woman is married, she relinquishes her home, control over the products of her labor all her life long accumulated social capital in the form of social relations kinships, friendships, neighborhood, and all the social support systems and trust that gave meaning to social life. She becomes uprooted from her social and cultural anchorage to join her husband's kin group, whom she had most probably never seen or met before, in unfamiliar social and physical environment (Kibreab 2008: 234–235).

Throughout the colonial and postcolonial period (up to the era of liberation struggle—1961–1991), women retained marginal positions in Eritrean society. As we shall see below, the status and participation of women in various sociocultural activities started to change during the liberation struggle. Despite the process of emancipation during the liberation struggle, the status of women within Eritrean society has not fully changed. Yet gender roles as prescribed by cultural norms and values have eroded over time. The erosion of these cultural norms can be attributed to several factors, which include the women's struggle for emancipation over the last decades and the prevalent ecological changes in the rural economy in which the struggle for survival has become prevalent. Contemporary Eritrean societies are trapped by changing ecologies and fading sustainability. Amid such changes, the most important priority of each Eritrean household becomes one of survival. Community members are preoccupied with basic issues that concern their survival rather than the dictates of patriarchal social norms and behaviors. In the Eritrean environment where societies are increasingly affected by hunger, poverty, famine, and territorial instability, questions of survival are becoming paramount, and people are increasingly developing negligence toward patriarchal and patrilocal cultural constraints. However, this does not mean that

Woman in a typical dress for Saho women.
(K. Kuluberhan)

patriarchal cultural values and norms are no longer in practice. Gender disparity is still of concern in the country.

FEMALE CIRCUMCISION AND INFIBULATIONS

As mentioned, female circumcision (also called Female Genital Mutilation) is practiced by all ethnolinguistic groups in the country with the exception of the non-Moslem Kunamas (Gebremedhin 2002: 118). Although the Eritrean Liberation Front—People's Liberation Front (EPLF) and later the Eritrean government (Proclamation 158/2007) banned the practices of female circumcision and infibulations, it is still a prevalent practice all over the country. The main feature of this practice is the partial or complete excision of parts of male and female genital organs. It is a practice that is deeply rooted in the cultures of the country and is especially considered as a cultural practice with symbolic values of identity and medical benefits based on traditional beliefs. Circumcision usually takes place during the early years of infancy. In every community, there are traditional and communally acknowledged practitioners. Infibulation is also an extreme form of circumcision. It involves the repeated hemming of parts of a female's genital organs (especially the vagina). Infibulation is practiced even after giving birth. The main rationale behind these practices is to achieve maximum sexual satisfaction for men, and to limit women's natural joy of sex. As in most patriarchal societies, men have more rights than women, and practices such as infibulation are designed to offer them sexual pleasures during intercourse. Yet, societies justify acts of circumcision and infibulation in assorted ways. For some societies, these practices are cultural rites that victims have to undergo in their transitional phases of life. For some societies the practices are a way of attaining cultural purification for women. Others justify it on the basis of their assorted traditional beliefs related to health, production, and reproduction (for more details, see Asefaw 2008; Abdulkadir 2008; and Gebremedhin 2002).

Eritrea has one of the highest rates of women undergoing circumcision rites in the world. Over 70 percent of the women in the country are believed to be circumcised. The types of circumcision might vary greatly from one cultural group to another. Surgeries of circumcision may result in the removal of part of the clitoris, the removal of the entire clitoris, the excision of the clitoris and its subordinate parts (such as the inner lips—*labia minora*), or infibulations—the removal of several external parts of the genitalia (including the clitoris) and closure of a greater part of the vaginal opening (Gebremedhin 2002: 119).

WOMEN IN THE LIBERATION STRUGGLE

Although the institutional alienation of women continued, Eritrea did ratify one of the most progressive and democratic constitutions in Africa during the federal period (1952–1962). For example, the Eritrean federal constitution provided the right to vote only to men (Killion 1998: 436). Therefore, women's participation in public decision-making and state affairs was still limited by patriarchal cultural and state institutions. Yet, thanks to the proliferating nationalist movements, a number of women (especially those who got a chance for basic education during the British Military Administration [BMA] and the federal period) started to actively participate in various areas of society once denied to them. For example, women were noticeably involved in protests against Ethiopian domination—such as in the students' and workers' strikes (Killion 1998: 436–437). Women also increasingly started to get involved in clandestine political activities. Moreover, a number of women started to break cultural norms and join cultural groups in various activities such as the performing arts—music, dance, drama, and theater; activities that were culturally considered almost as taboo for women.

The Eritrean liberation struggle that was launched in 1961 did not achieve remarkable success in changing gender relations until the 1970s. It was during this time that the Eritrean Liberation Front (ELF), and later the Eritrean People's Liberation Front (EPLF), started to consider the possible vital roles of women in the liberation struggle. Although not great numbers of women joined the combatant forces of the ELF until the early 1970s, the Front continued to recognize women's participation in the liberation struggle. By 1975, the ELF managed to create the General Union of Eritrean Women (GUEW). Owing to its unstable political structure and the obstacles created within its organizational structure during its attempts for women's emancipation, the ELF did not achieve notable success in stimulating the substantive participation of women.

Considering the social stratification (among the poor, middle, and rich) of households in Eritrean society, the EPLF started to apply socialist principles of land redistribution and reforms in which the status of women was addressed. Acknowledging
the role of women in the liberation struggle, and pushed by its Maoist principles, the
EPLF granted equal rights to Eritrean women in possessing land as well as in guaran-
teeing them equal opportunity to participate in the Eritrean liberation struggle. The
women's emancipation policy also became one of EPLF's most important goals in
its intended "social transformation." EPLF's attitude about the equality between men
and women attracted the country's women, who started to join the liberation fighters
in great numbers. Within the liberation army, the EPLF also applied principles of
emancipation in which women were considered equal to men. Based on these principles, women participated in all activities of the EPLF, including as members of the
combatant forces. They fought alongside men in various battles and constituted a critical part of the liberation army. Male EPLF members also performed various types of
labor that would otherwise be culturally unacceptable—such as cooking and fetching
water. By the end of the liberation struggle (1991) women comprised approximately
35 to 40 percent of the EPLF army (which was estimated at the time to be 100,000).
The EPLF also launched a new literacy campaign for its armed members and also
among the civilian population in areas that were under its control or influence. This
action facilitated its acceptance among rural people, particularly among Eritrean
women. The EPLF, considering the vital roles of women in the liberation struggle, created a new women's organization—the National Union of Eritrean Women (NUEW)
in 1979.

THE NUEW

Part of the EPLF's struggle for social change was its effort to emancipate women and
assure equal status between men and women. While elevating women from their
inferior status in Eritrean societies became one of the EPLF's successful initiatives,
the liberation struggle also incorporated other social transformations in its agendas.
The struggle for women's emancipation involved a series of attempts to alter "both
specific traditional legal disabilities against women, and to change the even more pervasive cultural norms which required women to remain in the social position inferior
to men" (Killion 1998: 436). Similar to the workers' organization, NUEW emerged
as a remarkable mass organization within the EPLF. In addition to its valuable contribution to the struggle for women's emancipation, the NUEW achieved success in
stimulating and organizing women to take part in the war for liberation.

Starting in 1978, the EPLF openly challenged traditional patriarchal and suppressive cultural norms and launched campaigns in favor of women's emancipation. As
part of its campaigns, the EPLF abolished early marriage and introduced equal rights
to divorce (Killion 1998: 438). It also abolished suppressive patriarchal rites such as
sexual abuses against women. At the same time, the Front launched literacy campaigns in rural areas that focused on transforming the attitudes of the rural population
toward women's status in the society. The Front provided and implemented policies of
emancipation within its organizational structures that served as a model for the civilian

population (Killion 1998: 438). It was on the basis of these policies of emancipation that the NUEW was created, and this organization served as an important tool for the EPLF's struggle for social change within its domains, among Eritreans in the diaspora, and populations under the "enemy" domains and influences. Women cadres, usually members of the *kifli hizbi* (Department of Civil Affairs), were dispatched to the rural areas where they played leading roles in launching literacy campaigns and in educating rural populations about issues of gender relations and disparities within the country's society. Paradoxically, despite its increasing campaigns for emancipation, the EPLF's leadership did not represent a significant number of women at least until the end of 1980s. Despite the few numbers of women who were involved in the leadership of the EPLF, the number of women joining the Front continued to increase in great numbers throughout the 1980s.

WOMEN AFTER INDEPENDENCE

After the independence of the country, the EPLF and later the Provisional Government of Eritrea (PGE) implemented gender policies that were consistent with its principles during the liberation struggle. It recognized the rights of women and the equality between men and women. Its Macro Policy, the National Charter, and the new constitution (ratified in 1997) also demonstrated its determination to achieve complete equality between men and women (Government of Eritrea 1994: 35–37). The government also ratified new conventions, including the Convention on the Elimination of All Forms of Discrimination Against Women (Kibreab 2008: 240). Furthermore, the government attempted new reforms such as "equal pay for equal work, equal rights in the family, and provision of gender sensitive services in health care and education of children and adults" (Kibreab 2008: 239).

The government showed determination in attempts to ensure active participation of women in the process of national political development. Hence, 30 percent of the seats in the National assembly are reserved for women. As stated in the Macro Policy of 1994 (Article 13.5), the government set guidelines for assuring gender equality in the country. The Transitional Government of Eritrea's (TGE) gender policy as presented in the Macro Policy follows:

a. All efforts will continue to be undertaken to sensitize and enhance the awareness of the society on the decisive role of women for the socioeconomic, political, and cultural transformation of the country.

b. The equal rights of women will be upheld and all laws that subtract from this right will be changed.

c. Participation of women in education and economic activities and employment will be expanded.

d. Appropriate labor saving technologies will be introduced to reduce the drudgery of women in the household and other activities (water, fuel, wood, childcare, etc.)

e. Mother childcare services will be improved and expanded (Government of the State of Eritrea 1994:43–44).

In principle, the government abolished all discriminatory formal and informal laws against women. Yet, in practice, not all institutional and cultural gender disparities have been eliminated (see Kibreab 2008: 241–257). A great majority of Eritrean women still live under conditions of subordination. Although rapid change was observed among women members of the liberation army, such change has been slow among the civilian populations. Only a few women have been able to ascend to high-ranking political official positions—as ministers, heads of institutions, and members of national councils.

The NUEW, which claims to be an independent organization, has been active in implementing equal gender rights. Among its goals are achieving equal access of women to public services; literacy for women; protecting children and fighting against child abuse; and assisting women in accumulating various skills that lead to employment. Although not much documented evidence has been available during this study, the NUEW claims that it has achieved notable success in helping needy women in various ways—such as by creating small self-help businesses. Yet observers imply that NUEW's claims might not be so accurate, although it definitely has achieved successes to a limited degree. On this issue, Matsuoka and Sorenson note as follows:

> Although we do not have hard data to support our observation, by interviewing local NUEW officers and participants in the programs at their business sites, we found that most of these ventures in rural areas were barely making ends meet and required constant credit to maintain their business. Women explained that they could not afford to rent a store in a prime location, nor could they afford to purchase a variety of goods to compete with other stores or have them delivered. They seem to face a lack of resources in many aspects (network, knowledge, skills, financial) (Matsuoka and Sorenson n.d.: 11).

In practice, most of the cultural constraints such as early arranged marriages and other forms of gender abuses are still prevalent in the country. The multicultural societies of Eritrea still practice patriarchal and partilocal norms that continue to deprive women equal status. Although formal government initiatives were aimed at bringing about rapid social transformation, they have not been fully implemented. Demobilized women members of the EPLF, who once enjoyed equal rights in the liberation army, suffered from cultural negligence in the civilian environment where gender relations had changed very little. In some cases, people started to categorize between the civilian and *tegadelti* (ተጋዳላቲ) (fighters) cultures. This categorization usually put *tegadelti* or ex-*tegadelti* women at the peripheral positions where their acceptance in the multicultural environment started to erode during the post-independence years. Most women *tegadelti* found it difficult to live in the patriarchal civilian cultures. Therefore, most of them who were demobilized from the army remained in cities and towns, and not many of them returned to their home villages. Faced with low opportunities for employment and other cultural constraints, these women continue to suffer from cultural exclusion and economic hazards.

Contemporarily, women in rural households are highly disadvantaged because of continued conscription of young people in the Eritrean Defense Forces (EDF) and growing rural poverty. Reporting on the situation of women and rural poverty in Eritrea, the International Fund for Agricultural Development (IFAD) notes as follows:

> Armed conflicts and mandatory military service take many men [and also women] away from their villages and their families. As a result, a large number of rural households are headed by women, many of whom are widows. These women bear the dual burden of producing food and providing care for their families. Households headed by women are disadvantaged: they cultivate less land and have fewer assets, including livestock, than those headed by men. Women are particularly disadvantaged during the period when land is prepared for cultivation, because they are not allowed to operate oxen teams for ploughing. They have to rely on help from male relatives and neighbours, who may not be available to do the work at the proper time (IFAD, November 2006: 2).

A great majority of Eritreans live below the poverty line. In addition to traditional barriers affecting women's abilities to earn a living, rural households headed by women are especially disadvantaged. Women who have access to job opportunities in urban areas also suffer from a lack of equal employment opportunities or earn unequal wages and, therefore, remain prone to poverty. Legal equality, as stated in the constitution and other legal decrees of the country, has brought little change to the lives of rural women, who still live under a patriarchal and patrilocal environment. In spite of "state laws," rural women are communally neglected in various ways—they still do not have the right to own land (the most important asset in rural Eritrea) and underage marriage prevails. As stated earlier, social, political, and economic equality of genders is still an ongoing process. In the multicultural and patriarchal society of Eritrea, equality between men and women as prescribed by the laws of the nation is not adequate. Social transformation, which was one of the main objectives of the Eritrean liberation struggle, may not be achieved without providing societies with basic education and effective protection against gender abuses. Moreover, a convenient educational, cultural, and economic environment should be created in which women could develop their own initiatives of change. Therefore, prospects for change remain unclear. If cultural constraints, the compulsory national service, high competition for the control of natural resources, and the consequences of the Ethio-Eritrea conflict (1998–2000) continue to affect women, emancipation might be an even slower process of change.

MARRIAGE

Generally, marriage is one of Eritrea's most important social institutions and a well-celebrated cultural event among all ethnolinguistic. Customs related to marriage have similarities and differences among Eritrean cultural groups. For most ethnolinguistic groups, marriage is a strong bond or alliance not only for the marrying couples but also for their respective families and relatives. Cultural norms and attitudes influence marriage bonds among all ethnolinguistic groups in the country. Each ethnolinguistic group's customs and communal laws have usually defined rules about marriage.

In general, marriage is considered by Eritrean societies as a vital institution in establishing strong family, kinship, and clan alliances, and in strengthening frail relations as well as healing blood feuds.

As in many patriarchal and patrilocal societies, typical marriages are arranged by families and not by the marrying couples. Moreover, except the Kunama, all Eritrean ethnolinguistic groups are patrilineal; hence, residence after marriage is based on a patrilocal system. Hence, the bride is required to move and reside in the locality where her husband resides. Among the Kunama, kinship lineage is matrilineal; hence, the groom may be required to move and settle in the locality where his bride resides. In most ethnolinguistic groups of Eritrea (save perhaps the Kunama), women do not have the privilege to choose their husbands. Their families (under considerations of various aspects such as dowry, interest in establishing a relationship with the family of the groom-to-be, and more) decide whom their daughters shall marry. In addition, most rural women marry at an early age (ranging between 12 and 18 years old). The type of arrangements of marriage may differ from one ethnolinguistic group to another.

Among the determinant elements of arranged marriages are issues related to dowry, bride wealth, and types of wedding festivities. Dowry plays a significant role among all ethnolinguistic groups in the country (except among the Afar). Among the Afar, bride wealth plays a predominant role in the establishment of marriage bond. Wedding styles may differ among the Muslim communities in the country. As in many parts of the Islamic world, Eritrean Muslim men may marry up to three or four wives (depending on their capability to support the families). However, economic burden has compelled practices of polygamy to be considerably reduced among most Muslim communities of Eritrea. Among the Tigre ethnolinguistic group, it is usually unacceptable to remarry the same woman after divorce. Or else, she has to get married to another man and then again get divorced for her first husband to remarry her. All communities in the country strongly discourage divorce. Although many ethnolinguistic groups in Eritrea are Muslims, their marriage practices may not necessarily be strictly Islamic. Practices of Islamic and traditional customs are usually mixed among most social groups in the country. Although there are harmonious cultural and ethnolinguistic interactions among the ethnolinguistic groups in Eritrea, interreligious (especially Muslim-Christian) marriages are uncommon.

Among the Tigrinya ethnolinguistic group, the typical marriage is performed by a communally acknowledged *qal-kidan* (ቃል-ኪዳን)—covenant, and is performed in a standard religious way (for details, see Favali and Pateman 2003: 175–176). Marriage among the Tigrinya is monogamous and most communities strongly discourage divorce and any acts leading to divorce. The wedding is arranged after both families agree to establish marriage bonds. Before the actual wedding day, they arrange an occasion known as *hitse* (ሕጸ)—engagement. During engagement, both families decide on a specific day for the wedding. They also agree on other aspects related to the wedding— such as how many people should be expected for the *arki-hilifot* (ዓርኪ-ሕ ልፎት)— festivities on the eve of the wedding day; types and amounts of gifts the family of the bride should receive; types of ornaments and clothes for the bride; the church where the covenant should take place; types of music and musicians for the wedding; and the number and type of animals to be slaughtered for the wedding. During all the procedures and negotiations that take place in *hitse*, the bride's family has the upper hand in presenting its wishes for the wedding. The groom's family and their delegates in *hitse* are expected to interact in manners of civility—polite physical and language expressions.

Preparation for the wedding involves a number of activities that go on for weeks, sometimes for months. Activities include brewing *suwa* (ሱዋ)—a beer-like type of alcoholic drink and *mes* (ሜስ)—a type of local alcoholic drink comprising fermented honey; milling, storing, and processing of grains as well as sending written or verbal invitations to people. On the eve of the wedding day, *arki-hilifot* (but this also depends on the agreements between the families) takes place at the household of the bride's family. During *arki-hilifot*, music and dancing performances continue for most of the night. Covenant takes place in the morning of the actual wedding day. Around midday of the same day, *werado-mera'a* (ወራዶ-መርዓ)—the guests and relatives of the groom's family, come to the bride's household in a celebratory manner, after which the elders of the community (as selected under agreements by both families) declare the marriage bond as legitimate—on the bases of the rules and regulations stated in their communal laws. Once the legal procedures are over, attendants of the wedding are supplied with food and drink. They usually eat in groups of eight people (in a *me'adi* (መአዲ)).

Local drinks such as *suwa* and *mes* are also served. The food ceremony is followed by music and dancing. Once the ceremony is over, the bride (especially in rural areas) is put on the back of a horse and is taken to the groom's household where the honeymoon takes place (usually for about two weeks to one month).

Marriage involves a contract acknowledged by the community (also by the church), material, or cash types of *gezmi* (ገዝሚ)—dowry offered by the bride's family to the couple, to the groom's family, or both. The types of dowry can vary but generally there are two common forms of dowry:

newedenan negwalnan (ንወድናን ንጓልናን), literally meaning "to our son and daughter"; hence, to the couple. This type of dowry is directly given to the newly married couple. As stated above, the type of dowry can differ—money, live animals, ornaments, and more.

worqi metfi'e hawi (ወርቂ መጥፍእ ሓዊ), literally meaning "gold for eradicating fire", or also referred to as *farshem* (ፋርሸም) which literally does not mean anything. This type of dowry involves offering cash by the bride's family specifically designed to help the groom's family cover their expenses during the wedding. This type of dowry that is preferably called *farshem* also signifies to the type of dowry given by the bride's family to the groom's family, the couple and relatives of the groom.

The bride's family can give to the groom's family one or more of the above-mentioned types of dowry. The newly married couple may temporarily settle in the family household of the groom or the bride. But they are expected to establish their own residence and move as soon as they can manage to do so. In some rural areas, they are considered fully emancipated once they establish their own *tisha* (ጥሻ)—local type

---

INFANT CARE

Among all ethnolinguistic groups of Eritrea, mothers are usually responsible for taking full care of infants and young children. In addition to their household tasks, they take care of their babies and children. Eritrean children usually have the freedom to go out and play around their homes. There is almost no danger for children who go out of their homes and play whatever games in their neighborhoods. Mothers usually carry their infants on their backs using a leather mat called *mahzel* (ማሕዘል). Mahzel is designed by craftswomen, and includes various types of beads, which serve as decoration and source of entertainment for the infant.

---

of residence house. Once emancipated, they then have the right to own land and other community services. Usually, the newlyweds prefer to have their *tisha* (it may not be as good a residence as that of other established families, but it also depends on their ability to afford having a residence), because then they can have access to communal properties such as a plot of farming land.

Unlike the Tigrinya, the honeymoon among the Kunama can take place for over a year, during which time the married couple live in the household of the bride's family. During the time of the honeymoon, the groom has to demonstrate to the bride's family that he is capable and productive. He is expected to work hard in a number of the household's activities, such as farming and other social duties. Once the bride's family is satisfied by the performance of the *solaba kisa* (groom), the honeymoon period comes to an end and the couple may start establishing its own household afterward.

The family is the fundamental unit among all ethnolinguistic groups in the country. Yet, social life is usually regulated by extended families, kinship, or lineage groups. Each single family may have a number of children (five or above). All able children take part in the household's labor. Grandparents are also part of their children's households. They are considered as knowledgeable, wise, and respected members of the households. Therefore, all members of the extended family are expected to treat their grandparents with respect and dignity. As we have seen in Chapter 5, among most ethnolinguistic groups (perhaps with the exception of the Kunama) women play a leading role only in household management while men work outside the "home" area—such as plowing farming land, raising livestock, and more. Women are responsible for cooking food, taking care of children, constructing temporary huts (for example, among the Tigre ethnolinguistic group), fetching firewood and water, and more.

As we have seen, although a woman plays a predominant role in household management, by custom, the head of the family unit and the household at large, as well as the "source of bread," is the father. The mother (sometimes with the help of her unmarried daughters) is responsible for various types of labor within the household, including preparing food for the family. Both parents have the responsibility of teaching their children social and cultural norms. Traditionally, women are the main players during all phases of pregnancy and maternity. There are traditional practitioners (women) who help mothers during pregnancy and maternity.

SOME ASPECTS OF MARRIAGE AMONG THE KUNAMA ACCORDING TO ORAL SOURCES

Before marriage, Kunama boys generally go through a series of initiation rituals after which they are acknowledged as having reached the stage of manhood. In other words, Kunama boys undergo difficult events that are socially accepted as tests to their manhood. The types of initiation include a boy's going a far distance from his family where he is expected to protect the livestock of his parents without the company of any family members. In general, the stage of initiation is designed to be a difficult test of manhood for the person who is expected to go through the process. A person is considered as a "man" only after having gone through stages of initiation. Initiation rituals may take years depending on the rules set by community figures. Once the *massasa* (a ceremony for people who successfully accomplished initiation rituals) is celebrated, a person's right to marry and establish his own family is acknowledged.

On the other hand, the first menstrual cycle demonstrates a girl's womanhood. Once the womanhood of the girl is confirmed, her family builds a house for her next to their residence where she has the right to have company of her male or/and female friends. During this stage, she also has the right to fall in love and choose her partner.

Unlike other ethnolinguistic groups, Kunama boys have the right to choose their partners. Hence, in many cases, arranged marriage systems are only optional. Once a young man is sure that he has chosen his partner, the first person whom he shall inform is his mother. The mother is responsible for facilitating arrangements, such as informing the father, grandmothers, and other close members of the family. Similarly, the mother of the groom-to-be has priority in commenting about whether the chosen bride-to-be is the right one for her son. If the families agree to establish blood relationships through their daughter/son, then the mother of the groom-to-be offers some gifts to the bride in the presence of her parents, especially her mother. This signifies that the families have agreed to the wedding of the couple and that the engagement has officially been declared.

Yet, both families have to establish a harmonious relationship and work together in various economic activities such as farming at least until the day of the wedding. The bride-to-be also offers some help to her future parents-in-law and so does the groom-to-be for his future parents-in-law.

Both families work hard to accumulate enough grain and other products that will help them celebrate the wedding. Once both families agree that they have accumulated enough resources for the wedding, they then set a date for the ceremony. The actual wedding ceremony takes place at the house of the groom and bride. Though the bride's family may contribute their material and moral assistance to the family of the groom during the wedding event, mostly the groom's family has the considerable task of arranging the wedding. During the wedding day, the ceremony usually starts at the house of the bride's family, where attendants of the wedding drink, eat, and dance for many hours. Then, the bride is taken to the house of the groom's family where festivities continue for the next day. During the wedding, the most common local drink is *daga* (a local type of beer).

Unlike most other ethnolinguistic groups in Eritrea, the dowry is paid by the family of the groom. The type of dowry usually comprises livestock—often four or five cows, about 25 to 30 goats, and some animals to be slaughtered during the wedding. Some families may also offer cash as dowry, or they may combine cash and livestock.

Unlike in Tigrinya communities, a Kunama woman's virginity does not play so pivotal a role in establishing her own family. Yet, virginity is a sign of honest, and women to be married often go through phases of "virginity inspection" by elderly women members of the community. A virgin bride is often preferred, and she receives extra gifts such as a live cow, an ox, or anything valuable from the family members of the groom. However, virginity does not affect the relationship of the couple.

As stated earlier, the honeymoon often takes place at the house of the groom's family. It takes up to one year during which time the groom has to work hard to demonstrate that he is capable of producing enough for the new family he intends to establish. He has to demonstrate this to the family of the bride. Once the families believe that the couple can be emancipated, they let the couple have their own dwelling and farming fields.

SOME ASPECTS OF MARRIAGE AMONG THE HEDAREB ACCORDING TO ORAL SOURCES

As in most Muslim communities, marriage among the Hedareb is a social and moral bonding that creates strong and extended family relationships. Although wealth and beauty may play roles in marriage arrangements, the most important aspect of all is the blood relationship that is to be established with the new couple. Marriage is often arranged, and couples may not have had chances to see each other or to have spent time with each other before marriage.

All members of the families have to agree on the marriage relationship of the new couple. First, the father of the groom-to-be has to make sure that he announces the need for his son's marriage. Then, once all members of the single family unit as well as close relatives agree on that proposal, the initiative of asking the bride's family falls in the hands of the father of the groom-to-be. Accompanied by people who act as "mediators," the father meets the family of the bride-to-be and formally asks for their daughter in marriage. If both sides agree, then both families decide on a day when the engagement ceremony shall take place. Without asking the groom and bride, both families decide on the date and procedures of the ceremony for engagement. Depending on the agreement of the families, the engagement ceremony takes place at the house of the bride where animals (often one or more goats) are slaughtered for the ceremony, and people celebrate it in a colorful manner. After the engagement, the couple is expected not to meet or see each other until the wedding day. In case of an accidental meeting, they are not expected to exchange verbal or physical greetings; they simply need to avoid talking to each other or even looking at each other.

The dowry, which is more of a bride-price, is given to the bride's family by the groom's family. There are a number of systems of dowry among the Hedareb. One of the most common ones is known as *diwane* (in which the groom's father gives some amount of cash and about 12–14 goats). The other form of dowry is known as *derfin* (in which the family of the bride receives five or more goats as a gift from the groom's family). Another type of dowry is known as *bitahat* (in which seven or more goats or other live animals are given to the bride's family by the groom's family). The Hedareb practice seasonal migration along the northwestern parts of Eritrea and as far as to parts of eastern Sudan. Therefore, the type and amount of cash paid as dowry often comprises Sudanese pounds and in some cases Eritrean Nakfa.

Dowry is shared between the bride's family and their close relatives. Some amount of dowry is also used for building the dwelling (huts or tents) of the bride. Depending on the strength of their relationship, the bride's family may also offer some gifts to the groom's father.

REFERENCES

Abdulkadir, Asia (2008). *Die Perzeption von Gewalt im Geschlechterverhältnis in Eritrea: Eine Untersuchung über die Gewalterfahrung Weiblicher Rekrutinnen*. Hamburg: Dr. Kovaó Verlag.

Asefaw, Fana (2008). *Weibliche Gentalbeschneidung: Hintergründe, Gesundheitliche Folgen und Nachhaltige Prävention*. Frankfurt am Main: Ulrike Helmer Verlag.

Bereketeab, Redie (2000). *Eritrea. The Making of a Nation 1890–1991*. Uppsala: Uppsala University Press.

Cliffe, Lionel, and Davidson, Basil (1988). *The Long Struggle for Eritrea*. Trenton, NJ: Red Sea Press.

Conti Rossini, Carlo (1916). *Principi di diritto consuetudinario dell' Eritrea: (Manuali coloniali pubbl. a cura del Ministero delle colonie)*. Roma: Tipografia dell'Unione editrice.

Fahlbusch, Erwin (ed.) (2001). *Encyclopedia of Christianity* (vol. II). Leiden: Brill Academic Publishers.

Favali, L. and Pateman, Roy (2003). *Blood, Land, and Sex: Legal and Political Pluralism in Eritrea*. Bloomington: Indiana University Press.

Gebre-Medhin Jordan (1989). Peasants and Nationalism in Eritrea: *A Critique of Ethiopian Studies*. NJ: Red Sea Press.

Gebremedhin, Tesfa G. (1996). *Beyond Survival: The Economic Challenges of Agriculture & Development in Post-independent Eritrea*. Lawrenceville, NJ: Red Sea Press.

Gebremedhin, Tesfa G. (2002). *Women, Tradition and Development in Africa: The Eritrean Case*. Lawrenceville, NJ: Red Sea Press.

Ghaber, Michael (1993). *The Blin of Bogos*. Bagdad, Iraq: (publishers, n.a.).

Haddas Eritra newspaper, May 2007–December 2009.

Hepner, Tricia Redeker (2009). *Soldiers, Martyrs, Traitors and Exiles: Political Conflict in Eritrea and the Diaspora*. Ethnography of Political Violence Series. Philadelphia: University of Pennsylvania Press.

IFAD (November 2006). *Enabling the Rural Poor to Overcome Poverty in Eritrea*. Rome: International Fund for Agricultural Development (IFAD). November.

Kibreab, Gaim (1987). *Refugees and Development in Africa: The Case of Eritrea*. Trenton, NJ: Red Sea Press.

Kibreab, Gaim (2008). "Gender Relations in the Eritrean Society." In: Gebremedhin, Tesfa G. and Tesfagiorgis, Gebre H. (ed.). *Traditions of Eritrea: Linking the Past to the Future*. Trenton, NJ: Red Sea Press, pp. 229–262.

Kifle, Temesgen (2003). *Return to and Demand for Education in Eritrea and the Role of International Remittances*. Bremen: Shaker Verlag.

Killion, Tom (1998). *Historical Dictionary of Eritrea*. Lanham, MD: Scarecrow Press.

Longrigg, Stephen Hemsley (1944). *A Short History of Eritrea*. Oxford: Clarendon Press

Markham, Clements (1868). "Geographical Results of the Abyssinian Expedition." In: *Journal of Royal Geographical Society*. 38, pp. 12–49.

Matsuoka, Atsuko and Sorenson, John (n.d.). "After independence: Prospects for Women in Eritrea," unpublished paper (available at: http://www.ifaanet.org/Economicr/Matsuoka_Atsuko.pdf).

Matzke, Christine (2003). *En-gendering Theatre in Eritrea. The Roles and Representations of Women in the Performing Arts*. Unpublished Ph.D. Dissertation: University of Leeds.

Miran, Jonathan (2005). "A Historical Overview of Islam in Eritrea." In: *Die Welt des Islams* 45(2): 176–215.

Müller, Tanja (2004). *The Making of Elite Women: Revolution and Nation Building in Eritrea*. London: Brill Academic Publishers.

Munzinger, Werner (1883). *Ostafrikanisce Studien: Mit einer Karte von Nord-Abyssinien und den Ländern am Mareb, Barka und Anseba*. Bassel: Schaffhausen.

Murtaza, Niaz (1998). *The Pillage of Sustainablility in Eritrea, 1600s-1990s: Rural Communities and the Creeping Shadows of Hegemony*. Westport, CT: Greenwood Press.

Nadel, Siegfried Frederick (1944). *Races and Tribes of Eritrea*. Asmara: British Military Administration—Eritrea.

National Statistics and Evaluation Office (NSEO) [Eritrea] and ORC Macro. 2003. *Eritrea Demographic and Health Survey 2002*. Calverton, MD: National Statistics and Evaluation Office and ORC Macro.

Papstein, R. (1995). *Eritrea: Tourist Guide*. Lawrenceville, NJ: Red Sea Press.

Plowden, Walter C. (1868). *Travels in Abyssinia and the Galla Country: With an Account of a Mission to Ras Ali in 1848*. London: Longmans.

Pollera, Alberto (1935). *Le poplazioni indigine dell'Eritrea*. Bologna: Cappelli Ed.

Rassam, Hormuzd (1869). *Narrative of the British Mission to Theodore, King of Abyssinia: With Notices of the Countries Traversed from Massowah—Through the Soodân, the Amhâra, and Back to Annesley Bay, from Mágdala*. London: Murray.

Saleh Mohammed, Abdul Kader (1984). *Die Afar-Saho-Nomaden in Nordost-Afrika*. (Ph.D. Dissertation): University of Bayreuth.

Smith-Simonsen, Christine (1997). *". . . all'Ombra della Nostra Bandiera": A Study on Italian Educational Activities in Colonial Eritrea 1890–1941*. Faculty of Social Science, University of Tromse: Unpublished M.A. Thesis.

Tesfagiorgis G., Mussie (2007). *A Fading Nature: Aspects of Environmental History of Eritrea (1980–1991)*. Felsberg: Edition Eins Printing Press.

Tesfagiorgis, Abeba (1992). *A Painful Season and a Stubborn Hope: The Odyssey of an Eritrean Woman in Prison*. Trenton, NJ: Red Sea Press.

Trimingham, John Spencer (1949). *Islam in the Sudan*. London: Frank Cass & Co. Ltd.

Trimingham, John Spencer (1965). *Islam in Ethiopia*. London: Frank Cass & Co. Ltd.

Tronvoll, Kjetil (1998). *Mai Weini; A Highland Village in Eritrea: A Study of the People, Their Livelihood, and Land Tenure During Times of Turbulence*. Lawrenceville, NJ: Red Sea Press.

UNDESF—United Nations Department of Economic and Social Affairs, Population Division (2007). *World Population Prospects: The 2006 Revision*. Vol 1: Comprehensive Tables. United Nations Publication.

Wilson, Amrit (1991). *The Challenge Road: Women and the Eritrean Revolution*. Trenton, NJ: Red Sea Press.

Woldemikael, Tekle M. (2005). "Eritrea's Identity as a Cultural Crossroads." In: Spickard, Paul R. (ed.). *Race and Nation: Ethnic Systems in the Modern World*. New York: Routledge Publishers, pp. 337–354.

Wylde, Augustus. B. (1888). *'83 to '87 in the Soudan, with an account of Sir William Hewett's mission to King John of Abyssinia* (2 Vols.). New York: Negro Universities Press.

Yatana Entertainment—Tigrinya cultural movie, 2008.

Education

BRIEF HISTORICAL OVERVIEW OF EDUCATION IN ERITREA

Prior to the introduction of modern education in the Eritrean region, traditional institutions of learning (such as churches, monasteries, and mosques) served as centers for education. Modern education was introduced to Eritrea with missionaries in the nineteenth century. The introduction of Christianity and Islam during their initial phases of development was an important factor in the expansion of education throughout the region. At least since the first decades of Christianity's expansion in the Aksumite Empire (see Chapter 2), the church started to become the center for formal education, and therefore, the introduction of Christianity in the region became a turning point in the development of formal education (Taye 1991: 2). Among those cited as responsible for the introduction of Christianity to the region, *Abba Selama Kesatie Berhan* ("the enlightener"—Frumentius's traditional reference), became the first educator in the royal court (Taye 1991: 3; Kifle 2003). With the increase of Christianity's expansion, religious institutions (which became important centers of learning) also increased in number. Church education, among its many other objectives, focused on producing educated and knowledgeable clergy and providing religious and secular education deemed necessary for the function of the church. Although church teachings also contained dogmatic principles, their contribution to the expansion of formal education was commendable. The church produced leading educators (based in churches and monasteries) who in turn provided remarkable contributions to the enlightenment of the people at large. The church usually served as an important institution linking the state and the people. It worked hand-in-hand with the state so that the state and church provided both secular and religious training for the people. Also as an important societal institution, the church accumulated substantial power, and so the church-state cooperation was not always without disadvantages for societies.

As in many parts of Africa, European missionary activities in the nineteenth century facilitated the introduction of modern education in the region. As mentioned earlier, various groups of missionaries, including the Lazarists and the Sons of St. Francis (see section on religion), became active in both the expansion of religion and in efforts to provide basic education to small parts of society. To help foster both of these goals, early translations (such as translations of the Gospels) appeared in local languages as early as the nineteenth century. In the twentieth century, a number of Catholic and Evangelical (Swedish) mission schools were opened in several parts of the country. The expansion of evangelical missionary activities in Africa brought some Swedish missionaries to Eritrea, where they established missionary schools and a printing press in the 1860s.

Eritrea became an Italian colony in 1890. During the first phase of colonialism in Eritrea the colonial government attempted the establishment and expansion of schools in the colony, yet it relied on the pre-existing and newly established missionary schools. During the early years of colonialism, the colonial government established tenuous relations with the French missionaries, especially with the Lazarists and the Charity Sisters (Smith-Simonsen 1997: 74–75). In 1895, the colonial government expelled these missionaries from Eritrea. It then focused on expanding the Italian language and basic local education relevant to its administrative functions, and so, preferred Italian mission schools. The Swedish missionaries, whom the colonial regime allowed to stay in the territory, also established a number of elementary schools in many towns and villages, including Belesa, Tseazzega, Adi Ugri (Mendefera), Ginda'e, and Assab (Smith-Simonsen 1997: 75–76). Among other subjects, languages such as Tigrinya and Amharic, as well as basic mathematics, geography, and history were taught at the Swedish missionary schools (Smith-Simonsen 1997: 76).

Confronted by the need for schools for white settlers in the colony, the Italian colonial government continued to establish more schools in different parts of the territory. Although small sections of the local populations also got access to education in schools that were reserved for "the Africans," the curriculum of these schools was purposely structured to meet only colonial requirements. First, schools for the local population provided education only up to grade four. Second, in these four grades, students were taught only basic skills such as Italian language and history—the contents of which usually reflected the discriminatory policies of the colonial state. Local languages were also systematically discouraged. On the other hand, schools that were reserved for white settlers provided education comparable to that of the homeland. The missionary schools, which usually implemented their own curriculum, were also ordered to follow state policies—providing education aimed at the indoctrination and subordination of local people. Starting in 1909, all missionary schools in Eritrea were made to provide the same education as provided by the state (Taye 1991: 23–25). As mentioned by Taye, education throughout the colonial period focused on creating a subordinate and obedient society. The following statement taken from a colonial textbook reserved for local populations clearly illustrates the aims and expectations of the education to be delivered by the colonial state:

O; Children of Eritrea, love the three colors of the Italian flag, because it is your flag, salute it, raise your right hand to it and promise it with faithfulness and honor. Love ... your teachers who teach you to love Italy, the common mother, be always obedient children. When you enter class in the morning, child, salute your king. He is the supreme head of the nation, the first citizen of Italy (quoted in Taye 1991: 27).

In general, the Italian colonial state did not provide any substantial education, and Eritreans were purposely deprived of their right to education. Throughout the Italian colonial era education remained at an elementary level. Even the few sections of society that had access to these elementary schools did not acquire any progressive knowledge. Some Eritreans served as administrative assistants and in other subordinate positions. All professional and skilled labor was reserved for Europeans, and most Eritreans became only sources of cheap labor and for the colonial army.

The British occupation of Eritrea (1941–1952) ushered in a marked change in the sphere of education. The British Military Administration (BMA) established the Department of Education (1942), which facilitated the expansion of education across the territory. Many schools were built in many parts of the country, including a Teachers' Training Institute in Asmara. Racial segregation in schools was abolished and Eritrean students were admitted to public schools. BMA also increased the level of education, and great numbers of students attended school at elementary and middle levels. The educational syllabus was also more detailed and adapted to local needs and conditions (Taye 1991: 51). Local languages (especially Tigrinya and Arabic) were encouraged to be taught as part of the curriculum and to be used as the medium of instruction in some elementary schools. In general, BMA's educational policies in Eritrea made a significant contribution to the development of education in Eritrea. The expansion of education during the period also contributed to the rise of Eritrean political consciousness.

After the establishment of the federation between Eritrea and Ethiopia, the Eritrean government, as provided by the constitution, attempted to ensure educational rights to all citizens. The government established the Department of Education with an aim of educational expansion and improving the quality of education. Educational structure was divided into three levels: elementary/primary; middle; and secondary. In addition to these schools, a few vocational training centers were also established. Secondary school education, which was not available during either the Italian or British periods, was now well established. A few secondary schools were opened in Asmara. Generally, education during the federal period showed steady progress (Taye 1991: 71–93).

Although education was affected by political developments in the 1960s, Eritrean education continued to grow, and educational development was faster in Eritrea than any other part of the region. A number of secondary schools were opened in different parts of the country. The enrollment of students also continued to increase in all levels of education. Moreover, Asmara University was opened in 1964 and began offering some courses at the level of diploma. The university continued to grow and by the 1970s a number of departments and a few faculties were opened. However, the steady growth of education in Eritrea was adversely affected during the 1970s and 1980s. During this period, warfare and famine affected the majority of the Eritrean population. Atrocities of war as well as prolonged warfare affected all societies of Eritrea: schools were destroyed; expansion of schools interrupted; people massacred in masses; and people, including teachers, either joined the liberation fronts or left the country to live as refugees elsewhere.

The Eritrean People's Liberation Front (EPLF) also introduced new policies aimed at the expansion of education in the country. However, owing to the destructive warfare and lack of resources, EPLF's educational policies focused primarily at fighting illiteracy. Some of its underground schools, such as the Zero School in Sahel, provided basic education mostly to orphans, refugees, and children whose parents were in the liberation army. The school provided elementary and middle levels of education and at times accommodated over 2,500 children. It also launched a number of literacy campaigns for its armed members and also for civilian populations in areas under its control.

EDUCATION AFTER INDEPENDENCE

Like most sectors of the country, the war during the liberation struggle (1961–1991) devastated the educational system of Eritrea. Most aspects of education in the country were crippled by the consequences of war and negligent policies. The Ethiopian occupation period was accompanied by systematic discouragement of educational development in the country and the infrastructure of education remained severely undeveloped.

Although the EPLF attempted widespread educational awareness campaigns from its strongholds, its programs were limited only to literacy activities. Higher education remained at the mercy of the ravages of war and Ethiopia's marginal policies throughout the decades of warfare.

After independence, the EPLF and later the Transitional Government of Eritrea (TGE) attempted progressive educational programs. In principle, education at the elementary and junior levels (for ages ranging between 7 and 13) was made compulsory. Immediately after the Eritrean government was established, it declared its intention to establish a policy of progressive public education by expanding education and educational opportunities to all Eritreans in a free and equal way; extending schools for infants; and creating a secured atmosphere for the progressive educational development of every Eritrean. Moreover, the government also implemented policies of "elementary education in mother tongues," a policy to provide all societies the opportunity to develop basic educational skills.

The Eritrean pre-university educational levels are divided into four groups: kindergarten; elementary (first–fifth grades); junior (sixth–seventh grades); and secondary (eighth–twelfth (formerly eleventh) grades). The concentration on illiterate populations is usually in rural areas where farming and pastoralist communities live.

In theory, all students who complete secondary school can enroll at the university or other vocational training centers. In practice, however, most secondary-school students who fail to get a passing grade at the university level are kept in the compulsory national service. The distribution and capacity of vocational training centers have also been limited by a lack of resources and skilled personnel. Although ambitious attempts have been made to achieve a progressive system of education, educational development in Eritrea is still in its preliminary stages. In practice, state policies have not yet produced a serviceable community initiative for educational development. As we shall see below, this can be attributed to many factors, some of which are the lack of career prospects for "the educated"; compulsory national service, which affects the

---

LIST OF THE MAIN SECONDARY SCHOOLS IN ASMARA

1. Asmara Red Sea Secondary School
2. Asmara Hafeshawi Secondary School
3. Barka Secondary School
4. Denden Secondary School
5. Enda Mariam Secondary School
6. Halay Secondary School
7. Ibrahim Sultan Secondary School
8. Sema'etat Secondary School, Also known as Santa Anna Secondary School.

   Note that there are also secondary schools in all major towns of Eritrea (Assab, Massawa, Dekemhare, Segeneity, Adi Keyyih, Akordat, Barentu, Tesseney, Keren, Adi Kwala, and Mendefera).

---

performance of students at all levels; an inadequate educational infrastructure; and lack of skilled educational personnel.

Yet the government has built over 380 new schools in various parts of the country and attempted renovation programs for schools pre-existing independence. In the early years of independence (1991–1992), there were 381 elementary schools with 150,982 pupils; 65 middle (junior) schools with 27,917 students; and 25 secondary schools with 27,627 students (Kifle 2003: 50). Throughout the 1990s, the number of students enrolled in public schools showed a sharp increase—in 2000, by approximately 265 percent at elementary levels and over 174 percent at secondary school levels. By 2000, the number of schools across the country increased to 655 elementary schools (with 295,941 pupils); 131 middle schools (with 74,317 students); and 38 secondary schools (with 59,626 students) (Kifle 2003: 50). The number of teachers also increased dramatically. The curriculum at all levels of education was revised (in accordance to the needs of the society), and new textbooks were published in 1994, 1995, and 1996. To upgrade teachers' knowledge and skill, the government provided summer training courses for them. It should also be noted that the trend of educational development in Eritrea during the post-independence shows that the number of schools owned by the government sharply increased while the total number of schools owned privately decreased by 14 percent in 2000 (Kifle 2003: 50). In general, the government showed remarkable determination in expanding equitable distribution of education throughout the 1990s.

The government implemented a policy aimed at environmental protection and rehabilitation that was mandatory for all secondary school students. Starting in 1994, all secondary school students were sent to different parts of the country to help during summer campaigns known as *keremtawi ma'etot* (ክረምታዊ ማእቶት)—to plant new trees (afforestation); to work in terracing of deforested landscapes (or other activities

Elementary and junior school graduation and a missionary college. (M. Tesfagiorgis)

aimed at soil conservation); to construct new roads; to contribute in the struggle against rural illiteracy; and so on. The *keremtawi ma'etot* program was also designed to improve students' knowledge about cultural, societal, and economic aspects of Eritrean communities as well as to teach them the basic ethics of work. This program involved (at least until the outbreak of the war between Eritrea and Ethiopia in 1998) over 35,000 students each summer.

Since 1998, upper levels of education in the country have been affected by the consequences of war and a lack of pragmatic policies. There has been only one university in the country (the University of Asmara), and post-secondary education has been limited at undergraduate levels. Recently, the government initiated new programs in which the faculties of the university were established as separate colleges and placed in different areas. The main former faculties of the University of Asmara, which are now established as colleges, include: the College of Arts and Social Sciences (located in Adi Keyyih), the College of Agricultural Sciences (located in Hamelmalo, Keren); the College of Natural Sciences (located at Mendefera); the College of Business and Economics (located in Halhale); the College of Nursing and Health Sciences (located in Asmara); the College of Marine Biology (located in Massawa); and the Orotta School of Medicine (located in Asmara). Some of these colleges also want to provide graduate studies. How successful their programs will be is a matter to be seen in the future. Although not formally announced, observers indicate that the Eritrean Institute of Technology (a newly founded college located at May Nefhi) is believed to be a replacement for the University of Asmara (was recently closed). This college has become the biggest educational institution in the country. Observers also note this college has the potential to accommodate over 6,000 students a year. Among the major

Students of Asmara University during graduation, 2003. (S. Tesfagiorgis)

constraints facing this college, observers indicate, are the tight state control and lack of adequate educational materials—such as books. The closing down of the University of Asmara has caused a lot of dissatisfaction with the Eritrean population, which is because the government has been perceived as acting coercively after the short-lived uprising of students at the university in 2001. The government imprisoned members of the Student Union of the University of Asmara (such as Mr. Semere Kesete, a law graduate from the same university) in 2001. They were imprisoned after they demanded pay for their summer services and better treatment of Eritrean students by government authorities.

Owing to government policies of interference, Eritrea has lost a great part of its university graduates during the last few years. Frustrated by government actions, many students that were sent to various universities in South Africa, Europe, and North America to pursue further education have not returned to their home country. Most of them remain in the host countries as refugees or legal immigrants.

Observers also note that the Eritrean government closed down the University of Asmara for fear of potential uprisings by university students. The displacement of former faculties of the university and re-establishing them as independent colleges at various locations, they point out, is a strategy to "divide and rule" the intellectual section of the population. Moreover, most of the faculties that have been established as independent colleges in many parts of the country have no recognition whatsoever by international institutions of higher education.

It has been argued by many people that the quality of education in the newly established colleges has also been undergoing a significant decline. Colleges such as May Neffhi have operated under tight military control over the last few years. Again, frustrated by the increasing interference of the government in the affairs of the University of Asmara, many faculty members of various departments of the university have already left the country to work in universities in Europe, North America, and Africa. As a result, most Eritrean colleges are compelled to rely on university instructors from other countries—predominantly India.

Eritrean societies remain patriarchal and traditional in practice, which ensure that men have considerable privileges in acquiring access to education, employment, and economic resources. Today, it is estimated that over 60 percent of Eritrean women are illiterate, while the literacy rate for men is approximately 34 percent.

REFERENCES

Bereketeab, Redie (2000). *Eritrea. The Making of a Nation 1890–1991*. Uppsala: Uppsala University Press.

Chelati Dirar, Uoldelul (2003). "Church-State Relations in Colonial Eritrea: Missionaries and the Development of Colonial Strategies (1869–1911)." In: *Journal of Modern Italian Studies*, 8 (3), pp. 391–310.

Cliffe, Lionel and Davidson, Basil (1988). *The Long Struggle for Eritrea*. Trenton, NJ: Red Sea Press.

Conti Rossini, Carlo (1913). *Schizzo del dialetto saho dell'alta assaorta in Eritrea*. Rome: Accademia dei Lincei.

Conti Rossini, Carlo (1916). *Principi di diritto consuetudinario dell' Eritrea: (Manuali coloniali pubbl. a cura del Ministero delle colonie)*. Roma: Tipografia dell''Unione editrice.

EPLF (1994). *A National Charter for Eritrea: For a Democratic, Just and Prosperous Future*. Nacfa: N.A.

Favali, L. and Pateman, Roy (2003). *Blood, Land, and Sex: Legal and Political Pluralism in Eritrea*. Bloomington: Indiana University Press.

Gebremedhin, Tesfa G. (1996). *Beyond Survival: The Economic Challenges of Agriculture & Development in Post-independent Eritrea*. Lawrenceville, NJ: Red Sea Press.

Gebremedhin, Testa G. (2002). *Women, Tradition and Development in Africa: The Eritrean Case*. Lawrenceville, NJ: Red Sea Press.

Government of the State of Eritrea (1994). *Macro-Policy*. Asmara: Government Press.

IFAD (November 2006). *Enabling the Rural Poor to Overcome Poverty in Eritrea*. Rome: International Fund for Agricultural Development (IFAD). November.

Kibreab, Gaim (1987). *Refugees and Development in Africa: The Case of Eritrea*. Trenton, NJ: Red Sea Press.

Kibreab, Gaim (2008). "Gender Relations in the Eritrean Society." In: Gebremedhin, Tesfa G. and Tesfagiorgis, Gebre H. (ed.). *Traditions of Eritrea: Linking the Past to the Future*. Trenton NJ: Red Sea Press, pp. 229–262.

Kifle, Temesgen (2003). *Return to and Demand for Education in Eritrea and the Role of International Remittances*. Bremen: Shaker Verlag.

Killion, Tom (1998). *Historical dictionary of Eritrea*. Lanham, MD: Scarecrow Press.

Longrigg, Stephen Hemsley (1944). *A Short History of Eritrea*. Oxford: Clarendon Press

Matsuoka, Atsuko and Sorenson, John (n.d.). "After independence: Prospects for Women in Eritrea" unpublished paper. (available at: http://www.ifaanet.org/Economicr/Matsuoka _Atsuko.pdf).

Miran, Jonathan (2005). "A Historical Overview of Islam in Eritrea." In: *Die Welt des Islams* 45(2): 176–215.

Müller, Tanja (2004). *The Making of Elite Women: Revolution and Nation Building in Eritrea*. London: Brill Academic Publishers.

Murtaza, Niaz (1998). *The Pillage of Sustainablility in Eritrea, 1600s–1990s: Rural Communities and the Creeping Shadows of Hegemony*. Westport, CT: Greenwood Press.

National Statistics and Evaluation Office (NSEO) [Eritrea] and ORC Macro. 2003. *Eritrea Demographic and Health Survey 2002*. Calverton, Maryland: National Statistics and Evaluation Office and ORC Macro.

O'Mahoney, Kevin (1982). *"The Ebullient Phoenix". A History of the Vicariate of Abyssinia* (vol. I). Asmara: Ethiopian Studies Centre.

O'Mahoney, Kevin (1987). *"The Ebullient Phoenix". A History of the Vicariate of Abyssinia* (vol. II). Asmara: Ethiopian Studies Centre.

O'Mahoney, Kevin (1992). *"The Ebullient Phoenix". A History of the Vicariate of Abyssinia* (vol. III). Adis Ababa: United Press.

Papstein, R. (1995). *Eritrea: Tourist Guide*. Lawrenceville, NJ: Red Sea Press.

Pollera, Alberto (1935). *Le poplazioni indigene dell'Eritrea*. Bologna: Cappelli Ed.

Smith-Simonsen, Christine (1997). *". . . all'Ombra della Nostra Bandiera": A Study on Italian Educational Activities in Colonial Eritrea 1890–1941*. Faculty of Social Science: Unpublished M.A. Thesis: University of Tromse.

Taye, Adane (1991). *A Historical Survey of State Education in Eritrea*. Asmara: EMPDA.

Tesfagiorgis, Abeba (1992). *A Painful Season and a Stubborn Hope: The Odyssey of an Eritrean Woman in Prison*. Trenton, NJ: Red Sea Press.

Trimingham, John Spencer (1949). *Islam in the Sudan*. London: Frank Cass & Co. Ltd.

Trimingham, John Spencer (1965). *Islam in Ethiopia*. London: Frank Cass & Co. Ltd.

UNDESF—United Nations Department of Economic and Social Affairs, Population Division (2007). *World Population Prospects: The 2006 Revision,* Vol 1: Comprehensive Tables. United Nations Publication.

Wilson, Amrit (1991). *The Challenge Road: Women and the Eritrean Revolution*. Trenton, NJ: Red Sea Press.

Woldemikael, Tekle M. (2005). "Eritrea's Identity as a Cultural Crossroads." In: Spickard, Paul R. (ed.). *Race and Nation: Ethnic Systems in the Modern World*. New York: Routledge Publishers, pp. 337–354.

CHAPTER 6

Culture

As is generally understood, culture designates to a commonly reflected quality of a person's, group's, or society's set of manners, behaviors, values, norms, arts, and more. As in most countries of Africa, Eritrea enjoys cultural diversity. Despite its small geographical size, Eritrea is occupied by multicultural societies. There are nine recognized languages and cultures in the country. The factors influencing Eritrean cultures include climate, geography, religion, and language. The geographical divisions of the country fall into two major zones—the *kebesa* (ከበሳ) (highlands); and the *quolla* (ቆላ) (lowlands). Also, the geographical "perception roughly coincides with the social organization and religious affiliation of the people of these two regions" (Kifleyesus 1997: 433). The highlanders (majority Christians) are mostly sedentary farmers whose affiliation to the "land" is crucial to their lives. As we have seen in chapter five, the lowlands are mainly occupied by an array of linguistic groups whose respective cultures can greatly vary. The lowlanders (majority Moslems) are predominantly pastoral communities who are concerned with raising livestock and grazing lands. The respective linguistic and economic activities of the Eritrean communities also reflect aspects of their cultures. Eritrea's proximity to the Arabian Peninsula as well as its strategic location at the Red Sea, which links it to the African and Arabian territories, also plays a pivotal role in shaping the culture of its inhabitants. In general, the current cultural diversity of Eritrea is the result continuous movement of people within the territory, region, and across the Red Sea.

Today there are no obvious class or caste structures (meaning caste as we know it from societies such as that of India) among the societies of Eritrea, although

economic, linguistic, religious, and ethnolinguistic factors are among the most important factors of social stratification among the Eritrean population. In fact, social and
economic caste systems have played a dominant role among some ethnolinguistic
groups in the country. The societies of these groups were divided into various unequal
social classes. For example, among parts of the Tigre-speaking communities the society was divided between the nobles and vassals. The social status was also inherent
(Favali and Pateman 2003). Among the Tigrinya, economic occupation played the role
of social caste. The society was divided into various social classes such as blacksmiths, goldsmiths, clergy, the social elite, and the *ghebar*s (ጓር—the farmers or the
laymen). Among almost all ethnolinguistic groups of Eritrea women have occupied
the lowest social rank.

Cultural aspects of most ethnolinguistic groups in Eritrea are based on their respective principles of customs and norms. For example, cultural practices related to marriage and inheritance may vary from one ethnolinguistic group to another. Most
ethnolinguistic groups preserve their respective customary principles through written
or oral forms. As stated in the preceding chapter, the Tigrinya of the highlands of
Eritrea preserve their customary principles in coded laws—the communal laws. The
communal laws of the highland communities, which deal with the overall aspects of
livelihood of these people, were transferred from one generation to the next through
oral tradition. Since the twentieth century, some of these laws have also been preserved in written form. The communal laws, which are still being used by a majority
of the highland traditional communities, reflect the *Tigrinya culture*. Most other communities in Eritrea also have similar communal laws that serve as guidelines of their
respective livelihoods and resource management.

Save for the critiques related to the meaning and applicability of terms such as clan,
kinship, and lineage, most ethnolinguistic groups of Eritrea are divided into clans and
kinships. Clan, kinship, and religion play predominant roles in the solidification of
endogamous or exogamous relationships of the society. For example, among the Tigre
ethnolinguistic group there are a number of clans, and members of the group identify
themselves with their respective clans such as the Maria, the Mensae, Beni Amer,
and Habab. Similarly, the Saho ethnolinguistic group is divided into numerous clans
such as the Tora, Assaworta, Irob, Menifere, and Hazo. The Bilen ethnolinguistic
group is divided into the major clans of the Tawqe and Traqe.

Among the Tigrinya ethnolinguistic group the so-called *enda* (house or a family
based on sib or kinship established by members claiming common ancestry) played
a similar role as clan. It is worth noting that the social structure of Eritrean society
has also been characterized by significant changes in the recent past. The Eritrean liberation struggle (also referred to as the Eritrean Revolution), which involved all parts
of the society, embarked on creating a society based on principles of equality. Therefore, classes such as the noble classes and social elites as well as gender gaps have
been abolished during the process of the revolution. Despite the impact of the Eritrean
Revolution, a number of customary practices that are rooted in the culture of the society are still prevalent. For instance, marriage and inheritance practices (especially in
the rural areas) are still based on customary principles and norms. Moreover, gender

gaps and the patriarchal nature of social structure continue to be prevalent among all social groups of the country.

The family is the most fundamental social unit among all Eritrean ethnolinguistic groups. Owing to variables such as rapid urbanization and war, the Eritrean family structure is showing noticeable change in which extended family structure is being substituted by more concentrated members of nuclear units. Yet, this change is not as exaggerated as it might seem, and so the extended family structure is still prevalent throughout the country. The nuclear family forms the basic unit of the social organization. The extended kin systems of families also continue to play important roles in shaping internal and external relationships of cultural groups. Grownup (adult) children usually stay with their nuclear and extended family circles, at least until they get married and establish families of their own.

Languages

Eritrean languages are classified into three major linguistic families: the Semitic also known as Ethio-Semitic (a subfamily cluster in the Afro-Asiatic languages); Cushitic; and Nilotic. All these families are among the subfamilies of the Afro-Asiatic language family. No matter the complexity and difficulty of methodological approaches applied in linguistic classifications, the Eritrean ethnolinguistic groups fall largely into three linguistic groups: the Semitic (comprising of Tigrinya, Tigre, and Rashaida); the Cushitic (comprising of Saho, Bilen, Afar, and Hedareb); and the Nilotic or Nilo-Saharan (comprising Kunama and Nara).

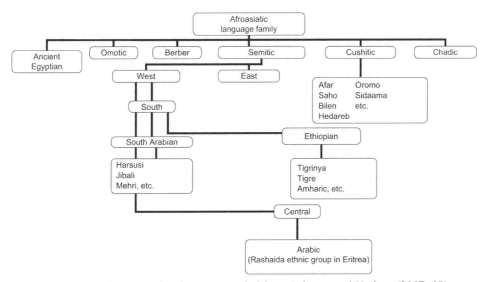

Major Afro-Asiatic language family tree compiled from Anbessa and Hudson (2007: 18)

BRIEF HISTORICAL OVERVIEW OF LANGUAGES IN ERITREA

The origin of most of these languages, especially Tigrinya and Tigre, is yet a cause of debate when it comes to comprehending the historical developments of local languages. It has been generally agreed that Tigrinya and Tigre in Eritrea (and some languages in Ethiopia, especially Amharic) allegedly descended from the major classical language of the region—Ge'ez. It is also generally believed that Ge'ez was introduced to the region by migrants (commonly known as the Habeshat) from south Arabia. However, this theory has been characterized by obscure evidence. Therefore, it is also most likely that the Eritrean region was the cradle of early Semitic and Cushitic languages. No matter its origins, Ge'ez had already become the major written and spoken language in the region in the first millennium B.C. The Ge'ez-speaking population in the region referred to themselves as *'ag'azyan* (ኣግኣዝያን). The Ge'ez language developed to a level of *lingua franca* for the greater part of the ancient civilizations in the Horn of Africa. Ge'ez also became the state language of the Aksumite Empire. After the fall of Aksum, Ge'ez is believed to have been greatly influenced by languages such as the Agau or Agew (Cushitic) languages for centuries to come. Yet, it remained a major written language for the entire region. It mainly served and still serves as a major liturgical language in all churches and monasteries. Thus, Ge'ez became and still is the classical language in liturgical contexts. Although Ge'ez has no mother-tongue speakers, the language is by no means dead. It still serves as a source of linguistic features, especially as a source of vocabulary for languages such as Tigrinya and Amharic. Tigre, another major Semitic language in Eritrea, is also akin to Ge'ez (particularly in syntactical and lexical linguistic features). A number of languages in the region still depend on the Ge'ez syllabi for their writing.

As we have seen in chapter 5, Italian colonial policies in Eritrea focused on introducing their own language and culture. Their educational policies intended to keep Eritreans in the periphery, while they also attempted to teach their language and history as part of the elementary literacy program. The colonial administration usually exploited linguistic and cultural diversity for its own political advantage. As in most parts of colonial Africa, whenever the opportunity arose they applied policies of "divide and rule," in which cultural and linguistic differences played pivotal roles. Their policies were designed to enhance colonial consolidation and not local development. The Italians attempted to provide elementary education in the Italian language. Moreover, the elementary education provided by the Italians was designed for the recruitment of people in preparation for low-level clerical jobs. A great part of the colonial education focused on producing obedient local workers to serve at the lowest levels of colonial administration. It barely made any attempt to recognize and encourage any of the local languages.

No matter the covert political agenda behind the Italian policy, it was only during the British occupation (1941–1952) that Tigrinya and Arabic were recognized as major working languages in the country. For the first time, these languages also started to become important political languages. Newspapers were published in Tigrinya (and also sections in Arabic), and Eritreans started to get involved in aspects of the political, economic, and social debates using their own languages. It is generally understood that the British encouraged the development of Tigrinya and Arabic mainly because these were the most widely spoken/understood languages and also both of these languages had a written tradition. The other Eritrean local languages did not have significant written traditions (see Hailemariam et al. 1999: 480).

During the federal period between Eritrea and Ethiopia (1952–1962), Tigrinya and Arabic continued as the official languages in Eritrea (at least until 1956 when Ethiopia started its encroachments against the federal agreements). However, English became the main medium of instruction in middle, secondary, and vocational training institutions (Negash 1999: 9–10). Although Italian had been the dominant language until the 1940s, it now became the medium of instruction only in specific schools owned by Italians.

Local languages were again suppressed after the federation between Eritrea and Ethiopia (1962–1991). Ethiopian occupation was characterized by the imposition of Amharic as the major language in Eritrea. In Ethiopia, Amharic was the official language although English was also the medium of instruction in middle and secondary schools as well as in institutions of higher education. Among other things, the introduction of Amharic as the official language instead of Tigrinya and Arabic irritated Eritreans who had already experienced many years of colonial suppression. The imperial government introduced various methods of language suppression—such as imposing censorship. Tigrinya, which was considered by the imperial government as the major rival for Amharic, was highly targeted—Amharic replaced Tigrinya in schools and governmental administration offices. To make matters worse, the Ethiopian state applied more extreme methods of suppression—"Tigrinya books that were considered "socially undesirable" or simply bad for "Ethiopia's unity" were burned, while political activists, and individual intellectuals and journalists who were opposed to the termination of the federation or were suspected of being critical or discontented with the intervention, were harassed and, in some cases, dismissed from civil service jobs as well" (Negash 1999: 10). Language suppression was only exacerbated during the *Dergue* rule. As in most other parts of the region, educational development was strictly limited during the *Dergue* period mainly because of the state of war and atrocious policies of suppression. Education and research conducted in Tigrinya or other local languages became almost impossible for most years under the *Dergue* rule.

During the liberation struggle, the Eritrean People's Liberation Front (EPLF) launched a massive campaign against illiteracy. It introduced successful literacy programs among the fighting ranks of the EPLF. Interestingly, although the EPLF published most of its literary works in Tigrinya and/or Arabic, at some point it also attempted to provide literacy as well as propaganda campaigns in other local languages through its trained cadres (commonly known as *jemahir*). Waves of literacy campaigns (aimed at the civilian population) were also launched in rural areas where the EPLF had full control or influence. Although its preceding organization (the Eritrean Liberation Front—ELF) adopted Arabic and Tigrinya as official languages, the EPLF did not specify any official language, a policy that continued after Eritrea's independence. This, according to the organization, signified that all Eritrean languages were treated equally. Yet, the EPLF's chief languages were Arabic and Tigrinya. For example, most of the EPLF's official publications, media, and other literary works were published in Tigrinya and/or Arabic (in some cases also in English) (Negash 1999: 58; Simeone-Senelle 2000).

BRIEF LANGUAGE PROFILE OF ERITREA

As stated, Eritrea is inhabited by a multicultural and multilingual society. It is worth noting that, in Eritrea, the name of all the ethnolinguistic groups and their respective languages (except in the case of the Rashaida who speak Arabic, and perhaps also the Hedareb who speak a variety of the Beja language) is the same or eponymous. To avoid confusion regarding the reference names, Tigrinya speakers usually use the term *biher* ("nation"/ethnolinguistic—ብሄር) as a prefix to signify an explicit reference to an ethnolinguistic group and not the respective language. For example, they say *bihere*-Tigrinya (the Tigrinya nation), *bihere*-Tigre (the Tigre nation), *bihere*-Saho (the Saho nation), and so on. The biggest ethnolinguistic group is Tigrinya (ca. 50%) followed by the Tigre ethnolinguistic group (ca. 31.4%) (Ghirmai 1999: 49). The other seven ethnolinguistic groups are distributed throughout (mostly the lowlands) of the country in smaller clusters. These are: the Saho (ca. 5%), Afar (ca. 5%), Hedareb (ca. 2.5%), Bilen (ca. 2%), Kunama (ca. 2%), Nara (ca. 1.5%), and Rashaida (ca. 0.5%).

Because of their mode of economy, common history, as well as their prevalent social, political, and cultural interactions, most ethnolinguistic groups in Eritrea are at least bilingual. Most members of ethnicities such as the Tigre, Saho, and Bilen also manage to speak Tigrinya as their second or third language. Moreover, Eritrea's long war of liberation, which involved a great majority of the country's population, contributed to multilingualism and cultural interaction among various groups in the country. Therefore, most people who were involved in the struggle in one way or another speak or understand Tigrinya (and many also speak Arabic). Arabic is the major language of the Holy book Quran, and most Muslim communities in Eritrea learn the language during basic Quran teachings in mosques and other Muslim community centers. Arabic schools, which provide basic literacy education, are also fairly distributed in areas predominantly inhabited by Muslim communities. Arabic has also served as the major written language in Islamic *shari'a* courts. Therefore, most Muslim communities in Eritrea have a fluent or rudimentary knowledge of Arabic.

As stated earlier, most Eritrean communities speak one or more languages of other ethnolinguistic groups in their surrounding areas. For example, most members of the Saho and Afar can communicate well with each other and they are also proficient in Arabic and/or Tigrinya (Negash 1999: 51). Similarly, the Bilen can communicate well in Tigrinya and/or Tigre. The Tigrinya-speaking groups who were involved in the liberation struggle may add other languages such as Tigre and/or Arabic. Also, a great majority of the Nara and the Hedareb ethnolinguistic groups speak Tigre as their first or second language. However, it should be noted that most of the local languages are used only for oral communication. The most frequently used written languages in the country are Tigrinya, Arabic, English, and to a limited extent, Italian. Although Tigrinya and Arabic are common written languages, English and Italian are used mostly in schools, and most speakers (apart from those who had advanced to an upper educational level) have rudimentary knowledge of these languages (see also Negash 1999: 51–52). Brief profiles of most languages spoken in Eritrea follow. But it is worth noting that we do not have detailed statistical or ethnographical information regarding most linguistic groups in the country. There is almost no precise official data regarding the number of speakers of each language and what is presented below is only an estimation made at various times. Hence, the data presented below are not exhaustive.

TIGRINYA

Tigrinya is the language of about half of Eritrea's population (approximately 2.1–2.5 million people) in the Eritrean plateau. It is also the third major language spoken in the northern provinces of Ethiopia (Tigray). In general, Tigrinya is spoken by over 5 million inhabitants in northern Ethiopia. All in all, Tigrinya is the chief language for about 6 million people in the Horn (particularly in Ethiopia and Eritrea), and over 3 million worldwide. Most Tigrinya-speaking communities are settled sedentary farmers or agro-pastoralists who occupy the highland plateaus of the country (mainly in the Zoba Ma'ekel and Zoba Debub provinces).

Tigrinya has a written tradition that can be traced back to the thirteenth century. The early written tradition of Tigrinya was concerned with the documentation of communal laws (for example, the case of the *sera'at* Logo-Sarda—ሰር ዓት ሎጐ–ሳርዳ). However, written tradition of the language was more elaborated and expanded through the European missionary activities in the nineteenth century. The first printing press, which also attempted publishing in Tigrinya, was established by the Lazarist Catholic missionaries in Massawa in 1863 (Tewolde Yohannes 2002: 15). European missionaries published a number of materials in Tigrinya in the nineteenth century.

TABLE 6.1.   Tigrinya Alphabet or the Fidel

	ግዕዝ	ካዕብ	ሳልስ	ራብዕ	ሓምስ	ሳድስ	ሳብዕ
	ä̱	u̱	i̱	a̱	e̱	ə̱	o̱
	ä	u	i	a	e	ə	o
IPA							
h	ሀ *hä*	ሁ *hu*	ሂ *hi*	ሃ *ha*	ሄ *he*	ህ *hə*	ሆ *ho*
l	ለ *lä*	ሉ *lu*	ሊ *li*	ላ *la*	ሌ *le*	ል *lə*	ሎ *lo*
ħ	ሐ *ħä*	ሑ *ħu*	ሒ *ħi*	ሓ *ħa*	ሔ *ħe*	ሕ *ħə*	ሖ *ħo*
m	መ *mä*	ሙ *mu*	ሚ *mi*	ማ *ma*	ሜ *me*	ም *mə*	ሞ *mo*
s	ሠ *sä*	ሡ *su*	ሢ *si*	ሣ *sa*	ሤ *se*	ሥ *sə*	ሦ *so*
r	ረ *rä*	ሩ *ru*	ሪ *ri*	ራ *ra*	ሬ *re*	ር *rə*	ሮ *ro*
s	ሰ *sä*	ሱ *su*	ሲ *si*	ሳ *sa*	ሴ *se*	ስ *sə*	ሶ *so*
ʃ	ሸ *shä*	ሹ *shu*	ሺ *shi*	ሻ *sha*	ሼ *she*	ሽ *shə*	ሾ *sho*
k'	ቀ *qä*	ቁ *qu*	ቂ *qi*	ቃ *qa*	ቄ *qe*	ቅ *qə*	ቆ *qo*

(*Continues*)

Table 6.1. Tigrinya Alphabet or the Fidel (*Continues*)

	ግዕዝ	ካዕብ	ሳልስ	ራብዕ	ሓምስ	ሳድስ	ሳብዕ
x'	ቔ x'ä	ቑ x'u	ቒ x'i	ቓ x'a	ቔ x'e	ቕ x'ə	ቖ x'o
b	በ bä	ቡ bu	ቢ bi	ባ ba	ቤ be	ብ bə	ቦ bo
t	ተ tä	ቱ tu	ቲ ti	ታ ta	ቴ te	ት tə	ቶ to
č	ቸ chä	ቹ chu	ቺ chi	ቻ cha	ቼ che	ች chə	ቾ cho
h	ሐ *hä*	ሑ *hu*	ሒ *hi*	ሓ *ha*	ሔ *he*	ሕ *hə*	ሖ *ho*
n	ነ nä	ኑ nu	ኒ ni	ና na	ኔ ne	ን nə	ኖ no
ɲ	ኘ ñä	ኙ ñu	ኚ ñi	ኛ ña	ኜ ñe	ኝ ñə	ኞ ño
ʔ	አ ʾä	ኡ ʾu	ኢ ʾi	ኣ ʾa	ኤ ʾe	እ ʾə	ኦ ʾo
k	ከ kä	ኩ ku	ኪ ki	ካ ka	ኬ ke	ክ kə	ኮ ko
x	ኸ xä	ኹ xu	ኺ xi	ኻ xa	ኼ xe	ኽ xə	ኾ xo
w	ወ wä	ዉ wu	ዊ wi	ዋ wa	ዌ we	ው wə	ዎ wo
ʕ	ዐ ʿä	ዑ ʿu	ዒ ʿi	ዓ ʿa	ዔ ʿe	ዕ ʿə	ዖ ʿo
z	ዘ zä	ዙ zu	ዚ zi	ዛ za	ዜ ze	ዝ zə	ዞ zo
ž	ዠ žä	ዡ žu	ዢ ži	ዣ ža	ዤ že	ዥ žə	ዦ žo
y	የ yä	ዩ yu	ዪ yi	ያ ya	ዬ ye	ይ yə	ዮ yo
d	ደ dä	ዱ du	ዲ di	ዳ da	ዴ de	ድ də	ዶ do
ǧ	ጀ ǧä	ጁ ǧu	ጂ ǧi	ጃ ǧa	ጄ ǧe	ጅ ǧə	ጆ ǧo
g	ገ gä	ጉ gu	ጊ gi	ጋ ga	ጌ ge	ግ gə	ጎ go
t'	ጠ t'ä	ጡ t'u	ጢ t'i	ጣ t'a	ጤ t'e	ጥ t'ə	ጦ t'o
č'	ጨ č'ä	ጩ č'u	ጪ č'i	ጫ č'a	ጬ č'e	ጭ č'ə	ጮ č'o
p'	ጰ p'ä	ጱ p'u	ጲ p'i	ጳ p'a	ጴ p'e	ጵ p'ə	ጶ p'o
s'	ጸ s'ä	ጹ s'u	ጺ s'i	ጻ s'a	ጼ s'e	ጽ s'ə	ጾ s'o
s'	ፀ *s'ä*	ፁ *s'u*	ፂ *s'i*	ፃ s'a	ፄ s'e	ፅ *s'ə*	ፆ s'o
f	ፈ fä	ፉ fu	ፊ fi	ፋ fa	ፌ fe	ፍ fə	ፎ fo
p	ፐ pä	ፑ pu	ፒ pi	ፓ pa	ፔ pe	ፕ pə	ፖ po
v	ቨ vä	ቩ vu	ቪ vi	ቫ va	ቬ ve	ቭ və	ቮ vo
kʷ	ኰ kʷä	ኵ kʷu		ኳ kʷa	ኴ kʷe	ኵ kʷə	
xʷ	ዀ xʷä	ዅ xʷu		ዃ xʷa	ዄ xʷe	ዅ xʷə	
qʷ	ቈ qʷä	ቍ qʷu		ቋ qʷa	ቌ qʷe	ቍ qʷə	
xʷ'	ቘ xʷä	ቝ xʷu		ቛ xʷa	ቜ xʷe	ቝ xʷə	
gʷ	ጐ gʷä	ጕ gʷu		ጓ gʷa	ጔ gʷe	ጕ gʷə	
hʷ	ኈ *hʷä*	ኍ *hʷu*		ኋ *hʷa*	ኌ *hʷe*	ኍ *hʷə*	
	ሏ lʷa	ሟ mʷa	ሯ rʷa	ሷ sʷa	ሿ šʷa	ቧ bʷa	
	ቷ tʷa	ቿ čʷa	ኗ nʷa	ኟ ñʷa	ኧ ʾəʷa	ዟ zʷa	
	ዷ dʷa	ጧ t'ʷa	ጯ č'ʷa	ጿ s'ʷa	ጷ s'ʷa	ፏ fʷa	

Note that the underlined alphabets are no longer in regular use by the Eritrean Tigrinya.

Although all Tigrinya-speaking communities can communicate without much difficulty, Tigrinya comprises various dialects with remarkable grammatical, phonetic, and
lexical differences. Dialectical differences can be identified in various Tigrinya-
speaking areas within Eritrea. There are also striking dialectical differences between
Tigrinya dialects spoken in northern Ethiopia and the Eritrean plateau. However, there
is no acknowledged standard Tigrinya dialect. The varieties of Tigrinya spoken in different areas of the whole region have also influenced other languages such as the
Cushitic languages. Tigrinya is heavily influenced by other languages, mainly by
Cushitic languages (for example, the Agau languages), especially on the syntax level.
Its morphological and lexical features are almost purely Semitic. On the lexical level,
Tigrinya has inherited remarkably lexical features of Ge'ez. Since the Italian colonial
period in Eritrea (1890–1941) and the British Military Administration (1941–1952),
Tigrinya has borrowed a significant number of Italian and English words.

As the Tigrinya writing system is different from Latin, it has been difficult to apply
the guiding rules of the International Phonetic Alphabet (IPA). Hence, as with some
other Semitic languages (such as Amharic), there is no standard Tigrinya transilitera-
tion system.

TIGRE

Tigre is the second major language in Eritrea. Tigre shares some commonalities with
Ge'ez and Tigrinya. It is a written language—using the Ge'ez syllabi. A number
of works related to Tigre religion and culture were also published by European
missionaries during the second half of the nineteenth century. It is spoken in large
parts of the Eritrean lowlands such as in the Semhar and Shi'eb plains, the Anseba
foothills, and the Barka lowlands as well as in the northern highlands. Tigre is
also spoken by small Beja (Beni Amer) communities who are distributed in
small groups in the eastern Sudan. Most of the Tigre-speaking communities are
pastoralists who roam around the western lowlands, northern highlands, and
eastern lowlands of the country. Although with significant dialectical differences, most
Tigre communities who live in various parts of Eritrea can communicate without
remarkable difficulties. Some of the Tigre dialects are: the western lowland and
northern highland Tigre dialects (mainly spoken by the Maria and Bet Asghede clans);
the Senhit and Anseba highlands (spoken by the Mensae triebes); and the eastern
lowlands (spoken by the Bet Abrehe and Bet Shakan clans). Tigre is closely related
to Tigrinya (structurally and grammatically) but with considerable influences from
Ge'ez and Arabic.

SAHO

Saho is one of the minority Cushitic languages in Eritrea. Its speakers inhabit the
southeastern escarpments as far as the southern Semhar Plains in the east and Adi Keyyih in the west. Saho-speaking communities are sometimes known by their Tigrinya
neighbors as *Shaho* (ሻሙ) or *Shihay* (ሻዮይ—singular)/*'Ashihu* (አሽሙ—plural). They
are mostly pastoralists who practice seasonal migration between the escarpments/

plateau and the eastern lowlands (as far as the Gulf of Zula). Small clusters of Saho-speaking communities are also distributed in various parts of the southern plateau and as far as parts of northern Tigray in Ethiopia (in the territories inhabited by the Irob clans). There are a number of Saho dialects, including the Assawerta, Minifere, Irob, and Hadu. "Depending on where they live, they are in contact with the Tigrinya, Tigre and Afar. They also speak Arabic which they use the vehicular variety" (Simeone-Senelle 2000).

AFAR

Afar is spoken by the Afar ethnolinguistic group in Eritrea, whose territory is commonly known as Dankalia. The Afar ethnolinguistic group and its language are known in Arabic as Danakil. Danakil also refers to the wide geographical area that extends from the south of Zula to as far as the borders with Djibouti and Ethiopia (along the Great East African Valley). Afar language is also spoken in Ethiopia and Djibouti. The overall Afar-speaking population in the Horn of Africa is estimated at 1,660,000—of these, about 445,000 live in Eritrea (Minahan 2002: 41). Afar and Saho languages share some commonalities not only because they belong to the same language family (Cushitic), but also because they share closely related linguistic features, especially vocabulary. The Afar depend on a subsistence pastoral economy for a living.

HEDAREB

Hedareb is another minority language (Cushitic) spoken by the Bejas in the northwestern parts of Eritrea and in some parts of eastern Sudan. The Hedareb language is also known by the speakers as *bedawye* or *te-bedawye*. In Sudan, this language is mostly known as Beja—an Arabic name for the language. There are some varieties of dialects such as the Halenga and Beni Amer. It is worth noting that considerable sections of the Hedareb have almost lost Beja as their mother tongue, rather many of them speak Tigre at a mother-tongue level. "The situation prevailing among the Beja seems to be that of bilingualism or multilingualism (Beja-tiger-Arabic)" (Simeone-Senelle 2000).

BILEN

As mentioned in the preceding section, the Bilen is a language spoken by the Bilen ethnolinguistic group, who refer to themselves as "Blin." The language is spoken almost exclusively in central Eritrea (in the territory that was commonly known as Bogos—along the Anseba in Senhit [including in Keren and its vicinities]). Its speakers are estimated to be ca. 90,000–100,000 (Lamberti 2003: 585). Bilen language belongs to a sub-Cushitic linguistic family known as Agau/Agaw. Bilen language is characterized by some dialectical variations mainly related to its lexicon and morpho-syntax (Lamberti 2003: 585). Cities and towns such as Keren are inhabited by multilingual groups. Some of the main languages spoken in these towns are Tigre, Bilen, Tigrinya, as well as Arabic.

KUNAMA

Kunama is one of the two Nilotic languages spoken in Eritrea. The language is spoken in particular territories, especially in the Gash-Barka area, with Barentu being the main town in the Kunama territory. Few Kunama-speaking groups are found in northern Ethiopia (in areas such as Tekezze and Setit). Some of the Kunama dialects include Aymasa, Barka, Bitama, Odasa, Setit, and Tika (Bender 1976: 10).

NARA

The Nara people are a minority group who inhabit territories north of the Kunama. Nara is the second Nilotic language spoken in Eritrea. Generally, although Nara and Kunama belong to the same linguistic family (unlike other languages such as Tigrinya and Tigre or Saho and Afar), there are only slight similarities between the two languages: usually related to phonology and syntax. The Nara language has been under continuous influence of Tigre. Therefore, most Nara-speaking communities also speak Tigre as their first or second language. Nara has mostly been a spoken language and there has not been an extensive Nara written tradition. Since the 1990s, attempts have been made by the Ministry of Education to strengthen the Nara written and spoken language.

ARABIC

The Rashaida communities (comprising about 0.5% of the Eritrean population) are the only mother-tongue speakers of Arabic in Eritrea. The Rashaida are nomadic pastoralists and traders who inhabit coastal areas north of Massawa. Yet, as Ge'ez is the language of the Eritrean churches, so also is Arabic in the Eritrean mosques. Arabic is considered to be the language of the Quran, and most Muslim communities who attend literacy education and Quran studies have to learn Arabic. Therefore, significant sections of the Eritrean population (especially the Muslim population) do speak and/or understand the Arabic language.

MULTILINGUALISM AND STATE LANGUAGE POLICIES

Concerns and debates related to multilingualism and state policies vis-à-vis nation building have been paramount in most African countries. These themes are also highly complex, especially where a territory encompasses remarkable geographical, cultural, and religious differences. The imposition of colonialism in Africa was characterized by the "scramble" for the continent among various European colonial powers. The scramble for Africa did not consider ethnolinguistic, religious, linguistic, cultural, and other factors of the local populations. Thus, colonialism resulted in the vertical division of many African ethnolinguistic groups. For example, the new colonial borders divided the Afar-speaking groups into three countries (Eritrea, Djibouti, and Ethiopia); the border also divided the Tigrinya-speaking and Saho-speaking populations between

Eritrea and Ethiopia. Similarly, most African ethno-cultural groups fell under the territorial and political divisions imposed by colonialism. Somalia is the only exception where there is a monolingual and ethnically uniform population (Habtemariam et al. 1999: 476).

After independence, most African countries inherited heterogeneous societies—with distinctive cultures and languages. One of the challenges most of these countries faced from the early years of their independence was how and which language to select as a national or official language. Although a number of African countries adopted the language of their former colonial powers (French or English) as an official language, many others struggled to adopt local language(s) as their national language.

After independence, Eritrea was also not relieved of the "official language" dilemma that most African countries had faced. Among other prevalent issues of debate during the drafting of the Eritrean constitution, intensive discussions took place regarding language policy (Negash 1999: 56–57). The debates mainly focused on pivotal questions such as: Should Eritrea have an official language? If yes, which language(s)? Why these language(s)? Could the state function better without having any "official" language(s) but by applying a *free languages policy*? (Negash 1999: 56–61). Language policy issues in post-independent Eritrea have been significantly debated. As stated in chapter two, Eritrea has been characterized by over a century's long history of colonialism and conflict. In addition to factors attached to language and cultural diversity, Eritrea's long history of colonialism and war has intensified the complexity of post-independence language policies. For the Eritrean government, education was considered an important instrument for sociocultural transformation. To achieve sociocultural change, new language policies were introduced.

Interestingly, unlike most African nations that either adopted the language of their former colonial power or applied the "national language policy," Eritrea chose to experiment somewhat by offering equal status to all languages in the country. In fact, "what distinguishes Eritrea, however, is not this multilingual and multicultural situation, that many countries, particularly in Africa possess, but rather the policy in defense and illustration of national cultures and languages led by the State, which is not regular, if not, it is exceptional" (Simeone-Senelle 2000 [translated from French]). One of the main aspects of educational policies was the introduction of "mother-tongue" education for elementary level pupils. Although the Eritrean model may differ in some ways, similar policies were already implemented in some African states such as Ghana and South Africa.

By implementing the "mother-tongue" educational system, the government intended to create a platform of progressive cultural change in which younger generations evolve with a common Eritrean identity based on communal and local knowledge as well as pride. In other words (as also demonstrated in various governmental plans), the main aim of mother-tongue education was to achieve national unity in a culturally diverse society. It justified its policies by arguing that mother-tongue education for young children fosters better learning enthusiasm for the children, while at the same time it helps to maintain cultural traditions of respective ethnolinguistic groups. However, the government also introduced Tigrinya, Arabic (the working languages of the state), and English as common and compulsory language courses to be taught in elementary schools. While Tigrinya and Arabic remained as compulsory subjects for elementary school pupils, English was chosen to be the medium of instruction for middle and above levels of education (see also Woldemikael 2003).

The main objective behind Eritrea's free language policy is also to deflect language discrimination among the vernaculars and offer a free platform for the development of all languages in the country. As we have seen earlier, to achieve this, the state introduced an educational policy in which the elementary level of education is taught in the mother tongue language. To achieve the intended goals in education, the development of languages, and cultural change, the Eritrean government started an ambitious program that prepared teaching materials, offered training to teachers, and prepared new school curriculums. The Department of Curriculum was founded within the Ministry of Education in the mid-1990s. The main objective of this department has been to prepare curriculum and teaching materials designed for a progressive and modern education. As stated by Woldemikael (2003: 182), the mother-tongue policy has been a form of social engineering that emphasizes "one state, one nation, and many languages."

In addition, several ethnolinguistic groups did not have their own written language; therefore, new written materials would be made available to implement the government policy. Describing the circumstances of this Department of Curriculum, Ministry of Education, Simeone-Senelle (2000) notes:

> The Department of Curriculum Branch, a large team that includes specialists in each national language, is responsible for carrying out this ambitious project. Among the tasks of the researchers include: not least that of the transition [of vernaculars] with no written tradition to a written language—which is the case with most vernacular languages [in the country], and also the development of an orthography [system]. Three writing systems are used by the languages: Ge'ez syllabi for Tigrinya, Tigre and Bilen, the Arabic alphabet for Arabic and Latin characters for other languages. Schools are opened that teach with the mother tongue language, and when resources permit, instruction is in mother tongue. Note that the war for independence and the war for defending the Eritrean territory since May 1998, schools have been permanently or temporarily deprived of teachers who could teach in mother tongues [trans. from French].

Yet the new policy was loaded with numerous sorts of challenges. First, a lack of both trained teachers as well as resources (including learning texts) created enormous obstacles. Hence, several ethnolinguistic groups (such as the Nara and Hedareb) did not enjoy the privileges of the policy for several years. Moreover, a number of Muslim communities, who either did not have a written language of their own or who saw one of the major working languages more important than theirs, were also puzzled as to whether to opt for Arabic as the language of instruction for their children or simply their respective mother tongue language. Eventually, many Christian communities opted for the Tigrinya language, and some Muslim communities opted for Arabic. This created perhaps undesired diversity (Woldemikael 2003: 177–189). In several cases, the new policy faced resistance from local communities. According to Woldemikael, local resistance to the policy of "mother-tongue" education in the Eritrean schools

> has to do more with seeking direct economic and political rewards and benefits from learning regional and international languages such as Arabic and English. In fact, one can make a compelling argument that other than Tigrinya and Arabic, which have been designated as working languages, there is hardly any material benefit attached to being literate in the other Eritrean languages. Since English, Tigrinya, and Arabic are widely used in official communication, a person knowing all or a combination of these languages has an advantage in gaining economic and political opportunities and rewards in the modern sector of Eritrean society. In fact, one can function effectively in the lower official circles of the Eritrean government knowing only Tigrinya but not knowing only Arabic or English. Tigrinya is the language of military training and communication. In the higher circles of the governmental hierarchy, however, English is an essential medium of internal and international communication. Thus, learning Tigrinya, English, and Arabic are advantageous in the job market as well as in governmental and international transactions (Woldemikael 2003: 210).

The major working languages in the country are Tigrinya and Arabic. Both of these languages played significant roles in the formation and development of the Eritrean national identity (Simeone-Senelle 2000). Both languages also have written traditions. English is usually understood in most areas of Eritrea, while Italian is widely used by the elderly, who somehow experienced direct or indirect impact of Italian colonialism in the country. In fact, English can also be considered as a third working language in the country. In most institutions of higher education (middle, secondary school level, and above) English serves as the main medium of instruction. It is also becoming an increasingly widely spoken foreign language in Eritrea. The frequent use of English benefits traders and other professionals. The economic and professional success of Eritreans in English-speaking countries is usually based on their school experience or the profession-related English they have learned in the country. English has not yet managed to become a *lingua franca*; however, most successful Eritreans do speak several languages, including English and Tigrinya.

Arabic is widely accepted because it is the language of the Holy Quran; hence, followers of Islam learn Arabic in mosques and possess considerable knowledge of the language. Amharic, the legacy of Ethiopia's rule, is also widely spoken, especially among returnees/deportees from Ethiopia who are ironically known as *'amiches* (አምችƷ)—an automobile company's name in Ethiopia. Yet, as bad memories of the atrocities committed during Ethiopian rule are still prevalent, not all people who master the language like to use it in their daily communication. Interestingly, while the Amharic language is not frequently used, Amharic music is preferred by a considerable number of Eritreans.

SOME COMMON TIGRINYA PHRASES

When visiting cultural groups, it is preferable to have at least a rudimentary knowledge of their respective languages. Eritreans usually provide generous compliments to strangers who demonstrate a basic knowledge of—or have at least some facility with—phrases in the local language(s). In the following section, we shall see a list of some useful vocabularies and phrases in Tigrinya.

TABLE 6.2. Some Useful Tigrinya Phrases

Seb (ሰብ)	man; human	*gemel* (ገመል)	camel	*megbi* (መግቢ)	food
Seb'ay (ሰብኣይ)	man; husband	*kelbi* (ከልቢ)	dog	*meste* (መስተ)	drink
sebeyti (ሰበይቲ)	woman; wife	*adgi* (ኣድጊ)	donkey	*bun* (ቡን)	coffee
gual (ጓል)	girl	*derho* (ደርሆ)	hen; chicken	*bani* (ባኒ)	bread
wedi (ወዲ)	boy	*be'eray* (በዕራይ)	ox	*mai* (ማይ)	water
geza (ገዛ)	house	*lam; lahmi* (ላም/ላሕሚ)	cow	*hamli* (ሓምሊ)	vegetables
telefon (ተሌፎን)	telephone	*begi'e* (በጊዕ)	sheep	*fruta* (ፍሩታ)	fruits
posta (ቡስጣ)	mail	*t'el* (ጤል)	goat	*komidere* (ኮሚደረ)	tomatoes
'awtobus (ኣውቶቡስ)	bus	*feres* (ፈረስ)	horse	*denish* (ድንሽ)	potatoes
'arat (ዓራት)	bed	*zeraf* (ዘራፍ)	giraffe	*shigurti* (ሽጉርቲ)	onions
t'awla/terepeza (ጣውላ/ጠረጲዛ)	table	*harmaz* (ሓርማዝ)	elephant	*selat'a* (ሰላጣ)	salad
qeshi (ቀሺ)	priest	*hebey* (ህበይ)	monkey	*zeyti* (ዘይቲ)	oil
harestay (ሓረስታይ)	farmer	*we'ag* (ወዓግ)	ape	*shikor* (ሽኮር)	sugar
guasa (ጓሳ)	shepherd	*t'elebedu* (ጤለበዱ)	antelope	*'enkwakuho* (እንቋቑሖ)	eggs
betekerestyan (ቤተክርስትያን)	church	*segen* (ሰገን)	ostrich	*s'muaq* (ጽሟቕ)	juice
mesgid (መስጊድ)	mosque	*mantile* (ማንቲለ)	rabbit	*shahi* (ሻሂ)	tea
'edaga (ዕዳጋ)	market	*temen* (ተመን)	snake	*manka* (ማንካ)	spoon
dekwan (ድኳን)	shop	*gobiye* (ጎብየ)	turtle	*farketa* (ፋርኬታ)	fork
muziqa (ሙዚቃ)	music	*'asa* (ዓሳ)	fish	*piyati* (ፒያቲ)	plate
werqi (ወርቂ)	gold	*'enqwi* (ዕንቍ)	beads	*c'ew* (ጨው)	salt
nehas (ነሃስ)	silver	*gereb* (ገረብ)	bush; tree	*shim'a* (ሽምዓ)	candle
jalba (ጃልባ)	boat	*tekli* (ተኽሊ)	plant	*mebrahti* (መብራህቲ)	light
merkeb (መርከብ)	ship	*'enbaba* (ዕንባባ)	flower; roses	*menber* (መንበር)	stool; chair
babur (ባቡር)	tram; train	*hus'a* (ሑጻ)	sand	*'ekli* (እኽሊ)	grain

TABLE 6.3. Examples of Greetings in Tigrinya

Hello	*selam* (ሰላም)
How are you (informal)	*kemey 'aleka* (ከመይ ኣለኻ) (m. sing); *kemey 'aleki* (f.) *kemey 'alekum* (m. polite); *kemey 'aleken* (f. polite)
Good day	*kemey we'ilka* (ከመይ ውዒልካ) (m. sing.)? *kemey we'ilki* (f. sing.)? *kemey we'ilkum* (m. pl. or polite form)?; *kemey we'ilken* (f. pl. or polite form)? [for farewell] *senay me'alti!* (ሰናይ መዓልቲ) or, *selam me'alti!* (ሰላም መዓልቲ)
Good evening!	*kemey 'amsika* (ከመይ ኣምሲኻ) (m. sing.)?; *kemey 'amsiki* (f. sing.)?; *kemey 'amsikum* (m. pl.)?; *kemey 'amsiken* (f. pl.)?
Good night!	*dehan heder* (ደሓን ሕደር) (m. sing.); *dehan hederi* (f. sing.); *dehan hederu* (m. pl. or polite form); *dehan hedera* (f. pl. or polite form)
My name is . . .	*simey. . .yebehal* (ስመይ. . .ይበሃል)
What is your name?	*menyu shimka* (መንዩ ሽምካ) (m. sing.)? *meyu shimki menta* (f. sing.); *men'yu shimkum* (m. pl. or polite sing.); *men'yu shimken* (f. pl. or polite form for sing.)
Thank you	*egziabher yihabeley* (እግዚኣብሔር ይሃበለይ) (or *yekeniyeley*[የቸንየለይ])
You are welcome!	*genzebka* (ገንዘብካ) (m. sing.); *genzebki* (f. sing.); *genzebkum* (m. pl. or m. sing. polite form); *genzebken* (f. pl. or f. sing. polite form)
Good-bye	*dehan kun* (ደሓን ኩን) (m.sing); *dehan kini* (f. sing.); *dehan kunu* (m. pl. or polite form for m. sing.); *dehan kuna* (f. pl. or polite form for f. sing.)

TABLE 6.4. Examples of Greetings in Tigre

Hello	*selamat* (ሰላማት) or *'aselam we'alekum* (ኣሰላም ወዓሊ ይኩም) (usual reply: *we'alekum 'aselam*)
How are you	*kafo heleka* (ከፎ ሀሊካ) (m.); *kefo heleki* (f.) *kafo helekum* (m. pl. or polite form); *kafo heleken* (f. pl. or polite form)
Good day	*kafo we'alka* (ከፎ ወዓልካ) (m. sing.); *kafo we'alki* (f. sing.); *kafo we'alkum* (m. pl. or polite form); *kafo we 'aken* (f. pl. or f. polite form)?
Good night!	*dehan maye* (ደሓን ማየ) (m. sing.)! *dehan mayay* (f. sing.); *dehan mayo* (pl.)
My name is. . .	*semye. . .'ebehal*
What is your name?	*semka menta*? (ስምካ መን'ታ) or *'aw haye men lebluka* (መን ል'ብሉካ) (m. sing.)?; *semki menta* (f. sing.); *semkum menta* (m. pl. or polite form)? *semken menta* (f. pl. or polite form)
Thank you	*shukran* (ሽኩራን) [also in Arabic]
You are welcome!	*'affon* (ዓፎን) [also in Arabic]
Good-bye	*'aw selamet* (ኣው ሰላመት) Or simply *selamet* (ሰላመት)

SLANG (TIGRINYA CONTEXT)

Slang refers to informal features of a language that are used by a certain social group or section of society. Although there are varieties of dialects of Eritrean languages, slang is usually a characteristic feature of language use among the younger generations. In Asmara, slang is known as *qwanqwa asmarino* (ቋንቋ ኣዝማሪኖ) "the language of the Asmarans." *Asmarino* slang comprises informal words and expressions that are not understood by most common Tigrinya speakers. Some of the *asmarino* terms and expressions are the result of vocabulary combinations from Arabic and Tigrinya, Tigre and Tigrinya, and so on. Other forms of slang include the use of Tigrinya but with inverted words and expressions or by putting an extra syllabus between formal Tigrinya words or alphabets. The following are some examples of *asmarino* slang vocabulary:

TABLE 6.5. Asmarino Slang Vocabulary

asmarino	**Formal Tigrinya**	**Meaning**
'amshi (ኣምሽ)	*kid* (ኪድ)	go away
bellit' (በሊጥ)	*gual* (ጓል)	girl
da'ewa (ዳዕዋ)	*shiger* (ሽግር)	problem; conflict
gahbba (ጋሕባ)	*faytot* (ፋይቶት)	prostitute
helwa (ሕልዋ)	*sebeqti* (ጽብቕቲ)	beautiful
hurmma (ሑርማ)	*gorzo* (ጎርዞ)	an adult girl
ju'e (ጁዕ)	*t'emiet* (ጥሜት)	hunger
me'ekkal (ምእካል)	*mebla'e* (ምብላዕ)	to eat
medek'al (ምድኻል)	*me'etaw* (ምእታው)	to enter
mederrab (ምድራብ)	*mehram* (ምህራም)	to beat; to hit
medurram (ምዱራም)	*medeqas* (ምድቃስ)	to sleep
mehebbay (ምሕባይ)	*meftaw; mefqar* (ምፍታው/ምፍቃር)	to love; to like
meherrab (ምህራብ)	*mehdam* (ምህዳም)	to escape; to run away
mejewa'e (ምጀዋዕ)	*met'may* (ምጥማይ)	to get hungry
mek'ellay (ምኽላይ)	*megdaf* (ምግዳፍ)	to leave aside
mekerrab (ምክራብ)	*memwat* (ምሟት)	to die
meshegag (ምሸጋግ)	*meskar* (ምስካር)	to get drunk
mesherrab (ምሸራብ)	*mestay* (ምስታይ)	to drink
meshewwaf (ምሸዋፍ)	*mer'ay* (ምርኣይ)	to see; to pay a look at
nejis (ነጂስ)	*'asha* (ዓሻ)	stupid

As stated, other forms of slang may include an inverted reading of terms and expressions. The following are some examples of this category.

TABLE 6.6. Some Terms of Tigrinya Slang Language with Inverted Word Orders

Formal Tigrinya	Slang	Meaning
kede (ከደ)	*deke* (ደከ)	He went.
mes'e (መጸ)	*s'eme* (ጸመ)	He came.
serhe (ሰርሐ)	*herse* (ሐርሰ)	He worked.
seteyet (ሰተየ)	*yetese* (የተሰ)	She drunk.
tezarebe (ተዛረበ)	*berezate* (በረዛተ)	He spoke.

Another form of slang is created by putting certain alphabets in between words or formal syllables. One of the common alphabets used for this purpose are the varieties of *ze* (ዘ). Thus, by putting the varieties of (ዘ)—ze (ዘ), zu (ዙ), zi (ዚ), za (ዛ), zie (ዜ), z (ዝ), and zo (ዞ), slang users make their language very incomprehensible for others. Let us look at some examples of this system of slang.

TABLE 6.7. Some Terms of Tigrinya Slang Language (with Informally Installed Radicals)

Formal Tigrinya	Slang	Meaning
'alewu (ኣለዉ)	*'azelezewuzu* (ኣዘለዘዉዙ)	They (m. pl.) are present.
bele (በለ)	*bezeleze* (በዘለዘ)	He said.
keydu (ከይዱ)	*kezeyzduzu* (ከዘይዝዱዙ)	He went.
serhe (ሰርሐ)	*sezerzheze* (ሰዘርዝሐዘ)	He worked.

REFERENCES

Bender, M. Lionel (ed.) (1976). *The Non-Semitic Languages of Ethiopia*. East Lansing: Michigan State University Press.

Carillet, Jean-Bernard and Phillips, Matt (2006). *"Lonely Planet": Ethiopia & Eritrea*. 3rd rev. ed., n.p.: Lonely Planet.

Conti Rossini, Carlo (1903). "Canti Populari Tigrai." In: *Zeitschrift für Assyriologie und Verwandte Gebiete*, 17, pp. 23–52.

Conti Rossini, Carlo (1904/05). "Canti Populari Tigrai." In: *Zeitschrift für Assyriologie und Verwandte Gebiete*, 18, pp. 320–386.

Conti Rossini, Carlo (1905/06). "Canti Populari Tigrai." In: *Zeitschrift für Assyriologie und Verwandte Gebiete*, 19, pp. 388–341.

Faitlovitch, Jacques (1911). "*Qene Habesha* [Habesha Poetry]." In: *Giornale della Società Asiatica Italiana*, 23, pp. 1–88.

Favali, L. and Pateman, Roy (2003). *Blood, Land, and Sex: Legal and Political Pluralism in Eritrea*. Bloomington: Indiana University Press.

Habtemariam, Asmerom (2009). "*Bahlen Hebreteseben* [Culture and Society]." In: *Haddas Ertra newspaper* (issue April 2, p. 4).

Hailemariam, Chefena; Kroon, Sjaak; and Walters, Joel (1999). "Multilingualism and Nation Building: Language and Education in Eritrea." In: *Journal of Multilingual and Multicultural Development*. Vol. 20 (6), pp. 475–492.

Kifleyesus, Abebe (1997). "Dyadic Relation and Market Transaction in an Environment of Economic Depression." In: *Cahiers d'études africaines*, Volume 37 (146), pp. 429–465.

Lamberti, Marcello (2003). "Bilin." In: Uhlig, Siegbert (ed.), *Encyclopaedia Aethiopica*. Vol. I, Wiesbaden, Harrassowitz Verlag, pp. 584–585.

Minahan, James (2002). *Encyclopedia of the Stateless Nations: Ethnic and National Groups around the World*. Vol. III. Westport/London: Greenwood Press.

Negash, Ghirmai (1999). *A History of Tigrinya Literature in Eritrea: The Oral and the Written (1890–1991)*. Trenton, NJ: Red Sea Press.

Negash, Ghirmai (2008). *"Oral Poetic Tradition of the Tigrinya."* In: Tesfa G. Gebremedhin and Gebre H. Tesfagiorgis (eds.) (2008). *Traditions of Eritrea: Linking the Past to the Future.* Trenton, NJ: Red Sea Press, pp.155–189.

Simeone-Senelle, Marie-Claude «Les langues en Erythrée», *Chroniques yéménites*, 8, Numéro 8, 2000, [Online source], URL: http://cy.revues.org/document39.html. Accessed on 19 August 2009.

Teferra, Anbessa and Hudson, Grover (2007). *Essentials of Amharic*. Cologne: Rüdiger Köppe Verlag.

Tewolde Yohannes, Tesfay (2002). *A Modern Grammar of Tigrinya*. Rome: Tipografia U. Detti.

Ullendorff, Edward (1985). *A Tigrinya Chrestomathy: Introduction—Grammatical Tables—Tigrinya Texts—Letters—Phrases—Tigrinya-English Glossary—Select Bibliography.* Stuttgart: Steiner Franz Verlag.

Woldemikael, Tekle M. (2003). "Language, Education, and Public Policy in Eritrea." In: *African Studies Review*, 46 (1), pp. 117–136.

Etiquette

Etiquette refers to the acknowledged codes of conduct of a society, group, or professional institution as generally prescribed in their cultural norms, customs, and behaviors. Etiquette is a sort of social convention that is usually understood by all members of a society without having had any prescribed formal education related to the code. In other words, etiquette also refers to a generally accepted set of rules and conventions that a society considers are important for interpersonal, intergroup, or intercultural interactions. Conventions related to etiquette are usually unwritten, and members of a society acquire knowledge of their respective society's etiquette through informal learning and other socialization agents—at home, church, mosque, peer-groupings, and other social institutions. Most important institutions of socialization in every culture play pivotal roles in transferring social norms, customs, and behaviors (of which etiquette constitutes a substantial part). Through regular customs and behaviors (etiquette), a society differentiates between what it considers are acceptable or unacceptable codes of conduct. Therefore, it is most important to learn a society's cultural etiquette and set one's norms in accordance with the hosting society. A visiting outsider should make every possible effort to understand a society's social norms and customs and provide his/her compliance by obeying those norms and customs.

MANNERS, NORMS, CUSTOMS, AND TRADITIONS

As stated earlier, Eritrea comprises diverse cultures. Therefore, the cultural norms, customs, and traditions of Eritrean society also reflect remarkable diversity. In multicultural societies such as Eritrea, it is difficult to present all the customs, norms, and traditions in a single work like this. However, there are some shared traditions among the cultural groups in the country. In the following sections, a brief description of cultural etiquette is presented to give the reader a general overview of cultural norms among Eritrean society.

GREETINGS AND BODY LANGUAGE

The art of greeting differs from one cultural group to another. Among the Tigrinya, for example, friends, relatives, guests, or people who simply know each other shake hands and also exchange kisses on both cheeks (usually three times). Shaking right hands is a common expression of greetings. But it is unacceptable to shake with the left hand. This applies to people between the same or opposite sex. It is also common to see men tapping or bumping each other with their right shoulders. Verbal greetings include longer discussions about family members, friends, or anyone both parties know. In rural areas, it is also common to exchange verbal greetings among people who may or may not know each other (regardless of where they meet). As their proverb demonstrates—*selamta nay egziher iyu* "greeting (literally, peace) is a gift from God"; members of the Tigrinya ethnolinguistic group like greeting anyone whom they encounter anywhere. This similar custom also exists among most ethnolinguistic groups of the country. In rural areas where modern communication technology is usually absent, these long greetings and long conversations especially help people to create an atmosphere conducive for exchanging actual information. In rural areas, especially among the agro-pastoral communities, it is common to see people spending several minutes (as part of their greetings) exchanging various forms of information on actual matters: such as about the location and circumstances of grazing lands, type and distribution of rainfall, and other types of news. Among the Saho, greetings include kissing each other's hands several times.

A great part of personal communication is conducted through verbal or written language. Yet body language also constitutes an important part of the communication system. Especially in rural areas where written language is almost nonexistent for daily communication, verbal and body language become the most important means of people's interaction. In verbal language the types of tone, cadence, and words used play decisive roles in determining the context of communication. Body language varies greatly because of the country's ethnolinguistic, cultural, and regional diversity. Yet, subtlety and curiosity constitute an important part of body language among all ethnolinguistic groups of the country.

Among the Tigrinya ethnolinguistic group, one can greet friends and strangers by making brief direct eye contact and a little bending of the head. At the same time, a person (from either of the greeting parties) wearing a hat normally removes it briefly. If both greeting parties are wearing hats, they normally remove them briefly and greet by bending their heads down a little bit. Removing the hat during greetings is considered a sign of respect. Raising the eyebrows briefly shows a sign of agreement or loyalty. Shaking the head right and left more than once is considered a sign of disagreement or disloyalty. In some places, this same body language may become a sign of surprise or amazement or shock.

Eye contact is a sensitive matter and people usually avoid staring at others. Direct and prolonged eye contact may convey a message of dissatisfaction, anger, or aggressiveness of the actor. Eye contact, especially between opposite sexes, may become a delicate sort of communication. Usually, women practice less frequent eye contact during communication.

Laughing and smiling are another common type of body communication. As stated earlier, Eritreans are very hospitable and friendly people. Therefore, smiling constitutes an important part of their friendly demeanor. Yet, laughing and smiling may not always be a sign of pleasure and happiness. Depending on the context and tone, people may demonstrate their negative feelings (anger, sadness, or discomfort) through assorted types of smiles and laughter. Therefore, it is usually advisable to learn the contexts of body communication to make a pleasant communication environment.

Unlike Western societies, body contact between opposite genders is usually not acceptable. Yet body contact between the same genders is considered a sign of harmony and friendship. Thus, it is common to see two men or two women holding hands or resting their hands on each other's shoulders in streets and other public places.

HOSPITALITY

Eritreans are very hospitable, sociable, and generous. Guests are generally treated in a very hospitable manner. Individuals, families, and communities provide their utmost attention and respect to guests (be they foreigners or visitors from within the society). During all times of communication and interaction with guests, Eritreans remain polite and accommodating. For example, a family unit that hosts guests presents its best provisions/accommodations to them. The household gives priority to serving food, drinks, and other amenities to the guests before its own family members. For instance, among the Tigrinya ethnolinguistic group, it is common to observe that children and women usually eat food after the guests have been served. Eritreans are also usually generous and ready to help in any way they can. Wondering about the generosity of the local people, Wylde (a European traveller to Eritrea in the nineteenth century) writes:

The people have been most kind, giving presents of milk and offering sheep. If I had taken all the animals offered [to] me at Wekeero [Wekiro] and on this trip I should have had a small herd by this time (Wylde 1888: I: 74).

The kind of hospitality mentioned by Wylde is a common practice among many communities in Eritrea. Offering gifts (including live animals) to newcomers is a common gesture of welcome. However, one should also be careful not to exploit the friendly and generous atmosphere. Being a selfish and exploitative person has possible negative consequences in personal interactions. A person without *'ib* (ዒ ብ) or *qal-'alem* (ቃል- ዓለም)—an act of showing a sort of countercare—is usually considered as selfish, a norm that is not approved of by Eritreans. As Denison and Paice (2002: 37) suggest, "It is vital, therefore, that any interaction you have to be a positive, two-way experience rather than one taking advantage of the other." Moreover, the Eritrean people give special respect to the elderly, disabled, and communal authorities. Therefore, it is typical to see (especially on public transports) riders offering their seats to the elderly and disabled. Offering your seat or helping the elderly/disabled in any way is considered a sign of civility and respect.

Unlike many Western societies, Eritreans keep close social relations, which they express in various ways. They usually exchange long and perhaps repetitive words of greetings and also show their warmth in facial and physical expressions. For example, it is quite normal to see friends or relatives (of the same sex) holding hands while walking or talking to each other. Although it might seem a sign of homosexuality in the Western world, Eritreans consider holding hands or putting their hands on the shoulders of a friend as intimate expressions of a normal friendship. Homosexuality is socially and legally not acceptable in Eritrean society. Homosexuals usually practice their sexual interactions in a highly covert atmosphere. They do not want to be openly identified by the public as homosexuals, and they make every possible effort to keep their lifestyle a secret.

EATING, DRINKING, AND SMOKING

Family members usually eat together off a large tray called (in Tigrinya) *me'adi* (መአዲ). Except in some restaurants, serving separate *me'adis*, or dishes, is not common among Eritreans. It is usually a hospitable gesture to say *tefeddel* (Arabic) or *nekedem belu/a* (ንቐድም በሉ/ላ—Tigrinya), "you are welcome to join me/us for meal," to any person who arrives during a *me'adi*. Depending on the mood of the invited person, he/she may reply in Tigrinya *kibret yihabeley* (ክብረት ይሃበለይ), "thank you for inviting," and then simply join the people who are eating; or he/she may say *buruk* (ብሩኽ), meaning "No, thank you, but let you have a blessed food." Among some members of the Tigrinya ethnolinguistic group, adults and young children usually eat in separate *me'adis*. If the family is hosting guests, children and, in some cases also women (including the hostess), have to wait until male adults are served. Similarly, among the Tigre ethnolinguistic group, the man of the house or only the male members of the household usually eat together. Among all ethnolinguistic groups in Eritrea, food is consumed by the right hand, and eating with the left hand is considered as a sign of impurity.

Among the Christian Tigrinya communities, *me'adi* comprises important codes of social norms. They believe that God and his apostles are watching during meals, and so apart from the woman who serves the dish, no significant physical movement during the *me'adi* is considered appropriate. Just before eating, the eldest person among the people around the *me'adi*, or in the household at large, leads a short prayer and gives a small slice of bread (*enjera*) to all attendants of the meal sitting around the *me'adi*. This is considered to be a sign of blessing. Each person in the *me'adi* is supposed to eat only from the portion of food located in front of him/her and shall not trespass in the portions of others.

As we shall see below, there are various types of local drinks. However, it is socially unacceptable to get drunk in public; especially for young people. Youngsters younger than 18 years old are also legally prohibited from alcoholic drinks. As in most parts of the Muslim world, alcoholic drinks are taboo in the Islamic societies of Eritrea. Similarly, smoking is also socially discouraged. Young smokers are usually shunned by members of the community. Normally, women in Eritrean society do not smoke and indulge their habit covertly; it is absolutely socially unacceptable for any woman to smoke in public. Illegal drugs are not tolerated in Eritrean society. Therefore, drug addiction and illegal drug trafficking are socially unacceptable and legally criminal acts.

VISITING

Unlike Western cultures, Eritreans often visit each other without any prior arrangements. Friends or relatives visit each other without expecting any invitation. The hosting individual or family would not be astonished about any sudden arrival of visitors. The hosting family may offer any kind of foods or drinks to visitors. Among other things, visitors may usually be offered tea, coffee, or food. Visitors may come with various gift items such as live animals (for example, chicken or sheep), sugar, tea, and so on.

DRESSING

Dressing styles vary greatly among Eritrean ethnolinguistic groups. Among the Tigrinya ethnolinguistic group, for example, dressing includes a variety of types, such as the *ejetebab* (እጀጠባብ)—a gownlike white dress for men; *zurya* (ዙርያ)—a gownlike white dress for women with various types of designs; *shifon* (ሽፎን)—a gownlike dress for women; and *tilfi* (ጥልፊ)—handmade gowns for women decorated with various designs. *Netsela* (ነጸላ)—a sheetlike white textile that is worn by men and women. As their proverb demonstrates—"May you fill your stomach with vegetables, but do not put bad clothes on yourself so that your enemy shall not be happy"—the Tigrinya usually wear clean clothes. Similar practices are also prevalent among most ethnolinguistic groups in the country. The Tigre men also usually dress in white costumes and white turbans. Among other lowland communities, women usually wear long dresses with bright and various types of colors. Although veiling is religiously encouraged among Muslim communities, only the Rashaida women practice veiling and regularly wear decorated scarves.

Types of dresses also signify individual or communal events. For example, among the Tigrinya ethnolinguistic group, *zurya* and *tilfi* types of dresses mark celebratory events such as weddings and other festivities, while complete black dress is considered a sign of mourning.

HAIRDRESSING

Traditional hairdressing is part of women's everyday cultural practices among most ethnolinguistic groups in the country. The styles of hairdressing and types of ornaments may differ greatly among the ethnolinguistic groups in the country. *Fegiret* and *qedamit*, types of hairstyle (where the hair is braided backward and sideways), are some of the most common types of hairdressing among the Tigre. Among the Kunama, unmarried and married women wear different types of hairstyles, usually with beads braided in their hair. Ornaments worn by the Kunama women are of different types of beads and iron bracelets. Kunama brides wear *samaydirga* (a type of ornament usually made of beads). It is also common to see Kunama men with beads attached to their long beards. Among the Tigrinya ethnolinguistic group, there are a number types of hairstyles such as *gamme* (ጋመ)—where hair is braided to the side and backwards; *albaso* (ኣልባሶ)—where hair is braided in few lines backward; *gilbich* (ግልብጭ)—where hair is braided in small lines and backward; *rubbo* (ሩቦ)—a hairstyle where the hair is braided in small lines; and *segem* (ሰገም)—a type of hairstyle similar to *rubbo*. Among the Tigrinya ethnolinguistic group, hairstyles also signify particular events. During celebratory events such as weddings and other cultural festivities, Tigrinya women usually wear *albaso* or *gilbich* hairstyles. During sad or mourning events, women either cover their hair with black scarves or wear a type of hairstyle known as *dirmim* (ድርምም)—where hair is braided in backward lines but all lines attach to each other at the edge. Hairstyles also signify individual marital status among the Tigrinya ethnolinguistic group. Unmarried women use the *gamme* hairstyle, while married women braid their hair in the form of *albaso*, *gilbitch*, and other styles.

ORNAMENTS, PIERCING, AND BODY DECORATION

Ornaments and types of piercing also differ from one ethnolinguistic group to another. As in most cultures of the world, women among Eritrean society are also obsessed with ornaments. Ornaments and jewelry include earrings, bracelets, arm and leg bands, and necklaces. Common ornaments are made of gold and silver. Among the Tigrinya ethnolinguistic group, there are various types of ornaments that are worn on the neck and ears. Body tattoos (such as on the neck, the forehead, and other body parts) are also considered an important component of body ornaments. Christian Tigrinya women usually tattooed with a sign of the cross on their foreheads. The common types of ornaments include *kutisha* (ኩትሻ)—a gold or silver design resembling a rose worn on ears; *gubagub* (ጉባጉብ)—similar design to *kutisha*; *stelini* (ስተሊኒ)—a coin-like design usually made of gold and worn on the neck; and other varieties. Among other ethnolinguistic groups such as the Saho and Tigre, gold in various designs is also worn by women.

Piercing is typical of most ethnolinguistic groups in Eritrea. For instance, the Saho and Tigre women practice piercing of the nose and ears. The Tigrinya women (and men in a much earlier time) only pierce their ears. Among the Tigrinya ethnolinguistic group, ornaments are usually worn only during "happy events." Piercing and body decoration may indicate transitional stages of life. For example, among the Tigrinya, the type of body decorations, tattoos, ornaments, and piercings clearly indicate if a person is married or not.

Body decoration may also include various types of tattoos. Traditionally, Tigrinya Christian women put a tattooed cross on their foreheads. They also tattoo themselves (usually legs and hands) with various designs using henna. The type of decorations commonly indicates special events—weddings, religious and other cultural festivities. Similarly, among the Saho and Tigre ethnolinguistic groups, women also decorate their bodies with various types of ear and nose piercings and henna tattooing. Usually married and unmarried women do not wear similar styles of henna tattooing. They also do not carry the same ornaments. Hence, body decorations usually signify a person's marital status and social standing.

FUNERAL CEREMONY

Most cultural communities in Eritrea practice certain rites and customs in their observances of death. Most of the rituals are associated with the religious beliefs of respective groups and their beliefs of life after death. In general, funeral customs and practices among the ethnolinguistic groups in Eritrea may vary considerably based on respective religious beliefs and cultures. For example, among the Muslim communities of Eritrea, usually only men attend burials, while there are no gender–based limitations among the Christian communities. In the following section, we will present a brief overview of a burial ceremony among the highland Tigrinya communities.

In the highlands of the country, where the majority of dwellers belong to the Orthodox *Tewahdo* Church, funerals reflect the beliefs and principles of the Orthodox Christian Church at large. The concept of death usually conveys an emotionally powerful message among the communities, and most members sympathize with the deceased and his/her family members. As a demonstration of their sympathies, members of the communities pay a moral and/or material contribution to the preparation of the ceremony.

If a person dies, *'awyat* (ኣውያት)—notice containing message that someone has died— is distributed all around. There are skilled messengers called *me'eweyti* (መእወይቲ) whose task is to transfer the message that someone has died and that the burial ceremony will take place at a specific place and time. In rural villages, the death of a person is usually declared by *'awyat*—in which someone stands in a strategic area (such as on the roof of a house or a nearby hill) and declares (in a loud voice) that the named person has died, and the funeral ceremony will take place at a specific place and time.

Burial preparation of the corpse also follows certain rituals. In many cases, before burial takes place, the corpse is "washed" using water and then clothed with clean white cloth known as *megnez* (መግነዝ) or in some places called *shama* (ሻማ). Covering the body is usually performed by elderly and skilled members of the community. In most cases, this process is accompanied by intensive prayers. Once the preparation for burying the corpse is accomplished, it is transported in a coffin or *qareza* (ቃሬዛ)—a traditional bed for transporting corpses to a church (thereby also to the cemetery) where the prolonged religious requiem Mass (known as *fithat*—ፍትሐት) takes place. *Fithat* may take a couple of hours, during which time attendants of the ceremony are expected to abstain from sobbing, wailing, or weeping. Priests lead the prayers and the locality-specific Christian rituals. The funeral ceremony may take place for any member of the community who dies after baptism. The usual practice of baptism takes place during infancy (younger than one-year old).

Attendants of the ceremony (sympathizers, relatives, and friends) come with *debes* (ደስስ)—material or cash contributions for the family of the deceased. *Debes* may include grains and other items. Any contribution related to readymade foodstuffs and drinks (such as coffee) is called *qwaret'a* (ቋሬጣ). *Qwaret'a* is usually consumed by the attendants of the ceremony just after the burial has taken place. Before the corpse is buried, it is placed in the center of a field near the church, around which mourners sit or stand. Depending on the popularity of the deceased, a genre of oral poetry called *melqes* (መልቀስ) can be performed in memory of the person. During the occasion of the actual burial of the corpse, most attendants express their farewell by loud wailing, sobbing, and weeping.

The traditional Tigrinya communities also practiced ceremonies for the memorial of the dead. Among these ceremonies are: *'asur* (ዓሱር)—memorial on the twelfth day after death; *'arba'a* (ኣርብዓ)—memorial on the fortieth day after death; *'amet* (ዓመት)—memorial at one year after death; and *teskar* (ተስካር)—elaborate memorial ceremony that might take place anytime after the twelfth day after death. It is worth noting that after independence these practices were largely discouraged by the government of the country. The government (through its media and agents) launched campaigns demonstrating that these practices were uneconomic and backward in nature. Despite these campaigns, traditions related to these practices have, by no means, faded away.

In some cases where the corpse of the deceased is not available—meaning if someone dies far away from the locality (such as in the diaspora)—members of the family or relatives may prepare *kala'ay qebri* (ካልኣይ ቀብሪ)—literally meaning "second funeral." Although prayers for the deceased may take place, no elaborate religious festivities are performed during this occasion. People gather and mourn for the dead; and *debes* as well as *qwaret'a* may also be collected during this occasion.

INITIATION CEREMONY

For most societies, *initiation* designates a universally or locally applied practice of a socially and culturally acknowledged observance. During initiations certain members or age groups of a community go through a transitional process to attain a new status in the society to which they belong. Initiation is also usually associated with a process of obtaining a social recognition of adulthood or any other status in a given society. Initiation ceremonies may be gender- age-, or "group"-based benchmarks. There are varieties of initiation ceremonies: religious, cultural, or any specialized customs. Religious initiations are associated to practices commonly associated with religious beliefs and religious rites of passage for a certain section of society. These practices include baptism, confirmation, priesthood, or any other related initiation. In diverse cultural practices such as those of Eritrea, it is difficult to present detailed practices of the initiation ceremonies. Therefore, in the following paragraphs, only aspects of initiation ceremony related to the Kunama ethnolinguistic group is presented.

The initiation ceremony among the Kunama ethnolinguistic group demonstrates rich cultural traditions. One of the initiation ceremonies is related to young members of the community who are shortly to become adults and have to go through a process of initiation to attain that status. The most widely practiced type of initiation ceremony among the Kunama is called *'anna 'ila* (Debesay 2008: 4a–4e). For the Kunama, to pass through the process of *'anna 'ila* means to demonstrate culturally accepted capabilities and skills for the adult members of the community to achieve a socially recognized status. Therefore, the initiation is a decisive test during the transitional period to adulthood.

There are skilled community members who lead the *'anna 'ila* initiation ceremony. Each household that claims that any of its members is to become an adult consults these community members. Until the candidate is taken away for the initiation, he is not given any prior notice as to when the initiation ceremony will take place. The leading members of the community set a fire using animal dung and read signs from the smoke: if the smoke does not make unusual movements caused by the wind, then it is considered as a good sign for conducting an initiation ceremony; if the smoke shows significant movements and waves, a different date is chosen for the event (Debesay 2008: 4a). Once the initiation is confirmed, all candidates are immediately brought from their homes to the site where the ceremony starts. They are brought to the site early in the morning. The ceremony sets forth a number of tough physical challenges for each candidate: tests against hunger, exhaustion, and for survival strategies. The initiation ceremony confronts candidates with trials during which they are required to accomplish long travels with little food and drink and with other varieties of obstacles that are culturally sanctioned (Debesay 2008: 4a–4e).

At the end of the ceremony candidates are usually taken to a river where they bathe and eventually get their hair shaved. After the above-mentioned procedures are accomplished, each candidate has to perform an oath where he attests he has never had sexual relations with anyone prior to the initiation. Initiation oaths have deep cultural impact. For instance, a candidate who performs a false oath is believed to be cursed: he would encounter evil experiences in life, including bearing disabled or dead progenies (Debesay 2008: 4c–4d). Therefore, participants of the initiation are culturally compelled to provide oaths based on truth. If any candidate is criticized for any culturally unacceptable practices or if anyone denies the oath, he may encounter punitive social challenges, including culturally based legitimate tortures.

All successful participants of the initiation ceremony are then taken home. They are accompanied by a person delegated by the leaders of the ceremony. Each household that sent candidate(s) to the ceremony usually prepares food and drinks for the "freshly baked" adults. They decorate their bodies with various ornaments— commonly with beads. Any person who passes through *'anna 'ila* initiation is considered to be an adult man. He has the right to get married and attend events that concern adult men in the community (Debesay 2008: 4c–4d).

COFFEE CEREMONY AMONG THE TIGRINYA

Coffee is cultivated in the eastern escarpment of the country. Yet, Eritrea imports large amounts of coffee from various areas. Prior to the Eritrean-Ethiopian conflict (1998–2000), coffee was usually imported from Ethiopia (for more information about Ethiopian coffee, see Belachew [2003] and Pankhurst [2003]). For many ethnolinguistic groups in Eritrea, coffee has been an important component of their drinks for centuries. Coffee is known by different names among the ethnolinguistic groups in the country. The Tigrinya name for coffee is *bun* (ቡን). Also for the Tigrinya, coffee has become an important component of their daily drinks. Moreover, coffee plays a considerable ceremonial role on many occasions. Moreover, coffee is still prepared in the traditional way and does not involve any substantial electronic machines.

Coffee among the Tigrinya is prepared by women and involves washing, roasting, grinding/crushing, and boiling of coffee beans. Important components of traditional coffee-making tools include: the *jebena* (ጀበና) also known as *jebenat* (ጀበናት)—a locally made (out of clay soil) small, long-necked pot designed for boiling coffee; *finjal* (ፍንጃል) (plural: *fenajil* [ፈናጅል])—small cups (but without handles) used mainly for drinking coffee; the *medegdeg* (መደግደግ) also known as *mendegdeg* (መንደግደግ)—a small wooden tool (and an iron pestle) used for crushing roasted coffee; and *ferniello* (ፈርኔሎ)—a traditionally designed stove for boiling coffee.

As stated earlier, preparation of the coffee ceremony is the task of women. The hostess preparing the coffee sits in front of the attendants (on a low stool) and puts all the

Jebena. A typical pot for boiling coffee. (M. Tesfagiorgis)

tools for making the traditional coffee around her. Attendants of the ceremony can observe the coffee-making process during all stages of the ceremony. Sometimes, the hostess spreads green grasses and leaves around the place where the coffee is prepared. This signifies a hope for a green and fertile year (but this also depends on the occasion when the ceremony takes place—for example, this practice is absent during occasions of mourning). Coffee beans are roasted on a small, flat tin called a *menkeshkesh* (መንከሽከሽ), which is known in some areas as *meshahshah* (መሻሕሻሕ). The roasted coffee is then passed on to the attendants of the ceremony to inhale a good deal of the aroma of the roasted coffee. After coffee aroma is dispersed throughout the room or hall where the ceremony takes place, *'et'an* (ዕጣን "incense") is also burned to fill the room with a much more beautiful smell and to create a relaxed atmosphere. It should be noted that incense is also a traditionally important part of rituals in Eritrean and Ethiopian churches.

Unless absolutely necessary, no physical movement or talking with "loud voice" (from attendants or anyone preparing the coffee) are considered appropriate during

Eritrean Tigrinya lady preparing traditional coffee ceremony. (M. Tesfagiorgis)

any phase of the coffee ceremony. Coffee is then usually boiled/brewed in three rounds known as: *'awel* (ኣወል)—first round; *kala'ay* (ካልኣይ)—second round; *berekka* (በረካ)—third round, but also literally meaning "blessings"; and in some households *dereja* (ደረጃ)—fourth round. Just before the coffee is poured, the eldest person in the ceremony leads short prayers and blessings. Then, *kursi-bun* (ቁርሲ, ቡን)—literally meaning coffee snacks (such as popcorn); *himbasha* (ሕምባሻ)—type of bread (usually decorated); *kicha* (ቂጫ)—type of bread; or *t'ayta* (ጣይታ)—slice of *enjera* are offered to all attendants of the ceremony. Once coffee is boiled in each round, the hostess slowly pours it on the *fenajil* and hands the coffee-filled small cups to people attending the ceremony. Attendants usually give their compliments to the hostess by saying *t'u'um* (ጥዑም) (delicious)! During all phases of the ceremony, attendants speak to each other in happy and friendly manners. They may talk on various issues that are of interest or concern to them. The whole ceremony may take more than an hour and a half. Attendants may leave after the third (*berekka*) round is brewed and consumed.

The coffee ceremony is prepared in most Tigrinya households on a daily basis; in some households, it is prepared more than one time a day. It is common to see neighbors inviting each other for a coffee ceremony. The coffee ceremony is, however, a ceremony beyond only drinking coffee. People use occasions of the coffee ceremony to meet and talk in a calm "coffee" atmosphere and discuss their concerns. During attempts of reconciliation between individuals and groups, the coffee ceremony is used to create an amiable atmosphere. The coffee ceremony is prepared in various other occasions such as weddings, epiphany, meetings, and other religious cultural festivities.

NAMES

Perhaps owing to the patriarchal nature of society, most ethnolinguistic groups use a patronymic system of naming. Therefore, European styles of surnames are not common in the region. Eritreans give their children their own respective names and their father's name as a surname; hence each child is given its own first name that is to be recognized as his/her legitimate name. Similar to the European naming system, middle names are also not used. For example, if a person is named *Mussie Tesfay Mehari, Mussie* is the first name of the person; *Tesfay* is his father's name and *Mehari* is his grandfather's name. In the European context, both names "Tesfay Mehari" may be used as surnames. Most Eritrean official name registrations include three names: first name, surname (father's first name), and grandfather's name. This helps in getting a detailed identification of the person. As stated earlier, the father's and grandfather's first names can mostly be used as surnames. In general, the regulations regarding surnames (as seen from the European naming systems) are quite complex.

TABOOS

Taboos refer to using or practicing anything that a society acknowledges as absolutely unacceptable. Aspects of taboos include practices that are universally accepted or are simply specific to a country and a cultural group. Among Eritrean society there are a number of practices or uses that are considered taboos by custom. Yet, it is worth noting that taboos may differ from one ethnolinguistic group to another. What is presented below refers only to general aspects; hence it is not an exhaustive list of taboos. It is also worth noting that each ethnolinguistic group in the country has its own culturally acknowledged taboos.

Generally, all types of crimes that are also considered by state law as illegal acts (such as murder, stealing, lying, bribing, or abusing anyone) are culturally considered as strict taboos among all ethnolinguistic groups of Eritrea. Anyone who commits these crimes faces strong social seclusion. Therefore, the commission of crimes is low in most parts of Eritrea. Records of crimes in most Eritrean cities and towns are also quite low. As a visitor to Eritrea exclaimed in 1999 "one can walk along the streets of Asmara with a bag full of dollars without been stolen or threatened of any crime." Among the Christian Tigrinya (especially in the Catholic section), anyone who commits any sort of crime is required to confess to religious figures. The religious figures or the church at large to which the offender belongs have to try attaining reconciliation between the delinquent and the victim (this also depends on the type of crime). In addition, the society's communal laws also clearly define each crime and its punishment. Offenders are not only discouraged by the communal and state laws but also by the consequences of social exclusions. The church, the mosque, the communal laws, and the society demonstrate strong resentment against offenders. Among the Muslim communities of Eritrea the social and communal treatment of offenders is similar to that of Tigrinya. The *shari'a* courts and Islamic community institutions strongly oppose acts of any type of crime.

Although women hold lower social status, Eritrean society considers abusing women as absolutely unacceptable. Among most cultural groups of Eritrea, it is unacceptable to have pre-marriage sexual interactions. No coarse language shall be used against women. As most Tigrinya communal laws describe it, "a woman's witness is her own tears," and so if a woman declares having been physically abused, she may not need any witness. Among the Tigre ethnolinguistic group, it is unacceptable for any stranger to immediately enter into a woman's domains within a household (Littmann 1910: 107). Yet, a woman among all ethnolinguistic groups in Eritrea is expected to behave as "reproductive mother and good wife." Therefore, it is taboo when a woman behaves differently—such as engaging in professions that expose her to wide publicity; to mention one (especially prior to the 1950s)—becoming a singer.

REFERENCES

Abdulkadir, Asia (2008). *Die Perzeption von Gewalt im Geschlechterverhältnis in Eritrea: Eine Untersuchung über die Gewalterfahrung Weiblicher Rekrutinnen*. Hamburg: Dr. Kovaó Verlag.

Asefaw, Fana (2008). *Weibliche Gentalbeschneidung: Hintergründe, Gesundheitliche Folgen und Nachhaltige Prävention*. Frankfurt am Main: Ulrike Helmer Verlag.

Belachew, Mekete (2003). "Coffee." In: Uhlig, Siegbert (ed.), *Encyclopaedia Aethiopica*. Wiesbaden: Harrassowitz Verlag, pp. 763–764.

Belcher, Wendy (2000). "After the Freedom: Post-War Cultural Production and National Identity in Eritrea." In: *Third Text: Socialist Eastern Europe*, 50 (Special Issue, Spring), pp. 87–125.

Carillet, Jean-Bernard and Phillips, Matt (2006). *"Lonely Planet": Ethiopia & Eritrea*. 3rd rev. ed., n.p.: Lonely Planet.

Conti Rossini, Carlo (1903). "Canti Populari Tigrai." In: *Zeitschrift für Assyriologie und Verwandte Gebiete*, 17, pp. 23–52.

Conti Rossini, Carlo (1904/05). "Canti Populari Tigrai." In: *Zeitschrift für Assyriologie und Verwandte Gebiete*, 18, pp. 320–386.

Conti Rossini, Carlo (1905/06). "Canti Populari Tigrai." In: *Zeitschrift für Assyriologie und Verwandte Gebiete*, 19, pp. 388–441.

Culture of Eritrea: http://en.wikipedia.org/wiki/Culture_of_Eritrea (access in August 2009).

Debesay, Santina (2008). *"Mewetag ab behere kunama* [Adulthood Initiation among the Kunama]." In: *Haddas Ertra Newspaper*, September 23, pp. 4a–4e.

Denison, Edward and Paice, Edward (2002). *Eritrea: The Bradt Travel Guide*. Chalfont: St. Peter, Bradt.

Faitlovitch, Jacques (1911). *"Qene Habe*sha [Habesha Poetry]." In: *Giornale della Società Asiatica Italiana*, 23, pp. 1–88.

Favali, Lyda and Pateman, Roy (2003). *Blood, Land, and Sex: Legal and Political Pluralism in Eritrea*. Bloomington, IN: Indiana University Press.

Gebremedhin, Tesfa G. (2002). *Women, Tradition and Development: A Case of Eritrea*. Trenton, NJ: Red Sea Press.

Gebremedhin, Tesfa G. and Tesfagiorgis, Gebre H. (eds.) (2008). *Traditions of Eritrea: Linking the Past to the Future*. Trenton, NJ: Red Sea Press.

Habtemariam, Asmerom (2009). *"bahlen hebreteseben* [Culture and Society]." In: *Haddas Ertra newspaper* (issue April 2, p. 4).

Kifleyesus, Abbebe (2005). "Food." In: Uhlig, Siegbert (ed.), *Encyclopaedia Aethiopica*. Vol. 2, Wiesbaden: Harrassowitz Verlag, pp. 560–565.

Kifleyesus, Abbebe (1997). "Dyadic Relation and Market Transaction in an Environment of Economic Depression." In: *Cahiers d'études africaines*, Volume 37 (146), pp. 429–465.

Kifleyesus, Abbebe (2002). "Muslims and Meals: The Social and Symbolic Function of Foods in Changing Socio-Economic Environments." In: *Africa*, Volume 72 (2), pp. 68–71.

Lamberti, Marcello (2003). "Bilin." In: Uhlig, Siegbert (ed.), *Encyclopaedia Aethiopica*. Vol. I, Wiesbaden: Harrassowitz Verlag, pp. 584–585.

Literature of Eritrea: http://en.wikipedia.org/wiki/Literature_of_Eritrea (access in August 2009).

Littmann, Enno (1910). *Publications of the Princeton Expedition to Abyssinia*. Vol. II, Late E. J. Brill: Leyden [Leiden].

Matzke, Christine (2002b). "Of *Suwa* Houses & Singing Contests: Early Urban Women Performers in Asmara, Eritrea." In: Banham, Martin, et al. (eds.). *African Theatre Women*. Oxford: James Currey, pp. 29–46.

Mercier, Jacques (1946). *Ethiopian Magic Scrolls*. New York: George Braziller.

Minahan, James (2002). *Encyclopedia of the Stateless Nations: Ethnic and National Groups Around the World*. Volume III, Westport/London: Greenwood Press.

Negash, Ghirmai (1999). *A History of Tigrinya Literature in Eritrea: The Oral and the Written (1890–1991)*. Trenton, NJ: Red Sea Press.

Negash, Ghirmai (2008). *"Oral Poetic Tradition of the Tigrinya."* In: Gebremedhin, Tesfa G. and Tesfagiorgis, Gebre H. (eds.) (2008). *Traditions of Eritrea: Linking the Past to the Future*. Trenton, NJ: Red Sea Press, pp. 155–189.

NgCheong-Lum, Roseline (2005). *Eritrea*. New York: Marshall Cavendish.

Pankhurst, Richard (1990). *A Social History of Ethiopia: The Northern and Central Highlands from Early Medieval Times to the Rise of Emperor Téwodros II*. Addis Ababa: St. Edmundsbury Press.

Pankurst, Rita (2003). "Cultural Role of Coffee in Ethiopia." In: Uhlig, Siegbert (ed.), *Encyclopaedia Aethiopica*. Wiesbaden: Harrassowitz Verlag, pp. 764–765.

Tesema, Asres (2006). *Teamot: kab tarik medrekawi senetebeb ertra* [The Taste: Aspects of Eritrean Performing Arts]. Asmara: Francescana Printing Press.

Tewelde, Teklemichael *Abba* (2009). *Meseretawi temherti qedus metshaf: gebbu'e arredade'an atekakeman metshaf qal egzi'abeher* [Basic Teachings of the Bible: For the Proper Understanding and Use of God's Words]. Asmara: Francescana Printing Press.

The Tigre culture and customs: http://awkir.com (access in August 2009).

Tronvoll, Kjetil (1998). *Mai Weini; A Highland Village in Eritrea: A Study of the People, Their Livelihood, and Land Tenure During Times of Turbulence*. Lawrenceville, NJ: Red Sea Press.

Wylde, Augustus. B. (1888). *'83 to '87 in the Soudan, with an account of Sir William Hewett's mission to King John of Abyssinia* (2 Vols.). New York: Negro Universities Press.

Yatana Entertainment—Tigrinya cultural movie, 2008.

Literature

Literature is a term usually associated with the written works of any society. In its narrower sense, the term may signify inscribed texts comprising the *littera* (Latin word for "letters"). In practical terms, however, the term can be used in different ways depending on a variety of contexts. Especially where there is limited or no written culture, literature shall embody the oral, written, and material culture that a society preserves, uses, and transfers as important components of its overall culture.

The literature of Eritrea comprises a mostly rich oral tradition as well as a written culture. The literature of Eritrea reveals the cultural attitudes of Eritrean society. Oral literature comprises poems, riddles, folklores, fables, customary rules of law, and more. Although writing was an important component of historical developments in the whole region, no great number of written local materials survived and/or appeared until the nineteenth century.

As mentioned earlier, Ge'ez was the main language of the Aksumite Empire. It also became the main language of literature in Eritrea and Ethiopia for many centuries afterward. Aksumite literature dealt with various aspects of society, including religion. Moreover, ecclesiastical and chronicle works were produced at various times during and after the Aksumite era. Ge'ez literature, especially the writing culture including Ge'ez *fidel* (ፊደል)—"alphabet" system—was inherited by the Semitic languages of Eritrea and Ethiopia—Tigrinya, Amharic, and Tigre languages and continued to dominate the field for many centuries prior to the nineteenth century. Ge'ez literature, inherited by Tigrinya and Tigre, includes linguistic aspects such as morpho-syntax

SOME TIGRINYA PROVERBS

ዘይናቱ ዝደሊ. ከም ሳእኒ. ይበሊ.።
zeynatu zedeli kem sa'eni yibeli
Anyone who desires the property of others becomes as insignificant as used shoes.

ፍረ ኣይካብ ባይታን ካብ ባይቶ።
fre aykab baytan kab bayto
Harvest does not come from the earth but from a just Assembly.

ንመሬት ኣይወሃባን ስድሪ።
nemeriet aywehaban sedri
Even an inch shall be given from the land.

ሓቂ ብእግራ እንተቐበርካያ ብርእሳ ትወጸእ።
haqi be'egra enteqeberkaya bere'esa tewes'e
However you bury truth by its feet, it unearths itself by its head

እንዳሰም'0 ዘደቀስ ነቅኒቃዮ ነይሰመ'0።
endasem'e zedeqeses neqniqayo neyseme'e
You cannot awake anyone who pretends to be asleep.

ዘብኢ. ክሳብ ዝጥዕሞ ይሕንክስ።
zeb'i kesab zete'mo yihenkes
A hyena crawls until it gets an opportunity.

ዝገብር ነዲኡ ነይነግር።
zegeber nedi'u neyneger
Someone who wants to take an action does not need to consult his mother.

መርገም ወላዲ እንተዘይቀተለ የዕነኒ።
mergem weladi entezeyqetele ye'neni
The nuisance of parents creates turbulence, otherwise it kills.

and vocabulary. Tigrinya became the main written language of literature in Eritrea (at least until the mid-twentieth century). To some extent Arabic also played an important role in Eritrea's literature. Yet, it was usually confined as a religious language for most Muslim communities of Eritrea.

Substantial studies about the history of Eritrea's literature have yet to be conducted. Regarding the history of Tigrinya literature, Ghirmai Negash's book (1999), *A History of Tigrinya Literature in Eritrea: The Oral and the Written 1890–1991* (Leiden: University of Leiden CNWS-Publications) is almost the only well studied and pioneer work available. Another important work is also presented by the same author (2008), "Oral Poetic Tradition of the Tigrinya," in a book compiled by Tesfa G. Gebremedhin and Gebre H. Tesfagiorgis (editors), *Traditions of Eritrea: Linking the Past to the Future* (Red Sea Press, Trenton, NJ). Both of the above-mentioned works present rich historical analysis of Tigrinya literature. Other works related to Eritrea's literature include a couple of oral literature collections by Carlo Conti Rossini, (*Traditional Tigrinya Proverbs and Songs* [1942]) and *The Tigrinya Oral Poetry* (1904–1906) (see also the bibliographic reference section), Johannes Kolmodin's book on *Traditions of Tseazzega and Hazzega* (1912), and Jacques Faïtlovitch's article on *The Habesha Poetry* (1911). In the following sections, we will examine (mostly on the bases of the works mentioned above) brief historical aspects of Tigrinya oral and written literature in Eritrea.

BRIEF HISTORICAL OVERVIEW OF TIGRINYA LITERATURE

As we have seen, Tigrinya inherited substantial linguistic elements from Ge'ez, including the Ge'ez letters or syllabic scripts. Although no conclusive evidence is available, it seems that Tigrinya has been one of the most important literary languages in the territory for many centuries. However, no definitive studies have been conducted regarding the history of Tigrinya literature prior to the nineteenth century. The available studies are usually from obscure sources. Yet, considering the important and obvious influence of Ge'ez on Tigrinya, it can be assumed that the Tigrinya written literature goes back centuries. In spite of this, however, Tigrinya literature continued to remain almost inactive until the 1940s. As Ghirmai elaborated very well, Tigrinya comprises oral and written literary tradition (for details see Negash 1999 and 2008). Although Tigrinya oral literature constitutes the most important part of the society's literary tradition, writing is also becoming an increasingly literary practice among Tigrinya society (especially since the nineteenth century).

Although some European travellers in the nineteenth century attempted to include Tigrinya themes in their works (such as short texts, religious excerpts and/or translations, and vocabulary lists), no substantial Tigrinya sources were produced until the colonial period. Around the 1860s, missionaries started to publish Tigrinya educational and religious texts, which played pivotal roles in reviving Tigrinya literature. Some of these missionaries produced Tigrinya texts related to linguistics, religion, health, and other subjects in context of the Eritrean society. In the 1890s, the renowned Tigrinya scholar Fisseha Giyorgis (who taught Tigrinya language in Italy for a few years and published a Tigrinya text about his experience there) also started to produce some works in Tigrinya. Fessega Giyorgis's works played an essential role in the revival of Tigrinya as a written literature (see Negash 1999: 77–87).

TIGRE TALE OF A HEN

A family had a chicken. Now [once], when guests came to them, they wished to kill the chicken, that is to say, in order to give a meal to the guests. But they did not find the knife with which to kill it; then they set the chicken free. When the chicken was free, it scratched the ground with its feet, and unearthed the knife. When its masters saw the knife, they killed the chicken with the knife which it had found itself, and they gave a meal to their guests. And they say as a proverb: "The chicken scraped out the instrument that killed it."

Source: Littman (1910: 18).

THE POWER OF A DICTATOR DOES NOT HAVE
A LIMIT! (A TIGRINYA TALE)

Once upon a time, wild animals including a young lion were living in a jungle. The lion in that jungle acted brutally against his neighbors. Everyone feared the lion because none of those animals knew what exactly he wanted from them. He would attack any member for reasons that were not known to anyone. The father of the young lion was living in a jungle that was located far away from the area. He was old, and all community members knew that he was seriously ill, and that he could die any time. He lived in a small cave that was located in a forest. His young boy who acted as an absolute dictator in this jungle never cared to pay him a visit. Instead, he asked one of the apes in that jungle to go and see his father after which he should bring news to the young lion dictator. The messenger kindly agreed that he could go and see the old lion. Yet, the dictator told the messenger "but once you see my father, and return here, never tell me whether he is alive or dead." Puzzled by the preconditions of the dictator, the messenger agreed and left to see the old lion. Upon his return, he was terrified what would happen if the dictator asked him as to what happened to his father. So, the messenger ape decided to shave half of his head on his way to the dictator. He did, and came to see the dictator. Upon his arrival, the dictator asked him, "is my father alive?" The messenger said "I would not have shaved half part of my head if he is alive!" "Then, he is dead?!" asked the dictator. The smart ape replies "I would not have left half of my head unshaved if he was dead!" The dictator was puzzled by the news the messenger ape brought, and tried to threaten the poor ape. Yet, the messenger ape had to stick into his puzzling answer. Finally, thinking the messenger ape would be of great value in getting more messages in the future, the dictator ordered him to stay in contact and set him free. [translation mine]

Message: Dictators do not even know what they exactly want, and do not know whom they employ.

Note: Part of this tale was also published by Gebreyesus, Yakob Abba (1949). *Tales, Fames and Proverbs of Precursors.* Asmara, Comboni School, p. 25.

In the twentieth century, Tigrinya literary works continued to grow, and a number of works were also published in the language. Authors such as Ghebremedhin Dighinei, Carlo Conti Rossini, Johannes Kolmodin, and Jacques Faïtlovitch published works—with their main focus on documenting Tigrinya oral traditions. The collections of Carlo Conti Rossini, Johannes Kolmodin, and Jacques Faïtlovitch contain songs and plain poems of several forms—love songs/poems, *melqes* (መልቀስ), and *massé* (ግጥ) (some examples of each of the above-mentioned styles are presented below). Detailed analyses regarding the above-mentioned literary works are presented by Negash (1999: 77–108). Although missionaries, European scholars, and local educators continued to contribute to Tigrinya literary progress, the rise of the Italian Fascist regime (in Eritrea between 1922 and 1941) introduced suppressive policies during which development of local literature was largely discouraged. Therefore, not many works related to Tigrinya literature were produced during these decades. The Fascist regime's educational policies in Eritrea focused on methods of indoctrination. Liberal literary works attempted by missionaries and the local elite as well as colonial studies on local literature were discouraged.

The main revival of Tigrinya literature started during the British occupation of Eritrea (1941–1952). The British Military Administration (BMA) in Eritrea abolished policies of color-bar (which was prevalent during the Italian colonial period). More-over, the BMA also established various new institutions and expanded existing institutions in various spheres such as education and civil administration. The expansion of education stimulated renewed interest in the local population. A number of educational centers were established for Eritreans. Moreover, unlike the Italian colonial administration, the BMA made ambitious efforts to publish newspapers in Tigrinya and Arabic. This increased public awareness and participation in developing local literature. In addition, the local newspapers served as legitimate platforms for local political and social debates.

Among the Eritrean educators in the 1940s, Ato Woldeab Woldemariam vigorously advocated for the standardization of the Tigrinya language and the development of Tigrinya literature. By 1942, he published a book titled *'arki tämäharay* (ዓርኪ ተመሃራይ)—"the student's friend." Moreover, he served as a well-regarded journalist, director, and editor of the Tigrinya newspaper known as *nay 'ertra sämunawi gazetta* (ናይ ኤርትራ ሰሙናዊ ጋዜጣ) "the Eritrean weekly gazette" that was controlled and published the BMA Ministry of Information, for which he worked until 1948 (for details on Woldeab's articles, see Aresie 1995). This newspaper also contained a section in Arabic; and the items covered in the newspaper were mainly educational, social, and political as well as a diverse genres of poetry (see Saulsberry 2001: 95–99; Negash 1999: 114–116). In 1944, the BMA also established a Tigrinya Language Council (comprising a president and a number of members), which aimed at modernizing and standardizing the grammar and usage of the Tigrinya language. The Council organized a number of seminars and workshops, and "the most recurrently debated topics were the linguistic history of Tigrinya; its future; correct usage of grammar; the necessity of safeguarding the 'purity' of the language, and also ways of adapting it to new technology and the necessity of 'borrowing' words from the English language for this purpose" (Negash 1999: 116).

Tigrinya literature continued to grow throughout the 1940s, and until the 1950s a number of Tigrinya books as well as novels were published. One of the early Tigrinya books was *zennan tärätin meselan qedamot* (ዝ ናን ተረትን ምስላን ቀዳ ሞት) "Legends, Stories and Proverbs of the Ancestors" by *Abba* Yacob Ghebreyesus. This book comprises about a hundred different types of stories, over 3,000 Tigrinya proverbs, and poems of various types. This book was intended to provide pupils with Tigrinya written material as well as to stimulate for further Tigrinya writing (for details, see Negash 1999: 130–132). At the same time, Tigrinya novels also started to appear in published form. Some examples (as also well presented in Negash's [1999] work) of the novels include: *nezetä 'askärä nehadä män'essäy zäre'i hadä zanta* (ንዝተዓስከረ ንጓሓደ መንእስይ ዘርኢ፣ ሓደ፡ ዛንታ።) "A Story of a Conscript" by Ghebreyesus Hailu (1949); *ne'egziabher zessä'ano nägär yälbon. tensa'en 'awätin* (ንእግዚኣብሔር ዝሰኣኖ ነገር የልቦን። ትንሳኤን ዓወትን) "Everything is Possible for God. Resurrection and Victory" by Zegga-Iyesus Iyasu (1949/50); and *wägahta natsinät* (ወጋሕታ ናጽነት) "Dawn of Freedom" by Teklai Zeweldi (1954). For further details on the above-mentioned literature, see Negash (1999: 75–145).

The Story of a Conscript is a novel about a group of Eritrean conscript soldiers (commonly known as *asker*) who were sent to Libya to serve the Italian colonial army where they were forced to fight for the Italians. One of the main actors in the novel returns home facing hardships in Libya. At home, he finds that his mother had died during his absence; and he expresses his deep grief against Italian rule and colonialism in the form of local oral poetry called *melqes* (see Negash 1999: 132–136). *Resurrection and Victory*, another book, is an allegory with "candidly didactic and moralistic" message (Negash 1999: 137). *Dawn of Freedom*, "chronicles how Italian colonialism came to Eritrea and how it ended up in attacking Ethiopia on the eve of W.W.II" (Negash 1999: 138).

Although Ethiopia applied oppressive language policies in Eritrea, Tigrinya literature continued to grow from the late 1950s. A significant number and variety of publications appeared in Tigrinya. The Eritrean struggle also stimulated interest in Tigrinya literature. Most of the publications from the Eritrean Liberation Fronts focused on resistance toward the occupation and oppression of the Ethiopian state. Discussing the large volume of Tigrinya written literature is out of the scope of this work; however, Negash (1999) presents a long list of the published works and a well-studied analysis on the subject.

A number of local authors have emerged after Eritrea's independence. Most of these authors write in local languages and their subject matter has been on diverse issues—ranging from history to fiction to translations. In addition, several local lexicons have also been published in local languages, which also help in facilitating the development of local literature.

ORAL LITERATURE

As stated, the Eritrean literary tradition comprises both written and oral literature. Although Arabic and Tigrinya have increasingly become the literary languages in the country, oral literature (especially where there has not been written tradition) is an important literary tradition among all ethnolinguistic groups of the country. Therefore, the Eritrean linguistic groups have a rich oral tradition by which they preserve and transfer their literary treasures. Again, because of the great diversity and depth of oral literature in Eritrea, only a brief overview of the Tigrinya oral literature and tradition is presented in the following paragraphs. As in all other ethnolinguistic groups of the country, oral literature has been an important component of tradition among the Tigrinya . Tigrinya oral literature comprises history, poetry, folklore, riddles, fables, and more. All these genres are significant sources in understanding the history and culture of Eritrean society.

ORAL HISTORY/TRADITION/LITERATURE

"Oral history" and "oral tradition" are terms that have mostly been used interchangeably though they may convey different meanings. Human beings, as makers of history and as victims of historical events, are capable of storing, analyzing, and passing on their historical experience from one generation to the next. Oral historical literature involves word of mouth or informants who speak about their experience, the experience of others, or about events that happened in their surroundings that affected them in positive or negative ways. Similarly, oral tradition chronicles the practices, norms, and values of a society that are transferred from one generation to the next (see also Tesfagiorgis G. 2007). Oral tradition is also a method of transferring (through "word of mouth") the history, literature, and other communal treasures of a society. Oral literature is an important component of Eritrea's history. Observing the rich oral traditions of the peoples such as the people of the Horn of Africa, Phillips and Carillet note as follows:

> In the West, culture is usually defined in terms of grandiose monuments, works of arts and sophisticated customs. In some countries, however, and particularly where the climate dictates a nomadic existence of its people, culture manifests itself not in enduring buildings and great writings, but in the spoken word, passed down from generation to generation (Phillips and Carillet 2006: 55).

The above statements also reflect facts about the rich oral traditions of Eritrean society. As mentioned earlier, all ethnolinguistic groups in the country have diverse oral traditions that preserve and transfer their history and sociocultural traditions. For example, most of the Eritrean communal laws were not compiled until the 1930s (although a few written records of communal codes might have also existed in scattered locations). In most cases the communities recorded, analyzed, and passed down these laws by word of mouth from generation to generation. The laws were transferred in the form of oral tradition for many centuries. Most communities in Eritrea trace their origins on the basis of oral history. No matter how accurate or scientific their narratives are, most communities give remarkable attention to their histories as passed on to them from the preceding generations.

As stated earlier, Eritrean oral literature consists of thousands of tales, fables, legends, riddles, proverbs or maxims, varieties of poetry, and more. Various types of local literature such as tales, legends, and poems have been told and retold among members of communities. Usually the elderly (men and women) are considered as ideal narrators of tales, maxims, and legends. Various forms of oral literature are told to entertain, convey sociopolitical messages, and teach community members as well as to transfer and preserve community customs. Usually there are several storytellers in a village. Traditionally, especially where there was no substantial modern communication technology, children of a village would love to spend hours with storytellers. By storytelling, the elderly teach and entertain children. Moreover, storytellers also play a significant role in socializing the children by teaching them their community's norms, morals, customs, and etiquette. These tales play a significant role in the art of communication and personal interaction among adults.

Maxims and tales are employed to clarify, describe, or summarize complex situations in a simple and compact form (see also Phillips and Carillet 2006: 55). Tigrinya has rich maxim tradition, and most Tigrinya speakers integrate maxims during their verbal interactions. Through maxims or tales, they offer advice, describe complex events, counsel friendly vigilance to avoid physical confrontation but still they can manage to throw a verbal attack at someone (usually without resorting to coarse language). Maxims and tales among the Tigrinya communities have the highly powerful effect of articulating complex interactions, ideas, and circumstances in simple terms.

Therefore, historians, anthropologists, archaeologists, ethnographers, and other specialists are strongly advised to integrate oral literature in their research methodologies when conducting studies in Eritrea.

TIGRINYA ORAL POETRY

The scope and nature of oral poetry in Eritrea may vary greatly from one ethnolinguistic group to another. Among the Tigrinya there are several genres of poetry. Girmai describes three main genres of oral poetry: *massé/'awlo* (ማሰ / ኣውሎ)—usually praise poems that are performed on special occasions such as weddings, community festivities, and religious rituals; *melqes* (poems during burial ceremonies) and *dog'a* (ዶግዓ)—poems for the dead (see Negash 2008: 156–189). To these could be added Tigrinya poetic songs, *fekera* (ፈኸራ)—a sort of epigram in which the actor boasts in a poetic art, as well as occasional verbal poetry, exchanges among individuals such as *yalaka* (ያላኸ)—sort of riddles by which individuals communicate in a poetic form. Each type of these oral poetries is usually performed for diverse rationale. All of these genres of poetry are usually performed in a gathering where any person claiming any sort of the above-mentioned genres is offered a live and open platform for participation. In general, oral poetry served and still serves as an important literary tradition among the Tigrinya. Poets used and still use distinct and specialized genres to transfer their messages among the communities (Negash 2008: 155–160).

In fact, poets did not and do not only serve as beloved entertainers but also as powerful artists who convey actual sociopolitical message(s) among the communities. Regarding the popularity, distribution, and limitations of poets during the nineteenth and twentieth centuries, Negash notes:

> It appears that hundreds of oral poets, performers, and singers were active in the Eritrean highlands of Hamasien, Akeleguzai and Seraye, and in Tigray, in Ethiopia . . . Some poets worked under the custodianship of chiefs, others operated on their own, and many moved from place to place as "beggar-wandering-poets" . . . Their status, in fact, was largely dependent on their ability and commitment to truthfully voice the concerns of their social base as such moments . . . Occasionally an oral poet could also be faced with adversity resulting from his or her performance. One common hazard was the possibility of being caught up in the dispute of rivaling chiefs. Another danger was becoming the source of fearful concern of despotic clan chiefs, traditional leaders, and colonial governors (Negash 2008: 156–157).

These communal artists are usually invited to events to practice their arts (as a form of entertainment as well as transferring messages to audiences). For instance, *massegnatat* (ማሰኛታት)—praise poets, are invited to attend a wedding and perform *massé*. During wedding events, these artists entertain audiences by offering spontaneous and literary poets. They also create oral poems designed to praise the newlyweds, their families, and relatives. At times, several *masségnatat* will exchange verbal poetry among each other—arguing, agreeing or seeking mobilization aimed at certain events of common concern. Moreover, *masségnatat* may perform their artistic poetry for various purposes such as cultivating a harmonious relationship with chiefs, supporting or criticizing chiefs or their strategies of governance, or simply to praise any person who may or may not have prevalent role chieftainship/governance—(for further details, see Negash 2008: 160–172).

Excerpt in Tigrinya language	Literal translation
"እንስቲ፡ ማይ፡ ጸዕዳ፡ እተወቕዓ፡ ምንታይ፡ ገቢረን።	Why should the women of May-Tsaeda be beaten?
ዘይ፡ ጸዕዳ፡ ጣፍ፡ ዝሀባ፡ ኃጊረን።	They baked and served bread out of white-*taff*.
እንስቲ፡ እገላከ፡ ምንታይ፡ ገቢረን።	And what did the women of Egela do?
ዳጉሳ፡ ዝሀባ፡ ኃጊረን።	They baked and served bread out of *dagusa*.
እንስቲ፡ ሐማሴን፡ ምንታይ፡ ገቢረን።	What did the women of Hamasien do?
ዘይ፡ ስርናይ፡ ዝሀባ፡ ኃጊረን።	They baked and served bread out of wheat.
በዓል፡ ኣሓ፡ ኣርሒቃ፡ ኣይተፍረን።	The shepherd, do not take the cattle far away,
በዓል፡ ነፍጢ፡ ኣብ፡ ማንቲ፡ ቀቅረን።	The gunman, squeeze them in a hollow.
በዓል፡ ቅርሺ፡ ኣዕሚቃ፡ ቅበረን።	The holder of cash, bury it deep in the ground.
እንድጎሪ፡ በረቆ፡ ብባሕሪ፡ ብሽርሬን	If it lightens in the direction of Bahri and Shire,
ገዛኢና፡ ንጉሥ፡ እኳ፡ ኣሎ፡ ኣይጸረን።	Our Emperor is still there, and has not yet attained intelligibility.

Source: Conti Rossini 1905/1906: 326

(Note that *taff* and *Dagusa* are types of grains used as staple food. Please also note that the Tigrinya version contains some orthographic errors.)

Through this *massé* poem, it can be assumed that the artist conveys two important messages. First, he appreciates the role of women and offers an opinion that they should be treated humanely. Second, he alerts the audience that they should be cautious of possible invasion from outside. By "Emperor" it seems that he points his finger toward the Ethiopian king or perhaps any warlord or governor from across the border. Also, by "the shepherd, do not take the cattle far away," it seems he wants to convey that cattle raids might take place and the audience should be alerted to it. He also advises the gunmen of the locality to preserve their ammunition, and those who possess cash to hide it in a safe place.

EXAMPLE OF *MELQES* POETRY

Excerpt of *melqes* performed by a certain Inday from Akrur for the deceased person called Amenay Tesfu	Literal translation
"ብላታ፡ ባ፡ ይኢ፡ ብላታ።፡	Belatta, indeed, blatta,
ብላታ፡ ጻድዋ፡ ሐሙ፡ ባሕታ።፡	*Belatta* Tsadwa, the father-in-law of Bahta,
ሐሙ፡ ሸንጋልባ፡ ይኢ፡ ሐሙ፡ ባሕታ።፡	The father-in law of Sengal and Bahta,
እዛ፡ ስልኪ፡ ዝብላዊ፡ ተራኢታ።፡	The so called wire is appearing,
ንምድሪ፡ክሎ፡ ዘይራ፡ እሃዛታ።፡	It has occupied the whole territory,
ብዙሕ፡እንጋ፡ ኢዩ፡ ረዳኢታ።፡	It has diverse purposes,
ገሊ፡ ከይተምጽእ፡ ንምሽታ።፡	It may cause something at the end of the day,
ምድሪ፡ ገደፍኩምዋ፡ ምጥዕምታ።፡ "	You left the earth while it was still suitable.

Source: Conti Rossini 1905/1906: 330

Note that *belatta* was one of the old military/administration titles during the last centuries.

As stated earlier, another genre of oral poetry is *melqes* (መልቀስ). It is practiced during funeral ceremonies. Artistic oral poets offer their poetry—in praise or memory of the deceased as well as their relatives (often for the dead). Through *melqes*, poets attempt to recall lifetime achievements and weaknesses of the deceased. This type of poetry is usually a source of remarkable information related to the deceased. Theoretically, attendants of the funeral ceremony are expected to stay silent during *melqes* performances. However, it is common to see that mourners accompany *melqes* performances by wailing and lamentation (see also Negash 2008: 161).

Through the above piece of poetry, the artist conveys his concerns about the expansion of information technology (particularly the expansion of telegraph and telephone lines) and considers this as a development with a negative impact on the territory. Although the author does not give a date and context to the poems, by reading the context, it can be assumed that this poem was performed around the end of nineteenth century or early twentieth century. By "wire," the artist seems to address the telephone/telegraph line was expanding into Eritrea during the 1890s, and he addresses his concerns about the circumstances.

Doga'a is another form of oral poetry that deals with the deceased in an "intermediate time after the death has taken place" and "allows relatively more room for lament several deaths together in one poem making it profoundly nostalgic and romantic" (Negash 2008: 161–162). According to Negash, some of the features of *doga'a* include fantastic linguistic lyricism; freer commentary on sociopolitical issues; and performances by experienced poets (Negash 2008: 162).

EXAMPLE OF *DOG'A* ORAL POETRY

Excerpt of *dog'a* in Tigrinya	**Literal translation**
"ኣይትመለስ፡ ናይ፡ ሰኑይ፡ መዓልቲ።	May the day of Monday never return
ጸሓይ፡ ተኸዲና፡ ለይቲ፤	When the sun was covered in dusk
ርኢኹሞዶ፡ ሕልፈት፡ ደገዝማቲ፤"	Have you witnessed the passing of the *Degezmati*

Source: Quoted in Negash 2008: 183

Note that *Degezmati* was a type of local military title

In the above-mentioned piece of *dog'a*, the artist seems to convey the message to his audience that the death of the chief (*degezmati*) has serious impact on the community. He expresses his feeling that after the death of the chief, things have become more fragile.

REFERENCES

Aresie, Tekwabo (1995). *Merutsat anqetsat ato weldeab weldemariam* [Selected Articles of Ato Woldeab—1941–1991]. Asmara: Hedri Publishers.

Belcher, Wendy (2000). "After the Freedom: Post-War Cultural Production and National Identity in Eritrea." In: *Third Text: Socialist Eastern Europe*, 50 (Special Issue, Spring), pp. 87–125.

Bender, M. Lionel (ed.) (1976). *The Non-Semitic Languages of Ethiopia.* East Lansing: Michigan State University Press.

Carillet, Jean-Bernard and Phillips, Matt (2006). *"Lonely Planet": Ethiopia and Eritrea.* 3rd rev. ed., n.p.: Lonely Planet.

Conti Rossini, Carlo (1903). "Canti Populari Tigrai." In: *Zeitschrift für Assyriologie und Verwandte Gebiete*, 17, pp. 23–52.

Conti Rossini, Carlo (1904/05). "Canti Populari Tigrai." In: *Zeitschrift für Assyriologie und Verwandte Gebiete*, 18, pp. 320–386.

Conti Rossini, Carlo (1905/06). "Canti Populari Tigrai." In: *Zeitschrift für Assyriologie und Verwandte Gebiete*, 19, pp. 388–341.

Culture of Eritrea: http://en.wikipedia.org/wiki/Culture_of_Eritrea (access in August 2009).

Denison, Edward and Paice, Edward (2002). *Eritrea: The Bradt Travel Guide.* Chalfont: St. Peter Bradt.

Ellingson, Lyold Schettler (1986). *Eritrea: Separatism and Irredentism (1941–1985).* Ph.D. Dissertation, Department of History: Michigan State University.

Faitlovitch, Jacques (1911). *"Qene Habesha* [Habesha Poetry]." In: *Giornale della Società Asiatica Italiana*, 23, pp. 1–88.

Favali, Lyda and Pateman, Roy (2003). *Blood, Land, and Sex: Legal and Political Pluralism in Eritrea.* Bloomington, IN: Indiana University Press.

Gebremedhin, Tesfa G. (2002). *Women, Tradition and Development: A Case of Eritrea.* Trenton, NJ: Red Sea Press.

Gebremedhin, Tesfa G. and Tesfagiorgis, Gebre H. (eds.) (2008). *Traditions of Eritrea: Linking the Past to the Future.* Trenton, NJ: Red Sea Press.

Gebreyesus, Yacob *Abba* (1949). *Zennan tereten qeddamot* [Legends, Stories and Proverbs of the Ancestors]. Asmara: Comboni School.

Habtemariam, Asmerom (2009). "*bahlen hebreteseben* [Culture and Society]." In: *Haddas Ertra newspaper* (issue April 2, p. 4).

Hailemariam, Chefena, Kroon, Sjaak, and Walters, Joel (1999). "Multilingualism and Nation Building: Language and Education in Eritrea." In: *Journal of Multilingual and Multicultural Development*, Vol. 20 (6), pp. 475–492.

Literature of Eritrea: http://en.wikipedia.org/wiki/Literature_of_Eritrea (access in August 2009).

Littmann, Enno (1910). *Publications of the Princeton Expedition to Abyssinia.* Vol. II, Leyden [Leiden]: Late E. J. Brill.

Matzke, Christine (2002a). "Comrades in Arts and Arms: Stories of Wars and Watercolours from Eritrea." In: Döring, Tobias (ed.). *African Cultures, Visual Arts, and the Museum: Sights/Sites Creativity and Conflict.* Amsterdam/New York: Editions Rodopi, pp. 21–54.

Matzke, Christine (2002b). "Of *Suwa* Houses & Singing Contests: Early Urban Women Performers in Asmara, Eritrea." In: Banham, Martin, et al. (eds.). *African Theatre Women.* Oxford: James Currey, pp. 29–46.

Matzke, Christine (2003a). "Engendering Theatre in Eritrea: The Roles and Representations of Women in the Performing Arts." In: Eva-Maria Bruchhaus (ed.). *Hot Spot Horn of Africa: Between Integration and Disintegration.* Münster: Lit Verlag, pp. 156–164.

Matzke, Christine (2003b). *En-gendering Theatre in Eritrea: The Roles and Representations of Women in the Performing Arts.* Unpublished Ph.D. Dissertation, School of English: University of Leeds.

Matzke, Christine (2004). "Shakespeare and Surgery in the Eritrean Liberation Struggle: Performance Culture in Orota." In: *Journal of Eritrean Studies* 3, 1, pp. 26–40.

Matzke, Christine (2008a). " 'Life in the Camp of the Enemy': Alemseged Tesfai's Theatre of War." In: Emenyonu, Ernest E. (ed.). *African Literature Today 26: War in African Literature Today.* Oxford: James Currey, pp. 15–32.

Matzke, Christine (2008b). "*Mahber Te'atr Asmera*—The Asmara Theatre Association, 1961–1974." in: Banham, Martin, James Gibbs, and Femi Osofisan (eds.). *African Theatre: Companies.* Oxford: James Currey, pp. 62–81.

Matzke, Christine (2008c). "The Asmara Theatre Association (1961–74): *Mahber Teyatr Asmera.*" In: Gibbs, James (ed.). *African Theatre Companies.* Leeds, James Currey, pp. 62–81.

Negash, Ghirmai (1999). *A History of Tigrinya Literature in Eritrea: The Oral and the Written (1890–1991).* Trenton, NJ: Red Sea Press.

Negash, Ghirmai (2008). *"Oral Poetic Tradition of the Tigrinya."* In: Gebremedhin, Tesfa G. and Tesfagiorgis, Gebre H. (eds.) (2008). *Traditions of Eritrea: Linking the Past to the Future.* Trenton, NJ: Red Sea Press, pp. 155–189.

Saulsberry, Nicole Denisen (2001). *The Life and Times of Woldeab Woldemariam (1905–1995).* Department of History, Stanford University.

Simeone-Senelle, Marie-Claude «Les langues en Erythrée», *Chroniques yéménites*, 8, Numéro 8, 2000, [Online source], URL : http://cy.revues.org/document39.html. Accessed on 19 August 2009.

Tesema, Asres (2006). *Teamot: kab tarik medrekawi senetebeb ertra* [The Taste: Aspects of Eritrean Performing Arts]. Asmara: Francescana Printing Press.

Tesfagiorgis G., Mussie (2007). *A Fading Nature: Aspects of Environmental History of Eritrea (1980–1991).* Felsberg: Edition Eins.

Tewelde, Teklemichael *Abba* (2009). *Meseretawi temherti qedus metshaf: gebbu'e arredade'an atekakeman metshaf qal egzi'abeher* [Basic Teachings of the Bible: For the Proper Understanding and Use of God's Words]. Asmara: Francescana Printing Press.

The Tigre culture and customs: http://www.awkir.com (access in August 2009).

Ullendorff, Edward (1985). *A Tigrinya Chrestomathy: Introduction—Grammatical Tables—Tigrinya Texts—Letters—Phrases—Tigrinya-English Glossary—Select Bibliography.* Stuttgart: Steiner Franz Verlag.

Woldemikael, Tekle M. (2003). "Language, Education, and Public Policy in Eritrea." In: *African Studies Review*, 46 (1), pp. 117–136.

Art and Aesthetics

Art is a term of diverse meaning and with no simple definition. In its general sense, art refers to any inventive work based on imaginary or real aesthetic ideals. As defined in the Encyclopedia Britannica, art designates "modes of expression that use skill or imagination in the creation of aesthetic objects, environments, or experiences that can be shared with others" (Encyclopaedia Britanica Ultimate Reference, DVD 2007 edition). Works that fall in the category of "art" include, but are not limited to: literary art such as poetic performances, drama, creative stories, and more; visual art such as paintings, drawings, imaginary and real designs, and more; plastic art, comprising sculpture, modeling, and design; architecture; performing art such as theater, drama, dance, and other artistic contests; and compositional art such as music (Encyclopedia Britannica online reference, 2007 edition). In general, human works of creativity based on aesthetic principles are what we consider artistic products. In one way or another, art reflects a society's culture in a tasteful manner. Art may be considered to be as old as human history because creativity and production have always accompanied human nature throughout history.

As in any other part of the world, art has also been an important part of the cultural tradition of Eritrean society. There is great diversity of artistic work in the country—ranging from fine visual art to diverse architecture. The National Museum of Eritrea (located in Asmara) also contains important ancient and contemporary artistic works. The types of artistic works may differ from one cultural group to another. It should be noted that no significant studies have yet been conducted on Eritrean art. Indeed, few studies so far rival the pioneering research of Christine Matzke's unpublished Ph.D. dissertation (*En*-gender*ing Theatre in Eritrea*) as well as her insightful chapters published in various books (see reference section), Asres Tessema's recent book in the Tigrinya language (*The History of Performing Arts in Eritrea*), and Ghirmai Negash's book (*The History of Tigrinya Literature*). Therefore, owing to limitations caused by lack of source materials, only an overview of Eritrean art is presented in the following sections.

THE FINE ARTS

As in every other part of the world, Eritrean visual art demonstrates a great variety of artistic works such as painting, sculpture, pottery, handicrafts, and more. Visual arts have a long tradition in Eritrea and are deeply rooted in the country's cultures. Early types of visual art include rock paintings, decorated pottery, and a variety of tools. Archaeological remains provide sufficient evidence that the above-mentioned types of art were well integrated in the culture of the region (for further details on ancient types of art, see Schmidt, Peter. Curtis, Matthew C., Zelalem Teka, et al. [2008]). Ancient rock art offered an array of paintings, engravings, and geometric and abstract designs (Peter Schmidt et al. 2008: 49). Early rock paintings constitute a remarkable slice of Eritrea's history. These paintings are distributed throughout many parts of Eritrea and provide an interesting insight on the socioeconomic and cultural testimonies of the prehistoric peoples of the area. Not only do these paintings provide historical value to prehistoric circumstances, but they also demonstrate the creativity and intellectual life of early civilizations of the whole region. Rock paintings clearly demonstrate the mode of life of prehistoric people. Most of the rock paintings are located in the southern parts of the Eritrean highlands.

Diverse religious paintings and sculptures have also been important components of visual art throughout history. Religious art expressed the respective cultural group's beliefs and spirituality. Yet, "although the two main religions in Eritrea are Christianity and Islam, artistic work relating to the latter has been scarce. The most abundant pictorial art in Eritrea is paintings associated with the Orthodox Church . . ." (Bairu 2008: 1999).

PAINTING

As stated earlier, religious paintings reflected the beliefs and the cultural depictions of "good and evil." As for the religious paintings of the Orthodox Church, most of the themes were associated with biblical figures such as saints, Christ, angels, and the Virgin Mary, and demonstrate various influences from such early Christian painting styles as Byzantine, Coptic, and Syrian (Bairu 2008: 199). Church paintings are usually characterized by splendid colors and straightforward messages to viewers. "They are intended to impress believers with human vision of heaven and hell. In other words, they educate the viewer in a direct way in visual form of the Christian message" (Bairu 2008: 199).

Although the styles are different, it seems the messages are easy and direct. Coptic religious art in the region is a common tradition. It is characterized by simplistic outlines and descriptive features. This art is the result of a number of influences, ranging from Hellenistic, Alexandrian, and local initiatives of creativity. The Eritrean/Ethiopian Coptic art also incorporates a great variety of textile designs. Most of the church paintings are influenced by the spiritual beliefs as prescribed in the Holy Bible and demonstrate little secular initiative of the artists. During the war of liberation, secular arts played a significant role as a tool for war propaganda, literacy campaigning, and entertainment.

Among the few artists who have provided a substantial contribution to "modern" Eritrean painting is Michael Adonai. Michael, who was born and raised in the Eritrean highlands, was influenced by his elder brother (Berhanne Adonai) who practiced secular arts. Michael joined the EPLF in 1977 and engaged himself in a number of artistic works. His main work focused on secular painting, although he also wrote several novels and short stories (Adonai 2007: 1-4). He took part in a number of art workshops and trained extensively in the field. Michael has demonstrated remarkable skill in modern art and has produced a considerable number of paintings. The artistic motif of Michael's works is usually associated with the various aspects of the liberation war and the post-liberation process of nation-building. Other renowned "modern artists" with a liberation war background include Elsa Yakob, Berhanne Adonai, Demoz Russom, Tirhas Iyassu, Fatma Suleman, and Fisehayye Zemichael. Other non-fighter painters include Ermias Ekube and Gidey Gebremichael (Matzke 2002a; 2002b).

As stated earlier, the main motif of artistic works during the struggle was the war. Hence, most paintings reflected realistic depictions of the struggle. Most of the images produced during the struggle portrayed social and military life under war—such as images of war heroes, the communal life of the fighters, and war atrocities committed by the Ethiopian army. A good example of such artistic works is the poster (1988) created by artist Elsa Yakob, entitled *The Tanks Crushed My Mom*. This painting depicts a crying young child (whose mother was just brutally murdered by Ethiopian soldiers) being comforted by an Eritrean fighter. Another painting (1984) by Yakob depicts a "Woman Hero" who holds a Kalashnikov in the left hand and stands ready to throw a hand grenade held in her right hand while in the midst of actual fighting. The painting conveys an important message: the heroism of Eritrean women in the struggle. Describing the styles of arts during the liberation struggle, Matzke (2002a: 40) notes:

> Two stylistic features are . . . notable in most of these works: the seeming absence of the Byzantine style utilized by the Orthodox Church, and the prevalence of a socialist aesthetic. Both aspects can easily be linked to the EPLF's need for redefinition at the time, and to their attempt at creating a new cultural identity. The Orthodox Church style of art was too closely associated with the repressive regime of the Ethiopian Emperor to be comfortably employed.

Recognizing the great importance of arts in the struggle, the EPLF established the so-called Division of Arts in 1978. This division was administered under the EPLF's Department for Political Orientation, Education and Culture. Some of the most innovative early members of this division were Berhanne Adonai, Haile Woldemichael, and Woldu Afeweki (Matzke 2002a: 33–34). All of these artists were engaged in a number of activities such as preparing teaching materials for the children at the Revolutionary School in Fah and producing artistic propaganda material for the EPLF. They also served as early teachers of arts in the EPLF. As we have seen earlier, other artists (most of them trained by these teachers) such as Michael Adonai, Demoz Russom, and Tirhas Iyasu joined this small group of EPLF artists and continued to actively produce art materials and literature throughout the years of struggle.

PERFORMING ARTS

In this section, performing arts refer to Eritrea's theater, drama, music, and dance. Performing arts in Eritrea are characterized by great diversity (with each ethnolinguistic group practicing its own traditions of performing arts). Traditional performing arts usually reflect the history as well as the social and political conditions of the people. Therefore, performing arts play an important role for people's cultural representation and sense of identity (Matzke 2003a: 159). Traditional performers such as poets, painters, dancers, storytellers, and musicians have always played decisive roles in preserving and transferring traditional performances. As well illustrated by Matzke, "traditional performing arts are dynamic and very alive in Eritrea. They constitute an integral part of social life and as such complement modern urban theatre practices" (Matzke 2003b: 13).

As stated earlier, performing arts have been an integral part of human history in the country. Yet, "modern" systems of performing arts such as theater and drama were only introduced in the country during the Italian colonial period (1890–1941) and were enhanced during British rule (1941–1952). In correlation to the increasing national consciousness and proliferation of political movements, new Eritrean theater groups and associations started to emerge in the 1940s. One the most influential theater associations was the *mahber tewase'o deqebbat,* (National Theater Association) (Ma.Te.De.) founded in 1944. Many members of this association were teachers (Matzke 2003a: 159; Tessema 2006: 172–183). Interestingly, most of the new theater associations albeit cultural barriers included women members who played decisive roles in performing arts. The performing arts continued to grow, and by the 1960s, there were a number of active theater associations such as the *mahber tiyater asmera* (ማሕበር ትያተር አስመራ) (Asmara Theater Association) (Ma.Te.A) and *mahber memeheyash hagerawi lemdi,* (ማሕበር ምም ሕደሽ ሃገራዊ ልምዲ) (Association for the Improvement of National Customs) (Me.M.Ha.L) (for further details, see Matzke 2003a; Matzke 2003b; Tessema 2006).

The Ethiopian occupation of Eritrea (1962) marked the beginning of the disintegration of local cultural associations. Most performers were affected by the political environment that was created after the annexation of Eritrea by Ethiopia. Many active members of the Eritrean theater and musical associations either joined the liberation struggle or left the country to live in exile. Ma.Te.A. was among the few Eritrean theater organizations that struggled hard to survive suppression throughout the 1960s. Alemayo Kahsay, a renowned comedian and singer-playwright, served as the head of this organization until it fragmented in the mid-1970s. One of the ways the Ethiopian administration frustrated the growth of performing arts in Eritrea was the introduction of even more stringent measures of censorship. .

All music, stage drama, comedy, and so forth were heavily censored by the authorities, and anyone who was suspected of sympathizing with the liberation struggle was detained or oppressed. For example, Yemane Barya, one of the most renowned Eritrean artists (a Tigrinya singer) was detained after he produced a song entitled *lula* (ሉላ), "diamond," in 1975. The authorities alleged that the song addressed Eritrea's political case although literally the song dealt with a girl whose boyfriend (lover) was forcibly taken away from her. After serving a prison term for some months, Yemane Barya managed to escape from Asmara and join the Eritrean Liberation Front (ELF). A number of the women who were active members of Ma.Te.A., such as Tsehaytu Beraki, also left Asmara to join the ELF; and later many others, such as Tebereh Tesfahuney, joined the Eritrean People's Liberation Front (EPLF). In such a way, local systems of performing arts were increasingly suppressed throughout Ethiopia's occupation of Eritrea.

On the one hand, Ethiopia's suppressive measures against Eritrean artists fragmented the urban performing arts. On the other hand, the exodus of professional urban performers who joined the liberation army stimulated vibrant cultural activities on the Liberation Fronts (first the ELF and later the EPLF). The ELF and EPLF founded respective cultural troupes. The main objectives of these cultural troupes were to:

- Provide performances to entertain the liberation armies
- Preserve "useful" cultural values and customs
- Serve as a means to disseminate campaigns and propaganda—to awaken popular awareness of the liberation struggle, to boost the morale of combatants and non-combatants alike, and more

Explaining the growth of cultural performances within the EPLF, Matzke (2003a: 160) notes:

The EPLF encouraged cultural work from 1975 onwards, in the form of a full-time central cultural troupe and innumerable smaller amateur ones in military units and non-combatant departments. These groups usually produced variety shows dominated by music, song and dance representing all Eritrean nationalities, as well as educational and political sketches. Stage drama became more prominent when a Section of Literature and Drama was introduced in 1981 as part of the Division of Culture in the Department of Political Orientation, Education and Culture. Women performers became increasingly prominent, but they never inhabited central positions as cultural officers in the Division of Culture.

The performing arts in the EPLF featured mainly songs, posters, music, drama, and dance related to all nationalities of the country. The Cultural Department of the EPLF was engaged in a number of artistic works, a great many of which reflected revolutionary themes. Drama performances included short and long tragedies, short comedies and comic sketches, some translated adaptations of European dramas—Shakespeare, Ibsen, and Gogol; and theoretical writings of some African works such as those of Ngugi wa Thiongo were also used (see Matzke 2008a; 2003b; Negash 1999).

Songs, much like the literature produced by the Eritrean liberation struggle, usually reflected an outraged reaction to Ethiopia's occupation and commented on timely military and political circumstances. Singing contests were also used for propaganda purposes. A number of singers and performers, notably Tekle Keflemaryam (commonly known as Wedi Tikul), Aklilu Foto (commonly known as Tefono), Tesfay Mehari (commonly known as Fihira), Abrehet Ankere, Berekti Weldeselassie (commonly known as Tanki), and many others produced revolutionary performances and played vital roles in stimulating popular awareness for the liberation struggle.

In general, the performing arts, or more broadly "culture," became an important tool of mobilization during the years of the liberation struggle. Moreover, it "began to be more aggressively promoted as 'revolutionary culture' in the field" (Matzke 2008a: 16). Note that the Eritrean liberation fighters referred to their area of operations as *meda* (ሜዳ) "field." Starting from the mid-1970s, the EPLF cultural troupes were organized almost at all military levels (such as at brigade and army division levels). A number of influential cultural troupes, including a Central Cultural Troupe (CCT), operated until the strategic retreat in 1978 when the EPLF focused almost entirely on defending its military positions. This status was then changed in the early 1980s when a new structure was needed, and the EPLF re-established the Central Cultural Troupe (Matzke 2008a: 15–20). Until the end of the conflict (1991) the CCT was a remarkably influential center of performing arts and literature. Cultural troupes under the CCT toured the country (where there was little Ethiopian control known by the fighters as "liberated areas") and provided cultural shows to combatants and civilians. The shows usually included music, dances, and drama that mostly reflected military and political events in the country.

Based in the Sahel Mountains (especially around the areas of Fah and Arrag), a number of professional artists and writers engaged in full-time production of revolutionary aesthetic works and literature as well as fighting in combat whenever the need arose. These artists included Alemseged Tesfai (by training a lawyer and historian but also a distinguished playwright), Angesom Isak (writer), Temesgen Tiku'e (writer), Mesgun Feraday (playwright), Solomon Dirar (writer), Isaias Tsegai (playwright) and Asmerom Habtemariam (journalist, poet, and comedian). This group produced a significant amount of literature. For example, one of Alemseged Tesfai's important works, *eti kalie kunat* (እቲ ካልእ ኩናት), "the other war," was widely performed in the theater (for further reading on the subjects, see Matzke [2008a] and Negash[1999: 180-186]).

Since independence, the performing arts have grown significantly. In fact, the performing arts have played a vigorous role in the nation-building process. A great deal of artistic production promotes a positive nationalist image—for military mobilization, the state's social and economic rehabilitation programs, and other national objectives. The development of arts in Eritrea has been characterized by diversity and interaction between different formats such as media, performing arts, films, photography, and handicrafts (Matzke 2002b: 27).

After independence, a number of initiatives were also taken to promote artistic works in Eritrea. For example, the Asmara School of Art was opened to train new artists. Renowned artists such as Fesehayye Zemichael and Berhanne Adonai teach in the school.

CINEMAS AND FILM PRODUCTION IN POST-INDEPENDENT ERITREA

As mentioned earlier, the introduction of "modern" performing arts in Eritrea is associated with Italian colonial rule in the country. Modernization and urbanization were characterized by the construction of cinema and theater houses in urban centers such as Asmara. The first cinema in Eritrea—*Teatro Asmara*, Asmara Theater—was constructed by the Italians in 1918. At present (2009) Asmara Theater no longer serves as a cinema but is used by various cultural groups as an important site for rehearsals of stage drama, music, and other performing arts. The construction of a number of other cinemas in Asmara continued throughout the 1920s and 1930s. By the 1930s, major towns in Eritrea also had cinemas or film houses. By 1940, there were at least three film houses in Massawa. Film venues were also constructed in the towns of Keren, Akordat, and Dekemhare. Most early cinemas and theater houses were used for performances related to stage drama, comic sketches, music performances (such as orchestra recitals). All in all there were about ten cinemas countrywide.

However, not all Eritreans under Italian colonial rule were privileged to enjoy watching and/or performing in modern arts. Owing to the policies of segregation introduced by the state, most of the urban zones that contained cinema houses were reserved for Europeans. For example, Asmara had three settlement zones: the zone reserved only for Italians (mainly central parts of the town); the zone reserved only for the *mista* (for Europeans and other nationalities); and the zone reserved purely for the indigenous population (Checchi 1910: 67). Indigenous people were not permitted into any zone that was reserved for Europeans (for further reading on urban life during the Italian period, see Locatelli 2004). Yet, the theaters and cinema houses built by the Italians are valued additions to a great architectural heritage. Even currently (2009), most of the cinemas built in the 1920s and 1930s are serving as important institutions for the performing arts. Some of most remarkable cinemas in Eritrea are:

- Cinema Roma (located in Asmara, constructed in 1937)
- Cinema Hamassien (located in Asmara, constructed in 1939 [?])
- Cinema Impero (located in Asmara, constructed in 1937)
- Cinema Capitol (located in Asmara, constructed in 1937)
- Cinema Odeon (located in Asmara, constructed in 1938)

British rule in Eritrea (1941–1952) was characterized by the abolition of "color bar" and the relative liberalization of social institutions. The expansion of educational and public institutions increased the momentum of political and cultural development. Schools began to be the main centers of change, including the transformation of the performing arts in Eritrea. Most early theater and other cultural associations were composed of teachers and students. These theater associations also played defining roles in shaping national consciousness and identity. The Eritrean cinemas served as important centers for cultural activities throughout the decades. Even since independence, these cinemas have continued to play dynamic roles as centers for theater and other performing arts.

As stated earlier, Eritrean cinemas presented shows related to stage dramas, orchestra, and European films during the Italian period. Throughout the post-Italian period, the cinemas presented European, Indian, and American films. Even during the period of Ethiopian rule in Eritrea, there were no local movies, and the cinemas usually screened foreign movies. During the period of the 1970s and throughout the 1980s, Indian movies became extremely popular with the public. Indian movies such as *Mother India* and others were the most well-received shows in Eritrea, particularly Asmara.

Film production, especially documentaries and drama recordings, was already in place during the liberation struggle. Documentary films of the time were produced in the various languages of the country. Following the lead of other performing arts, documentary films were used for specific nationalistic purposes such as campaigning and mobilization. Some of the above-mentioned plays such as *eti kalie kunat*, "the other war," *sedrabet* (ስድራቤት), "family," as well as recordings of numerous-stage performances (mostly musical and dance) were also reproduced in films.

As stated earlier, the performing arts have shown significant improvement since Eritrea's independence. There have also been new advancements in the sphere of film production. Under its Cultural Affairs Bureau, the Eritrean ruling party established the Film and Drama Branch. Since its establishment, this branch has been fully engaged in filmmaking and the documentation of stage dramas. Although all Eritrean films are produced in local languages (mostly in Tigrinya), several of them contain English subtitles. By 1997, a number of local films and new drama recordings appeared in Eritrean cinemas. Some of the movies presented in Eritrean cinemas have included *barud 77* (ባሩድ 77) ("The 1977's Gunpowder") and *eta adde* (እታ አደ) ("The Mother"). For the first time in their history, Eritrean cinemas are showing predominantly local movies and dramas. Eritreans started to fill cinemas to watch movies in their own native language(s). A number of the more popular films focus on themes of Eritrea's liberation war, resistance, and patriotism. However, since 2001, filmmaking has focused on themes of love and sexuality, traditions, and more. As of 2009, there are about 100 films known to the author, and the number of Eritrean films may be higher. Yet, it should be noted that the quality of most of the films is still poor. The Eritrean film industry may also need to establish training centers for filmmaking to help produce higher-quality films.

HANDICRAFTS

Most types of handicrafts involve artistic creativity in transforming and processing raw materials into tools and goods. In Eritrea, handicrafts comprise an important source of various types of products. In rural areas, especially, primary work tools are the product of handicrafts. The principal handicrafts in Eritrea are pottery, woodwork, ironwork, leatherwork, blacksmithing/jewelry, basketry, and more. Although a great variety of handicraft works are produced to satisfy of local needs, their designs originate with the individual creativity of each artisan. Each ethnolinguistic group in Eritrea has its own specialized art of handicraft. A number of lowland groups comprise

Hand-crafted products. (M. Tesfagiorgis)

A variety of hand-crafted products. (M. Tesfagiorgis)

Meblie Kursi or Winchihti, a traditional tool for serving snacks. (M. Tesfagiorgis)

skilled artisans in basketry and other household tools made of local raw materials (commonly from *laka* (ላካ)—palm tree leaves). Highlanders have skilled artisans such as blacksmiths, ironworkers, pottery makers, and others.

Handicraft works reflect economic, cultural, and religious aspects of a society. Therefore, there are diverse handicraft arts among Eritrean society. The type and function of a particular handicraft generally determines whether the artisans are part-time or full-time producers. Most often, an artisan involved in the production of handicrafts invests labor on either a seasonal or year-round basis. Although greater varieties of handicraft works are created by skilled artisans, people who are engaged in certain types of works, such as farming, may produce their own equipment—such as plow tools. Handicraft production usually involves gender-based labor. For example, *sife* (ስፈ) (special designs related to basketry, mats, trays, and more), pottery, textile designs, spinning, and weaving are performed by women. Handicrafts related to woodworking and ironworking are usually performed by men. Leatherworks and

Moseb, a traditional tool for storing food, and also serves as tray or dining table. (M. Tesfagiorgis)

Hand-crafted products at the Akordat Market, 2009. (S. Tesfagiorgis)

jewelry designing may involve both genders. Among the Eritrean ethnolinguistic groups, there are certain skilled individuals who make their living on their handicraft skills, including blacksmiths, tanners, potters, and textile weavers.

The art of handicrafts in the Horn of Africa in general and Eritrea in particular has a long history. Based on the available archaeological findings, we can surmise that the technology of handicrafts in the territory has long been practiced in human history. Fragmented pottery shards (with or without designs) and other types of artifacts indicate that handicraft works were well known during the prehistoric periods. For example, pottery works excavated at Yeha (modern-day Tigray, Ethiopia) indicate that handicrafts, particularly ceramic works, were developed around sixth–fifth century B.C. (Amborn 2005: 999). Ancient ceramic artwork was centered on the productionof jars and bowls. Moreover, ironworking seems to have started as early as the time of ceramic productions. Various iron tools were produced by the ancient populations of the region.

LEATHERWORK

Tanning is one of the most integrated handicrafts among all the ethnolinguistic groups in Eritrea. Most local peasants and pastorals, regardless of gender differences, engage in producing leather products necessary to their daily activities—such as household leather utensils. For some Eritrean ethnolinguistic groups, leatherworks such as mats and a number of other items comprise their household tools. Hides of cattle are usually efficiently transformed into a number of tools. A number of their commodities are fashioned from leather arts. For instance, among the Tigrinya ethnolinguistic group, a typical rural household would possess leatherworks such as stools, musical instruments, mats, and containers such as a *harbbi* (ሓርቢ.)—a sort of tiny sack usually used as a milk container; a *delmi* (ደልሚ.)—a type of sack usually used for containing water; and a *loqota* (ለቖታ)—a leather sack for containing grain. Leatherworks are made by men and/or women, depending on the type of leather goods being produced, and depending on which cultural group is the producer. Depending on the particular cultural tradition, hides are used for various purposes: for making sandals and shoes, as mats, tents, bags, belts, yarns, processed sacks, clothing, and more.

POTTERY

Pottery (ceramics) comprises one of the most important technological arts in Eriteria. Refined earthenware ceramic technology developed with the artistic creativity of the peoples of Eritrea for most of their history. Great numbers of traditional household tools are formed from pottery works. For instance, most commodities in the Tigrinya communities are made of pottery. Among the traditional pottery tools of the Tigrinya ethnolinguistic group are the *jebena/jebenat* (ጀበና/ጀበናት) (coffee pot); the *'etro* (ዕትሮ)—water or *suwa* container; the *sarma* (ሳርማ)—*suwa* or water container; the *qura'e* (ቁራዕ)—a sort of traditional pot for cooking various types of food, including meat and vegetables; the *t'sahli* (ጻሕሊ.)—traditional tool for making stews; the *mogogo* (ምጎጎ)—traditional stove; and so on. The art of pottery among the Eritrean ethnolinguistic groups reflects their respective traditions. A great majority of potters are women. Most pottery works are made out of clay soil. The art, modeling, and design of all pottery works among the Eritrean ethnolinguistic groups are made by hand. This means that all types of pottery involve intensive work for the production of each tool.

IRON/METALWORK

It is evident that metalworking has a long tradition among the Eritrean ethnolinguistic groups. Although we do not have conclusive evidence as to exactly when ironworking became an important component of handicraft technology in the region, there are indications that local iron tools were already in production during the early Aksumite era.

Blacksmiths played valuable roles in the social, economic, and military history of the region. They produced various articles that served as both economic and military instruments, which include: plowshares and other farming equipment, sickles, axes, hammers, and various kinds of household tools. For military or hunting purposes, blacksmiths produced a number of tools, including spears, swords, and knives. Blacksmiths developed their own ways of iron smelting and mastered ironworking in accordance to local needs. Regrettably, blacksmiths usually occupied a lower social rank among the Tigrinya, which was mainly because of the traditional belief that blacksmiths possessed undesirable supernatural powers. Based on the fanciful belief that blacksmiths could turn into flesh-eating animals during darkness, people usually

Young man in Medeber workshop. (S. Tesfagiorgis)

avoided social contacts with them (see also Pankhurst 1990: 222–224). Therefore, blacksmiths were sometimes unjustifiably condemned by communal beliefs and suffered social exclusion and humiliation. Although prejudices against blacksmiths varied from region to region and from community to community, generally they were considered an excluded caste within any given community.

Modern Eritrean metal forgers and blacksmiths are engaged in metalworking; and they possess finely honed skills. In fact, they produce most of their community's ironwork. Thanks to the expertise of these professionals, metal waste is quite minimal in Eritrea. Metal tools are repaired, recycled, or modified in utilizable fashion. A good example of an ironwork site in Eritrea is the Medeber Metal Market in Asmara. In Medeber (a Tigrinya term literally meaning "junkyard"), almost all sorts of metal bits are processed to eventually serve as functional tools—such as making metal coffee pots and stoves, chairs, desks, doors, shovels, axes, plowshares, and more. Most of the local weapons such as swords, spears, daggers, and so on are also produced by these skilled blacksmiths. Medeber is a handicraft market as well as a site where impressive creativity, innovation, and teaching of Eritrean metalworkers takes place. Observing the creative art of Medeber, Belcher notes:

> Perhaps the most prevalent Eritrean self-identification is of being a mechanically minded people . . . In a country that has had almost every inch bombed, there is much scrap metal available and the artisans of Medeber are busy making domestic goods from bomb casings, old tires, barrels, tanks, wire and tin cans. Part ingenuity, part the necessity of poverty, Medeber is a lesson in the art of transforming tragedy into utility" (Belcher 2000: 94–95).

SCULPTURE/MONUMENTS

Sculpture is one of the least practiced art forms in Eritrea. The renaissance of sculptural art took place during the war of liberation, especially starting in the 1970s. The main actors of the revival of sculpture in Eritrea were a few members of the liberation struggle who also engaged in artistic works such as painting and music. Among the most renowned EPLF (Eritrean People's Liberation Front) sculptors are Fessehaye Zemichael and Elsa Yacob (Matzke 2002: 35–39). Through their paintings and sculptures, these fighters attempted to reflect the contemporary ramifications of the liberation struggle. However, there is no thriving practice of sculptural art in the country.

Monument sculptures are also relatively minimal in Eritrea. There are only a few monuments distributed in Eritrean cities and towns. For example, in Asmara, there is a monument resembling plastic sandals. The sculptured sandals represent the type worn by the liberation fighters. In Massawa, a monument of three tanks has been erected to commemorate the liberation struggle.

Although Eritrean history is characterized by war and resistance, there are almost no memorial sculptures to honor the sacrifices of this history. "One finds no larger-than-life sculptures of weary but determined fighters, no triumphal arches, no eternal flames, no empty tombs . . . Eritrean monuments are less about trying to preserve its materiality" (Belcher 2000: 97). Here and there, tombs and "martyrs' cemetery"

Monument of a tank. (J. Miran)

monuments and sculptures can be found. But their small number and limited distribution do not appropriately venerate the hard-won independence of the country.

BASKETRY

Basketry is usually an exclusive task of women. Especially in the lowlands of Eritrea, where there is abundant material for basket-weaving, women engage in making a variety of food containers. *Laka*—leaves of the palm tree—is the main material for basketry. Women weave various sorts of baskets, sometimes with decorative designs. A number of articles are produced by these women, such as *zenbil* (ዘንቢል)—a type of container for transporting fruits, vegetables, and other foodstuffs; *mekoster* (መኰስተር)—dusters of various kinds; *borsa* (ቦርሳ)—bags, and more.

ARCHITECTURE

There are two main types of traditional architecture (housing) in the Eritrean plateau—the *hidmo* (ህድሞ) and the *agudo* (አጉዶ) or *tikul* (hut). The *hidmo* is widespread in the Hamasien and Akele Guzay provinces. It is a rectangular-shaped, flat-roofed

Early architecture: Torino Hotel, Massawa. (J. Miran)

traditional dwelling, and it is made of wood, earth, stone, and mud. The pillars are made of strong juniper or olive tree trunks. The size of a *hidmo* house is measured by the number of *maybets* (ማይቤት) (the area between two vertically erected pillars). *Hidmo* houses are usually separated into two sections—*wushate* (ውሻጠ) "kitchen" and *mederibet* (ምድሪ ቤት) "living room." Although the *hidmo* type of housing can be found here and there in the western parts of the central plateau, the most common type of houses in this area are well-constructed cylindrical huts, usually made of stone and clay. In recent times, a *mereba'e* (መረባዕ) house (usually rectangular with stonewalls, cement floors, and a corrugated iron roof) has become a predominant type of housing

A building of Turkish architecture. (J. Miran)

Italian-built fortification building in Akordat. (S. Tesfagiorgis)

in all the provinces of the central plateau. As most of the pastoral communities establish temporal settlements, they construct temporary dwellings such as huts and *Agnet* (a hut-style housing made of mats and cattle skins).

Local architecture dates back to ancient times. Although archaeology has yet to proclaim anything definitive about features of the architecture, ancient city-states such as Adulis, Metera, and Kohayto were characterized by sophisticated systems of architecture. Based on archaeological remains, these cities were constructed of stone-walled buildings and perhaps had remarkable local villas and monumental structures. The Aksumite architecture (first to seventh century A.D.) was also characterized by magnificent architecture. This was reflected in the buildings of early churches such as the Enda Mariyam Siyon of Aksum and the remains of ancient villas in Metera. Ancient architecture also reveals that there was a complex social structure with features of remarkable stratification.

Eritrean buildings, especially on the coast of the Red Sea (Massawa), were heavily influenced by Ottoman architecture. The Turks, who occupied Massawa and its vicinities for about 300 years, introduced new architectural designs to the area in their superb and extravagant mosques, palaces, and small dwellings. Ottoman architecture in the area seems to have incorporated ancient Byzantine (Mediterranean) elements as well as Islamic (Middle Eastern) features.

"Modern" architecture was introduced to Eritrea by the Italians. Therefore, the modern urban architecture of Eritrea strongly reflects its colonial heritage. For example, Asmara was "modernized" during the Italian colonial period. Impressed

Typical Italian architecture in a street in Asmara. (J. Miran)

by the fascinating architectural development of the city, the Italian colonizers used to call Asmara *Piccola Roma* "little Rome." Especially during the reign of Benito Mussolini, Asmara was transformed into a modern city with magnificent buildings such as cafés, restaurants, cinemas, museums, municipality buildings, and government palaces (for further details about Asmara's architecture, see Denison; Naigzy et al [2003]).

One of the most impressive buildings to visit in Asmara is the National Museum of Eritrea. Located near the center of the city, the National Museum of Eritrea was opened in 1992. Since its establishment, this museum has exhibited archaeological and historical collections related to all the people of Eritrea. It strives to identify, study, interpret, and preserve archaeological, ethnographic, and natural historical findings from the region's antiquity. The museum also conducts its own archaeological surveys and excavations in the country. The museum contains a considerable number and type of artifacts dealing with the ancient and modern history of Eritrea and the region at large.

REFERENCES

Adonai, Michael (2007). *Michael Adonai and Painting*. Unpublished biography, posted at http://www.adonaiartwork.com/images/stories/archive/Michael_Adonai_and_painting_.pdf (accessed on May 2009, [Text in Tigrinya]).

Amborn, Hermann (2005). "Handicrafts." In: Uhlig, Siegbert (ed.), *Encyclopaedia Aethiopica*. Vol. 3, Wiesbaden: Harrassowitz Verlag, pp. 999–1003.

Bairu, Zerabruk (2008). "Traditional Art in Eritrea." In: Gebremedhin, Tesfa G. and Tesfagiorgis, Gebre H. (eds.). *Traditions of Eritrea: Linking the Past to the Future*. Trenton, NJ: Red Sea Press, pp. 190–228.

Belcher, Wendy (2000). "After the Freedom: Post-War Cultural Production and National Identity in Eritrea." In: *Third Text: Socialist Eastern Europe*, 50 (Special Issue, Spring), pp. 87–125.

Carillet, Jean-Bernard and Phillips, Matt (2006). *"Lonely Planet": Ethiopia and Eritrea.* 3rd rev. ed., n.p.: Lonely Planet.

Checchi, Michele (1910). *Asmara*. Roma: n.a.

Denison, Edward and Paice, Edward (2002). *Eritrea: The Bradt Travel Guide*. Chalfont: St. Peter Bradt.

Denison, Edward; Yu Re, Guang and Gebremedhin, Naigzy (2003). *Asmara: Africa's Secret Modernist City*. London: Merrell; illustrated edition.

Encyclopaedia Britanica Ultimate reference (DVD 2007).

Gebremedhin, Tesfa G. (2002). *Women, Tradition and Development: A Case of Eritrea*. Trenton, NJ: Red Sea Press.

Gebremedhin, Tesfa G. and Tesfagiorgis, Gebre H. (eds.) (2008). *Traditions of Eritrea: Linking the Past to the Future*. Trenton, NJ: Red Sea Press.

Habtemariam, Asmerom (2009). *"bahlen hebreteseben* [Culture and Society]." In: *Haddas Ertra newspaper* (issue April 2, p. 4).

Littmann, Enno (1910). *Publications of the Princeton Expedition to Abyssinia*. Vol. II, Leyden [Leiden]: Late E. J. Brill.

Locatelli, Francesca (2004). *Asmara During the Italian Period: Order, Disorder and Urban Identities—1890–1941*. (Ph.D. Dissertation), SOAS, University of London.

Matzke, Christine (2002a). "Comrades in Arts and Arms: Stories of Wars and Watercolours from Eritrea." In: Döring, Tobias (ed.). *African Cultures, Visual Arts, and the Museum: Sights/Sites Creativity and Conflict*. Amsterdam/New York: Editions Rodopi, pp. 21–54.

Matzke, Christine (2002b). "Of *Suwa* Houses & Singing Contests: Early Urban Women Performers in Asmara, Eritrea." In: Banham, Martin, et al. (eds.). *African Theatre Women*. Oxford: James Currey, pp. 29–46.

Matzke, Christine (2002c). "Of *Suwa* Houses and Singing Contests: Early Urban Women Performers in Asmara, Eritrea." In: Banham, Martin; Gibbs, James; Osofisan, Femi; Gasthg and Plastow, Jane (eds.). *African Theatre: Women*. Oxford: James Currey, pp. 29-46.

Matzke, Christine (2003a)."Engendering Theatre in Eritrea: The Roles and Representations of Women in the Performing Arts." In: Eva-Maria Bruchhaus (ed.). *Hot Spot Horn of Africa: Between Integration and Disintegration*. Münster: Lit Verlag, pp. 156–164.

Matzke, Christine (2003b). *En-gendering Theatre in Eritrea: The Roles and Representations of Women in the Performing Arts*. Unpublished Ph.D. Dissertation, School of English: University of Leeds.

Matzke, Christine (2004). "Shakespeare and Surgery in the Eritrean Liberation Struggle: Performance Culture in Orota." In: *Journal of Eritrean Studies* 3, 1, pp. 26–40.

Matzke, Christine (2008a). "'Life in the Camp of the Enemy': Alemseged Tesfai's Theatre of War." In: Emenyonu, Ernest E. (ed.). *African Literature Today 26: War in African Literature Today*. Oxford: James Currey, pp. 15–32.

Matzke, Christine (2008b). *"Mahber Te'atr Asmera*—The Asmara Theatre Association, 1961–1974." In: Banham, Martin, James Gibbs, and Femi Osofisan (eds.). *African Theatre: Companies*. Oxford: James Currey, pp. 62–81.

Matzke, Christine (2008c). "The Asmara Theatre Association (1961–74): *Mahber Teyatr Asmera*." In: Gibbs, James (ed.). *African Theatre Companies*. Leeds: James Currey, pp. 62–81.

Negash, Ghirmai (1999). *A History of Tigrinya Literature in Eritrea: The Oral and the Written (1890–1991)*. Trenton, NJ: Red Sea Press.

Negash, Ghirmai (2008). *"Oral Poetic Tradition of the Tigrinya."* In: Gebremedhin, Tesfa G. and Tesfagiorgis, Gebre H. (eds.) (2008). *Traditions of Eritrea: Linking the Past to the Future.* Trenton, NJ: Red Sea Press, pp. 155–189.

NgCheong-Lum, Roseline (2005). *Eritrea.* New York: Marshall Cavendish.

Pankhurst, Richard (1990). *A Social History of Ethiopia: The Northern and Central Highlands from Early Medieval Times to the Rise of Emperor Téwodros II.* Addis Ababa: St. Edmundsbury Press.

Pankurst, Rita (2003). "Cultural Role of Coffee in Ethiopia." In: Uhlig, Siegbert (ed.), *Encyclopaedia Aethiopica.* Wiesbaden: Harrassowitz Verlag, pp. 764–765.

Schmidt, Peter, Curtis, Matthew C., et al. (2008). *The archaeology of ancient Eritrea.* Trenton, NJ: Red Sea Press.

Tessema, Asres (2006). *Teamot: kab tarik medrekawi senetebeb ertra* [The Taste: Aspects of Eritrean Performing Arts]. Asmara: Francescana Printing Press.

The Tigre culture and customs: http://www.awkir.com (access in August 2009).

Tronvoll, Kjetil (199). *Mai Weini; A Highland Village in Eritrea: A Study of the People, Their Livelihood, and Land Tenure During Times of Turbulence.* Lawrenceville, NJ: Red Sea Press.

Yatana Entertainment—Tigrinya cultural movie, 2008.

Music

In Eritrea, each ethnolinguistic group has its own form of music; hence, there is a great diversity in the art of musical performance. But there are also some common musical traits among the various ethnolinguistic groups in the country. Unfortunately, comprehensive studies related to the arts and music in Eritrea have yet to be conducted. The available source materials are slight and do not present an in-depth analysis of most ethnolinguistic music in the country. The book by Mariana Valentini, *Traditional Musical Instruments in the Eritrean Highlands* (published in 2004), is one of the few comprehensive published studies on the subject. In the following sections, a brief overview is presented of religious, secular, traditional, and folk musical instruments and performances in the highlands of Eritrea.

Traditional musical instruments comprise a unique system of modalities called *qinit* (ቅኒት). The modalities are classified according to the sounds of the instruments. According to Valentini (2004), there are four distinct types of modes:

> *Idiophones:* Types of musical instruments that produce sounds without any strings or membranes. These instruments include sacred instruments such as the *tsenat-sil* (ጸናጽል)—sistrum/rattles and the *moquomya* (መቋምያ)—long sticks used for leaning and maintaining dance rhythm.

> *Chordophones:* Types of musical instruments that produce their sounds by using one or more strings. In Eritrea, these instruments include the *kerar* (ክራC)—a

five- or six-string lyre); *wat'a* or *chira-wat'a* (ዋጣ/ጭራ–ዋጣ)—a single string lute; *begena* (በገና)—a ten or more string lyre, which resembles the *kerar* but is bigger in size.

Aerophones: Types of musical instruments that produce sounds through vibrating air. The type of traditional instruments in this category include the *shambeqo* (ሻምብቆ)—a bamboo flute comprising four or more holes; *embelta* (እምብልታ)—a metal or bamboo flute similar to *shambeqo* but without holes; and *meleket* (መለኸት)—a long flute-like trumpet.

Membranophones: Types of musical instruments that are usually associated with various kinds of drums. The types of traditional instruments in this category are the *kebero-betekerestiyan* (ከበሮ–ቤተክርስትያን)—church hand drums; *kebero* (ከበሮ)—secular hand drums; and *negarit* (ነጋሪት)—a type of small drum played by a hard stick to make secular announcements and proclamations.

SACRED MUSIC

Secular, particularly Christian, musical tradition goes as far back as at least to the era of Aksum (around the sixth century A.D.). As noted by Matzke, "The Ethiopian [and Eritrean] Christianity developed unique worship practices including a distinct church music and music notation, a chanted liturgy and religious dancing for the priests" (Matzke 2003b: 40). Sacred music dealt with religious songs, including the *psalms of David* and religious *zema* (ዜማ)—liturgical chants—in the Aksumite churches. During the Aksumite era, the famous church musician Saint Yared became renowned for his musical and religious performances in the Christian Orthodox church. "He was the saint of all musicians, and it is thought that he was the author of many and of all the church hymns written for different times of the year" (Valentini 2004: 10). He became a legendary saint with great musical capabilities and liturgical recitations. Saint Yared's main musical genres/modes fall into three categories: the *ge'ez* (ግዕዝ)—a type of genre that offers thanks and honor to the Father; *'ezl* (እዝል)—a type of genre that offers an honor to the Son; and the *'araray* (አራራይ)—a type of genre that offers an honor to the Holy Spirit (Valentini 2004: 10–11). All musical genres of the territory are believed to be based on the above-mentioned categories. Saint Yared is believed to have had divinely inspired musical capabilities during the time he composed the sacred songs (collectively known as *mahlet* [ማኅሌት]). Like religious painting, religious music also prospered with the expansion of Christianity in the region. Even after the fall of Aksum, the tradition of religious music was maintained and continues to this day. Some of the main instruments used for sacred music follow.

kebero-betekeristyan (church drum): This type of *kebero* is a two-sided hand drum and is larger than the one used for secular music. The size of the drum may be irregular. Some of the smallest drums of this kind may be up to 60 centimeters high; the height of similar but bigger drums may reach over a meter (Valentini 2004: 52). Although the two ends of the drum are covered by an oxskin of high quality, the rest of the drum parts may be covered by textiles of splendid colors interwoven with strings made of leather. The handles of the drum are also made of leather. Both sides of the *kebero* are designed to produce different sounds; hence, the area size of one side

Kebero-betekerestyan: Church drum. (M. Tesfagiorgis)

of the *kebero* are designed to produce different sounds; hence, the area size of one side is usually bigger than the other. It is played by hitting both sides; and priests play this drum by putting it on the ground or by hanging it on their shoulders. According to Valentini (2004), the production of such a drum requires certain religious rituals. For example, it involves the scarifying of a selected (*'awlie* [አውልዕ] wild olive or *'awhi* [አውሒ]—*Cordia Africana*, or any other type of plant) tree accompanied by a sacred ceremony; the branches and trunks of the tree are also not wasted and are used to make other instruments such as crosses and *moqomyas*. The ritual also involves the slaughtering of an ox. While the meat of the ox is consumed by all attendants of the ritual, its skin in used to produce a drum (for more details, see Valentini 2004: 53–54).

tsenatsil (sistrum): A small rattle used as a musical instrument usually with a wooden handle, U-shaped metal frame made of iron, silver, or copper; two or three metal wires connecting the two frames; and comprising some iron discs. During musical performances, the sistrum is shaken to produce various forms of sounds. It is commonly used during liturgical chanting.

met'qi'e (መጥቀዕ)—stone bells: These types of bells are made up of flat and resonant stones. Usually three flat and strong stones are hung on a horizontal wooden trunk. The player of *met'qi'e* hits the stones with round, hard stones to produce a simple musical sound. The function of these stones is equivalent to modern church bells. These traditional bells have been in use for many centuries although they are rarely used nowadays (for further details, see Valentini 2004: 38–40).

Church tsenatsil. (M. Tesfagiorgis)

Moqomya. (M. Tesfagiorgis)

Sacred music is performed during religious festivities such as *fasika* (Easter), *timket* (Epiphany), and *meskel* (the feast of the True Cross). During these festivities, varieties of musical genres and dances are performed—all of which are related to praising, honoring, and giving glory to God. The musical instruments are accompanied by *zema* (long religious hymns or songs) and religious dances.

During religious festivities, mainly priests and members of the clergy play music and dance, but this does not mean that non-priests do not take part in the dancing and singing contests. Describing the Orthodox Christian musical performances during *meskel* (a religious ceremony that takes place on September 27), Valentini (2004) notes:

> They [priests] dance with the cheberos [kebero-betekerestian] hanging from their necks and resting a wooden stick (moquomias) on their shoulder. If the moquomya is held with the right hand, the tzenatsel [tsenatsil] is played with the left, and vice versa: their particular choice of position depends on the various churches. The priests who play the tzenatsel and hold the moquomiya place themselves in two lines, one facing the other. Each line is made up of approximately ten priests—one next to each other; whilst singing, they start the first steps of the dance by placing the weight of their bodies first on the right foot; then on their left: both steps last the same length of time and they always move on the strong beat of the music; similarly the moquomiya is moved forward (on the strong beat) and then back again on the one shoulder (on the weak beat); at times they even wave it right and then left, all this while the other hand plays the tzenatsel, first towards the ground (on the strong beat) and forward, the towards the sky (on the weak beat) (Valentini 2004: 14).

Kebero-betekeristyan is also played during the sacred chant. Two or more *kebero-betekiristyan* players hang the big drums on their shoulders and perform different tempos of beats. The singing, drumming, and *tsenatsil* contests may be accompanied by a variety of body movements. For instance, *kebero-betekiristyan* players may perform jumping and dancing, while attendants may clap their hands in accordance with the variety of rhythms performed. The whole dancing and singing contests provide an impressive and celebratory atmosphere. It should be noted that all the songs and chants during the celebrations are held in the language of the liturgy—Ge'ez. Yet, many churches also recruit young boys and girls as religious singers. Although these singers may sing some extracts of choirs in Ge'ez, most of the choirs played by the young singers are performed in the local language (Tigrinya). These young singers may also use modern musical instruments such as a piano.

SECULAR MUSIC

Similar to sacred music, traditional secular music (especially among the Tigrinya ethnolinguistic group) was limited to some minority groups of performers commonly known as *hamien* (ሓሜን)—wandering singers and *wat'ot* (ዋጦት)—wandering musicians. These performers played music on particular festive occasions such as weddings and other communal celebrations. *Hamien* performers were usually invited to play their singing contests during social occasions such as wedding and baptism ceremonies. They usually got no formal training apart from their own performance experience in villages and towns. Most of the time, these performers had the freedom to practice their own art during musical performances. They decided which music to play for which audiences. In addition to the agreed-upon compensation, these artists usually solicit individuals among the audience to get extra remuneration. Interestingly, women were not encouraged to play any traditional musical instruments until recently, and most performing groups consisted of men. Women music artists usually received dejection by members of the communities. As we shall see below, most women who became *hamien* or *wat'ot* were relegated to the lowest caste—at least until the 1940s.

Performing secular music was not a popularly chosen profession. Eritrean societies usually associated professions related to music with *hamien* or *wat'a*, and so professionals were usually "looked down upon as a caste, even if admired for their artistry. Their mastery of language was especially appreciated which was often more important than their musical talent" (Matzke 2003: 55–56).

FOLK MUSICAL INSTRUMENTS
The kerar

The *kerar* is commonly a five-stringed lyre, comprising five notes. But modern *kerar* may comprise more than five notes and also electronic parts. The sound-box, the frames/pillars, and the beam of the instrument are usually made up of wood. The two

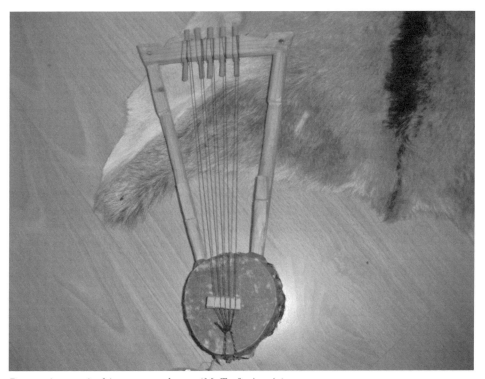

Decorative musical instrument, kerar. (M. Tesfagiorgis)

frames of the instrument are of the same size and length. The strings are stretched from the bottom of the sound-box to the horizontal beam to which the strings are attached.

The *kerar* is one of the most popular traditional musical instruments in Eritrea. Unlike players of the guitar and other instruments in the West, players of the *kerar* do not get formal training. Rather, they learn to play the instrument on their own initiative and through non-formal training with experienced players. Its name may vary, but the *kerar* is one of the most widely used instruments among the Eritrean ethnolinguistic groups.

In the Eritrean highlands, the *kerar* is the most popular instrument of the local population. Similar to *wat'a* professional players, professional *kerar* players also possess great oral poetry skills. They may compose their own songs or replay traditional melodies. Among the Tigrinya, professional *kerar* players are invited to almost all secular festivities. For example, *kerar* musicians play a significant role in *guayla* (ጓይላ)—traditional music and dance at wedding ceremonies.

The wat'a/chira-wat'a

In many cases the names *chira-wat'a* and simply *wat'a* are used to refer to the instrument and a professional player, respectively. Yet, many also use *wat'a* as an eponymous name for the instrument and a professional player. It is a type of lute comprising a single string. The string of *wat'a* is made of *chira feres* (ጭራ ፈረስ)—horsehair, and it is usually polished by *'et'an* (ዕጣን)—incense. By polishing the string of *wat'a* with a solid but soft *'et'an*, artists attempt to produce acoustically better sounds. The sound-box of *wa'ta* is a square or a diamond shape. The size of the sound-box may differ greatly from region to region. It is made of high-quality goat- or sheepskin. Most other parts of the instrument are made of selected types of wood. Some of the typical parts of *wat'a* are: the string-bridge, spike/beam, and peg. The *wat'a*-bow (which also comprises string) is an extra part of the instrument. Although it may vary from region to region, the most preferred type of wood for making *wat'a* include *awli'e* (wild olive) and *tsihdi* (ጽሕዲ)—*Juniperus procera*. It is typical to observe various types of decorations on the instrument, and they reflect individual views or expressions of artists or the makers of the instrument.

Like the European viola, *wat'a* players produce a variety of tones by placing and moving the fingers at various locations on the string. Performers of *wat'a* are men and are highly skilled traditional entertainers. They are also great poetic artists, and they are usually invited to any occasion to perform their art. Sometimes, they are even invited to funeral ceremonies to accompany mourners through their artistic performances (for details on the instrument and performers, see Valentini 2004: 69–72).

The embelta

The *embelta* is a type of flute with hand holes but is usually longer than a normal *shambeqo* (flute). The length of the *embelta* may differ from region to region. The length of the *embelta* may range between 65 centimeters to 1.5 meters. Like the *meleket*, the *embelta* is a ceremonial, but not frequently used, musical instrument. It is played in a group of at least three professionals. Each of the *embeltas* played by the

Wata players at Bahti Meskerem, Asmara. (J. Miran)

three professionals are known by different names: *shankit* (ሻንኪት)—the shortest; *defen* (ድፈን)—the middle-sized; and *debai* (ደባይ)—the longest (for more details, see Valentini 2004: 94).

The shambeqo

The *shambeqo* is a local type of flute usually made from the stalk of a local plant of the same name as the instrument. It is cylindrical in shape; comprises four finger holes; and reaches up to 60 centimeters in length. It is a type of solo instrument that individual players use for personal or group entertainment. Sometimes, this instrument may also accompany the *embelta* and/or the *meleket* during festive events. However, unlike the *kerar* and the *wat'a*, this instrument is slowly disappearing from the Eritrean musical scene.

The meleket

Although it has a long history in the region, the *meleket* is a rarely used instrument in the country. It is a type of trumpet with a long tube, covered by leather, without hand holes, and a conical-shape at the end. It was usually used for secular celebrations or as an escorting instrument for communal or state decrees and proclamations. The instrument is usually made of metal. In some places, the *meleket* could also be made of wood or from bamboo trees. According to Valentini (2004), this instrument is almost extinct from Eritrea, and there are only two instruments and players in the whole country.

The kebero

The *kebero* is a type of traditional drum with a cylindrical form. The two ends of the drum are covered by an oxskin of high quality attached by interwoven strings made of leather. The handle is also usually made of leather. It is one of the most frequently used musical instruments in Eritrea, especially among the Tigrinya ethnolinguistic group. It is played at almost every secular festive event. The player usually suspends the handle around his/her neck and plays with both hands. It may be accompanied by the *kerar* or the *wat'a* or any other local musical instrument. During *guayla*, good *kebero* players show impressive body movements such as jumping. During *guayla*, the number of *kebero* players may roughly range between two and five. The beat of all these players is usually the same and will match the dance rhythm.

The negarit

The *negarit* is a type of small drum that consists of a hollow hemisphere covered by high-quality skin. It is played by wooden sticks and produces an intense, high-pitched sound. This kettledrum was also used for state or communal purposes—such as for conveying messages for proclamations, decrees, or as an alert against raids and attacks from invaders. The drum was usually used by officials and community figures and not for popular entertainment. Today, the instrument is rarely used for its earlier function.

SECULAR MUSIC DURING THE LIBERATION STRUGGLE

As stated earlier, the history of aesthetic performances in Eritrea is one of the country's least studied subjects. Although the EPLF made a number of half-hearted studies on the arts—such as drama, music, and dancing—almost no detailed information is yet available. Among the few pioneering works related to the history of the performing arts in Eritrea is the Ph.D. dissertation of Matzke (2003)—*En-gendering Theatre in Eritrea: The Roles and Representations of Women in the Performing Arts* (see bibliography section). Matzke's study specifically examines the role of women in the Eritrean performing arts and provides an excellent overview of the history of the performing arts in the country.

Secular music showed a remarkable revival during the Eritrean liberation war. As part of their struggle to achieve sociocultural transformation, the liberation fronts (ELF and EPLF) established a number of departments to institute change and to guide in various activities in the country. Music also played a valuable role in mobilization and propaganda throughout the liberation struggle. Above all, the cultural

---

THE ERITREA CULTURAL EXPO

Eritrea organizes a cultural festival every year that represents all ethnolinguistic groups. Various cultural shows (usually running for one week during July or August), such as dance, music, and drama are presented in the festival. The festival also presents such things as art exhibitions and industrial fairs. Similar annual festivals also take place in the diaspora. Eritreans in different parts of the world organize annual festivals that comprise cultural shows and contests.

---

performances during the liberation struggle played a critical role in the development of the Eritrean "folk culture." Both the ELF and the EPLF established cultural troupes and embarked on ambitious attempts aimed at using music for a sociocultural and political transformation as well as for propaganda. Their cultural troupes toured throughout the areas that were under their military domains. Moreover, the cultural troupes also organized shows abroad (for the Eritrean diaspora). Generally, the audiences for the cultural performances organized by the liberation fronts were their respective fighters, civilians in the "liberated areas," and Eritreans living abroad (such as in Sudan and Europe).

Cultural performances organized by the EPLF broke the traditional gender barriers, and now women became contributing members of the performing arts. Women singers and musicians who were involved in the performing arts even before the struggle (such as Tebereh Tesfahunei and Tsehaytu Beraki) served as catalysts for the movement and as role models for young women artists. Many other experienced artists also joined the ELF and/or EPLF and contributed a great deal to the development of the performing arts during the struggle. Some of these performers included: Bereket Mengisteab, Asmerom Habtemariam, and Idris Mohammed Ali (Matzke 2003: 157–158).

Starting in the mid-1970s, the EPLF established a number of cultural troupes, including the so-called *qeyyahti embaba* (ቀያሕቲ ዕምባባ), "the Red Flowers." The Red Flowers was established at the EPLF strongholds, especially in the *Sewra* School (Revolutionary boarding school for children). The *Sewra* School was also known as Zero (an eponymous name for the place where the school was located). The cultural troupe was comprised mainly of children, commonly known as *fitewrari* (ፊተውራሪ)—a traditional military title, but in this case literally meaning "vanguard." The Red Flowers was among the most beloved cultural troupes of the time. Through performing arts, young artists "enjoyed themselves and had the time of their life. They were also encouraged to tend the more creative aspects of their character from which they undeniably benefited in their adult life" (Matzke 2003: 151). Their performances touched on various subjects, including entertainment and culture as well as aspects related to atrocities of war committed on the children of Eritrea.

In addition, several EPLF infantry brigades also established their own respective cultural troupes. The numerous cultural troupes in the EPLF were known by various names (such as *gujile bahli Hilal*). Later, an umbrella of the cultural troupes of the

Excerpt in Tigrinya language	Literal translation
"ጸላኢና ክይሰጕመ ስድሪ	Before our enemy steps in,
ተዘቢጡ ኣካሉ ክቾሪ	to beat him and disable him,
ጸልማት ክቅንጠጥ ክወግሓልና ምድሪ	to let the darkness fade and the dawn comes,
በረኻ ሰፊርና ክነፍሪ	to be fruitful, we have settled in the wilderness,
ብጸተይ ብጸተይ ሃየ ንበገስ ናባና እያ ሃገር	my comrades, the country is for us,
ኤርትራ ኣንቲ ሸዊት ለምለም	Eritrea, you are so gorgeous,
ክትለብሲ ኢኺ ሓርነት ዘለኣለም"	You will be achieving an everlasting freedom (Song by Wedi Tikul, 1987).

Front was established under the collective name of *Maekelay Bahli Wedeb* (ማእከላይ ባህሊ ውድብ), "the central cultural troupe of the organization." During all the years of fierce fighting in the Sahel Mountains and in the Barka Lowlands (1978–1985), these cultural troupes supported the fighting forces with morale and artistic innovations.

Aron Abraham, one of the renowned Eritrean Tigrinya singers since the liberation struggle during singing in a concert. (M. Tesfagiorgis)

TABLE **6E1** Eritrean artists evolved during the Eritrean Revolution

Artists' given names	Nickname	Sex	Main profession	Main language of arts
Abdela Ali	-	M	singer	Saho
Abeba Haile	-	F	singer/musician	Tigrinya
Abrar Osman	-	M	singer/musician	Saho/Tigrinya
Abrehet Ankere	Gual Ankere	F	singer	Tigrinya
Abrehet Berhane	-	F	singer/musician	Tigrinya
Adem Fayid Amer	-	M	singer	Nara
Adem Hamed	-	M	singer/musician	Hedareb
Ahmed Mohammed Osman	Wedi Sheikh	M	singer	Tigre
Aklilu Foto	Tefono	M	singer/musician	Tigrinya
Alemseged Tesfay	-	M	play writer/ composer	Tigrinya
Alganesh Yemane	Industry	F	singer	Tigrinya
Ali Mohammed	Ya'asina	M	singer	Saho
Almaz Yohannes	Aga Wegahta	F	singer	Tigrinya
Atsede Mesfin	-	F	singer/writer	Tigrinya
Bekita Ali	-	F	singer	Tigre
Berekti Woldeselassie	Tanki	F	singer	Tigrinya
Berhanne Adonai	-	M	painter	variety
Dashim Misghena	-	M	singer/musician	Tigrinya
Dehab Faytinga	Faytinga	F	singer	Kunama
Demoz Russom	-	M	stage designer/ painter	variety
Elsa Kidane	-	F	singer	Tigrinya
Elsa Yakob	-	F	painter/sculpture	variety
Estifanos Abraha	Zemach	M	singer/musician	Tigrinya
Fatma Suleman	-	F	singer/artisan	Saho/Afar
Gebreselassie	-	M	singer	Tigrinya
Habte Gebreyesus	Wedi Shawel	M	singer/comedian	Tigrinya
Helen Meles	-	F	singer	Tigrinya
Isayas Tseggai	-	M	composer/play writer	Variety
Kedija Adem	-	F	singer	Tigre
Kibra Mesfin	-	F	singer/writer	Tigrinya
Mekonnen Sereqe	Bitibito	M	singer/comedian	Tigrinya
Melekin Atombos	-	M	singer	Bilen
Michael Adonai	-	M	painter/writer	variety

(*Continues*)

TABLE 6E1 Eritrean artists evolved during the Eritrean Revolution (*Continues*)

Artists' given names	Nickname	Sex	Main profession	Main language of arts
Misgun Zerai	Wedi Feraday	M	composer/play writer	Variety
Mohammed Osman	-	M	singer	Tigre
Mulugeta Beyin	Wedi Zager	M	singer/musician	Tigrinya
Nechi Fesehatsiyon	-	F	actress	Tigrinya
Ogbagaber	-	M	singer/musician	Tigrinya
Solomon Tsehaye	-	M	play writer	variety
Teages Firezgi	-	M	singer	Bilen
Tekle Kiflemaryam	Wedi Tekul	M	singer/musician	Tigrinya
Tesfay Mehari	Fihira	M	singer/musician	Tigrinya
Tsegai Gebrehiwot	-	M	choreographer	variety
Tsehaytu Beraki	-	F	singer	Tigrinya
Zahra Ali	-	F	singer	Tigre
Zeineb Beshir	-	F	singer/musician	Tigre
Alex Kahsay	-	M	singer	Tigrinya
Aron Abraham	-	M	singer	Tigrinya

The EPLF also considered culture as an important tool for preserving folk tradition as well as fueling and strengthening the ventures of the masses for achieving national freedom. Therefore, although cultural activities were a morale-boosting source of entertainment, their principal function was to be a persuasive tool of propaganda throughout the struggle. Most messages conveyed through cultural activities were "revolutionary" in nature and focused on winning maximum popular awareness and support for the struggle. Amid the diversity of languages and cultures, the continuous environment of war, drought, famine, and other massive challenges, music served as an important language of revolutionary communication throughout the liberation struggle.

During the early phases, most members of the cultural troupes of the EPLF did not have adequate training or enough musical instruments. Most of them started with traditional instruments such as the *kerar* and the *kebero*. But gradually, although on a limited scale, the EPLF cultural troupes started to make modern musical instruments of their own. Moreover, material and cash remittances from Eritreans living abroad also contributed a great deal to the development of cultural activities in *meda* (the field where the war was mostly fought).

By the end of the 1980s, the troupes had already produced professional artists who had contributed a great deal to the mobilization and recruitment of new fighters. The EPLF's radio broadcast (known as *demtsi hafash* [ድምጺ ሓፋሽ] "voice of the masses") delivered timely news and music produced in the war zone, which in turn served as an important source of information and entertainment for the civilian population. Table 6E1 shows some of the renowned professionals who evolved during the liberation struggle. Note that some of the artists on the list are martyrs who died during or after the war of liberation.

Perhaps one of the amazing developments during the liberation struggle was the establishment of an exclusive cultural troupe for the Ethiopian prisoners of war who were kept in the strongholds of the EPLF. The EPLF accommodated thousands of prisoners of war in the Sahel Mountains. In 1981, the EPLF allowed the establishment of a cultural troupe for the Ethiopian prisoners of war, and until 1985 the troupe rose to a noteworthy prominence in the field. Interestingly, the cultural troupe for the prisoners of war presented its performances not only to the prisoners but also for the overall public in the field and the civilian population in some liberated areas. "A men-only troupe, since female soldiers were not recruited to the Ethiopian army, they nonetheless played a crucial role concerning the representation of women, and the context of 'en-gendering' theatre [also music] in the field" (Matzke 2003: 256). Most of the shows organized by this troupe were adapted to appeal to diverse Ethiopian cultures. This cultural troupe was eventually disbanded in 1991 (just after the independence of Eritrea). As with most Ethiopian prisoners of war, members of this cultural troupe were set free to join their families in Ethiopia.

MUSIC AFTER INDEPENDENCE

In general, the performing arts continued to show significant progress during post-independence Eritrea. In fact, one of the few sectors with an exceptional record of development is the theater/music industry. Amid economic and political challenges, many new artists (musicians/singers/actress) have evolved since Eritrea's independence. A number of post-independence musical and theater bands also comprised professionals who served with the ELF/EPLF.

After Eritrea's independence, the EPLF (later the ruling party—Peoples Front for Democracy and Justice [PFDJ]) established a department for cultural development. The new department, called PFDJ Cultural Affairs, concerned itself with the organization of cultural activities throughout the country. It established several music and drama bands and started various projects aimed at the preservation and development of Eritrean cultures. Most of the PFDJ bands comprised professionals who grew as artists during the liberation struggle. It organized a number of cultural events (such as at the annual Expo Festival) and rewarded a national prize for artists, called the Raimoc Prize, for outstanding performers. Among the main music/theater bands under the umbrella of PFDJ Cultural Affairs or fully/partly supported by this department were: Shushan, Bana Harenet, and Sebrit.

Interestingly, during the Eritrea-Ethiopia border conflict (1998–2000), the bands under the umbrella of PFDJ Cultural Affairs served almost the same role as in the field during the liberation struggle. With the idea of providing entertainment and morale for the fighting army in the front lines, the PFDJ bands and cultural troupes conducted extensive cultural tours. Many professional artists also turned to producing propaganda works.

Table 6E2   Post-independence Eritrean singers/musicians

Artist's given names	Nickname	Sex	Main profession	Main language of arts
Dawit Shilan	-	M	singer	Tigrinya
Fitsum Yohannes	-	M	singer	Tigrinya
Isaac Simon	-	M	singer	Tigrinya
Kahsai Berhe	-	M	singer	Tigrinya
Sami Berhanne	-	M	singer	Tigrinya
Teame Woldemichael	-	M	singer	Tigrinya
Temesgen Gebreyesus	Taniqo	M	singer	Tigrinya
Tesfalem Arefaine	Korchach	M	singer	Tigrinya
Tesfalidet Mesfin	-	M	singer	Tigrinya
Tesfay Mengesha	-	M	singer	Tigrinya
Tesfay Ner'e	-	M	singer	Tigrinya
Yohannes Tikabo	Wedi Tikabo	M	singer	Tigrinya

As with most sectors, post-war political developments in Eritrea greatly affected the country's performing arts. The arrest of political figures as well as artists and journalists in 2001 resulted in a regrettable situation. Many professional artists were discouraged by the ongoing suppressive political environment, and many left the country to go elsewhere to live as immigrants. Yet the performing arts have shown resilient progress amid the uncertain political atmosphere. A number of new professional musicians and singers have emerged since 2000, and music, theater, and film production have resumed. Perhaps owing to the political situation, the content of most of the new songs is related to social issues such as love, family, and feelings of freedom. During the liberation struggle, the bulk of the songs dealt with the affairs of the struggle and the nation. Table 6E2 shows a list of some Tigrinya music artists who became famous during the post-independence years.

Most of these artists have published more than one music albums; their music has dominated public entertainment. Since 2008, a national music competition project called *shingrwa* has also become increasingly popular. It is a sort of talent show (similar to the German "Super Star" shows) that is broadcast on national television. The objective of this project is to discover and recruit new professional singing stars.

REFERENCES

Bairu, Zerabruk (2008). "Traditional Art in Eritrea." In: Gebremedhin, Tesfa G. and Tesfagiorgis, Gebre H. (eds.). *Traditions of Eritrea: Linking the Past to the Future.* Trenton, NJ: Red Sea Press, pp. 190–228.

Belcher, Wendy (2000). "After the Freedom: Post-War Cultural Production and National Identity in Eritrea." In: *Third Text: Socialist Eastern Europe*, 50 (Special Issue, Spring), pp. 87–125.

Carillet, Jean-Bernard and Phillips, Matt (2006). *"Lonely Planet": Ethiopia and Eritrea.* 3rd rev. ed., n.p.: Lonely Planet.

Conti Rossini, Carlo (1903). "Canti Populari Tigrai." In: *Zeitschrift für Assyriologie und Verwandte Gebiete*, 17, pp. 23–52.

Conti Rossini, Carlo (1904/05). "Canti Populari Tigrai." In: *Zeitschrift für Assyriologie und Verwandte Gebiete*, 18, pp. 320–386.

Conti Rossini, Carlo (1905/06). "Canti Populari Tigrai." In: *Zeitschrift für Assyriologie und Verwandte Gebiete*, 19, pp. 388–341.

Culture of Eritrea: http://en.wikipedia.org/wiki/Culture_of_Eritrea (access in August 2009).

Denison, Edward and Paice, Edward (2002). *Eritrea: The Bradt Travel Guide*. Chalfont St. Peter, Bradt.

Faitlovitch, Jacques (1911). "*Qene Habe*sha [Habesha Poetry]." In: *Giornale della Società Asiatica Italiana*, 23, pp. 1–88.

Favali, Lyda and Pateman, Roy (2003). *Blood, Land, and Sex: Legal and Political Pluralism in Eritrea*. Bloomington, IN: Indiana University Press.

Gebremedhin, Tesfa G. (2002). *Women, Tradition and Development: A Case of Eritrea*. Trenton, NJ: Red Sea Press.

Gebremedhin, Tesfa G. and Tesfagiorgis, Gebre H. (eds.) (2008). *Traditions of Eritrea: Linking the Past to the Future.* Trenton, NJ: Red Sea Press.

Habtemariam, Asmerom (2009). "*bahlen hebreteseben* [Culture and Society]" in: *Haddas Ertra newspaper* (issue April 2, p. 4).

Matzke, Christine (2002a). "Comrades in Arts and Arms: Stories of Wars and Water-colours from Eritrea" in: Döring, Tobias (ed.). *African Cultures, Visual Arts, and the Museum: Sights/Sites Creativity and Conflict.* Amsterdam/New York: Editions Rodopi, pp. 21–54.

Matzke, Christine (2002b). "Of *Suwa* Houses & Singing Contests: Early Urban Women Performers in Asmara, Eritrea." In: Banham, Martin et al. (eds.). *African Theatre Women.* Oxford: James Currey, pp. 29–46.

Matzke, Christine (2003a). "Engendering Theatre in Eritrea: The Roles and Representations of Women in the Performing Arts." In: Eva-Maria Bruchhaus (ed.). *Hot Spot Horn of Africa: Between Integration and Disintegration.* Münster: Lit Verlag, pp. 156–164.

Matzke, Christine (2003b). *En-gendering Theatre in Eritrea: The Roles and Representations of Women in the Performing Arts.* Unpublished Ph.D. Dissertation, School of English, University of Leeds.

Matzke, Christine (2004). "Shakespeare and Surgery in the Eritrean Liberation Struggle: Performance Culture in Orota." In:*Journal of Eritrean Studies* 3, 1, pp. 26–40.

Matzke, Christine (2008a). " 'Life in the Camp of the Enemy': Alemseged Tesfai's Theatre of War." In: Emenyonu, Ernest E. (ed.). *African Literature Today 26: War in African Literature Today.* Oxford: James Currey, pp. 15–32.

Matzke, Christine (2008b). "*Mahber Te'atr Asmera*—The Asmara Theatre Association, 1961–1974." In: Banham, Martin, James Gibbs and Femi Osofisan (eds.). *African Theatre: Companies.* Oxford: James Currey, pp. 62–81.

Matzke, Christine (2008b). "The Asmara Theatre Association (1961–74): *Mahber Teyatr Asmera*" in: Gibbs, James (ed.). *African Theatre Companies.* Leeds, James Currey, pp. 62–81.

Mercier, Jacques (1946). *Ethiopian Magic Scrolls*. New York: George Braziller.

Negash, Ghirmai (1999). *A History of Tigrinya Literature in Eritrea: The Oral and the Written (1890–1991)*. Trenton, NJ: Red Sea Press.

Negash, Ghirmai (2008). *"Oral Poetic Tradition of the Tigrinya."* In: Gebremedhin, Tesfa G. and Tesfagiorgis, Gebre H. (eds.) (2008). *Traditions of Eritrea: Linking the Past to the Future*. Trenton, NJ: Red Sea Press, pp.155–189.

NgCheong-Lum, Roseline (2005). *Eritrea*. New York: Marshall Cavendish.

Tesema, Asres (2006). *Teamot: kab tarik medrekawi senetebeb ertra* [The Taste: Aspects of Eritrean Performing Arts]. Asmara: Francescana Printing Press.

The Tigre culture and customs: www. awkir.com (access in August 2009).

Tronvoll, Kjetil (199). *Mai Weini; A Highland Village in Eritrea: A Study of the People, Their Livelihood, and Land Tenure During Times of Turbulence*. Lawrenceville, NJ: Red Sea Press.

Valentini, Mariana (2004). *Strumenti Musicali Tradizionali dell'Altopiano Eritreo* (Traditional Musical Instruments in the Eritrean Highlands). Asmara: Francescana Printing Press.

Yatana Entertainment—Tigrinya cultural movie, 2008.

Food

Food constitutes any substance that is consumed by living things and serves as a source of energy and pleasure. For human beings, the main sources of food are usually animals and plants. Throughout history, human beings have sought food production in assorted ways. Early humans depended on hunting and gathering to acquire food. Modern man has managed to achieve remarkable success in the production of food. Some of the most profitable means of food production are farming, animal husbandry, fishing, and more. Means of food production may vary from society to society. Some of the decisive factors for the diversity and nature of food production are technology, culture, geography and environment/ecology. Most cultures have their own traditions related to food production, preparation, and consumption. Therefore, most cultures have their unique traditional or local cuisine. Also, most cultural groups usually have their own traditions related to gastronomical practices—such as food cooking, dietary habits and norms, as well as knowledge. In the following sections, we will see some particularities related to Eritrean cultural foodstuffs and customs of consumption.

THE ERITREAN ECOLOGY OF FOOD

As in most third world countries, the Eritrean ecology of food is mainly based on subsistence crop and animal byproducts. Food production in the fashion of industrial capitalism is not yet substantial. Therefore, one of the main characteristic features of locally produced food is its organic nature. Mainly owing to lack of capital, most farming and pastoral communities in the country tend to depend entirely on pure natural resources for producing food. Fertilizers, pesticides, and inorganic supplies have not been widely available to farmers and pastorals.

In the Eritrean highlands, some of the most important grains that serve as sources of traditional diets are *meshela* (መሽላ)—*Sorghum bicolor*; barley, maize, *taff* (ጣፍ)— *Eragorostis abyssinica*; millet; wheat; and pulses. Other sources of food include nuts, vegetables (such as onions, pepper, cabbages, potatoes, and tomatoes), and fruits. Wild fruits such as *beles* (በለስ)—fruit of prickly pears, wild berries, leaves and wild vegetables, and roots are also used as supplements to the common diet during various seasons. Animal byproducts also comprise important sources of food throughout the country. The main types of domestic animals raised in the region are cattle, goats, and sheep.

The most favored food grains are *taff*, barley, and wheat. These grains are usually regularly available to rich peasants while poor peasants usually depend on food from the end products of sorghum, millet, and maize. The type and geography of distribution of these products varies based on factors such as altitude, climate, rainfall, and regional ecologies. Therefore, there are certain grains that are specific to the highlands (such as barley and *taff*). Grains such as millet and sorghum are usually cultivated in areas of lower altitude. Similarly, certain types of cattle such as the *Barka* and *Bishar* varieties are tended in the lowlands; and the zebu type of livestock is the preferred variety in the highlands. While the highlands are preferred for tending sheep, goats are raised in lower and middle altitudes.

Pastoral farming is practiced in various regions of the country. It is characterized by the movement of pastorals and their animals in search of seasonal grazing. The main pastoral zones in the country are the northern highlands, southwestern, and eastern lowlands. Ethnolinguistic groups greatly dependent on pastoral activities for living are the Afar, part of the Rashaida, part of Tigre, and Hedareb. Other ethnolinguistic groups in the country practice mixed farming—they tend livestock and farm grains. Therefore, although livestock play significant roles in food production for the nomadic pastoralist section of the population, farming, and tending a limited number of livestock is the preferred economic activity for several ethnolinguistic groups of the country.

The food ecology is also affected by seasonality. Various food items are produced in different seasons. Except for the eastern escarpments where rain falls throughout the year, there are four seasons in the country: *hagay* (ሓጋይ) literally "dry season or winter"— between November and March; *tsediya* (ጸድያ) literally "spring"—between April and June; *keremti* (ክረምቲ) literally "rainy season or summer"—rainy season between July and September; and *qew'i* (ቀውዒ) literally "fall"—between September and November. During *hagay*, semi-sedentary farmers and pastoral communities move from one ecological area to another in search of grazing lands for their livestock and for farming. During *hagay*, rain falls in the eastern lowlands and escarpments. So farmers and pastorals from the Anseba territories, the plateau, and southern escarpments move toward the eastern escarpments and eastern plains to practice subsistence farming. Starting from *tsediya* up to *qew'i*, they retreat to their sedentary settlements in the plateau, western lowlands, and northern highlands.

FOOD PREPARATION AND RECIPES

There are diverse traditions of food and its preparation among the various cultural groups in the country. Discussing aspects of traditional food for all ethnolinguistic groups of the country is beyond the scope of this work. Therefore, the following is a description of food preparation among the highland population of the country.

Wushat'e and keshine

Among the Tigrinya, food is prepared and preserved at a specific place within the *hidmo* (ሀድሞ) dwelling called the *wushat'e* (ውሻጠ). *Hidmo* is a type of traditional dwelling with stone walls and a roof made of tree trunks, branches, and earth. But food is usually consumed in the *medribet* (part of the dwelling that serves as a living room; and where the family's hearth is located). Usually the *wushat'e* (a separate room in the *hidmo* dwelling) is reserved for women who prepare, preserve, and serve food. The *wushat'e* also serves as an important room for women to dress their hair, enjoy their *tish* (a sort of traditional sauna), and so on. Men are usually not supposed to do food-related works in general and within the *wushat'e* in particular. The social life of a family unit in a *hidmo* dwelling is usually centered around the hearth. As an anthropologist put it when referring to the Amhara food tradition (which is akin to that of the Tigrinya), "the hearth is . . . the basis of the nuclear family. The use of parent-child kinship terminologies refers to family members who share space around the hearth and where the older generation feeds the younger one" (Kifleyesus 2005: 561). The *wiushate* comprises important tools for preparing food. Some of the main tools are the *mogogo* (ሞጎጎ) (a traditional stove for baking *enjera* [እንጀራ]—a pancake-like soft bread); *moqlo* (መቅሎ)—traditional stove for baking a type of local bread called *kicha* (ቅጫ); and also for roasting grains; *tsahli* (ጻሕሊ) (a small pot for cooking sauce);cooking hearth; and more.

Modern dwellings (such as *mereba'e* [መረባዕ]) usually do not incorporate a *wushat'e*. The *merebaba'e* is a type of dwelling with stone walls and a roof covered with corrugated iron sheets. A typical Tigrinya modern household uses a *keshine* (ክሽን) (perhaps originating from the Italian term *cucina*, literally meaning "kitchen") not only for preserving and cooking foodstuffs, but also as a central place for a family's economic and social life. The *keshine* is usually a separate room where members of a family spend the bulk of their day—for food preparation and consumption and more. The coffee ceremony also usually takes place in the kitchen or *medribet* (ምድረቤት), where family members and neighbors entertain themselves, hair is dressed, and so on. Therefore, the kitchen is basically the central place for the creation and development of strong ties among members of a family unit. But note that, although the economic function of the *keshine* and the *wushat'e* are similar, their social functions may somehow differ.

As stated earlier, the preparation of food is the exclusive task for women. Women's ability to prepare various types of dishes is usually communally acknowledged. This is to say that each woman's skills in preparing delicious food as well as making efficient cooking tools plays a decisive role in her social contacts. The communities also use some criteria to appraise a woman's cooking and housewifely skills. For example, a

Geat or porridge, typical foodstuff for the Tigrinya. (M. Tesfagiorgis)

woman with professional skills of cooking and good household management is called *wehalle* (ወሓለ). A woman with poor cooking and housekeeping skills is called *besero* (በሰሮ) or *ge'ezeyti* (ግዕዝይቲ).

The common diet comprises a single staple-food crop that is consumed almost daily. Before the grain is ready to be consumed as food it passes through an involved process. The crops are ground to produce flour. Traditionally, grinding grains is performed by hand, and it has been an exclusive task for women. Women use grinding stones called *met'han* (መጥሓን). End products of this process are usually *enjera* and a variety of bread.

COMMON BEVERAGES

There are a great variety of traditional beverages in the country. Most cultural groups have their own specialties. Yet, alcoholic beverages are often specialties of the Christian section of society. As in most parts of the Islamic world, alcoholic drinks are taboo for Eritrean Muslims.

The most popular traditional alcoholic beverages are *suwa* and *mes*. *Suwa* is a specialization of the Tigrinya (and also of the Ethiopian Amhara) ethnolinguistic group. It is a combination of water and bread (made from various grains such as millet and sorghum). *Mes* is a type of alcoholic mead made of fermented honey. It is homemade, and its strength may vary from brewer to brewer.

CONSUMPTION OF FOOD

Among most ethnolinguistic groups of the country, food is normally served three times a day: *quesi* (ቁርሲ) "breakfast"; *mesah* (ምሳሕ) "lunch"; and *derar* (ድራር) "dinner." Various kinds of snacks are also consumed at different times of the day. Snacks may include *qursi bun* (ቁርሲ ቡን) "coffee snacks" or *t'e'amot* (ጠዓሞት), literally meaning "afternoon snacks." The meals are served for lunch and dinner. Although warm food is preferred, the Eritrean manner of eating is to use fingers.

The varieties of bread and *enjera* are eaten with different kinds of stews, commonly known as *tsebhi* (ጸብሒ). Yet, *enjera* comprises the main component of all the common dishes. Another ingredient of the common dishes is *berbere* (በርበረ) (spiced chili flour). Variations of menu and dishes depend on the economic capability of each household. Therefore, while rich households consume variable stews and favored grains, poor households depend on limited stews such as *shiro* (ሽሮ). The ingredients of stews may also greatly vary substantially, depending on the economic means of the household. Good stews usually comprise *tesmi* (ጠስሚ)—a spiced butter; an item not easily affordable in poor households. The inter-household variations in content and type of foodstuffs reflect the economic and/or social distinctions.

COMMON DISHES

There are great varieties of local dishes across the country. Interestingly, dishes are usually known not by the type of bread, but by the types of stews eaten with the bread. Some of these dishes are *zegni* (ዘግኒ)—cooked meat with varieties of spices; *tsebhi-derho* (ጸብሒ ደርሆ)—chicken stew; *shiro*—a paste-like thick puree; *t'ebsi* (ጥብሲ)—roasted meat; *tsebhi-bersen* (ጸብሒ ብርስን)—lentil sauce; *'alicha* (ኣልጫ)—cooked vegetables or meat without *berbere*; and varieties of broths.

In the lowlands (especially where the Tigre are the dominant ethnolinguistic group), the main dish is called *akkelet* (ኣከለት)—similar to porridge. It is made from wheat, barley or sorghum. Some of the main ingredients for this dish include *hesas* (ሕሳስ)—butter, *berbere*, and yoghurt.

DISHES WITH MEAT

Meals featuring meat are usually favored dishes, and the symbolic value of meat is greater than non-meat meals. Therefore, meat meals are usually occasional dishes. For most farming and pastoral communities, meat consumption is confined to Christian and Muslim holidays and other cultural festivities. The symbolic value of meat emanates from resource scarcity and its value as a source of physical energy. Hence, meat-based food is considered vital for regaining and sustaining health. For example, as a priority, meat dishes are given to sick persons, women during pregnancy and after delivery, and so on. Therefore, animals are slaughtered not only during festive religious and cultural occasions, but also during times of sickness in which meat plays quasi-medical and health-strengthening roles (Kifleyesus 2005: 263). As mentioned earlier, Eritreans observe strict food taboos. Therefore, most cultures in Eritrea do not eat animal meat such as pigs (wild or domestic), donkeys, horses, snakes, snails, and more. The source of meat for the common dishes is usually from domestic animals such as goats, sheep/lamb, cows, oxen/calf, and chicken. Lamb stew is favored in the highlands and goat stew is common in the lowlands. Christians (especially members of the Orthodox *Tewahdo* Church and Catholic Church) abstain from eating meat during religious fasting.

Zegni

Zegni is one of the most popular dishes in the Eritrean highlands. It is a type of meat stew with *berbere*. *Zegni* is a spicy stew and comprises a number of ingredients such as onions, garlic, pepper, oil, *t'esmi*, tomato paste, and so on. The following is a recipe for *zegni*. Please note that the recipe provided below is not precise, and the amount and type of items mentioned may differ from one household to another.

Type of meats may vary. But beef and lamb are common meats for *zegni*.

400–600 g meat (cut into small pieces)

500–700 g hacked red onions

30–60 g sunflower oil

3–4 tablespoons of *t'esmi*

40–60 g *berbere*

30–60 g tomato paste (but many people also prefer *zegni* without tomato)

3–6 pieces of crushed garlic

1–2 teaspoons of salt

0.5–1.0 liter water

First, the hacked red onions and sunflower oil are fried until the onions become golden (with moderate heat for five to seven minutes). *Berbere* is then added and fried with the onions and oil for several more minutes. Tomato paste may be included before meat is added. All of these ingredients are then fried in a covered pan for at least ten minutes with moderate heat. A small amount of water might be added during the cooking process. Pepper, garlic, and salt are then added. The pan is then left to boil on low or moderate heat for about fifty minutes until all the ingredients are well mixed to form a good flavor, and the meat is well cooked.

Tsebhi-derho

Chickens are raised within the household and the courtyard of the house. Usually women tend to be the ones who take care of chickens within the household. *Tsebhi-derho* is one of the favorite dishes in the region. Chicken meat is usually eaten during meals marking special occasions. Hence, unlike Western cultures, chicken meat is not an "everyday" meal, and for some ethnolinguistic groups, it is considered a delicacy. For some ethnolinguistic groups, preparing a meal of chicken demonstrates the need to create, formalize, or strengthen relations between hosts and guests (see also Kifleyesus 2005: 564). The following is a recipe for *tsebhi-derho*. Please note that the recipe provided below is not precise, and the amount and type of items mentioned may differ from one household to another.

1 frying chicken cut into 12 pieces

500–1,000 g hacked red onions

30–60 g sunflower oil

3–5 tablespoons of *t'esmi*

2–4 pieces of crushed garlic

40–60 g *berbere*

3–8 g varieties of spices such as pepper, cayenne, ginger

Typical dehro stew. (M. Tesfagiorgis)

30–60 g tomato paste (note that some people prefer without tomato)

1–2 teaspoon salt

0.3–0.5 liter water

12 boiled eggs

The preparation of *tsebhi-derho* is usually a longer process and involves slaughtering, plucking the feathers, cutting into particular pieces, and washing the chicken (commonly with lemon and/or salt). Slaughtering is the task of men while all other activities for preparing *tsebhi-derho* are the tasks of women. Based on traditional beliefs, the chicken is usually cut into twelve particular pieces. According to some oral sources, the twelve pieces represent the twelve biblical apostles of Christ. Moreover, twelve hard-boiled eggs are also added to the stew to represent all the apostles. As part of their socialization process, girls learn from their mothers the correct way of cutting the chicken into twelve pieces. To prepare *tsebhi-derho*, first, hacked red onions and sunflower oil are fried until the onions become golden (with moderate heat for five to seven minutes). *Berbere* is then added and fried with the onions and oil for several more minutes. Tomato paste may be included before the pieces of *derho* are added. All of these ingredients are then fried in a covered pan for at least ten minutes on low heat. A small amount of water might be added repeatedly during the cooking process. Pepper, garlic, and salt are then added. The pan is then left to boil on low or moderate heat for about fifty to sixty minutes until all the ingredients are well mixed to form a good flavor, and the chicken is well cooked. Note that some people prefer cooking *tsebhi-derho* with *t'esmi* rather than oil.

T'ebsi

This type of dish comprises roasted beef, lamb, or goat meat. The fried meat is then consumed with *enjera* or other common types of bread. Cooking *t'ebsi* is perhaps one of the easiest tasks in food preparation. The following is a recipe for *t'ebsi*. Please note that the recipe provided is not precise, and the amount and type of items mentioned may differ from one household to another.

500–1,000g meat cut into consumable size

100–300 g hacked red onions

4–5 tablespoons of sunflower oil or *t'esmi*

2–5 pieces of crushed garlic

5–10 g various spices (such as pepper and rosemary)

1–2 slashed tomatoes

1–2 teaspoons of salt

0.2–0.4 liters of water

1–2 pieces of green chili

First, onions and oil/*t'esmi* are fried for two to five minutes in a moderate heat. Tomato is then added and fried together for an additional two to four minutes. Meat is then added in the pan. After three or so minutes, garlic and green chili (cut into small pieces or simply chopped in two parts each) and other spices are put in the same pan. A little water might be added several times to keep it boiling properly. Finally, salt is added and the stew is left boiling in a covered pan for fifteen to twenty minutes, depending on the strength of heat.

DISHES WITHOUT MEAT

The Eritrean food culture is also known for its various stews of vegetable bowls and legumes. Among the most common non-meat dishes are *alicha* (ኣልጫ), *shiro*, *tsebhi-bersen* (ጸብሒ-ብርስን), *tumtumo* (ትምትሞ), and a number of vegetable bowls. The consumption and preparation of these stews may differ from season to season. For example, in some rural areas wild vegetables might be commonly used during the rainy season, while end products of legumes and pulses (such as *shiro* and *tem-tumo*) might constitute important parts of dishes during the dry season. Pulses such as beans and peas are ground to produce flour. The flour is then mixed with various types of spices, including red peppers, dried and crushed garlic, salt, and more. Thick or soup-like stews are then prepared using these ingredients.

The most widely consumed foodstuffs include legume products. Meals with legumes and pulses are routinely part of the society's diet for most of the year. Even when other meals (such as meat dishes) are available, legume stews are eaten as sidedishes, and so they somehow serve the role of vegetables (Kifleyesus 2005: 562). Roasted legumes and varieties of grains called *qolo* (ቆሎ) are also used as supplementary or snack food for most of the year. Occasionally, most households also consume boiled legumes and grains called *t'et'eqo* (ጥጥቖ). Food made out of end products of beans or peas such as *hel-bet* (ሕልበት)—a porridge-like thick paste—is consumed by the Christian highlanders on an occasional basis. Some of the common non-meat dishes in Eritrea follow.

Shiro

Shiro is a type of common stew (a puree-like sauce), and it is frequently consumed by most Eritreans. The main ingredient of *shiro* is chickpeas flour. It is mixed with a variety of ingredients such as dried onions, salt, garlic, ginger, *berbere*, and more. Depending on regional variation, there are two main types of *shiro*: with *berbere* and without *berbere*. It is commonly eaten during Christian Lent and Islamic Ramadan. The following is a recipe for *shiro*. Please note that the recipe provided is not preciese, and the amount and type of items mentioned may differ from one household to another.

20–50 g hacked red onions

2–3 tablespoons of sunflower oil or *t'esmi* (during non-Lent days)

1–2 smashed tomatoes

0.5–1 liter water

4–6 tablespoons of *shiro* flour

1–2 teaspoons of salt

1–2 pieces of smashed garlic

½–2 pieces of green chili (cut into small pieces or simply cut in two or three pieces)

First, onions and oil/*t'esmi* are fried for two to five minutes on a moderate heat. Tomato is then added and fried together for an additional two to four minutes. Water is added to the pan. After the water starts to boil, *shiro* flour is added in small amounts, and should be well mixed with the water. Mixing *shiro* and the other ingredients is important so that the ingredients are well distributed in the pan. After three to five minutes, garlic and green chili (cut into small pieces or simply chopped in two parts each) and other spices are put in the same pan. Finally, salt is added and the stew is left to boil in a covered pan for 25 to 45 minutes. Once the stew is ready, it is consumed with *enjera*.

Tsebhi-bersen

Tsebhi-bersen is a type of common stew, and it is frequently consumed by most Eritreans. The main ingredient of *tsebhi-bersen* is lentil seeds and tomatoes. It is mixed with a variety of ingredients such as onions, salt, garlic, *berbere*, and more. Like *shiro*, it is commonly eaten during periods of Lent. The following is a recipe for *tsebhi-bersen*. Please note that the recipe provided below is not precise, and the amount and type of items mentioned may differ from one household to another.

200–300 g hacked red onions

1–3 tea cups of lentil seeds

2–4 tablespoons of sunflower oil

2–3 smashed tomatoes

1–2 teaspoons of salt

1–2 pieces of smashed garlic

0.3–0.5 liters of water

First, onions and oil are fried for two to five minutes on a moderate heat. Tomato is then added and fried together for an additional two to four minutes. Lentils seeds are then added in the pan and are mixed well with the other ingredients. After three to five minutes, water, garlic, and other spices are put in the same pan. Finally, salt is added and the stew is left to boil in a covered pan for 25 to 45 minutes. Once the stew is ready, it is consumed with *enjera*.

Fruits

Eritrea has rich fruit variety. Fruit constitutes an important supplementary diet for most Eritreans. Wild fruits (some of which are probably not known to people who never have been to the country) are also commonly used as sources of food. Yet, fruit production is usually confined to particular gardens in specific areas such as the Ala Plains, Gash plantations, and other riverine areas. Other types of fruits—oranges, papayas, bananas, and mangos—are produced in different parts of the country. Interestingly, fruits are used as symbolic items for friendship. During visits, people offer each other various types of fruits. Offering fruit is considered as a sign of friendship as well as a sign of demonstration for good wishes to the host. Therefore, it is common to see people (especially in urban areas) offering bananas, oranges, mangos, and other fruit to the sick or to friends during their visits.

SOME ASPECTS OF FOOD CONSUMPTION AND TABLE MANNERS

As stated earlier, members of a household or people who come together for a meal share the same dish or bowl. Table manners may differ from one cultural group to another. In some areas, gender may also play a role in the etiquette of food consumption. Women and children, especially where guests or strangers are present, share food from a separate dish. Among most societies of the Horn of Africa, including Eritrea, "the shared meal represents the unity of the family that gathers to eat it, but the manner in which it is served and eaten also speaks of the division between more important and less important household members" (Kifleyesus 2005: 564). Therefore, the manners of sharing food among members of a household may sometimes be unequal. For example, among the Tigrinya ethnolinguistic group, traditionally women and children usually receive the smallest shares of a household's meal. However, this does not mean that the Tigrinyas are anti-children or anti-women. In fact, children are well treated and are considered the most important members of the household. Similarly, although women traditionally do not possess equal rights and the status of men, they are culturally the most respected members of the society. Rather, these matters of inequality are simply rooted in the "male-dominated" customs in which men usually get priorities most often.

Most cultural groups in the region show great respect for food. Among the Tigrinya, food consumption comprises blessings and particular manners of eating. The eldest person of the group around the dish is expected to lead prayers and blessings before and after eating. All the people who share the same dish are also expected to stay as calm and silent as possible during the time of the meals. Food is eaten with the right-hand fingers, chewing food should be done with a closed mouth and only on one side of the jaws. Chewing on both sides of the jaw at the same time (called *adraga-meheyak*—አድራጋ ምሕያኽ) is considered to be a bad habit. Consumers from the same dish or the same drink usually offer their compliments to the woman or women who cook the food by saying *t'u'um* (ጥዑም) "delicious."

TABOO FOODSTUFFS

Any types of foodstuffs and drinks that a cultural or religious group considers to comprise unacceptable dietary contents are deemed taboo. A society's designation of certain food and drink as taboo may also be based on health, religious beliefs, and other reasons. Some types of foods may become taboo on an occasional basis such as during days of Lent, pregnancy, and other cultural occasions. In most cases, taboo food and drink among Eritrean societies are related to religious beliefs. Most types of food that are considered taboo by a large section of Eritrean Christians are usually based on a set of religious rules and dictates (such as in the Old Testament of the Holy Bible). Muslim communities also pay close observance to the Islamic set of laws related to the *halal* (foodstuffs usually containing meat must be prepared in comportment with Islamic law so that consumption is permitted) and *haram* (types of food that are not necessarily prepared in a manner prescribed by Islamic law, which prohibits consumption). Some types of food are taboo not because of any religious reasons, but simply because a society does not "by custom" accept them as types of food that fall within the range of that society's definition of accepted foodstuffs. For example, the consumption of worms and insects as well as birds of quite small size is considered taboo in most Eritrean communities.

As in several parts of the world, pork and any swine byproducts are strongly prohibited by the Eritrean Muslim and Orthodox *Tewahdo* Christians. For these societies swine or pig is considered an impure animal. For the Orthodox Church pork is prohibited mainly based on the tenets mentioned in the Old Testament. Although hare can be eaten by several communities in Eritrea, some communities, such as the Hedareb, and among some members of the Orthodox Christian Tigrinya, do consider eating hare a taboo. Among the Tigre (although it also depends from community to community), it is taboo to eat things such as an unborn or an aborted animal (this also applies to the Tigrinya and some other ethnolinguistic groups), or other animal organs such as the heart, lungs, tongue, and bladder (Littmann 1910: II: 236–238). Animal organs such as kidney, intestine, and stomach are, however, an important part of the diet among the Tigrinya communities, although it might be taboo among other ethnolinguistic groups. Yet, most ethnolinguistic groups in Eritrea consider eating organs such as animal brains as abnormal.

Among some communities it is also quite unusual to eat dwarf or disabled wild or domestic animals. Although camel meat is eaten by several ethnolinguistic groups, it is taboo to do so among the Tigrinya ethnolinguistic group. Eating the flesh of animals such as dogs, donkeys, mules/horses, cats (domestic animals), hyenas, leopards, rhinoceros, wild pigs, crocodiles, frogs, crabs, mice, primates, wolf, jackals, foxes, turtles, snails, serpents/snakes, lizards, chameleons, eagles, vultures, and ostriches (wild animals) is taboo for most members of the Eritrean society. The practice of cannibalism carries a strong taboo for all ethnolinguistic groups. Moreover, most of the Christian Tigrinya section of the Eritrean society (especially members of the Orthodox *Tewahdo*; however, the Catholic sections may be allowed to consume fish once a week during Lent) abstain from consuming meat of any kind and dairy products for most of Wednesdays and Fridays as well as common Christian fasting dates (especially Lent). Fasting periods among the Christian and Muslim communities of Eritrea are strictly regulated—as to the timing and types of food consumption. Fasting is usually practiced by all Christian and Muslim adults.

The consumption of all sorts of insects is taboo for most cultural groups (although locusts may be eaten by some communities in the country). Moreover, eating any part of a living animal is unacceptable by all cultural groups in the country.

REFERENCES

Belcher, Wendy (2000). "After the Freedom: Post-War Cultural Production and National Identity in Eritrea." In: *Third Text: Socialist Eastern Europe*, 50 (Special Issue, Spring), pp. 87–125.

Carillet, Jean-Bernard and Phillips, Matt (2006). *"Lonely Planet": Ethiopia and Eritrea*. 3rd rev. ed., n.p.: Lonely Planet.

Culture of Eritrea: http://en.wikipedia.org/wiki/Culture_of_Eritrea (access in August 2009).

Denison, Edward and Paice, Edward (2002). *Eritrea: The Bradt Travel Guide*. Chalfont St. Peter, Bradt.

Gebremedhin, Tesfa G. (2002). *Women, Tradition and Development: A Case of Eritrea*. Trenton, NJ: Red Sea Press.

Gebremedhin, Tesfa G. and Tesfagiorgis, Gebre H. (eds.) (2008). *Traditions of Eritrea: Linking the Past to the Future*. Trenton, NJ: Red Sea Press.

Habtemariam, Asmerom (2009). *"bahlen hebreteseben* [Culture and Society]." In: *Haddas Ertra newspaper* (series April 2, p. 4).

Kifleyesus, Abebe (1997). "Dyadic Relation and Market Transaction in an Environment of Economic Depression." In: *Cahiers d'études africaines*, Volume 37 (146), pp. 429–465.

Kifleyesus, Abebe (2002). "Muslims and Meals: The Social and Symbolic Function of Foods in Changing Socio-Economic Environments." In: *Africa*, Volume 72 (2), pp. 68–71.

Kifleyesus, Abbebe (2005). 'Food'. In: Uhlig, Siegbert (ed.), *Encyclopaedia Aethiopica*. Vol. 2, Wiesbaden: Harrassowitz Verlag, pp. 560–565.

Littmann, Enno (1910). *Publications of the Princeton Expedition to Abyssinia*. Vol. II, Leyden [Leiden]: Late E. J. Brill.

NgCheong-Lum, Roseline (2005). *Eritrea*. New York: Marshall Cavendish.

Pankhurst, Richard (1990). *A Social History of Ethiopia: The Northern and Central Highlands from Early Medieval Times to the Rise of Emperor Téwodros II*. Addis Ababa: St. Edmundsbury Press.

The Tigre culture and customs: www. awkir.com (access in August 2009).

Tronvoll, Kjetil (1998). *Mai Weini; A Highland Village in Eritrea: A Study of the People, Their Livelihood, and Land Tenure During Times of Turbulence*. Lawrenceville, NJ: Red Sea Press.

Yatana Entertainment—Tigrinya cultural movie, 2008.

Leisure and Sports

There are diverse sport and leisure activities throughout Eritrea. Some of the leisure activities, especially in towns, are watching films and dramas in cinemas, shopping, a variety of sport activities, relaxing at cafés, and more. In rural areas, leisure and sport activities are quite limited, which can be attributed to the more impoverished way of life. Yet, there are a multitude of traditional sports for youth of all ages. In big cities, such as Asmara, there are diverse leisure venues, which include sports, recreation clubs, and bars.

OFFICE, SHOPPING, AND MARKET BARGAINS

Office hours in Eritrea are between 7:00 and 12:00 hours; and 14:00 and 18:00 hours. The time between 12:00 and 14:00 hours is usually considered as lunchtime. Most government or private offices remain closed during lunch hours. It is also common to see employees taking longer tea breaks in between. Break hours occur on Fridays (when Muslim members of the communities go to the mosque for their weekly worship). During official or work visits to government private offices, politeness and respect are expected. It is also advisable to use polite language, including pronouns or demonstratives during conversations.

In most Eritrean towns, marketing takes place once a week, usually on Saturdays. Most of the time, shopping takes place either in open squares or in big verandahs where various items are sold. But there are also small shops well distributed in cities and towns that usually contain various trading items. Usually there are separate market squares for livestock and other market items. Traders in open markets do not put prices on items, which means they are open for bargaining; it is quite common to bargain on prices of items in any market across the country.

The most popular sports in Eritrea are cycling, athletics, volleyball, and football (soccer). There are also a number of other traditional types of sports related to respective ethnolinguistic groups and communities.

Buyers and sellers of items in a part of small open market in Agordat. (S. Tesfagiorgis)

CYCLING

As stated earlier, cycling is one of the most popular sports in the country. There are cycling clubs in most towns. Indeed, cycling in Eritrea may-be considered as one of the most widely followed sports in Sub-Saharan Africa. A great majority of Eritrean youth are fond of cycling. Hence, sports clubs usually field a cycling team; in many cases, women also become members and take part in cycling races. At the national level, there is a Cycling Federation that is mainly responsible for organizing interclub and interregional cycling in the country. It organizes a number of cycling tours in the country every year.

The history of cycling in Eritrea can be traced back to the Italian colonial period. But it gained momentum in the 1940s when the first cycling tour was organized by an Italian community in Asmara. This tour (which was also known as *Giro di Eritrea* "Tour of Eritrea"), in which over 30 cyclists participated, was the first of its kind. In 1947, a second cycling tour was conducted in which many new cyclists took part. Until the 1960s, cycling clubs were mostly sponsored in sports clubs in urban centers. However, several Eritrean cycling clubs were also established in the 1960s. One of the renowned cycling clubs of the time was the May Leham Club. This club comprised Eritrean cyclists, and it took part in several cycling races and was one of the favorite Eritrean cycling clubs by far. The Dog'li Cycling Club of Asmara was also extremely popular. Some renowned cyclists in the 1970s were Abraham Teklehaimanot, Zeregaber Gebrehiwet, and Yemane Negasi. Despite political instabilities and conflicts, cycling remained one of the most active sports in the country throughout the 1980s.

After Eritrea's independence, cycling became even more popular, and a number of new cycling clubs cropped up around the country. Eritrea organizes an annual cycling tour race that attracts the participation of a great number of professional cyclists. Throughout the 1990s, there were a number of popular cyclists in the country, including Samuel Zecharias and Yemane Teskeste. Among the most renowned cyclists currently in Eritrea are Merhawi Gebrehiwet, Dawit Haile, Michael Tekle, Michael Teklu, and Michael Tekle. Some of the cycling clubs in Eritrea are the Asbeko Cycling Club, the EriTel, the Adulis Cycling Club, the Mereb Cycling Club, and the Debub Cycling Club.

National cycling races take place within the city of Asmara, on the Asmara-Keren, Asmara-Massawa, or Asmara-Dekemhare roads. During cycling events, fans from various areas in the country gather along the cycling roads to provide moral support and admire their favorite cyclists. Eritrea also participated in various international cycling races. Some of the international regular cycling tours in which Eritrea took part are: the Tour of Italy and *Tour de France*. Eritrea also hosted a number of regional and international cycling tours.

FOOTBALL (SOCCER)

Another popular sport in Eritrea is soccer. There are over 150 soccer clubs in the country; however, many of these soccer clubs are small. There are soccer clubs in most Eritrean towns. The Eritrean National Federation of Sports is responsible for organizing soccer matches on the national level. Other small interclub premier leagues arrange matches almost regularly. Football games are usually watched by thousands of Eritrean fans, and the media usually provides full coverage.

The Eritrean National Football Team (ENFT) was established in 1996. This team comprises professional players and is administered directly by the National Football Federation (NFF). Immediately after its establishment, the NFF attained membership in the Confederation of African Football (CAF). Since 2000, the National Football Team has participated in a series of African qualifying matches. In 2008, Eritrea also participated in a number of qualifying matches for the World Cup (FIFA)—against the national teams of Kenya, Ghana, Angola, Nigeria, and Sudan. In 2009, most members of the ENFT refused to return to their country after they took part in the matches organized by the Council for East and Central Africa Football Association (CECAFA). They applied for asylum in Kenya, and the United Nations Higher Commissioner for Refugees (UNHCR) in cooperation with the Kenyan government, is believed to have granted them political asylum.

As of 2009, the ENFT comprises two goalkeepers, at least seven defenders, at least ten modifiers, and at least eight forwarders. There are at least ten prominent football clubs in Eritrea. Some of these football clubs are: al-Tahrir Club, the Red Sea, Edaga Hamus Club, Midelaw Megbi Club, May Temenay Club, Denden, Hentsa, and Adulis. Followed by Adulis, the Red Sea Foot Ball Club is by far the most popular and dominant club in the country. All these clubs take part in nationwide leagues and championships; the most important level of football is the Eritrean Premier League. The Premier League is the highest football division in the country.

Despite the great popularity of football, there are few sport venues in the country. In Asmara, there are two significant football stadiums—the Denden Stadium and Asmara Stadium (also commonly known as Cicero). There is also a third stadium called Bahti Meskerem Stadium, but it does not accommodate football activities. Rather it is usually used as a site for national festivities such as *meskel* (the feast of the True Cross) and Independence Day. Other cities in Eritrea also have one or two stadiums each. In general, the number of football stadiums and football facilities are not adequate countrywide.

VOLLEYBALL AND OTHER SPORTS

Volleyball is another sport that is becoming increasingly popular in Eritrea. There are volleyball teams in almost every school and town. Women are also increasingly becoming active participants in national and international volleyball matches. Organized under the Eritrean National Volleyball Federation (ENVF), a great number of volleyball clubs participate in annual national championships.

Athletics is also becoming an increasingly trendy sport in the country. Eritrea has participated in a number of international championships such as the Olympics in Sydney (Summer 2000) and Athens (Summer 2004). During the Olympia in Athens, Eritrea won a bronze medal for the 10,000 meters race. Zeresenay Tadesse, one of the most renowned athletes in Eritrea, won the medal. Since 2000, Eritrea has cultivated a number of other promising athletes, such as Yonas Kifle and Nebiat

Eritrean athletes during a festive sport event. (M. Tesfagiorgis)

Habtemariam. Mebrahtom Kiflezghi (Eritrean-American athlete) has also become a successful long-distance runner in the United States. In 2009, Mebrahtom Kiflezghi won the New York City Marathon (2:09:15 hours) and became the first American citizen to win this marathon since 1982.

Although not as popular, a number of other sport arts are also practiced in schools and other leisure centers, such as swimming, bowling, horse racing, golf, and tennis. Most schools also include "sports" as a teaching subject. Some sports venues in Asmara are the Asmara Bowling Center, Asmara Gymnasium, Sembel Residential Housing Tennis Court, Boce-Filgia Volley-ball and Basket-ball, Asmara Swimming Pool, and Asmara Fitness Center. There are a number of recreation clubs in the city, including the Warsay Recreation Club, Shamrock Disco Club, Intercontinental Hotel, Aybay Hotel, Aguadu Night Clubs, and more. Apart from the above-mentioned types of sports, Eritreans also play traditional games such as *bucha* (resembling discus throwing) and *shakwi* (resembling hockey). These types of sports are widely popular in rural areas.

REFERENCES

Carillet, Jean-Bernard and Phillips, Matt (2006). *"Lonely Planet": Ethiopia and Eritrea.* 3rd rev. ed., n.p.: Lonely Planet.

Culture of Eritrea: http://en.wikipedia.org/wiki/Culture_of_Eritrea (access in August 2009).

Denison, Edward; Yu Re, Guang; and Gebremedhin, Naigzy (2003). *Asmara: Africa's Secret Modernist City.* London: Merrell; illustrated edition.

Maps of the World: http://www.mapsofworld.com/eritrea/sports/
NgCheong-Lum, Roseline (2005). *Eritrea*. New York: Marshall Cavendish.
Wapedia-Eritrea: http://wapedia.mobi/en/Eritrea?t=4.

Traditional (Herbal) Medicine

INTRODUCTION

What is traditional medicine? Simple question but difficult to answer! The term "traditional medicine" is not well defined, and it is a subject that is often complicated. Some people associate this subject with an array of themes that have to do with *shamanism* and *witchcraft*. To differentiate these terms, some scholars prefer to use expressions such as "folk medicine," "local medicine," "herbal medicine," or "indigenous medicine." The World Health Organization (WHO) defines traditional medicine as "the sum total of knowledge, skills and practices based on the theories, beliefs and experiences indigenous to different cultures that are used to maintain health, as well as to prevent, diagnose, improve or treat physical and mental illnesses" (WHO Online Fact sheets: No. 134). In most parts of the world, people accumulate a good deal of knowledge related to their respective environments and often manage to deal with common diseases using resources exploited from their natural environment. Traditional medicine usually develops as a distinct method and discipline of practice that has evolved and been practiced for generations. As defined by WHO, it is the sum total of medical experience, observations, skills, and more that a given society distills over many centuries.

All traditional medicine deals with the prevention and treatment (cure) of diseases. Traditional medicine is sometimes seen by some people as a superstitious and negative practice. However, it can be argued that not all traditional medical practices are harmful. For instance, in areas where there is a lack of "modern" medicine, traditional medical practices such as midwifery play crucial roles. As is modern medicine, traditional medicine is concerned with preventing and healing disease. Traditional healers are specialists concerned with healing practices for one or more types of diseases. Their experience and observances often result in precise knowledge of common diseases and their treatments. Most communities worldwide use certain herbal treatment for diseases—good examples can be found in traditional medicine in China, India, and the Arab world. In many communities where health infrastructure is still at a primary or below primary condition, such as the Eritrean modern health system, traditional medicine offers a practical alternative. In many African countries, especially places prone to war (for example, the Democratic Republic Congo) or with an underdeveloped health infrastructure, traditional medicine plays an undeniable role in saving lives. In many parts of the world, traditional medicine is cheaper than modern medicine and so a great majority of these populations financially depend on traditional healing practices for their primary health requirements. Interestingly, in some countries where a great majority of the populations have access to modern medicine, herbal medicine is often more expensive than modern medical care.

TRADITIONAL MEDICINE IN ERITREA

Eritrean society has a long history of practicing traditional/herbal medicine that also has links to local cultural values and beliefs. In this context, traditional medicine is concerned with types of medical treatments and practices that are based on customary knowledge. Owing to poor health-care facilities in rural Eritrea, a great majority of the population are still reliant on traditional medicine. Traditional medical practices are quite varied based on cultural diversity. While a majority of traditional healers deal with human diseases, some also specialize in the treatment of animal diseases. In general, medical practices are concerned with the treatment of diseases, disease prevention, and the promotion of spiritual and physical well-being of community members.

Traditional healers are respected by all communities, and their medical skills are often associated with supernatural gifts. Most traditional healers are also keenly aware of their skills, and they usually never publicize secrets of their medical practices. In most cases healers transfer their skills only to their closest family members (usually to their first-born child) orally. In this way, traditional medical practices are transferred from one generation to the next. In other words, traditional medical practices are usually confined to specific families. Observing the features of traditional medicine and local drugs in Ethiopia (which is the same also in Eritrea), Deribe Kassaye et al. (2006) describe the following:

> Healers obtain their drugs mainly from natural substances and in descending order of frequency these constitute plants, animals and minerals. Drugs are prepared in various dosage forms including liquids, ointments, powders and pills. Drugs are also prescribed in a nonformulated form and additives are usually incorporated and more than one drug is used in a single dosage form. Drugs were administered using different routes, the main ones being, topical, oral and respiratory. When side effects became severe, antidotes were claimed to be used. The healers imposed restriction when certain types of drugs were taken by patients. Drugs are stored usually in containers such as bottles, papers, pieces of cloth, leaves and horns, and were kept anywhere at home (Deribe Kassaye et al 2006: 128).

PREVENTION/PRESERVATION

Traditional medicine comprises a number of elements designed for maintaining sanitation, sterilization, as well as for disease prevention. Among the most frequently used methods of preservation and sanitation are drying, salting, boiling, heating, and

TABLE **6H1** Some local plants used for medical purposes

Local name	Scientific name	Purpose
shibti (ሽብጢ)	*Phytolacca dodecandra*	Sanitation
meqi'e (መቒዕ)	*Balanites aegyptica*	Sanitation
grawwa (ግራዋ)	*Vernonia amigdalina*	Sanitation
segemo (ሰገሞ)	*Vernonia abyssinica*	Sanitation
lehtit (ልሕቲት)	*Genus malva*	Treatment for intestinal diseases and abdominal pains
sono (ሶኖ)	*Sonna Alexandria/Cassia alexandria*	Treatment for abdominal pains
kerbe (ክርበ)	*Commiphora erythraea/ Commuphora abyssinica*	Treatment for abdominal pains and intestinal diseases
'ere (ዕረ)	*Aloecalidophylla*	Treatment for intestinal illnesses and other variety types of infections
besenna (ብሰና)	*Albezia anthelminitica*	Treatment against parasites, especially tapeworm
shlan (ሽላን)	*Anethum graveolens*	Treatment against abdominal pains
qemida (ቀሚዳ)	*Clematis hirsute*	Treatment against communicable diseases

Source: Adapted from Andemariam (2008: 106; 110–111)

smoking. Traditional ways of food preservation, particularly meat and bread, vary. Yet, drying is one of the most typical methods of preservation. Meat is cut into slices and sundried to become *quanta* (ቋንጣ) and *enjera* (local bread) to become *korensho* (ኮረንሾ). Varieties of grains are also dried and ground for preservation purposes (see Gebremichael 2008: 102–109). Salting is the standard way of meat preservation.

Another method of disinfection is smoking. Containers for milk and other liquids are smoked. Specific plants are used for this purpose—for example, the African olive (*Olia Africana*). This method is designed to prevent microorganisms (such as bacteria and parasites). Communicable diseases such as typhus are prevented by soaking clothes in boiling water. This practically kills disease-carrying organisms such as lice. In addition, exposing blankets and other clothes to sunlight is also used as a means to prevent microorganisms (Gebremichael 2008: 103–104). Prevention techniques also involve cleaning clothes using extracts of certain plants, such as *shibti* (ሽብጢ)— *Phytolacca dodecandra*.

During epidemic outbreaks of animal or human diseases, Eritreans also practice quarantine methods. For example, any animal bought from a different market and brought to a village usually requires a medical checkup by a practitioner. Unless confirmed as healthy by a village practitioner, new animals are usually kept away from preexisting herds. Also, animal quarantine practices often follow legal procedures as prescribed in communal laws.

CURATIVE PRACTICES
Psychiatric Illnesses and Treatments

Based on their respective beliefs, Eritrean communities also practice prevention through assorted beliefs and cultural rituals. Religions also play great roles in shaping traditional healing practices. Praying, oblations, and fasting are some of the practices used to prevent illnesses. For example, people wear an object called a *kitab* (ክታብ), or "amulet" that is used for the purpose of protection from illnesses in connection with the *buda* (ቡዳ), "evil eye," or wild animal attacks (such as against snake bites). There are also a number of cultural rituals and scarifications practiced for disease prevention (Deribe Kassaye et al. 2006: 129; Gebremichael 2008: 124–128). Spiritual healing is usually associated with highly learned Orthodox *Tewahdo* Christian clergymen commonly known as *debteras* (ደብተራ), or the Muslim *kalechas*. These healers are usually concerned with mental illnesses that are often associated with evil spirits. Healers practice intensive prayers and use the "powers of holy water" called *may chelot* (ማይ ጨሎት), or *tsebel* (ጸበል), and *kitab* for treating mental disorders. Prayers attributed to these types of healing are called *degam* (ድጋም), and are performed by the *debteras* on behalf of their patients. *Kitabs* associated with mental healing vary, but the common ones are amulets that contain secretly written scripts. These scripts are believed to have the power to expel evil spirits (see also Deribe Kassaye et al. 2006: 129). Eritrean Christians widely believe in the healing powers of "holy water." Therefore, religious institutions often prescribe patients to undergo certain religious rituals, such as bathing in or drinking from *may chelot*. There are a number of *may chelot* venues throughout the country. To mention a few: the Gaber Der'anto of Mendefera; Abba Meta'e of Guh Che'a; and the Abuna Tekle of Kurbarya (Dekemhare). There are also a number of other natural sources such as hot springs that are widely considered as sites with healing powers. An example of such a site is the May Wu'uy hot spring, located near the village of Gahtelay, at the foothills of the eastern escarpments.

Traditional healers handle varieties of diseases and bodily injuries. Diseases handled by these healers "range from simple headache to psychosomatic illnesses" (Gebremichael 2008: 101). Most medical herbs used by traditional healers are extracts from the natural resources that can be found in their respective localities. Traditional practitioners include bonesetters, skin disease healers, psychiatrists, hematologists and surges, spiritual healers, and witches. Discussing whether all practices of traditional medicine are useful or harmful is out of the scope of this work, although Gebremichael (2008) provides insightful information on the subject. Some of the common traditional medical practices in Eritrea follow.

DISEASES RELATED TO INTERNAL BODY ELEMENTS AND TRADITIONAL HEALING

Traditional herbal medicine in Eritrea deals with a variety of diseases, including respiratory disorders, tuberculosis, intestinal parasites and diseases, liver disorders, skin diseases, malaria, sexually transmitted diseases, and more. Most of these diseases are treated by healers who use plants as their primary resource for providing treatments. Diagnosis usually depends on physical examinations and questioning patients (Deribe Kassaye et al. 2006: 129). Drug dosages are prepared by the healers themselves, and their preservation depends entirely on individual experiences of the practitioners. Some of the common diseases treated by traditional healers are *hanat* (ሓናት) "tonsil"; *hebet* (ሕበጥ) "swellings"; *qertset* (ቅርጸት) "abdominal pains"; *nefyo* (ነፍዮ) "measles"; *tektekta* (ትኽትኽታ) "dry coughing"; and *wese'at* (ውጽኣት) "diarrhea" (see also Gebremichael 2006: 106–118).

Hanat is a common disease of many Eritreans. To treat it, healers use special types of soils and plants, usually mixed with water, and apply them to the external parts of the swelling. Viral diseases such as measles are also a great concern to the population at large. Traditional healers provide valuable advice to patients with measles. For example, they advise them "to avoid direct sunlight exposure and spare themselves from irritation of the eyes" (Gebremichael 2008: 117). Moreover, healers provide medical help deemed necessary for disinfection and sanitation to patients with measles. Dry coughing is usually treated with a combination of plant and animal resources. A certain vegetable locally known as *adri* (ኣድሪ)—*Brassica carinata* (similar to mustard)—is mixed with milk and garlic to heal diseases related to the respiratory system, such as coughing (Gebremichael 2008: 117). *Adri* is actually one of the most practical healing plants to use against various microbial infections. For example, it is also used to treat diseases such as diarrhea and gastrointestinal infections.

SURGERY

Traditional medical practices in Eritrea also comprise a number of health operations. Traditional surgeries include bone setting, *mahgoma* (ማሕጎማ) "bloodletting"; *mehras* (ምሕራስ) "midwifery"; *metkosa* (መትኮሳ) "skin burning"; and *mekenshab* (ምክንሻብ) "circumcision." It is worth noting that although some traditional healers might combine knowledge of one or more healing practices (such as surgical and other nonsurgical body healings), traditional surges are people who often specialize in one of the traditional surgical practices mentioned above.

BONE FRACTURE FIXING AND DENTAL EXTRACTION

Known as *wegiesa* (ወጊሳ), "repairer," or in some areas *sefeyti* (ሰፈይቲ), "tailors," these healers usually deal with injuries related to bone fractures. Using local resources, these healers fix broken bones and treat diseases of the mouth and teeth. In other words, the healers serve as socially acknowledged orthopedists. Their healing methods include a thorough survey of the injury and the affected bone and the careful setting of bone fractures. Most rural villages have one or more *wegiesas*. Most of the medical resources used by these healers are extracts from natural resources that surround them. Traditional practitioners are also experienced at extracting teeth, but this procedure is done without anti-pain drugs. Unwanted teeth are usually pulled by the healers regardless of how dire the consequences might be. Yet, "one worrisome aspect of the traditional extraction and care of teeth is infection. It can lead to health complications of various magnitudes . . ." (Gebremichael 2008: 119).

BLOODLETTING

Bloodletting is one of the oldest surgical methods in the country. Known as *hagwamo* (ሓጓሞ), these practitioners are concerned with various diseases such as *mende'at* (መንደዓት)—a type of tuberculosis characterized by swellings—as well as a variety of other diseases associated with the muscles attached to the spinal cord. "The main rationale behind bloodletting is to cause the patient to bleed, and through the flow of "bad blood, to ascertain riddance of illness" (Gebremichael 2008: 121). Practitioners make an incision in the affected area and apply blood suction, usually using an animal horn. The broader end of the horn is placed on the incised part and sucks the "bad" blood by way of mouth (placed at the narrower part of the horn). This practice is, however, widely opposed by modern medical practitioners, mainly because it involves greater risk for the transfer of infectious diseases such as HIV/AIDS.

SKIN BURNING

This practice is also prevalent throughout the country. Affected body parts such as the chest and abdomen are purposely burned by healers using hot sticks and other hot objects. Diseases treated with this method also include rheumatism, facial paralysis, jaundice, and snake and scorpion bites (adapted from Gebremichael 2008: 120–121). How effective this treatment can be is still a matter of debate. Apart from treating diseases, skin burning is also used for decorative or customary purposes. Many communities also use the same system to imprint clan symbols or other brands on their animal herds.

MIDWIFERY

Midwifery is another important and commonly practiced part of traditional medicine. Midwives are commonly known in Tigrinya as *mehresti* (መሕረስቲ), "traditional birth attendants." These practitioners have no formal education on the subject, and their medical knowledge is acquired through experience. They have also earned remarkable trust and acknowledgment by their respective communities. Midwives provide primary health care and consultancy to women—from the time of pregnancy to delivery. A great majority of women bear their children in the company of midwives rather than in hospitals. This is simply because the health infrastructure, especially in rural Eritrea, has yet to develop. Therefore, communally acknowledged midwives play crucial roles all over Eritrea.

REFERENCES

Abdulkadir, Asia (2008). *Die Perzeption von Gewalt im Geschlechterverhältnis in Eritrea: Eine Untersuchung über die Gewalterfahrung Weiblicher Rekrutinnen.* Hamburg: Dr. Kovaó Verlag.

Asefaw, Fana (2008). *Weibliche Gentalbeschneidung: Hintergründe, Gesundheitliche Folgen und Nachhaltige Prävention.* Frankfurt am Main: Ulrike Helmer Verlag.

Carillet, Jean-Bernard and Phillips, Matt (2006). *"Lonely Planet": Ethiopia and Eritrea.* 3rd rev. ed., n.p.: Lonely Planet.

Culture of Eritrea: http://en.wikipedia.org/wiki/Culture_of_Eritrea (access in August 2009).

Denison, Edward and Paice, Edward (2002). *Eritrea: The Bradt Travel Guide.* Chalfont St. Peter: Bradt.

Deribe Kassaye, Kebede; Amberbir, Alemayehu; Getachew, Binyam and Mussema, Yunis (2006). "A historical overview of traditional medicine practices and policy in Ethiopia." In: *Ethiopia Journal of Health Development.* 20(2), pp. 127–134.

Faitlovitch, Jacques (1911). "*Qene Habe*sha [Habesha Poetry]." In: *Giornale della Società Asiatica Italiana,* 23, pp. 1–88.

Favali, Lyda and Pateman, Roy (2003). *Blood, Land, and Sex: Legal and Political Pluralism in Eritrea.* Bloomington, IN: Indiana University Press.

Gebremedhin, Tesfa G. and Tesfagiorgis, Gebre H. (eds.)(2008). *Traditions of Eritrea: Linking the Past to the Future.* Trenton, NJ: Red Sea Press.

Gebremichael, Andemariam (2008). "Traditional Health Practices in Eritrea." In: Tesfa G. Gebremedhin, Tesfa and Tesfagiorgis, Gebre H. (eds.). *Traditions of Eritrea: Linking the Past to the Future.* Trenton, NJ: Red Sea Press, pp.101–130.

Littmann, Enno (1910). *Publications of the Princeton Expedition to Abyssinia.* Vol. II, Leyden [Leiden]: Late E. J. Brill.

Tronvoll, Kjetil (199). *Mai Weini; A Highland Village in Eritrea: A Study of the People, Their Livelihood, and Land Tenure During Times of Turbulence.* Lawrenceville, NJ: Red Sea Press.

World Health Organization, Fact sheet Number 134: http://www.who.int/mediacentre/factsheets/fs134/en/index.html (accessed on February 2010).

CHAPTER 7

Contemporary Issues

In the 1980s and early 1990s, the Eritrean case, particularly the destructive war for independence was seen as one of the urgent regional and international causes for self-determination. The liberation struggle under the EPLF (currently the People's Front for Democracy and Justice—PFDJ) had to demand the lives of about 70,000 Eritrean fighting members and tens of thousands of Eritrean civilians. Hundreds of thousands of Eritreans who experienced the brutal consequences of the war also left their homes to live as refugees elsewhere on the globe. After such a prolonged and destructive liberation struggle, Eritreans finally achieved their independence militarily in 1991 (and legally in 1993 through an internationally supervised free and fair referendum). Eritrea then became the newest nation on the continent. Immediately after the independence of the country, the peoples of Eritrea, who suffered from the consequences of the conflict for many years, engaged themselves in the reconstruction of their country and continued to dream of a peaceful life. For most Eritreans, independence of their country signified a better future for a peaceful and harmonious life. In fact, this was also what the EPLF and later the PFDJ promised them.

The Eritrean revolution (1961–1991) came with numerous promises of peace and stability for the people. The revolution propagated that an independent Eritrea would immediately strive to achieve sustainable economic, social, and political development. Eritreans, whether at home or abroad, fought by all means necessary to achieve this end. Without the support of the Eritrean masses, the liberation organizations—the Eritrean Liberation Front (ELF) and the EPLF would never have survived the conflict. The EPLF, which achieved widespread popular support, especially depended on the masses for most of its supplies. For example, wherever they went, its fighters were supported and fed by the rural dwellers who saw the revolution as the only means to end the suffering they had endured all of their lives. Through its awareness campaigns, the EPLF also filled them with promises and hope for a better future. Have the promises been fulfilled or betrayed? Has the revolution achieved its intended social, economic, and political transformation, or has it simply been a failure? What happened to the dream for self-reliance and the achievement of food security? Do Eritreans live in a liberal political environment? Why is there a remarkable exodus of Eritrean youth to Europe and the Middle East? These are the questions that occupy most Eritreans in the diaspora and at home. Free contemporary cyberspace discussions also focus on these above questions.

Among the most pressing issues in contemporary Eritrea are internal political dynamics, food insecurity, massive population displacement and migration, as well as health threats such as epidemic diseases. As we have seen in chapter three, the current political situation of the country is by no standard sustainable. Chronic internal instability as well as a lack of a constitutional political structure have caused considerable discontent among the Eritrean population. In addition, the government's suppression of freedom of the press and speech, its denial of religious rights and freedom of movement, as well as human rights abuses have been cited by national and international organizations as the most concerning issues in the country.

As mentioned earlier, after Eritrea's independence, the popular dream was focused on the establishment of a constitutional and democratic state. Although the former EPLF and the current PFDJ, which controls almost all of the political and economic aspects of the country, promised to establish a democratic regime, the Eritrean constitution that was approved in 1997 has not yet been implemented. The government is also continuously accused by national and international organizations of practicing gross human rights violations. No governmental democratic elections have taken place since the formal independence of the country. Today, Eritrea is almost isolated from most international political communities. Owing to the current state of affairs, almost no international NGO or aid agency is actively engaged whatsoever in the country. Most former high officials as well as independent journalists and religious activists have been jailed. Many of these prisoners will stay in custody for unknown periods of time. None of the "political prisoners" has been presented in a legal court, and no one knows the conditions or whereabouts of the prisoners. Generally, some of the most pressing political issues for Eritrea's public are economic mismanagement, unstable relations with neighboring countries, lack of sufficient food supplies, and violations of fundamental human rights.

AN OVERVIEW OF CONTEMPORARY ERITREAN POLITICS

As with most Sub-Saharan African countries, Eritrea is characterized by unstable political circumstances and economic hazards. The current political system of the country is based on a single-party system. Although the government initially advocated for the establishment of a politically pluralist state, it has not yet come into effect.

Apart from the PFDJ there is no other active political party in the country. The president of the country, who is also the head of the PFDJ, plays his roles both as the head of the state and the government. Although the PFDJ calls itself as a "front for democracy," the government has not yet established a democratic political infrastructure. The country's politics are dominated by the PFDJ. All other political institutions have been banned or expelled from the country. Despite early promises for general democratic elections, the country has not held any democratic governmental elections since 1993.

Since its independence, Eritrea has gone through two paradoxically different systems of political regimes. Following its independence, the country attempted to establish a pluralist political structure characterized by democratic rule of law. The masses were mobilized to achieve sustainable political and economic development. For the first time in their history the people voted in a democratic referendum and declared their independence. The popular referendum provided a great deal of expectation for citizens, and they hoped that Eritrea would eventually form a democratic system of rule in which their individual voices would be heard. Therefore, the initial phase of Eritrea's independence displayed an image showing an African "triumph and bacon of hope" (Mengisteab and Yohannes 2005: 35). The positive image of Eritrea was formed on the basis of its sociopolitical achievements during the revolution. The fact that the EPLF managed to cultivate mass support and implement self-reliant policies in the field of struggle made most observers and the country's masses hope for a successful sociopolitical transformation in post-independent Eritrea.

However, coupled with the unexpected tensions with its neighbors, and particularly the destructive border conflict with Ethiopia (1998–2000), the dream for the establishment of a democratic state started to fade. Rather, the political decision making of governmental affairs started to fall exclusively into the hands of the PFDJ and the head of state. The government also began to apply suppressive actions against individuals and institutions who openly expressed their political opinions. For example, the government imprisoned political figures who demanded political reform in 2001. A group of high-ranking government officials collectively known as G-15—including Haile Woldetinsae (Deru'e), Petros Solomon, Beraki Gebreselassie, Mahmud Ahmed Sherifo, Mesfin Hagos, Ogbe Abraha, and Astier Fisehatsion—were imprisoned without any charges based on legal grounds. Although the government informally charged these officials with forms of treason, it has not presented them to a legal court to this day. Similarly, international organizations and Eritrean civic movements continuously report that thousands of Eritreans are kept in underground prisons across the country.

The Eritrean constitution was drafted and ratified in 1997. But although the new constitution was planned to be put into effect in 1998, the government has placed its implementation on hold for an unknown period of time. Hence, Eritrea has no constitutional government. Although the government attempted to reform a number of legal codes, the administration of justice has mainly been based on laws that were in place from previous regimes. As a signatory to a number of international laws, Eritrea is principally required to institute major global laws such as human and political rights of its citizens. However, as stated earlier, the country is repeatedly and bitterly criticized for violating established international laws—particularly related to human and political rights.

FREEDOM OF THE PRESS

The public press emerged in Eritrea mainly during the British Military Administration (BMA) of the country in the 1940s. Throughout the Italian colonial rule (1890–1941), the formation of the Eritrean press was strictly controlled. Moreover, the fact that the colonial state did not provide an adequate educational infrastructure to the citizens further impeded the process of developing a free press in the country. The British rule in Eritrea was characterized by the expansion of formal education, growth of national political consciousness, as well as support for the Eritrean press. During this period, Eritreans were allowed to express their political, cultural, and economic views through the press media. Newspapers were published in Tigrinya and Arabic, and citizens used these newspapers as convenient platforms for expressing their views. The relative freedom of press created during the British rule also resulted in the expansion of local literature.

However, the gradual process of press development in Eritrea was again curtailed during the Ethiopian occupation period (1962–1991). Freedom of press in the country was adversely affected during the Dergue regime (1974–1991). Local languages and newspapers were discouraged in assorted ways (see chapter six).

After independence, the Eritrean government demonstrated on various occasions that freedom of press would be an integral part of the country's political transformation. It encouraged private and institutional agencies to actively participate in the development of press media. In principle, the government also showed tolerance toward public criticisms that appeared in the private press. By 2000, encouraged by the promises of the government for the development of a free press, a number of private newspapers had emerged. Individuals and groups who were university graduates, students, and veteran members of the EPLF launched their own independent newspapers. Among the most prominent private newspapers were Setit, Meqalih, Qeste-Demenna, Zemen, and Tsigenai. All these newspapers focused on serving the public by providing actual information related to various internal aspects of the country. By 2000, these newspapers had become important sources of information for the public. During the Eritrea-Ethiopia border conflict (1998–2000), these newspapers served as relatively credible sources of information on issues related to the war and internal developments within the country. Their distribution also grew and they became accessible to most dwellers of towns and cities of Eritrea. During the political friction among members of the PFDJ in 2001, private newspapers played an important role in providing information reflecting views of members of the G-15 and the nonreformist members of the government. Some of the newspapers also published interviews with members of the G-15.

However, in September 2001, the Eritrean government cracked down on private journalists and shut down all private newspapers. Although the majority of the journalists were arrested by the government, a few managed to flee the country. The government alleged that these journalists and members of the G-15 were a grave threat to the national security of the country. Yet, to this day (October 2009), the government has not presented any of them in a public court. Not much is known about the condition or the whereabouts of the detained journalists, although some nonofficial reports disclose that a number of them have died in prison.

Today, there is no privately owned media in Eritrea. The only legal media sources are the single government-owned newspaper (called *Haddas Ertra*), the single national television (called *ERI-TV*), the single radio broadcast (called *Dimtsi Haffash*), and a few Internet cafés where the public receives limited access to information. According to reports by Reporters Without Borders (2008), Eritrea is ranked among the countries with the least freedom of the press (as the 137th country on the index list), just after North Korea (Reporters Without Borders: Press Freedom Index 2008).

CIRCUMSTANCES OF HUMAN RIGHTS IN ERITREA

As stated earlier, Eritrea has continuously been criticized by national and international organizations for violating the fundamental human rights of its own citizens. Based on numerous human rights reports by institutions such as Amnesty International and Human Rights Watch, Eritrea applies repressive policies that violate the fundamental rights of its population. The Eritrean judiciary system is still weak, owing to the lack of constitutional rule of law as well as a lack of personnel. Therefore, especially since 2001, it has repeatedly been reported that innocent people are detained without legal trial procedures, tortured, killed, as well exploited for as forced labor and military conscription (see also Tronvoll 2009; Kibreab 2009).

FREEDOM OF MOVEMENT

According to reports of human rights activists, one of the issues related to human rights violation in Eritrea is lack of freedom of movement, especially for people ranging of age between the ages of 18 and 40 (although the age range appears sometimes as between 18 and 50). According to the available reports, Eritreans whose ages fall in the above-mentioned age range suffer from freedom of movement within the country. People are asked to have travel permissions wherever they intend to travel. All members of the national service are required to have permission papers called *menqesaqesi wereqet* (መንቀሳቀሲ ወረቐት) to travel within the country. Movement outside the country is also highly restricted, especially for Eritrean youth. Concerning Eritrea's lack of freedom of movement, the Human Rights Watch reports as follows:

> The government does not issue travel documents or exit visas to Eritreans eligible for national service therefore men younger than 50 (or even 55) and women younger than 47 are confined to the country. Children older than 14 are also not allowed to travel outside Eritrea. Despite these restrictions, increasing numbers of Eritreans are fleeing the country, braving the government's shoot-to-kill policy at the borders

---

SOME INTERNATIONAL AIRLINES WITH REGULAR FLIGHTS TO ERITREA

- Lufthansa Airlines: Flight usually via Frankfurt (and sometimes Rome). There is a local Lufthansa branch office in Asmara.
- Yemenia Airlines: Flights usually via Sena'a, Yemen (and via Rome to Frankfurt)
- Egypt Air: Flights usually via Cairo

---

rather than endure the unending toil and abuse inflicted during their national service (Human Rights Watch, 2009).

FREEDOM OF RELIGIOUS WORSHIP

Human rights organizations also harshly criticize the Eritrean government for applying repressive policies against religious institutions and groups. In principle, the Eritrean government recognizes four religious faiths: Islam, Orthodox *Tewahdo* Christianity, Roman Catholicism, and Lutheranism. Any other religious gathering or worship is considered by the government as an "illegal" act. This, as demonstrated by the Eritrean president, is because the "new" religions, such as the growing Pentecostal religious movement or Jehovah's Witnesses, "do not bring anything good to the existing religious beliefs" but create disarray within the existing religious institutions (president's interview in the local media, 2008). Hence, according to the president, it was for the safety of the above-mentioned four religious institutions that the government intervened. But, seen from a human rights point of view, it is also a grave violation of fundamental rights to abuse innocent people simply because of their faith.

Religious leaders and individual worshipers have also been cracked down on and arrested for unknown periods of time. The way they are treated in prison, according to human rights reports, is terrifying. Many are detained in shipping containers and are made to suffer from maltreatment by government authorities. The Human Rights Watch notes as follows:

> Persons arrested for their religious affiliations and practices suffer the same torture and abuse as other prisoners, sometimes with the express intent of compelling them to renounce their religions. International religious organizations estimate that a minimum of between 2,000 and 3,000 Eritreans are incarcerated solely because of their religious practices and affiliations (Human Rights Watch, 2009).

In addition to the above-mentioned violations, the government is also accused of interfering in the church affairs of the very religious institutions it recognizes. For example, it has been reported that the dismissal of the Orthodox *Tewahdo* Church's overall religious figure, his Holiness Patriarch Antonios in 2006, was orchestrated by the government. Patriarch Antonios has also been under house arrest since 2006. However, the government has not yet justified its actions or interference in the affairs of the

Orthodox *Tewahdo* Church. Since the arrest of his Holiness patriarch Antonios, the Eritrean Orthodox *Tewahdo* Church has been going through an unfortunate fragmentation, especially among the Eritrean diaspora.

NATIONAL SERVICE AND ITS IMPLICATIONS

Although post-independent Eritrea initially showed optimistic determination for reconstruction and economic rehabilitation, it also continued to create a highly militarized society. Already in 1991, the Eritrean government issued a new proclamation (National Service Proclamation 11/1991) obliging all citizens (between ages 18 and 45) to take part in the compulsory national service program. The National Service Proclamation 11/1991 declared that citizens should serve in the compulsory service program for 18 months. As detailed by the proclamations and decrees of the government, the national service consisted of compulsory military training for six months and 12 months service in development schemes and/or military commitments. Under Proclamation 11/1991, certain members of the population were exempted from the service. Among others, under Article 5, the Proclamation exempted people who were engaged in self-administered trading activities (but only those who owned licenses for their business). Under Article 7, the Proclamation exempted married women and single mothers. Article 8 of the Proclamation exempted people with family responsibilities (sole breadwinners of a household) and so forth.

The main objective of the national service, as also stated by government authorities, was for the formation of a secular and socially integrated Eritrea. As part of its "nation-building" strategies, the government considered the national service program as a means to transfer its political and social values to the next generation. The Eritrean government, which is mainly formed on the scaffolding of the liberation front, particularly the EPLF, believes that it has to "bestow" the main sociopolitical values that were achieved during the liberation war to the younger generation. Hence, the national service program has been considered as an important channel in transferring EPLF's values to the younger generation and to the overall population. As argued by a PFDJ cadre, the national service program was considered a good platform for the young generation to easily learn the basic values of the EPLF, such as "hard work," *nih* (being tough), *habbo* (fortitude; perseverance), and *senni menkas* (courageousness). On the other hand, the government's intention is also believed to have been to create a society that bypasses ethnolinguistic and religious parochialisms. Therefore, if people from all ethnolinguistic groups are taken to the same training center and share common experiences during their national service period, the government believes, they could eventually develop values that transcend their ethnolinguistic and religious affiliations. This, according to the perception of the government, would facilitate the creation and strengthening of a common national identity.

In 1995, the Eritrean government replaced National Service Proclamation 11/1991 with a new revised decree under Proclamation 82/1995. The proclamation provided that people with disabilities, EPLF veteran fighters, and young mothers would be exempted from the National Service (article 15). Moreover, full-time students were also temporarily exempted until they finished school. A number of exemptions that were provided under Proclamation 11/1991 were, however, abandoned. Interestingly, this Proclamation also includes a couple of somewhat bolder objectives for the national service program. For example, under Chapter 2 (Art. 5) of Proclamation 82/1995, the government elaborates some of the objectives of the National Service. One of the statements under this article reads as follows: "To establish a strong defense force to ensure a free and sovereign Eritrea." With this statement, the government clarified that the national service program was not only for the creation of common national identity and integrity, but also for the establishment of a "strong defense force."

Based on the proclamations mentioned above, the government started to implement the national service program in forms of rounds. The draft rounds of conscription were regulated to take place in intervals of six months. The first round of national service conscripts were sent to the Sawa military training camp in July 1994. The second, third, fourth, and fifth rounds of conscripts were sent to Sawa in January 1995, June 1995, January 1996, and July 1996, respectively. Through 1998 (the seventh round), Eritrea had already recruited about 115,000 conscripts (see Hughes 2004: 24). To date (November 2009), the country continues to recruit using the same method.

In addition to the problem of massive conscription, Eritrea lacks governing rules and regulations for the national service. Literally, the government does not even follow the laws provided by the national service proclamations. As a result, there has not been any significant demobilization of the army since the mid-1990s. This means that although members of the national service should be demobilized after serving for 18 months as provided by the proclamations, it has not taken place. Hence, most conscripts are still serving in the army and other various governmental schemes—some for over 10 years now, but they are still compelled to stay in the army. It is worth noting that no members of the national service get any compensation or salary for their unlimited services apart from a little monthly pocket money ranging from 150 to 500 Nakfa (equivalent to U.S.$9 to U.S.$33.3). Owing to the dramatic increase in prices of goods and services in Eritrea, the above-mentioned amount cannot help conscripts buy basic supplies let alone feed families. How can 18 months of army duty be turned into endless service? This dilemma has created grave dissatisfaction among recruits. On various occasions, the government has attempted to justify national service by alleging that the country is under security threats, and so it needs a standby army. Yet, there has not been any legitimate military threat since the end of the actual border conflict with Ethiopia in 2000. Of course, as is the case with a number of its neighbors, Eritrea finds itself in a "no war, no peace" political environment with Ethiopia. However, this cannot be a justifiable reason as to why the government continues to practice forced conscription and keeps such a large army.

According to reports, the government also applies suppressive measures against deserters or anyone who fails to perform national service. On the government's treatment of the Eritrean youth in general and the conscripts in particular, EMDHR notes:

> There are no clear laws and a regulation governing the whole military system—a law that precisely limits the powers and responsibilities of military commanders, and that protects the rights of ordinary servicemen ... What one normally learns

in the system is how to become "fearful and obedient" to immediate military commanders. Hence, the massive youth outflow is the immediate result, and a clear sign of an utter defiance against the ill-practiced military service in particular and the increasing militarization of the nation in general.

Unwilling to reconsider its ill-practiced military conscription, the government of Eritrea sadly resorted to the least effective method of securing compliance—intimidation against and violent coercion upon Eritrea's youth. It opted to employ routine propaganda campaigns against young draft evaders with an effort of labeling them as "tourists but not refugees" or "traitors who failed to fulfill their national obligations." Moreover, it introduced or otherwise endorsed "arbitrary torture" and "prolonged imprisonments without trial," a "shoot-to-death" on site policy against those who are found to flee the country; and it even goes to the extent of arresting parents of the missing children—an utterly irresponsible and flawed measure which seriously continue to undermine Eritrea's long-stayed rich culture of treating the elders with respect and dignity (EMDHR 2008: 2).

Although the first few rounds of the national service comprised great numbers of volunteers, prevalent suppressive government measures resulted in a dramatic decrease of volunteers. Hence, the government resorted to additional measure for conscription—*giffa* (raids and roundups in search of new recruits). Especially after 2000, the government distributed armed forces everywhere, including in cities such as Asmara, and grabbed potential conscripts, deserters, or anyone who did not comply with national service calls. It became the army's common practice to simply seize people in streets and public places and take them off to national service. Armed battalions garrisoned within cities and towns such as Asmara continued to hunt young people throughout the years after the border war with Ethiopia. Forced conscription, suppressive measures against members of the national service and postponement of national service for unknown periods of time resulted in popular dissatisfaction and resentment against the government.

"FLEEING ERITREA!": NEW TRENDS OF MIGRATION

There has been an exodus of Eritreans to Sudan and Ethiopia for the last few years to live there as refugees. Many also made their way to Europe and the Middle East. Great numbers of these refugees are deserters from the army. Moreover, the imposition of the government's movement restrictions has also provoked massive illegal border crossings by Eritreans. For the first time in history, great numbers of Eritreans are now living in refugee camps in northern Ethiopia and at the Shimelba Refugee Camp in Tigray.

Other refugees who flee Eritrea are distributed in various camps in Sudan, such as the Shegerab Refugee Camp. Eritrean refugees arrive at these camps almost daily. In the Shimelba Refugee Camp alone, the number of Eritrean refugees is roughly estimated to be between 15,000 to 17,000, while the number of refugees in Sudan is much higher. Based on the United Nations Higher Commission for Refugees (UNHCR) estimate, about 500–800 Eritreans enter Sudan as refugees monthly, and there are about

100,000 Eritrean refugees in Eastern Sudan (BBC [Africa] broadcast, Monday, November 23, 2009, 1530GMT).

Sarcastic as it also sounds, Eritrea accuses foreign governments and international organizations such as the United States and the United Nations of "orchestrating" a planned exodus of Eritreans from their home country. Eritrea alleges that the UN and other powerful states are behind the plots. Yet, the government does not prove its accusations in any formal way. For example, the Eritrean Minister of Information, Mr. Ali Abdu, on the one hand, denies the massive exodus of Eritreans to Sudan, and on the other hand, he accuses the UN for getting involved in human trafficking from Eritrea. In an interview with a BBC correspondent on November 23, 2009, the minister says "remember that the UN agencies including sometimes UNHCR are involved in human trafficking and human trafficking networks of mafia groups" (BBC [Africa] broadcast, Monday, November 23, 2009, 1530GMT).

Although refugees receive limited assistance by the hosting governments as well as international humanitarian organizations such as the UNHCR, the International Rescue Committee (IRC) and International Committee of the Red Cross (ICRC), they live under appalling conditions. Women and children in those refugee camps are reported to be the most especially disadvantaged. Owing to lack of enough food, poor security, and deteriorating health conditions, the lives of great numbers of refugees are threatened.

REFUGEES BETWEEN LIFE AND DEATH: FACING THE DESERT, THE SEA, AND THE GUN

Faced with horrific living conditions in the camps, many Eritrean refugees take another life-threatening step of migration—crossing the Sahara Desert to arrive at Libya, crossing the Mediterranean Sea in "boats," crossing the Egyptian-Israeli borders by foot, and so forth. The result of such actions is usually terrifying. Many refugees die in the desert for lack of food and drink, many languish in the Mediterranean Sea, a number of these refugees are also killed by border guards (example, at the borders between Egypt and Israel), yet many others suffer from brutal atrocities of human traffickers.

In addition, many Eritrean refugees are ill-treated by hosting countries such as Libya and Egypt. In many cases, these poor refugees are grabbed from anywhere in Libya and Egypt, put in prisons, and eventually deported back to Eritrea (see ICRC 2007). Note that deported refugees usually face severe punishments in their homeland. Many also languish in prisons. In the last few years, the world media partially covered the conditions of migrants to Europe and the Mediterranean world. The media coverage showed deteriorating conditions of refugees on the sea and national borders.

Refugees who finally manage to arrive in Europe, especially Malta and Italy, are also living under destitute conditions. Those who attempt further migration to other countries in Europe usually face deportation to the primary hosting country. Lack of employment, substantial aid, and other related factors are among the most pressing concerns of refugees in Europe (see Kidane and Lenoir 2009).

FOOD INSECURITY AND THE THREAT OF HUNGER AND FAMINE IN ERITREA

As discussed in chapter four, over 80 percent of the Eritrean population is dependent on farming and/or animal husbandry for a living. These economic activities are based on traditional ways of production and are labor-intensive activities. Farming requires the tilling of land, methodical care of cultivated grains, and harvesting. All these activities are conducted by human labor. Similarly, animal husbandry (pastoralism) also demands intensive human labor. Among other things, pastoralism in Eritrea is characterized by seasonal migration of animals and their owners in search of pastures. Continuous ecological adversities as well as the fragile nature of ecosystems in the pastoral zones usually compel pastoral communities to adjust, change, or abandon their economic strategies. Among the common strategies of pastoralist communities is the dispersion of herds of animals. By dispersion, they attempt to maximize the survival chances of their herds. In a nutshell, they live under prevalent struggle for survival. Most of their strategies require the availability of enough personnel from each pastoral household for herding.

Explaining Eritrea's contemporary economic difficulties, Mengisteab and Yohannes (2005) note the following:

> Eritrea's economy, like the economies of most other post-colonial African countries, faces many fundamental problems, including lack of capable and selfless leaders, a shortage of a skilled workforce, internal economic and social fragmentation, political instability, poor institutional infrastructure, a lack of adequate transportation and communication networks, asymmetrical trade relations, and debilitating debt. Additionally, the country's economy is beset by structural problems emanating mainly from three ill-conceived policy measures, comprising the ruling party's engagement in business activities, state of control of the country's human resources and the country's land tenure system (Mengisteab and Yohannes 2005: 97).

Obviously, the backbone of these economic systems has been the working human force, hence the youth. As mentioned above "lack of a skilled workforce" and "state control of the country's human resources" are among the critical factors of food insecurity. The fact that a great majority of the youth are either kept in the Eritrean army or has left the country to live as refugees elsewhere has created immense economic disorder, especially in rural Eritrea. Most Eritrean households lack enough labor to produce food. Therefore, sustainability of food production in the country has continuously been compromised. Most villages in Eritrea comprise mostly the elderly, widows, children, or disabled people who usually fail to produce enough food. In addition to consecutive droughts for the last several years as well as the lack of foreign aid, these communities are frequently threatened from epidemic hunger and famine. The government imposes high restriction on private property rights. Although peasants have usufruct rights, land and related resources are owned by the state. Even during good rainy seasons, Eritrea has been unable to produce enough food supply.

Apart from some help offered to the needy families of martyred ex-fighters and orphans, there is no government help for the vulnerable sections of society. Even then, most of the fund has been collected from remittances by members of the diaspora community—contributions for helping orphans and families of martyrs. Although approved by law in 2005, the pension policies have not yet been implemented by the government. "Social safety nets remain based on extended family networks and associated with customary laws. Private remittances from members of the diaspora are an indispensable source of income for a large number of Eritreans residing in the country" (Gütersloh: Bertelsmann Stiftung [2009], *BTI 2010—Eritrea Country Report*).

The economic performance of the country has not been satisfactory. Most private business has not been able to function properly. This may be attributed to the absence of free market–based economic principles. In general, the private sector has been crippled by a list of problems such as lack of capital, unavailability of free and competitive economic foundations, and persistent monopoly of resources by companies run under the PFDJ. Regarding the economic situation of the country, Bertelsmann Transformation Index (2009) notes:

> Eight years after the end of the war with Ethiopia, per capita GDP has remained stagnant. The availability of statistical data and their reliability remains unsatisfactory, as there is a lack of transparency on the part of the government. During the period of review, the budget deficit further increased, there was an extreme lack of hard currency and the shortage of daily consumer goods continued. During 2008, there was an extreme scarcity of kerosene for cooking purposes, forcing the population to rely on charcoal and wood, which will have a long-term negative impact on the environment. As the extremely high rate of militarization was maintained (at least 600,000 conscripts serve in the army or perform national service), the labor market was severely disturbed, and it was impossible to produce accurate unemployment rates. There are still no statistical data on unemployment. Undermining the government's claim of self-reliance, the population was partially malnourished and relied much on imported consumer goods sold at prices as much as two or three times as high as world market prices (Gütersloh: Bertelsmann Stiftung [2009], *BTI 2010—Eritrea Country Report*).

HEALTH ISSUES

Eritrean health infrastructure was greatly damaged during the war for liberation. The war caused severe damage to health facilities and medical supplies. A majority of health professionals left the country during the war, and many also joined the liberation struggle. There have been considerable attempts to reconstruct and rehabilitate the health infrastructure and services in the country during the post-independence period. However, the health system in Eritrea is still in desperate conditions. The number of health service–providing institutions as well as qualified personnel has been inadequate. The lack of skilled manpower, inadequate medical supplies, and a medical infrastructure in disrepair are still some of the main problems of the Eritrean health sector.

The goal of the country's health services is to provide primary health care. Even at this basic level, health services in the country fail. As of 2002, the country's Ministry of Health runs 23 hospitals, 52 health centers, and 255 health stations (NSEO and ORC Macro 2003: 4). Yet, there has been a commendable increase of health-providing institutions since independence. Part of the Ministry of Health's focus has been the provision of primary health centers to fight endemic diseases such as malaria and HIV/AIDS, as well as improving maternal and child health care services. Although considerable achievements have been reported, health services in Eritrea are still inadequate at all levels. The quality and coverage of health systems are operated with considerable deficiencies. Regarding Eritrea's health care situation, NESO and ORC Marco wrote in 2003:

> Health services are still inadequate for the population, a problem common to most African countries: there is, for example, a shortage of skilled medical personnel, medications, and equipment. In 2000, the ratio of population per physician was 13,144, while the ratio of population per nurse was 2,804 [based on WHO sources]. Another problem is the uneven distribution of medical facilities. There is high concentration of health facilities in urban areas, especially in the capital city, Asmara. Traditional healers are still consulted in Eritrea, especially in the rural areas. In this respect, although the MOH [Ministry of Health] has made efforts to improve the health situation through educational campaigns directed to eradicate harmful traditional practices, such as female circumcision, it appears that there are still problems in this area. Also, the health system of Eritrea provides only limited services on reproductive health and family planning (NSEO and ORC Macro 2003: 4–5).

The health care system is also affected by the country's political developments after 2001. The exodus of a great number of Eritreans also comprises health care professionals and young scholars.

ERITREA'S FOREIGN RELATIONS DURING THE POST-WAR PERIOD

Eritrea's foreign relations with many countries, especially in the post-war period, have been erratic and rough. Since 1994, Eritrea has experienced conflicts with almost all of its neighboring countries. Her relations with Sudan remain unpredictable, although relations have improved in recent years. Her relations with Ethiopia and Djibouti are still under strained conditions. Eritrea's relations with the Arab World are often mixed. The fact that it established relations with Israel during the post-independence period created suspicion from many Arab countries. The country has good diplomatic relations with the State of Qatar.

Eritrea has a hostile image among many Western governments. Several of these countries either broke off their diplomatic relations with Eritrea. Many embassies of countries of the West either closed their offices or reduced their diplomatic interactions with the government of Eritrea. However, the European Union (EU), which on many occasions has demonstrated that the gross violations of human rights in the country were among the main concerns for its diplomatic relations with Eritrea, has been reluctant to refuse financial aid to the regime in Eritrea. For example, while the government in Eritrea has been bitterly criticized by several member states as well as the United States for violating human rights, the EU launched a financial aid package for Eritrea in September 2009. The package comprised 122 million Euro, which the EU and Eritrean government agreed to spend on development programs (see European Commission—External Cooperation Programs, 2009).

Especially since the border conflict period, the Eritrean government has cultivated tense and hostile relations with Western NGOs, and (in public) it has rejected any foreign aid that would have gone to assisting sections of the population that are vulnerable to hunger. The Eritrean government claims that it has achieved almost all economic needs to be self-reliant in food production. Therefore, many Western NGOs and active Western institutions that were engaged in the country were expelled from Eritrea in 2005 and after. Therefore, there are almost no NGOs that are actively participating in the struggle for achieving food security.

ERITREA-UNITED STATES RELATIONS

The relations between the United States and Eritrea have been uneasy, especially since the border conflict with Ethiopia. Eritrea repeatedly accused the United States for favoring Ethiopia during the conflict as well as supporting Ethiopia's stand after the Eritrea-Ethiopia Border Commission (EEBC) passed its resolution. Ethiopia refused to concede the decision. Therefore, this was considered as a violation of the rules of the EEBC, hence the international law. Eritrea sent its appeals to the UN Security Council and other Western powers that the international community should compel Ethiopia to acknowledge the EEBC decision. However, Ethiopia continued its stand, although it formally declared that it accepted the decision—but only "in principle." It demanded further dialog on the issue while Eritrea refused any dialog saying that both countries had signed agreements that empowered the EEBC decision to be binding and final. The stalemate continued while Ethiopia failed to abide by the EEBC ruling for delimitation of the border between the two countries. The Eritrean government, particularly the president of the country, sent a number of requests to the United Nations Security Council to take actions against Ethiopia. Although the UN formally requested Ethiopia to acknowledge the EEBC ruling, it failed to take action against Ethiopia. This inaction increased Eritrea's frustration with the UN, and the president of the country started to overtly criticize the UN and other Western powers such as the United States (for a historical analysis and detailed information between the United States and Eritrea, see Mengisteab and Yohannes 2005).

In the meantime, the United States also accused Eritrea of sponsoring Islamic military insurgents in Somalia and other parts of the Horn of Africa. Diplomatic tensions between the two governments have continued to worsen throughout the years. By 2007, the United States, on the recommendation of the State Department (especially on the proposal of Dr. Jandayi Frazer, United States Assistant Secretary of State for African Affairs), considered putting Eritrea on the list of countries that were believed to be supporters of state-sponsored terrorism. This increased the degree of tension between the two countries.

While the border issue between Eritrea-Ethiopia remained formally unresolved, the Somali Islamic Courts Union (SICU), especially the al-Shabab Islamist groups in Somalia attempted persistent military insurgencies to occupy large parts of Somalia. The al-Shabab are Islamist insurgency groups who are engaged in war (a form of jihad) against the "enemies of Islam," including the Transitional Federal Government of Somalia (TFGS). Threatened by the advancement of these Islamists, Ethiopia invaded Somalia in July 2006. The Ethiopian army attacked the Islamist groups, and splintered the al-Shabab into a number of smaller units. Eritrea protested that the Ethiopian invasion of Somalia was a gross violation of international law. The Eritrean government also bitterly condemned the United States for supporting Ethiopia's military actions in Somalia. Ethiopia, backed by the United States, continued the war until 2009. However, the Islamist insurgents reorganized themselves and have continued to attack government positions in most parts of southern Somalia.

As some observers stated, the war in Somalia also resembled a proxy war between Ethiopia and Eritrea. Eritrea was accused by the United States and Ethiopia for providing military assistance to the al-Shabab groups. Eritrea was also accused of receiving and training militant Islamic groups in the country. Eritrea continued to deny the allegations by the United States and Ethiopia. For example, during his recent interview with Aljazeera (on February 20, 2010), President Isaias Afeweki states:

> We don't believe religion is an alternative or substitute for political, social, economic problems in any one country or any society. We have never entertained the idea of Sharia being a solution or Islam being a solution as many may like to appreciate. How possibly could one blame Eritrea for sympathising or supporting one group over another in Somalia? We have never done that (Aljazeera, 2010).

The United States Secretary of State, Hillary Clinton, accused Eritrea of supporting the al-Shabab during her visits to a number of African countries in August 2009. Secretary Clinton warned Eritrea that if it continues to support military insurgents in Somalia, the United States might take action. Eritrea has continued to deny the allegations.

Based on the issues of the al-Shabab and Somalia, the United States and Eritrea have continued tense relations in recent years. In the meantime, Eritrea has strengthened its relations with Iran. This move has increased the mistrust from the United States and other Western countries. Eritrea has continued to confront Western organizations such as the UN in various ways. For example, the Eritrean government has refused to allow free movement of members of the UN peacekeeping forces in the country—United Nations Mission to Ethiopia and Eritrea (UNMEE). It also refused to supply them with fuel and other basic commodities. By 2007, tensions rose between the peacekeepers and the Eritrean government. The UNMEE, restricted by the government limits imposed upon it, left the country in 2008. Eritrea also expelled most of the key members of UNMEE from the country.

Unable to demarcate the Eritrea-Ethiopia border on the ground, the EEBC closed the mandate in November 2007. Although Eritrea considers the decision of the EEBC as a virtual demarcation, Ethiopia has not yet agreed to the provisions of the EEBC decision. Eritrea considers that the main force behind the war and post-war crisis is the United States. The president of Eritrea also accuses the United States of instigating the border war with Ethiopia. During his interview with Aljazeera (on February 20, 2010), he states:

> This border issue war was a senseless conflict instigated by the United States in the first place, for the record. And we went to arbitration, and arbitration was done, almost eight years now, 2002. And the decision was taken, and that decision is blocked by the United States. It is not blocked by Ethiopia. Ethiopia does not have the resource and the means to block any decision of arbitration and implementation. It is a cover up for the failures of the misguided policies of the United States in the Horn of Africa for the last 20 years (posted by Aljazeera, February 22, 2010).

UN SANCTIONS AGAINST ERITREA

As mentioned earlier, Eritrea has been considered by most Western governments as a principal source of instability in the Horn of Africa. The government is believed to have supported a number of opposition forces from countries in the Horn of Africa. For instance, Eritrea is accused of supplying arms to Oromo, Amhara, Somali, and Tigrean opposition groups. A number of reports showed that these opposition forces have established their camps and offices within Eritrea, and that the Eritrean government provides them with arms and training.

Eritrea's involvement in the peace negotiations in the Sudan and Chad have also been presented as sources of dissatisfaction by many Western governments. Since the civil war in Sudan, Eritrea has been involved in the peace negotiations between the Sudanese government and its factions. It has been acting as broker or mediator for peace between the forces in Sudan.

Allegations that Eritrea supports militant Islamic insurgents in Somalia have mounted recently. The African Union (AU), which deployed over 4,000 peacekeeping troops in Somalia, has also been concerned by Eritrea's alleged involvement in Somalia. In May 2009, the AU appealed to the United Nations Security Council that Eritrea deserved sanctions. The AU, the United States, and other members of the United Nations Security Council fiercely accused Eritrea of providing weapons and other logistical support for Islamist groups in Somalia. The issue of Eritrea became one of the main themes of discussion in the United Nations Security Council.

On December 23, 2009, members of the United Nations Security Council reached a consensus to impose an arms embargo and other sanctions on Eritrea. The Security Council adopted Resolution 1907, imposing sanctions against Eritrea. The United Nations Security Council passed Resolution 1907 by 13 of the 15 voting member states. The Security Council justified the sanction as a response to Eritrea's failure to comply with the organization's orders on issues of the border conflict between Eritrea and Djibouti as well as Eritrea's support of Islamic military insurgents in Somalia.

Based on the United Nations' arguments, Eritrea has become a threat to international peace and security. The UN sanction against Eritrea

1. places an arms embargo on Eritrea,
2. imposes travel bans of Eritrea's top officials, and
3. freezes the assets of Eritrea's senior political and military officials.

UN sanctions against Eritrea created mixed reaction within the Eritrean population, especially among people in the diaspora. For many opposition groups, the UN-imposed "targeted" sanctions against the leadership in Eritrea were in fact needed and expected. For the supporters of the regime, the UN sanctions against Eritrea are "illegal." Hence, throughout the last weeks of February 2010, there were demonstrations against the sanction in several cities in North America and Europe. Opposition groups protested that the main organ behind these demonstrations has been the government in Eritrea. Human rights activists and opposition groups also argued that the Eritrean government orchestrated these demonstrations.

REFERENCES

Amnesty International (2007). Report: Eritrea: http://archive.amnesty.org/report2007/eng/Regions/Africa/Eritrea/default.htm (accessed on November 3, 2009).

Amnesty International (Dec. 2008). Eritrean Asylum-seekers Face Deportation from Egypt: http://www.amnesty.org/en/news-and-updates/news/eritrean-asylum-seekers-face-deportation-egypt-20081219 (accessed on October 2, 2009).

BBC (Africa) broadcast, Monday, November 23, 2009 1530GMT.

Christian Solidarity Worldwide (2008?). Help Stop Forcible Return of Eritrean Refugees: http://www.csw.org.uk/urgentactioneritrearefugees.htm (accessed on November 4, 2009).

EMDHR—Eritrean Movement for Democracy and Human Rights (2008). *Eritrea: Youth and Militarization* (A discussion paper presented to the European Union Delegation), July 1, 2008, Brussels, Belgium: also posted at: http://meseley.net/index.php?option=com_content&view=article&id=67:youth-militarization-eritrea&catid=4:featured-articles&Itemid=4 accessed on November 8, 2009).

European Commission—External Cooperation Programs (2009): http://ec.europa.eu/development/geographical/methodologies/strategypapers10_en.cfm (accessed on March 3, 2010).

Fortress Europe (September 2007). Libya: 600 Eritrean Refugees fear deportation: http://fortresseurope.blogspot.com/2006/01/libya-600-eritreans-refugees-fear.html (accessed on October 20, 2009).

Gütersloh, Bertelsmann Stiftung (2009). *BTI 2010—Eritrea Country Report*: http://www.bertelsmann-transformation-index.de (accessed on March 7, 2010).

Hadgu, Mussie (2009a). Eritrea: A Country in Overall Crisis; NGOs and Food Aid: http://asmarino.com/en/eyewitness-account/91-i-eritrea-a-country-in-overall-crisis-ngos-and-food-aid- (accessed on March 15, 2009).

Hadgu, Mussie (2009b). Eritrea: A Country in Overall Crisis; Land Expropriation: http://asmarino.com/en/eyewitness-account/91-i-eritrea-a-country-in-overall-crisis-ngos-and-food-aid- (accessed on March 29, 2009).

Hadgu, Mussie (2009c). Eritrea: A Country in Overall Crisis; Copying Strategies in Hard Times: http://asmarino.com/en/eyewitness-account/133-iii-eritrea-a-nation-in-overall-crisis-coping-strategies-in-hard-times- (accessed on April 18, 2009).

Hughes, Howard (2004). *Eine Volksarmee besonderer Art—der Militärkomplex in Eritrea* [*A Particularly People's Forces—the Eritrean Military Complex*]. Appeared in 2004—Translated extracts into German by Berger, Christian: http://www.connection-ev.de/pdfs/eri_militaer.pdf (accessed on August 12, 2009).

Human Rights Watch (2009). *UPR Submission: Eritrea.* April: http://lib.ohchr.org/HRBodies/UPR/Documents/Session6/ER/HRW_ERI_UPR_S06_2009.pdf (accessed on November 5, 2009).

ICRC (2007). Eritrean Refugees in Libya Facing Torture/Forcible Return to their Homeland: http://www.ihrc.org.uk/show.php?id=2835 (accessed on June 19, 2009).

Kibreab, Gaim (2008). *Critical reflections on the Eritrean War of Independence: Social Capital, Associational Life, Religion, Ethnicity and Sowing Seeds of Dictatorship.* Trenton, NJ: Red Sea Press.

Kibreab, Gaim (2009). "Forced Labour in Eritrea." In: *Journal of Modern African Studies,* 17 (1), pp. 41–72.

Kidane, Nanu and Lenoir, Gerald (November 2009). African Immigrants and Refugees in Europe: http://www.asmarino.com/en/news/369—african-immigrants-and-refugees-in-europe-part-1 (part I and II, accessed on November 10, 2009).

Mengisteab, Kidane and Yohannes, Okbazghi (2005). *Anatomy of an African Tragedy: Political, Economic and Foreign Policy Crisis in Post-Independence Eritrea.* Trenton, NJ: The Red Sea Press.

National Statistics and Evaluation Office (NSEO) [Eritrea] and ORC Macro (2003). *Eritrea Demographic and Health Survey 2002.* Calverton, MD: National Statistics and Evaluation Office and ORC Macro.

Rena, Ravinder (2005). "Challenges for Food Security in Eritrea—A Descriptive and Qualitative Analysis." In: *African Development Review,* Vol. 17, No. 2 [Abidjan (Ivory Coast])], pp. 193–212 (also posted at: http://www.afdb.org/fileadmin/uploads/afdb/Documents/Publications/00688249-EN-VOL17-2.PDF (accessed on July 18, 2010).

Reporters Without Borders: Press Freedom Index 2008: http://www.rsf.org/Only-peace-protects-freedoms-in.html (accessed on October 20, 2009).

Tronvoll, Kjetil (2009). *The Lasting Struggle for Freedom in Eritrea: Human Rights and Political Development, 1991–2009.* Oslo, HBO AS, Haugesund.

UNHCR (April 2009). Eligibility Guidelines for Assessing the International Protection needs of Asylum-Seekers from Eritrea: http://www.unhcr.se/Pdf/Positionpaper_2009/Guidelines_Eritrea_April_09.pdf

Aljazeera (2010, Feb. 20): http://english.aljazeera.net/programmes/talktojazeera/2010/02/201021921059338201.html (access on March 8, 2010).

Glossary

'Et'an (ዕጣን) is a Tigrinya term for varieties of incense. Incense is considered a valuable item and is associated with assorted rituals and ceremonies, such as church services. The Eritrean region is believed to have been one of the earliest sites of incense for ancient Egypt.

Afar (ዓፋር) is the language and name of an ethnolinguistic group in Eritrea, Djibouti, and Ethiopia. In Eritrea, the Afar people inhabit the southeastern parts of Eritrea (at the Southern Red Sea Zone), in the region commonly known as Danakil or Dankalia. The Afar territory is characterized by an extremely hot climate. The Afar people are Muslims by religion and a great majority practice nomadic pastoralism as an economic activity. Their social organization is characterized by major clan and subclan divisions.

Agro-pastoralism is an economic activity in which people practice mixed farming and animal herding. Agro-pastorals often have one or more fixed settlements and pasturelands where they send their animal herd for seasonal grazing. A majority of Eritreans practice agro-pastoralism as their main economic activity.

Agudo (ኣጉዶ) is a type of local dwelling that literally means "hut." It is found most often in the lowlands of Eritrea; however, this type of dwelling is also not uncommon in parts of the highlands. It is a dome-shaped, grass-hatched dwelling with stone, wood, or earth walls.

Albaso (ኣልባሶ) is a type of hairdressing of Tigrinya women in which the hair is braided in a few lines. It is usually a style associated with celebratory events such as weddings.

329

Awli'e (ኦውሊ.ዕ), or *Olea Africana*, is a type of common plant in the Eritrean highlands. It is usually a small- or medium-sized multistemmed tree. This tree has remarkable economic and health values for rural communities. It is used for making farming tools and musical instruments. It is also usually used for constructing dwellings such as *hidmo* houses.

Azmera (ኣዝመራ) is a short rainy season in the Eritrean highlands (usually between March and May). During this period, a number of long cycle crops such as sorghum and millet grains are sown. This season is also an important part of the year for most pastoral communities simply because it provides water and fodder for their livestock. Failure of *azmera* rainfall is usually accompanied by major natural resource disorders in rural Eritrea.

Ba'ekel (ባዕከል) is a local term for a less productive type of soil and farming plots. Plots in this classification are usually characterized by soils that have less water-absorption capacity and are low in nutrient contents.

Bahri (ባሕሪ) is a Tigrinya term that translates as "sea," but it also denotes rich pasture and farming areas located at the eastern escarpments of Eritrea. Farming and pastoral communities migrate to and from these areas on a seasonal basis.

Baito (ባይቶ) is a Tigrinya term that literally means "assembly." Especially in rural (highland) Eritrea, *baito* signifies a village assembly that comprises democratically elected members whose tasks vary from responsibilities related to land redistribution to village administration. Depending on the prefix used (such as *hagerawi* "national" and *zobawi* "provincial") *baito* also refers to the state's legislative bodies.

Banda, a term usually synonymously used with "*askaries,*" refers to irregular Eritrean native army units under the service of the Italian colonial government in the country. During its early rule, the colonial government recruited native militias called *banda* under the leadership of local chiefs such *Degiat* Bahta Hagos and Abera Kasa. During Italian colonialism, Eritrea became a major source of colonial soldiers. Italy used tens of thousands of Eritreans during its conflicts in Libya and Ethiopia.

Beles (በለስ), or *Opuntia ficus-indica* or cacti, is a common drought-resistant type of plant in the Eritrean highlands and eastern escarpments. The plant falls under the family of Cactaceae and grows mostly in temperate areas. In Eritrea, while the fruits of these trees are important components of diet for rural communities, the stems of these plants are also used as forage for livestock.

Beni Amer (ብንዓምር) is a mixture of sociolinguistic groups in Eritrea. The Beni Amer is believed to have origins from Tigre, Beja, and other groups. They occupy parts of the Eritrean western lowlands as well as parts of eastern Sudan. The Eritrean Beni Amer speak mainly Tigre language.

Bilen (Blin) (ቢለን) is an ethnolinguistic group in Eritrea. The Bilen are almost equally divided between Christians and Muslims. They occupy areas in the Anseba Valley (particularly the town of Keren and its surroundings) where they practice animal herding and farming as their main economic activities. The Bilen speak the Bilen language and are divided into clans, the Tarqe and Tewqe being the major ones.

Bodu (ቦዱ) is a local term for a highly productive type of soil and farming plots. Plots in this classification are usually characterized by soils that have high water-absorption capacity and rich nutrient contents.

Buda (ቡዳ), a Tigrinya term that translates as "evil eye," refers to people who are believed to have uncommon powers usually demonstrated with their sight. They are believed to have unusual power of transferring evil spirits to others.

Debes (ደስስ) is a Tigrinya term that refers to the material or cash tribute as well as moral consolation given to members of a deceased's household by relatives and other members of the community. *Debes* may be given during or after the funeral ceremony.

Debteras (ደብተራ) (sing. *debtera*) are learned individuals among the clergy of the Orthodox *Tewahdo* Church, whose spiritual practices are believed to have powers in curing diseases such as mental illnesses and other afflictions. *Debteras* are also considered to be highly professional church chanters and sacred musicians. They perform a number of other job functions such as teachers (religious teachings), scribes, and astrologers.

Desa (ደሳ), also known in some areas as *shehena*, is a type of land tenure system in the Eritrean highlands. In the *desa* system of land tenure, village communities collectively posses lands; redistribution of arable lands takes place every six to seven years.

Dirmim (ድርምም) is a type of hairdressing of Tigrinya women in which the hair is braided in many tiny lines. It is usually associated with sorrowful occasions such as mourning events.

Dominale, a semantic form of an Italian term *demaniale* that means "state property," refers to the land that was owned by the colonial government in Eritrea. It comprised land concessions for lease.

Duka (ዱኽ) is a Tigrinya term for the most productive type of soils and farming plots. Plots in this classification are usually characterized by soils that have high water-absorption capacity and rich nutrient contents.

Enda (እንዳ) is a Tigrinya term referring to a family kinship unit of a given Tigrinya group who claim common ancestry. The number of families and individual members of *enda* varies, but this kinship unit serves as an economic and social group to which many single family units are attached; hence, it serves as an umbrella organization for many family units. The *enda* is a social organization system from which descent is traced. Based on this social organization, land is shared or administered among members on the bases of communal systems of tenure; territories are defined among a number of *enda* villages on the basis of this social organization system; and other social rights of each member family are surpassed by the *enda*.

Enjera (እንጀራ) is a pancake-like local bread used as a staple food in large parts of northeast Africa (Eritrea, Ethiopia, and Somalia). In Somalia, it is known as *canjeroo,* in Eritrea and Ethiopia, it is known as *enjera* or *ingera* or *tayta* [Tigrinya]. Some of the main grains for making *enjera* are *taff* (*Eragrostis tef*), sorghum, and maize. But *enjera* can also be made from a variety of other grains. It is consumed with a number of local stews.

Equub (ዕቁብ) is an age-old system of association used for credit saving as well as social and financial networking among the Tigrinya (mostly administered by women) and other ethnolinguistic groups in northeast Africa. Members usually have monthly meetings at which they contribute a specific amount of cash to a common fund. Each member receives back contributed savings in a rotating manner. For centuries, this system has served as a sort of insurance organization.

Fithat (ፍትሓት) is a term that refers to the religious requiem mass for the dead. It is the requiem that often takes place immediately before the burial ceremony and usually comprises prolonged prayers and rituals.

Gamme (ጋመ) is a type of hairdressing of Tigrinya women in which hair is braided in many tiny lines (to the side and back). It is usually a form of coiffeur for unmarried women.

Gezmi (ገዝሚ), a Tigrinya term for "dowry," is a common cultural practice among most ethnolinguistic groups in the country. *Gezmi* refers to the material or cash gifts (among the Tigrinya communities) given by the family of the bride to the family of the groom, or to the newly married couple. There are a variety of types of dowries used throughout the country.

Ghebar (ገባር) refers to any emancipated member of a village community who cultivates and works on his share of plots of community land, and has established his own dwelling in the village. However, the term has often been used to differentiate between the *tegadalay,* "fighter" (during the Eritrean liberation struggle), and the civilian. No matter a civilian's occupation, the Eritrean fighters referred to any person who was not conscripted to the liberation army as *ghebar.*

Guayla (ጓይላ) refers to traditional dancing and singing usually accompanied by musical instruments that take place during wedding ceremonies or other social festivities. During *guayla,* people express their happiness through repeated dancing. Among the Tigrinya, particular individuals (called *abo guayla* "the *guayla* father") are elected by attendants of the ceremony to administer the occasion. *Abo guaylas* are often responsible for maintaining order at the occasion, and they decide who dances when.

Gulhay (ጉልሓይ), a term that is translated as "Rinderpest," is one of the most deadly animal diseases in any part of Eritrea. It is a viral and highly contagious animal plague, primarily of cattle, characterized by severe fever, diarrhea, and ulceration of the alimentary tract. It is caused by *paramyxovirus* (a type of virus belonging to the genus *morbillivirus*). This disease is believed to have been introduced to the region during the early years of Italian expansion in Eritrea (1887–1888).

Gulti chewa (ጉልቲ ጨዋ) is a term that refers to the old tenure system in the Eritrean highlands in which charter plots of land were allotted to noblemen and other community figures.

Gulti seb (ጉልቲ ሰብ) is a term that refers to the old tenure system in the Eritrean highlands in which charter plots of lands were granted to individuals.

Gulti tsadkan (ጉልቲ ጻድቃን) is a term that refers to the old tenure system in the Eritrean highlands in which charter plots of land were allotted to monasteries, churches, or convents.

Hadega ghebar (ሓደጋ ገባር) a Tigrinya term that translates as "*ghebar's* danger" refers to the land (under the *shehena* or *desa* tenure system) formerly occupied by the deceased or migrated individuals and then confiscated by the village community. The land is then redistributed to accommodate newly married couples ready to establish their own *tisha* (dwelling and land rights), and also to the descendants of the village returning after a period of absence to claim rights in their original villages.

Hagay (ሓጋይ) is the dry season (roughly in the central and northern highlands and western lowlands from November to March/April; in the eastern lowlands from April to September).

Hamien (ሓሜን) is a Tigrinya term (often derogatory) that refers to wandering secular singers. These singers are highly skilled professionals. Their linguistic and musical skills are usually highly appreciated by all communities; however, these artists also often occupy the lowest ranks in society.

Hedareb (ሕዳርብ) is an ethnolinguistic group located in the northwestern parts of Eritrea. In Eritrea, the Hedareb language is often the same as the ethnolinguistic group. However, the language of the Hedareb is also known as *To-bedawi* (a major language of the Beja people in Sudan). The Hedareb people are divided into clans (such as the Labat and Halenqwa) and are believed to be direct descendants of the Beja clans. These people are located in the western parts of the Barka lowlands and the northwestern parts of the Sahel Mountains and are predominantly agro-pastorals.

Hidmo (ሀድሞ) is a type of local dwelling mainly for the Tigrinya ethnolinguistic group. It is rectangular in shape, with stone walls, a flat roof made of tree branches and earth, and is normally divided into two areas—*wushate* (a kitchen section) and *medri bet* (an open living room).

Hitse (ሕጸ) is a Tigrinya term that translates as the German term *die Verlobung* (engagement). The traditional *hitse* occasion is characterized by a series of procedures and agreements between the families of the bride-to-be and the groom-to-be.

Hiza'ety (ሕዛእቲ), the term translates as "reserve," but it refers to grasslands, forestlands, or sacred lands allotted for communal use.

Hurum meriet (ሕሩም መሬት) refers to highly restricted village (communal) lands. These lands include areas of cemeteries, around churches, meeting squares, and water sources. Based on the communal laws of Eritrean highland communities, any resource located in *hurum meriet* shall not be exploited without the collective consent of the village community.

Jeberti (ጀበርቲ) is a name for the minority Muslim section of the Tigrinya ethnolinguistic group (in Eritrea and parts of Tigray).

Jebha (ጀብሃ) is a popular name for the Eritrean Liberation Front (ELF).

Jerif (ጀሪፍ) is a Tigrinya term for plots of land that are irrigated from river sources, such as gorges. These plots are considered to be among the most productive types of plots.

Kebesa (ከበሳ) is a Tigrinya popular term for Eritrea's highlands. This geographical zone comprises the provinces that were previously known as Akkele Guzay, Seraye, and Hamassien.

Keremti (ክረምቲ) is the Tigrinya name for the rainy season (roughly in the central and northern highlands and western lowlands—June to September; in the eastern lowlands—December to March).

Kitab (ኪታብ) refers to various types of small amulets that contain holy prayers, images of saints, or items that are believed to have powers against diseases and wild animal attacks. These amulets are usually leather-covered scrolls and are prescribed by traditional healers such as the *debteras*.

Kunama (ኩናማ) is an ethnolinguistic group in Eritrea and Ethiopia. The Kunama people speak a Nilo-Saharan language also called Kunama. They are mostly Christians and Muslims. There are also members of this society who follow their traditional religions. They occupy the Gash-Setit (southwestern, in and around the town of Barentu) part of Eritrea, and the Kunama land is some of the most fertile areas in the country. Most Kunamas are sedentary farmers and pastoralists.

Laka (ላኽ) is a Tigrinya term for dried leaves of the doum palm trees. *Laka* is used for making handicraft works, particularly basketry items.

Ma'ekelay alet (ማእከላይ ዓሌት) is a Tigrinya term that translates as "race in the middle" or "people in the middle" and refers to newcomers—nonindigenous people residing in a village who usually did not have land possession rights.

Mahgoma (ማሕጎማ) a Tigrinya term that refers to a particular type of traditional medical surgery. This practice deals with "bad" bloodletting from an injured or affected area of the body.

Massé (ማሰ) is a type of genre in Tigrinya oral poetry by which oral poets compose praise poems. *Massé* is often performed during special occasions such as wedding ceremonies and other communal festivities.

May chelot (ማይ ጨሎት) a Tigrinya term that literally means "holy water" is either ordinary water blessed by a clergy or water that is located in sites that are recognized by communities as sacred and holy places. *May chelot* is believed to have healing powers, especially in treating mental illnesses.

Meda (ሜዳ), a term that is translated as "field," is also used to refer to areas of operation for the Eritrean liberation fighters during the war of independence. Liberation fighters collectively called all of their strongholds, as well as other areas of operation, *meda*.

Medri worki (መሬት ወርቒ), a term that is translated as "land of gold," refers to rights of selling and purchasing of land on conditional bases or on communally acknowledged legal agreements.

Mehresti (መሕረስቲ), a term that literally translates as "tiller-makers," also often refers to midwives with traditional knowledge and practices of midwifery. Usually, *mehresti* do not have a formal education, but through experience, they have earned the trust of the people in their respective communities. They provide primary medical assistance to pregnant women and are the main actors during delivery.

Melqes (መልቀስ) is a type of genre in Tigrinya oral poetry by which oral poets compose poems during burial ceremonies. *Melqes* often deals with oral poems composed in memory (or in praise) of the deceased and usually serves as an artistic way of telling important biographical parts of the deceased person's life.

Memasahty (መማሳሕቲ) refers to particular village elders who are democratically elected by a village community in the Eritrean highlands. Their main task is to attain fair distribution of land among members of a village community.

Mereba'e (መረባዕ) is a type of local dwelling that is increasingly becoming a popular type of house, especially in rural Eritrea. It is rectangular in shape and built with corrugated iron-sheets, wood, cement, and stones.

Mes (ሜስ) is a type of local beer/mead made of water and honey.

Met'qi'e (መፕቀዕ) is the name for specific types of stone bells that are used as instruments for sacred music.

Metahet (መታሕት) is a popular term for Eritrea's lowlands. This geographical zone comprises the eastern and western lowlands of the country. Areas with less altitude than 1,500 meters above sea level fall in this category (lowlands).

Metkosa (መትኮሳ) a Tigrinya term that refers to a particular type of traditional medical surgery. This practice deals with burning of skin at an injured or affected area of the body.

Metseltsal (ምጸልጸል), a term that translates as "getting rid of," was also a policy implemented by the Eritrean government in the 1990s. Under this policy, the government forced thousands of Eritrean workers to give up their jobs. The government alleged that those workers were unskilled.

Naibs (ናይብ) was a name given to some Beja aristocrats who served as Turkish local deputies or governors of Massawa and Hergigo (sixteenth–nineteenth centuries). They served in the role of viceroy for the Ottoman caliphate.

Nara (ናራ) is an ethnolinguistic group in Eritrea. The Nara people are Muslims who speak a Nilo-Saharan language, also called Nara; they are divided into clans. They occupy parts of the Gash-Barka area where they practice farming and animal herding as major economic activities.

Pastoralism is an economic activity in which people practice animal herding as their main source of livelihood or income. In the case of Eritrea, most rural communities in the lowlands practice pastoralism as their main economic activity. Pastoralists move their animal herd to seasonal pasture areas. Some of the popular animals that are tended by these pastorals are goats, sheep, camels, and cattle.

Qal-kidan (ቃል-ኪዳን) is a Tigrinya term that translates as "convention" and refers to the matrimonial agreement between a man and woman. *Qal-kidan* takes place on the wedding day and serves as a formal contract, on the basis of which the married couple maintain their respective and family rights within the village community.

Qew'i (ቀውዒ) is a name for the harvesting season or the "fall" (in the highlands: between October and December).

Qeyyahti embaba (ቀያሕቲ ዕምባባ) is a name that translates as "red flowers." This was a name given to one of the cultural troupes of the Eritrean People's Liberation Front (EPLF). Most members of this troupe were young boys and girls.

Qolla (ቆላ) is a Tigrinya name for geographical areas with tropically hot climates (average temperature ranges between 26 and 27°C = 78.8°F to 80.6°F). The average elevation of *qolla* areas is about 1,000 meters above sea level.

Quanta (ቋንጣ) is a Tigrinya term for sundried meat. However, *quanta* also refers to a type of stew made of dried meat.

Qwanqwa asmarino (ቋንቋ ኣዝማሪኖ) is the urban slang language used by young people, typically living in Asmara.

Rashaida (ራሻይዳ) is an ethnolinguistic group in Eritrea and some other coastal areas of northeast Africa. The Rashaida, who speak Arabic as their mother tongue, migrated to Eritrea in the nineteenth century from the Arabian Peninsula. They are mostly pastorals and transborder traders.

Restegnatat (ርስተኛታት) is a Tigrinya term that refers to all members of an *enda* who are acknowledged by village communities as inheritors of land—people who belong to families in the same kinship system (especially in the *resti-tsilmi* tenure system).

Resti (ርስቲ) is a Tigrinya term that translates as "possession; personal property." However, the same term is often associated with land possession rights. *Resti* refers to land and other property that is handed over to the next person by inheritance. Land allotted to individuals or individual family units was often owned by the kinship group called *enda*.

Resti gulti (ርስቲ-ጉልቲ) was a type of land tenure in the Eritrean/Ethiopian highlands in which land was allotted to individuals, notables, churches, and so on; and owners enjoyed absolute ownership rights.

Resti tsilmi (ርስቲ-ጽልሚ) refers to a type of land tenure system in the Eritrean highlands in which land was allotted to individual and family unit members of an *enda* kinship group. Land possession was passed down to *restegnatat* through patrilineal lineage lines. Selling of land under this tenure system was highly restricted.

Saho (ሳሆ) is the language and name of an ethnolinguistic group in Eritrea. Saho people occupy the southeastern escarpments and the eastern slopes of southern highlands. The Saho are predominantly Muslims by religion and they practice nomadic pastoralism as an economic activity. Their social organization is characterized by clan and subclan divisions.

Sedentary farming is a system in which farming communities have fixed settlements all year round. In this system, no transhumant farming is practiced.

Sefeyti (ሰፈይቲ) is a Tigrinya term that translates as "tailors," but it also refers to traditional healers who, through experience, specialize in surgery related to bone setting.

Sehdi (ጽሕዲ), or African Juniper (*Juniperous procera*), is a medium-sized, fragrant, and multistemmed tree that is native to the east African mountains. It is also widely distributed in the Eritrean highlands. It is used for making tools; it is also usually used for constructing dwellings such as *hidmo* and *mereba'e* houses.

Shehena (ሽሕና) is a Tigrinya term that translates as "brother's land"; it is a communal or *desa* type of land tenure in the southern highlands of Eritrea.

Shifta (ሽፍታ) is a Tigrinya term that translates as "outlaw; bandit; robber; plunderer" and refers to a widespread practice in Eritrea during the 1940s and 1950s. Most *shifta* activities during that time had political and economic motives.

Suwa (ስዋ) is a type of local beer made of grains, herbs, and water; it is a common beer for the Tigrinya people in Eritrea and Tigray/Ethiopia. Known as *tella, suwa* is also a common local beer among the Amhara of Ethiopia.

Taff (ጣፍ), or *Eragrostis tef*, is a type of grain that grows mostly in northeast Africa (particularly Ethiopia and Eritrea). It is widely cultivated and used as a staple food grain.

Teskar (ተስካር) refers to a memorial feast for the dead. *Teskar* may take place between two weeks and one or more years after death.

Tigre (ትግረ) is the second-largest ethnolinguistic group in Eritrea. Tigre people, who speak the Tigre language, occupy large territories in the western and eastern lowlands as well as the northern highlands of Eritrea. A majority of the Tigre people are Muslims, but there are minority Christians. The social organization of most Tigre communities is based on clans and subclans.

Tigrinya (ትግርኛ) is the largest ethnolinguistic group in Eritrea. The Tigrinya people, who speak the Tigrinya language, occupy most parts of the Eritrean highlands and parts of northern Ethiopia (particularly Tigray). Most Tigrinya people are followers of the Christian Orthodox *Tewahdo* (also known as Coptic Christianity). There are also minority followers of Catholicism, Islam (see Jeberti), and Protestanism among the Tigrinya people.

Tisha (ጥሻ) refers to the land and settlement rights allotted to emancipated members of a village community. Land rights were usually granted to emancipated members of a given community, often to people who established their habitation (*tisha*).

Transhumance is a seasonal migration of farming, pastoral, or agro-pastoral communities to and from pasture and farming lands. Transhumant communities may or may not have fixed settlement areas.

Tsebel (ጸበል) refers to holy water or food often blessed by priests. *Tsebel* is believed to have powers attributed to preventing and healing diseases.

Tsebhi (ጽብሒ) is the collective name for varieties of local stews.

Tsediya (ጸድያ) is the name of the "spring" season; the months prior to *keremti* (rainy season).

Tsenatsil (ጸናጸል) is the name of sistrum-like rattles that are used as musical instruments for sacred music.

Tsimdi (ጽምዲ) is a term that translates as "pair"; it also refers to an area that a farmer can plow in a single day using a pair of oxen (approximately 0.25 ha.). The term is often considered as a local measurement for plots of farming land.

Walaka (ዋላኽ) is a Tigrinya term for a clay type of soils that are characterized by a high capacity of water storage and fertile and loamy features. *Walaka* soil is also often used for tool making—such as varieties of local pots and stoves.

Warsay (ዋርሳይ) is a Tigrinya term that translates as "inheritor," but it is often popularly used as a collective name for members of the Eritrean national military service. It refers to all members of the army who were recruited after Eritrea's independence.

Wat'ot (ዋጦት) is a Tigrinya term (often derogatory) that refers to wandering secular musicians. These musicians are often highly skilled professionals. Their musical skills are highly appreciated by all communities; however, these artists also often occupy the lowest ranks in society.

Wehalle (ወሃለ) is a Tigrinya term that translates as "skilled; professional"; it also refers to women with professional skills for cooking and household management.

Wofera (ወፈራ) refers to communal work on land such as the construction of houses and other activities in which individual or collective members of a village volunteer to perform certain task(s).

Wotsel (ወጸል) is a local name for farming plots that are characterized by highly degraded soils.

Zurya (ዙርያ) is a term that translates as "round; circle"; it also refers to a type of traditional dress for Tigrinya women. *Zurya* is white gown-like cloth made of cotton and is often decorated with designs on some of its parts.

Facts and Figures

COUNTRY INFORMATION

TABLE A.1   Basic Facts and Figures

Location	Northern part of the "Horn of Africa," bounded by the Red Sea to the east, Sudan to the north and west, Djibouti to the south, and Ethiopia to the southwest.
Local Name	Hagere Ertra (Tigrinya)
Government	Transitional, single-party
Capital	Asmara
Head of State	Isaias Afeweki
Head of Government	Isaias Afeweki
National Holiday	Independence Day, May 24 (1993)
Major Political Parties	Peoples Front for Democracy and Justice (PFDJ)

Source: CLA Factbook

DEMOGRAPHICS

TABLE A.2. Basic Facts and Figures

Population	5,647,168 (2009 est.)
Population by age	
0–14	42.8%
15–64	53.7%
65+	3.6%
Median age	18.4
Population growth rate	2.577 (2009 est.)
Population density	125 people per sq. mile
Infant mortality rate	43.33 deaths per 1,000 live births
Ethnolinguistic groups	Tigrinya, Tigre, Kunama, Afar, Saho, Bilen, Nara, Hedareb, Rashaida
Religions	Muslim, Coptic Christian, Roman Catholic, Protestant
Language	Afar, Arabic, Bilen, Hedareb, Kunama, Nara, Saho, Tigre and Tigrinya working languages: Arabic and Tigrinya
Voting age	18 years
Voter participation	n/a
Literacy	59%
Life expectancy (average)	61.78
Fertility rate	4.72 children per woman (2009 est.)

GEOGRAPHY

TABLE A.3. Basic Facts and Figures

Land area	45,174 sq. miles
Arable land	5%
Irrigated land	81 sq. miles (2003)
Natural hazards	Frequent droughts, locust swarms
Environmental problems	Deforestation, desertification, soil erosion, overgrazing
Major agricultural products	Sorghum, lentils, corn, cotton, tobacco, livestock, goats, fish
Natural resources	Gold, potash, zinc, copper, salt, possibly oil and natural gas, fish

ECONOMY

TABLE A.4. Basic Facts and Figures

GDP	$1.65 billion (2008)
GDP per capita	$292 (2008)
GDP by sector	Agriculture—17.3%; industry—23.2%; services—59.5% (2009 est.)
Labor force	Agriculture—80%; industry/service—20% (2004 est.)
Unemployment	n/a
People below poverty line	50% (2004 est.)
Major industries	Food processing, beverages, clothing and textiles, light manufacturing, salt, cement
Exports	$12 million (2009 est.)
Imports	$590 million, (2009 est.)
Export goods	Livestock, sorghum, textiles, food, small manufactured goods
Import goods	Petroleum products, machinery, food, manufactured goods

COMMUNICATIONS AND TRANSPORTATION

TABLE A.5. Basic Facts and Figures

Electricity production	271 million kWh (2007 est.)
Electricity consumption	228 million kWh (2007 est.)
Telephone lines	40,400 (2008)
Mobile phones	108,600 (2008)
Internet users	200,000 (2008)
Roads	2,485 miles (2000)
Railroads	190 miles (2008)
Airports	4 (2009)

MILITARY

TABLE A.6. Basic Facts and Figures

Defense spending (% of GDP)	6.3% (2006 est.)
Armed forces	201,750 active; 120,000 reserve (2007)
Manpower fit for military service	834,018 males; 887,495 females (2009 est.)

TABLE B. Eritrea: Other Key Facts

Infant mortality rate	45.24 deaths/1,000 live births (2007 estimates)
Life expectancy	59.55 years (2007 estimate)
Literacy rate	58.6% (2003 estimate)
Net primary school enrollment/attendance (2000–2005)	67%
People living with HIV/AIDS	60,000 (2003 estimates)
Human poverty index (HP-1) rank	70

Source: Adapted from Epstein, Irvin (2008). *The Greenwood Encyclopedia of Children's Issues Worldwide.* Westport: Greenwood Press, p. 183.

TABLE C. Some of the Larger Islands of Eritrea

Island	**Area (in km^2)**
Dahlak Kebir	642.95
Norah	103.39
Halba	78.30
Goba Baka	48.15
Howakil	41.40
Erwa	33.91
Naheleg	31.38
Harmil	21.60
Harat	20.24
Isratu	17.99
Adjuz	13.95
Serabay	13.50
Aucan	13.28
Dehel	11.70
Dar Dase	11.03
Total	**1102.77**

Source: Compiled from Ministry of Education (1995). *Geography for Grade 11.* Curriculum Development Division, Asmara, p. 16.

TABLE D. Distribution and Altitude of Major Mountains in Eritrea

Name of Mountain	Altitude in Meters	Geographical Location
Aderba	1,483	Western lowlands
Amba Debresina	2,615	Northern highlands
Amba Hamid	1,143	Western lowlands
Amba Metera	2,224	Central plateau
Amba Saim	2,737	Central plateau
Amba Soira	3,013	Central plateau
Amba Tarika	2,775	Central plateau
Amba Tekera	2,579	Central plateau
Amba Tekilo	1,973	Central plateau
Arato	2,549	Central plateau
Armaso	2,409	Central plateau
Aykuno	1,484	Western lowlands
Biru	1,280	Danakil depression
Debra Mark	2,034	Northern highlands
Debra Sala	2,035	Northern highlands
Debre Musa	2,284	Northern highlands
Dubbi	1,250	Danakil depression
Engershatu	2,575	Northern highlands
Fengaga	2,549	Northern highlands
Hager Nues	2,770	Northern highlands
Keru	1,317	Western lowlands
Meteten	2,724	Central plateau
Ona	2,241	Northern highlands
Romelo	2,130	Danakil depression
Saber	2,596	Northern highlands
Tala	2,310	Central plateau

Source: Compiled from Ministry of Education (1995). *Geography for Grade 11.* Curriculum Development Division, Asmara, pp. 41–52.

TABLE E. Distribution of Land Use and Land Cover Types

Land use	Area in Hectares	Share of the Total Land
Cultivated land	1,084,821	8.9%
Grazing and browsing land	5,984,799	49.1%
Forest land	53,000	0.44%
Unproductive land	243,780	2.0%
Wood land and shrubs	670,395	5.5%
Uncultivable land	4,030,902	33.07%

Source: Adapted from Srikanth, R. (2003). "Challenges of Environmental Management in Eritrea: A Case Study." In: *African Journal of Environmental Assessment and Management-RAGEE*, 6, p. 63.

TABLE F. Eritrea: Geographical Information

Time zone	Standard time is GMT/UTC +3 – 8 hours ahead of U.S. Eastern Standard Time
Local time	No change of hours throughout the year
Geographical location	Roughly between 12° and 18° north, and 36° and 44° east *or* at longitude 39° 00´ east of Greenwich and latitude 15° 00´ north of the Equator

TABLE G. Administrative Divisions of Eritrea as of December 2008

Administrative Zones	Major Sub-Zones	Major Cities and Towns	Zone Administrator
Southern Zone (*zoba debub*)	Mendefera, Addi Keyyih, Adi Kwala, Areza, Debarewa, Dekemhare, Senafe, Segeneiti, Tserona, May Mene, and Kudo Abu'ur	Addi Keyyih, Mendefera (capital), Segeneiti, Dekemhare, May Edaga, May Mine, Adi Kwala, Debarewa, and Senafe	Mustofa Nurhussien
Gash Barka Zone (*zoba Gash-Barka*)	Agordat, Mensura, Molki, Mogolo, Gulij and Omhajer, Shambuko, Barentu, Tesseney, Gash *la'elay*, Deghe, Gogne, Hykota, and Logo 'Anseba	Agordat, Barentu (capital), Tesseney, Hykota, Gogne, Omhajer, and Gulij	Kahssai Gebrehiwot (*Kisha*)
Anseba Zone (*zoba 'Anseba*)	Geleb, Asmat', Elabered, Hagaz, Habero, Kerkebet, Keren, Sela, Halhal, and Adi Tekelezan	Keren (capital), Adi Tekelezan, Serejeka, Hagaz, and Glass	Selma Hassan

TABLE G. Administrative Divisions of Eritrea as of December 2008 (*Continued*)

Administrative Zones	Major Sub-Zones	Major Cities and Towns	Zone Administrator
Central Zone (*zoba Ma'ekel*)	Composed of former Hamassien Province— major sub-zones include Gala Nefhi, Serejeka, and Berik	Asmara (capital; also Serejeka, Hembirti, Nefasit, Beleza, Emba Derho, Tse'azzega, and Adi Teklay	Semere Russom
Southern Red Sea Zone (*zoba Debubawi Keyyih Bahri*)	Are'eta, Central Dankalia, Assab, and Southern Dankalia	Assab, Tio, Beylul, and Iddi Irafayle	Sigereda Woldegiorgis
Northern Red Sea Zone (*zoba Semienawi Keyyih Bahri*)	Massawa, Irafayle, Gela'elo, Shi'eb Shebbah, Dahlak Archipelagoes, Ginda'e, Foro, Hergigo (Dekono), Nakfa, Afabet, and Karura	Nakfa, Karura, Marsa Teklay, Shieb, Massawa, Ghinda'e, Dongolo, and Hergigo (Dekono)	Abdella Mussa

Sources: Compiled from Doornbos, Martin and Tesfa, Alemseged (eds.) (1999). *Eritrea: Prospects for Reconstruction and Development.* Lawrenceville, NJ: Red Sea Press, pp. 239–324.

TABLE H. Eritrean Ministries (2008)

Ministry	Current Minister
Ministry of Agriculture	Mr. Arefaine Berhe
Ministry of Defense	General Sebhat Efrem
Ministry of Education	Mr. Osman Saleh Mohammed (*acting*)
Ministry of Energy and Mines	Mr. Tesfai Gebreselassie
Ministry of Finance and Development	Mr. Berhane Abrehe
Ministry of Fisheries and Marine Resources	Mr. Ahmed Haj Ali
Ministry of Foreign Affairs	Mr. Osman Saleh Mohammed
Ministry of Health	Mr. Salih Meki
Ministry of Information	Mr. Ali Abdu
Ministry of Justice	Ms. Fozia Hashim
Ministry of Labor and Human Welfare	Ms. Askalu Menkerios
Ministry of Land, Water and Environment	Mr. Woldemichael Gebremariam
Ministry of National Development	Dr. Woldai Futur
Ministry of Public Works	Mr. Abraha Asfaha
Ministry of Tourism	Ms. Amna Nurhusien
Ministry of Trade and Industry	Dr. Giorgis Teklemichael
Ministry of Transport and Communications	Mr. Woldemichal Abraha

Source: Ministry of Information (Eritrea), http://www.shabait.com (accessed March 2010).

TABLE I. Members of the G15

Name	Position in the Eritrean Government (1991–2001)	Membership of Political Organization	Detained Since	Place of Detention
Adhanom Gebremariam	Governor of *zoba* Debub Southern Zone— (especially Seraye); Eritrean Ambassador to Scandinavian Countries; and Eritrean Ambassador to Nigeria	Member of the EPLF	Not detained	In Europe since 2001 (founder of the Eritrean Democratic Movement [EDM])
Aster Fesehatzion	Member of PFDJ-CC; General Director of Social Affairs in the Ministry of Labor and Social Welfare	Member of the EPLF since 1974; EPLF Political Commissioner	2001	Unknown
Aster Yohannes (non-member, but associated to G-15)	Head of one of the local companies under the Commercial wings of the Ministry of Fisheries	EPLF— She joined the organization in 1979 and worked in different departments of the organization	2003	Unknown
Beraki Gebreselassie	Minister of Information; and Eritrean Ambassador to Germany	Member of the EPLF since 1971; member of EPLF-CC; founder of the EPLF Revolutionary School	2001	Unknown
Birhane Gebregziabher (Major General)	Member of the PFDJ-CC; Commander in the Eritrean Defence Forces (EDF)	Active member and Commander of the EPLF army since 1972 and member of the EPLF-PB	2001	Unknown
Germano Nati	Member of the PFDJ-CC; and Administrator of *zoba* Gash-Setit	Politician and active member of the EPLF since 1976	2001	Unknown
Haile Woldetinsae (Duru'e)	Minister of Finance; and Minister of Foreign Affairs (1997–2001)	Member of the ELF (1966); member of the EPLF Political-Bureau (PB), EPLF-CC, and Head of Cadre School (EPLF)	2001	unknown
Hamid Himed	Member of PFDJ-CC; Department Head at the Ministry of Foreign Affairs; Ambassador to Saudi Arabia; and Zone Administrator	Active member of the EPLF in the Middle East	2001	Unknown

Name	Position	Membership	Year detained	Status
Istifanos Siyum (Brigadier General)	Member of PFDJ-CC; Secretary of Finance; and Head of EDF Department of Finance	Active member of the EPLF since 1975	2001	Unknown
Mahmud Ahmed Sherifo	Member of PFDJ-CC; Minister of Foreign Affairs; and Minister of Local Government	Member of the ELF 1966–1970; and active member of the EPLF since 1970; member of EPLF-PB	2001	Unknown
Mesfin Hagos	Minister of Defense and Administrator of *zoba* Debub (Southern Zone)	Founding member of the EPLF and EPLF; Chief of Staff	Not detained	In Germany since 2001
Miriam Hagos	Head of Eritrean Cinemas	EPLF/PFDJ. Returned from USA to join the EPLF in 1977. She worked in different departments of the EPLF, mainly the Department of Information	2001	Unknown
Mohammed Berhan Bilata	Member of PFDJ-CC; Mayor of Mendefera (1991–1993); Mayor of Adi Keyyih (1993–1996); and administrator of Dekemhare subzone.	Active member of the ELF (1964–1991); and member of the EPLF	Not detained	In Sweden since 2001
Ogbe Abraha (General)	Member of the PFDJ-CC; Minister of Trade and Industry; Minister of Labor and Social Welfare; and Chief of Staff of the EDF	Member of the EPLF since 1972; Military Commander and member of the EPLF-PB	2001	Unknown
Petros Solomon	Minister of Defense; Minister of Foreign Affairs; and Minister of Marine Resources	Member of the EPLF since 1972; and member of the EPLF-PB	2001	Unknown
Saleh Kekiya	Member of the PFDJ-CC; Office of President's Director; Eritrean Ambassador to Sudan; Mayor of Assab City; and Minister of Transport and Communication	Member of the EPLF since 1976; and member of the EPLF-CC	2001	Unknown
Senait Debessai (non-member, but associated to G-15)	Member of the Executive Committee of the National Union of Eritrean Women	Active member of the EPLF/PFDJ. She joined the EPLF in 1976 and worked in various departments of the EPLF—Department of Healthcare and Member of the EPLF Cultural Troupe	2003	Unknown

Source: Compiled from Connell, Dan (2005). *Conversation with Eritrean Political Prisoners.* Trenton, NJ: Red Sea Press.

TABLE J. The Proliferation of Eritrean Opposition Organizations (since 1998)

Name of Opposition Organization	Year Established
Alliance of Eritrean National Forces	1999
Committee for Eritrean Unity	2004
Eritrean Afar Federal Alliance	2004
Eritrean Alliance Initiative Movement	2001
Eritrean Congress Party	2005
Eritrean Democratic Alliance	2005
Eritrean Democratic Assembly	2005
Eritrean Democratic Congress	2004
Eritrean Democratic League	2005
Eritrean Democratic Party	2004
Eritrean Federal Democratic Movement	2002
Eritrean Independent Democratic Movement	2000
Eritrean Independent Democratic Party	2003
Eritrean Islamic Front (Sword of Truth)	2002
Eritrean Islamic Movement	2004
Eritrean Islamic Reform Movement	2003
Eritrean Islamic Salvation Movement	1998
Eritrean Liberation Front—National Congress	2003
Eritrean Liberation Front—United National Organization	2001
Eritrean Liberation Front—Central Council (merger of several ELF groups)	2002
Eritrean National Alliance	2002
Eritrean National Democratic Front	2001
Eritrean People's Congress	1998
Eritrean People's Democratic Front	2004
Eritrean People's Liberation Front—Democratic Party	2002
Eritrean People's Movement	2004
Eritrean People's Party	2005
Eritrean People's Revolutionary Front	2003
Eritrean Salvation Congress	2004
Eritrean Social Democratic Party	2001
Freedom Now Action Movement	2005
Movement for Democratic Change for Eritrea	2002
Movement of Nationals for Democratic Government	2005
Red Sea Afar Democratic Organisation	1999
Renaissance Party	2005

Sources: Compiled from Iyob, Ruth (2004). "Shifting Terrain: Dissidence versus Terrorism in Eritrea." In: *Terrorism in the Horn of Africa: United States Institute of Peace* Special Report No. 113.; Markakis, John (1998). "The Nationalist Revolution in Eritrea." *The Journal of Modern African Studies*, Volume 26, (I), pp. 51–70; Alliance of Democratic forces, http://www.fas.org/irp/world/para/aenf.htm (accessed in March, 2010), RSADO, http://www.arhotabba.com/rsado.html (accessed in March, 2010); EDP, http://www.selfidemocracy.net/ (accessed in March, 2010).

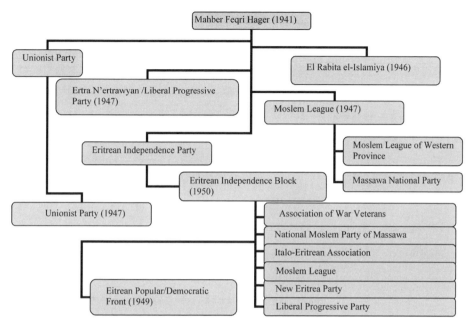

Figure 1: Propagation of Eritrean political parties in the 1940s

Sources: Compiled from Negash, Tekeste (1997). *Eritrea and Ethiopia: The Federal Experience*. Uppsala: Nordiska Afrikainstitutet, pp. 37–68; from Killion, Tom (1998). *Historical Dictionary of Eritrea*. London: The Scarecrow Press, and partly adapted from Bereketeab, Redie (2000). *Eritrea: The Making of a Nation, 1890–1991*. Uppsala: Uppsala University Press, pp. 144–160.

TABLE **K.** Eritrea's Membership to Regional and International Organizations

Organizations

United Nations (UN); African Union (AU); and The Common Market for Eastern and Southern Africa (COMESA)

TABLE L. Land Use Classification (Area in Hectares) (1998)

S. No.	Use	Area in Hectares	Percent Share of the Total Area
1	Suitable for cultivation	3.1 million	25
2	Area under cultivation	522,161	4.21
3	Area under cereals	477,043	3.85
4	Area under pulses	6,942	0.056
5	Area under food grains	483,985	3.90
6	Area under oil seeds	16,177	0.13
7	Area under fruits and vegetables	22,000	0.18
8	Irrigated area	22,000	0.18

Source: Adapted from Haile, Solomon (2002). "Dryland Farming Systems and Coping Strategies in Eritrea." In: Dryland Coordination Group (ed.). *Sustainable Livelihoods of Farmers and Pastoralists in Eritrea: Proceedings from a Workshop Organized by DGG Eritrea* (Asmara, November 28–29, 2002), p. 61.

TABLE M. Crop Production in Eritrea, 1997–2004 (tons)

	1997	1998	1999	2000	2001	2002	2003	2004
CEREALS								
Sorghum	55,316	269,772	207,197	52,370	78,759	28,434	64,061	44,646
Maize	6,406	28,986	15,899	4,054	9,051	3,008	4,456	3,164
Wheat	5,131	22,945	19,010	10,579	25,423	2,637	3,442	5,053
Barley	16,085	56,605	31,835	25,786	44,934	9,736	8,576	11,134
Pearl millet	4,332	44,183	17,829	1,515	18,174	4,931	11,748	7,118
Finger millet	3,156	7,622	5,402	2,716	12,093	865	5,187	4,436
Taff	4,150	18,706	13,147	10,415	19,551	3,191	7,161	7,574
Hanfez	4,504	8,992	8,508	3,197	11,067	1,728	1,313	1,859
Total	**99,080**	**457,811**	**318,827**	**110,632**	**219 052**	**54,530**	**105 944**	**84,984**
OTHER FOOD CROPS								
Peas	175	398	581	1,670	1,130	2,797	60	91
Chick peas	492	1,783	2,793	2,972	8,284	225	1,600	3,459
Horse beans	176	659	3,301	1,420	4,022	445	600	603
Green peas	364	399	718	722	2,730	3,484	N/A	N/A
Haricot bean	0	36	36	0	36	0	0	31
Lentils	1	0	272	116	211	110	100	86
Total	**1,208**	**3,275**	**7,701**	**6,900**	**16,413**	**7,061**	**2,360**	**4,270**

Source: Adapted from FAO/WFP (2005). *Crop and Food Supply Assessment Mission to Eritrea: Special Report* (January 2005). Also posted at http://www.fao.org/docrep/007/j3959e/j3959e00.htm#3 (accessed on 20 November 2009).

TABLE N. Estimated Livestock Population in Eritrea (2003)

Region	Cattle	Sheep	Goats	Camels
Anseba	218,923	124,300	620,023	25,266
Debub	490,093	614,069	706,409	19,382
Gash Barka	917,344	675,268	1,745,784	113,263
Maekel	40,505	149,927	23,556	0
Northern Red Sea	178,532	462,333	994,596	107,032
Southern Red Sea	82,060	103,047	571,417	53,971
Total	**1,927,457**	**2,128,944**	**4,661,785**	**318,914**

Source: Adapted from FAO/WFP (2003). *Crop and Food Supply Assessment Mission to Eritrea: Special Report* (November 2003). Also posted at http://www.fao.org/DOCREP/006/J0981E/J0981E00.HTM#3 (accessed on 20 November 2009).

TABLE O. Estimated Value of Imports, 2000–2004

Year	Imports (million US$ c.i.f)		
	Food	Total	% food
2000	117.3	421.6	28%
2001	76.4	393.0	19%
2002	94.5	400.2	24%
2003	116.4	456.3	26%
2004	123.4	425.5	29%

Source: Adapted from FAO/WFP (2005). *Crop and Food Supply Assessment Mission to Eritrea: Special Report* (January 2005). Also posted at http://www.fao.org/docrep/007/j3959e/j3959e00.htm#3 (accessed on 20 November 2009).

TABLE P. Eritrea's Economic Indicators (2002–2006)

	2002	**2003**	**2004**	**2005**	**2006**
Population (mn.)	4.304	4.412	4.522	4.635	4.747
Population growth (%)	2.5	2.5	2.5	2.5	2.4
GDP (US$bn. at current prices)	0.635	0.584	0.635	0.970	1.018
GDP per capita (US$ at current prices)	147.5	132.4	140.4	209.2	241.5
GDP growth at constant prices (%)	0.7	3.0	3.5	4.8	2.0
Current account balance (US$mn.)	28	23	30	36	(7)
Inflation rate (%)	16.9	22.7	25.1	12.4	16.5
Exchange rate: annual average Nakfa per US$*	13.958	13.878	13.788	14.500	15.400

*The official exchange rate is 15 Nakfa per US$.

Source: table adapted from the World Bank Group (http://devdata.worldbank.org/AAG/eri_aag.pdf, accessed on May 5, 2009)

TABLE Q. Approximate Land Use in Eritrea as of 2004

Type of Land Use	Area per 1,000 ha	Percentile of the Country's Total Landmass
Cropland	439	3.5
Rainfed	417	
Irrigated	22	
Plantations	10	
Grazing land	7,000	56.4
Vegetation	737	5.9
Highland forestland	53	
Bush and woodland	674	
Urban land	13	0.1
Unused or barren land	4,243	34.1
Overall total	12,432	100

Source: Compiled and adapted from the Ministry of Agriculture, Eritrea (2004). *National Report.* Asmara, pp. 53–54.

TABLE R. Railroad Construction in Eritrea

Year	Line	Distance in Kilometers
1887–1888	Massawa—Saati	27
1904	Massawa—Ghindae	75
1910	Ghindae—Nefasit	26
1911	Nefasit—Arborebue	10
1911	Arborebue—Asmara	13
1922	Asmara—Keren	100
1928	Keren—Agordat	86
1929	Agordat—Tessenei	103

Source: Adapted from Tesfagiorgis G., Mussie (2007). *A Fading Nature: Aspects of Environmental History of Eritrea.* Felsberg: Edition Eins, p. 156; and compiled from Killion, Tom (1998). *Historical Dictionary of Eritrea.* London: The Scarecrow Press, 352–353.

TABLE S. Census and Estimation Figures of Eritrean Population Growth, 1942–2005

Year	Population
1942	807, 393
1943	835,017
1944	858,489
1950	1,103,607
1960	1,420,000
1970	1,831,000
1980	2,382,000
1990	2,881,000
2000	3,809,000
2005	4,286,000

Source: The figures for 1942 are derived from WO/32/10235 B.M.A. *Half-yearly Report,* June 1942, p. 77, for 1943 are derived from WO/32/10235, B.M.A. *Annual Report,* December 1943, p. 31, for 1944 are derived from WO/32/10235, BMA *Annual Report,* Jan.–Dec. 1944, p. 68, for 1950 are derived from FO/371/90314, BMA, *Eritrea Annual Report for 1950,* Dec. 1950, p. 59; and figures after 1950 are derived from the estimations made by the UN, "World Population Prospects: The 1996 Revision," United Nations, 1997; and Population Division of the Department of Economic and Social Affairs of the United Nations Secretariat, World Urbanization Prospects: The 2003 Revision. Part One: Urban and Rural Areas, also posted at http://www.uneca.org (accessed on 26.02.2009).

TABLE T. Some Monasteries in Eritrea

Name of Monastery	Location, Administrative Zone
Debre Bizen	Bizen, Zoba Ma'ekel
Debre Sina	
Debre Libanos/Debre Hawaryat	Hamm (Tserona), Zoba Debub
Abune Libanos	Derechen, Zoba Debub
Enda Maryam	Ayla, Zoba Debub
Abune Buruk	Meraguz, Zoba Debub
Debre Tsige	Tekela, Zoba Debub
Enda Selassie	Damba, Zoba Ma'ekel
Abune Endrias	Sef'a, Zoba Debub
Abune Yonas/Debre-Dehan	Kohayin, Zoba Debub
Debre Menkeryos	Zoba Debub
Debre Maryam	Kohayin, Zoba Debub
Kinfe-Michael	Tsaeda Emba, Zoba Anseba
Abune Esiet	Zadekolom, Zoba Debub
Abune Yohannes	Tedrer, Zoba Debub
Maryam Kuskwam	Tselima, Zoba Debub

Sources: Compiled from Killion, Tom (1998). *Historical Dictionary of Eritrea.* London: The Scarecrow Press, pp. 149–152; Pankhurst, Richard (1997). *The Ethiopian Borderlands: Essays in Regional History from Ancient Times to the End of the 18th Century.* Lawrenceville: Red Sea Press, pp. 22, 37, 38; and Pankhurst, Richard (1967). *The Ethiopian Royal Chronicles.* Oxford: Addis Ababa, pp. 125–129.

TABLE U. Distribution of Eritrean Ethnolinguistic Groups Over the Different Climatic Zones of Eritrea

Name of Ethnolinguistic Group	Approx. Population (%)	Settlement Zone	Religion	Main Economic Activities
Tigrinya	50.0	Central and southern plateau	Christianity and minority Islam[*]	Farming; agro-pastoralism
Tigre	31.0	Eastern lowlands; northern highlands, western lowlands	Islam	Nomadic pastoralism; agro-pastoralism
Saho	5.0	Eastern eascarpments and foothills	Islam	Nomadic pastoralism; agro-pastoralism
Afar	5.0	Eastern lowlands and southeastern coastal plains (Danakil Depression)	Islam	Nomadic pastoralism; fishing and trading
Hedareb/Beni Amer	2.5	Western lowlands	Islam	Nomadic pastoralism
Bilen	2.1	Northern parts of central highlands (formerly known as Bogos territory)	Islam and Christianity	Agro-pastoralism
Kunama	2.0	Western lowlands	Islam and Christianity	Sedentary farming; and agro-pastoralism
Nara	1.5	Western lowlands	Islam	Agro-pastoralism; subsistence farming; and nomadic pastoralism

Source: Adapted and modified from Murtaza, Niaz (1998). *The Pillage of Sustainability in Eritrea, 1600s–1990s: Rural Communities and the Creeping Shadows of Hegemony.* London: Greenwood Printing Press, p. 33; UNICEF (1995). *Children and Women in Eritrea.* Asmara, p. 12.

[*]Note that the highlands of Eritrea are predominantly occupied by Tigrinya Christian farming communities. There are minority Muslims, mainly the *Jeberti* (Tigrinya speakers), as well as *Asaorta-Sahos* (in places such as Senafe and Adi Qeyyih).

TABLE V. Enrollment by Level of Education and by Sex 1991/92–1999/00

	Pre-elementary		Primary Elementary (1–5)		Middle (6–7)		Secondary (8–11)	
Year	Total	Female	Total	Female	Total	Female	Total	Female
1991/92	6,461	3,319	150,982	69,236	27,917	13,503	27,627	13,346
1992/93	7,031	3,605	184,656	82,421	28,431	13,379	31,531	14,390
1993/94	7,748	3,839	208,199	92,536	32,781	14,652	32,756	13,324
1994/95	8,032	3,930	224,287	99,743	34,995	15,685	36,728	14,631
1995/96	8,180	3,979	241,725	108,254	39,751	18,103	39,188	15,475
1996/97	7,443	3,652	240,737	108,487	47,460	20,721	40,594	16,332
1997/98	9,300	4,617	247,499	111,930	57,152	24,154	41,615	16,417
1998/99	11,581	5,413	261,963	118,385	67,021	29,290	47,533	17,756
1999/00	11,885	5,704	295,941	133,045	74,317	33,284	59,626	22,093

Source: Adapted from Kifle, Temesgen (2003). *Return to and Demand for Education in Eritrea and the Role of International Remittances.* Bremen: Shaker Verlag, p. 63.

TABLE W. Eritrea Pupils-Teacher Ratio by Level of Education and Administrative Region, 1999/00

	Pupil-teacher ratio		
Zone	Elementary	Middle	Secondary
Anseba	47	55	61
Southern Red Sea	32	48	39
Southern	52	63	77
Gash-Barka	45	47	49
Central	46	56	52
Northern Red Sea	44	51	42

Source: Adapted from Kifle, Temesgen (2003). *Return to and Demand for Education in Eritrea and the Role of International Remittances.* Bremen: Shaker Verlag, p. 54.

Holidays

Post-independent Eritrea adopted the Gregorian (European) calendar as its official calendar. Hence, public holidays and official festivities are celebrated on the basis of the Gregorian calendar. However, a great majority of religious holidays are also celebrated on the basis of the ancient liturgical (Ge'ez or Alexandrian/Julian) as well as Muslim calendars. Adherents of the Orthodox *Tewahdo*, the Roman Catholic and Lutheran religions, follow the Ge'ez calendar while Eritrean Muslim populations celebrate their holidays on the basis of the lunar calendar. Therefore, there are three applicable calendars in Eritrea: the Gregorian calendar (which is used for official purposes), the Ge'ez calendar (which is used by great majority of Christian populations), and the lunar calendar (used by the Muslim sections of the Eritrean population).

As in most parts of the Muslim world, Islamic holidays and festivals take place on the basis of lunar observances; hence, they change almost every year. The Ge'ez calendar follows characters closely related to the ancient Egyptian solar year. The Ge'ez calendar year comprises 12 months of 30 days each as well as 5 extra days known as *pagume* (ጳጉመ) or *pagumen* (ጳጉሜን). "The years are in groups of four. Each of the four years, called *zämän* [ዘመን] (lit. "time," receives the name of an Evangelist (Mathew, Mark, Luke . . .) " (Fritsch and Zenetti 2003: 668). Unlike the Gregorian calendar (reformed by Pope Gregory XIII in 1582), the Ge'ez calendar is mostly similar to the Julian system; however, it also differs some from the Coptic and Julian calendars (see also Fritsch and Zenetti 2003: 668). In the following sections, the Tigrinya names of months of a calendar year are presented. Please note that each New Year starts on the 1st of September of the Ge'ez calendar (11th of September of the Gregorian calendar).

TABLE 1. Months of the year

Month name in Tigrinya	Translation	Meaning
መስከረም	*meskerem*	September
ጥቅምቲ	*teqemti*	October
ሕዳር	*hedar*	November
ታሕሳስ	*tahsas*	December
ጥሪ	*tiri*	January
የካቲት/ለካቲት	*yekatit/lekatit*	February
መጋቢት	*megabit*	March
ሚያዝያ	*miyazya*	April
ግንቦት	*genbot*	May
ሰነ	*sene*	June
ሓምለ	*hamle*	July
ነሓሰ	*nehase*	August
ጳጉመን	*pagumen*	(five extra days between September 6 and 11)

TABLE 2. Tigrinya Names of Days of the Week

Day name in Tigrinya	Translation	Meaning
ሰኑይ	*Senuy*	Monday
ሰሉስ	*selus*	Tuesday
ረቡዕ	*rebu'e*	Wednesday
ሓሙስ	*hamus*	Thursday
ዓርቢ	*'arbbi*	Friday
ቀዳም	*qedam*	Saturday
ሰንበት	*senbbet*	Sunday

The Ge'ez symbols and systems of numerals that are also applied in the Julian calendar are different than the Arabic, or common numerals. The following are some of the Ge'ez numerals used in the Eritrean traditional calendar:

TABLE 3. Ge'ez Numerals

Symbol of number	Translation	Meaning
፩	*hade* (ሓደ)	one
፪	*kelette* (ክልተ)	two
፫	*selestte* (ሰለስተ)	three
፬	*'arba'ette* (ኣርባዕተ)	four
፭	*hammushte* (ሓሙሽተ)	five
፮	*shedushtte* (ሽዱሽተ)	six
፯	*show'ate* (ሸውዓተ)	seven
፰	*shemontte* (ሸሞንተ)	eight
፱	*tishi'atte* (ትሽዓተ)	nine
፲	*'assertte* (ዓሰርተ)	ten
፳	*'esra* (ዕስራ)	twenty
፴	*selasa* (ሰላሳ)	thirty
፵	*'arbe'a* (ኣርብዓ)	forty
፶	*hamsa* (ሓምሳ)	fifty
፷	*sessa* (ስሳ)	sixty
፸	*seb'a* (ሰብዓ)	seventy
፹	*semanya* (ሰማንያ)	eighty
፺	*tes'a* (ተስዓ)	ninety
፻	*mi'etti* (ምእቲ)	one hundred
፻፼	*hade shih* (ሓደ ሽሕ)	one thousand

The liturgical seasons are also different than the Gregorian one, and so "the whole year is organized according to an either four-fold or three-fold basic structure in which the liturgical seasons are set" (Fritsch and Zenetti 2003: 669). The common fourfold liturgical seasons in Eritrea and Ethiopia are:

1. ቀውዒ (*qew'i*): The Windy/Harvest Season—between the Ge'ez calendar of September 26 and December 25. Note that in Amharic, this season is called መጸው (*mes'ew*).

2. ሓጋይ (*hagay*): The Dry Season—between December 26 and March 25 of the Ge'ez calendar.

3. ጸደይ (*sedey*): The Sowing Season—between March 25 and June 25 of the Ge'ez calendar.

4. ክረምቲ (*keremti*): The Rainy Season—between June 26 and September 25 (Fritsch and Zenetti 2003: 669).

The year begins on September 1 of the Ge'ez calendar, and every month of the year is characterized by a number of liturgical holidays as designated in the Ge'ez calendar such as the following:

1. ቅዱስ ዮሓንስ "Saint John" (September 1 to 7)
2. መስቀል "the Cross/The finding of the True Cross" (two weeks after Saint John, September 17)
3. ዘካርያስ "Zechary" (September 8–9)
4. ስብከት (*sebket*) "the Preaching" (the Sunday between December 8 and 14)
5. ኖላዊ (*nolawi*) "shepherd" (between December 24 and 27)
6. ልደት (*leddet*) "the Nativity; Christmas" (between December 29)
7. ጥምቀት (*timqet*) "the Holy Epiphany" (January 11)
8. ግዝረት (*gezret*) "Jesus's Circumcision" (January 6–7)
9. ናዝሬት (*nazret*) "Nazreth" (between the Monday following the first Sunday after Christmas to January 10)
10. አስተርእዮ (*aster'eyo*) "Epiphany" (between January 11 and 13)
11. ሰሙነ-ሕማማት (*semune-hemamat*) "the Holy Week" (the week before the Easter Sunday). The Holy Week also comprises a number of liturgical festivities such as ሓሙስ ጸግቦ (*hamus segbbo*) "the Satiety Thursday", ዓርቢ ስቅለት (*'arbbi seqllet*) "Good Friday" (on Friday of the *semune-hemamat*; the hole day of prayers and oblations, usually April 9) and ሆሳእና (*hosa'enna*) "Palm Sunday" (on the Saturday before Easter, usually April 4)
12. ፋሲካ (*fasika*) "Easter" (= *tensa'e* is one of the major feasts among the Christian population. It is celebrated between March 26 and April)
13. ትንሳኤ (*tensa'e*) "the Resurrection" (April 11)
14. ዕርገት (*'erget*) "the Christ's Ascension" (May 20). For further details, see Fritsch and Zenetti (2003: 669).

The Ethiopian/Eritrean Ge'ez calendar year is characterized by a number of liturgical cycles of holidays and colorful festivities such as the Epiphany, Easter, and monthly cycles for the commemorations of a number of saints and holy men such as St. Peter, St. John, St. Joseph, Abune Aregawi, as well as Our Lady Mary. The following are some of the main events of cyclical liturgical festivities among the Christian populations of the country (see also Fritsch and Zenetti 2003: 669–672). Note that the dates of festivities provided in the parentheses are based on the Ge'ez calendar. One can add usually eight days to the Ge'ez calendar to convert the date to Gregorian calendar although this method may sometimes be wrong.

1. ጸንስታ (*senseta*) "St. Mary's Conception" (celebrated on August 7)
2. ልደታ (*leddeta*) "St. Mary's Nativity" (celebrated on May 1)

3. በአታ (*be'ata*) "St. Mary's entry [to the Temple]" (celebrated in December and February 12)

4. ማርያም ግንቦት (*maryam genbbot*) "St. Mary of May" (similar to *leddeta*, but celebrated in a traditional way with prayers, singing, and oblations signifying the coming *keremti* season and wishing for a good rainy season)

5. ፍልሰታ (*felseta*) "the Assumption" (celebrated on August 16)

6. ስላሴ (*selassie*) "Trinity" (celebrated in December and January 7)

7. በዓለ እግዚአብሔር (*be'ale egziabher*) "the Commemoration for the Father" (celebrated on October and March 29)

8. በዓለ ገብሪኤል (*be'ale gebriel*) "the Commemoration for St. Gabriel" (celebrated on December 19)

9. መድኃኔ ዓለም (*medhanie 'alem*) "the Savior's Day" (on October 27)

10. ቅዱስ ጊዮርጊስ (*qeddus giyorgis*) "St. George" (on November 23)

11. በዓለ ሚካኤል (*be'ale mika'el*) "St. Michael's Day" (celebrated on November 12 and June 12)

12. ኪዳነ ምሕረት (*kidane mehret*) "the Covenant of Mercy" (celebrated on February 16)

13. አቡነ አረጋዊ (*abune aregawi*) "the Aregawi"—one of the main saints (celebrated on October 14)

14. ቅዱስ ዮሴፍ (*qeddus yosief*) "St. Joseph" (26 October)

15. ቅዱስ ጴጥሮስ (*qeddus petros*) "St. Peter" (On July 5)

16. ዮሃንስ ወልደ ነጕድጓድ (*yohannes welde negodgwad*) "St. John, the Son of the Thunder" (January 12)

17. አቡነ ተክለሃይማኖት (*abune teklehaymanot*) (one of the local saints, commemorated in August, January and May 24)

18. በዓለ መንፈስ ቅዱስ (*be'ale menfes qeddus*) "the Feast of the Holy Pentecost" (celebrated on May 30)

19. ደብረ ታቦር (*debre tabor*) "the Feast of Transfiguration" (celebrated on August 13)

20. አቡነ ያዕቆብ (*abune yakob*) "day of de Jacobis"—in commemoration of one of the local saints—on June 18)

The liturgical year of the Ge'ez calendar is also characterized by a number of fasting days and seasons. The fasting periods are closely attended by most Christian sections of the population. "People observe the fast until the noon or later, not absorbing any food or drink, and abstain the whole day (i.e., not eating any food of animal origin). Fasting implies that married people also observe sexual abstinence" (Fritsch and Zenetti 2003: 670). During longer periods of fasting, people abstain from consuming animal byproducts such as meat, milk, eggs, and butter while they can resort to "vegetarian" types of foodstuffs. During fasting periods, people usually attend liturgical services. The following are some of the most important fasts practiced in Ethiopia and Eritrea (note that the dates ate based on the Ge'ez calendar):

1. ጾመ-ነነዌ (*some-nenewie*) "Jonah's Fast" (takes place between February 2 and 4)
2. ጾመ-ነብያት (*some-nebiyat*) "the Holy Nativity Fast" (takes place between November 17 and December 28)
3. ጾመ-ሃዋርያት (*some-huwaryat*) "the Apostles' Fast" (takes place between on June 8 or 9 and July 5)
4. ጾመ-ፍልሰታ (*some-felseta*) "St. Mary's Fast" (takes place between August 1 and 15)
5. ጾመ-አርብዓ/ዓቢዪ ጾም (*some-'arbe'a / 'abiyi som*) "the Forty Days Fast/the Great Fast" (starts on February 1 and continues for 55 days).

THE ISLAMIC HOLIDAYS

Islamic holidays in Eritrea follow the usual Hijira calendar, which is about ten days shorter than the Roman calendar. Based on the Islamic calendar and practice, holidays are determined on the basis of lunar observances—the signings of the moon. The main Islamic holidays are the following:

1. *Ramadan* (fasting that takes place on the month 9 of the lunar calendar)
2. *Lailat al-Miraji* (Ascension of the Prophet)
3. *Id al-adha* (the Festival of Sacrifice)
4. *Id al-fitir* (Festivity ending the Ramadan)
5. *Id mawlid al-Nabi* (the birthday of the Prophet) (see also Phillips and Carillet 2006: 261).

THE SECULAR HOLIDAYS

The country also celebrates national holidays, all based on the Gregorian calendar. Among the most important public holidays are the following:

1. Independence Day (May 24)—a one week of colorful celebrations across the country. The festivities are accompanied by music, theater, and various performances.
2. Martyrs' Day (June 20)—countrywide events in commemoration of the fallen heroes of the county. People light candles and pay tribute to the martyrs by visiting *mekaber harbegnatat*—"Martyrs' Cemetery."
3. Beginning of the Liberation Struggle (September 1)—this day signifies the beginning of the Eritrean 30 years of liberation war. The first bullet was fired on September 1, 1961, and this marks the start of liberation struggle in Eritrea.

4. International Women's Day (March 8)—Women's Day, as in most parts of the world, is celebrated in Eritrea in a colorful manner. The Eritrean Womens' Association also prepares festive events during the day.

5. International Worker's Day (May 1)—also called May Day, Eritrea celebrates this holiday. However, mostly the working classes take active roles during the festivities.

6. The *Fenkil* Day (Liberation of Massawa) (May 10) — the liberation of Massawa, May 10, 1990 marks an important event in Eritrea's history. On that day, the liberation fighters fought bitter battles at the Red Sea coasts of Eritrea and liberated the port city of Massawa. The annual *fenkil* festivities take place in Massawa.

REFERENCES

Fritsch, Emmanuel and Zenetti, Ugo (2003). "Calendar." In: Uhlig, Siegbert, *Encyclopaedia Aethiopica*, Vol. I, Wiesbaden, Harrassowitz Verlag, pp. 668–672.

Phillips, Matt and Carillet, Jean-Bernard (2006). *Ethiopia and Eritrea: Country Guide*. Lonely Planet Publications: Chalfont St Peters.

Organizations

There are many national and international religious, humanitarian, and professional organizations in many parts of the country. There are also a number of associations related to music, theater, and sports. A great majority of the main organizations in Eritrea are based in Asmara. Among the most important organizations in Eritrea are the following:

ASSOCIATIONS AND UNIONS

Eritrean Association for the Blind
P.O. Box 615
Asmara,
Eritrea
Tel: (+291-1) 12 24 35
Fax: (+291-1) 12 24 35

Eritrean War Disabled Fighters Association
P.O. Box 5613
Asmara,
Eritrea
Tel: (+291-1) 12 29 67
Fax: (+291-1) 12 08 20

National Confederation of Eritrean Workers (NCEW)
P.O. Box 1188
Asmara
Eritrea
Tel: (+291-1) 12 12 69
Fax: (+291-1) 12 66 69

National Union of Eritrean Women (NUEW)
Box 239, Roosevelt St, No. 12
P.O. Box 239
Asmara
Eritrea
Tel: (+291-1) 12 54 44 / 12 06 28
Fax: (291-1) 120628, 11-89-11

National Union of Eritrean Youth and Students
P.O. Box 1042
Asmara
Eritrea
Tel: (+29-1-1) 12 59 81 / 12 34 19

Planned Parenthood Association of Eritrea
P.O. Box 226
Asmara
Eritrea
Tel: (+291-1) 12 73 33
Fax: (+291-1) 12 01 94

PROFESSIONAL UNIONS

The Association of Eritreans in Agricultural Sciences
P.O. Box 4826
Asmara,
Eritrea
Tel: (+291-1) 11 95 22

The Eritrean Islamic Relief Association
P. O. Box 4479
Asmara,
Eritrea
Tel: (+291-1) 12 79 26

The Eritrean Medical Association
P.O. Box 9145
Asmara,

Eritrea
Tel: (+291-1) 15 01 75
Fax: (+291-1) 15 02 34

The Eritrean Nurses Association
P. O. Box 7996
Asmara,
Eritrea
Tel: (+291-1) 12 22 80
Fax: (+291-1) 12 41 94

The Eritrean Pharmaceutical Association
P. O. Box 5415
Asmara,
Eritrea
Tel.: (+291-1) 12 0 2 93
Fax: (+291-1) 12 6 4 55

The Eritrean Red Cross Society
P. O. Box 575
Asmara,
Eritrea
Tel: (+291-1) 15 16 93
Fax: (+291-1) 15 05 49

The Eritrean Teachers' Union
P. O. Box 954
Asmara,
Eritrea
Tel: (+291-1) 12 55 44

Religious Institutions

The Eritrean Catholic Church
P.O. Box 244
Asmara,
Eritrea
Tel: (+291-1) 12 02 06
Fax: (+291-1) 12 65 19

The Eritrean Evangelical Church
Geza Kenisha quarter, 905
Street number: 137, House number 4
Asmara,
Eritrea
Tel: (+291-1) 12 07 11
Fax: (+291-1) 12 00 62

The Eritrean Mufti Office
P.O. Box 2884
Asmara,
Eritrea
Tel: (+291-1) 12 09 45
Fax: (+291-1) 12 20 79

The Eritrean Orthodox *Tewahdo* **Church**
Warsay Street
House number 728
Asmara,
Eritrea
Tel: (+291-1) 18 42 90
Fax: (+291-1) 18 21 95

Economic Organizations and Financial Institutions

Commercial Bank of Eritrea
P.O. Box 219
Asmara,
Eritrea
Tel: (+291-1) 12 18 44
Fax: (+291-1) 12 48 49

Eritrean Development and Investment Bank
P.O. Box 1266
Asmara,
Eritrea
Tel: (+291-1) 12 67 77
Fax: (+291-1) 20 19 76
Website: http://www.shaebia.org/new-hcb.html

Eritrean National Chamber of Commerce
P.O. Box 856
Asmara,
Eritrea
Tel: (+291-1) 12 15 89
Fax: (+291-1) 12 01 38

Housing and Commercial Bank of Eritrea
P.O. Box 235
Asmara,
Eritrea
Tel: (+291-1) 12 03 50
Fax: (+291-1) 12 04 01

National Insurance Corporation of Eritrea
Bdho Avenue 171

P.O. Box 881
Asmara,
Eritrea
Tel: (+291-1) 12 30 00
Fax: (+291-1) 12 32 40
Website: http://www.nice-eritrea.com

The Eritrean Free Zone Authority
P.O. Box 9150
Asmara,
Eritrea
Tel: (+291-1) 20 08 12
Fax: (+291-1) 20 27 78

The Himbol Financial Services
P.O. Box 1113
Asmara,
Eritrea
Tel: (+291-1) 12 07 88
Fax: (+291-1) 12 10 58

The National Bank of Eritrea
P.O. Box 849
Asmara,
Eritrea
Tel: (+291-1) 12 30 33
Fax: (+291-1) 12 31 62

The Red Sea Trading Corporation
P.O. Box 332
Asmara,
Eritrea
Tel: (+291-1) 12 78 46 / 12 43 88
Fax: (+291-1) 12 43 53

OFFICES AND BRANCHES OF INTERNATIONAL ORGANIZATIONS IN ERITREA

Catholic Relief Services
P. O. Box 8016
Asmara,
Eritrea
Tel: (+291-1) 15 12 82
Fax: (+291-1) 15 05 11

Food and Agricultural Organization of the United Nations (FAO)
P. O. Box 4908

Asmara,
Eritrea
Tel: (+291-1) 15 17 53
Fax: (+291-1) 15 17 38

Oxfam Great Britain
P. O. Box 4118
Asmara,
Eritrea
Tel: (+291-1) 12 51 92
Fax: (+291-1) 12 51 90

Save the Children of the United Kingdom
P.O. Box 4118
Asmara,
Eritrea
Tel: (+291-1) 15 17 72
Fax: (+291-1) 12 51 90

Swiss Agency for Development and Cooperation
P.O. Box 3099
Asmara,
Eritrea
Tel: (+291-1) 18 48 68
Fax: (+291-1) 18 27 35

The Caritas International
P.O. Box 1990
Asmara,
Eritrea
Tel: (+291-1) 12 50 00
Fax: (+291-1) 12 00 70

The Delegation of European Commission to Eritrea
P. O. Box 5710
Asmara,
Eritrea
Tel: (+291-1) 12 65 66
Fax: (+291-1) 12 65 78

United Nation Children's Fund (UNICEF)
P. O. Box 2004
Asmara,
Eritrea
Tel: (+291-1) 15 15 39
Fax: (+291-1) 15 11 99

United Nations Development Program (UNDP)
P. O. Box 5366
Asmara,
Eritrea
Tel: (+291-1) 15 11 66
Fax: (+291-1) 15 10 81
Website: http://www.er.undp.org/contacts.html

United Nations Higher Commission for Refugees (UNHCR)
P. O. Box 1995
Asmara,
Eritrea
Tel: (+291-1) 12 72 11
Fax: (+291-1) 12 79 01

United Nations Mission in Ethiopia and Eritrea (UNMEE)
P.O. Box 5805
Asmara,
Eritrea
Tel: (+291-1) 15 19 08
Fax: (+291-1) 15 19 89
Website: http://www.un.org/en/peacekeeping/missions/unmee/

United Nations Population Fund (UNFPA)
P. O. Box 5366
Asmara,
Eritrea
Tel: (+291-1) 15 11 10
Fax: (+291-1) 15 16 48

World Food Program (WFP)
P. O. Box 1229
Asmara,
Eritrea
Tel: (+291-1) 15 16 23
Fax: (+291-1) 15 12 39

World Health Organization (WHO)
P. O. Box 5561
Asmara,
Eritrea
Tel: (+291-1) 15 16 13
Fax: (+291-1) 15 13 22

GOVERNMENT MINISTRIES

Ministry of Agriculture
P.O. Box 124
Asmara,
Eritrea
Tel: (+291-1) 18 14 99 / 18 13 24 / 12 03 95
Fax: (+291-1) 18 14 15

Ministry of Defense
P.O. Box 629
Asmara,
Eritrea
Tel: (+291-1) 16 05 59 / 16 05 51 / 16 05 52
Fax: (+291-1) 16 05 50 / 18 13 91

Ministry of Education
P.O. Box 5610 /1056
Asmara,
Eritrea
Tel: (+291-1) 11 30 44 / 12 63 53
Fax: (+291-1) 11 38 66

Ministry of Energy and Mines
P.O. Box 5285
Asmara,
Eritrea
Tel: (+291-1) 11 68 72 / 12 15 41
Fax: (+291-1) 12 76 52 / 12 76 52

Ministry of Finance
P.O. Box 895
Asmara,
Eritrea
Tel: (+291-1) 11 67 92 / 20 08 19 / 12 77 55
Fax: (+291-1) 11 78 85 / 12 79 47

Ministry of Fisheries
P.O. Box 923
Asmara,
P. O. Box 27
Massawa
Eritrea
Tel: (+291-1) 11 42 71 / 55 29 85 (Massawa office)
Fax: (+291-1) 11 21 85 (Asmara) / 55 21 77 (Massawa office)

Ministry of Foreign Affairs
P.O. Box 190
Asmara,
Eritrea
Tel: (+291-1) 11 38 11 / 12 51 53
Fax: (+291-1) 12 37 88 / 12 51 41

Ministry of Health
P.O. Box 212
Asmara,
Eritrea
Tel: (+291-1) 11 28 77 / 20 29 17
Fax: (+291-1) 12 52 62

Ministry of Justice
P.O. Box 241
Asmara,
Eritrea
Tel: (+291-1) 12 49 16 / 20 29 10 / 12 49 16
Fax: (+291-1) 11 18 22

Ministry of Labor and Human Welfare
P.O. Box 5252
Asmara,
Eritrea
Tel: (+291-1) 15 17 50 / 15 18 46
Fax: (+291-1) 15 02 00

Ministry of Land, Water and Environment
P.O. Box 976
Asmara,
Eritrea
Tel: (+291-1) 12 67 12
Fax: (+291-1) 12 32 85

Ministry of National Development
P.O. Box 1386
Asmara,
Eritrea
Tel: (+291-1) 12 33 56
Fax: (+291-1) 12 56 79

Ministry of Public Works
P.O. Box 841
Asmara,
Eritrea
Tel: (+291-1) 12 24 77
Fax: (+291-1) 12 06 61

Ministry of Tourism
P.O. Box 1010
Asmara,
Eritrea
Tel: (+291-1) 12 69 97
Fax: (+291-1) 12 69 49

Ministry of Trade and Industry
P.O. Box 1844
Asmara,
Eritrea
Tel: (+291-1) 11 39 10 / 12 61 55
Fax: (+291-1) 12 14 62 / 12 02 45

Ministry of Transport and Communications
P.O. Box 204 / 6465
Asmara,
Eritrea
Tel: (+291-1) 11 04 44 / 18 52 51
Fax: (+291-1) 12 70 48 / 18 46 90

FOREIGN EMBASSIES AND CONSULAR REPRESENTATIONS IN ERITREA

Embassy of China
P.O. Box 204
Asmara,
Eritrea
Tel: (+291-1) 18 52 72
Fax: (+291-1) 18 93 61
Website: http://chinese-embassy.com/chinese-embassy-in-eritrea.htm

Embassy of Djibouti
P.O. Box 7702
Asmara,
Eritrea
Tel: (+291-1) 12 59 90
Fax: (+291-1) 12 62 13

Embassy of Egypt
P.O. Box 5570
Asmara,
Eritrea
Tel: (+291-1) 12 36 06
Fax: (+291-1) 12 32 94

Embassy of France
P.O. Box 209
Asmara,
Eritrea
Tel: (+291-1) 12 65 99
Fax: (+291-1) 12 32 88
Website: http://www.diplomatie.gouv.fr/en/country-files_156/eritrea_205/index.html

Embassy of Germany
P.O. Box 4974
Asmara,
Eritrea
Tel: (+291-1) 18 66 70
Fax: (+291-1) 18 69 00
Website: http://www.asmara.diplo.de/Vertretung/asmara/de/Startseite.html

Embassy of Italy
P.O. Box 220
Asmara,
Eritrea
Tel: (+291-1) 12 07 74 / 12 01 60 / 12 02 15
Fax: (+291-1) 12 11 15
Website: http://www.ambasmara.esteri.it/Ambasciata_Asmara

Embassy of Norway
P.O. Box 5801
Asmara,
Eritrea
Tel: (+291-1) 12 16 09 / 12 21 38
Fax: (+291-1) 12 21 80

Embassy of Russia
P.O. Box 5667
Asmara,
Eritrea
Tel: (+291-1) 12 74 16 / 12 72 62
Fax: (+291-1) 12 71 64

Embassy of Saudi Arabia
P.O. Box 5599
Asmara,
Eritrea
Tel: (+291-1) 18 78 90
Fax: (+291-1) 18 78 82

Embassy of South Africa
P.O. Box 11447
Asmara,

Eritrea
Tel: (+291-1) 15 25 21
Fax: (+291-1) 15 25 16

Embassy of Sudan
P.O. Box 246
Asmara,
Eritrea
Tel: (+291-1) 11 55 46
Fax: (+291-1) 11 55 39

Embassy of the Netherlands
P.O. Box 5860
Asmara,
Eritrea
Tel: (+291-1) 12 76 28
Fax: (+291-1) 12 75 91

Embassy of the United Kingdom
P.O. Box 5584
Asmara,
Eritrea
Tel: (+291-1) 12 01 45
Fax: (+291-1) 12 01 04 / 18 80 31

Embassy of the United States of America
P.O. Box 211
Asmara,
Eritrea
Tel: (+291-1) 12 00 09
Fax: (+291-1) 12 22 68
Website: http://eritrea.usembassy.gov/

Embassy of Yemen
P.O. Box 5566
Asmara,
Eritrea
Tel: (+291-1) 12 43 76
Fax: (+291-1) 12 37 95

Qatar Embassy
P.O. Box 9315
Asmara,
Eritrea
Tel: (+291-1) 15 89 97
Fax: (+291-1) 15 89 95

CONSULATES ADMINISTERED
BY HONORARY APPOINTEES

The Consulate of Belgium
P.O. Box 3446
Asmara,
Eritrea
Tel: (+291-1) 12 11 35
Fax: (+291-1) 12 11 39

The Consulate of Canada
P.O. Box 3962
Asmara,
Eritrea
Tel: (+291-1) 18 18 55
Fax: (+291-1) 18 64 99

The Consulate of India
P.O. Box 1491
Asmara,
Eritrea
Tel: (+291-1) 18 67 42
Fax: (+291-1) 18 66 33

The Consulate of Japan
P.O. Box 5399
Asmara,
Eritrea
Tel: (+291-1) 12 65 60
Fax: (+291-1) 12 65 50

The Consulate of Sweden
P.O. Box 5560
Asmara,
Eritrea
Tel: (+291-1) 12 23 02
Fax: (+291-1) 12 22 88

The Consulate of Turkey
P.O. Box 4173
Asmara,
Eritrea
Tel: (+291-1) 12 75 12
Fax: (+291-1) 12 23 77

Directory of some crucial local telephone numbers (for international calls, add country dialing code (0029-1-1) to the given numbers.

HOSPITALS AND CLINICS IN ASMARA

Berhan Clinic	16-16-09
St. Mary Psychiatry	15 37 56
Halibet Hospital	18 54 00
Orota Hospital	20 29 14
Hazhaz Hospital	16 16 89
Emergency, also Fire Brigade	20 20 99 / 20 22 60
Sembel Polyclinic	15 01 75 / 15 02 34
Ambulance	12 22 44

POLICE (AND STATIONS)

1st Police Station (Carcelli)	11 62 19
2nd Police Station	11 49 42
3rd Police Station	16 19 44
Asmara main police headquarter	12 77 99
Traffic Police	12 05 55

DIRECTORY OF SOME HOTELS IN ERITREA

Asmara

Albergo Italia	12 07 40
Allascala Hotel	15 15 40
Ambassador Hotel	12 65 44
Bologna Hotel	18 66 90
Central Hotel (Asmara)	12 00 41
Crystal Hotel	12 09 44
Embasoira Hotel	12 32 22
Expo Hotel	18 42 42
Hotel Asmara Palace	15 37 00
Khartoum Hotel	12 13 94
Lion Hotel	15 95 72
Nyala Hotel	12 31 11
Savannah International Hotel	20 21 41 / 11 61 83
Selam Hotel	12 72 44
Sun Shine Hotel	12 78 80 / 12 78 74

Massawa

Bailul Hotel	55 19 05
Central Hotel	55 20 02
Dahlak Hotel	55 29 80
Gurgusum Hotel	55 29 11
Hamassien Hotel	54 70 11
Red Sea Hotel	55 28 39
Torino Hotel	55 28 55

Keren

Awet Hotel	40 11 76
Hotel Hollywood	40 16 21
Hotel Wedeb	40 16 20
Keren Hotel	40 10 14
Sarinna Hotel	40 02 30
Shigey Hotel	40 19 71

Assab

Kebal International	66 17 00
Ras Gombo Hotel	66 09 42

SELECTED OFFICIAL GOVERNMENT WEBSITES

Alenalki—pro-government media foundation: http://www.alenalki.com/

Meadna—pro-government website: http://www.meadna.com/

Ministry of Tourism—The State of Eritrea: http://www.shaebia.org/mot.html

Shabait—the Official Website of the Ministry of Information, The State of Eritrea: http://www.shabait.com/

Shaebia—official website of the PFDJ: http://www.shaebia.org/artman/publish/index.shtml

SELECTED WEBSITES OF ERITREAN OPPOSITION GROUPS IN THE DIASPORA

Awate: http://www.awate.com/portal/

Eritrean Movement for Democracy and Human Rights (EMDHR): http://www.meseley.net/

Meskerem—"The Eritrean Political Opposition": http://www
.meskerem.net/

Nharnet—ELF Revolutionary Council: http://www.nharnet.com/

The Asmarino Independent: http://asmarino.com/home

The Assenna Media Foundation for Freedom of Expression:
http://assenna.com/

Annotated Bibliography

GEOGRAPHY

Abdul-Haggag, Y. (1961). *A Contribution to the Physiography of Northern Ethiopia*. London:, Athlone Press, 153 pages. This book contains important geographical information on Eritrea and Northern Ethiopia. Detailed geographical aspects of Eritrea are well presented in this study. Among the book's most important themes are the diversity and nature of Eritrean landscapes, climate, relief and rainfall, features of human settlement, and diversity of natural resources. Although the book does not present complete geographical features of Eritrea, it does provide important information about Eritrean and Ethiopian geography for general readers.

Boerma, Pauline A. (1999). *Seeing the Wood for the Trees: Deforestation in the Central Highlands of Eritrea since 1890*. (Ph.D. Dissertation), Environmental Change Unit, School of Geography, University of Oxford. This study deals with Eritrean geography, particularly with the history of forestry in Eritrea. Based on archival and library works, this study provides interesting insights on Eritrea's forestry history since the colonial period.

Lätt, Louise (2004). *Eritrea Re-Photographed: Landscape Changes in the Eritrean Highlands 1890–2004—An Environmental-Historical Study Based on the Reconstruction of Historical Photographs*. (MSc Thesis), University of Bern. This unpublished thesis provides interesting historical analysis of the Eritrean landscape and forestry since the Italian colonial period. Among other themes, Lätt, based on photographical information, presents historical analysis on landscape and forestry changes in the Eritrean highlands.

Ministry of Education (1995). *Geography for Grade 11*. Curriculum Development Division, Asmara. This textbook provides basic geographical information on Eritrea. Among the textbook's main geographical themes are the geological events of Eritrea, Eritrean landscape, climate, rainfall, vegetation, agriculture, and mineral resources.

Murtaza, Niaz (1998). *The Pillage of Sustainability in Eritrea, 1600s–1990s: Rural Communities and the Creeping Shadows of Hegemony*. London, Greenwood Printing Press, 224 pages. This book presents a comprehensive and remarkable history of the relationship among the environment, state, and society in Eritrea. It also delivers a significant examination of the historical relationship between the state actors, environment, and society and how state actors affected local communal ways of living through time and space.

Naty, Alexander (2002). "Environment, Society and the State in Western Eritrea." In: *Africa: Journal of International African Institute*. 72, pp. 569–97. This article provides a critical examination of the relationship among the state, environment, and society of a particular region in Eritrea—the Gash-Barka geographical area. It sheds important light on the relationship between state and local actors, and the complex relationships between anthropogenic *vis-à-vis* environmental variables. Based on historical, anthropological, and environmental sources, the study closely examines the relationship between the above-mentioned actors and discusses how the overall interactions resulted in ecological adversities in the study area.

Tesfagiorgis, Mussie G. (2007). *A Fading Nature: Aspects of Environmental History of Eritrea*. (Ph.D. dissertation), Felsberg, Edition Eins, 237 pages. This study focuses on the environmental history of Eritrea (1800–1991). Broadly, it is concerned with the examination of the triangular relationship between rural populations, natural resources, and state power. The relationship between these variables has been shaped by factors such as a commercial nexus governed by customary and state laws, by the physical landscape, and by inequalities of power. It examines the nature and course of the continuous struggle where rural populations, institutions and agencies, and "nature" all played roles in shaping the choices, options, strategies, and tactics available to rural communities of Eritrea; as well as the examination of how the state's role changed at specific points in time.

HISTORY

Connell, Dan (1993). *Against All Odds: A Chronicle of the Eritrean Revolution*. Philadelphia: Red Sea Press, 325 pages. The book provides excellent narratives regarding the course and aftermath of the Eritrean liberation struggle through the 1970s, 1980s, and 1980s.

Gebre-Medhim, Jordan (1989). *Peasants and Nationalism in Eritrea: A Critique of Ethiopian Studies*. Trenton, NJ: Red Sea Press, 220 pages. The book deals with a number issues regarding Eritrea's political and social history. Gebre-Medhim examines the nature and course of developments of the Eritrea-Ethiopian Federation (1952–1962), the Eritrean liberation struggle, and the rise of nationalism in Eritrea. The author provides an insightful critique of Ethiopian history and politics. Based on historical, anthropological, and political sources, the book presents a remarkable history of the relationship between peasants, nationalism, and rural development in Eritrea. Among some of the main themes of study are:

Eritrea-Ethiopian politics since British rule; the *shifta* movements and atrocities in Eritrea (1940s and 1950s); and traditional systems of land tenure.

Iyob, Ruth (1995). *The Eritrean Struggle for Independence: domination, resistance, Nationalism (1941–1993)*. Cambridge, Cambridge University Press, 216 pages. This work provides an excellent presentation and analysis of Eritrea's political history, especially for the period of liberation struggle (1961–1991). It examines the rise and development of Eritrean nationalism and provides a comprehensive presentation of Eritrean nationalist movements. The author also provides regional and international contexts of the Ethiopian-Eritrean federation and the Eritrean liberation struggle. Some of the main themes examined in the work are: "regional hegemony in the post-World War II order," "the origins of the Eritrean conflict," "the federation years: 1952–1962," and Eritrean nationalist movements and liberation struggle fronts.

Kibreab, Gaim (1987). *Refugees and Development in Africa: The Case of Eritrea*. Trenton, NJ: Red Sea Press. This work presents detailed analysis of the situation of Eritrean refugees in Sudan. It traces the origins of refugees and assesses the overall situation of their livelihoods in Sudanese refugee camps. Some of the most interesting issues presented in this book include: the refugee households and their economic situations; refugees and settlement issues; and the persistent struggle of refugees in securing self-reliant strategies of survival.

Killion, Tom (1998). *Historical Dictionary of Eritrea*. London: The Scarecrow Press, 535 pages. This volume presents a rich historical guide of Eritrea. The entries presented in the volume are significantly useful for all those who seek knowledge about Eritrea's history. It covers a long historical period (1600s–1990s), and entries deal with diverse themes such as biographies, place names, historical events, and historical institutions. This volume is highly recommended as a source for various aspects of Eritrean history, society, and politics.

Locatelli, Francesca (2004). *Asmara During the Italian Period: Order, Disorder and Urban Identities—1890–1941*. (Unpublished Ph.D. Dissertation), SOAS, University of London. This dissertation examines the impact of colonial rule in Eritrea in regard to the growth of the city of Asmara during the period of Italian colonialism, 1890–1941. The main focus of the study is the social history of Asmara, with a particular focus on the relationship between the colonizers and the colonized in urban Eritrea. Some of the main themes of the study include: Italian colonial racial theories and aspects of their implementation in Eritrea; ethnographic survey of Asmara's dwellers during the colonial period; law, order, and crime in the colonial capital of Asmara; gender relations and prostitution in colonial Asmara; and the history of Italian settlers in Asmara.

Longrigg, Stephen H. (1945). *A Short History of Eritrea*. Oxford: Clarendon Press, 188 pages. The author of this work (who served as brigadier in the British army in Eritrea) provides the "British" view of Eritrea's history. His presentation provides helpful historical information about Eritrea. The book presents Eritrea's history to the 1940s.

Mesghenna, Yemane (1988). *Italian Colonialism: A Case Study of Eritrea, 1869–1934: Motive, Praxis, and Result*. Lund: University of Lund Press, 253 pages. This study provides excellent accounts of Eritrea's economic history during the Italian colonial period. The author provides insightful information on colonial economic policies and practices in Eritrea.

This well-presented research unearths Italy's major economic policies and their implementations in colonial Eritrea.

Miran, Jonathan (2009). *Red Sea Citizens: Cosmopolitan Society and Cultural Change in Massawa*. Bloomington: Indiana University Press, 400 pages. The book is "grounded in innovative scholarship that seeks to historicize the social, cultural, and religious connections and exchanges across the Indian Ocean world. This book examines how a particular historical conjuncture of amplified global interactions in the second half of the nineteenth century formed and transformed society, culture, and notions of identity in the Red Sea port town of Massawa in present-day Eritrea. Miran reconstructs the social, urban, religious, and cultural history of a cosmopolitan community in a period of sweeping economic and social change and demonstrates how different forms of capital (economic, social, cultural, symbolic) were converted and reconverted in the process of social integration, the construction of urban power, and communal authority, as well as the definition of a new moral order. Making use of a rich and wide variety of European, Arabic-language sources, and oral data, the book reveals complex identities and relationships in Massawa by moving between local, regional, and macroregional scales of analysis and interpretation" (quoted from online summary of Western Washington University at: http://onlinefast.org/wwutoday/facstaff/publications/5405).

Negash, Tekeste (1997). *Eritrea and Ethiopia: The Federal Experience*. Uppsala: Nordiska Afrikainstitutet, 234 pages. The book examines the establishment, course, and fall of the Eritrean-Ethiopian federation (1952–1962). Based on archival sources, the book presents historical versions of the federal experience and the causes of the Eritrean conflict.

Negash, Tekeste (1987). *Italian Colonialism in Eritrea—1882–1941: Policies, Praxis and Impact*. Uppsala: University of Uppsala, 217 pages. Based on archival sources, this work examines the economic, educational, and social policies of the colonial state in Eritrea, and assesses the overall impact of colonialism. The work also provides insightful perspectives on of theory of colonialism. While the author dismisses the conventional versions of colonial motives, he argues that the "fifty years of colonial rule [in Eritrea] were neither long enough nor sufficiently profound to bring about a political transformation that could be described in terms of Eritrean nationalism." Among the main themes in the study are: "the political economy of colonialism," "the ideology of colonialism: educational policy and praxis," "the ideology of colonialism: native policy," local response to Italian colonialism, and "colonial impact on Eritrean society."

Pateman, Roy (1990). *Eritrea: Even The Stones are Burning*. Lawrenceville, NJ: Red Sea Press, 278 pages. The book deals with Eritrea's history with special focus on Ethiopia's occupation of the country and the response of Eritreans to the occupation. Some of the subjects examined in the book include: aspects of foreign intervention in the region, the impact of war and famine during the liberation struggle; the impact of military rule in Eritrea; and the impact of reforms (especially land reform) by the Eritrean liberation forces.

Reid, Richard (2007). "The Trans-Mereb Experience: Perceptions of the Historical Relationship Between Eritrea and Ethiopia." In: Journal of Eastern African Studies, 1 (2), pp. 238–255. This article provides an excellent insight on Eritrea's history and politics since the war for liberation. The author makes a comparative assessment between the perceptions of

Eritrea nation-state during the liberation struggle and post-independent Eritrea as well as its position in international politics. He also examines the widening divisions between the Eritrean generations—the generation during and after the war.

Schmidt, Peter. Curtis, Matthew C, et al. (2008). *The Archaeology of Ancient Eritrea*. Trenton, NJ: Red Sea Press, 395 pages. The study provides an excellent archaeological overview of Eritrea. The book contains results of archaeological research conducted by staff members and students of the Department of Archaeology and Anthropology, University of Asmara (1993–2008). The themes covered in the work are diverse, covering prehistory and ancient history of Eritrea. The research sites presented in the work include: the greater Asmara area, Metera, Keskese, Gulf of Zula, Quhaito, and Adulis.

Sherman, Richard (1980). *Eritrea: The Unfinished Revolution*. New York: Praeger Publishers, 199 pages. This book presents a comprehensive history of Eritrea with special focus on the roots and developments of the Eritrean struggle for liberation in the 1960s and 1970s.

Selassie, Bereket Habte (1989). *Eritrea and the United Nations and Other Essays*. Trenton, N.J.: Red Sea Press, 177 pages. This book examines Eritrea's political history. It provides excellent accounts and analysis of political developments that led to the Eritrea-Ethiopia Federation and liberation struggle. The book comprises topics on issues of self-determination and international involvement in the Horn during the Cold War, the role of the UN, and more.

Taddia, Irma (1986). *L'Eritrea colonia (1890–1952): paesaggi, strutture uomini del colonialismo* [Colonial Eritrea—1890–1952: Landscape, Structure and the Men of Colonialism]. Milan: Franco Angeli Press, 429 pages (text in Italian) . With this book, Taddia provides an in-depth analysis of the history of Italian colonialism in Eritrea. Taddia's book also offers an excellent perspective of the social history of colonialism in Eritrea. In addition, this book examines Italian land, agricultural, and economic policies in the colony.

Tafla, Bairu (2004). "Eritrea: Remote Past and Present." In: *Journal of Eritrean Studies*, 3 (1), pp. 82–98. This article provides an important synopsis of Eritrean history from the ancient to the modern periods.

Tafla, Bairu (2007). *Troubles and Travels of an Eritrean Aristocrat: A Presentation of Kantiba Gilamika'el's Memoirs*. Shaker Verlag GmbH, 128 pages. This book deals with the biographical history of an Eritrean notable. It also provides an interesting historical reflection of political, social, and cultural events in the second half of nineteenth-century Eritrea. Moreover, the book depicts the nature of Italian colonialism in Eritrea and Ethiopia's political situation under Emperor Menelik's reign.

Tesfay, Alemseged (2001). *Aynefelale: ertra 1941–1950 (ኣይንፈላለ)* [*Let Us Stay United: Eritrea from 1941 to 1950*]. Asmara, Hidri Publishers, 603 pages. The work analyzes complex historical developments in Eritrea during the British occupation period. The author examines socioeconomic and political processes of change during this period and provides excellent historical accounts related to the process of development of Eritrean nationalism. Some of the historical themes treated in the work are: the emergence and development of political parties, aspects of economic circumstances under British rule in the country; the Eritrean question during post-World War II. It provides an excellent study of the origins and growth of the prolonged Eritrean struggle for independence. The book is written in the Tigrinya language, although an English translation of the work is also expected to appear in the near future.

Tesfay, Alemseged (2005). *Federeshin ertra mes ityopiya: kab matienzo kesab tedla (1951–1954)* (ፌደረሽን ኤርትራ ምስ ኢትዮጵያ ፡ ካብ ማቴንዞ ክሳብ ተድላ—1951–1954) [*The Federation of Eritrea with Ethiopia: From Matienzo to the reign of Tedla (1951–1954)*]. Asmara; Hidri Publishers, 655 pages. Based on archival, library, and oral sources, this work provides detailed analysis of Eritrean history during the Ethiopian-Eritrean federation. The author presents significant new historical sources and accounts of Eritrea's history during the federal period. Among other subjects treated in the book are: the historical backgrounds for the establishment of the Ethiopian-Eritrean federation; the federal constitution; the Eritrean economic and sociopolitical situation before and during the federal period; the growth of the national labor class; the establishment of the General Union of Eritrean Labor Syndicates; and Ethiopia's intervention in the affairs of Eritrean government and its aftermath. The book is written in the Tigrinya language; an English translation of the work is also expected to appear in the near future.

Trevaskis, Gerald Kenedy Nicholas (1960). *Eritrea: A Colony in Transition—1941–52.* London: Oxford University Press, 137 pages. This book presents first-hand accounts of Eritrean history during the British occupation period. The author attempts to provide useful accounts of the sociopolitical history of the country. Some of the main themes examined are "the British impact on Eritrea;" the origins and growth of Eritrean national consciousness; Eritrea's political fate after the British rule; and the establishment of the Ethiopian-Eritrean federation.

Uoldelul Chelati Dirar (2007). "Colonialism and the Construction of National Identities: The Case of Eritrea." In: *Journal of East African Studies*, 1 (2), pp. 256–276. This article analyzes the relationship between the colonial state's systems, structures, strategies of rule as well as its juridical systems of justice, and the implications on colonial subjects. It provides excellent perspectives on the colonial system of subjugation and the new molding of local identities. The article also provides an insightful analysis of the correlation between the colonial system of rule and the growth of the "Eritrean elite."

Yohannes, Okbazghi (1991). *Eritrea: A Pawn in World Politics*. Gainesville: University of Florida Press, 331 pages. This work provides a comprehensive examination of Eritrea's political history in regional and international contexts. The author argues that the prolonged conflict in Eritrea was the result of political developments on the regional and international level during the Cold War. The author asserts that Eritrea was denied its independence in the 1950s because of "collusion" between Ethiopia and other Western countries, mainly the United States. Among the main themes examined in this work are the development of Eritrean nationalism; the Eritrean questions in the post-World War II period; "the struggle over Eritrea in the United Nations"; the Ethiopian-Eritrean federation; "the evolution of Ethio-American connection"; and "the Ethiopian devolution and the Ethio-Soviet connection." The book also provides an excellent perspective on the diplomatic history of the Horn of Africa during the Cold War era.

GOVERNMENT AND POLITICS

Bereketeab, Redie (2000). *Eritrea: The Making of a Nation, 1890–1991*. Uppsala: Uppsala University Press, 344 pages. This work provides an excellent perspective on the origins and developments of Eritrean nationalism and collective identity. "This book examines the century-long process of the making of the Eritrean nation. Developments that culminated in the emergence of the State of Eritrea in 1991 are investigated and elaborated as they are traced from their beginnings in 1890, when Italy declared the creation of its new Colony of Eritrea. The study argues that the act of territorial delineation initiated the creation of Eritrea, followed by various phases of transformation that shaped its formation. This century-long process is divided into three distinct periods, Italian rule, the British administration and Ethiopian rule" (extracted from the book). Some of the main themes analyzed in the work include "the synopsis of pre-colonial history"; "territorial integration: the birth of Eritrea"; economic developments and nationalism under the Italian colonial rule; the emergence of political and legal institutions during the British Military Administration (1941–1952) and the national liberation movements and nation building.

Ellingson, Lloyd (1977). "The Emergence of Political Parties in Eritrea (1941–1950)." In: *Journal of African History*, 18 (2), pp. 261–281. This article examines major political developments in Eritrea with special focus on the development of Eritrean political consciousness and the emergence of numerous political parties in the country. Among other subjects of the article are: issues related to the proliferation of political views and parties and the contribution of Italian communities in Eritrea to local politics.

Hepner, Tricia Redeker (2009). *Soldiers, Martyrs, Traitors and Exiles: Political Conflict in Eritrea and the Diaspora*. Ethnography of Political Violence Series, Philadelphia: University of Pennsylvania Press, 272 pages. This work examines how the Eritrean revolution shaped the livelihoods of Eritrean communities in the diaspora (particularly in the U.S.). It critically assesses the nature and depth of Eritrean trans/national features of the Eritrean revolution and provides excellent first-hand accounts and narratives of people whose lives have greatly been affected by war, migration, and human rights abuses. It further provides a critical assessment of Eritrea's post-independence political developments.

Kibreab, Gaim (2008). *Critical Reflections on the Eritrean War of Independence: Social Capital, Associational Life, Religion, Ethnicity and Sowing Seeds of Dictatorship*. Trenton, NJ: Red Sea Press, 450 pages. This work critically examines the internal political developments of Eritrea's war of independence (1961–1991) and establishes links to Eritrea's post-independence political environment. The work focuses on "the social capital" and political developments of the country. Among many other themes examined in the work are: the relationship between foreign occupation and social capital and associational life in Eritrea; nature and development of political frictions and military conflicts among various members of the Eritrean liberation organizations; and a critical overview of the civil war in Eritrea. The author further argues that the political developments of post-independent Eritrea cannot be pragmatically understood without critical understanding of political developments during the Eritrean conflict.

Kibreab, Gaim (2009). *Eritrea: A Dream Deferred*. London: James Currey Publishers, 446 pages. This book provides an interesting account of the history and politics of post-independent Eritrea. It illustrates how things went wrong during the post-independence period, and why the rule of law and justice has not yet been prevalent practices in the post-conflict political environment of Eritrea.

Mengisteab, Kidane and Okbazghi Yohannes (2005). *Anatomy of an African Tragedy: Political, Economic and Foreign Policy Crisis in Post-Independence Eritrea*. Trenton, NJ: Red Sea Press, 310 pages. This book presents an analytical study of Eritrean post-independence politics. The work examines post-independence Eritrea's policies and praxis related to its economy, internal politics, and foreign relations.

Pool, David (2001). *From Guerrillas to Government: The Eritrean People's Liberation Front*. Athens: Ohio University Press, 206 pages. The work examines the formation of the Eritrean liberation fronts, with particular focus on the Eritrean People's Liberation Front (EPLF) and its transformation into a single ruling party in post-independent Eritrea.

Reid, Richard (2003). "Old Problems in New Conflicts: Some Observations on Eritrea and its Relations with Tigray, from Liberation Struggle to Inter-State War." In: *Africa*, 73 (3), pp. 369–401. This article presents an interesting examination of the historical relationship between Eritrea and Ethiopia (particularly the respective ruling parties). The author provides a sound explanation of the complex relationship between the Tigrean and Eritrean liberation fronts with particular references to issues of nationality/identity, ethnicity, frontiers, and sovereignty.

Selassie, Bereket Habte (2003). *The Making of the Eritrean Constitution: The Dialectic of Process and Substance*. Lawrenceville, NJ: Red Sea Press, 326 pages. "Written by a scholar and practitioner who led the process of constitution drafting in the newly independent Eritrea from 1994 to 1997, this book analyzes the process from beginning to end, recording in concise summaries the intensive public debates held in village and town meetings during that three-year period" (quoted from publisher's review).

Wrong, Michela (2005). *I Didn't Do It For You: How the World Used and Abused a Small African Nation*. London: Fourth Estate, 464 pages. This well-written book presents a comprehensive history of Eritrea since the colonial period. The author provides interesting historical insights on how foreign powers (the United States, Britain, the Soviet Union, and Ethiopia) established their political interests in the country, and how the country and its people were used and ignored during all the troubled years of internal crisis and foreign interventions. The book also provides interesting narratives of historical accounts for the periods during and after the Eritrean liberation struggle. The work contains remarkable information on diplomatic and political history of the northeast African region.

ECONOMY

Favali, L. and Pateman, Roy (2003). *Blood, Land, and Sex: Legal and Political Pluralism in Eritrea*. Bloomington: Indiana University Press, 304 pages. This volume presents a detailed assessment of Eritrean communal laws, natural resources (land), and gender relations through various times in history. It presents significant analysis of the relationship and impact of communal laws on traditional systems of land tenure, gender relations, and local strategies of conflict (blood feud) resolutions. Some of the main themes of study in this work are: systems of land tenure in the Eritrean highlands; legal and ethnolinguistic pluralism; crimes and traditional ways of settlement; marriage and gender; and female circumcision.

Tesfai, Alemseged and Martin Doornbos (1999). *Post-Conflict Eritrea: Prospects for Reconstruction and Development.* Lawrenceville, NJ: Red Sea Press, 362 pages. This book examines the main issues of Eritrea's post-independence experiences and prospects for national reconstruction and rehabilitation. Some of the main topics presented in the book are: assessment of ongoing (1991–1999) reconstruction programs; challenges of reintegration for returned refugees and ex-combatants; issues of infrastructural development and food security; and issues of governance.

Zekarias, Ambaye (1966). *Land Tenure in Eritrea (Ethiopia).* Addis Ababa, N.A., 150 pages. This book offers a detailed study of Eritrea's traditional systems of land tenure. The author also provides an interesting analysis of the traditional link between man and the land in the Eritrean highlands. The book presents remarkable historical, social, and economic accounts related to Eritrea's rural communities.

SOCIETY

Dirar, Uoldelul Chelati (2003). "Church-state relations in colonial Eritrea: Missionaries and the development of colonial strategies (1869–1911)." In: Journal of Modern Italian Studies, 8 (3), pp. 391–310. This article examines the complex nature of the relationship between the state and the church in Eritrea (1890–1911). It provides an interesting historical assessment on how the colonial state and the church interacted between themselves and the local populations.

Ghaber, Michael (1993). *The Blin of Bogos.* Bagdad, Iraq (publishers, n.a.), 70 pages. This work is one of the few studies of the history of the Bilen ethnolinguistic group of Eritrea. Based on oral history and archival/library sources, the book provides a comprehensive history of the Bilen since the nineteenth century. Among other themes, the book presents the impact of trans-border raids as well as the impact of Egyptian and Italian occupation on the Bilen communities of Eritrea.

Miran, Jonathan (2005). "A Historical Overview of Islam in Eritrea." In: *Die Welt des Islams* 45(2), pp. 177–215. Reprinted in an anthology, Andrew Rippin (ed.), *World Islam: Critical Concepts in Islamic Studies*, Volume III (London and New York: Routledge, 2008), pp. 195–224. This detailed survey article is the first of its kind to examine the history of Islam in the territory that became known as Eritrea in northeast Africa in 1890. It especially covers the period from the beginning of the nineteenth century to the turn of the twenty-first century and serves as an introduction to a hitherto poorly covered subject aiming to stimulate more research into specific themes and questions. The survey is organized chronologically and is based on an assorted combination of known and untapped sources. The article covers themes such as the role of the Sufi orders in the spread of Islam in the nineteenth century, the relationship between Muslim leaders and Italian authorities in the Italian colonial period (1885–1941), the flourishing of Islamic educational, legal, and political institutions under the British in the 1940s, as well as the complex relationship between the development of "Eritrean Islam" and the Eritrean national liberation struggle (1960s–1991).

Mohammed, Abdul Kader Saleh (1984). *Die Afar-Saho-Nomaden in Nordost-Afrika.* (Ph.D. Dissertation): University of Bayreuth, 276 pages. This study analyzes the historical, social, economic, and political aspects of the Afar and Saho ethnolinguistic groups in Eritrea. Based on archival, library and oral sources, the book provides excellent ethnographical information about the Saho and Afar populations of Eritrea.

Müller, Tanja (2004). *The Making of Elite Women: Revolution and Nation Building in Eritrea.* London: Brill Academic Publishers, 306 pages. This work examines the impending of elite women in Eritrea since the decades of liberation struggle. The book presents a variety of subjects such as Eritrea's history, political developments, as well as sociocultural aspects of Eritreans; however, the main focus of the study is on aspects related to the process of emancipation of Eritrea's women.

Nadel, Siegfried Frederick (1944). *Races and Tribes of Eritrea.* Asmara, British Military Administration—Eritrea, 133 pages. This book provides a general overview of Eritrea's ethnography. It is divided into various sections based on geography and explores the social, economic, and political organizations of various ethnolinguistic groups and clans of Eritrea.

Taye, Adane (1991). *A Historical Survey of State Education in Eritrea.* Asmara: EMPDA, 146 pages. The book provides a useful history of education in Eritrea. It deals with aspects of church education as well as the history of formal education since the Italian colonial rule in Eritrea.

Trimingham, John Spencer (1965). *Islam in Ethiopia.* London: Frank Cass & Co. Ltd, 299 pages. This volume examines the history of Islam in Ethiopia and Eritrea and its impact on various sections of northeast African populations. It provides an interesting account of historical events related to Islam in the region.

Tronvoll, Kjetil (1998). *Mai Weini; A Highland Village in Eritrea: A Study of the People, Their Livelihood, and Land Tenure During Times of Turbulence.* New Jersey: Red Sea Press, 311 pages. This study examines peasant livelihood and their traditional systems of economic and social organizations. The author analyzes how kinship structures and social networks helped the peasants' survival during natural adversities and famine.

CULTURE

Iyob, Ararat (1999). *Blankets of Sand: Poems of War and Exile.* Lawrenceville, NJ: Red Sea Press, 68 pages. An excellent book of poetry related to various aspects of Eritrea—war, social, and cultural life under war, and the overall impact of war on Eritrea's people.

Cantalupo, Charles (ed.) (1999). *We Have Our Voice: Selected Poems of Reesom Haile.* Lawrenceville: Red Sea Press, 244 pages. This book presents selected Eritrean poems by the late Dr. Reesom Haile. The subject deals with diverse issues related to Eritrea.

Cantalupo, Charles and Ghirmai Negash (eds.) (2006). *Who Needs a Story? Contemporary Eritrean Poerty in Tigrinya, Tigre and Arabic.* Asmara: Hidri Publishers, 137 pages.

The book presents an exciting anthology of Eritrean (Tigrinya, Tigre, and Arabic) poems dealing with subjects such as the diaspora, Eritrea's aspirations for development, and aspects of the national liberation struggle.

Denison, Edward; Yu Re, Guang; and Naigzy Gebremedhin (2003). *Asmara: Africa's Secret Modernist City*. London: Merrell; illustrated edition, 240 pages. Based on archival and contemporary first-hand information, this book presents an excellent illustration of Asmara's modern architecture.

Haile, Reesom (2000). *We Invented the Wheel*. Trenton, NJ: Red Sea Press, 226 pages. This book is an excellent collection of poems related to various aspects of Eritrean culture, politics, and more.

Negash, Ghirmai (1999). A *History of Tigrinya Literature in Eritrea: The Oral and the Written (1890–1991)*. Trenton, NJ: Red Sea Press, 236 pages. This pioneering and original work offers a comprehensive history of Tigrinya literature in Eritrea. It provides excellent historical analysis of both oral and written literary traditions of the Tigrinya in Eritrea.

Negash, Ghirmai (2008). *"Oral Poetic Tradition of the Tigrinya."* In: Tesfa G. Gebremedhin and Gebre H. Tesfagiorgis (eds.) (2008). *Traditions of Eritrea: Linking the Past to the Future*. Trenton, NJ: Red Sea Press, pp. 155–189. This article deals with the study of various types of oral literature among the Tigrinya population. It presents comprehensive analysis of various genres of oral poetry and assesses their cultural values for the highland population of Eritrea.

Matzke, Christine (2002). "Of *Suwa* Houses & Singing Contests: Early Urban Women Performers in Asmara, Eritrea." In: Banham, Martin, et al. (eds.), *African Theatre Women*. Oxford: James Currey, pp. 29–46. This article presents a comprehensive analysis of the historical aspects of the performing arts in Eritrea, with special reference to early women artists. Basing his study on oral and archival sources, the author presents excellent accounts of the history of Eritrea's performing arts.

Matzke, Christine (2003). *En-gendering Theatre in Eritrea: The Roles and Representations of Women in the Performing Arts*. Unpublished Ph.D. Dissertation, School of English, University of Leeds. This study examines the history of theatre in Eritrea in relation to the role of women in shaping the country's culture, particularly the performing arts (1930s–1991). It is the first attempt of its kind and provides an excellent account and analysis of Eritrea's historiography of the performing arts.

Tesema, Asres (2006). *Te'amot: kab tarik medrekawi sne tebeb ertra* (ጠዓሞት፡ካብ፡ታሪኽ፡መድረኻዊ ስነጥበብ፡ኤርትራ) [*The Supper: Historical Aspects of Eritrean Performing Arts*]. Asmara: Francescana Printing Press, 340 pages. This pioneering work deals with the historical developments of the performing arts in Eritrea. It provides a detailed historical assessment of early and modern aspects of the performing arts (theatre and music) in the country, and illuminates the contributions of performing arts in preserving and transforming Eritrea's cultures and traditions. Among the most important themes presented in the book are: features of early music and performance in Eritrea; the introduction of modern arts in Eritrea; the impact of modern arts on traditional arts; performing arts during the Italian colonial period; and early associations and cultural troupes of Eritrea. The book is written in the Tigrinya language, and it is hoped there will be an English version in the future.

Tesfa G. Gebremedhin and Gebre H. Tesfagiorgis (eds.) (2008). *Traditions of Eritrea: Linking the Past to the Future*. Trenton, NJ: Red Sea Press, 189 pages. "The book is intended to serve two

related purposes: first, to document and analyze selected traditional legacies and cultural practices in Eritrea, and second, to establish the linkage of those legacies and practices to Eritrea's
current and prospective socio-economic developmental goals . . . The book is aimed at an inter-
disciplinary and general audience interested in Eritrea's traditions and its relevance to development issues and concerns . . . " (quoted from the publisher). Among the main studies presented
in this work are: "customary laws in Eritrea"; "traditional institutions of democratic governance
in Eritrea"; oral poetic tradition of the Tigrinya"; and "traditional art in Eritrea."

Valentini, Mariana (2004). *Strumenti Musicali Tradizionali dell'Altopiano Eritreo (Traditional
Musical Instruments in the Eritrean Highlands)*. Asmara: Francescana Printing Press, 109
pages. This pioneering work explores various traditional musical instruments in the highlands
of Eritrea. It may serve as a significant source material for those interested in the music and traditions of the Eritrean highland population. The book is written in both Italian and English.

Yohannes, Tesfay Tewolde (2002). *A Modern Grammar of Tigrinya*. Tipografia U. Detti: Rome.
This book presents the comprehensive grammar of the Tigrinya language—phonology, mor-
phology, and syntax. It is obviously one of the best grammar books available for advanced
Tigrinya language students.

SHORT BIBLIOGRAPHY ON USEFUL OLD TRAVEL AND COLONIAL SOURCES

Acton, Roger (1868). *The Abyssinian Expedition and the Life and Reign of King Theodore*.
London, 1868.
Alvarez, Francisco [Transl. by Lord Stanley—1970]. *Narrative of the Portuguese Embassy to
Abyssinia during the Years 1520–1527*. Repri. New York.
Baldrati, Isaia (1903). *Mostra agricola della colonia Eritrea: catalogo illustrativo*. Florence.
Baldrati, Isaia (1928). *Note ecologiche sulla colonia Eritrea*. Pisa.
Beccari, Camillo (1912). *Il Tigre: Descritto da un Missionario Gesuita del Osecolo XVII*.
Rome.
Bechtinger, J. (1870). *Ost-Afrika: Erinnerungen und Miscellen aud dem Abessinischen
Feldzuge*. Wien.
Bent, Theodore (1896). *The Sacred City of the Ethiopians*: *Being a Record of Travel and
Research in Abyssinia in 1893*. London.
Blanc, Henry (1868). *A Narrative of Captivity in Abyssinia: With Some Account of the Late
Emperor of Theodore, His Country and People*. London.
Blanford, W. T. (1870). *Observations on the Geology and Zoology of Abyssinia: Made during
the Progress of the British Expedition to that Country in 1867–68*. London.
Borsari, Ferdinanddo (1890). *Le Zone Colonizzabili dell'Eritrea e delle Finitime regioni etio-
piche*. Milan.
Bruce, James (1790). *Travels to discover the source of the Nile, in the years 1768, 1769, 1770,
1771, 1772, and 1773* (5 vols.). London.
Checchi, Michele (1910). *Asmara*. Rome.
Commissariato Keren (1928). *Note sul Commissariato regionale di Cheren*. Cheren.
Conti Rosini, Carlo (1916). *Principi di diritto consuetudinario della colonia Eritrea*. Rome.
Conti Rossini, Carlo (1955). *Croquis de Massouah: Cote d'Abyssinie*. Paris.
Corni, Guido (1929). *Tra Gasc e Setit: Note di Viaggio*. Rome.

d'Abbadie, Antoine (1868). *L'Abyssinie st le roi Theodore*. Paris.

Danielli, G. and Marinelli (1912). *Risultati scientifici di un viaggio nella Colonia Eritrea*. Florence.

de Almeida, Manoel de [Transl. by C.F. Beckingham and G.W.B. Huntingford—1954]. *Some Records of Ethiopia, 1593–1646: Being Extracts from the History of high Ethiopia or Abissinia Together with Bahrey's History of the Galla*. London.

De Cosson, Emilius A. (1877). *The Cradle of the Blue Nile: A Visit to the Court of King John of Ethiopia (Vols. I–II)*. London.

Dufton, Henry (repr. 1970). *Narrative of a Journey Through Abyssinia, in 1862–3*. Westport.

Gioli, G. Bartolemmei (1906). *Agricoltura e Colonizzazione nell'Eritrea*. Rome.

Gobbat, Samuel (1834). *Journal of a Three Years' Residence in Abyssinia: In Furtherance of the Objectives of the Church Missionary Society*. London, 1834.

Hartmann, Robert (1883). *Abyssinien und die Übrigen Gebiete der Ostküste Afrikas*. Leipzig.

Hotten, John C. (1868). *Abyssinia and Its People: Or Life in the Land of Prester John*. London.

Kolmodin, Yohannes (1912). *Traditions de Tsazzega et Hazzeg*. Rome.

Littman, Enno (1910). *Publications of the Princeton Expedition to Abyssinia: Tales, Customs, Names and Dirges of the Tigre Tribes*. Leyden.

Markham, Clements (1868). "Geographical Results of the Abyssinian Expedition." In: *Journal of Royal Geographical Society*. 38, pp. 12–49.

Markham, Clements (1869). *A History of the Abyssinian Expedition*. London.

Martini, Ferdinando (1896). *Nell'Africa Italiana: Impressioni e Ricordi*. Milan.

Mulazzani, A. *Geografia della colonia Eritrea*. Firenze, N.d.

Munzinger, Werner (1859). *Über die Sitten und das Recht der Bogos*. Winterthur.

Munzinger, Werner (1869). "Narrative of a Journey Through the Afar Country." In: *Journal of Royal Geographical Society*. 39, pp. 188–232.

Munzinger, Werner (1883). *Ostafrikanisce Studien: Mit einer Karte von Nord-Abyssinien und den Ländern am Mareb, Barka und Anseba*. Bassel.

Parkyns, Mansfield (1853). *Life in Abyssinia*. (Vols. I and II). London.

Plowden, Walter (1868). *Travels in Abyssinia and the Galla Country: With an Account of a Mission to Ras Ali in 1848*. London.

Portal, Gerald H. (1892). *My Mission to Abyssinia*. London.

Rassam, Hormuzd (1869). *Narrative of the British Mission to Theodore, King of Abyssinia: With Notices of the Countries Traversed from Massowah—Through the Soodân, the Amhâra, and Back to Annesley Bay, from Mágdala*. London.

Rodén, K. G. (1913). *Le tribù dei Mensa: Storia—Leggi e costumi*. Stockholm.

Rohlfs, Gerhard (1869). *Im Auftrag Sr. Majestät des Königs von Preußen mit dem englischen Expeditionscorps in Abessinien*. Bremen.

Rohlfs, Gerhard (1882). *Meine Mission nach Abessinien: Auf Befehl Sr. Maj des Deutschen Kaisers Unternommen*. Leipzig.

Salt, Henry (1815). *A Voyage to Abyssinia and Travels to the Interior of the Country*. London.

Schoefeld, Emil Dagobert (repr. 1904). *Erythräa und der ägyptische Sudan*. Berlin.

Schoeller, Max (1895). *Mitteilungen über meine Reise in der Colonia Eritrea*. Berlin.

von Heuglin, Theodor (1858). "Die Habab-länder am Rothen Meere." In: *Mittheilungen aus Justus Perthes' Geog. Anst*. 4, pp. 370–72.

von Heuglin, Theodor von (1861). *Reisen in Nord-Ost-Afrika zwischen Chartum und dem Rothen Meere bis Suakin und Massaua*. Gotha.

von Heuglin, Theodor von (1868). *Reise nach Abessinien, den Gala-Länden, Ost-Sudan und Chartum in den Jahren 1861 und 1862*. Jena.

von Heuglin, Theodore (1861). "Ein Arabischer Schriftsteller über die Beja-Länder" in: Bruno Hassenstein (ed.). *Zwischen Chartum und dem Rothen Meere bis Suakin und Massaua: Eine Vornehmlich zum Verfolg der v. Heuglinschen Expedition Bestimmte Karte, (Geographische Mitteilungen)*. N.p.

von Heuglin, Theodore (1877). *Reise in Nordost-Afrika: Schielderungen aus dem Gebiete der Beni Amer und Habab*. Braunschweig.

von Katte, A. (1838). *Reise in Abyssinian im Jahr 1836*. Stuttgart.

Winstanley, W. (1881). *A Visit to Abyssinia: A visit to Abyssinia—An Account of Travel in Modern Ethiopia*. London.

Wylde, Augustus B. (1888). *'83–'87 in The Soudan: With an Account of Sir William Hewett's Mission to King John*. London.

Wylde, Augustus B. (1901). *Modern Abyssinia*. London.

Thematic Index

Index